# STUDY GUIDE AND
# SELF-EXAMINATION REVIEW

FOR
MODERN SYNOPSIS OF
COMPREHENSIVE TEXTBOOK OF

# PSYCHIATRY/IV

## SECOND EDITION

# STUDY GUIDE AND SELF-EXAMINATION REVIEW

FOR
MODERN SYNOPSIS OF
COMPREHENSIVE TEXTBOOK OF

# PSYCHIATRY/IV

## SECOND EDITION

## HAROLD I. KAPLAN, M.D.

Professor of Psychiatry, New York University School of Medicine;
Attending Psychiatrist, University Hospital of the New York University Medical Center;
Attending Psychiatrist, Bellevue Hospital, New York, New York

## BENJAMIN J. SADOCK, M.D.

Professor and Vice Chairman, Department of Psychiatry,
New York University School of Medicine;
Attending Psychiatrist, University Hospital of the New York University Medical Center;
Attending Psychiatrist, Bellevue Hospital, New York, New York

WILLIAMS & WILKINS
Baltimore • Hong Kong • London • Sydney

*Editor:* Sara A. Finnegan
*Associate Editor:* Victoria M. Vaughn
*Design:* Joanne Janowiak
*Development Editor:* Anne D. Craig
*Illustration Planning:* Lorraine Wrzosek
*Production:* Raymond E. Reter

**Library of Congress Cataloging in Publication Data**

Kaplan, Harold I., 1927-
  Study guide and self-examination review for Modern synopsis of Comprehensive textbook of psychiatry/IV.
  Rev. ed. of: Study guide and self-examination review for Modern synopsis of Comprehensive textbook of psychiatry/III. c1983.
  Includes index.
  1. Mental illness—Examinations, questions, etc. 2. Psychiatry—Examinations, questions, etc. I. Sadock, Benjamin J., 1933-    . II. Kaplan, Harold I., 1927-    . Modern synopsis of Comprehensive textbook of psychiatry/IV. III. Kaplan, Harold I., 1927-    . Study guide and self-examination review for Modern synopsis of Comprehensive textbook of psychiatry/III. IV. Title. V. Comprehensive textbook of Psychiatry/IV. [DNLM: 1. Mental Disorders—examination questions. 2. Psychiatry—examination questions. WM 100 K172m Suppl.]
  RC454.K36 1985      616.89′0076      84-26943
  ISBN 0-683-04508-3

88  89  90  91
10  9  8  7  6

*Dedicated to our wives,*
Nancy Barrett Kaplan
and
Virginia Alcott Sadock

# Preface

This is the second edition of the *Study Guide and Self-Examination Review for the Modern Synopsis of the Comprehensive Textbook of Psychiatry* to appear within 2 years. Significant changes have been made to improve this edition so that it further meets the needs of medical students, psychiatrists, neurologists, and other physicians who require a review of the behavioral sciences and psychiatry.

Among the new changes introduced in this edition are the following: The authors have added new questions, modified the previously included questions, and increased the total number of questions from 905 in the first edition to 1171 in this edition. Each chapter now begins with a brief overview that describes the material covered and refers the student to the area in the *Modern Synopsis* from which the questions are derived. All answers have been carefully researched and made more complete. Not only is the correct answer discussed, but each incorrect answer is carefully defined. A bibliography of review articles on the subject covered in each section has been added and an index has been included. Finally, certain phrases in the answers are italicized in order to emphasize the main idea encompassed by the question.

This book forms part of a tripartite effort by the editors to provide for both student and practitioner a thorough educational system to facilitate the learning of psychiatry.

At the head of this system is the *Comprehensive Textbook of Psychiatry*, which is global in depth and scope and is designed and used by psychiatrists, behavioral scientists, and all others in the mental health field. Next is the *Modern Synopsis of the Comprehensive Textbook of Psychiatry*, a shortened and highly modified version, especially helpful to medical students, psychiatric residents, and, for quick reference purposes, to the practicing psychiatrist. The *Study Guide and Self-Examination Review for the Modern Synopsis of the Comprehensive Textbook of Psychiatry*, consisting of multiple choice questions and answers derived from the *Modern Synopsis*, forms the last part of the triad.

The *Study Guide* will be especially useful for students preparing for certification examinations, such as the National Board of Medical Examiners (NBME), the American Board of Psychiatry and Neurology (ABPN), and the Federation Licensing Examination of the Commission on Foreign Medical Graduates (FLEX). It will also be useful to physicians who wish to update their general psychiatric knowledge or who wish to identify areas of weakness and areas of strength. The allocation of questions has been carefully weighted, with subjects of both clinical and theoretical importance taken into account.

To use this book most effectively, the student should attempt to answer each question in a particular chapter. By allowing about 1 minute to answer each question, the time constraints of an actual examination can be approximated. The answers should then be verified by referring to the corresponding answer section in each chapter. Careful reading of the answer will provide the student with more than enough data to understand how the question was formulated. The student can refer to the appropriate page in the *Modern Synopsis* for a more extensive and definitive discussion of the material. We wish to thank Robert J. Campbell, M.D. and his publishers for giving us permission to derive some of the definitions used in this text from his book—the fifth edition of the *Psychiatric Dictionary* published by Oxford University Press.

Several persons helped in the preparation of this book. Linda Didner Platt was especially helpful in the coordination of every aspect of production, Brian E. Shaw and Judy Rivera provided valuable literature research, and Anne Craig and her associates at Williams & Wilkins provided important editorial assistance.

Virginia A. Sadock, M.D., Associate Professor of Psychiatry and Director of Graduate Education in Human Sexuality, played a key role in planning and implementation. She made many contributions to this book, drawing upon her extensive experience as an educator and teacher of undergraduate, graduate, and postgraduate students in psychiatry. We are deeply appreciative of her outstanding help and assistance.

Peter Kaplan, M.D., Resident in Psychiatry at New York University Medical Center, assisted the authors throughout the project and was instrumental in the preparation and production of this book. He provided new material on the recent advances in psychiatry, particularly in the field of psychopharmacology, which is his area of expertise. He was especially helpful in the development of case history questions, and he ably represented the psychiatric residents' viewpoint.

Rebecca Jones, M.D., Fellow in Psychiatric Education at New York University Medical Center, helped to integrate the nomenclature of the American Psychiatric Association's *Diagnostic and Statistical Manual of Mental Disorders (DSM-III)* with the text and was most helpful throughout. We also wish to thank the following NYU medical students for their help in reviewing this book from the vantage point of the medical student: John Kanegaye, Louis Cornacchia, Laura Bernays, Nick Restifo, and Elizabeth Eden.

Finally, we should like to express our sincere gratitude to Robert Cancro, M.D., Professor of Psychiatry and Chairman of the Department of Psychiatry at New York University School of Medicine, for his continued support and encouragement for all of our projects.

# Contents

# 1

# The Life Cycle

Human behavior, the main concern of psychiatry, is an exceedingly complex process that reflects the interaction of many divergent variables. In fact, the specific determinants of normal and abnormal human behavior are not yet fully understood. During the past decade, concepts and theories of psychic functioning have undergone constant modification to accommodate the rapid accumulation of data derived from the behavioral sciences. Concurrently, it has become increasingly apparent that behavioral determinants operate on several levels and must be considered within a sociocultural and psychological frame of reference, as well as a physiological one.

Understanding the life cycle is essential to an understanding of psychiatry. *Homo sapiens* go through an extended cycle that begins with fertilization and pregnancy and continues on to birth, infancy, childhood, immaturity, maturity, old age, and death. Maturation goes through various phases, which start both physically and psychologically with enormous dependence on the parenting figure. The goal is toward increasing independence. Increasing physical and psychological maturation accompanies cognitive, emotional, and cultural development. Various theorists have studied these phases of maturation; foremost among them have been Sigmund Freud, Erik Erikson, Daniel Levinson, Theodore Lidz, and Jean Piaget.

In the *Study Guide*, as well as in *Modern Synopsis-IV*, the life cycle is divided into various periods of development called *stages*: infancy, toddler, preschool, juvenile, pre-adolescence, adolescence, young adulthood, mid-adulthood, and late adulthood.

Students should review Chapter 1, "The Life Cycle," in *Modern Synopsis-IV* and should then check their understanding of the subject by studying the following questions and answers.

# Questions

**DIRECTIONS:** Each of the statements or questions below is followed by five suggested responses or completions. Select the *one* that is *best* in each case.

**1.1.** According to Kübler-Ross, the dying person experiences five psychological stages before death. These stages include all of the following *except*

A. denial
B. anger
C. bargaining
D. depression
E. projection

**1.2.** The defense mechanisms that are used by the average 50-year-old man or woman include all of the following *except*

A. dissociation
B. repression
C. sublimation
D. altruism
E. splitting

**1.3.** Stranger anxiety and separation anxiety emerge at the age of

A. 2 months
B. 4 months
C. 6 months
D. 8 months
E. 10 months

**1.4.** The concept that each stage of the life cycle has characteristic tasks or challenges for a person and that those issues must be satisfactorily resolved in order for development to proceed smoothly is known as the

A. developmental level
B. individuation process
C. maturational state
D. epigenetic principle
E. psychosexual development

**1.5.** Infancy is said to end when a child is able to

A. creep
B. stand without assistance
C. control his or her anal sphincter completely
D. speak
E. climb stairs

**1.6.** Consistent and affectionate maternal behavior during infancy will provide the child with a continuing sense of

A. trust
B. autonomy
C. initiative
D. industry
E. identity

**1.7.** Competition for the exclusive possession of the parent of the opposite sex and rivalry with the same-sex parent are characteristic of the age period between

A. 1 and 3 years
B. 3 and 6 years
C. 6 and 10 years
D. 10 and 13 years
E. 13 and 18 years

**1.8.** Gender identity not only is clearly evident but also is firmly established by age

A. 1 year
B. 3 years
C. 5 years
D. 7 years
E. 9 years

**DIRECTIONS:** For each of the incomplete statements below, *one* or *more* of the completions given is correct. Choose answer:

A. if only **1, 2,** and **3** are correct
B. if only **1** and **3** are correct
C. if only **2** and **4** are correct
D. if only **4** is correct
E. if all are correct

**1.9.** The subphases for the separation-individuation process include

1. differentiation
2. practicing period
3. rapprochement
4. consolidation

**1.10.** Old age is frequently marked by

1. more problems for women than for men
2. the impact of the loss of reproductive capacity
3. the loss of positions of authority
4. more logical and abstract thinking

**1.11.** Which of the following statements about young adulthood are true:

1. It is the most poorly defined of all developmental periods.
2. The major task is establishing personal identity.
3. The most important decisions affecting one's life are made during this time.
4. The major defense mechanism used is altruism.

**1.12.** Normal adolescence is marked by which of the following events:

1. Dissolution of ties to parents
2. Episodes of depression
3. Occasional delinquent acts
4. Vulnerability to crisis

**1.13.**   Infants are born with which of the following reflexes:
1. Moro reflex
2. Rooting reflex
3. Babinski reflex
4. Exogenous smiling reflex

**1.14.**   Which of the following sensations can be differentiated by the infant:
1. Smell of bananas
2. Sour taste
3. Smell of rotten eggs
4. Sweet taste

**DIRECTIONS:** Each group of questions below consists of five lettered headings followed by a list of numbered words or statements. For each numbered word or statement, select the *one* lettered heading that is most closely associated with it. Each lettered heading may be selected once, more than once, or not at all.

### Questions 1.15–1.19
A. 4 weeks
B. 16 weeks
C. 28 weeks
D. 40 weeks
E. 12 months

**1.15.**   Grasping and manipulation

**1.16.**   Ocular control

**1.17.**   Verbalization of two or more words

**1.18.**   Standing with slight support

**1.19.**   Sitting alone

# Answers

# The Life Cycle

**1.1. The answer is E** (*Synopsis*, ed. 4, page 7).

The correct answer, *projection*, is not related to the five stages of Kübler-Ross and is the unconscious defense mechanism in which a person attributes to another the ideas, thoughts, feelings, and impulses that are part of his or her inner perceptions but are personally unacceptable. This defense mechanism is used in paranoid thinking.

According to Kübler-Ross, the dying person experiences five psychological stages before death: denial, anger, bargaining, depression, and acceptance. Those stages are not necessarily sequential, however, and a person may shift back and forth among the stages at any time.

*Denial*, the first stage of dying, is accompanied by refusal to believe that the patient is going to die or has a fatal illness. *Anger*, the second stage, is characterized by the patient venting feelings of frustration about death onto the family, friends, and physician. In the third stage, known as *bargaining*, the patient promises something, such as giving a donation to charity, in exchange for a respite from death or a change in the diagnosis of the illness. *Depression*, the fourth stage, ranges from feelings of sadness about events to acute suicidal impulses or attempts. In the fifth and last stage, called *acceptance*, the patient is able to deal with impending death.

**1.2. The answer is E** (*Synopsis*, ed. 4, page 7).

According to Melanie Klein, *splitting* is not a defense mechanism but is an ego mechanism in which the object is perceived as either all good or all bad; it is a mechanism used against ambivalent feelings toward the object. It is also used by children and by patients in borderline states.

A 50-year-old person is in mid-life, which is marked by the use of certain defense mechanisms. Specifically, the defenses that dominate during those years are dissociation, repression, sublimation, and altruism. Splitting is not one of these defenses.

*Dissociation* is an unconscious defense mechanism involving the segregation of any group of mental or behavioral processes from the rest of the person's psychic activity. It may entail the separation of an idea from its accompanying emotional tone, as seen in dissociative disorders. *Repression* is an unconscious defense mechanism in which unacceptable mental contents are banished or kept out of consciousness. A term introduced by Freud, it is important in both normal psychological development and in neurotic and psychotic symptom formation. *Sublimation* is an unconscious defense mechanism in which the energy associated with unacceptable impulses or drives is diverted into personally and socially acceptable channels. Unlike other defense mechanisms, sublimation offers some minimal gratification of the instinctual drive or impulse. *Altruism* is a regard for and dedication to the welfare of others. In psychiatry the term is closely linked with ethics and morals. Freud recognized altruism as the only basis for the development of community interest; Bleuler equated it with morality.

**1.3. The answer is D** (*Synopsis*, ed. 4, page 5).

The infant develops stranger anxiety and separation anxiety at *8 months* of age. *Separation anxiety* is excessive anxiety about separation from significant others, such as worries that harm will befall attachment figures if the subject is separated from them. *Stranger anxiety* occurs when the infant is separated from the natural caretaker and placed in the care of a new person.

**1.4. The answer is D** *Synopsis*, ed. 4, page 7).

Erik Erikson first described the *epigenetic principle*, a principle that maintains that each stage of the life cycle is characterized by events or crises that must be satisfactorily resolved in order for development to proceed smoothly. The epigenetic model states that if resolution is not achieved within a given life period, all subsequent stages will reflect that failure in the form of physical, cognitive, social, or emotional maladjustment.

*Developmental level* refers to the chronological age divisions from infancy to old age. *Individuation* is a Jungian term that refers to the process of the person developing a healthy, integrated, individual personality. *Maturation* is a general term that refers to the state of the person being fully developed biologically, psychologically, and socially. *Psychosexual development* refers to the psychic development of a person's sexuality throughout the life cycle. Freud defined its stages as oral, anal, phallic, latency, and genital.

**1.5.  The answer is D** (*Synopsis*, ed. 4, page 3).

Infancy is considered to end when the use of language develops. It refers to the period from birth until about 18 months of age. During the first month of life, the infant is termed a neonate or newborn. The child crawls at *40 weeks*, stands without assistance at *52 weeks*, develops meaningful speech and language at *15 months*, climbs stairs at *2 years*, and controls his or her anal sphincter completely at *3 years*. There are variations in these figures among different children.

**1.6.  The answer is A** (*Synopsis*, ed. 4, page 5).

According to Erikson, the development of what he termed *basic trust* is a result of consistent and affectionate maternal behavior during infancy. There is an extreme sensitivity to the mother; both the overt and the more subtle aspects of maternal behavior profoundly affect the infant. The dependency on others is total, a fact that has important psychological effects. *Autonomy* is a stage in which children gain the ability to control their muscles, their impulses, themselves, and ultimately their environment. *Initiative* provides the freedom and opportunity for children to begin motor-play gymnastics and intellectual questioning of those around them. During the period of *industry*, children learn to reason deductively in that they are concerned with the details of how things are made, how they work, and what they do. *Identity* is that stage when individuals develop a sense of who they are, where they have been, and where they are going. *Trust* extends through the first year of life, *autonomy* through the second and third years, *initiative* through the fifth year, and *identity* roughly through age 18.

**1.7.  The answer is B** (*Synopsis*, ed. 4, page 5).

The Oedipus complex develops between the ages of *3 and 6 years*. It is the constellation of feelings, impulses, and conflicts in the developing child that concern sexual impulses and attraction toward the opposite-sex parent and aggressive, hostile, or envious feelings toward the same-sex parent. Real or fantasied threats from the same-sex parent result in the repression of these feelings. The development of the Oedipus complex coincides with the phallic phase of psychosexual development. One of Freud's most important concepts, the term was originally applied only to males.

**1.8.  The answer is B** (*Synopsis*, ed. 4, page 5).

Gender identity is firmly established by age 2½ or 3. *Gender identity* is an inner sense of maleness or femaleness, as distinct from sexual identity, which is biologically determined. Cultural definitions of attitudes and behavior patterns associated with masculinity and femininity exert a developmental influence on gender identity. *Gender role* is the public declaration of gender identity; that is, the image of maleness or femaleness that the person presents to others. It may not coincide with gender identity. A *gender identity disorder* is a psychosexual disorder that causes the person to feel discomfort and inappropriateness about his or her anatomical sex. If the person's sex was wrongly determined before the age of 2½, as sometimes happens with ambiguous external genitalia, a gender identity disorder usually develops.

**1.9.  The answer is E (all)** (*Synopsis*, ed. 4, page 2).

Margaret Mahler described the separation-individuation process, resulting in a person's subjective sense of separateness from the surrounding environment. The separation-individuation phase of development begins in the fourth or fifth month of life and is completed by age 3.

Mahler delineates four subphases of the separation-individuation process: (1) *Differentiation*: the child is able to distinguish between self and other objects. (2) *Practicing period*: in the early phase, the child discovers his or her ability to physically separate from the mother by crawling and climbing, but still requires the mother's presence for security. The later phase is characterized by free, upright locomotion (7 to 10 months until 15 to 16 months). (3) *Rapprochement*: increased need and desire for the mother to share the child's new skills and experiences and a great need for the mother's love (16 until 25 months). (4) *Consolidation*: achievement of a definite individuality and attainment of a certain degree of object constancy (25 to 36 months).

**1.10.  The answer is B (1, 3)** (*Synopsis*, ed. 4, page 31).

A primary task of old age is the need to adapt to major losses, such as work, friends, or a spouse. Old age may present *special difficulties for women*, who are widowed longer than men, institutionalized more frequently, and usually poorer financially than men of the same age. For both sexes there is the *giving up of authority* and the questioning of competence, the reconciliations with significant others and with one's achievements and failures, and the resolution of grief over the death of others and of the approaching death of self.

Erikson described this period as a stage of *integrity versus despair*. Persons at this stage who can look back on their lives with satisfaction, who can pause to reflect on the past and take time to enjoy their grandchildren, manifest a sense of integrity. At the other end of the scale are those persons whose lives consist of a series of missed opportunities and mistakes that cannot be undone; they are filled with despair at the thought of what might have been.

Old age is also marked by the emergence of new issues. Many of these issues are related to the physical manifestations that accompany the aging process—a decline in physical health and reduced sensory acuity. Negative stereotypes about being old—held by society and the elderly themselves—are important aspects of this period. *Logical and abstract thinking processes are not affected* by old age and may vary from person to person. The *loss of reproductive capacity* in women who have already had children does not appear to have a major impact on their identity as they grow older.

**1.11.   The answer is B (1, 3)** (*Synopsis*, ed. 4, page 6).

*The most poorly defined of all developmental periods* is the period of young adulthood. It is a stage of life that extends from the early twenties until the early or middle thirties. This is the stage, characteristically, when *most of the important decisions are made* that will affect the remainder of one's life. These decisions include courtship and marriage, choice and entry into a job or profession, the establishment of enduring friendships, and a sacrifice of activities that were considered play. The major issue of this period that must be resolved is that of *intimacy*. Erikson identified the crisis of this period as being one of *intimacy versus isolation*. During this phase, the person must learn to share with and care about another person. If this goal is not accomplished, the person develops a sense of isolation and a feeling of being alone.

*Identity*, and the task of establishing personal identity—the sense of who a person is and where that person is going—usually develops between the ages of 12 to 18 years. *Altruism* is the regard for and dedication to the welfare of others. In psychiatry the term is closely linked with ethics and morals. Freud recognized altruism as the only basis for the development of community interest; it has also been equated with morality. It is more commonly used later in life than in young adulthood.

**1.12.   The answer is E (all)** (*Synopsis*, ed. 4, page 6).

Early adolescence (12 to 15 years) is marked by *increased anxiety and depression*, acting-out behavior, and *occasional delinquent acts*. Teenagers, for example, obtain about 300,000 legal abortions and give birth to about 600,000 babies per year. There is a diminution in sustained interest and creativity; there is also *dissolution of intense ties to siblings, parents, and parental surrogates*. Middle adolescence (14 to 18 years) is marked by efforts at mastering simple issues concerned with object relationships. The late adolescent phase (17 to 21 years)—which is marked by resolution of the separation-individuation tasks of adolescence—is characterized by *vulnerability to crisis*, particularly with respect to personal identity.

If adolescence does not proceed normally, a problem encountered may be an identity disorder. This disorder is characterized by a chaotic sense of self and a loss of the sense of personal sameness, usually involving a social role conflict as perceived by the actual person. Such conflict occurs when adolescents feel unwilling or unable to accept or adopt the roles they believe are expected of them by society. The identity disorder is often manifested by isolation, withdrawal, rebelliousness, negativism, and extremism.

**1.13.   The answer is A (1, 2, 3)** (*Synopsis*, ed. 4, page 3).

Infants are born with a number of reflexes, many of which were once needed for survival. Experts assume that the genes carry messages for those reflexes. Among the reflexes are the *Moro reflex*—flexion of the extremities when startled; the *rooting reflex*—turning toward the touch when the cheek is stroked; and the *Babinski reflex*—spreading of the toes with an upgoing big toe when the sole of the foot is stroked.

Infants are also born with an innate reflex pattern, endogenous smiling, which is unintentional and is unrelated to outside stimuli. *Exogenous smiling* occurs by the age of 16 weeks as a reaction to outside stimuli.

**1.14.   The answer is E (all)** (*Synopsis*, ed. 4, page 5).

Infants are able to differentiate among various sensations. Babies as young as 12 hours old gurgle with satisfaction when *sweet-tasting sugar water* is placed on the tongue, and they grimace at the *sour taste of lemon juice*. Infants smile at the *smell of bananas* and protest at the *smell of rotten eggs*. At 8 weeks of age, they can differentiate between the shapes of objects and colors. Stereoscopic vision begins to develop at 3 months of age.

**1.15–1.19.** **The answers are 1.15–C, 1.16–A, 1.17–E, 1.18–E, and 1.19–D** (*Synopsis*, ed. 4, page 5).

Most of the developmental landmarks are readily observed. Examples of some major developmental events and their approximate time of appearance are *ocular control*, 4 weeks; *balance*, 16 weeks; *grasping and manipulation*, 28 weeks; *sitting alone*, creeping, poking, and ability to say one word, 40 weeks; *standing with slight support*, cooperation in dressing, and *verbalization of two or more words*, 12 months; and use of words in phrases, 18 months. Growth is so rapid during infancy that developmental landmarks are measured in terms of weeks.

## References

Erikson E H: *Childhood and Society.* W W Norton, New York, 1950.

Levinson D J, Gooden W L: The life cycle. In *Comprehensive Textbook of Psychiatry*, ed 4, H I Kaplan, B J Sadock, editors, p 1. Williams & Wilkins, Baltimore, 1985.

Lidz T: *The Person: His and Her Development Throughout the Life Cycle.* International Universities Press, New York, 1983.

Neugarten B L, editor: *Middle Age and Aging: A Reader in Social Psychology.* University of Chicago Press, Chicago, 1968.

Sze W, editor: *The Human Life Cycle.* Jason Aronson, New York, 1975.

# 2

# Science of Human Behavior: Contributions of the Biological Sciences

If the physician is to transcend the role of clinical technician, some insight must be acquired about the nature of the contributions of the biological sciences to the basic determinants of behavior. Admittedly, much of the data derived from the basic behavioral sciences has yet to be effectively translated into psychiatric knowledge. Nevertheless, these data form the cornerstone of current research in psychiatry, which, in turn, will determine the future progress of this discipline.

It is important to be aware of the biological factors that are relevant to the understanding of behavior. In addition, basic concepts of psychopharmacology should be studied with specific reference to the clinical use of psychopharmacological agents. Genetic factors are crucial in understanding research and clinical practice. The interaction between genetic inheritance and environmental events is one of the most significant issues in psychiatry today.

This chapter of the *Study Guide* covers both genetics and the biological basis of psychopharmacology. Students should review Chapter 2 (Section 2.1, which covers genetics, and Section 2.2, which covers the basic science of psychopharmacology) in *Modern Synopsis-IV* and should then check and expand their understanding of the subject by studying the following questions and answers.

# Questions

**DIRECTIONS:** Each of the statements or questions below is followed by five suggested responses or completions. Select the *one* that is *best* in each case.

**2.1.** 5-Hydroxyindoleacetic acid (5-HIAA) is the chief metabolite of

A. melatonin
B. serotonin
C. histamine
D. tryptophan
E. tyramine

**2.2.** The over-all risk for developing schizophrenia in a person whose sibling is schizophrenic is about

A. 1 percent
B. 5 percent
C. 10 percent
D. 20 percent
E. 40 percent

**2.3.** In counseling two married schizophrenic patients who wish to have a child, the therapist would inform them that the risk of their offspring becoming schizophrenic is

A. 10 percent
B. 20 percent
C. 30 percent
D. 40 percent
E. 60 percent

**2.4.** Studies of monozygotic twins with all forms of affective disorders show a concordance rate of

A. 5 percent
B. 10 percent
C. 35 percent
D. 70 percent
E. 85 percent

**2.5.** The region of the brain with the highest concentration of dopamine is the

A. fornix
B. mammillary body
C. preoptic region
D. corpus striatum
E. hypothalamus

**2.6.** Enkephalin is a(n)

A. opiate-like peptide
B. tricyclic antidepressant
C. lithium salt
D. adrenergic agent
E. monoamine oxidase inhibitor (MAOI)

**2.7.** The dietary amino acid precursor of serotonin is

A. neurotensin
B. phenylalanine
C. tyramine
D. tryptophan
E. glycine

**2.8.** Neuroleptics are most effective for which of the following schizophrenic symptoms:

A. Hallucination
B. Poverty of speech
C. Affect disturbance
D. Intellectual performance
E. Negativism

**2.9.** Schizophrenia is thought to be genetically transmitted by which of the following mechanisms:

A. Autosomal dominant disorder
B. Autosomal recessive disorder
C. Sex-linked disorder
D. Genetic heterogeneity
E. None of the above

**2.10.** Psychedelic drugs most commonly produce

A. delusions
B. distortions of perception
C. loosening of associations
D. auditory hallucinations
E. word salad

**2.11.** Dopamine regulates which of the following substances:

A. Thyrotropin
B. Prolactin
C. Substance P
D. Norepinephrine
E. Bradykinin

**2.12.** In relatively high doses, the drug levodopa can cause which of the following syndromes:

A. Abnormal involuntary movements
B. Bronchoconstriction
C. Orthostatic hypotension
D. Carcinoma of the breast
E. Galactorrhea

**2.13.** A selective lesion in the hippocampus results in which of the following:

A. Loss of ability to form new memories
B. Psychic blindness, oral hyperactivity, hypersexuality, and hyperphagia
C. Involuntary movements, depression, and a sensation of *déjà vu*
D. Placidity and docility
E. Fear and rage

**2.14.** The pedigree chart shown on the facing page illustrates a particular type of genetic inheritance known as

A. dominant
B. Y-linked
C. X-linked
D. recessive
E. none of the above

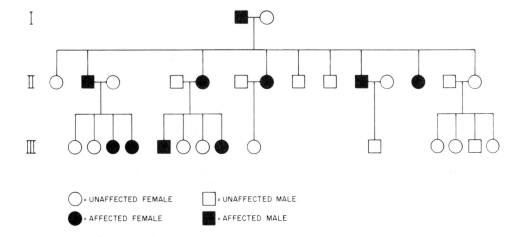

○ = UNAFFECTED FEMALE    □ = UNAFFECTED MALE

● = AFFECTED FEMALE    ■ = AFFECTED MALE

**DIRECTIONS:** For each of the incomplete statements below, *one* or *more* of the completions given is correct. Choose answer:

> A. if only **1**, **2**, and **3** are correct
> B. if only **1** and **3** are correct
> C. if only **2** and **4** are correct
> D. if only **4** is correct
> E. if all are correct

**2.15.** Twin studies in relation to the occurrence of schizophrenia have demonstrated

1. what is inherited
2. a higher concordance rate for monozygotic twins than for dizygotic twins of schizophrenic parents
3. the role of environmental factors
4. higher concordance rates in more severe types of schizophrenia than in less severe types

**2.16.** Bipolar (manic-depressive) disorders have which of the following characteristics, as compared with unipolar disorders:

1. Earlier age of onset
2. Higher risk in females
3. Better response to lithium treatment
4. Affected relatives may have both unipolar and bipolar disorders

**2.17.** The sex chromosomes are involved in which genetic disorders:

1. Klinefelter's syndrome
2. Alzheimer's disease
3. Turner's syndrome
4. Down's syndrome

**2.18.** Monoamine oxidase inhibitors (MAOI's) act by causing within the nerve terminals an accumulation of

1. norepinephrine
2. dopamine
3. serotonin
4. acetylcholine

**2.19.** $\beta$-Endorphin

1. is released during stressful stimuli
2. binds to lymphocytes
3. has an opiate-like action
4. is a pituitary hormone

**2.20.** The neurotransmitter dopamine plays an important role in which of the following disorders:

1. Parkinson's disease
2. Diabetes insipidus
3. Schizophrenia
4. Narcolepsy

**2.21.** Which of the following have been suggested as genetic markers for vulnerability to affective disorders:

1. Glucose-6-phosphate dehydrogenase (G6PD)
2. Color blindness
3. X-linked dominant factor
4. Monoamine oxidase

| Directions Summarized | | | | |
|:---:|:---:|:---:|:---:|:---:|
| A | B | C | D | E |
| 1, 2, 3 | 1, 3 | 2, 4 | 4 | All are |
| only | only | only | only | correct |

**2.22.** Huntington's disease is characterized by

1. an average age of onset in the mid-forties
2. an *in utero* screening test for the affected fetus
3. a 50 percent risk of inheriting the disease from an affected parent
4. a neurological test for a gene carrier

**2.23.** Which of the following statements apply to alcoholism:

1. Severe drinking problems are more common in sons of alcoholic parents.
2. Sons of alcoholic parents adopted away are less apt to become alcoholics.
3. Alcoholism is less common in women than in men.
4. Persons with the enzyme alcohol dehydrogenase are predisposed to drink more.

**2.24.** Androgen insensitivity syndrome is a term applied to individuals

1. with male (XY) chromosomal constitution
2. whose tissues do not respond to testosterone
3. who have the external genitalia of normal females
4. who consider themselves to be female

**2.25.** Male homosexuals

1. show no evidence of chromosomal abnormality
2. show monozygotic twin concordance for homosexuality
3. show no increase in homosexuality among dizygotic twins over general population statistics
4. are not causally influenced by parental rearing practices

**2.26.** Unipolar disorder has been associated with which of the following:

1. Early onset
2. Family history of depression
3. Alcoholism
4. Sociopathy

**2.27.** Parents of bipolar (manic-depressive) patients show a higher incidence of

1. bipolar disorder
2. unipolar disorder
3. schizoaffective disorder
4. schizophrenic disorder

**2.28.** Twin studies in affective disorders show that

1. unipolar twin pairs have a higher concordance rate than bipolar twin pairs
2. a bipolar twin may have a unipolar twin
3. bipolar probands have few or no unipolar relatives
4. unipolar symptoms may be a manifestation of the bipolar phenotype

**2.29.** Intelligence quotient (I.Q.) scores

1. show close correlation with genetic closeness in families
2. are similar among twins
3. are relatively stable into advanced years
4. are not affected by social deprivation

**2.30.** Both tricyclics and monoamine oxidase inhibitors (MAOI's)

1. facilitate synaptic action of norepinephrine
2. produce hypertension
3. act synergistically when given together
4. are not commonly used simultaneously by U.S. physicians

**2.31.** Phenothiazines

1. block dopamine receptors
2. exert an antiemetic effect
3. have anticholinergic effects
4. cause hypertension

**2.32.** Research into benzodiazepine receptors reveals that

1. benzodiazepines facilitate the synaptic action of $\gamma$-aminobutyric acid (GABA)
2. there are two types of benzodiazepine receptors
3. different benzodiazepines may compete for the same receptor site
4. sedating effects of benzodiazepines are unrelated to receptor site binding

**2.33.** Extrapyramidal effects of phenothiazines result from

1. a blockade of dopamine receptors
2. competition of phenothiazines with dopamine receptor sites
3. dopamine receptor supersensitivity
4. impaired dopamine system

**2.34.** Which of the following neurotransmitters are most common (up to 40 percent) at the synapses of the central nervous system:
1. Glycine
2. Norepinephrine
3. $\gamma$-Aminobutyric acid
4. Acetylcholine

**2.35.** The chief metabolites of norepinephrine are
1. normetanephrine and vanillymandelic acid (VMA)
2. homovanillic acid (HVA)
3. 3-methoxy-4-hydroxyphenylglycol (MHPG)
4. 5-hydroxyindoleacetic acid (5-HIAA)

**2.36.** Secretion of hormones, appetitive controls, autonomic responses, and control of emotions are under close regulation of which of the following centers of the brain:
1. Medulla oblongata
2. Limbic system
3. Cerebellum
4. Hypothalamus

**2.37.** 3-Methoxy-4-hydroxyphenylglycol (MHPG) is
1. the major metabolite of norepinephrine in the brain
2. formed from the action of monoamine oxidase on norepinephrine
3. measured to predict the response of patients to antidepressants
4. excreted in the urine

**2.38.** There is a cross-tolerance between alcohol and which of the following drugs:
1. Barbiturates
2. Meprobamate
3. Diazepam
4. Chlordiazepoxide

**2.39.** Tardive dyskinesia
1. involves a hypermotility of the facial muscles
2. follows prolonged phenothiazine treatment
3. may result from tricyclic antidepressant treatment
4. does not involve the extremities

# Answers

# Science of Human Behavior: Contributions of the Biological Sciences

**2.1. The answer is B** (*Synopsis*, ed. 4, page 24).

The chief metabolite formed from *serotonin* is 5-hydroxyindoleacetic acid (5-HIAA), although a limited amount is metabolized to the alcohol 5-hydroxytryptophol.

*Melatonin* is formed by the mammalian pineal gland and appears to depress gonadal function in mammals. *Histamine* is a neurotransmitter and depressor amine derived from histidine. It is a powerful stimulant of gastric secretion and a constrictor of bronchial smooth muscle. It acts as a vasodilator of capillaries and arterioles, and causes a fall in blood pressure as a result. *Tryptophan* is an amino acid precursor of serotonin and reduces sleep latency time. *Tyramine* is a sympathomimetic amine having an action in some respects resembling that of epinephrine. It is present in certain foods, such as ripe cheese, herring, and red wine. A patient receiving a monoamine oxidase inhibitor (MAOI) should avoid foods high in tyramine, because a hypertensive crisis may develop as a result of the interaction.

**2.2. The answer is C** (*Synopsis*, ed. 4, page 10).

A person whose sibling develops schizophrenia has an *over-all expectancy rate of 10 percent* for developing that illness, compared to about a 1 percent rate in the general population.

**2.3. The answer is D** (*Synopsis*, ed. 4, page 11).

The highest empirical risk of developing schizophrenia for offspring of two schizophrenic parents is *40 percent*. If one parent is schizophrenic, the risk is in the 10 to 15 percent range. Often, it is only the brother or sister of one of the couple who is ill; assurance can be given to the couple that the risk for their children is probably in the 2 to 3 percent range, not appreciably greater in absolute value than for the general population.

**2.4. The answer is D** (*Synopsis*, ed. 4, page 12).

Studies of twins with all forms of affective disorders indicate a concordance rate of about *70 percent* in monozygotic pairs. There is a greater risk in monozygotic twins than in dizygotic twins.

**2.5. The answer is D** (*Synopsis*, ed. 4, page 19).

The *corpus striatum* is part of the basal ganglia and is the area of the brain with the highest concentration of dopamine. The corpus striatum is made up of the caudate nucleus, putamen, and globus pallidus, which are large subcortical nuclear masses. Two types of diseases are associated with diseases of the corpus striatum: abnormal involuntary movements known as dyskinesias (akathisia, dystonia, and the parkinsonian syndrome) and disturbances of muscle tone, such as hypotonia or rigidity.

The *hypothalamus* is the region of the brain that is important in the coordination of behavior. Such behavior as feeding or aggression is related to hypothalamic stimulation. The *mammillary bodies*, the *preoptic region*, and the *fornix* are anatomical regions of the brain that send fibers to and from the hypothalamus.

**2.6. The answer is A** (*Synopsis*, ed. 4, pages 19 and 26).

Enkephalins are *opiate-like peptides* that are found in many parts of the brain and that bind to specific receptor sites. They are opiate-like because they decrease pain perception. They also serve as neurotransmitters.

*Adrenergic agents* are drugs that cause the liberation of norepinephrines. *Lithium* is a drug effective in the treatment of the manic phase of bipolar affective disorder and a mood-stabilizing drug when used chronically in bipolar disorder. It may also be an effective antidepressant in a subgroup of depressed patients.

The two major classes of antidepressant drugs are the monoamine oxidase inhibitors (MAOI's) and the tricyclic antidepressants. *MAOI's* comprise a group of agents that have widely varying chemical structures but that have in common the ability to inhibit monoamine oxidase. Inhibition of that enzyme results in an accumulation of the monoamines norepinephrine, dopamine, and serotonin within nerve terminals. At a certain point, the amines start leaking out into the synaptic cleft, so that the drugs facilitate the actions of all monoamines. The *tricyclic antidepressants* are potent inhibitors of the reuptake inactivation mechanism of catecholamine and serotonin neurons. The ability of those drugs to inhibit the reuptake process accounts for their antidepressant activity.

**2.7.   The answer is D** (*Synopsis*, ed. 4, pages 23 and 24).

*Tryptophan*, the dietary amino acid precursor of serotonin, is hydroxylated by the enzyme tryptophan hydroxylase to form 5-hydroxytryptophan. 5-Hydroxytryptophan is decarboxylated to serotonin. When parkinsonian patients are treated with L-dopa, dopamine is formed not only in dopamine neurons but also in serotonin neurons and may displace serotonin, so that dopamine becomes a false transmitter in brain serotonin neurons of those patients, with unknown consequences. Serotonin is destroyed by monoamine oxidase, which oxidatively deaminates it to the aldehyde, just as the enzyme does with the catecholamines.

*Neurotensin* is a neurotransmitter and an amino acid peptide that can lower blood pressure; it acts as an analgesic when injected directly into the brain. *Phenylalanine* is an amino acid in proteins that, when not present in infants, causes mental retardation. *Glycine* is an amino acid that also has been shown to be a neurotransmitter.

*Tyramine* is a sympathomimetic amine that has an action similar to epinephrine. It is present in ripe cheese, herring, and other foods.

**2.8.   The answer is A** (*Synopsis*, ed. 4, page 27).

Neuroleptics are most effective in the treatment of schizophrenia and in relieving the positive (more obvious) symptoms of schizophrenia, including *hallucinations*, delusions, and major thought disorders. They are much less effective in dealing with the negative (less obvious) symptoms of schizophrenia, such as *poverty of speech, affect disturbance, intellectual performance*, and *negativism*.

*Poverty of speech* is speech that is quantitatively adequate but qualitatively inadequate because it imparts minimal, vague, or repetitious information. Replies to questions are brief and unelaborated, and little or no unprompted additional information is provided. It occurs in major depression, schizophrenia, and organic mental disorders. *Negativism* is verbal or nonverbal opposition or resistance to outside suggestions and advice. It is commonly seen in catatonic schizophrenia in which the patient resists any effort to be moved or does the opposite of what is asked.

**2.9.   The answer is D** (*Synopsis*, ed. 4, page 9).

*Genetic heterogeneity* (different modes of inheritance for different subjects) is hypothesized as the mode of genetic transmission of schizophrenia. There is no good evidence to support any simple mono or multiple allele mode of inheritance. An example of an *autosomal dominant disorder* is Huntington's disease; an *autosomal recessive disorder* is phenylketonuria (PKU). Such disorders as hemophilia and night blindness are known to be *sex-linked*; that is, related to the X chromosome.

**2.10.   The answer is B** (*Synopsis*, ed. 4, page 28).

Psychedelic drugs rarely produce hallucinations but usually just elicit *distortions of perception*. The psychedelic drugs comprise a wide range of chemical structures that produce a strikingly similar set of profound subjective effects. Although the psychological effects of lysergic acid diethylamide (LSD) and mescaline were initally likened to a model schizophrenia, the symptoms elicited by LSD do not mimic schizophrenia well. For instance, psychedelic drugs produce primarily perceptual alterations in the visual sphere, but schizophrenic hallucinations are auditory.

*Delusion* is a false belief that is firmly held, despite objective and obvious contradictory proof or evidence and despite the fact that other members of the culture do not share the belief. *Loosening of associations* is a characteristic schizophrenic thinking or speech disturbance involving a disorder in the logical progression of thoughts, manifested as a failure to adequately verbally communicate. Unrelated and unconnected ideas shift from one subject to another. *Hallucinations* are false sensory perceptions occurring in the absence of any relevant external stimulation of the sensory modality involved. An *auditory hallucination* is a hallucination of sound. *Word salad* is an incoherent, essentially incomprehensible mixture of words and phrases commonly seen in far-advanced cases of schizophrenia.

**2.11.   The answer is B** (*Synopsis*, ed. 4, page 22).

*Prolactin*, the hormone that causes lactation, is produced by the anterior pituitary and is under close control of dopamine in the hypothalamus. Phenothiazines can cause lactation as a side effect. Other psychiatric disorders, such as amenorrhea associated with affective disorders, are accounted for by neurohumoral changes. Fluctuation in prolactin serum levels may be of some clinical help in assessing some drugs' effects on dopaminergic pathways.

*Thyrotropin* is a hormone produced by the anterior pituitary gland and is under the control of a negative-feedback system by thyroid hormone. Thyrotropin causes an increase in thyroid hormone synthesis. *Substance P,* next to enkephalin, is the most studied brain peptide. Its localization throughout the brain resembles that of neurotensin and enkephalin. Substance P is the sensory transmitter of pain. The blockade of its release in the spinal cord by opiates may account in part for analgesia, at least as mediated at the spinal cord level. *Norepinephrine* (NE) is synthesized by the conversion of dopamine, using the enzyme dopamine B-hydroxylase (DBH), an enzyme that is present in NE specific vesicles at the synaptic clefts of the neurons. *Bradykinin* was first discovered in the plasma, although it probably serves functions in the intestine as well as the brain. Bradykinin is the most potent pain-producing substance known.

**2.12.   The answer is A** (*Synopsis,* ed. 4, page 22).

In high doses levodopa (L-dopa) can produce a tardive dyskinesia-like syndrome with *abnormal involuntary movements.* This is thought to be caused by L-dopa's dopaminergic agonistic activity.

*Bronchoconstriction* is controlled by $B_2$-receptors and is not associated with L-dopa, but does occur with adrenergic blocking agents, such as propranolol. There are many agents that cause orthostatic hypertension. L-Dopa has no such activity. Any drug that interferes with adrenergic neuronal function, such as clonidine, is capable of producing *orthostatic hypotensive* effects. Some drugs are associated with an increased risk of *carcinoma of the breast,* but L-dopa does not seem to be one of these agents. Reserpine has been reported to increase approximately 3-fold the incidence of breast cancer. *Galactorrhea* is a continued discharge of milk from the breasts after the child has been weaned. It is a rare side effect of phenothiazines.

**2.13.   The answer is A** (*Synopsis,* ed. 4, page 21, 157, 165, and 780).

Lesions of the hippocampus interfere with encoding memory; that is, the *ability to make new memories.*

Bilateral temporal lobe destruction, involving total ablation of the amygdaloid complex and destruction of major sections of the hippocampus, produces the Klüver-Bucy syndrome. The syndrome includes the following changes in behavior: (1) hypermetamorphosis, in which the patient demonstrates an inability to ignore stimuli and explores all objects regardless of their novelty; (2) *psychic blindness,* in which vision is physically intact but there is inability to discriminate between objects in a meaningful fashion, such as food and a menacing animal; (3) *oral hyperactivity,* in which compulsive licking, biting, and examination of all objects by mouth occurs; (4) placidity and docility, in which there is no evidence of fear or anger reactions; (5) altered sexual behavior, such as *hypersexuality,* is manifest without regard to gender or species of partner; and (6) altered dietary habits, in which *hyperphagia* is seen. The Klüver-Bucy syndrome is rare in humans, but has been produced experimentally in monkeys. Uncinate fits are a constellation of changes seen in temporal lobe epilepsy that arise from involvement of the uncus. They are characterized by olfactory aura, *involuntary movements,* and sensations of *déjà vu* and may resemble the changes of behavior seen in schizophrenia. Fear, rage, and depression may also occur. It has been reported that such changes can be produced by electrical stimulation of limbic structures. *Placidity and docility* can be produced by lesioning both amygdalae. *Fear and rage* can be produced by a lesion in the ventromedial hypothalamic nuclei.

**2.14.   The answer is A** (*Synopsis,* ed. 4, page 14).

The *dominant* mode of inheritance, in which each child of an affected parent has a 50 percent chance of receiving a particular gene, is illustrated. The pedigree chart is of a family affected by Huntington's disease.

In *sex-linked inheritance,* a gene is located on a sex chromosome, *Y-linked* or *X-linked* but usually on the X chromosome. *Recessive* inheritance requires that a pair of genes consist of both genes of one type (homozygosity) for a trait to be apparent. If one of the pair is dominant, the recessive gene's effect will not be apparent.

**2.15.   The answer is C (2, 4)** (*Synopsis,* ed. 4, page 10).

Twin studies have not given definitive answers to *what is inherited,* how it is inherited, and *what the significant environmental factors are.* Nevertheless when their data are combined with the data of other research designs, they have been useful for their contribution to the search for genetic markers. *Monozygotic* rates for schizophrenia are significantly higher than the *dizygotic* rates, and they are *higher for the co-twins of more seriously ill patients* than for co-twins of patients with milder cases.

**2.16.   The answer is E (all)** (*Synopsis,* ed. 4, page 12).

Bipolar disorders are more common in females, who have a *higher risk* in most surveys, as do relatives of probands with early onset and a preponderance of manic symptoms. Cases with *early age onset* appear to have a higher genetic risk, and they also seem to show a *better response to lithium treatment.* It has also been noted that the *affected relatives of bipolar patients are both unipolar and bipolar* in type, whereas affected relatives of unipolar patients are only of the recurrent unipolar depression variety.

**2.17. The answer is B (1, 3)** (*Synopsis*, ed. 4, pages 16 and 17).

*Klinefelter's syndrome* is marked by the presence of an extra X sex chromosome, so that there is an XXY karyotype. The syndrome is occasionally marked by various degrees of weak libido, mental subnormality, and nonspecific personality disorders, ranging from inadequate personality to schizophrenic-like behavior. The XXY karyotype occurs as frequently as 2 to 3 per 1000 male newborns.

*Turner's syndrome* is usually marked by the absence of the second sex chromosome, leaving 45 chromosomes—instead of the normal 46—with a single X gene. Turner's syndrome is represented by females with various physical symptoms, such as short stature, webbing of the neck (lymphedema) shield-like chest, and streaked gonads with primary amenorrhea. Sexual immaturity and body defects do not seem to result in any emotional disturbance; in fact, these girls and women have been described as resilient to adversity, stable in personality, and maternal in temperament. Turner's syndrome is comparatively rare in living infants—about 1 in 2500—although the karyotype is frequent in abortions.

*Down's syndrome* is a form of mental retardation caused by a chromosomal abnormality (trisomy 21), formerly referred to as mongolism. *Alzheimer's disease* is a chronic organic mental disorder of unknown cause characterized by progressive mental deterioration with diffuse cerebral atrophy. In DSM-III, it is called primary degenerative dementia.

**2.18. The answer is A (1, 2, 3)** (*Synopsis*, ed. 4, pages 25 and 26).

Monoamine oxidase inhibitors (MAOI's) comprise a group of agents that have widely varying chemical structures but that have in common the ability to inhibit the enzyme monoamine oxidase. Monoamine oxidase deaminates naturally occurring catecholamines, such as *norepinephrine, dopamine,* and *serotonin.* Inhibition of that enzyme results in an accumulation of the monoamines (catecholamines) norepinephrine, dopamine, and serotonin within nerve terminals. At a certain point, the amines start leaking out into the synaptic cleft, so that the drugs facilitate the actions of all monoamines.

It is felt that many depressions are associated with an absolute or relative deficiency of catecholamines, particularly norepinephrine, at functionally important receptor sites in the brain. MAOI's are thus employed as antidepressants in that they raise the level of catecholamines.

*Dopamine* is also a catecholamine neurotransmitter, which is the precursor of norepinephrine, and is itself synthesized by the decarboxylation of dopa. It is hypothesized that the specific behavioral symptoms of schizophrenia are related to a functional excess of structurally normal dopamine.

*Norepinephrine* is a catecholamine neurotransmitter substance liberated by adrenergic postganglionic neurons of the sympathetic nervous system. It is the precursor of epinephrine and is present in the adrenal medulla. It is also found in many areas of the brain. A disturbance in its metabolism at important brain sites has been proposed as an important factor in the causation of affective disorders.

*Serotonin* is 5-hydroxytryptamine (5-HT), an endogenous indolamine synthesized from dietary tryptophan and found in the gastrointestinal tract, the platelets, and the central nervous system. There is compelling evidence that this monoamine serves as a neurotransmitter substance in the central nervous system. It may play an important role in such diverse functions as sleep, sexual behavior, aggressiveness, motor activity, perception (particularly pain), and mood. Dysfunction in central serotonergic systems has been proposed as a cause or factor in various mental disorders, including schizophrenia and the affective disorders.

*Acetylcholine* is believed to be the sole mediator at autonomic synapses and in the transmission of the nerve impulse from motor nerve to skeletal muscle. It had been suggested that acetylcholine was also the sole mediator for central synaptic transmission, but more recent work suggests that serotonin and norepinephrine are more likely the central synaptic neurotransmitters.

**2.19. The answer is E (all)** (*Synopsis*, ed. 4, pages 19 and 20).

β-Endorphins are endogenous morphine-like substances that occur naturally in the brain or *pituitary* and mimic the effects of *opiates.* They are assumed to be neurotransmitters or neuromodulators and are believed to be involved in the mechanisms of pain perception. Several different endorphins have been discovered, among them the enkephalins. Some researchers believe that a certain level of functioning endorphins is necessary for psychological homeostasis; they believe that both mental disorder and addiction may represent some abnormality in endorphins or their metabolism or may represent some abnormality in the brain receptors that would ordinarily respond to them.

β-Endorphin is *released during stress stimuli* together with adrenocorticotropic hormone (ACTH). It is not clear whether the peripheral target organ of β-endorphin, like ACTH, is the adrenal cortex. High affinity binding sites for β-endorphin not responding to opiate drugs have been identified on *lymphocytes*. Indeed, it is probable that the opiate-like action of β-endorphin is an epiphenomenon and that the physiological role of β-endorphin as a pituitary hormone is not related to any opiate-like effects.

**2.20.   The answer is B (1, 3)** (*Synopsis*, ed. 4, pages 22 and 26).

Dopamine is implicated in both Parkinson's disease and schizophrenia. *Schizophrenia* is a disorder associated with excessive functional levels of dopamine in the central nervous system. It has been observed that phenothiazines and butyrophenones alleviate schizophrenic symptoms by blocking dopamine receptors, thus decreasing the effects of dopamine.

Schizophrenia is a mental disorder characterized by disturbances in thinking, mood, and behavior. The thinking disturbance is manifested by a distortion of reality, sometimes with delusions and hallucinations, accompanied by a fragmentation of associations that results in characteristic disturbances of speech. The mood disturbance includes ambivalence and inappropriate or constricted affective responses. The behavior disturbance may be manifested by apathetic withdrawal or bizarre activity.

*Parkinson's disease* is marked by extrapyramidal dyskinesia characterized by resting tremor, rigidity, bradykinesia, and postural abnormalities. Primary parkinsonism—also called paralysis agitans, Parkinson's disease, and idiopathic parkinsonism—is a disorder of middle or late life, typically with a gradual progression and a prolonged course. Its cause is unknown. A parkinsonian syndrome may develop during the course of therapy with antipsychotic phenothiazine or butyrophenone drugs. There are several discrete dopamine pathways that degenerate in Parkinson's disease, accounting for major symptoms of the condition. Restoration of the depleted dopamine by treatment with its amino acid precursor dihydroxy-L-phenylalanine (L-dopa) greatly alleviates the symptoms of Parkinson's disease.

*Diabetes insipidus* is not a behavioral syndrome. It is marked by the chronic excretion of very large amounts of pale urine of low specific gravity, accompanied by extreme thirst; it ordinarily results from inadequate output of pituitary antidiuretic hormone, although it may be mimicked as a result of excessive fluid intake in emotionally disturbed individuals.

*Narcolepsy* is a sleep disorder characterized by recurrent, brief, uncontrollable episodes of sleep.

**2.21.   The answer is A (1, 2, 3)** (*Synopsis*, ed. 4, page 13).

In a number of studies, evidence for linkage of bipolar illness with *color-blindness* loci on the *G6PD* locus has been found.

Stemming from the observation that affective disorder is more common in women, there have been attempts to establish a locus on the X chromosome for a gene transmitted as an *X-linked dominant factor*; such a pattern would preclude father-to-son transmission. Because such transmission does occur, presumably in the absence of assortative mating, there must clearly be families in which the X-linked pattern does not obtain.

No definitive genetic markers for vulnerability to affective disorders have been currently identified, although a recent report suggests increased cholinergic receptor (binding site) activity in fibroblasts taken from the skin of patients and ill relatives.

*Monoamine oxidase* activity in blood platelets has been shown to be low in some schizophrenics and their relatives.

**2.22.   The answer is B (1, 3)** (*Synopsis*, ed. 4, page 14).

Huntington's disease is a classical example of a dominantly inherited disease with neurological and psychiatric symptoms and a variable age of onset. Although some cases appear in early adulthood or in late middle life, the *mid-forties is the average age of onset*. Unless a parent has died young, there will be a family history in the direct line, and each child of an affected parent will have a *50 percent risk of inheriting the gene*. Naturally, the older the children in question are without becoming ill, the lower their remaining risk becomes. Nevertheless, with *no reliable biochemical or neurological test available in the preclinical stages* for gene carriers, such persons may have to decide on marriage and parenthood while they are still in doubt as to their own status. Huntington's disease is one of the conditions for which linkage with DNA fragment polymorphisms is being sought. There is *no in utero screening test* available through amniocentesis.

**2.23.   The answer is B (1, 3)** (*Synopsis*, ed. 4, page 13).

Alcoholism is influenced by both heredity and environment. Some data suggest an overlap of depression and alcoholism in daughters raised by their own alcoholic parents, and other data suggest a possible spectrum, with early onset depression in women and increase in alcoholism and sociopathy without depression in male first-degree relatives. *Severe drinking problems are more common in sons of alcoholic parents than in controls, even when both groups were separated from their biological parents early in life. Sons are no more apt to become alcoholic if reared by their alcoholic parents than if adopted away. Alcoholism is much less common in women*, a fact that is reflected in the comparatively lower rates for daughters of alcoholic parents.

Aside from the cultural influences, alcoholism may be determined by metabolic differences. An atypical form of alcohol dehydrogenase (an enzyme normally present in all persons that reduces alcohols to aldehydes), as found in many Japanese persons, may cause flushing after ingestion of alcohol. Possibly, *this atypical form may make such a person drink less.*

**2.24.   The answer is E (all)** (*Synopsis*, ed. 4, page 15).

Individuals with androgen insensitivity syndrome *have a male (XY) chromosomal constitution whose tissues do not respond to testosterone.* This may be due to the absence of cellular receptors for testosterone or to a deficiency of 5-$\alpha$-reductase, an enzyme that converts testosterone to its active form. They *have the external genitalia and appearance of normal females*, are usually raised as girls, and *consider themselves to be female.* Conversely, females (XX) with adrenogenital syndrome are influenced by fetal androgens, so that their genitalia are masculinized. They often exhibit tomboyish, although not homosexual, behavior.

**2.25.   The answer is A (1, 2, 3)** (*Synopsis*, ed. 4, page 15).

*Chromosomal abnormalities are not found in male homosexuals. Twin studies showed monozygotic twin concordance rates, with dizygotic co-twins showing no increase over general population statistics.* These studies were interpreted as suggesting a gene-controlled disarrangement in psychosexual maturation patterns. Homosexuality would be part of the personality structure, rather than physically determined in this formulation. An ability to perceive and respond to sexual stimuli, to recognize satisfaction and success in heterosexual performance, and to use those experiences as integrating forces may be crucial to sexual role development. Vulnerability factors in these areas *may influence sexual choice, which is then reinforced accidentally or by family* or social surrounding. A few monozygotic twin pairs discordant for homosexual behavior also showed important intrapair similar-

ities, principally in psychological test findings that indicated sexual and body-image confusion.

Recent evidence has shown that, when given a challenge dose of progesterone, some homosexual men have a greater decrease in testosterone than a control group of heterosexual men.

**2.26.   The answer is E (all)** (*Synopsis*, ed. 4, page 12).

In some cases, unipolar illness has been associated with *early onset* and a *family history of depression, alcoholism*, and *sociopathy*. It has been described as more common in women. Sometimes the depression may manifest itself in the form of alcoholism, especially in males. When the patient stops drinking, a depressive clinical picture may develop weeks, months, or even years after total abstinence.

**2.27.   The answer is A (1, 2, 3)** (*Synopsis*, ed. 4, page 12).

Adult bipolar probands who had been adopted early in life show an increased incidence of affective disorder—*bipolar, unipolar, and schizoaffective*—equal to that shown in biological parents of bipolar nonadoptees. Their incidence of affective disorder is also higher than in their own adoptive parents or in control groups consisting of biological and adoptive parents of normal adoptees.

The parents of bipolar patients did not show a higher incidence of *schizophrenic disorder.*

**2.28.   The answer in C (2, 4)** (*Synopsis*, ed. 4, page 11).

Twin studies of affective disorders found that twins were either both *unipolar* or both *bipolar.* Bipolar monozygotic pairs had a *higher concordance rate* (about 70 percent) than unipolar pairs (45 percent). Some bipolar twins, however, had *unipolar co-twins*, which coincided with many family studies where *bipolar probands had an excess of unipolar relatives.* These observations have prompted investigators to consider that unipolar symptoms may sometimes be a manifestation of the *bipolar phenotype*, with the manic symptoms not expressed.

**2.29.   The answer is A (1, 2, 3)** (*Synopsis*, ed. 4, page 14).

Intelligence quotients (I.Q.) scores show remarkable *correlation with genetic closeness* within families. Other findings regarding the role of genetics in intelligence are the *similarity of performance I.Q. in twin pairs; the stability of similarities in twins' I.Q., even into advanced years*; and the possibility of gene linkages or biological associations.

I.Q. scores are lower in *socially deprived* children from low socioeconomic groups.

### 2.30. The answer is E (all) (*Synopsis,* ed. 4, page 26).

Both the tricyclic antidepressants and the monoamine oxidase inhibitors (MAOI's) *facilitate synaptic actions of norepinephrine* in the sympathetic system. This action can give rise to major side effects associated with enhanced sympathetic function. In some patients these drugs *produced marked hypertension.* Because the two classes of drugs facilitate norepinephrine effects in different ways, they enhance the activities of each other in a *synergistic fashion.* Severe, even fatal, hypertensive crises have occurred in patients treated simultaneously with MAOI's and tricyclic antidepressant drugs. *In the United States, caution is used in prescribing these two classes of drugs simultaneously,* although in Europe they are commonly prescribed with apparently few side effects.

### 2.31. The answer is A (1, 2, 3) (*Synopsis,* ed. 4, page 26).

The phenothiazines *block dopamine receptors,* and this mechanism may lead to extrapyramidal side effects, such as a parkinsonian syndrome and dyskinesias. In addition, they produce several other clinical effects, which vary among the drugs. Phenothiazines elicit postural hypotension, and some drugs are quite sedating. Most phenothiazines exert an *antiemetic effect* by acting directly on the chemoreceptor trigger zone in the brain stem. Many of the side effects of the phenothiazines are due to their *anticholinergic effects.* Anticholinergic effects include dry mouth, blurred vision, constipation, urinary retention, delayed ejaculation, and cutaneous flushing. They *do not cause* the side effect of *hypertension.*

### 2.32. The answer is A (1, 2, 3) (*Synopsis,* ed. 4, page 29).

Research into benzodiazepine receptors has demonstrated that there are *two types of receptors called type I and type II.* The type I receptors are postsynaptic, and the type II receptors are presynaptic. The most widely employed therapeutic benzodiazepines do not differ markedly in their effects on type I and type II receptors, but they *may compete for the same receptor site.* The relative potencies of benzodiazepines in competing for binding sites parallel closely their pharmacological activity. In addition, the *sedating effects of benzodiazepines are related to receptor site binding.* The benzodiazepines *facilitate the synaptic action of $\gamma$-aminobutyric acid* (GABA), which is an inhibitory neurotransmitter.

### 2.33. The answer is E (all) (*Synopsis,* ed. 4, page 26).

The extrapyramidal side effects of phenothiazine drugs result from their capacity to *blockade dopamine receptors* in the corpus striatum, the area of the brain with highest concentration of dopamine. In response to this blockade, the dopamine system may overcompensate, and a functional excess of dopamine may occur. The phenothiazines also have a molecular configuration similar to dopamine and *compete with dopamine at dopamine binding sites.* After prolonged phenothiazine use, the dopamine receptor site may become *supersensitive to dopamine or may degenerate.* In either case there is an *impaired dopamine system,* and the extrapyramidal symptoms that resemble Parkinson's disease develop. In Parkinson's disease there is a deficiency of dopamine presumed to result from the degeneration of dopamine neurons in the corpus striatum. Treatment involves the use of the exogenous dopamine precursor levodopa.

### 2.34. The answer is B (1, 3) (*Synopsis,* ed. 4, page 19).

The major neurotransmitters in the central nervous system (CNS) are glycine and $\gamma$-aminobutyric acid (GABA). In various brain regions, *GABA* probably accounts for transmission at between 25 and 40 percent of synapses. GABA inhibits the firing of neurons and is, therefore, a major inhibitory transmitter. In the spinal cord and brain stem, the amino acid *glycine,* in addition to its other metabolic functions, seems to be a prominent inhibitory transmitter at about the same percentage (25 to 40 percent) of synapses as GABA. *Norepinephrine* and *acetylcholine* account for only a small percentage of synaptic transmission in the CNS.

### 2.35. The answer is B (1, 3) (*Synopsis,* ed. 4, page 23).

The primary metabolites of norepinephrine (NE) are *normetanephrine, vanillylmandelic acid* (VMA), and *3-methoxy-4-hydroxyphenylglycol* (MHPG). These metabolites are produced using two enzymes, monoamine oxidase (MAO) and catechol-*O*-methyltransferase (COMT). These products of NE breakdown leave the cerebrospinal fluid (CSF) and are excreted in the urine.

There are a number of assays that are of clinical interest. In particular, one looks at MHPG level as an indicator of NE turnover, which appears to correlate to clinical stages of certain affective disorders.

*Homovanillic acid* (HVA) is one of three breakdown products of dopamine. Also produced in smaller quantities are 3,4-dihydroxyphenylacetic acid (DOPAC) and VMA. These byproducts exit from the central nervous system and may be blocked by the preadministration of probenecid (a benzoic acid derivative used in the treatment of gout and to increase serum concentrations of penicillin), which will result in CSF levels being a good index of dopamine turnover.

*5-Hydroxyindoleacetic acid* (5-HIAA) is the major metabolite of serotonin (5-HT). 5-HIAA is a breakdown product of 5-HT by the enzyme MAO, resulting in the production of this metabolite. The CSF levels following preadministration with probenecid is a clinically useful measure of serotonin metabolism.

**2.36.   The answer is C (2, 4)** (*Synopsis*, ed. 4, page 21).
The *limbic system* and *hypothalamus* are associated with appetitive drives, autonomic nervous system modulation, control of emotions (i.e. anger), secretion of hormones, and memory. The medulla oblongata and the cerebellum are not associated with those functions.

The *medulla oblongata* has a number of ascending and descending spinal pathways and is the primitive center of the brain stem that regulates vital functions, such as respiration and facial nerve nuclei. The *cerebellum*, which is part of the brain stem, is structurally similar to the cerebrum in that it has a cortex of gray matter and an interior of both white matter and nuclei. Its major functions are involved in movement and coordination.

**2.37.   The answer is E (all)** (*Synopsis*, ed. 4, page 23).
3-Methoxy-4-hydroxyphenylglycol (MHPG) is the *major metabolite of norepinephrine in the brain.* It is formed from the action of *monoamine oxidase on norepinephrine.* MHPG can diffuse from the brain to the general circulation and is *excreted in the urine.* Urinary MHPG is used as a *biochemical measure of depression.* Low urinary MHPG excretion is believed to represent decreased central norepinephrine activity, a state associated with clinical depression.

**2.38.   The answer is E (all)** (*Synopsis*, ed. 4, page 29).
Pharmacologically, there is considerable cross-dependence and cross-tolerance among such drugs as *alcohol, barbiturates, meproba-* *mate, chlordiazepoxide,* and *diazepam.* Cross-dependence and cross-tolerance are defined as the ability of one drug to suppress the manifestations of physical dependence produced by another and to maintain the physically dependent state. This suppression may be partial or complete. The withdrawal symptoms (which are the symptomatic expression of physical dependence), are similar and include insomnia, tremulousness, anxiety, convulsions, and a confusional psychosis associated with delusions and hallucinations. One can relieve withdrawal symptoms from one drug by the administration of any of the others. For instance, diazepam is highly effective in treating the symptoms of delirium tremens or of barbiturate withdrawal.

**2.39.   The answer is A (1, 2, 3)** (*Synopsis*, ed. 4, page 27).
Tardive dyskinesia is a late-appearing extrapyramidal syndrome associated with antipsychotic drug use. It consists of slow, rhythmical, automatic, stereotyped movements in one or more muscle groups *anywhere in the body.* It is most often characterized by repetitive *involuntary movements of the tongue, lips, and mouth* (buccolingual masticatory dyskinesia [BLM syndrome]). In younger patients in particular, choreoathetoid movements of the trunk and limbs are also a part of the clinical picture. The mechanism of neuroleptic-induced dyskinesias appears to be related to a defect in the dopamine system secondary to prolonged phenothiazine use. Even though tardive dyskinesia *follows prolonged phenothiazine use,* use of a different phenothiazine or the same phenothiazine in increased dosage and butyrophenones may relieve the associated symptoms. Because phenothiazines and butyrophenones appear to block dopamine receptors, this outcome seems to suggest that the mechanism responsible for tardive dyskinesia is an overcompensation of dopamine systems to the dopamine receptor blockade. It appears that after prolonged exposure to phenothiazines, dopamine receptors may become supersensitive to the effects of dopamine. Although neuroleptic agents may be the most likely drugs to be associated with the syndrome, it is known to be *induced also by the tricyclic antidepressants.*

## References

Gottesman I I, Shields J: *Schizophrenia and Genetics: A Twin Study Vantage Point.* Academic Press, New York, 1972.

Klein D F, Gittelman R, Quitkin F, Rifkin A: *Diagnosis and Drug Treatment of Psychiatric Disorders.* Williams & Wilkins, Baltimore, 1980.

President's Commission for the Study of Ethical Problems in Medicine and Biomedical and Behavioral Research: *Screening and Counseling for Genetic Conditions.* US Government Printing Office, Washington DC, 1983.

Rainer J D: Genetics and psychiatry. In *Comprehensive Textbook of Psychiatry,* ed 4. H I Kaplan, B J Sadock, editors, p 25. Williams & Wilkins, Baltimore, 1985.

Snyder S H: Basic Science of psychopharmacology. In *Comprehensive Textbook of Psychiatry,* ed 4, H I Kaplan, B J Sadock, editors, p 42. Williams & Wilkins, Baltimore, 1985.

# 3

# Science of Human Behavior: Contributions of the Psychological Sciences

The psychological sciences are fundamental to an understanding of human behavior and psychiatry. Perception and cognition are normal psychological phenomena that are affected in all forms of emotional disorders. In schizophrenia, for example, disturbances of perception are essential features of the syndrome. The concepts of Jean Piaget are crucial to a knowledge of cognitive development, and the interaction between cognitive function and the emotions is basic to an understanding of mental illness. Psychological learning theory has been applied most successfully in the treatment of emotional disorders, many of which result from faulty or impaired learning. Cognitive therapy, behavioral therapy, and biofeedback are examples of therapies based on learning theory. Ethology is discussed because of the relevance of data about animal behavior to an understanding of human behavior; especially relevant are developmental theories, which are intrinsic to the study of child psychiatry.

This chapter covers the topics discussed above, and the reader should refer to Chapter 3, "Contributions of the Psychological Sciences," in *Modern Synopsis-IV*. In particular, Section 3.1 on perception and cognition, Section 3.2 on Jean Piaget, Section 3.3 on learning theory, and Section 3.4 on ethology are relevant for an in-depth understanding of this area. Studying the questions and answers that follow will enable students to assess their knowledge of these subjects.

# Questions

**DIRECTIONS:** Each of the statements or questions below is followed by five suggested responses or completions. Select the *one* that is *best* in each case.

**3.1.** According to Piaget, an important process that develops during the concrete operational stage is the

A. ability to reason about reasoning or thinking
B. ability to make and follow rules
C. ability to distinguish between the ideal self and real self
D. use of phenomenological causality as a mode of thinking
E. attainment of object permanence

**3.2.** What is the final stage of Piaget's description of cognitive development:

A. Formal operational
B. Concrete operational
C. Sensorimotor
D. Epigenesis
E. Preoperational

**3.3.** The following are all examples of instrumental conditioning *except*

A. primary reward conditioning
B. escape conditioning
C. avoidance conditioning
D. secondary reward conditioning
E. classical conditioning

**3.4.** The concept of operant conditioning was developed by

A. William James
B. Hans Selye
C. O. Hobart Mowrer
D. Bhurrus F. Skinner
E. Neal Miller

**3.5.** The best-known projective test in psychiatry to determine an individual's personality in terms of his or her perceptual predisposition is the

A. Rorschach Test
B. Minnesota Multiphasic Personality Inventory
C. California Personality Inventory
D. Draw-A-Person Test
E. Stanford-Binet

**3.6.** Which of the following statements best describes the long-term effects of 6 months of total social isolation in monkeys:

A. They are able to make a remarkable social adjustment through the development of play.
B. They assume postures that are bizarre and schizoid.
C. They rarely exhibit aggression against age-mates who are more physically adept.
D. They are both abnormally aggressive and abnormally fearful.
E. There is a total unresponsiveness to the new physical and social world with which they are presented.

**3.7.** The figures below depict an experiment that interferes with the normal social interaction among monkeys. *A* and *B* represent, respectively, the two stages that occur in sequence when the infant is separated from the mother as illustrated. They are

A. yearning and resolution
B. despair and acceptance
C. protest and despair
D. conflict and resolution
E. none of the above

A

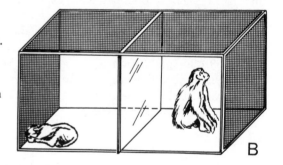

B

**DIRECTIONS:** For each of the incomplete statements below, *one* or *more* of the completions given is correct. Choose answer:

A. if only **1, 2,** and **3** are correct
B. if only **1** and **3** are correct
C. if only **2** and **4** are correct
D. if only **4** is correct
E. if all are correct

**3.8.** In order to shape behavior, one must do which of the following:

1. Specify the desired response
2. Identify the steps leading to the terminal response
3. Reinforce behavior immediately after the response
4. Vary the reinforcement frequency

**3.9.** In learning theory, the extinction of a response

1. causes learned behavior to occur less frequently
2. occurs when performance is not consistently reinforced
3. is a type of nonreinforcement
4. is related to stimulus similarity

**3.10.** Which of the following indicate the concept of object permanence:

1. Looking for a toy that has been hidden
2. Strong attachment to parents
3. Existence of object even though not present to the senses
4. Learning through trial-and-error experience

**3.11.** The following substances have been implicated in enhancing memory:

1. Endorphins
2. Chlorpromazine
3. Norepinephrine
4. Propranolol

**3.12.** Which of the following stages of cognitive development are *correctly* matched with an occurrence during that stage:

1. Sensorimotor period—construction of object concepts
2. Preoperational period—comprehension of causality
3. Concrete operational period—making and following rules
4. Formal operational period—capacity to abstract

**3.13.** By use of a conditioning technique, neurophysiologist Ivan Pavlov produced the abnormal phenomenon labeled

1. response by analogy
2. stimulus generalization
3. discrimination
4. experimental neurosis

**3.14.** According to B. F. Skinner, some key concepts in operant conditioning are

1. reinforcement
2. response frequency
3. shaping
4. chaining

**3.15.** In a famous study of induced anaclitic depression in monkeys by Harry Harlow, it was found that

1. at initial separation, the rhesus infants exhibited a protest stage
2. the protest stage changed to despair
3. the phenomenon of detachment was far less common and far less intense in monkey infants than in human infants
4. play was almost abolished during a 3-week period of maternal separation, but after maternal reunion it rose rapidly

**3.16.** Which of the following statements about perception are true:

1. An experience that predisposes a person to certain types of perception is called a set.
2. Ambiguous stimuli cause greater perceptual variations than do nonambiguous stimuli.
3. The meaning attributed to a particular stimulus is a function of the ambiguity of the stimulus.
4. Projective tests are most often used to test perceptual distortions.

**3.17.** Data from the studies of behavioral rehabilitation of induced animal psychopathology showed which of the following:

1. After 6 months of social isolation, there is no objective record of monkey psychopathology being cured by time.
2. Contact with surrogates changed the isolated monkeys from animals devoid of security into animals capable of maintaining some social contacts when with their confreres.
3. Infantile or abnormal behaviors were progressively reduced under conditions of social behavior therapy.
4. Isolated monkeys exposed to surrogate maternal figures eventually achieved the full gamut of monkey realization by establishing active, sex-typed play and appropriate sexual responsiveness.

**3.18.** Punishment

1. is a negative reinforcement
2. can decrease a response
3. causes avoidance responses
4. increases the probability of a response recurring

# Answers

## Science of Human Behavior: Contributions of the Psychological Sciences

**3.1.   The answer is B** (*Synopsis*, ed. 4, page 37).

The *ability to make and follow rules* occurs during the stage of concrete operations. At that time, syllogistic or deductive reasoning occurs. During the concrete operational stage, children also learn to engage in a form of deductive reasoning that allows them to begin to acquire and abide by rules, and they learn to quantify their experience.

The *ability to reason about reasoning or thinking* occurs during the formal operational period, as does the *ability to distinguish between the ideal self and the real self*. The *use of phenomenological causality as a mode of thinking* is seen during the preoperational period. The *attainment of object permanence* occurs during the sensorimotor period.

(See the table on page 27 for an overview of the major developmental stages of the life cycle.)

**3.2.   The answer is A** (*Synopsis*, ed. 4, page 33).

The final developmental stage that Piaget defines is the period of *formal operations* (from about 11 to about 15 years). The child develops true abstract thought during that time and is able to make hypotheses and test them logically.

The critical achievement of the *sensorimotor period* (birth to 2 years) is the construction of object concepts. Objects and one's sense of their permanence are constructed during the first year or so of life by the progressive coordination of sensorimotor schemata—elementary concepts—that result from the infant's actions on the world and from his or her growing mental abilities and motor skills.

During the *preoperational stage* (2 to 5 years), children begin to give evidence of having attained a new, higher order level of mental functioning. These characteristics are shown not only in the child's language but also in his or her play, dreams, and imitative behavior. These behaviors are symbolic. They are processes by which the child re-presents objects and activities in their absence. The attainment of object permanence, which involves representation by means of visual images, marks the transition from sensorimotor to preoperational or intuitive intelligence.

Toward the age of 5 or 6, children give evidence of having attained another, higher level system of mental structures that Piaget called *concrete operations*. These operations enable children to engage in syllogistic reasoning, which in turn permits them to acquire and to follow rules. In addition, concrete operations enable young people to construct unit concepts (a unit, such as a number, is both like and different from every other number) and thus to quantify their experience. This period of development is characterized by the construction of what may be called the lawful world.

*Epigenesis* is a term introduced by Erik Erikson to refer to the stages of ego and social development during the various stages of the life cycle.

**3.3.   The answer is E** (*Synopsis*, ed. 4, pages 39 and 40).

*Classical conditioning* is not an example of instrumental conditioning. In classical conditioning, also called Pavlovian conditioning and respondent conditioning, a neutral stimulus is repeatedly paired with a stimulus (the unconditioned stimulus) that naturally elicits a response (the unconditioned response) until the neutral stimulus (the conditioned stimulus) comes to elicit that response (now the conditioned response) by itself.

Instrumental conditioning is an experimental technique in which a freely moving animal produces behavior that is instrumental in producing a reward. For instance, a cat must learn to lift a latch in order to escape from a box; a monkey in an experimental chair must press a lever to effect the presentation of food.

There are four kinds of instrumental conditioning: (1) *Primary reward conditioning*—The simplest kind of conditioning. The learned response is instrumental in obtaining a biologically significant reward, such as a pellet of food or a drink of water. (2) *Escape conditioning*—The animal learns a response that is instrumen-

**Life Cycle in Development Stages**

| Age (yr) | Epigenetic Stages of Erickson | Psychosexual Stages of Freud | Stages of Cognitive Development of Piaget | Major Emotional and Developmental Disorders |
|---|---|---|---|---|
| 0–1 | Trust vs. mistrust: Basic feelings of being cared for by outer-providers | Oral (merges into oral sadistic) | *Sensorimotor:* Infant moves from an indifferent stage to awareness of self and the outside world. Object constancy not yet developed (birth to 2 yr) | Rumination, pylorospasm. Stranger anxiety at 8 months, infantile autism, failure to thrive |
| 1–3 | Autonomy vs. shame, doubt (begins at 18 mo): Rebellion, clear-dirty issues, compulsive behavior | Anal (divided into anal-explusive and anal-retentive) | | Sleep disturbances, pica, negativism, temper tantrums, toilet-training problems. Night terrors, separation anxiety, phobias |
| 3–7 | Initiative vs. guilt: Competitiveness develops, self-confidence emerges | Phallic (includes urethral eroticism and Oedipal-Electra complex) | *Preoperational thought:* A prelogical period in which thinking is based on what child wants, not what is (3–7 yr) | Somnambulism. School phobias, encopresis, enuresis, dyslexia, gender identity disorders. Tics |
| 7–13 | Industry vs. inferiority: Peer relations important, risk-taking behavior begins | Latency | *Concrete operations:* Object constancy develops. child appears rational and able to conceptualize shapes and sizes of observed objects (7–13 yr) | Psychosomatic disorders, personality disorders, neurotic disorders, antisocial behavioral patterns, anorexia nervosa, bulimia |
| 13–18 | Identity vs. role diffusion: Develops sense of self, role model important | Genital phase | *Formal operations:* Person is able to abstract and can deal with external reality. Can conceptualize in adult manner and evaluate logically. Ideals develop (12 or 13 yr through adulthood) | Suicidal peak in adolescents, schizophrenia, identity crisis. Neurotic disorders |
| Early adult-hood | Intimacy vs. isolation: Love relationships, group affiliations important | Genital phase consolidation | | Anxiety states. Bipolar disorder |
| Middle adult-hood | Generativity vs. self-absorption or stagnation: Contributing to future generations, acceptance of accomplishments | Maturity | | Mid-life crisis. Dysthymia |
| Late adult-hood | Integrity vs. despair: Learning to accept death, maintaining personal values | | | Highest suicide rates, organic mental disorders |

tal in getting it out of some place that it prefers not to be. (3) *Avoidance conditioning*—The kind of learning in which a response to a cue is instrumental in avoiding a painful experience. A rat on a grid, for example, may avoid a shock if it quickly pushes a lever when a light signal goes on. (4) *Secondary reward conditioning*— The kind of learning in which there is instrumental behavior to get at a stimulus that has no biological utility itself but that has in the past been associated with a biologically significant stimulus. For example, chimpanzees learn to press a lever to obtain poker chips, which they insert in a slot to secure grapes. Later, they work to accumulate poker chips even when they are not interested in grapes.

**3.4.   The answer is D** (*Synopsis,* ed. 4, page 41).

Operant conditioning originated with the psychologist *B. F. Skinner.* Operant refers to a class of responses emitted by the organism, rather than elicited by some known stimulus. Operant responses are also frequently called voluntary behavior, as opposed to involuntary or reflex behavior. Reflex responses are elicited as in classical conditioning and are called "respondents." Thus, respondents, such as pupillary reflexes, are differentiated from operants. An example of an operant response is reaching for a telephone.

*William James,* in the late 1800s, formulated a new theory of emotions by asserting that emotions follow behavior. He challenged the notion that emotions produce behavior. For example, he would argue that when people trip and begin to fall, they thrust out their hands to protect themselves before the emotion is labeled as fear.

*O. Hobart Mowrer* enunciated what is now known as the frustration-aggression hypothesis of aggression and violence. He asserted that aggression and violence were the inevitable results of being blocked or frustrated in an attempt to achieve a desired goal.

*Hans Selye* described the body's physiological-hormonal reaction to major stress and called it the general adaptation syndrome during which the body passes through the alarm reaction, resistance, and, finally, the exhaustion stage.

*Neal Miller* synthesized psychoanalytic and behavioral theory by taking Freud's ideas and translating them into a language and method of experimental research in behavior and learning theory.

**3.5.   The answer is A** (*Synopsis,* ed. 4, pages 31 and 32).

The *Rorschach Test* is a projective psychological test in which subjects are asked their associations in response to a series of 10 inkblot

pictures. It is the best known of the projective tests.

The *Minnesota Multiphasic Personality Inventory* (MMPI) is a questionnaire consisting of true-false statements that are coded in various scales that assess different dimensions of personality structure. A measure of the closeness of fit with various psychiatric diagnostic categories can then be made. The test is for persons aged 16 and over. It is not a projective test. The *California Personality Inventory* consists of 17 scales developed for normal populations for use in guidance and selection. Examples include socialization, dominance, and responsibility. It, also, is not a projective test.

The *Draw-A-Person Test* is a graphomotor test in which the person is asked to draw a person and then to draw a person of the opposite sex to the one in the first drawing. It is interpreted as a projection of body image. Interpretative principles rest largely on the assumed functional significance of each body part. It is sometimes useful for detecting brain damage. It is a less used and less widely known projective test than the Rorschach. The *Stanford-Binet* is primarily a verbal test of intellectual functioning that is administered individually to children and adults. It emphasizes problem-solving and is one of the most widely used I.Q. tests.

**3.6.   The answer is D** (*Synopsis*, ed. 4, pages 49, 50, and 51).

The long-term effects of 6 months of total social isolation produce adolescent monkeys that are both *abnormally aggressive and abnormally fearful.* The isolates *aggress against agemates who are far more physically adept.*

Infant monkeys that survive a 3-month, rather than a 6-month, total social isolation can make a *remarkable social adjustment through the development of play.* When allowed to interact with equal-age normally reared monkeys, the isolates play effectively within a week.

Monkeys totally isolated for a 12-month period are *totally unresponsive to the new physical and social world* with which they are presented. These isolates are devoid of social play or strong emotion. Totally isolated monkeys exhibit a depressive-type posture, including self-clutch, rocking, and depressive huddling. Partially isolated monkeys assume, with increasing frequency, *postures that are more schizoid,* such as extreme stereotypy and sitting at the front of the cage and staring vacantly into space.

**3.7.   The answer is C** (*Synopsis,* ed. 4, page 51).

The initial reaction of the infant monkey to separation from the mother is the strongly emotional *protest stage,* which is characterized by upset and continuous agitation on the part of the infant. When the separation is prolonged beyond 2 or 3 weeks, the infant's behavior changes to reflect the onset of the *despair stage*, in which the deprived monkey engages in less activity, little or no play, and occasional crying. There is a parallel here to separation among humans and the occurrence of grief that sometimes is reflected in initial protest and later in despair.

**3.8. The answer is A (1, 2, 3)** (*Synopsis,* ed. 4, page 42).

In order to shape behavior, the experimenter must *specify the response* that is desired from the organism. By clearly defining the terminal response, the experimenter must then *identify the steps by which this terminal response will be shaped.* By successive approximation—that is, leading the organism to the desired behavior—shaping occurs.

For example, if experimenters wish a pigeon to peck at a translucent plastic key on a wall of an experimental box, they most likely start by reinforcing the pigeon for facing the particular wall on which the key lies. Then they reinforce the pigeon when it moves toward the wall, when it ultimately pecks at the wall, and, finally, when the pigeon pecks at the plastic key. The terminal response of key pecking was shaped from a large number of possible responses.

It is critical in shaping that the *reinforcement occur immediately after the response,* inasmuch as a delay in reinforcement may be accompanied by other responses that are not desired, and these responses, in turn, may be accidentally reinforced. The *reinforcement should not vary,* but should be consistent with the response desired.

**3.9. The answer is A (1, 2, 3)** (*Synopsis,* ed. 4, page 39).

Extinction of a learned response is a process by which *behavior occurs less frequently.* It is a *type of nonreinforcement* and *occurs when performance is not consistently reinforced.*

*Stimulus similarity* causes generalization to occur that is different from extinction. Generalization allows for new types of behavior to occur in a setting in which they have not previously been reinforced.

**3.10. The answer is A (1, 2, 3)** (*Synopsis,* ed. 4, page 36).

A sense of object permanence occurs during the first year or so of life. As children gain better control over their heads, eyes, and hands, they can begin to coordinate touching and seeing. They can begin to look at the objects they touch and to touch the objects they see. In this way,

they begin to coordinate visual and tactile schemata to form elaborate object concepts that are both seeable and touchable.

By the end of the first year, the child's sense of objects as permanent has advanced to the point where he or she will *look for objects, such as toys, even when they are hidden.* The *object exists even though it is not present to the senses.*

The *attachment of a child to a parent* presupposes object permanence. The object will continue to exist when it is no longer present to the senses. True attachment to parents apparently does not happen until the last trimester of the first year of life.

A second consequence of the construction of object permanence has to do with the child's self-concept. Just as the infant begins to construct object concepts, so does he or she construct a concept of the self as object. This object self is primarily a body self, consisting of the parts of the body the child can see, activate, and manipulate.

*Trial-and-error learning* is a type of learning based on positive or negative outcome that reinforces random behavior by the organism. According to Piaget, when the child touches one object to get another, these actions are part of an organized whole and are not random isolated acts.

**3.11. The answer is B (1, 3)** (*Synopsis,* ed. 4, pages 44 and 45).

*Endorphins* and catecholamine agonists, such as amphetamine, epinephrine, *norepinephrine,* and dopamine, can facilitate performance and improve learning and memory.

Conversely, antagonists of catecholamine metabolism, such as reserpine, *chlorpromazine,* and *propranolol,* measurably interfere with processes of learning and memory.

Much of the foundation for these observations derives from detailed studies and experiments concerning the effects of chemical agents on learning and memory. Recently, it has been found that anterograde amnesia can be caused by triazolam and, to a lesser extent, by other benzodiazepines.

**3.12. The answer is E (all)** (*Synopsis,* ed. 4, pages 36 and 37).

In the *sensorimotor period,* children gain better control over their heads, eyes, and hands; they can begin to coordinate touching and seeing. They begin the *construction of object concepts.* In the *preoperational period, phenomenalistic causality* occurs, which refers to the concept that events that happen together cause one another. The child at the *concrete operational stage* arrives at a concept of a lawful self as one who can *make and follow rules.* Children who become overly invested in this facet of themselves may show obsessive-compulsive symptoms, whereas children who resist this facet often seem willful and immature. In the *formal operational period*, the child develops true *abstract thought*. The formal operations are more abstract than are the concrete operations, and they make up a second-order system that operates on the first.

**3.13.   The answer is D (4)** (*Synopsis*, ed. 4, page 46).

Normal phenomena described by Pavlov include the following: *response by analogy*, in which animals respond to stimuli similar to the stimulus to which they were conditioned; *stimulus generalization*, which is the basis of higher learning in that similarities between objects are learned through generalization; and *discrimination*, which consists of learning to differentiate between similar stimuli, also the basis of higher learning.

**3.14.   The answer is E (all)** (*Synopsis*, ed. 4, pages 41 and 42).

According to B. F. Skinner, a key concept in operant conditioning is that of *reinforcement*. In operant conditioning, the words positive reinforcement are used to describe an event consequent upon a response that increases the probability of this response recurring. A negative reinforcement is an event likely to decrease the probability of this response's recurrence. In operant conditioning, *shaping* refers to the experimenter establishing a chosen type of behavior. *Response frequency* refers to the frequency with which a response is emitted and is a clear, observable measure of behavior. Skinner observed that personality descriptions are couched in frequency terms; to say that a person is an enthusiastic skier, an inveterate gambler, or hostile reduces to a statement the perceived frequency with which a certain class of behavior is emitted. *Chaining* refers to responses that are built on one another to form a pattern of behavior.

**3.15.   The answer is E (all)** (*Synopsis*, ed. 4, pages 51 and 52).

Harlow's study showed that, *at initial separation, the rhesus infants exhibited a protest stage*, which included aggressive attempts to regain maternal contact, plaintive vocalization, and a persistent pattern of nondirected behavior. This stage *progressed to despair* during the subsequent 48 hours. The most dramatic indicator of this despair stage was the almost total suppression of play. Associated with this suppression was a marked decreasing of vocalization and movement. *Play, although almost abolished during the 3-week separation, resumed rapidly after*

*reunion with the mother*. The separated monkey infants typically reattached to the monkey mother vigorously and rapidly when the separation phase ended. In contrast, John Bowlby noted that when many human children are reunited with their mothers, their responses are often those of rejection, termed by Bowlby, the *detachment* stage.

In Harlow's study of monkeys, the age chosen to begin experimental maternal deprivation was 6 months, which was the age at which play appeared to be maximally matured. The separation was obtained by physically preventing the infant monkeys from being able to touch their mothers or return from their play area into the home area where their mothers could be seen. All monkeys tested in their situation showed a nearly complete picture of human anaclitic depression. Anaclitic depression is the term used by René Spitz to refer to the syndrome shown by infants who are separated from their mothers for long periods of time. In Spitz's series, the reaction occurred in children who were 6 to 8 months old at the time of separation, which continued for a practically unbroken period of 3 months.

**3.16.   The answer is E (all)** (*Synopsis*, ed. 4, pages 31 and 32).

Perception is the conscious awareness of elements in the environment by the mental processing of sensory stimuli. The term is sometimes used in a broader sense to refer to the mental process by which all kinds of data—intellectual and emotional, as well as sensory—are organized meaningfully.

*An experience that predisposes a person to certain types of perception is called a set. The more ambiguous the stimulus, the more its perception is determined by the set* or proclivities of the subject. Also, the stronger the set, the more it determines the person's perception. *The meaning attributed to a particular stimulus by a person is a function of the ambiguity of the stimulus* and the strength of that person's set.

The major application of these principles in psychiatry has been in *projective testing*, in which ambiguous stimuli are presented to individuals and their responses are analyzed in terms of their emphasis and patterning. Extrapolated from this analysis is a description of the person's *personality in terms of his or her perceptual proclivities*.

**3.17.   The answer is A (1, 2, 3)** (*Synopsis*, ed. 4, pages 52 and 53).

In monkeys isolated for a 6-month period of time, *time alone does not cure the behavioral deficits*. In fact, with increased time, behavioral deficits remain in an exaggerated form.

When monkeys who had been in total isolation for 6 months were paired with a warm, surrogate model of a monkey mother made of wire and cloth, the monkeys subsequently showed a marked decrease in self-directed disturbance behavior. There was also an increase in frequency of environmental exploratior and peer contact. Data of this type appeared to indicate that *experience with the surrogate provided considerable social security to the isolated monkey*; however, data obtained from those studies also showed that surrogate contact failed as a total rehabilitation process. *The isolated monkeys were never able to realize their full potential*, in particular with regard to active and appropriate sexual responsiveness.

Social behavior therapy of monkeys consists of placing 6-month isolated monkeys with normal "therapist" monkeys each day for 2 hours of social interaction. At the end of a 12-month period of therapy, no differences existed between isolated and control monkeys in the observed frequency of behavioral norms. Social behavior therapy was *effective in reducing abnormal behavior*, such as self-clasp, huddle, and stereotyped movement.

**3.18. The answer is A (1, 2, 3)** (*Synopsis*, ed. 4, page 41).

Punishment is a *negative reinforcement*, which means that it *decreases* the probability of a specific response recurring. Any behavior that serves to avoid or escape the punishment is strengthened; therefore, punishment causes *avoidance responses* to occur.

Positive reinforcement is the opposite of negative reinforcement in that it *increases*, rather than decreases, the probability of a specific response recurring.

## References

Bachrach A J: Learning theory. In *Comprehensive Textbook of Psychiatry*, ed 4, H I Kaplan, B J Sadock, editors, p 184. Williams & Wilkins, Baltimore, 1985.

Bowlby J: *Attachment and Loss: I. Attachment.* Basic Books, New York, 1969.

Chapman L J, Chapman J P: *Disordered Thought in Schizophrenics.* Appleton-Century-Crofts, New York, 1973.

Ginsburg H P: Jean Piaget. In *Comprehensive Textbook of Psychiatry*, ed 4, H I Kaplan, B J Sadock, editors, p 178. Williams & Wilkins, Baltimore, 1985.

Kietzman M L, Spring B, Zubin J: Perception, cognition, and information processing. In *Comprehensive Textbook of Psychiatry*, ed 4, H I Kaplan, B J Sadock, editors, p. 157. Williams & Wilkins, Baltimore, 1985.

Liben L: *Piaget and the Foundations of Knowledge.* Erlbaum Associates, Hillsdale, NJ, 1983.

Skinner B F: *Science and Human Behavior.* Macmillan, New York, 1953.

Suomi S J: Ethology: Animal models. In *Comprehensive Textbook of Psychiatry*, ed 4, H I Kaplan, B J Sadock, editors p 226. Williams & Wilkins, Baltimore, 1985.

# 4

# Science of Human Behavior: Quantitative and Experimental Methods in Psychiatry

Epidemiology is the study of health conditions in a population in relation to any conceivable factors existing in or affecting that population which may influence the origin of the health state or affect its distribution in that population. The object of such study is to ameliorate any factors that contribute to ill health, to enhance any that contribute to health, and to draw generalizations from studies that can be applied to other populations to contribute to health in general. From the point of view of pure or basic science, the objective of the promotion of health is not essential to epidemiology; but as a derivative of the public health movement, epidemiology has always had a large element of applied science in its conceptual base. In practice, the promotion of health and the alleviation of disease states are accepted as parts of its logic.

Psychiatric epidemiology is that part of general epidemiology concerned with the pattern of occurrence of mental disorders, the ecological and human factors that influence those patterns, and the outcomes of attempts to alter them. Psychiatric epidemiology is the scientific basis of public health psychiatry and preventive psychiatry.

Sensory deprivation is a type of perceptual isolation or deprivation produced by reducing the absolute intensity of stimuli reaching the subject. It can occur experimentally or as a result of environmental factors, such as solitary confinement, shipwreck, or becoming a prisoner of war. It can cause various abnormalities in perception and reality testing. Sensory deprivation is valuable to study because it teaches how sensory input is related to mental illness.

The reader should refer to Chapter 4 of *Modern Synopsis-IV*, "Quantitative and Experimental Methods in Psychiatry," which covers epidemiology and sensory deprivation. Other epidemiologic studies are covered in Chapter 38, "Conditions Not Attributable to a Mental Disorder" and in Chapter 39, "Community Psychiatry Concepts."

# Questions

**DIRECTIONS:** Each of the statements or questions below is followed by five responses or completions. Select the *one* that is *best* in each case.

**4.1.** In order to provide information regarding a planned modification of circumstances to lower the incidence of disease in a given population, the method most used is

A. preventive trials
B. primary prevention
C. secondary prevention
D. tertiary prevention
E. community prevention

**4.2.** A short-lived syndrome characterized by severe decompensation of personal functioning in a patient recently discharged from a hospital is called the

A. general-adaptation syndrome
B. survivor syndrome
C. social breakdown syndrome
D. culture-specific syndrome
E. episodic-dyscontrol syndrome

**4.3.** The term used by Emil Durkheim to explain suicide as a result of a decreased sense of community affiliation is

A. egoistic
B. altruistic
C. anomie
D. epigenesis
E. none of the above

**4.4** The so-called cardiac psychosis is believed to result most often from which of the following factors:

A. Hemodynamic physiology
B. Medication
C. Pain
D. Sensory deprivation
E. Prior mental illness

**4.5.** The prevalance rate refers to the

A. proportion of a population that has a condition at one moment in time
B. number of persons who acquire a disorder during a year's time
C. risk of acquiring a condition at one moment in time
D. extent of the standard deviation of a disorder
E. rate of first admissions to a hospital for a disorder

**4.6** In the Stirling County study by Alexander Leighton, all of the following were found *except*

A. only 20 percent of the population were free of psychiatric symptoms
B. men showed more disorders than did women
C. psychophysiological symptoms were found in over 50 percent of the population
D. psychiatric disorders increased with age
E. mental health was related to economic status

**DIRECTIONS:** For each of the incomplete statements below, *one* or *more* of the completions given is correct. Choose answer:

A. if only **1, 2,** and **3** are correct
B. if only **1** and **3** are correct
C. if only **2** and **4** are correct
D. if only **4** is correct
E. if all are correct

**4.7.** In studying epidemics of disease, the proportion of a population affected by a disease over a period of time depends primarily on the

1. length of time between exposure and onset
2. type of immunity
3. method of transmission
4. genetic marker

**4.8.** Sensory deprivation has been postulated to play a role in

1. long-haul trucking
2. the psychoanalytic office
3. brainwashing
4. athletic competition

**4.9.** Sensory deprivation is considered an important element in

1. deafness
2. delirium tremens
3. cataract delirium
4. deterioration of the chronic back-ward patients

**4.10.** The figures below on national health expenditures from 1970 to 1982 indicate which of the following:

1. Approximately 10 percent of the U.S. gross national product is spent on health care.
2. Hospital costs have risen at a greater rate than physician fees.
3. More money is spent by the private sector on health costs than by the public sector.
4. The annual percentage change of medical care service has decreased in the decade between 1972 to 1982.

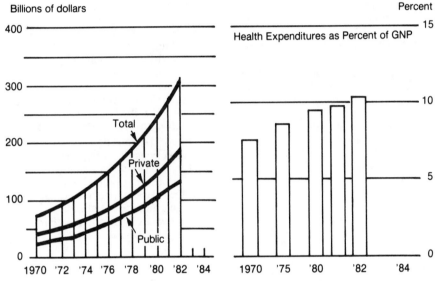

National health expenditures: 1970 to 1982.
(Source: Chart prepared by US Bureau of the Census.)

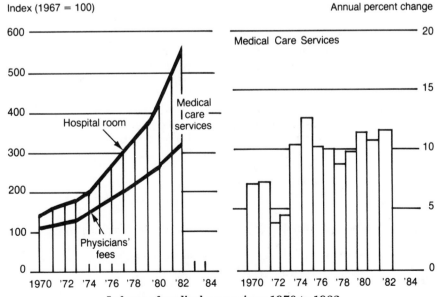

Indexes of medical care prices: 1970 to 1982.
(Source: Chart prepared by US Bureau of the Census.)

| Directions Summarized | | | | |
|---|---|---|---|---|
| A | B | C | D | E |
| 1, 2, 3 | 1, 3 | 2, 4 | 4 | All are |
| only | only | only | only | correct |

**4.11.** Which of the following factors are involved in preventing mental deterioration in the hospitalized geriatric patient:
1. Hearing aids
2. Night lights
3. Clean eyeglasses
4. Quiet environment

**4.12.** Included in the drift hypothesis are which of the following concepts:
1. There is an increased frequency of various mental disorders in central urban areas.
2. Schizophrenics slide down the socioeconomic scale.
3. Schizophrenics migrate into poverty-stricken living areas.
4. Mental illness is unaffected by socioeconomic status.

**4.13.** The famous New Haven study by Hollingshead and Redlich concluded that
1. position in the class structure is related to the prevalance of treated mental illness
2. diagnosis is unrelated to the class structure
3. position in the class structure is related to social factors in the development of psychiatric disorders.
4. mobility in the class structure is not related to the development of psychiatric disorders.

**4.14.** Which of these statements about class status and cultural characteristics as described by Hollingshead and Redlich are correct:
1. Class I persons do not often have family relations that are cohesive or stable.
2. Class II persons are marked by some education beyond high school.
3. More class IV persons do not make sacrifices to get ahead.
4. Acting out of hostility is characteristic of class V persons.

**DIRECTIONS:** Each set of lettered headings below is followed by a list of numbered words or phrases. For each numbered word or phrase, select

A. if the item is associated with **A** *only*
B. if the item is associated with **B** *only*
C. if the item is associated with *both* **A** *and* **B**
D. if the item is associated with *neither* **A** *nor* **B**

**Questions 4.15–4.19**
The following attitudes toward health issues are characteristic of which socioeconomic class:
A. Lower class
B. Upper middle-class
C. Both
D. Neither

**4.15.** More able to delay gratification

**4.16.** Seek health care earlier

**4.17.** Pregnancy is a time of crisis

**4.18.** Longer hospital stay

**4.19.** No contraceptive use

# Answers

# Science of Human Behavior:
# Quantitative and Experimental
# Methods in Psychiatry

**4.1.   The answer is A** (*Synopsis,* ed. 4, pages 56 and 58).

Planned *preventive trials* determine whether a planned modification of circumstances actually lowers the incidence of disease. They provide more information than any other method about causes of disease.

Another form of preventive trial occurs when a major reform is introduced with the intent of preventing a specific form of disorder. It cannot be designed to include a control group because the reform involves the reorganization of all the mental health services of a *community.*

Encompassed within the scope of prevention in psychiatry are measures to prevent mental disorders (*primary prevention*); measures to limit the severity of illness, as through early case finding and treatment (*secondary prevention*); and measures to reduce disability after a disorder (*tertiary prevention*). An example of primary prevention is prenatal parent training groups, of secondary prevention is psychotherapy, and of tertiary prevention is social skills rehabilitation training of schizophrenic patients.

**4.2.   The answer is C** (*Synopsis,* ed. 4, page 56).

The *social breakdown syndrome* is a short-lived breakdown in personal and social functioning that affects chronically ill mental patients who have been discharged from mental hospitals. The syndrome starts in the community and ends shortly after the patient is readmitted to the hospital.

The *general-adaptation syndrome* was described by Hans Selye; it is the body's reaction to stress and is characterized by three stages: alarm, resistance, and exhaustion.

The *survivor syndrome* is a type of posttraumatic stress disorder. Any number of symptoms may occur, including depression, insomnia, anxiety, psychosomatic illnesses, and nightmares, that are believed to be based on guilt feelings over being a sole survivor or nearly sole survivor of a disaster in which others perished who were emotionally close, such as patients, siblings, spouse, or friends.

*Episodic dyscontrol* is a syndrome consisting of violent outbursts with loss of control over aggressive behavior upon minimal provocation, often related to alcohol ingestion or occurring in a setting of alcoholism, and frequently with a history of hyperkinesis and truancy in childhood. Aurae and postictal states are seen in some cases. Functional abnormalities of amygdalar or other limbic regions are suspected in such cases, but often cannot be demonstrated.

*Culture-specific syndromes* are behavior disorders that appear to be limited to certain societies and have no counterpart in current Western nosology. Among such syndromes are *amok, koro, latah, piblokto,* and *Wihtiko psychosis.*

**4.3.   The answer is C** (*Synopsis,* ed. 4, page 58).

Emil Durkheim investigated suicide, using a sociological model, and suggested that suicide is the result of society's strength or weakness of control over the person. *Anomie* or anomic suicides occur when the relationship between a person and his or her sense of community affiliation is decreased or shattered. *Altruistic* suicides are required by society, such as the ritual of hara-kiri. *Egoistic* suicides occur in isolated individuals. *Epigenesis* is Erik Erikson's term for the developmental stages in the life cycle.

**4.4.   The answer is D** (*Synopsis,* ed. 4, page 62).

The so-called cardiac psychosis is not related to the actual state of the patient's *hemodynamic physiology* or *medication,* but results from *sensory deprivation.* The well-meaning physician's hospital orders may turn out to be a sentence of sensory deprivation, with excessive or too long-enduring absolute bed rest, silence, and no visitors. In the cardiac psychosis, patients may be found wandering in the corridors—usually at night, when the wards have become quiet—confused, thinking they are at home, and being unable to find a familiar room. Sensory deprivation has caused their hold on reality to become weakened, and the loss of reality is the psychotic process.

**4.5.    The answer is A** (*Synopsis,* ed. 4, page 56).

Prevalence rate refers to the *proportion of a population that has a condition at one moment in time.* The proportion of a population that *begins an episode of a disorder during a year's time* (new cases) is called the annual incidence rate. In a stable situation, the prevalence rate is approximately equal to the annual incidence rate times the average duration, measured in years, of the condition. The *risk of acquiring a condition* at some indefinite time in the future represents the accumulation of age-specific annual incidence rates over a period of time.

*Standard deviation* (SD) is a statistical measure of variability within a set of values so defined that, for a normal distribution, about 68 percent of the values fall within one SD of the mean, and about 95 percent lie within two SD's of the mean. It is sometimes represented by $\sigma$, the Greek letter sigma.

The *rate of first admissions* to a hospital is the ratio of all first admissions to the average general hospital during a particular year.

**4.6.    The answer is B** (*Synopsis,* ed. 4, pages 866 and 867).

Alexander H. Leighton headed a psychiatric epidemiologic study of Stirling County in Canada. The Stirling County study found that *only about 20 percent of the population could be said* with certainty *to be free of symptoms of mental disorder. Women showed considerably more psychiatric disorder than did men.* In terms of symptom categories, the survey found that *66 percent of the men and 71 percent of the women suffered from psychophysiological symptoms.* Psychoneurosis was found in 44 percent of the men and 64 percent of the women. Age was found to be a factor, *with psychiatric disorders increasing with age.* The study also disclosed *a linear relation between mental health and economic position.*

**4.7.    The answer is A (1, 2, 3)** (*Synopsis,* ed. 4, p. 55).

Disease epidemics over a period of time depend on such factors as the *length of time between exposure and onset of disease* for the particular illness under question, and the *method of transmission of the disease.* The epidemic ends when the supply of susceptible persons in the population is exhausted. Also, the scope of the epidemic depends on the prior history of the disease in the population, the *type of immunity* resulting from having the disease, and any immunizing measures that may have been used. Studying the pattern of a particular epidemic

may help determine the causative agent when that is not known.

*Genetic markers* are determinants that enable a cell to be identified.

**4.8.    The answer is A (1, 2, 3)** (*Synopsis,* ed. 4, pages 59, 61, and 62).

Sensory deprivation is a lack of external stimuli and the opportunity for the usual perceptions. Sensory deprivation may be produced experimentally or may occur in real-life contexts—for example, deep-sea diving, solitary confinement, loss of hearing or eyesight—and may lead to hallucinations, panic, delusions, and disorganized thinking.

*Athletic competition* is the antithesis of sensory deprivation and sensory isolation.

Instances of aberrant mental behavior in explorers, shipwrecked sailors, and prisoners in solitary confinement have been known for centuries. Toward the end of World War II, startling confessions, induced by *brainwashing* in prisoners of war, caused a rise of interest in the psychological phenomena brought about by deliberate diminution of sensory input in the human being.

The dangers of *long-haul trucking over monotonous superhighways* have been recognized as being related to inherent sensory deprivation and its symptoms. Increased accident rates and errors in judgment in boring assembly-line work have been similarly implicated. It is becoming increasingly understood that automation for greater production, with the elimination of supposedly distracting stimuli on the remaining workers, carries its price in sensory deprivation symptoms and human fallibility.

A patient being *psychoanalyzed* is in a kind of sensory deprivation room (soundproofing, dim lights, couch) and is encouraged to free associate and otherwise invite primary process mental activity.

**4.9.    The answer is E (all)** (*Synopsis,* ed. 4, pages 62 and 63).

An important feature in the care of some patients is to avoid sensory deprivation, especially in hospitalized patients and in those with severe handicaps, such as blindness, *deafness,* and paralysis.

The element of sensory deprivation is surely important in *delirium tremens,* in which the best sedative is a sympathetic, attentive nurse. Sensory deprivation is probably also a vital factor in the deterioration of the *chronic back-ward patient.*

The mental disturbance that sometimes follows operations for cataract or other eye disorders, and that is characterized by confusion and disorientation, has been known for years as *cataract delirium.*

**4.10. The answer is A (1, 2, 3)** (*Synopsis,* ed. 4, pages 874 and 875).

*Approximately 10 percent of the U.S. gross national product* of approximately 300 billion dollars *is spent for health care.* Mental illness makes up a large proportion of that figure. In general, general medical care services and *hospital costs have risen at a far greater rate than physician's fees. More money is spent by the private sector on health costs than by the public sector.*

The annual percentage change of medical care service has *increased* in the decade between 1972 to 1982.

**4.11. The answer is A (1, 2, 3)** (*Synopsis,* ed. 4, pages 62 and 63).

Hospitalized geriatric patients have many special limitations. These include restricted visual fields and other visual faults, confinement in bed, tactile restriction to bedsheets, dulled taste and smell perceptions, unfamiliar hospital sounds, minimal kinesthetic stimulation, and restricted social environment. These patients need a great deal more light, including *night lights,* and those over age 85 need 8 times as much as normal. Their *eyeglasses* should be cleaned frequently, and their *hearing aids* should be more freely furnished and regular attention paid to their batteries. Food for the elderly should be spiced and seasoned more than usual. Their calendars and clocks should be large and prominent, and the clocks should chime. Also, rooms and corridors should be painted in attractive and different colors for better orienting value and to increase the pattern of sensory input. Additionally, television sets and radios are helpful, and nothing can match the value of attending people—the ministering nurse, friends, relatives, and hospital volunteers. Unless the above needs are attended to, mental functioning may deteriorate becaue of sensory deprivation. A *quiet environment* of itself is isolating and is undesirable.

**4.12. The answer is A (1, 2, 3)** (*Synopsis,* ed. 4, page 58).

Epidemiologic studies show a *high incidence of mental illness in the slums of large urban communities.* The drift hypothesis, formulated by Farin and Dunham, suggests that many impaired persons *slide down the socioeconomic scale* because of their illness and that they move, *migrate,* or drift geographically to the slums of the central cities. Schizophrenics show marked downward social mobility because they are often unable to work or are unemployed. Mental illness of all types *is affected by socioeconomic status.* Mental disorders have a high frequency in poorer areas of the city.

**4.13. The answer is B (1, 3)** (*Synopsis,* ed. 4, page 865).

Hollingshead and Redlich conducted a survey of New Haven, Connecticut, and its surrounding region during parts of 1950 and 1951. The project was primarily concerned with determining the relation of social class to the prevalence of treated illness.

The data accumulated by the study proved the following:

1. *Position in the class structure is related to the prevalence of treated mental illness.*

2. *Position in the class structure is related to the type of diagnosed psychiatric disorders.*

3. *Position in the class structure is related to social and psychodynamic factors in the development of psychiatric disorders.*

4. *Mobility in the class structure is related to the development of psychiatric difficulties.*

Analysis of the data revealed definitive relationships between social class and various aspects of the psychiatric process, beginning with the nature of the initial referral for treatment. For example, referrals to private physicians were greater in the higher social groups than in the lower ones.

**4.14.   The answer is E (all)** (*Synopsis,* ed. 4, page 866).

The summary of the class structure and cultural characteristics of subjects in the New Haven study is listed in the table below.

### Class Status and Cultural Characteristics of Subjects in the New Haven Study

| Class | Class Status and Cultural Characteristics | Class | Class Status and Cultural Characteristics |
|---|---|---|---|
| I | Class I, containing the community's business and professional leaders, has two segments: a long established core group of interrelated families and a smaller upward-mobile group of new people. Members of the core group usually inherit money along with group values that stress tradition, stability, and social responsibility. Those in the newer group are highly educated, self-made, able, and aggressive. *Their family relations often are not cohesive or stable.* Socially, they are rejected by the core group, to whom they are, however, a threat by the vigor of their leadership in community affairs. | | less satisfaction with present living conditions and less optimism than in class II. |
| II | Class II is marked by *at least some education beyond high school* and occupations as managers or in the less-ranking professions. Four of five are upward mobile. They are joiners at all ages and tend to have stable families, but they have usually gone apart from parental families and often from their home communities. Tensions arise generally from striving for educational, economic, and social success. | IV | In class IV, 53 percent say they belong to the working class. Seven of 10 show no generational mobility. Most are content and *make no sacrifices to get ahead.* Most of the men are semiskilled (53 percent) or skilled (35 percent) manual employees. Practically all the women who are able to hold jobs do so. Education usually stops shortly after graduation from grammar school for both parents and children. Families are much different from those in class III. Families are larger, and they are more likely to include three generations. Households are more likely to include boarders and roomers. Homes are more likely to be broken. |
| III | Class III males for the most part are in salaried administrative and clerical jobs (51 percent) or own small businesses (24 percent); many of the women also have jobs. Typically, they are high-school graduates. They usually have economic security but little opportunity for advancement. Families tend to be somewhat less stable than in class II. Family members of all ages tend to join organizations and to be active in them. There is | V | Class V adults usually have not completed elementary school. Most are semiskilled factory workers or unskilled laborers. They are concentrated in tenement and cold-water-flat areas of New Haven or in suburban slums. There are generally brittle family ties. Very few participate in organized community institutions. Leisure activities in the household and on the street are informal and spontaneous. Adolescent boys frequently have contact with the law in their search for adventure. There is a struggle for existence. There is much resentment, expressed freely in primary groups, about how they are treated by those in authority. There is *much acting out of hostility.* |

**4.15–4.19.   The answers are 4.15–B, 4.16–B, 4.17–A, 4.18–A, and 4.19–D** (*Synopsis,* ed. 4, page 876).

The socioeconomic status of the patient influences attitudes toward physical and mental health as illustrated in the table below.

### Attitudes toward Health Issues

| Lower Class | Upper-Middle Class |
|---|---|
| Look for immediate solutions | More able to delay gratification |
| Negative view on life | More positive view of life |
| Low contraceptive use | High contraceptive use |
| Seek health care later | Seek health care earlier |
| Longer hospital stays | Shorter hospital stays |
| See pregnancy as a time of crisis | Pregnancy seen as normal event |

# References

Hollingshead A B, Redlich F C: *Social Class and Mental Illness.* John Wiley & Sons, New York, 1958.

Regier D A, Burke J D: Epidemiology. In *Comprehensive Textbook of Psychiatry,* ed 4, H I Kaplan, B J Sadock, editors, p 295. Williams & Wilkins, Baltimore, 1985.

Solomon P, Kleeman S T: Sensory deprivation. In *Comprehensive Textbook of Psychiatry,* ed 4, H I Kaplan, B J Sadock, editors, p 321. Williams & Wilkins, Baltimore, 1985.

Srole L, Langner T S, Michael S T, Opler M K, Rennie T A C: *Mental Health in the Metropolis: The Midtown Manhattan Study.* McGraw-Hill, New York, 1962.

Wilson L M: Intensive care delirium. The effect of outside deprivation in a windowless unit. Arch Intern Med *130:* 225, 1972.

# 5

# Theories of Personality and Psychopathology: Classical Psychoanalysis

Sigmund Freud's role in explaining the motivaton of behavior within the framework of his classical psychoanalytic theory was preeminent in the evolution of the psychodynamic approach in psychiatry. In addition to a comprehensive theory of personality, Freudian psychoanalysis provides a method for treatment and research. Classical psychoanalysis has undergone some modifications that reflect recent developments in ego psychology and the further refinement and elaboration of concepts concerning the structure of the psychic apparatus. On the whole, however, the basic concepts of psychoanalysis, as they were originally elaborated by Freud, remain relatively unchanged and represent the approach of many psychiatrists in the United States today.

Erik Erikson brought Freud's psychoanalytic theory out of the bounds of the nuclear family, focusing his interest on the wider milieu of the social world, where children interact with peers, teachers, national ethics, and expectations. He added to Freud's theory of infantile sexuality by concentrating on the child's development beyond puberty. Erikson also took the focus of psychoanalysis from pathology to health, providing a picture of how the ego can usually develop in a healthy way if it is given the right environment.

The reader is referred to Chapter 5 of *Modern Synopsis-IV*, "Classical Psychoanalysis," which covers the work of Freud and Erikson, and should then assess his or her knowledge by answering the following questions.

# Questions

**DIRECTIONS:** Each of the statements or questions below is followed by five suggested responses or completions. Select the *one* that is *best* in each case.

**5.1.** Autonomous functions of the ego include all of the following *except*

A. language
B. intelligence
C. perception
D. repression
E. motor development

**5.2.** Erik Erikson coined the term "identity crisis" to describe the stage occurring during

A. childhood
B. adolescence
C. young adulthood
D. middle adulthood
E. late adulthood

**5.3.** A male office worker steals supplies from the office and, when confronted with the evidence, states, "Well, everybody does it, and you can't fire me. I quit." Which of the following mechanisms are being used:

A. Denial and rationalization
B. Rationalization and identification with the aggressor
C. Identification and undoing
D. Projection and identification with the aggressor
E. Intellectualization and denial

**5.4.** The defense mechanism by which the emotional component of an unacceptable idea or object is transferred to a more acceptable one is known as

A. substitution
B. rationalization
C. projection
D. displacement
E. sublimation

**5.5.** At the end of the oedipal stage, when a boy, whose main source of love is his mother, becomes like his father—the powerful rival for the mother—the boy is using which defense mechanism:

A. Introjection
B. Identification
C. Denial
D. Incorporation
E. Undoing

**5.6.** All the following statements are true about the pleasure and reality principles *except*

A. the pleasure principle is inborn
B. the pleasure principle is modified by the reality principle
C. the reality principle is largely an unlearned function
D. the reality principle is related to the maturation of ego functions
E. the pleasure principle persists throughout life

**5.7.** Psychoanalytic treatment as formulated by Freud includes all of the following *except*

A. instinct theory
B. free association
C. libido theory
D. unconscious motivation
E. collective unconscious

**5.8.** Freud considered which of the following factors to be most important in the development of adult neurotic disorders:

A. Hereditary susceptibility
B. Unfavorable childhood experiences
C. Precocious sexual activity
D. Interpersonal difficulties during adolescence
E. None of the above

**5.9.** The most important defense mechanism in the development of neurotic symptoms is

A. suppression
B. inhibition
C. resistance
D. repression
E. regression

**5.10.** The process of condensation in dreams refers to

A. the combination of several attitudes into one image
B. ascribing unacceptable impulses to another person in the dream
C. the transferring of one emotion to its symbolic representation
D. giving the dream a sense of coherence
E. the direct expression of repressed impulses

**5.11.** The defense mechanism through which reasoning or logic is used in an attempt to avoid confrontation with an objectionable impulse and thus defend against anxiety is

A. altruism
B. repression
C. regression
D. projection
E. intellectualization

**5.12.** The defense mechanism in which one attributes one's own unacknowledged feelings to others is known as

A. introjection
B. denial
C. projection
D. displacement
E. reaction formation

**5.13.** Which of the following neuroses is characterized by rumination, doubting, and intruding thoughts:

A. Phobic disorder
B. Hypochondriasis
C. Depressive disorder
D. Obsessive-compulsive disorder
E. None of the above

**5.14.** All the following statements are true about dreams *except*

A. dreams have a definite but disguised meaning
B. dreams are a normal manifestation of unconscious activity
C. dreams represent wish-fulfillment activity
D. the core meaning of the dream is expressed by its manifest content
E. nocturnal sensory stimuli may be incorporated into the dream

**5.15.** The defense mechanism involving the separation of an idea or memory from its attached feeling tone is known as

A. alienation
B. isolation
C. sublimation
D. altruism
E. regression

**5.16.** The major defense mechanism used in phobia is

A. projection
B. identification
C. displacement
D. undoing
E. reaction formation

**5.17.** A young boy experiences pain at the dentist's office. The next day, he makes believe that he is the dentist extracting a tooth from his friend. The defense mechanism operating here is

A. symbolization
B. regression
C. isolation
D. identification with the aggressor
E. all of the above

**5.18.** The defense mechanism involving the separation of an idea or memory from its attached feeling tone and known as isolation is found most clearly in

A. obsessive-compulsive neurosis
B. anxiety disorder
C. pain disorder
D. dissociative disorder
E. dysthymic disorder

**DIRECTIONS:** For each of the incomplete statements below, *one* or *more* of the completions given is correct. Choose answer:

A. if only **1, 2,** and **3** are correct
B. if only **1** and **3** are correct
C. if only **2** and **4** are correct
D. if only **4** is correct
E. if all are correct

**5.19.** Erikson's locomotor-genital stage is characterized by which of the following:

1. Control of sphincter muscles
2. Interest in parent of the opposite sex
3. Indecision and confusion
4. Learning becomes instructive

**5.20.** Secondary gain refers to which of the following:

1. Gaining attention or sympathy
2. Monetary compensation
3. Protection
4. Reduction of conflict

**5.21.** Which of the following statements about Freud's view of hypnosis are true:

1. It helps patients to rid themselves of their symptoms.
2. Symptom relief is transitory.
3. Relief depends on the personal relationship between patient and physician.
4. Hypnosis can induce abreaction.

| **Directions Summarized** | | | | |
|---|---|---|---|---|
| A | B | C | D | E |
| 1, 2, 3 | 1, 3 | 2, 4 | 4 | All are |
| only | only | only | only | correct |

**5.22.** According to Freud, a man may fall in love with a particular type of woman for which of the following reasons:

1. She resembles the man's idealized self-image.
2. She resembles someone who took care of him when he was a boy.
3. She provides him with narcissistic gratification.
4. There is a sexual resemblance between them.

**5.23.** Which of the following statements apply to the unconscious:

1. Its elements are inaccessible to consciousness.
2. It is characterized by primary process thinking.
3. It is associated with the pleasure principle.
4. It is closely related to the instincts.

**5.24.** What characteristics describe Erikson's standing stage:

1. Paranoid fears of unseen and hostile people
2. Sexual fantasies that are accepted as unrealizable
3. Repressed and denied wishes
4. Feeling of emptiness

**5.25.** According to Freud's structural theory of the mind, the psychic apparatus is divided into the

1. id
2. ego
3. superego
4. unconscious

**5.26.** Which of the following statements are true about the development of a neurosis:

1. There is an inner conflict between drives and fears.
2. Sexual conflicts are involved.
3. Repression has made the conflict unconscious.
4. Neurosis can be traced to childhood.

**5.27.** Industry versus inferiority is characterized by

1. eagerness and curiosity
2. self-indulgence
3. expanded desires
4. confidence in ability to use adult materials

**5.28.** Erikson's generativity versus stagnation is characterized by

1. interests outside the home
2. establishing and guiding the next generation
3. self-absorption
4. bettering society

**DIRECTIONS:** Each set of lettered headings below is followed by a list of numbered words or phrases. For each numbered word or phrase, select

A. if the item is associated with **A** *only*
B. if the item is associated with **B** *only*
C. if the item is associated with *both* **A** *and* **B**
D. if the item is associated with *neither* **A** *nor* **B**

**Questions 5.29–5.32**
A. Conversion type of hysteria
  (conversion disorder)
B. Dissociative type of hysteria
  (dissociative disorder)
C. Both
D. Neither

**5.29.** Fugue states

**5.30.** Symbolic representation

**5.31.** Only occurs in women

**5.32.** Bodily symptoms that resemble those of physical disease

**DIRECTIONS:** Each group of questions below consists of five lettered headings followed by a list of numbered words or statements. For each numbered word or statement, select the *one* lettered heading that is most closely associated with it. Each lettered heading may be selected once, more than once, or not at all.

**Questions 5.33–5.37**
A. Rationalization
B. Projection
C. Denial
D. Reaction formation
E. Sublimation

**5.33.** A 45-year-old man who is having problems at work begins to complain that his boss "has it in for me."

**5.34.** A 34-year-old married woman who finds herself strongly attracted to a friend of her husband is very nasty to that friend.

**5.35.** A 35-year-old gambler loses $500 at the race track, but says he is not upset because "I would have spent the money on something else anyway."

**5.36.** A 42-year-old man is discharged from a cardiac intensive care unit after suffering a severe myocardial infarction, but continues to smoke 2 packs of cigarettes a day.

**5.37.** A 30-year-old man finds his greatest source of relaxation by going to watch football games.

**Questions 5.38–5.42.** Match each of
Erik Erikson's developmental stages,
listed below, with the correct psychosocial
crisis:

A. Basic trust versus mistrust
B. Integrity versus despair
C. Generativity versus stagnation
D. Intimacy versus isolation
E. Identity versus role of confusion

**5.38.** Oral-sensory (infancy)

**5.39.** Maturity

**5.40.** Adulthood

**5.41.** Young adulthood

**5.42.** Puberty and adolescence

**Questions 5.43–5.47**

A. Oral stage
B. Anal stage
C. Phallic stage
D. Latency stage
E. Genital stage

**5.43.** The main objective is to establish a
trusting dependent relationship with sustaining
objects.

**5.44.** The main objective is to focus erotic
interest in the genital area and genital
functions.

**5.45.** The main objective is striving for
separation and control.

**5.46.** The main objective is the
establishment of mature, heterosexual object
relationships.

**5.47.** The main objective is the further
integration of oedipal identifications and
sex roles.

# Answers

# Theories of Personality and Psychopathology: Classical Psychoanalysis

**5.1. The answer is D** (*Synopsis*, ed. 4, page 78).

Autonomous ego functions are based on rudimentary apparatuses that are present at birth. They develop outside the conflict with the id. Heinz Hartmann has included *perception*, intuition, comprehension, thinking, *language*, some phases of *motor development*, learning, and *intelligence* among the functions of this conflict-free sphere.

*Repression* is a mechanism of defense employed by the ego to help mediate conflict between the ego, superego, and id. It is not considered an autonomous ego function. Repression is defined as an unconscious defense mechanism in which unacceptable mental contents are banished or kept out of consciousness.

**5.2. The answer is B** (*Synopsis*, ed. 4, page 90).

According to Erik Erikson, identity crisis normally occurs during *adolescence*. It is characterized by a moratorium—the suspension between the morality learned by the child and the ethics to be developed by the adult. The indecision and confusion of that period often cause young people to cling to each other in a clannish manner.

Erikson accepted Freud's theory of infantile sexuality, but he also saw developmental potentials at all stages of life. His model of the life cycle consisted of eight stages, extending from birth into old age. Erikson believed that there was a dominant issue or maturational crisis arising during each period.

**5.3. The answer is B** (*Synopsis*, ed. 4, page 80).

The office worker is controlling guilt feelings by *rationalization*, a process that involves justifying unacceptable and irrational behavior by a plausible but invalid excuse for stealing. By turning from the victim role (the one who is fired) to quitting (firing himself), the worker is *identifying with his boss, whom he views as an aggressor.*

*Identification with the aggressor* is a process

by which individuals incorporate within themselves the mental image of a person who represents a source of frustration from the outside world. A primitive defense, it operates in the interest and service of the developing ego. *Rationalization* is a mechanism in which irrational or unacceptable behavior, motives, or feelings are logically justified or made consciously tolerable by plausible means. Ernest Jones introduced the term.

*Denial* is a mechanism in which the existence of unpleasant realities is disavowed. The term refers to a keeping out of conscious awareness any aspects of either internal or external reality that, if acknowledged, would produce anxiety. *Undoing* is a mechanism by which a person symbolically acts out in reverse something unacceptable that has already been done or against which the ego must defend itself. A primitive defense mechanism, undoing is a form of magical expiatory action. Repetitive in nature, it is commonly observed in obsessive-compulsive disorder. *Projection* is an unconscious defense mechanism in which a person attributes to another those generally unconscious ideas, thoughts, feelings, and impulses that are personally undesirable or unacceptable. Projection protects the person from anxiety arising from an inner conflict. By externalizing whatever is unacceptable, the person deals with it as a situation apart from himself or herself. *Intellectualization* is a mechanism in which reasoning or logic is used in an attempt to avoid confrontation with an objectionable impulse and thus defend against anxiety. It is also known as brooding compulsion and thinking compulsion. *Identification* is a mechanism by which individuals pattern themselves after another person; in the process, the self is more or less permanently altered.

**5.4. The answer is D** (*Synopsis*, ed. 4, page 80).

*Displacement* is a mechanism by which the emotional component of an unacceptable idea or object is transferred to a more acceptable one.

*Substitution* is a mechanism in which a person replaces an unacceptable wish, drive, emotion, or goal with a more acceptable one. *Rationalization* is a mechanism in which irrational behavior is justified. *Projection* is an unconscious mechanism in which a person attributes to another impulses that are personally undesirable. *Sublimation* is a mechanism in which the energy associated with unacceptable impulses or drives is diverted into personally and socially acceptable channels. Unlike other defense mechanisms, sublimation offers some minimal gratification of the instinctual drive or impulse.

**5.5.   The answer is B** (*Synopsis*, ed. 4, page 80).

The classic example of *identification* occurs toward the end of the oedipal stage, when a boy, whose main source of love and gratification is his mother, identifies with his father. The father represents the source of frustration, being the powerful rival for the mother; the child cannot master or run away from his father, so he is obliged to identify with him.

*Introjection* is the unconscious, symbolic internalization of a psychic representation of a hated or loved external object with the goal of establishing closeness to and constant presence of the object. It is considered an immature defense mechanism. In the case of a loved object, anxiety consequent to separation or tension arising out of ambivalence toward the object is diminished; in the case of a feared or hated object, internalization of its malicious or aggressive characteristics serves to avoid anxiety by symbolically putting those characteristics under one's own control. *Denial* is an unconscious mechanism in which unpleasant realities are disavowed. *Incorporation* is a primitive unconscious defense mechanism in which the psychic representation of another person or aspects of another person are assimilated into oneself through a figurative process of symbolic oral ingestion. It represents a special form of introjection and is the earliest preoedipal mechanism of identification. *Undoing* is an unconscious defense mechanism by which a person acts out in reverse something unacceptable.

**5.6.   The answer is C** (*Synopsis*, ed. 4, page 73).

The demands of external reality, called the reality principle, necessitate the postponement of immediate pleasure, with the aim of achieving perhaps even greater pleasure in the long run. *The reality principle is largely a learned function*, not an unlearned one; therefore, *it is closely related to the maturation of ego functions*, and it may be impaired in a variety of mental disorders

that are the result of impeded ego development.

*The pleasure principle*, which Freud considered to be *largely inborn*, refers to the tendency of the organism to avoid pain and to seek pleasure through tension discharge. In essence, the *pleasure principle persists throughout life*, but it must be *modified by the reality principle*.

**5.7.   The answer is E** (*Synopsis*, ed. 4, page 65).

Classical or orthodox psychoanalysis has been dependent in large part on Freud's *libido and instinct theories*. Libido theory derives from the investigation of the various manifestations and complex development of the original sexual instinct. Psychoanalysis is based on the investigative technique of *free association*, in which patients seek to verbalize without reservation, censorship, or guidance the passing contents of their minds. This method yielded Freud the data used to formulate such key concepts as *unconscious motivation*.

The *collective unconscious* is a term introduced by Jung; it consists of those psychic contents outside of the realm of awareness that are common to humankind in general. Transcending cultural differences, it is derived from the heritable collective experience of the species.

**5.8.   The answer is B** (*Synopsis*, ed. 4, page 69).

Freud proposed that, because childhood experiences remain so intensely vivid, they must exert a predisposing influence in relation to the development of psychoneurosis. He had discovered that his patients' train of memory extended well beyond the traumatic event that had precipitated the onset of illness. He found that his patients were able to produce memories of their childhood experiences, of scenes and events that they thought had long been forgotten. This discovery led to the conclusion that frequently these memories had been inhibited because they involved sexual fantasies or painful incidents in the patients' lives. Actual *precocious sexual activity* was relatively unimportant. Freud continued to acknowledge the role of *heredity* in determining a person's future susceptibility to neurosis, but he assigned most of the responsibility for neurosis *to unfavorable childhood experiences*. The *role of interpersonal factors* in mental disorders was developed by psychoanalytic workers, such as Harry Stack Sullivan, who came after Freud.

**5.9.   The answer is D** (*Synopsis*, ed. 4, page 69).

In a broad sense, Freud considered *repression* to be at the core of symptom formation and the development of all neuroses. Freud discovered, early in his practice, that his patients were often unwilling or unable to recount memories that later proved to be significant. He defined this reluctance as *resistance*. Later, he found that, in the majority of his patients, resistance was due to active forces in the mind (of which the patients themselves were often unaware) that led to the exclusion from consciousness of painful or distressing material. Freud described this active force as repression.

*Suppression* is a conscious act of controlling and inhibiting an unacceptable impulse, emotion, or idea. Suppression is differentiated from repression in that repression is an unconscious process. *Inhibition* is not a defense mechanism. It is the conscious or unconscious restraining of an impulse or desire. It may interfere with or restrict specific activities. *Regression* is a defense mechanism in which a person undergoes a partial or total return to earlier patterns of adaptation. Regression is observed in many psychiatric conditions, particularly schizophrenia.

**5.10.   The answer is A** (*Synopsis*, ed. 4, page 75).

Condensation is the mechanism by which several unconscious wishes, impulses, or *attitudes are combined and expressed in a single image*. In a young boy's dream, for example, an attacking monster may represent not only the dreamer's father but also some aspects of his mother, and the monster may stand for his own primitive impulses as well.

**5.11.   The answer is E** (*Synopsis*, ed. 4, page 80).

*Intellectualization* is a defense mechanism in which reasoning is used to avoid confrontation with an objectionable impulse.

*Altruism* is the regard for and dedication to the welfare of others. In psychiatry, the term is closely linked with ethics and morals. Freud recognized altruism as the only basis for the development of community interest; Bleuler equated it with morality. *Repression* is the defense mechanism in which unacceptable impulses are kept out of consciousness. *Regression* is the mechanism in which a person undergoes a return to earlier patterns of adaptation. *Projection* is the mechanism in which a person attributes to another those impulses that are personally unacceptable.

**5.12.   The answer is C** (*Synopsis*, ed. 4, pages 79 and 80).

Attributing one's own unacknowledged feelings to others is known as *projection*. A systematic and comprehensive study of the defen-

ses employed by the ego was presented for the first time by Anna Freud's contribution, *The Ego and the Mechanisms of Defense*. Miss Freud maintained that everyone, normal as well as neurotic, employs a characteristic repertoire of defense mechanisms to varying degrees.

*Introjection* is the unconscious, symbolic internalization of a psychic representation of an object. *Denial* is the unconscious disavowal of external reality. *Displacement* is a defense mechanism by which the emotional component of an unacceptable idea is transferred to a more acceptable one. *Reaction formation* is an unconscious defense mechanism in which a person develops a socialized attitude or interest that is the direct antithesis of some infantile wish or impulse that he or she harbors either consciously or unconsciously. It is considered to be one of the earliest and most unstable defense mechanisms.

**5.13.   The answer is D** (*Synopsis*, ed. 4, page 83).

The *obsessive-compulsive disorder* is characterized by persistent or urgently recurring thoughts (rumination) and repetitively performed behavior that bear little relation to the patient's realistic requirements and that are experienced as ego-dystonic. The thoughts are not experienced as voluntarily produced but, rather, as thoughts that invade consciousness and are felt to be senseless or repugnant. The behaviors are repetitive and seemingly purposeless and are performed according to certain rules or in a stereotyped fashion. The behavior is not an end in itself, but is designed to produce or to prevent some future event. The activity is not realistic, however, and may be clearly excessive. Other symptoms are a strong tendency to ambivalence, a regression to magical thinking (particularly in relation to the obsessional thoughts), and indications of rigid and destructive superego functioning.

*Phobic disorder* is an anxiety disorder characterized by intense specific fear of an object or situation. It is also called phobic neurosis. Phobic disorder is frequent in childhood. In DSM-III the phobic disorders include agoraphobia with and without panic attacks, social phobia, and simple phobia. *Hypochondriasis* is a somatoform disorder characterized by excessive, morbid anxiety about one's health. The term is derived from the belief that the state was caused by some dysfunction in the hypochondrium, especially the spleen. Hypochondriacal patients exhibit a predominant disturbance in which the physical symptoms or complaints are not explainable on the basis of demonstrable organic findings and are apparently linked to psychological factors. This disorder is also known as hypochondriacal neurosis. *Depressive disorder*, depressive neurosis, or as it is called in DSM-III, dysthymic disorder, is an affective disorder characterized by depressed mood. It is a chronic disturbance of mood, of at least 2 years' duration, that is not of sufficient severity and duration to meet the criteria for a major depressive episode. The depressed mood may be characterized by the individual as feeling sad or "down in the dumps." The mood or loss of interest or pleasure may be relatively persistent or intermittent and separated by periods of normal mood, interest, and pleasure, which may last a few days to a few weeks.

**5.14.   The answer is D** (*Synopsis*, ed. 4, page 74).

Freud first became aware of the significance of dreams in therapy when he realized that, in the process of free association, his patients frequently described their dreams of the night before or of years past. He then discovered that these dreams had a *definite meaning, although it was disguised.* He also found that encouraging his patients to free-associate to dream fragments was more productive than their associations to real-life events, insofar as it facilitated the disclosure of the patients' unconscious memories and fantasies.

In *The Interpretation of Dreams*, published in 1900, Freud concluded that a dream, like a neurotic symptom, is the conscious expression of an unconscious fantasy or wish that is not readily accessible in waking life. Although dreams were considered one of the *normal manifestations of unconscious activity*, they were shown later to bear some resemblance to the pathological thoughts of psychotic patients in the waking state. The dream images *represent unconscious wishes* or thoughts disguised through symbolization and other distorting mechanisms.

According to Freud, the manifest dream was the dream itself as reported by the dreamer. *The manifest dream in itself is not intelligible* as far as gaining new information about the patient is concerned. In the process of analysis of the manifest dream, however, information concerning the patient, which would otherwise be inaccessible, is obtained. This information that lies behind the dream is termed the latent dream-thoughts. The technique by which the latent dream-thoughts are derived from the manifest dream is called dream interpretation. The process by which the latent dream-thoughts become the manifest dream in the dreamer's mental life is called the dream work. *Nocturnal sensory stimuli* may be incorporated into the dream and can also be interpreted through free-association.

**5.15.   The answer is B** (*Synopsis*, ed. 4, page 80).

*Isolation*, in psychoanalysis, is a defense mechanism involving the separation of an idea or memory from its attached feeling tone. Unacceptable ideational content is thereby rendered free of its disturbing or unpleasant emotional charge. *Sublimation* is a defense mechanism in which energy is diverted into socially acceptable channels. *Regression* is a defense mechanism in which a person undergoes a return to earlier patterns of adaptation.

*Alienation* is not a defense mechanism. It is a psychiatric term used variously to describe a person's feelings of detachment from self or society, to denote one's avoidance of emotional experiences, or to describe a person's efforts to become estranged from his or her own feelings. *Altruism* is the regard for and dedication to the welfare of others.

**5.16.   The answer is C** (*Synopsis*, ed. 4, page 83).

A phobia is an abnormal fear reaction caused by a paralyzing conflict resulting from an increase of sexual excitation attached to an unconscious object. The fear is avoided by *displacing* the conflict onto an object or situation outside the ego system. Displacement is a transferring of an emotion from an original idea to which it was attached to another idea or object.

*Projection* is a defense mechanism in which thoughts, feelings, and impulses that are undesirable are transferred to another person. *Identification* is a defense mechanism by which individuals pattern themselves after another person. *Undoing* is an unconscious defense mechanism by which a person symbolically acts out in reverse something unacceptable. *Reaction formation* is an unconscious defense mechanism in which a person develops a socialized attitude or interest that is the direct antithesis of some infantile wish.

**5.17.   The answer is D** (*Synopsis*, ed. 4, page 80).

*Identification with the aggressor* is a defense mechanism by which individuals incorporate within themselves the mental image of a person who represents a source of frustration from the outside world. The young boy is identifying with the dentist who has caused him pain, and by taking on that role, he plays a make-believe game of extracting his friend's tooth.

*Symbolization* is a mechanism in which one idea or object comes to stand for another. *Regression* is a mechanism in which a person undergoes a return to earlier patterns of adaptation. *Isolation* is a mechanism involving the separation of an idea or memory from its attached feeling tone.

**5.18.   The answer is A** (*Synopsis*, ed. 4, page 83).

The *obsessive-compulsive* neurosis comes about as a result of the separation of affects from ideas or behavior by the defense mechanisms of undoing and isolation, by regression to the anal-sadistic level, or by turning the impulses against the self. As a defense against a painful idea in the unconscious, the affect is displaced onto some other indirectly associated idea, one more tolerable which in turn becomes invested with an inordinate quantity of affect.

*Anxiety disorder* is a disorder in which anxiety is the most prominent disturbance or in which the patients experience anxiety if they resist giving in to their symptoms. In DSM-III the anxiety disorders include phobic disorder, anxiety state, obsessive-compulsive disorder, post-traumatic stress disorder, and atypical anxiety disorder. *Pain disorder* is a disorder characterized by the complaint of pain. Pain may vary with intensity or duration and may range from a slight disturbance of social or occupational functioning to total incapacity and need for hospitalization. *Dissociative disorder* is a mental disorder characterized by a sudden, temporary alteration in consciousness, identity, or motor behavior. In DSM-III the dissociative disorders include psychogenic amnesia, psychogenic fugue, multiple personality, and depersonalization disorder. *Dysthymic disorder* is an affective disorder characterized by depressed mood. It is also known as depressive neurosis.

**5.19.   The answer is C (2, 4)** (*Synopsis*, ed. 4, page 90).

During the locomotor-genital stage, children move out into the world, where their *learning becomes instructive*; they grab at such instruction with eagerness and curiosity. Children show their first initiative at home, however, where they express passionate *interest in the parent of the opposite sex*.

During the muscular-anal stage, children learn to *control their anal sphincter muscles. Indecision and confusion* often cause young people in the stage of puberty and adolescence to cling to each other in a clannish manner.

**5.20.   The answer is A (1, 2, 3)** (*Synopsis*, ed. 4, page 82).

Secondary gain is the obvious advantage that a person gains from being ill, such as gifts, *attention*, and release from responsibility, *protection*, or *monetary compensation. Reduction of conflict* is not considered secondary gain; rather, according to Freud, it is known as primary gain.

Each form of illness has its characteristic form of secondary gain. For example, gaining attention through dramatic acting out, and, at times, deriving material advantages, is characteristic of hysteria. In obsessive-compulsive disorder, there is frequently a narcissistic gain through pride in illness.

**5.21.   The answer is E (all)** (*Synopsis*, ed. 4, page 67).

Freud's initial intent regarding hypnosis was to cause *patients to rid themselves of symptoms* by hypnotic suggestion. Although each patient did, indeed, behave as though the symptoms no longer existed, the symptoms returned during the waking experience. Because these beneficial effects were *transitory*, lasting only as long as the patient remained in contact with the physician, Freud suspected that *relief was dependent on the personal relationship between patient and physician.*

Later Freud turned to the cathartic method, in conjunction with hypnosis, to retrace the history of the symptoms to its traumatic origin. Accordingly, hypnotic treatment was modified with *the goal of inducing abreaction*. In the process of abreacting, the patient not only recalls but also relives the repressed material, which is accompanied by the appropriate affective response.

**5.22.   The answer is A (1, 2, 3)** (*Synopsis*, ed. 4, page 72).

A woman may be chosen by a man in adult life because *she resembles the man's idealized self-image* or his fantasied self-image, or because *she resembles someone who took care of him during the early years of his life*. Persons who have an intense degree of self-love, especially certain beautiful women, have, according to Freud, an appeal over and above their esthetic attraction. Such women supply for their lovers the *narcissism* that they were forced to give up in the process of turning toward object love (love for another).

The fourth reason is incorrect because Freud's notion of *sexual resemblance* is specifically referring to homosexual love. This is another example of narcissistic object choice, but because it refers to homosexuality, it does not answer the question directly.

**5.23.   The answer is E (all)** (*Synopsis*, ed. 4, pages 73 and 74).

Ordinarily, the repressed ideas and affects of the unconscious are *inaccessible to consciousness* because of the censorship or repression imposed by the preconscious. These repressed elements may attain the level of consciousness when the censor is overpowered (as in psychoneurotic symptom formation), relaxes (as in dream states), or is fooled (as by jokes).

The unconscious is associated with the form of mental activity that Freud called the *primary process*, or *primary process thinking*. Characteristically seen in infancy (and dreams), the primary process is marked by primitive, prelogical thinking and by the tendency to seek immediate discharge and gratification of instinctual demands. Consequently, the unconscious is also closely related to the *pleasure principle*, the principle by which the id seeks immediate tension reduction by direct or fantasied gratification. Similarly, the id also contains the mental representatives and derivatives of the *instinctual drives*, particularly those of the sexual instinct.

**5.24.    The answer is A (1, 2, 3)** (*Synopsis*, ed. 4, page 91).

During the standing stage, as described by Erikson, in which children are attempting to become upright, they experience in a new way their sense of smallness by comparison with the environment around them. *Paranoid fears of unseen and hostile people* can come into being as the children begin to develop feelings that they are not in control of their own feces. Others can condemn the feces that seemed acceptable when leaving the body, and a doubt begins that what one produces and leaves behind is inadequate. As *sexual fantasies are accepted as unrealizable*, some children may punish themselves for these fantasies by fearing harm to their genitals. They may *repress their wishes and begin to deny them* under the brutal assault of the developing superego.

During the lying and sitting stage, infants may experience a *feeling of emptiness*, starved not just for food because the nipple is taken away, or not there when they want it, but for sensual and visual stimulation as well.

**5.25.    The answer is A (1, 2, 3)** (*Synopsis*, ed. 4, page 76).

According to Freud's structural theory of the mind, the psychic apparatus is divided into three provinces: *id, ego, and superego*. The main distinction among these different functions lies between the ego and the id. The id is the locus of the instinctual drives. It is under the domination of the primary process; therefore, it operates in accordance with the pleasure principle, without regard for reality. The ego, however, represents a more coherent organization whose task it is to avoid unpleasure and pain by opposing or regulating the discharge of instinctual drives, in order to conform with the demands of the external world. In addition, the discharge of id impulses is opposed or regulated by the third structural component of the psychic apparatus,

the superego, which contains the internalized moral values and influence of the parental images.

The *unconscious* apparatus in psychoanalysis is the topographical division of the mind in which the psychic material is not readily accessible to conscious awareness by ordinary means. Its existence may be manifested in symptom formation, in dreams, or under the influence of drugs. The theories about the conscious, preconscious, and unconscious divisions of the psychiatric apparatus predated by many years Freud's structural hypotheses.

**5.26.    The answer is E (all)** (*Synopsis*, ed. 4, page 81).

The development of a neurosis is tied to certain conditions. These conditions are characterized by an *inner conflict between drives and fears* that prevents drive discharge. *Sexual drives are involved in their conflict*. According to Freud's theory, in order for a neurosis to develop, the inner conflict has not been worked through to a realistic solution. Instead, the drives that seek discharge have been expelled from consciousness through repression or through another defense mechanism. *This repression, however, has merely rendered the drives unconscious*; thus, it has not deprived them of their energy. Consequently, the repressed tendencies—or the disguised neurotic symptoms—have fought their way back into consciousness. Further, a rudimentary neurosis based on the same type of conflict existing in early childhood may be a condition under which an adult neurosis may develop, and thus *neurosis may be traced to childhood*.

**5.27.    The answer is D (4)** (*Synopsis*, ed. 4, page 90).

The stage of industry versus inferiority, which runs from ages 6 to 11, is characterized by the child's *confidence in his or her ability to use adult materials*. During this period of latency, the child is learning, waiting, and practicing to be a provider.

*Eagerness and curiosity* are characteristics of the initiative versus guilt stage. In intimacy versus isolation, young adults either become *self-indulgent and self-interested* or will share themselves in intense, long-term relationships. In initiative versus guilt, children develop a division between their *expanded desires* and their exuberance at unlimited growth.

**5.28.    The answer is E (all)** (*Synopsis*, ed. 4, pages 90 and 91).

The generativity versus stagnation stage spans the middle years of life. Generativity is characterized by *interests outside the home*, by *establishing and guiding the oncoming generation,* and by the *betterment of society.* Even a childless couple or person can be generative. When adults live only to satisfy their day-to-day personal needs, however, and to acquire comforts and entertainment for themselves, they become immersed in the *self-absorption* that is called stagnation.

**5.29–5.32.  The  answers  are  5.29–B, 5.30–A, 5.31–D, and 5.32–A** (*Synopsis*, ed. 4, page 82).

Hysterical states are described in two major forms depending on whether conversion symptoms or dissociative reactions are predominant.

*Conversion disorder* is a *symbolic representation* of physical conflict in terms of motor or sensory manifestations. The symbolization is the means by which repressed instinctual tendencies (over-intense libidinal stimulation) gain external expression. In other words, according to DSM-III, the predominant disturbance is the loss of or alteration in physical functioning that suggests physical disorder but that, instead, is apparently an expression of psychological conflict or need. The symptom has a symbolic value that is a representation and partial resolution of the underlying psychological conflict. *The most classic conversion symptoms are those suggesting neurological disorders,* such as paralysis, aphonia, seizures, anesthesia, blindness, parathesias, and coordination disturbances. There is no definite information available with regard to the sex ratio in this disorder. It is *seen in both men and women,* although apparently one particular conversion symptom, globus hystericus—the feeling of a lump in the throat that interferes with swallowing—is more common in women. Usually, conversion symptoms develop in a setting of intense psychological stress, and have both an abrupt onset and resolution. Prolonged loss of function may produce real and serious complications, such as contractures or disuse atrophy from conversion paralysis.

*Dissociative disorder* is a group of disorders characterized by sudden, temporary alteration in the normally integrated functions of consciousness, identity, or motor behavior. Included in this group are psychogenic amnesia, *psychogenic fugue,* multiple personality, and depersonalization disorder. If the alteration occurs in consciousness, important personal events cannot be recalled. Either the individual's usual identity is temporarily forgotten and a new identity is assumed, or the usual feeling of one's own reality is lost and is replaced by a sense of unreality. If the alteration is one of motor behavior, there is also a concurrent disturbance in consciousness or identity, such as in the wandering seen in psychogenic fugue. Other forms of dissociative phenomena that have been described include various trance states. Automatic writings, Ganser's syndrome, and some forms of mystical states of experience also occur.

Dissociation encompasses the segregation of any group of mental processes from the rest of the psychic apparatus; dissociation generally means a loss of the usual interrelationships between various groups of mental processes, with resultant almost independent functioning of the one group that has been separated from the rest. Dissociative hysterical symptoms are characterized by the fact that a group of recently related mental events—which may be memories, feelings, or fantasies—are beyond the patient's power of conscious recall, but still remain psychically active and ultimately capable of conscious recovery.

**5.33–5.37.  The  answers  are  5.33–B, 5.34–D, 5.35–A, 5.36–C, and 5.37–E** (*Synopsis*, ed. 4, page 80).

*Projection* is an unconscious defense mechanism in which a person attributes to another those generally unconscious ideas, thoughts, feelings, and impulses that are personally undesirable or unacceptable. Projection protects the person from anxiety arising from an inner conflict. By externalizing whatever is unacceptable, the person deals with it as a situation apart from himself. *Reaction formation* is an unconscious defense mechanism in which a person develops a socialized attitude or interest that is the direct antithesis of some infantile wish or impulse that the person harbors either consciously or unconsciously. One of the earliest and most unstable defense mechanisms, it is closely related to repression; both are defenses against impulses or urges that are unacceptable to the ego. *Rationalization* is an unconscious defense mechanism in which irrational or unacceptable behavior, motives, or feelings are logically justified or made consciously tolerable by plausible means. Ernest Jones introduced the term. *Denial* is a defense mechanism in which the existence of unpleasant realities is disavowed. The term refers to a keeping out of conscious awareness any aspects of either internal or external reality that, if acknowledged, would produce anxiety. *Sublimation* is an unconscious defense mechanism in which the energy associated with unacceptable impulses or drives is diverted into personally and socially acceptable channels. Unlike other defense mechanisms, sublimation offers some minimal gratification of the instinctual drive or impulse.

**5.38–5.42.  The  answers  are  5.38–A, 5.39–B, 5.40–C, 5.41–D, and 5.42–E** (*Synopsis*, ed. 4, pages 89, 90, and 91).

Erikson is probably best known for his positing of eight stages of ego development, which cover the entire life-span from birth to death. These stages, which roughly parallel Freud's psychosexual stages, have both positive and negative aspects, are marked by emotional crises, and are very much affected by the person's particular culture and by that person's interaction with the society to which he or she belongs.

**Erikson's Developmental Stages and Psychosocial Crises**

| Developmental Stage | Psychosocial Crisis |
| --- | --- |
| I. Oral-sensory (infancy) | Basic trust versus mistrust |
| II. Muscular-anal (early childhood) | Autonomy versus shame, doubt |
| III. Locomotor-genital (play age) | Initiative versus guilt |
| IV. Latency (school age) | Industry versus inferiority |
| V. Puberty and adolescence | Identity versus role confusion |
| VI. Young adulthood | Intimacy versus isolation |
| VII. Adulthood | Generativity versus stagnation |
| VIII. Maturity | Integrity versus despair |

**5.43–5.47. The answers are 5.43–A, 5.44–C, 5.45–B, 5.46–E, and 5.47–D** (*Synopsis*, ed. 4, pages 70, 71, and 72).

These stages represent Freud's psychosexual developmental stages.

The *oral stage* is the earliest stage in psychosexual development, lasting from birth to 18 months of age. During this period, the oral zone—mouth, lips, tongue and related structures—is the center of the infant's needs, perceptions, modes of expression, and pleasurable erotic experiences. The objectives of the oral stage are (1) to form a *trusting dependent relationship* with sustaining objects and (2) to establish comfortable expression and gratification of oral libidinal needs without excessive conflict or ambivalence from oral sadistic wishes. Successful resolution of the oral stage enables individuals to give to and receive from others without excessive dependence or envy, and gives them the capacity to trust themselves and others.

The *anal stage* follows the oral stage; it begins at approximately 12 to 18 months of age when there is maturation of neuromuscular control over sphincters, particularly the anal sphincter. During this time, the child acquires the physiological potential for voluntary control over retention or expulsion of feces. This period continues until about 3 years of age. The anal stage is essentially a period of striving for *independence and separation from parental control*. The child tries to achieve autonomy without shame or self-doubt. Successful resolution of the anal state provides the basis for later independence and personal autonomy.

The *phallic stage* (from 3 to 5 years of age) is characterized by a primary focus of sexual interest, curiosity, and pleasurable experiences in the penis in boys and the clitoris in girls. There is increased genital masturbation during this stage, with concomitant guilt and castration anxiety. During this phase, the oedipal involvement and conflict are established. The primary objective is to focus *erotic interest on the genital area* and genital functions. This lays the foundation for the establishment of core gender identity.

The *latency stage* is a stage of relative quiescence of the sexual drive during the period from the resolution of the oedipal complex until pubescence (from age 5 to 6 years until age 11 to 13 years). Friendships during latency tend to be with those of the same sex. Libidinal and aggressive energies are sublimated into learning and play activities and also into developing proficiency in dealing with persons and things in this environment. The main objective of this period is the integration of *oedipal identifications* and the consolidation of sex role identity.

The *genital stage* is the final step in the psychosexual development of the person. It begins with the onset of puberty and extends through adolescence into young adulthood. Along with a physiological maturation of the genital and endocrine systems, there is an intensification of libidinal drives. The primary objectives of the genital period are separation and independence from parents and the establishment of *mature, nonincestuous, heterosexual object relationships*. Related objectives of this period include the achievement of a sense of personal identity, acceptance of adult roles, and the development of mature, meaningful goals and values.

## References

Coles R: *Erik H. Erikson: The Growth of His Work.* Little, Brown, Boston, 1970.

Freud S: *Standard Edition of the Complete Psychological Works of Sigmund Freud.* Hogarth Press, London, 1953–1966.

Kohut H: *The Restoration of the Self.* International Universities Press, New York, 1977.

Meissner W W: Classical psychoanalysis. In *Comprehensive Textbook of Psychiatry,* ed 4, H I Kaplan, B J Sadock, editors, p 337. Williams & Wilkins, Baltimore, 1985.

Zetzel E R, Meissner W W: *Basic Concepts of Psychoanalytic Psychiatry.* Basic Books, New York, 1973.

# 6

# Theories of Personality and Psychopathology: Cultural and Interpersonal Schools

At various stages in the evolution of psychoanalysis, several of Freud's colleagues expanded or revised his formulations. At times, these modifications were subsequently incorporated into the body of psychoanalytic theory; however, other innovations produced schisms within the Freudian movement and, in some instances, led to the establishment of new schools of psychoanalysis.

Among the most prominent of these early dissenters were Alfred Adler and Carl Jung, both of whom rejected Freud's belief that sexuality plays a unique role in normal and pathological human behavior. Jung's rejection of Freud's libido theory led to the elaboration of a rather mystical psychoanalytic system. Adler turned to the sociocultural determinants of behavior. Social, cultural, and interpersonal behavioral determinants were also emphasized in the so-called culturalist theories of Karen Horney and Harry Stack Sullivan, among others. Concomitantly, these workers deemphasized the biological instinctual drives, particularly sexuality, as dominant determinants of behavior.

Other theories of psychopathology did not evolve as direct offshoots of Freudian psychoanalysis. Among these is the theory of Adolf Meyer, who conceived of normal as well as abnormal behavior as deriving from a series of adaptive reactions to the environment.

All of these theories have limitations; no single theory has, as yet, been universally accepted by psychiatrists and psychoanalysts. Nevertheless, the various theories of personality and psychopathology are the foundations upon which the practice of psychiatry rests. Each of these theories contains insights that merit consideration because they enhance one's understanding of the complexities of normal and abnormal human behavior. Furthermore, they provide useful theoretical frameworks around which the psychiatrists' clinical work can be organized. Methods of psychiatric assessment, as well as the various treatment methods, have evolved from these models, as have current hypotheses to explain the dynamics of the various psychiatric disorders. The different disorders are described according to different psychodynamic theories, another indication of the diversity of theoretical orientation that is characteristic of psychiatry today.

The reader is referred to Chapter 6 of *Modern Synopsis-IV*, which covers the cultural and interpersonal theories of personality and psychopathology. After reading that chapter, the reader can assess his or her knowledge by studying the questions and answers that follow.

# Questions

**DIRECTIONS:** Each of the statements or questions below is followed by five suggested responses or completions. Select the *one* that is *best* in each case.

**6.1.** Psychobiology is best characterized by which of the following concepts:
A. Analysis of the ego through interpretation of defense mechanisms
B. Biographical study and common-sense understanding of patients
C. Primary understanding of the biological and biochemical origin and treatment of mental illness
D. Emphasis of genetic factors in mental illness and the use of drugs in psychiatry
E. Psychological factors affecting physical illness

**6.2.** Alienation from self is a concept developed by
A. Sigmund Freud
B. Harry Stack Sullivan
C. Eric Berne
D. Karen Horney
E. Alfred Adler

**6.3.** Play therapy was most often used by
A. Sigmund Freud
B. Wilhelm Reich
C. Karen Horney
D. Melanie Klein
E. Harry Stack Sullivan

**6.4.** The term "habit training" was coined by
A. Adolf Meyer
B. Carl Jung
C. Otto Rank
D. Bhurrus F. Skinner
E. Joseph Wolpe

**6.5.** The self-system refers to Sullivan's concept of the
A. unconscious
B. personality
C. libido
D. defense mechanisms
E. Oedipus complex

**DIRECTIONS:** For each of the incomplete statements below, *one* or *more* of the completions given is correct. Choose answer:

A. if only **1, 2,** and **3** are correct
B. if only **1** and **3** are correct
C. if only **2** and **4** are correct
D. if only **4** is correct
E. if all are correct

**6.6.** Wilhelm Reich's technique of character analysis is based on which of the following hypotheses:
1. The analysis of resistance is the analyst's prime function, and interpretation is the analyst's chief tool.
2. Incestuous wishes are at the core of character formation.
3. Certain resistances are inherent in the character structure of the neurotic patient.
4. Children express real-life experiences through symbolic play.

**6.7.** Karen Horney's contribution to psychology included
1. actual self
2. idealized self
3. real self
4. oedipal conflict

**6.8.** The concept of birth trauma, as developed by Otto Rank, refers to which of the following concepts:

1. The mother's painful experience at the time of delivery
2. The transference
3. The Oedipus complex
4. The source of primal anxiety

**6.9.** Wilhelm Reich's concept of character includes which of the following:

1. Character is an armoring of the ego.
2. Punishment over sexual activity impacts on character formation.
3. Elasticity determines the difference between the healthy and the neurotic character.
4. The death instinct affects character formation.

**6.10.** According to Jung, archetypes

1. are instinctual patterns
2. express themselves in representational images
3. are organizational units of the personality
4. manifest themselves as mythological images

**6.11.** According to Alfred Adler, the helplessness of the infant accounts for which of the following:

1. Feelings of inferiority
2. Wanting to be perfect
3. Fantasied organic deficits
4. Compensatory strivings

**6.12.** The concept of masculine protest

1. was introduced by Alfred Adler
2. is a universal human tendency
3. refers to the female or passive role
4. is an extension of Adler's ideas about organ inferiority

**6.13.** In contrast to classical Freudian psychoanalytic theory, Melanie Klein maintained that

1. a 2-year-old child could be analyzed
2. depression occurs in the first year of life
3. aggressive drives are more important than sexual drives
4. the oedipal conflict has its onset in the earliest months of life

**6.14.** According to Sullivan, anxiety

1. occurs in an interpersonal context
2. results from feelings of disapproval from a significant adult
3. is accompanied by somatic symptoms
4. results in restriction of functioning

**DIRECTIONS:** Each group of questions below consists of five lettered headings followed by a list of numbered words or statements. For each numbered word or statement, select the *one* lettered heading that is most closely associated with it. Each lettered heading may be used once, more than once, or not at all.

### Questions 6.15–6.19
Match each characteristic with its accompanying term, as described by Karen Horney:
A. Externalization
B. Compartmentalization
C. Alienation
D. Automatic control
E. Supremacy of the mind (intellectualization)

**6.15.** Avoidance of experiencing emotional conflict

**6.16.** Experience of self as unconnected parts

**6.17.** Unconscious check of feelings and impulses

**6.18.** Experience of inner processes or feelings occurring outside of self

**6.19.** Achievement of relief from tension by blurring genuine wants, feelings, and beliefs

### Questions 6.20–6.24
A. Shadow
B. Anima
C. Animus
D. Persona
E. Collective unconscious

**6.20.** Face presented to the outside world

**6.21.** Another person of the same sex as the dreamer

**6.22.** A man's undeveloped femininity

**6.23.** A woman's undeveloped masculinity

**6.24.** Mythological ideas and primitive projections

# Answers

# Theories of Personality and Psychopathology: Cultural and Interpersonal Schools

**6.1.   The answer is B** (*Synopsis*, ed. 4, page 111).

Psychobiology is a term introduced by Adolf Meyer. It emphasizes the importance of *biographical study so that one may comprehend the person as a whole*. The immediate goal is to identify motives or indications for the psychiatric examination. In identifying important details of the patient's life history through a biographical study, the clinician records the most obvious related personality items, factors, and reactions.

In addition, a careful study should be made of the physical, neurological, genetic, and social status variables, as well as of the correlations between these variables and personality factors. Also, differential diagnosis and a therapeutic schedule should be formulated for each case.

*Analysis of the ego through interpretation of defense mechanisms* is a concept of psychoanalysis. A *primary understanding of the biological and biochemical origin and treatment of mental illness, the emphasis of genetic factors in mental illness, and the use of drugs in psychiatry* are concepts of psychopharmacology. *Psychological factors affecting physical illness* are the concerns of psychosomatic medicine.

**6.2.   The answer is D** (*Synopsis*, ed. 4, pages 95 and 96).

Alienation from self is a concept developed by *Karen Horney* to describe the various neurotic mechanisms, such as distorted self-image, self-hatred, and estrangement of one's own feelings, which all combine to lead to alienation. Such alienation of one's own feelings is characteristic of obsessive-compulsive disorders. Certain organs and body areas, or even the entire body, are often perceived as if they did not belong to the person or as if they were different from the usual. Some manifestations are objectively observable; others are subjective and subtle.

*Sigmund Freud* developed psychoanalysis; *Harry Stack Sullivan* conceptualized the interpersonal theory of psychiatry; *Eric Berne* developed transactional analysis; and *Alfred Adler* is best known for his concept of the inferiority complex.

**6.3.   The answer is D** (*Synopsis*, ed. 4, page 108).

*Melanie Klein* developed an analytical play technique, referred to as play therapy. Analagous to the free-association technique, which is the basis of the analysis of adults, play therapy is used as the basis of analysis with children. Used with children, the process is one in which the children reveal their problems on a fantasy level with dolls, clay, and other primitive-type toys. The therapist intervenes opportunely with helpful explanations about each child's responses and behavior, using language that is geared to the child's comprehension.

*Sigmund Freud* is known as the father of psychoanalysis, and he set forth the psychosexual stages of development: oral, anal, phallic, latency, and genital. *Wilhelm Reich* is best known for his concept of character armor, *Harry Stack Sullivan* for his interpersonal school of psychiatry, and *Karen Horney* for her emphasis on environmental and cultural factors in the genesis of neurosis.

**6.4.   The answer is A** (*Synopsis*, ed. 4, page 111).

*Adolf Meyer* used the term habit training to explain the process of therapy by which the main goal is to aid patients' adjustment by helping them to modify unhealthy adaptations. In the process of habit training the psychiatrist always emphasizes patients' current life situations using a variety of techniques, such as guidance, suggestion, re-education and direction.

*Meyer* is known for his concepts of psychobiology, *Carl Jung* developed the school known as analytic psychology, and *Bhurrus F. Skinner* and *Joseph Wolpe* are known for their work in learning theory and behavior therapy, respectively. *Otto Rank* focused on the analytic aspects of what he called the birth trauma.

**6.5.   The answer is B** (*Synopsis*, ed. 4, page 99).

Sullivan's self-system refers to the concept of *personality*, which begins to develop in infancy and becomes a technique for avoiding anxiety. The self-system is a reflection of both maternal and paternal attitudes and of any accumulated sets of experiences that begin in infancy and continue for a long period of time.

The *unconscious*, in psychoanalysis, is the topographic division of the mind in which the psychic material is not readily accessible to conscious awareness by ordinary means. Its existence may be manifested in symptom formation, in dreams, or under the influence of drugs. The *libido*, in psychoanalysis, is the psychic energy associated with the sexual drive or life instinct. *Defense mechanisms* are unconscious processes acting to relieve conflict and anxiety arising from one's impulses and drives. The *Oedipus complex* is the constellation of feelings, impulses, and conflicts in the developing child that concern sexual impulses and attraction toward the opposite-sex parent and aggressive, hostile, or envious feelings toward the same-sex parent. Real or fantasied threats from the same-sex parent result in the repression of those feelings. The development of the Oedipus complex coincides with the phallic phase of psychosexual development. One of Freud's most important concepts, the term was originally applied only to males.

**6.6.   The answer is A (1, 2, 3)** (*Synopsis,* ed. 4, pages 109 and 110).

Wilhelm Reich's most enduring contribution to psychoanalysis is the technique of character analysis. He hypothesized that *certain resistances are inherent in the character structure of the neurotic patient.* These resistances become evident in the patient's specific ways of acting and reacting and may take many forms, such as extreme passivity, ingratiation, argumentativeness, arrogance, distrust, and certain motor activities. In Reich's psychoanalytic treatment, the analyst actively concentrated, through *analysis and interpretation, on the patient's character defenses.* He also believed that *incestuous wishes are at the core of character formation.*

Melanie Klein developed an analytic technique, referred to as play therapy, in which *children express real-life experiences through symbolic play.*

**6.7.   The answer is A (1, 2, 3)** (*Synopsis,* ed. 4, page 93).

Crucial to the understanding of Karen Horney's theory of self are the triple concepts: the actual self, the real self, and the idealized self. The *actual self* refers to the whole person, as that person really exists at any point in time. The *real self* is the person's potential for further growth and development. The person the neurotic believes himself or herself to be—the result of identification with an idealized image of what

the person feels he or she should be—is the *idealized self.*

The *oedipal conflict* is a term formulated by Sigmund Freud to describe the conflict in the developing child that concerns sexual impulses and attraction toward the opposite-sex parent.

**6.8.   The answer is D (4)** (*Synopsis,* ed. 4, page 106).

Otto Rank hypothesized that the birth process is *the source of primal anxiety,* which is then subject to repression. Inasmuch as a subsequent desire to return to the position of original or primal pleasure gives rise to anxiety, so does any change from a pleasurable to a painful situation.

Rank maintained that the circumstances of birth are deeply imprinted on the psyche of the infant and often reappear in symbolic form in psychiatric patients. He stated that childhood was devoted to the mastery of the birth trauma, although the original or primal anxiety was displaced onto other situations and objects. Although he described the birth process as a *painful experience for the mother,* his concept of birth trauma did not relate to the mother's experience but to that of the infant.

*The transference* is an unconscious tendency of a person to assign to others in the person's present environment those feelings and attitudes originally linked with significant figures in the person's early life. It is a crucial process in psychoanalysis. The development of the *Oedipus complex* coincides with the phallic phase of psychosexual development. As formulated by Freud, it encompasses sexual impulses and attraction toward the opposite-sex parent.

**6.9.   The answer is A (1, 2, 3)** (*Synopsis,* ed. 4, page 109).

Wilhelm Reich viewed character as a defensive structure, an *armoring of one's ego,* both against instincts within and the world without. As a result, a defense develops that prevents flexibility, producing a loss in psychic and physical elasticity. This prevention or, rather, the degree of persisting *elasticity determines the difference between the healthy and neurotic character.*

Reich viewed the inevitable frustrations of incestuous wishes as the core of character formation. Character formation, according to Reich, represents an attempt to end these conflicts. *Punishment over sexual activity impacts on character formation.*

Reich disagreed strongly with Freud's concept of *the death instinct,* and he was particularly opposed to Freud's reference to the death instinct as the basis for masochistic phenomena.

**6.10.    The answer is E (all)** (*Synopsis*, ed. 4, page 102).

Jung believed archetypes to be *instinctual patterns*. All psychic energy is transmitted in forms of experience, behavior, and emotion, which *express themselves in representational or mythological images*. Thus, the archetypes represent the basic motivations and drives that become *organizational units of the personality*.

**6.11.    The answer is E (all)** (*Synopsis*, ed. 4, page 104).

According to Alfred Adler, infants are born with certain *feelings of inferiority*. As a result, they have a need to strive for superiority, *perfection*, and totality. He classified these strivings under the heading of the inferiority complex, which comprises the newborns' feelings secondary to their *real or fantasied organic or psychological deficits. Compensatory strivings* refer to the person's attempt to overcome feelings of inferiority.

**6.12.    The answer is E (all)** (*Synopsis*, ed. 4, page 105).

*Alfred Adler* introduced the concept of masculine protest, which represents the *universal human tendency* to move from *a female or passive role* to a masculine or active role. The doctrine *is an extension of his ideas about organ inferiority*. Adler regards this concept as the main force in neurotic disease. It represents the distorted perception of sex differences caused by the striving for superiority. If it takes an active force in women, they attempt from an early age to usurp the male position. They become aggressive in manner, adopt masculine habits, and endeavor to domineer everyone about them. The masculine protest in a male indicates that he has never fully recovered from an infantile doubt as to whether he was really male. He strives for an ideal masculinity, invariably perceived as the self-possession of freedom and power.

**6.13.    The answer is E (all)** (*Synopsis*, ed. 4, page 107).

In contrast to classical Freudian psychoanalytic theory, Melanie Klein maintained that *2-year-old children could be analyzed* without the aid of their parents. She described the formation of a primitive superego during the first and second years, and she believed that *aggressive drives are more important than sexual drives* during this stage of development. She traced the onset of the *oedipal conflict to the earliest months of life*, as well as maintained *that depression occurs in the first year of life*.

**6.14.    The answer is E (all)** (*Synopsis*, ed. 4, pages 98 and 99).

As with other concepts developed by Sullivan, anxiety is seen as an interpersonal phenomenon and is defined as the response to the *feelings of disapproval from a significant adult*. Therefore, it occurs only in an *interpersonal context*, even if the other person is not real but a fantasied image.

Feelings of disapproval can be communicated and interpreted by the person in a variety of ways, sometimes false. A distressing feeling, such as anxiety, *is accompanied by somatic symptoms* and psychological feelings of doom, which cannot be tolerated by the person for long.

Sullivan views the development of personality as a process of learning to cope with anxiety by using adaptive maneuvers and defense techniques designed to gain approval from significant people in one's life. When the person feels the anxiety is becoming too widespread, he or she will try to limit opportunities for the further development of such anxiety. *Such limitation results in restriction of functioning* that includes only those patterns of activity that are familiar and well established.

Other terms associated with Sullivan are (1) prototaxic thinking, which refers to primitive, illogical thought processes and (2) parataxic distortion, which refers to distortions in judgment or attitude in interpersonal relations based on patterns set by earlier experience.

**6.15–6.19.    The answers are 6.15–E, 6.16–B, 6.17–D, 6.18–A, and 6.19–C** (*Synopsis*, ed. 4, page 95).

Karen Horney uses the term supremacy of the mind or intellectualization to refer to the use of intellect in *avoiding emotionally conflicting experiences*. Logic and reasoning are associated with this mechanism, which can prevent free association in therapy, as well as trigger panic when the person is abruptly threatened with loss of control by being forced to let go in sexual activity or when anesthetized or intoxicated.

Compartmentalization refers to psychic fragmentation or the *experience of self as consisting of unconnected parts* that should be kept together.

Automatic control is an *unconscious mechanism that checks feelings and impulses* and their expression. These impulses and feelings tend to be expressed somatically.

*Experiences of inner processes or feelings occurring outside of self* refer to externalization. In active externalization, the feelings toward oneself are experienced as feelings toward others; in passive externalization, feelings toward others are experienced as being directed by others toward oneself.

Alienation from self is an active defensive measure that *achieves relief of tension by blurring genuine wants, feelings, and beliefs* that conflict with neurotically idealized qualities. This process produces the repression, inhibition, blocking, or dissociation of one's own feelings, so that they no longer seem effective, familiar, or convincing to the patient.

**6.20–6.24. The answers are 6.20–D, 6.21–A, 6.22–B, 6.23–C, and 6.24–E** (*Synopsis*, ed. 4, pages 102 and 103).

With the term "persona," Jung denotes the disguised or masked attitude assumed by a person, in contrast to the more deeply rooted personality components. Such persons put on a mask, corresponding to their conscious intentions, that makes up the *face presented to the outside world.* Through their more or less complete identification with the attitude of the mind, they deceive other people, and often themselves, as to their real character.

The shadow is represented in dreams as an-

*other person of the same sex as the dreamer.* According to Jung, one sees much in another person that does not belong to one's conscious psychology, but which comes out from one's unconscious.

In Jung's terminology, anima and animus are archetypal representations of potentials that have not yet entered conscious awareness or become personalized. Anima is *a man's undeveloped femininity.* Animus is *a women's undeveloped masculinity.* These concepts are universal basic human drives from which both conscious and unconscious individual qualities develop. Usually, they appear as unconscious imagery of persons of the opposite sex.

The collective unconscious is defined as the psychic contents outside the realm of awareness that are common to mankind in general. Jung, who introduced the term, believed that the collective unconscious is inherited and derived from the collective experience of the species. It transcends cultural differences and explains the analogy between ancient *mythological ideas and the primitive projections* observed in some patients who have never been exposed to those ideas.

# References

Adler A: *The Individual Psychology of Alfred Adler: A Systematic Presentation in Selections from His Writings,* H L Ansbacher, R R Ansbacher, editors. Basic Books, New York, 1956.

Groesbeck C J: Carl Jung. In *Comprehensive Textbook of Psychiatry,* ed 4, H I Kaplan, B J Sadock, editors, p 433. Williams & Wilkins, Baltimore, 1985.

Horney K: *The Neurotic Personality of Our Time.* W W Norton, New York, 1937.

Jung C G: *Two Essays on Analytical Psychology.* Princeton University Press, Princeton, 1966.

Kernberg O: Melanie Klein. In *Comprehensive Textbook of Psychiatry,* ed 4, H I Kaplan, B J Sadock, editors, p 441. Williams & Wilkins, Baltimore, 1985.

Klein M: *The Psycho-Analysis of Children.* Hogarth Press, London, 1954.

Meyer A: *Collected Papers of Adolf Meyer,* 4 vols. Johns Hopkins Press, Baltimore, 1948–1952.

Reich W: *Character Analysis.* Farrar, Straus & Young, New York, 1949.

Sullivan H S: *The Interpersonal Theory of Psychiatry.* W W Norton, New York, 1953.

Symonds A, Symonds M: Karen Horney. In *Comprehensive Textbook of Psychiatry,* ed 4, H I Kaplan, B J Sadock, editors, p 419. Williams & Wilkins, Baltimore, 1985.

Weiner M: Other psychodynamic schools. In *Comprehensive Textbook of Psychiatry,* ed 4, H I Kaplan, B J Sadock, editors, p 451. Williams & Wilkins, Baltimore, 1985.

Zaphiropoulos M: Harry Stack Sullivan. In *Comprehensive Textbook of Psychiatry,* ed 4, H I Kaplan, B J Sadock, editors, p 426. Williams & Wilkins, Baltimore, 1985.

# 7

# Diagnosis and Psychiatry: Examination of the Psychiatric Patient

Diagnosis may be defined as the recognition of signs and symptoms of disordered functions and their classification into entities that are associated with a predictable outcome. The role of diagnosis in psychiatry, however, is not quite analogous to its place in other fields of medicine, because in contrast to the medical disorders, the etiology of many of the psychiatric syndromes is not yet understood, and treatment is often empirical. Thus, formal diagnosis in psychiatry does not always implicate specific etiological factors, nor does it always facilitate treatment decisions. Despite these limitations, accurate assessment does play an important role in psychiatry. Clinical experience has shown that, on the basis of such assessment, it is possible, with respect to certain diagnostic entities, to predict the patient's response to therapy with a fair degree of accuracy. For example, the symptoms of many schizophrenic patients improve with appropriate antipsychotic medication, whereas certain hyperactivity disorders in children are likely to respond to treatment with amphetamines. Clearly, accurate assessment in such cases is required in order to choose appropriate pharmacological therapy, as well as to differentiate between those patients who require drugs and those who may be treated exclusively with psychotherapy.

The psychiatrist's principal diagnostic tool for the accumulation of the complex information on which the final assessment of the patient is based is the psychiatric examination, which comprises, in turn, a mental status examination and a psychiatric history. The purpose of the mental status examination is to assess current psychopathology. Therefore, it is designed specifically to elicit evidence of disturbances in thought processes and affect, in communication, and in social adaptation. The psychiatric history provides the psychiatrist with a longitudinal view of the personality development and the genesis of the psychopathology of the patient.

Psychological tests of intelligence may perform an important diagnostic function. The psychiatrist's estimate of this important psychological parameter on the basis of data elicited through the interview may not be reliable. The patient's performance on standardized intelligence tests, however, usually provides valid and reliable information in this regard. Once these test findings are available, the psychiatrist can distinguish between the patient whose pathological behavior is due to a basic intellectual deficiency and the patient whose impaired functioning may be attributed to psychiatric disorders. When brain damage is suspected but cannot be clinically demonstrated unequivocally, psychological tests may be of value in determining whether organic factors are operative in the genesis of the patient's pathological behavior. When brain damage is subtle, mild, and diffuse, has developed slowly, or occurs in a "silent" area of the brain, the resultant deficit may not be clearly apparent from the patient's daily behavior; nor is it likely to emerge clearly in the course of the psychiatric interview.

Finally, medical illness may produce psychiatric symptoms similar to symptoms that are psychological in origin. When evidence indicates that the behavioral disorders which have become evident in the course of the psychiatric examination may be due to organic factors, a medical or neurological evaluation and appropriate laboratory procedures, such as an electroencephalogram, are required for the establishment of definitive diagnosis.

Readers should refer to Chapter 7 of *Modern Synopsis–IV*, "Diagnosis and Psychiatry: Examination of the Psychiatric Patient," which covers the areas mentioned above. Then, by studying the questions and answers below, they can gain an accurate assessment of their understanding in this area.

# Questions

**DIRECTIONS:** Each of the statements or questions below is followed by five suggested responses or completions. Select the *one* that is *best* in each case.

**7.1.** The most important initial task of the doctor doing the psychiatric interview is to

A. make a diagnosis
B. establish rapport
C. give advice
D. reassure the patient
E. develop a treatment plan

**7.2.** The first sign of beginning cerebral disease is impairment of

A. immediate memory
B. long-term memory
C. remote memory
D. recent memory
E. none of the above

**7.3.** A stress interview is characterized by

A. intimidation of the psychiatrist by the patient
B. the anxiety produced in both doctor and patient
C. confrontation of the patient by the psychiatrist
D. the destructive effect it has on the patient's psyche
E. the use of the Social Readjustment Rating Scale

**7.4.** The most likely diagnosis of a 43-year-old college professor who drew the following figure on the Draw-a-Person Test is

A. obsessive-compulsive personality
B. depressive neurosis
C. organic brain damage
D. conversion disorder
E. mania

**7.5.** A first-year female psychiatric resident complaining of "anxiety attacks" is seen by a psychiatrist. During the interview she states that she is afraid that one of her patients may attack her. She then goes on to say, "This is a fear that many of the other residents share." An appropriate response by the evaluating doctor would be as follows:

A. You are being hysterical.
B. You cannot let fear control your life.
C. These fears may be justified, so we should discuss this to help you understand and deal with this problem.
D. You may need further training so that you do not get into these dangerous situations.
E. You need a tranquilizer.

**7.6.** Asking patients what they would do if they found a stamped, addressed letter in the street is an example of testing for

A. impulse control
B. judgment
C. insight
D. abstract thinking
E. intelligence

**7.7.** The correct formula for determining intelligence quotient (I.Q.) is

A. $\text{I.Q.} = \dfrac{CA}{MA} \times 100$

B. $\text{I.Q.} = CA \times MA \times 100$

C. $\text{I.Q.} = \dfrac{MA}{CA} \times 100$

D. $\text{I.Q.} = CA \times MA \div 100$
E. none of the above

**7.8.** A 23-year-old heterosexual male, during his first meeting with a female psychiatrist, suddenly states, "All women are whores and I am wasting my time talking with you." The patient gives a history of having had long-term sexual relationships with two women over the last 4 years, which he says were enjoyable. He describes normal feelings of intimacy toward his present partner. The treating doctor's best response is as follows:

A. You are expressing latent homosexual impulses.
B. These feelings are oedipal in nature.
C. Your feelings of hostility toward women will make it impossible for us to work together.
D. Why do you have these feelings?
E. You are bringing on feelings of fear in me.

**7.9.** An idea of reference is an example of a disturbance in

A. thought
B. intelligence
C. memory
D. perception
E. language

**7.10.** Which of the following indicates a language impairment:

A. Incoherence
B. Word salad
C. Clang association
D. Neologism
E. All of the above

**7.11.** A 43-year-old woman with progressive systemic lupus erythematosus has been responding poorly to treatment. Her doctor notes that she appears to be depressed and, as her physician, is concerned that she may commit suicide. The best treatment strategy for this patient is for the physician to

A. reassure the patient that she will get well
B. request psychiatric hospitalization
C. discuss the patient's mood and ask directly about any suicidal thoughts
D. immediately put the patient on high-dose antidepressant medication
E. avoid any further questioning of the patient

**7.12.** In taking the patient's history of later childhood (from puberty through adolescence), the psychiatrist should pay especially careful attention to

A. toilet training
B. thumb sucking
C. nightmares
D. social relationships
E. head banging

**7.13.** In taking a mental status examination, vocabulary, academic achievement, and a good knowledge base are the best guide to which of the following functions:

A. Intelligence
B. Attention
C. Memory and orientation
D. Abstract thinking and calculating
E. Judgment and insight

**7.14.** A good test for recent memory is to ask patients

A. their date of birth
B. what they had to eat for their last meal
C. the name of the hospital they are in
D. who is the president of the United States
E. to subtract 7 from 100

**7.15.** The medication most commonly used in the drug-assisted psychiatric interview is

A. meprobamate
B. diazepam
C. sodium amytal
D. phenothiazine
E. chloral hydrate

**DIRECTIONS:** For each of the incomplete statements below, *one* or *more* of the completions given is correct. Choose answer:

A. if only **1, 2,** and **3** are correct
B. if only **1** and **3** are correct
C. if only **2** and **4** are correct
D. if only **4** is correct
E. if all are correct

**7.16.** The reaction of the patient toward the psychiatrist

1. may be affected by previous experiences with nonpsychiatric physicians
2. is affected by the patient's cultural background
3. is related to the patient's view of authority figures in childhood
4. is influenced by the psychiatrist's attitude

**7.17.** Word-association tests may indicate

1. blocking
2. clang associations
3. perseveration
4. unusual responses

**7.18.** The Bender-Gestalt Test is used mainly to test for which of the following:

1. Perceptual acuity
2. Motor activity
3. Organic defects
4. Reaction time

**7.19.** In interpreting the Thematic Apperception Test (TAT), the examiner

1. notes with whom the patient identifies
2. may assume that all the figures are representative of the patient
3. can elicit data pertaining to different areas of the patient's functioning
4. can infer motivational aspects of behavior

**7.20.** A parapraxis is

1. an example of an intrapsychic conflict
2. the repetition of a special phrase unrelated to an outside stimulus
3. likely to occur in everyday normal conversation
4. pathognomonic of schizophrenia

**7.21.** Psychiatric interviews under hypnosis

1. can enable the patient to recall forgotten facts
2. can create undue anxiety
3. may increase resistance
4. can force the patient to reveal secrets

**7.22.** Objective personality tests

1. are typically pencil-and-paper tests
2. present ambiguous stimuli
3. are easily subjected to statistical analysis
4. allow for projection

**7.23.** If a patient is asked to subtract 7 from 100 and to keep subtracting 7's, which of the following are being tested:

1. Intelligence
2. Concentration
3. Anxiety
4. Mood

**7.24.** Important events of early childhood (through age 3) include

1. attitude and feelings of the child's parents toward toilet training
2. bed-wetting experiences
3. stranger anxiety
4. masturbation

**DIRECTIONS:** Each group of questions below consists of five lettered headings followed by a list of numbered words or statements. For each numbered word or statement, select the *one* lettered heading that is most closely associated with it. Each lettered heading may be used only once, more than once, or not at all.

**Questions 7.25–7.29**
A. Hyperthyroidism
B. Hypothyroidism
C. Porphyria
D. Hepatolenticular degeneration
E. Pancreatic carcinoma

**7.25.** Jaundice, fear of doom

**7.26.** Dry skin, myxedema madness

**7.27.** Kayser-Fleishcher rings, brain damage

**7.28.** Abdominal crises, mood swings

**7.29.** Tremor, anxiety, and hyperactivity

**Questions 7.30–7.34**
A. Autistic thinking
B. Magical thinking
C. Perseveration
D. Intellectualization
E. Tangential thinking

**7.30.** Giving the same answer to different questions

**7.31.** Numerous digressions so that the goal idea is never reached

**7.32.** Common in children and in obsessive-compulsive disorders

**7.33.** An idea that is divorced from any emotional content

**7.34.** Preoccupation with daydreams, fantasies, and reveries

**Questions 7.35–7.41**
A. Axis I
B. Axis II
C. Axis III
D. Axis IV
E. Axis V

**7.35.** A 12-year-old acting as president of the class

**7.36.** Affective disorder

**7.37.** Death of a spouse

**7.38.** Schizophrenia

**7.39.** Peptic ulcer

**7.40.** Schizoid personality

**7.41.** Inability to take care of self

# Answers

## Diagnosis and Psychiatry: Examination of the Psychiatric Patient

**7.1.   The answer is B** (*Synopsis*, ed. 4, page 112).

The most important role of the physician doing an initial psychiatric interview is to *establish rapport*. Failure of the physician to establish a good relationship will cause difficulties in communication, and an accurate assessment of the patient will be difficult to obtain. Good rapport increases the likelihood of enlisting the patient's cooperation in all aspects of care. The physician-patient relationship is the keystone of the practice of medicine.

*Making a diagnosis* and *developing a treatment plan* are of obvious importance, but without a good doctor-patient relationship those tasks are made complicated. *Advice giving* and *reassurance* play more of a role in the ongoing relationship with the patient than they do in the initial interview.

**7.2.   The answer is A** (*Synopsis*, ed. 4, page 134).

Memory impairment, most notably *immediate or short-term memory*, is usually the first sign of beginning cerebral disease.

Memory is a process by which anything that is experienced or learned is established as a record in the central nervous system, where it persists with a variable degree of permanence and can be recollected or retrieved from storage at will. Short-term memory is the reproduction, recognition, or recall of perceived material after a period of 10 seconds or less has elapsed after the initial presentation. *Recent memory* covers a time period from a few hours to a few weeks after the initial presentation. *Long-term memory or remote memory* is the reproduction, recognition, or recall of experiences or information that was experienced in the distant past. This function is usually not disturbed early in organic brain disease.

**7.3.   The answer is C** (*Synopsis*, ed. 4, page 114).

The stress interview is a type of interview in which the patient is intentionally *confronted* and pressured, and the usual ways of reducing anxiety during the session are deliberately avoided. Such interviews may be useful in diagnosis, but their repeated use is generally contraindicated in the course of psychotherapy. One situation in which the stress interview may be used is with certain patients who are monotonously repetitious or who show insufficient emotionality for motivation. Apathy, indifference, and emotional blunting are not conducive to a discussion of personality problems. In patients with such reactions, stimulation of emotions can be constructive. These patients may require probing, challenging, or confrontation to arouse feelings that further their understanding.

The *Social Readjustment Rating Scale*, devised by T. H. Holmes, quantifies life events, assigning a point value to life changes that require adaptation. Research indicates a critical level at which too many of these events happening to a person during a 1-year time span puts him or her at great risk of illness.

The stress interview is not related to *intimidation* of any kind, nor should it be *destructive*. *Anxiety* may be present in both doctor and patient during any initial interview.

**7.4.   The answer is C** (*Synopsis*, ed. 4, pages 131 and 132).

The Draw-a-Person Test (DAPT) was first used as a measure of intelligence with children; however, it is a very good screening technique for patients with *brain damage*. The test is easily administered, usually with the instructions, "I'd like you to draw a picture of a person; draw the best person you can." After the completion of the first drawing, the patient is asked to draw a picture of a person of the opposite sex to that of the first drawing.

A general assumption is that the drawing of a person represents the expression of the self or of the body in the environment. Interpretive principles rest largely on the assumed functional significance of each body part.

The DAPT might be of benefit in other mental disorders, but it should be used with other psychological tests to confirm the diagnosis. *Obsessive-compulsive* patients generally attend to every detail in the DAPT, especially buttons and other small items; *manic patients* may produce a large, expansive-looking drawing that fills the whole page. The DAPT would be of little use in the diagnosis of *depression* or *conversion disorder*, but body-image distortions may be revealed in these disorders with this test.

**7.5. The answer is C** (*Synopsis*, ed. 4, page 113).

The psychiatrist's function is to try to separate irrational fears from realistic ones. The doctor should try to encourage the resident to explore her feelings in order to make an accurate assessment. The resident may have *rational fears that can be explored by discussion of these feelings.*

The doctor's response in *calling the resident hysterical* has no basis in fact, and she may be expressing genuine rational fears. That response is an attack on the resident and may cause her to become defensive. The response, "*You cannot let fear control your life,*" is also an inappropriate one. It is judgmental, antagonistic, and counterproductive to any type of rapport that the physician is trying to establish. The response that the fear of danger is due to the resident's inexperience or *lack of training* or both may only prove to generate anger. It is a weak, impractical attempt to solve the problem. This statement is also premature in nature in that the problem has not yet been examined in depth. The use of an antianxiety agent is sometimes helpful in the treatment of anxiety. Yet, without a careful psychiatric examination there is no way to determine if the resident may be suffering from one of a number of other conditions with similar symptoms, such as panic attacks or simple phobias that are treated differently. *Giving any patient potent anxiolytics without first having a good working diagnosis and plan is contraindicated.*

**7.6. The answer is B** (*Synopsis*, ed. 4, page 125).

*Judgment* may include subtle manifestations of behavior that are harmful to the patient and contrary to acceptable behavior in the culture. Examples of impairment should be noted. Tests for judgment include patients' predictions of what they would do in imaginary situations; for instance, what would they do if they found a stamped, addressed letter in the street. Good judgment would be to mail the letter; poor judgment would be to open and read it. *Impulse control* is the ability to resist an impulse, drive, or temptation to perform some action. *Insight* is a conscious recognition of one's own condition. In psychiatry, it more specifically refers to the conscious awareness and understanding of one's own psychodynamics and symptoms of maladaptive behavior. It is highly important in effecting changes in the personality and behavior of a person. Intellectual insight refers to knowledge of the reality of a situation without the ability to successfully use that knowledge to effect an adaptive change in behavior. Emotional insight refers to a deeper level of understanding or awareness that is more likely to lead to positive changes in personality and behavior. *Abstract thinking* is thinking characterized by the ability to assume a mental set voluntarily, to shift voluntarily from one aspect of a situation to another, to keep in mind simultaneously various aspects of a situation, to grasp the essentials of a whole and to break a whole into its parts, to abstract common properties, to plan ahead, to assume make-believe attitudes, and to think or act symbolically. It is also called abstract attitude and categorical attitude. The capacity for abstract thinking is frequently impaired in patients with organic mental disorders. *Intelligence* is the capacity for learning; the ability to recall, integrate constructively, and apply what is learned; and the capacity to understand and to think rationally.

**7.7. The answer is C** (*Synopsis*, ed. 4, page 128).

Intelligence quotient (I.Q.) is the ratio between mental age and chronological age × 100

$$\left(I.Q. = \frac{MA}{CA} \times 100\right).$$

When mental age continues to increase in proportion to chronological age, the I.Q. provides an index of relative brightness that can be used to compare children of different ages. For example, a 10-year-old child who scores a mental age of 13 on a test would have an I.Q. of 130.

**7.8. The answer is D** (*Synopsis*, ed. 4, page 120).

The doctor should try to *encourage the patient to express his angry feelings* in order to get to the causes of those hostile thoughts. That will allow the physician to plan a treatment program that will deal with the patient's feelings during the course of therapy.

The *diagnosis of homosexuality is premature* and may be inaccurate. It is an inappropriate interpretation and may have nothing to do with the patient's personal experiences with women. It may also cause the patient to reject his doctor's attempt to interact with him. The interpretation about the patient having an *oedipal conflict* is also premature. The doctor telling the patient that *she cannot work with him* provides the ultimate therapeutic rejection to the patient and only further reinforces the patient's problems. It is totally inappropriate during the first psychiatric interview for the treating physician to discuss her *countertransference fears* with the patient.

**7.9.   The answer is A** (*Synopsis*, ed. 4, pages 124 and 125).

An idea of reference is a misinterpretation of incidents and events in the outside world as having a direct personal reference to oneself. It is a disturbance of *thought* that affects communication or thinking content.

*Intelligence* is the capacity for learning; the ability to recall, integrate constructively, and apply what one has learned; and the capacity to understand and to think rationally. *Memory* is the process whereby what is experienced or learned is established as a record in the central nervous system (registration), where it persists with a variable degree of permanence (retention) and can be recollected or retrieved from storage at will (recall). *Perception* is the conscious awareness of elements in the environment by the mental processing of sensory stimuli. The term is sometimes used in a broader sense to refer to the mental process by which all kinds of data—intellectual and emotional, as well as sensory—are organized meaningfully. A *language disorder* is a disturbance of speech or writing characterized by failure to follow semantic and syntactic rules. Examples include incoherence, clang association, word approximation, and neologism.

**7.10.   The answer is E** (*Synopsis*, ed. 4, page 124).

Language impairments reflect disordered mentation. They include incoherent or incomprehensible speech, word salad, clang associations, or neologisms. *Incoherent speech* is communication that is disorganized or disconnected. *Word salad* is an incoherent mixture of words or phrases. *Clang associations* are speech patterns directed by the sound of a word, rather than by its meaning, e.g. punning or rhyming. A *neologism* is a new word or phrase created by the patient.

**7.11.   The answer is C** (*Synopsis*, ed. 4, page 117).

Patients with chronic illness and deteriorating health often become depressed. The doctor must take any suicidal ideation seriously and must carefully evaluate all depressed patients for suicidal risk. Most patients who have suicidal ideation will feel better when their physician *directly asks about any suicidal thoughts*. There is good evidence that the risk of suicide does not in any way increase with direct questioning

about suicide. *Specific questions should not be avoided.* It is imperative to have a clear picture of the patient's psychiatric status in order to decide on an appropriate therapeutic plan.

*Reassurance, hospitalization, and antidepressant medication* should not be utilized unless indicated.

**7.12.   The answer is D** (*Synopsis*, ed. 4, page 122).

Later childhood extends from puberty through adolescence. *Social relationships* are especially important during this period. The following areas should be explored: attitudes toward siblings and playmates, number and closeness of friends, whether the patient is a leader or follower, social popularity, and participation in group or gang activities.

*Toilet training, thumb sucking, nightmares,* and *head banging* usually occur in early childhood.

**7.13.   The answer is A** (*Synopsis*, ed. 4, page 119).

The patient's *intelligence* may be roughly estimated by a number of intellectual functions tested for or observed during a mental status examination. A person's ability to articulately use language, past and present academic performance, and general fund of knowledge are good indicators of intellectual ability. When a patient's differential diagnosis includes a possible organic component or mental retardation, however, formal psychological testing is necessary to accurately assess his or her intellectual activity.

*Attention* is the conscious and willful focusing of mental energy on one object of a complex experience. *Memory* is that process by which what is experienced or learned is established as a record in the central nervous system, where it persists with a variable degree of permanence and can be recollected or retrieved from storage at will. *Orientation* is the state of awareness of oneself and one's surroundings in terms of time, place, and person. *Abstract thinking* is characterized by the ability to grasp the essentials of a whole and to break a whole into its parts. In psychiatry, *calculation* refers to the ability to do simple arithmetic. *Insight* refers to a person's understanding of one's own psychodynamics and symptoms of maladaptive behavior. *Judgment* refers to the ability to evaluate choices within the framework of a given set of values for the purpose of electing a course of action.

**7.14.   The answer is B** (*Synopsis*, ed. 4, page 120).

Recent memory is the ability to remember what has been experienced within the past few hours, days, or weeks. It is assessed by asking patients to describe how they spent the last 24 hours, such as *what they had to eat for their last meal.*

Remote memory or long-term memory is the ability to remember events in the distant past. Memory for the remote past can be evaluated by inquiring about important dates in the patient's life, such as *date of birth.* The answers must be verifiable.

To test patients' orientation to place, one can inquire whether patients know where they are; for instance, to *ask the name of the hospital they are in.* Concentration may be tested by *subtracting 7 from 100* serially. If patient cannot do this task, it is important to distinguish whether anxiety or some disturbance of mood or consciousness seems to be responsible for the difficulty. To test a patient's general knowledge or fund of information, one can ask such questions as *who is the president of the United States.* It is important to ask questions that have some relevance to the patient's educational and cultural background.

**7.15.   The answer is C** (*Synopsis*, ed. 4, pages 114 and 115).

*Sodium amytal* is the drug most commonly used in the drug-assisted psychiatric interview. It can be of use with patients who have difficulty expressing themselves freely or who are suppressing anxiety-provoking material. In narcotherapy, regularly scheduled interviews are conducted using sodium amytal as an adjunctive agent. The drug-assisted interview can also be of help in differentiating organic from psychogenic disease. For example, a patient suffering from a paralyzed right arm may move it normally during an amytal interview, thus pointing toward a functional rather than organic cause.

*Meprobamate, diazepam,* and *chloral hydrate* are antianxiety agents used as sedatives or hypnotics. The *phenothiazines* are neuroleptics or major tranquilizers used in the treatment of schizophrenic disorders.

**7.16.   The answer is E (all)** (*Synopsis*, ed. 4, page 112).

The reaction of patients toward the psychiatrist is *influenced by the psychiatrist's style, orientation, and attitude.* If patients believe that they will lose their doctor's respect as they expose their problems, they may be unwilling to disclose such material. If, in their *previous experiences with doctors* (psychiatric or nonpsychiatric), patients felt ridiculed or their problems were minimized, that experience would influence what they do or do not tell the psychiatrist.

Transference is a process in which patients unconsciously and inappropriately displace onto persons in their current life those patterns of behavior and emotional reactions that originated with significant *authority figures from their childhood.* The reaction of patients toward the psychiatrist will be influenced by these original reactions. Differences in the social, educational, and intellectual backgrounds of each patient and the interviewer may also interfere with the development of rapport. It is an obvious advantage for the psychiatrist to acquire as much understanding and familiarity as possible with *a patient's cultural background.*

**7.17.   The answer is E (all)** (*Synopsis*, ed. 4, pages 130 and 131).

The word-association test consists of presenting stimulus words to patients and having them respond with the first word that comes to their mind. Complex indicators include *clang associations, blocking, perseveration* of earlier responses, *unusual responses,* repetition of the stimulus word, apparent misunderstanding of the word, and unusual mannerisms or movements accompanying the response. The clinician may repeat the list, following the initial administration, asking patients to respond with the same words used previously. This technique may reveal discrepancies between the first and second test administrations that may provide additional clues to unconscious conflicts or disturbances of thinking.

**7.18.   The answer is A (1, 2, 3)** (*Synopsis*, ed. 4, page 131).

The Bender-Gestalt Test is mainly a screening device for studying *perceptual acuity, motor activity,* and *organic defects.* The test is most frequently used by clinicians because it is viewed generally by patients as nonthreatening, and it is ideal for allowing the patient to discharge anxiety through motor activity.

*Reaction time* is the length of delay between application of stimulus and appearance of response. In word association tests, for example, a long reaction time signals an emotional conflict. Reaction time is not of major significance in the Bender-Gestalt Test.

**7.19.   The answer is E (all)** (*Synopsis*, ed. 4, pages 129 and 130).

In interpreting the Thematic Apperception Test (TAT), the examiner *will note with whom the patient identifies* through the major figure or figures of the story. The characteristics of this figure *may be representative of the patient,* in that the patient will attribute onto the figure his or her own wishes, strivings, and conflicts. The story itself *can elicit data pertaining to different areas of the patient's functioning* by analysis of the representation of the subject. The figures closest to the subject in age, sex, and appearance will most probably have more acceptable and conscious traits and motives attributed to them. In contrast, the more unacceptable and unconscious traits and motives will probably be attributed to figures most unlike the subject.

The TAT is generally most useful as a technique for *interpreting motivational aspects of behavior.*

**7.20.   The answer is B (1, 3)** (*Synopsis*, ed. 4, page 146).

A parapraxis is a faulty act, such as a slip of the tongue, misplacing an article, or momentarily forgetting a name or fact. Freud described a parapraxis as *part of normal thinking* that *occurs in everyday normal conversation*; however, it is also an example of *intrapsychic conflict.* According to Freud, the conflict creates anxiety, and the mind uses repression as a defense against the anxiety, which then expresses itself in the parapraxis or distorted expression.

A parapraxis is *not pathognomonic of schizophrenia.* The *repetition of a special phrase unrelated to outward stimuli* is known as perseveration.

**7.21.   The answer is A (1, 2, 3)** (*Synopsis*, ed. 4, page 115).

Psychiatric interviews under hypnosis may be of value for certain patients who are unable to discuss important conflicts easily. Hypnosis *can enable the patient to recall forgotten facts* and memories and to talk freely about these recollections, which may otherwise have been difficult to discuss because of feelings of anger, anxiety, or shame. A premature confrontation of conflicts under hypnosis *can create undue anxiety* and *may increase resistance*, although patients may be told after the hypnotic interview that they will recall only the memories they consciously wish to discuss.

Patients *cannot be forced to reveal secrets* under hypnosis.

**7.22.   The answer is B (1, 3)** (*Synopsis*, ed. 4, page 127).

Objective personality tests *are typically pencil-and-paper tests* based on items and questions having obvious meanings. The advantage of objective personality tests is to furnish the clinician with numerical scores and profiles *easily subjected to mathematical or statistical analysis.*

In contrast, projective tests present stimuli, the meaning of which is not immediately ob-

vious; that is, some degree of *ambiguity* forces subjects to *project their own needs* into or onto an amorphous, somewhat unstructured situation. Projective tests are not easily subjected to statistical analysis.

**7.23.   The answer is E (all)** (*Synopsis*, ed. 4, page 125).

*Concentration* is a major function tested by asking the patient to subtract 7 from 100 and keep subtracting 7's. Sometimes, however, *anxiety* or some disturbance of *mood* or consciousness may be responsible for the patient's difficulty with this task. If the patient cannot perform the task because of limited *intelligence*, an easier task, such as 4 times 9 or 5 times 4, can be given. Concentration is often used synonymously with attention.

**7.24.   The answer is E (all)** (*Synopsis*, ed. 4, page 122).

Early childhood extends from birth through age 3. The following events should be examined: feeding habits, including whether or not the patient was breast-fed or bottle-fed; walking; talking; and teething. Language development, motor development, signs of unmet needs, sleep patterns, object constancy, *stranger anxiety*, and separation anxiety should also be discussed. *Toilet training*, including the age of training and *the parents' and patient's attitudes and feelings* about it, is important during this period. Symptoms of behavior problems, such as thumb sucking, temper tantrums, tics, head banging, rocking, night-terrors, fears, *bed wetting* or bed soiling, nail biting, and *masturbation* should also be inquired about. The examiner should try to determine the personality of the child, including the child's shyness, restlessness, overactivity, being withdrawn, or studiousness; whether the patient was outgoing, timid, athletic, or friendly; and what were his or her patterns of play and reactions to siblings. Early or recurrent dreams or fantasies should also be explored.

**7.25–7.29.   The answers are   7.25–E, 7.26–B, 7.27–D, 7.28–C, and 7.29–A** (*Synopsis*, ed. 4, pages 140 and 141).

The table on the facing page gives some examples of medical problems that may present as psychiatric symptoms.

**Some Examples of Medical Problems That May Present as Psychiatric Symptoms**

| | Sex and Age Prevalence | Common Medical Symptoms | Psychiatric Symptoms and Complaints | Impaired Performance and Behavior | Diagnostic Problems |
|---|---|---|---|---|---|
| Hyperthyroidism (thyrotoxicosis) | Females 3:1, 30 to 50 | *Tremor*, sweating, loss of weight and strength | *Anxiety* if rapid onset; depression if slow onset | Occasional *hyperactive* or grandiose behavior | Long lead time; a rapid onset resembles anxiety attack |
| Hypothyroidism (myxedema) | Females 5:1, 30 to 50 | Puffy face, *dry skin*, cold intolerance | Anxiety with irritability, thought disorder, somatic delusions, hallucinations | *Myxedema madness*; delusional, paranoid, belligerent behavior | Madness may mimic schizophrenia; mental status is clear, even during most disturbed behavior |
| Porphyria—acute intermittent type | Females, 20 to 40 | *Abdominal crises*, paresthesias, weakness | Anxiety—sudden onset, *severe mood swings* | Extremes of excitement or withdrawal; emotional or angry outbursts | Patients often have truly neurotic life styles; crises resemble conversion reactions or anxiety attacks |
| Hepatolenticular degeneration (Wilson's disease) | Males 2:1, adolescence | Liver and extrapyramidal symptoms, *Kayser-Fleischer rings* | Mood swings—sudden and changeable; anger—explosive | Eventual *brain damage* with memory and I.Q. loss; combativeness | In late teens, may resemble adolescent storm, incorrigibility, or schizophrenia |
| Pancreatic carcinoma | Males 3:1, 50 to 70 | Weight loss, abdominal pain, weakness, *jaundice* | Depression, *sense of imminent doom* but without severe guilt | Loss of drive and motivation | Long lead time; exact age and symptoms of involutional depression |

**7.30–7.34. The answers are 7.30–C, 7.31–E, 7.32–B, 7.33–D, and 7.34–A** (*Synopsis*, ed. 4, pages 147 and 148).

Perseveration is the pathological *repetition of the same response to different stimuli*; for example, giving the same answer to different questions. It is seen in organic mental disorders and schizophrenia. Tangential thinking is a disturbance in which the person replies to a question in an oblique or *digressive manner, so that the central or goal idea is not communicated.* Magical thinking is the idea that thinking something is the same thing as doing it or causing it to happen. It is the belief that a thought, word, or gesture can lead to the fulfillment of certain wishes or the warding off of certain evils. It *occurs normally in children* and in dreaming. Pathologically, it *occurs in obsessive-compulsive disorders.* Intellectualization is an unconscious defense mechanism in which reasoning or logic is used to ward off anxiety about an objectionable impulse or emotion. *The idea is divorced from any emotional content.* Autistic thinking is a form of thinking in which the thoughts are narcissistic and egocentric, with emphasis on subjectivity, rather than objectivity, and without regard for reality. The term is used interchangeably with autism and dereism. Persons who are *preoccupied with daydreams, fantasies, or reveries* are engaged in autistic thinking.

**7.35–7.41. The answers are 7.35–E, 7.36–A, 7.37–D, 7.38–A, 7.39–C, 7.40–B, and 7.41–E** (*Synopsis*, ed. 4, page 126).

DSM-III uses a multiaxial classification scheme that consists of five axes. The clinician records the findings on one or all of the various axes listed below.

Axis I consists of all the clinical syndromes, such as *affective disorders, schizophrenia,* and anxiety, among others. It excludes the personality disorders and the specific developmental disorders, which are recorded on Axis II. Axis II covers all the personality disorders, such as *schizoid*, paranoid, borderline, and so on. Pervasive developmental disorders and infantile autism are recorded here. Axis III consists of any existing medical or physical illness, i.e. epilepsy, cardiovascular disease, or gastrointestinal disease. *Peptic ulcer* is coded on this axis. Axis IV refers to psychosocial stressors—for example, divorce, injury, death of a loved one—relevant to the illness. A rating scale with a continuum of 1 (no stressors) to 8 (catastrophic stressors) is used. The *death of a spouse* is a catastrophic psychosocial stressor. Axis V relates to the highest level of functioning exhibited by the patient during the previous year, i.e. social and vocational functioning, leisure-time activities. A rating scale with a continuum of 1 (superior functioning) to 7 (grossly impaired functioning) is used. *A 12-year-old girl acting as president* of the class is functioning on a superior level. The *inability of a patient to take care of himself or herself* would be grossly impaired functioning.

# References

American Psychiatric Association: *Diagnostic and Statistical Manual of Mental Disorders*, ed 3. American Psychiatric Association, Washington, DC, 1980.

Benton A L: Psychological testing for brain damage. In *Comprehensive Textbook of Psychiatry*, ed 4, H I Kaplan, B J Sadock, editors, p 535. Williams & Wilkins, Baltimore, 1985.

Carr A C: Psychological testing of personality. In *Comprehensive Textbook of Psychiatry*, ed 4, H I Kaplan, B J Sadock, editors, p 514. Williams & Wilkins, Baltimore, 1985.

Deutsch F, Murphy N F: *The Clinical Interview*. International Universities Press, New York, 1955.

Filskov S B, Boll T J: *Handbook of Clinical Neuropsychology*. Wiley-Interscience, New York, 1981.

Ginsberg G: Psychiatric interview. In *Comprehensive Textbook of Psychiatry*, ed 4, H I Kaplan, B J Sadock, editors, p 482. Williams & Wilkins, Baltimore, 1985.

Hall R C W, Gardner E R, Popkin M D, LeCann A F, Stickney S K: Unrecognized physical illness prompting psychiatric admission: A prospective study. Am J Psychiatry *138:* 629, 1981.

Hollender M H, Wells C E: Medical Assessment in psychiatric practice. In *Comprehensive Textbook of Psychiatry*, ed 4, H I Kaplan, B J Sadock, editors, p 543. Williams & Wilkins, Baltimore, 1985.

Lewis N D C: *Outlines for Psychiatric Examinations*, ed 3. New York State Department of Mental Hygiene, Utica, NY, 1943.

Matarazzo J D: Psychological assessment of intelligence. In *Comprehensive Textbook of Psychiatry*, ed 4, H I Kaplan, B J Sadock, editors, p 502. Williams & Wilkins, Baltimore, 1985.

Webb L J, DiClemente C C, Johnstone E E, Sanders J L, Parley R A, editors: *DSM-III Training Guide*, Brunner/Mazel, New York, 1981.

# 8

# Clinical Manifestations
# of Psychiatric Disorders

A thorough knowledge of signs and symptoms of psychiatric illness is fundamental to proper diagnosis, treatment, and evaluation of treatment. It delineates the kinds of information the psychiatric examination is expected to produce and the kind of data the student must look for.

Psychiatric symptoms are characterized by disturbances at many levels of psychological functioning. Some behavioral parameters are more vulnerable to psychiatric disorders than are others. The most striking indices of psychiatric illness include thought disorders (which subsume disturbances in association, memory, judgment, and consciousness) and distortions in perception; psychomotor disturbances; disturbances in object relationships; psychophysiological disorders; and pathological manifestations of affect, such as anxiety, depression, euphoria, and ambivalence. In addition, psychiatric disorders also manifest themselves in more subtle ways, such as work inhibitions, and in an impairment of creative and sexual functioning.

The psychiatric examination is designed to bring to light all the patient's psychopathological manifestations and to underscore his or her specific vulnerabilities. Once these data are at hand, the psychiatrist can formulate more specific hypotheses concerning the possible determinants of the patient's illness and can plan an appropriate treatment program. It should be noted, however, that the psychiatrist's formulations should include an assessment of the assets, as well as the liabilities of the patient. In other words, if therapy is to be effective, the psychiatrist's awareness of the patient's potential capacity for constructive change and growth must remain in the forefront. For, essentially, the fulfillment of this potential is the goal of psychiatric treatment.

The reader should refer to Chapter 8 of *Modern Synopsis-IV*, "Clinical Manifestations of Psychiatric Disorders," which covers the clinical manifestations of psychiatric disorders and the typical signs and symptoms of psychiatric illness. By studying the following questions and answers, the student can check his or her understanding of the subject.

# Questions

**DIRECTIONS:** Each of the statements or questions below is followed by five suggested responses or completions. Select the *one* that is *best* in each case.

**8.1.** Compensating for a loss of memory by filling in the gaps with imagined or distorted experiences is known as

A. malingering
B. primary gain
C. blocking
D. hysteria
E. confabulation

**8.2.** Alexithymia is

A. feelings of intense rapture
B. psychopathological sadness
C. being unaware of one's moods
D. the expression of one's feelings
E. the inability to relate to others

**8.3.** Selective inattention refers to

A. compliant responses to ideas
B. blocking out things that generate anxiety
C. focusing on certain portions of experience
D. artificially induced modification of
   consciousness
E. distractibility

**8.4.** In hysterical neurosis (conversion disorder),

A. any type of loss of sensation can occur
B. the perceptual disturbances follow
   recognizable neuroanatomical
   distributions
C. a diminution of sensation is less common
   than total anesthesia
D. sensory loss does not occur
E. glove-and-stocking distribution does not
   occur

**8.5.** The mental representation of a scene or occurrence that is unreal but is either expected or hoped for is known as a

A. unio mystica
B. obsession
C. delusion
D. fantasy
E. illusion

**8.6.** The error of perception in which there is a false response to a real sensory stimulation is known as

A. delusion
B. hallucination
C. hypnagogic phenomenon
D. illusion
E. unconscious repression

**8.7.** An abnormal sense of well-being is known as

A. eupraxia
B. euergasia
C. euthanasia
D. euthymia
E. euphoria

**8.8.** A disharmony between the emotional feeling tone and the idea, thought, or speech accompanying it is known as

A. blunted affect
B. inappropriate affect
C. flat affect
D. labile affect
E. appropriate affect

**8.9.** The mental process in which one compares or evaluates alternatives within the framework of a given set of values in order to elect a course of action is known as

A. thinking
B. obsessing
C. anosognosia
D. judgment
E. none of the above

**8.10.** A false belief that is firmly held, despite objective and obvious contradictory proof or evidence and in the face of reason, is known as a

A. delusion
B. obsession
C. hallucination
D. illusion
E. compulsion

**8.11.** The separation of a group of mental processes from the rest of the psychic functioning is known as

A. displacement
B. disposition
C. command automatism
D. condensation
E. dissociation

**8.12.** A phobia of death is known as

A. coprophobia
B. thanatophobia
C. algophobia
D. xenophobia
E. peccatophobia

**8.13.** The mystical experience is characterized by all of the following *except*

A. ineffability
B. noesis
C. transiency
D. confusion
E. passivity

**8.14.** The three essential processes that determine memory are registration, recall, and

A. forgetting
B. retention
C. consciousness
D. repression
E. amnesia

**8.15.** The disturbance in thought in which a patient believes that thinking something is the same thing as doing it or that thinking something may cause it to happen is known as

A. neologism
B. autistic thinking
C. magical thinking
D. tangentiality
E. circumstantiality

**8.16.** Loss of normal speech melody is known as

A. stuttering
B. stammering
C. aphonia
D. dysprosody
E. dyslexia

**8.17.** The disturbance in stream of thought in which there is an involuntary and sudden cessation or interruption of thought processes because of unconscious emotional factors is known as

A. rumination
B. obsessing
C. perseveration
D. verbigeration
E. blocking

**8.18.** Rapid verbalizations causing a shift from one idea to another are known as

A. muddled speech
B. pressure of speech
C. blocking
D. clang associations
E. flight of ideas

**8.19.** A 55-year-old man who shows signs and symptoms of a major depression complains that his "brain is infected and is rotting away." This is an example of

A. somatic delusion
B. delusion of grandeur
C. nihilistic delusion
D. delusion of poverty
E. magical thinking

**DIRECTIONS:** For each of the incomplete statements below, *one* or *more* of the completions given is correct. Choose answer:

A. if only **1, 2,** and **3** are correct
B. if only **1** and **3** are correct
C. if only **2** and **4** are correct
D. if only **4** is correct
E. if all are correct

**8.20.** Violent behavior may be caused by
1. a seizure disorder
2. perverse sexual impulses
3. alcohol intoxication
4. prolonged benzodiazepine use

**8.21.** Examples of cries for help include which of the following:
1. Firesetting
2. Hyperkinetic behavior
3. Physical complaints
4. Enuresis

**8.22.** Which of the following are characteristic of a child's devising of an imaginary companion:
1. It usually occurs between the ages of 3 and 6.
2. It appears after a traumatic event.
3. It can assuage loneliness.
4. The imaginary child may be used as a scapegoat.

**8.23.** An agitated and fearful 30-year-old truck driver appears in the emergency room complaining, "I feel bugs crawling under my skin." On examining the patient, the physician finds superficial irritation caused by scratching but no physical basis for the patient's complaint. In order to determine the cause of the symptom, the examining physician should be aware that a common cause of that symptom complex is
1. amyl nitrite
2. alcohol
3. barbiturates
4. cocaine

**8.24.** Free association is
1. an artificial and deliberate disturbance in association
2. a process that suspends the demands of logic and reality
3. unpredictable
4. similar to loosening of associations

**8.25.** Ideas of reference are characterized by which of the following:
1. The patient attaches personal significance to neutral remarks.
2. The defense of projection is involved.
3. They are frequently found in paranoid patients.
4. They occasionally occur in normal persons.

**8.26.** Which of the following are characteristic of anaclitic depression:
1. It may occur as early as the first year of life.
2. It begins with an initial phase of despair.
3. It is equivalent to a state of mourning.
4. Most victims die from the disorder.

**8.27.** A 25-year-old woman who complains that things often feel unreal—"as if I were in a movie"—may be exhibiting a symptom that is associated with which of the following disorders:
1. Anxiety disorder
2. Affective disorder
3. Drug abuse disorder
4. Schizophrenic disorder

**DIRECTIONS:** Each group of questions below consists of five lettered headings followed by a list of numbered words or statements. For each numbered word or statement, select the *one* lettered heading that is most closely associated with it. Each lettered heading may be selected once, more than once, or not at all.

### Questions 8.28–8.31
A. Motor aphasia
B. Sensory aphasia
C. Nominal aphasia
D. Syntactical aphasia

**8.28.** Inability to comprehend meaning of words

**8.29.** Ability to speak is lost

**8.30.** Inability to arrange words in proper sequence

**8.31.** Difficulty in finding correct name for an object

### Questions 8.32–8.35
A. Dysphoria
B. Euthymia
C. Elation
D. Grief

**8.32.** Normal mood

**8.33.** Associated with increased motor activity

**8.34.** An unpleasant mood

**8.35.** Mood appropriate to real loss

### Questions 8.36–8.39
A. Neologism
B. Word salad
C. Circumstantiality
D. Tangentiality

**8.36.** Incoherent mixture of words or phrases

**8.37.** New words created by the patient

**8.38.** Nongoal-directed associations

**8.39.** Digression of inappropriate thoughts

### Questions 8.40–8.43
A. Hypnagogic hallucination
B. Hypnopompic hallucination
C. Haptic hallucination
D. Visual hallucination

**8.40.** Crawling sensation on skin

**8.41.** Phantom limb

**8.42.** Occurs while falling asleep

**8.43.** Macropsia

**Questions 8.44–8.48**

A. Amnesia
B. Paramnesia
C. Both
D. Neither

**8.44.** Partial inability to recall prior experiences

**8.45.** Exaggerated retention

**8.46.** Confabulation

**8.47.** *Déjà vu*

**8.48.** Hypermnesia

**Questions 8.49–8.53**

A. Autism
B. Aphasia
C. Mutism
D. Slowed associations
E. Flight of ideas

**8.49.** Depression

**8.50.** Catatonia

**8.51.** Organic brain disease

**8.52.** Schizophrenia

**8.53.** Mania

# Answers

# Clinical Manifestations
# of Psychiatric Disorders

**8.1. The answer is E** (*Synopsis*, ed. 4, page 161).

The correct answer, *confabulation*, is the unconscious filling in of memory gaps by imagined experiences. It is characteristic of diffuse organic brain disease. These recollections change from moment to moment and are easily induced by suggestion. A simple test for confabulation is to ask the hospitalized patient, "Where were you last night?" This question is usually sufficient to elicit the phenomenon if it is present.

*Malingering* is feigning disease in order to achieve a specific goal, e.g. to avoid an unpleasant responsibility. There is no memory loss in the malingerer. *Primary gain* is a psychoanalytic term that refers to the reduction of anxiety achieved by a defense mechanism or the relief from tension or conflict through the development of a neurotic illness. *Blocking* is the involuntary cessation or interruption of thought processes or speech because of unconscious emotional factors. It is also known as thought deprivation. *Hysteria* is the diagnostic category for a neurosis involving a sudden impairment of function in response to emotional stress. In DSM-III it is divided into two types: conversion type and dissociative type. In the conversion type there is functional impairment in one of the special senses or in the voluntary nervous system; the dissociative type is manifested by an alteration in state of consciousness or by such symptoms as amnesia, disorientation, fugue, somnambulism, or multiple personality.

**8.2. The answer is C** (*Synopsis*, ed. 4, page 176).

Alexithymia is the inability or *difficulty in describing or being aware of one's emotions or moods*. It is common in depressive states.

*Feelings of intense rapture* are known as ecstasy and are seen in mania and certain mystical states. *Psychopathological sadness* is seen in depression; the *inability to relate to others* is a common manifestation of many emotional disorders, and in general the *expression of one's feelings* is characteristic of normal mental functioning.

**8.3. The answer is B** (*Synopsis*, ed. 4, page 176).

Selective inattention refers to the *blocking out of things that generate anxiety*. It differs from *distractibility*, which is the inability to focus attention.

Suggestibility is manifested by the *compliant and uncritical response to an idea* or influence. *Artificially induced modifications of consciousness* may be produced by hypnosis or drugs. Attention is the amount of effort exerted in *focusing on certain portions of experience*. The term is used synonymously with concentration.

**8.4. The answer is A** (*Synopsis*, ed. 4, page 162).

In DSM-III, hysterical neurosis is referred to as a conversion disorder where any modality of perception may be disordered and *any type of loss of sensation can occur*.

*Total anesthesia can occur, but diminution in sensation is more common.* These perceptual disturbances *do not follow recognizable neuroanatomical distributions, but involve*, rather, a part of a limb (*glove-and-stocking distribution*), half the body, and the mucus membranes (vagina, rectum, nose, mouth, and pharynx). Peculiar to the hysterical anesthesias is the simultaneous *involvement of all forms of sensation*, superficial and deep, without the sensory dissociation that frequently characterizes organic sensory disturbances. If the sensory loss is limited to half the body, it is found to stop exactly at the midline, a condition contrary to the normal cutaneous innervative overlapping. Similarly, psychogenic loss of sensation is attested to by the hysteric's perception of the tuning fork on only one side of the sternum or on only one side of the head, an obvious impossibility in view of the normal bone conduction of vibrations.

**8.5. The answer is D** (*Synopsis*, ed. 4, page 150).

The correct answer, *fantasy*, is a mental representation of a scene or occurrence that is perceived as unreal but is either expected or hoped for. There are two types of fantasies—creative and daydreaming. Creative fantasy prepares for some later action. It may begin in inspirational moments that are deeply rooted in the unconscious; however, it is then elaborated automatically and translated to a realistic program of action. In daydreaming fantasies, wishes are not fulfilled. Daydreams have a tendency to diminish with psychological and biological maturation. They are replaced by real satisfactions in the environment.

An *obsession* is a persistent and recurrent idea, thought, or impulse that cannot be eliminated from consciousness by logic or reasoning. Obsessions are involuntary and ego-dystonic. An *illusion* is the perceptual misinterpretation of a real external stimulus. In *unio mystica* there is a sense of mystic unity with an infinite power and a quality of timelessness, in which minutes and centuries are one and in which past and present are one. This state tends to occur in settings of exhaustion and toxicity in which full alert consciousness is impaired. It also seems to represent psychological regression at its most extreme. A *delusion* is a false belief that is firmly held, despite objective and obvious contradictory proof or evidence and despite other members of the culture not sharing the belief.

**8.6.   The answer is D** (*Synopsis*, ed. 4, page 163).

In an *illusion* there is a perceptual misinterpretation of a real external sensory experience. Schizophrenic patients may misperceive the rustle of leaves as people talking about them.

*Repression* is an unconscious defense mechanism that eliminates unacceptable ideas, fantasies, affects, or impulses from consciousness. Repressed material is not subject to voluntary recall, but it may emerge in disguised form. A *hallucination* is a false sensory perception occurring in the absence of any relevant external stimulation of the sensory modality involved. A *hypnagogic phenomenon* is a hallucination occurring while falling asleep and is ordinarily not considered pathological. A *delusion* is a false, fixed belief that is not in keeping with the patient's culture.

**8.7.   The answer is E** (*Synopsis*, ed. 4, page 165).

An abnormal sense of well-being is known as *euphoria*, especially when it occurs in an inappropriate setting. Although it is usually psychogenic, it can be observed in organic brain disease. *Eupraxia* is a term that refers to the normal ability to perform coordinated movements. *Euergasia* is a word used by Adolf Meyer to mean normal mental functioning. *Euthymia* refers to normal mood. *Euthanasia* is the intentional putting to death by artificial means of persons with incurable or painful disease.

**8.8.   The answer is B** (*Synopsis*, ed. 4, page 176).

Affect is the feeling tone associated with an idea or thought. *Inappropriate affect* is the dis-

harmony between the emotional feeling tone and the idea, thought, or speech accompanying it.

*Appropriate affect* is present when the emotional tone is in harmony with the accompanying idea, thought, or speech. *Blunted affect* is a disturbance in affect manifested by a severe reduction in the intensity of externalized feeling tone. *Labile affect* is characterized by changeability from one moment to the next. *Flat affect* is an absence or near absence of any signs of affective expression accompanying an idea, thought, or speech.

**8.9.   The answer is D** (*Synopsis*, ed. 4, page 153).

The mental process by which one compares or evaluates alternatives within the framework of a given set of values in order to elect a course of action is known as *judgment*. If the course of action chosen is consonant with reality or with mature adult standards of behavior, judgment is said to be intact or normal; judgment is said to be impaired if the chosen course of action is frankly maladaptive, results from impulsive decisions based on the need for immediate gratification, or is otherwise not consistent with reality as measured by mature adult standards.

*Thinking* is the mental process of knowing and becoming aware. One of the ego functions, it is closely associated with judgment. *Obsessing* is thinking of an idea that repetitively and insistently forces itself into consciousness even though it is unwelcome. Its function is to diminish anxiety; it represents an unconscious conflict and may be a symptom of obsessive-compulsive disorder. *Anosognosia* is an unawareness or nonacceptance of a neurological deficit.

**8.10.   The answer is A** (*Synopsis*, ed. 4, pages 152 and 153).

A false belief that is firmly held, despite objective and obvious contradictory proof of evidence and in the face of reason, is a *delusion*. Although it is true that some superstitions and religious beliefs are held despite the lack of confirmatory evidence, such culturally engendered concepts are not considered delusions. What is characteristic of the delusion is that it is not shared by others; rather, it is an idiosyncratic and individual misconception or misinterpretation. Further, it is a thinking disorder of enough import to interfere with the subject's functioning, because in the area of the delusion the subject no longer shares a consensually validated reality with other people.

An *obsession* is a persistent and recurrent idea, thought, or impulse that cannot be eliminated from consciousness by logic or reasoning. Obsessions are involuntary and ego-dystonic. A *hallucination* is a false sensory perception occurring in the absence of any relevant external stimulation of the sensory modality involved. An *illusion* is a perceptual misinterpretation of a real external stimulus. A *compulsion* is an uncontrollable, repetitive, and unwanted urge to perform an act. It serves as a defense against unacceptable ideas and desires, and failure to perform the act leads to overt anxiety.

**8.11.    The answer is E** (*Synopsis*, ed. 4, page 156).

*Dissociation* is a mechanism in which there is a loss of the usual consistency and relatedness between various groups of mental processes, resulting in apparent independent functioning of one of them. It accounts for the symptoms in dissociative disorders, such as amnesia, fugue, and multiple personality.

In trance states, which may occur spontaneously in depersonalization disorders or in response to hypnotic suggestion, an apparently sleeping subject may express the dissociative state in the form of automatic writing; that is, subjects may express in written form ideas and feelings that they will not recognize as their own when the trance state is ended. The performance of automatic writing and other actions during a trance state, in response to a command or a suggestion, is called *command automatism*. A command automatism may manifest itself after the trance state is presumably over as a posthypnotic suggestion.

*Condensation* is a mental process in which one symbol stands for a number of components. *Displacement* is an unconscious defense mechanism by which the emotional component of an unacceptable idea or object is transferred to a more acceptable one. *Disposition* is the sum total of a person's inclinations as determined by his or her mood.

**8.12.    The answer is B** (*Synopsis*, ed. 4, page 151).

The correct answer is *thanatophobia*. A phobia is an excessive and irrational fear of some situation, object, or activity that causes avoidance behavior to occur. According to DSM-III all phobias are divided into three groups: (1) social phobia, which involves fears of being observed by others, such as public speaking; (2) agoraphobia, which involves the fear of leaving one's home or being in an open place; and (3) simple phobia, which relates to specific objects or anything that is not covered in (1) or (2) above.

The table below lists a variety of phobias with the Latin or Greek prefix.

**8.13.    The answer is D** (*Synopsis*, ed. 4, page 150).

The mystical experience may occur in a variety of different circumstances and is characterized by certain distinguishing qualities. *Confusion*, which is a disordered orientation in relation to time, place, or person, is not considered characteristic of the mystical experience, because it is inconsistent with the sense of immense illumination and mystic unity that pervades the experience.

The *ineffability* of the mystical experience renders the person incapable of describing the phenomenon to one who has never experienced it. *Noesis* refers to the person feeling an immense illumination or revelation that may be accompanied by a sense of authority and the conviction that one is privileged to lead and command. At the same time, the mystical state imposes a certain *passivity* or abeyance of will, as if the person were in the grip of a superior power to whose direction he or she is highly responsive. The actual mystic state is of a *transient* nature, lasting only momentarily or persisting for an hour or two. On cessation, the feelings aroused by the experience may be only imperfectly reproduced in memory, yet are unforgettable and highly treasured.

Types of Phobias

| Phobia | Dread of | Phobia | Dread of |
| --- | --- | --- | --- |
| Acro- | High places | Nycto- | Darkness, night |
| Agora- | Open places | Patho- (noso-) | Disease, suffering |
| *Algo-* | Pain | *Peccato-* | Sinning |
| Astra- (astrapo-) | Thunder and lightning | Phono- | Speaking aloud |
| Claustro- | Closed (confined) places | Photo- | Strong light |
| *Copro-* | Excreta | Sito- | Eating |
| Hemato- | Sight of blood | Tapho- | Being buried alive |
| Hydro- | Water | *Thanato-* | Death |
| Lalo- (glosso-) | Speaking | Toxo- | Being poisoned |
| Myso- | Dirt, contamination | *Xeno-* | Strangers |
| Necro- | Dead bodies | Zoo- | Animals |

**8.14.  The answer is B** (*Synopsis*, ed. 4, page 160).

Memory is based on three essential processes: (1) registration, the ability to establish a record of an experience in the central nervous system; (2) *retention*, the persistence or permanence of a registered experience; and (3) recall, the ability to arouse and report in consciousness a previously registered experience.

A good memory involves the capacity to register data swiftly and accurately, the ability to retain those data for long periods of time, and the capacity to recall them promptly in relation to reality-oriented goals.

Although a good memory is one of the factors in the complex of mental capacities that make up intelligence, phenomenal feats of memory are occasionally encountered in settings of apparent mental retardation. These feats of memory usually involve rote memory, the capacity to retain and reproduce data verbatim, without reference to meaning. In logical memory, however, problem solving in relation to a reality-oriented goal is paramount.

In addition to quantitative, there are also qualitative differences in memory. Some persons are particularly well endowed with visual memory and can recall images with virtual hallucinatory intensity. They are called eidetic persons, and the reproduced memories are called eidetic images. This eidetic capacity tends to occur in childhood and subside with age, so that it is rare after adolescence.

*Consciousness* is involved with individuals' clarity of awareness about themselves and their surroundings, including the ability to perceive and process ongoing events in light of past experiences, future options, and current circumstances. *Repression* is the banishing from consciousness of ideas or impulses that are unacceptable to it. *Amnesia* is a disturbance in memory manifested by partial or total inability to recall past experiences. *Forgetting* is the inability to retain or recall registered information.

**8.15.  The answer is C** (*Synopsis*, ed. 4, page 147).

*Magical thinking* refers to the belief that specific thoughts, verbalization, associations, gestures, or postures can in some mystical manner lead to the fulfillment of certain wishes or the warding off of certain evils. This type of thinking may occur normally in superstitious or religious beliefs that are appropriate in specific sociocultural settings. Young children are prone to this form of thinking as a consequence of their limited understanding of causality. It is a prominent aspect of obsessive-compulsive thinking. It achieves its most extreme expression in schizophrenia.

A *neologism* is a new nonsensical word or phrase whose derivation cannot be understood. Neologisms are often seen in schizophrenia. *Autistic thinking* is a form of thinking in which the thoughts are largely narcissistic and egocentric, with emphasis on subjectivity, rather than objectivity, and without regard for reality. *Tangentiality* is a disturbance in which the person replies to a question in an oblique, digressive, or even irrelevant manner and the central or goal idea is not communicated. Failure to communicate the central idea distinguishes tangentiality from *circumstantiality*, in which the goal idea is reached in a delayed or indirect manner.

**8.16.  The answer is D** (*Synopsis*, ed. 4, page 146).

Loss of normal speech melody is known as *dysprosody*. A disturbance in inflection and rhythm results in a monotonous and halting speech pattern, which occasionally suggests a foreign accent. It can be the result of an organic brain disease, such as Parkinson's syndrome, or it can be a psychological defensive device seen in some schizophrenics. As a psychological device it can serve the function of maintaining a safe distance in social encounters.

*Stuttering* is a speech disorder characterized by repetitions or prolongations of sounds, syllables, and words or by hesitations and pauses that disrupt the flow of speech. It is also known as *stammering. Aphonia* is a loss of one's voice. *Dyslexia* is a specific learning disability syndrome involving an impairment of the ability to read that is unrelated to the person's intelligence.

**8.17.  The answer is E** (*Synopsis*, ed. 4, page 148).

*Blocking* consists of sudden suppressions in the flow of thought or speech in the middle of a sentence. Commonly, the patient is unable to explain the reason for the interruption, which is usually the result of an unconscious mental intrusion. When, with conscious effort, the patient endeavors to continue the thought, new thoughts may crop up that neither the patient nor the observer can bring into connection with the previous stream of thought. The complete blanking out of the flow of thought, the effort to renew it, and the inability to account for the interruption create an unpleasant feeling state within the patient. Blocking is also known as thought deprivation. Although the phenomenon occurs intermittently in normal persons and in a variety of diagnostic categories, it occurs most strikingly in schizophrenia.

*Rumination* refers to a type of thinking in which an idea is repetitively thought about in the same way or in different ways, but it is always the same idea. It is common in obsessive-compulsive disorders. *Obsessing* is a state in which the patient is beset with irresistible ideas or feelings or both. *Perseveration* is the pathological repetition of the same response to different stimuli. *Verbigeration* is the meaningless and stereotyped repetition of words or phrases. Both perseveration and verbigeration are symptoms of schizophrenia.

**8.18. The answer is E** (*Synopsis*, ed. 4, page 178).

The correct answer, *flight of ideas*, refers to rapid verbalizations with shifts from one idea to another that are difficult, if not impossible, for the examiner to follow. It occurs in manic episodes.

Other disturbances in speed of associations and flow of speech are described below. *Clang associations* are words similar in sound but not in meaning that call up new thoughts. *Blocking* is an interruption in the train of thinking that is unconscious in origin. *Pressure of speech* is voluble speech that is difficult to interpret. Volubility or logorrhea is copious, but coherent, logical speech. Poverty of speech is a restriction in the amount of speech used. *Muddled speech* is fluent speech in which elements of different thoughts are muddled together.

**8.19. The answer is A** (*Synopsis*, ed. 4, pages 178 and 179).

*Somatic delusions* are false fixed beliefs, often of a bizzare nature, that involve the functioning of the body.

Other disturbances in content of thought are described below. *Magical thinking* is a belief that thoughts, words, or actions can prevent an occurrence by some mystical means. A delusion is a false belief, not consistent with the patient's intelligence and cultural background, that cannot be corrected by reasoning. Types of delusions include the bizzare delusion, an absurd, false, belief; the mood-congruent delusion, a delusion whose content is mood appropriate; the mood-incongruent delusion, a delusion whose content is mood inappropriate; the *nihilistic delusion*, a false feeling that self, others, or the world is nonexistent; the *delusion of poverty*, a false belief that one lacks material possessions; the systemized delusion, a false belief united by a single event or theme; and the *delusion of grandeur*, an exaggerated conception of one's importance.

**8.20. The answer is E (all)** (*Synopsis*, ed. 4, pages 169 and 170).

*Alcohol intoxication* is an important contributor to violent behavior. The amphetamines, cocaine, a variety of hallucinogens, the barbitu-

rates, and the prolonged use of *benzodiazepines* have also been implicated in episodes of violent dyscontrol. Violence may occur as a manifestation of a *seizure disorder*, particularly when the temporal lobe is involved. To make the diagnosis, one has to demonstrate temporally related electroencephalographic abnormalities. Violence, such as rape, may be connected with *perverse sexual impulses*. The act of rape is essentially an expression of rage and the wish to dominate the victim. In rape, male sexuality is always in the service of nonsexual needs. Sadistic and masochistic fantasies may also inadvertently lead to violence, as in the accidental suicides of patients with bonding fantasies (autoerotic asphyxiation).

**8.21. The answer is E (all)** (*Synopsis*, ed. 4, page 166).

A cry for help is the term used to convey a person's need for attention and care when that person is unable or unwilling to directly express the need, which is then expressed by other forms of behavior. Typical cries for help in children include *hyperkinetic behavior, firesetting*, accident proneness, and *enuresis*. The adolescent may indulge in conspicuous displays of antisocial behavior that compel the adult world to pay attention. All too often, these cries for help are not recognized as signs of emotional disorders, and they are dealt with punitively. Older persons often seek out their physicians with *physical complaints* because they do not know how else to express their cries for help.

**8.22. The answer is E (all).** (*Synopsis*, ed. 4, page 152).

Children who develop an imaginary companion usually do so *between the ages of 3 and 6*. The companion often develops *after a traumatic event occurs*, such as the birth of a sibling or the death of a grandparent. The imaginary companion may be a simple double who helps *assuage loneliness* or a *scapegoat* who is the recipient of endless scoldings and punishments for misbehavior.

Once emotional maturation develops, however, the need for the companion subsides and is gradually forgotten. The imaginary companion can be likened to a transitional object. Persistent attachment to the transitional object into adolescence is evidence of a maturational lag.

**8.23. The answer is C (2, 4)** (*Synopsis*, ed. 4, page 165).

Hallucinations of touch are known as haptic hallucinations. They commonly occur in *alcohol* withdrawal states, such as delirium tremens, and in *cocaine addiction*. They may take the form of a creeping sensation under the skin that is called formication.

Prolonged heavy use of *barbiturates* may be associated with an amnestic syndrome, characterized by impairment of short-term memory. *Amyl nitrite* is a vasodilator used in the treatment of angina pectoris. It has become a drug of abuse among some persons who believe erroneously that it heightens sexual sensations.

**8.24.   The answer is A (1, 2, 3)** (*Synopsis*, ed. 4, page 147).

Free association is a psychoanalytic technique devised by Sigmund Freud. It involves the uninhibited or uncensored reporting of all thoughts regardless of whether or not the patient considers them relevant. The associations, according to Freud, are not really free, but are governed by the unconscious and reveal intrapsychic conflicts. The patient is encouraged to verbalize all thoughts to the analyst without any holding back or censorship of any kind and *to suspend the demands of logic and reality* throughout the session. The normal thought process is *artificially and deliberately disrupted*. As a result, the flow of associations develops qualities of *unpredictability*; that is, the flow is unrelated to reality.

In the *loosening of associations*, the flow of thought is haphazard, purposeless, illogical, confused, incorrect, abrupt, and bizarre. It occurs spontaneously and is a symptom of schizophrenia.

**8.25.   The answer is E (all)** (*Synopsis*, ed. 4, page 152).

Ideas of reference or referential thinking refers to misinterpretation of incidents and events in the outside world as having a direct *personal reference* to oneself. Occasionally observed in *normal persons*, ideas of reference are frequently seen in *paranoid patients*. If present with sufficient frequency or intensity or if organized and systematized, they constitute delusions of reference. The major defense mechanism employed in referential thinking is *projection*, in which the person attributes to others the ideas or feelings that are unacceptable to the self.

**8.26.   The answer is B (1, 3)** (*Synopsis*, ed. 4, page 167).

Anaclitic is a term referring to an infant's dependence on his or her mother for a sense of well-being. Anaclitic depression can be demonstrated by infants *during the first year of life* who are deprived of love and attention from a mother or mothering figure.

Infants experience a number of changes when separated from their mothers for a prolonged period. First, there is an *initial phase of protest*, characterized by intense crying and struggling. If deprivation continues, a second phase of despair results. Struggling decreases and crying is softer than before. Staff of a children's hos-

pital may misinterpret this phase as a state of diminished distress. It is equivalent, however, to *a state of mourning*. A third phase, detachment, follows in which the infants withdraw from human relationships and become preoccupied with inanimate objects or their own body parts, engaging in masturbation, fecal smearing, head banging, or rocking. They may stop eating and waste away, *a state called marasmus from which most victims die*. It should be noted that most infants do not reach the state of marasmus.

**8.27.   The answer is E (all)** (*Synopsis*, ed. 4, page 171).

The complaints of things seeming unreal or unnatural are symptoms of derealization. It is most commonly seen in *anxiety disorders, affective disorders, schizophrenia*, and during *drug intoxication*.

Derealization is a mental phenomenon characterized by the loss of the sense of reality concerning one's surroundings. The patient says, in effect, "This environment is not dangerous to me because this environment does not really exist." Derealization includes distortions of spatial and temporal relationships so that an essentially neutral environment seems strangely familiar (*déjà vu*) or strangely unfamiliar (*jamais vu*), or otherwise strange and distorted. Like depersonalization, to which it is closely related, derealization can be either partial or complete, transient or long-lasting. Similarly, it may occur in hysterical neuroses or as part of the aura of epilepsy, but derealization, too, tends to be most complete and persistent in schizophrenic states.

**8.28–8.31.   The answers are 8.28–B, 8.29–A, 8.30–D, and 8.31–C** (*Synopsis*, ed. 4, page 178).

Aphasias are due to organic brain disorders. Motor aphasia is a disturbance of speech in which understanding remains, but the *ability to speak is lost*. Sensory aphasia is characterized by a *loss of ability to comprehend the meaning of words* or the use of objects. Nominal aphasia is marked by *difficulty in finding the correct name for an object*. Syntactical aphasia is the *inability to arrange words in proper sequence*.

**8.32–8.35.   The answers are 8.32–B, 8.33–C, 8.34–A, and 8.35–D** (*Synopsis*, ed. 4, page 176).

Mood is defined as a pervasive or sustained emotion. Various moods are described below.

A dysphoric mood is an *unpleasant mood* or feeling. A euthymic mood is a *normal-range mood*. Expansive mood is the expression of one's feelings without restraint. Irritable mood is displayed when one is easily annoyed and provoked to anger. Elation is an air of confidence and enjoyment *associated with increased motor activ-*

*ity.* Exaltation is intense elation with feelings of grandeur. Ecstasy is a feeling of intense rapture. Grief or mourning is *sadness appropriate to a real loss.*

**8.36–8.39. The answers are 8.36–B, 8.37–A, 8.38–D, and 8.39–C** (*Synopsis*, ed. 4, page 178).

Some disturbances in structure of the use of language and thought associations are outlined below.

A neologism is a *new word or words created by the patient* for psychological reasons. A word salad is an *incoherent mixture of words and phrases.* Circumstantiality is the *digression of inappropriate thought* into ideational processes, but the patient eventually gets from the desired point to the desired goal. Tangentiality is the *inability to have goal-directed association* of thought; the patient never gets from the desired point to the desired goal. Incoherence is the running together of thoughts with no logical connection, resulting in disorganization. Perseveration is the psychopathological repetition of the same word or idea in response to different questions. Condensation is the fusion of various concepts into one.

**8.40–8.43. The answers are 8.40–C, 8.41–C, 8.42–A, and 8.43–D** (*Synopsis*, ed. 4, page 179).

Hallucinations are false sensory perceptions not associated with real external stimuli. The various types are outlined below.

Hypnagogic hallucination is a *false sensory perception occurring while falling asleep.* Hypnopompic hallucination is a hallucination occurring while awakening from sleep. Auditory hallucination is a false auditory perception. Visual hallucination is a false visual perception. Macropsia is seeing objects larger than they actually are or seeing large objects which are not there. Olfactory hallucination is a false perception in smell. Gustatory hallucination is a false perception of taste, such as unpleasant taste due to an uncinate fit. Tactile or haptic hallucination is a false perception of movement or sensation, as from an amputated limb (also known as *phantom limb*), or as a *crawling sensation on the skin* (also known as formication).

**8.44–8.48. The answers are 8.44–A,** 8.45–D, 8.46–B, 8.47–B, and 8.48–D (*Synopsis*, ed. 4, pages 179 and 180).

Memory is that function by which information stored in the brain is later recalled to consciousness. Disturbances of memory include:

Amnesia—the *partial or total inability to recall past experiences.*

Paramnesia—the falsification of memory by distortion of recall. Forms of paramnesia include *fausse reconnaissance*, false recognition; retrospective falsification, recollection of a true memory to which the patient adds false details; *confabulation*, unconscious filling of gaps in memory by imagined or untrue experiences that the patient believes but that have no basis in fact; *déjà vu*, the illusion of visual recognition in which a new situation is incorrectly regarded as a repetition of a previous memory; *déjà entendu*, the illusion of auditory recognition; and *jamais vu*, the false feeling of unfamiliarity with a real situation one has experienced.

*Hyperamnesia*—an *exaggerated degree of retention* and recall.

**8.49–8.53. The answers are 8.49–D, 8.50–C, 8.51–B, 8.52–A, and 8.53–E** (*Synopsis*, ed. 4, pages 148 and 149).

In *depressed states*, the patient's speech may be halting, and the flow of associations is slowed up—not intermittently in response to hallucinatory or delusional intrusions, or by blocking—but as an ongoing consequence of sadness. The range of thoughts is limited to a perseverative repetition of the patient's pessimism and despair. Mutism is the absence of speech and is seen in *catatonic* schizophrenia. In *manic states* pressure of speech—voluble speech difficult for the listener to interrupt—occurs. Pressure of speech may progress to flight of ideas, a nearly continuous high-speed flow of speech. The patient leaps rapidly from one topic to another, each topic being more or less meaningfully related to the preceding topic or to adventitious environmental stimuli, but the progression of thought is illogical, and the goal is never reached. Autism is a form of thinking seen in *schizophrenia* characterized by preoccupation with fantasy and without regard for reality. *Organic brain disease* is a major cause of disturbance in the flow of speech. Aphasia is a disturbance of language output, resulting almost always from damage to the left side of the brain.

## References

Barsky A J, Klerman G L: Hypochondriasis, bodily complaints and somatic styles. Am J Psychiatry *140:* 273, 1983.

Cavenar J O, Brodie H K H: *Signs and Symptoms in Psychiatry.* J B Lippincott, Philadelphia, 1983.

Fenichel O: *Psychoanalytic Theory of the Neuroses.* W W Norton, New York, 1945.

Linn L: Clinical manifestations of psychiatric disorders. In *Comprehensive Textbook of Psychiatry*, ed 4, H I Kaplan, B J Sadock, editors, p 550. Williams & Wilkins, Baltimore, 1985.

Slater E, Roth M: *Mayer-Gross' Clinical Psychiatry*, ed 3. W B Saunders, Philadelphia, 1969.

# 9

# Classification in Psychiatry

In general, classifications are a device for reducing complexity by noting the similarities in a given mass of observations and then grouping them abstractly in order to deal with them more easily as a conveniently small number of things. A multitude of concrete observations must be brought to some kind of order and simplification if they are to constitute a subject of effective communication that can be handled by logic or if they are to serve the needs of knowledge.

In psychiatry, a major historical advance was made by Emil Kraepelin, who described in the 19th century a classification of syndromes associated with a predictable outcome, on the basis of clusters of clinical symptoms. Kraepelin's delineation of dementia precox—the syndrome now identified as schizophrenia—as distinct from other forms of psychosis was a crucial contribution toward this end. Equally significant was Freud's concept of the neuroses as a single diagnostic category that encompassed clinical disorders with widely divergent symptomatology, such as hysteria, obsessive-compulsive disorders, and phobias, which had previously been regarded as unrelated disorders; furthermore, this formulation led to important therapeutic advances, as well as conceptual clarity.

In 1980 another major advance occurred when the third edition of the American Psychiatric Association's *Diagnostic and Statistical Manual of Mental Disorders* (DSM-III) was published. That nomenclature represented a major change in psychiatric thinking; classification of the disease states became more descriptive and more in accordance with the medical model, and reliability between observers concerning different disorders was increased, because sets of highly structured criteria were available for replication.

The student needs to be aware, however, that there was—and continues to be—much disagreement within the profession about DSM-III and its contents. In *Modern Synopsis-IV*, an attempt has been made to set forth those areas of disagreement where relevant; however, an attempt has also been made to avoid the nosological disagreements that would serve only to confuse the reader.

Throughout the *Study Guide*, the reader will find tables listing the DSM-III diagnostic criteria for mental disorders, which represent the current thinking in the field and are criteria with which each student must be totally familiar.

The student should read Chapter 9 of *Modern Synopsis-IV*, "Classification in Psychiatry," and should then review the questions and answers that follow.

# Questions

**DIRECTIONS:** Each of the statements or questions below is followed by five suggested responses or completions. Select the *one* that is *best* in each case.

**9.1.** All the following are classified as paraphilias *except*

A. fetishism
B. homosexuality
C. exhibitionism
D. sexual sadism
E. transvestism

**9.2.** Korsakoff's psychosis is also known as

A. alcohol withdrawal delirium
B. alcohol amnestic disorder
C. alcohol idiosyncratic intoxication
D. alcohol dependence
E. alcohol intoxication

**9.3.** All the following are psychosexual disorders *except*

A. gender-identity disorder
B. inhibition of sexual desire
C. ego-dystonic homosexuality
D. paraphilias
E. hysteria

**9.4.** All the following are classified as personality disorders *except*

A. schizoid
B. explosive
C. paranoid
D. borderline
E. avoidant

**9.5.** The following are all somatoform disorders *except*

A. somatization disorder
B. conversion disorder
C. psychogenic pain disorder
D. dissociative disorder
E. hypochondriasis

**DIRECTIONS:** For each of the incomplete statements below, *one* or *more* of the completions given is correct. Choose answer:

A. if only **1, 2,** and **3** are correct
B. if only **1** and **3** are correct
C. if only **2** and **4** are correct
D. if only **4** is correct
E. if all are correct

**9.6.** Which of the following statements apply to the classification of affective disorders:

1. The essential feature is a disturbance of mood.
2. Bipolar disorder is a major affective disorder.
3. Depression is classified as either a single-episode disturbance or a recurrent disturbance.
4. Affective disorders are not accompanied by psychotic features.

**9.7.** The reliability of a classification of mental disorders is

1. the extent to which the classification of a disorder enables users to communicate to colleagues
2. the extent to which users will achieve the same diagnosis in a series of cases
3. confirmed by the agreement among physicians in classifying a single case
4. the extent to which subjects can be discriminated from each other

**9.8.** The third edition of the American Psychiatric Association's *Diagnostic and Statistical Manual of Mental Disorders* (DSM-III)

1. is generally atheoretical with regard to etiology
2. attempts to describe the manifestations of mental disorders while only rarely attempting to account for how the disorders evolve
3. requires a set of essential criteria to be met in order to make a diagnosis
4. is not a multiaxial system

**9.9.** Predictive validity

1. is the extent to which knowledge that a person has a particular mental disorder is useful in predicting the future course of an illness
2. is related to the practical purpose of management and treatment
3. was the basis on which Kraepelin distinguished manic-depressive psychosis from dementia precox
4. is relevant to the demonstration of the specificity with which persons with bipolar, as opposed to unipolar, depression respond to treatment with lithium carbonate

**9.10.** Anxiety disorders are characterized by which of the following:

1. Anxiety disorders differ from phobic disorders in that only the phobia is characterized by fear of a specific object.
2. The predominant disturbance is the experience of anxiety itself.
3. If anxiety is episodic, it is classified as panic disorder.
4. Trying to resist giving in to the symptoms of the disorder creates anxiety.

**9.11.** Tobacco dependence is classified as a psychiatric disturbance because

1. there are few serious medical complications of long-term use
2. there is an inability to control use
3. there are often interpersonal problems between smokers and nonsmokers
4. a withdrawal syndrome develops

**9.12.** Substance use disorders are classified according to

1. a minimal duration of use
2. social complications of use
3. a pathological pattern of use
4. the presence of either tolerance or withdrawal

**9.13.** Which of the following statements about stress and its relationship to mental disorders are accurate:

1. Stress can be a significant contributor to the development or exacerbation of a mental disorder.
2. In DSM-III, stress is coded on Axis III on a seven-point scale.
3. A person's prognosis may be better when a disorder develops after a marked stress than when it develops after a minimal stress.
4. Stress should not be evaluated in terms of its effect on the average person.

**9.14.** Which of the following statements about organic mental disorders are true:

1. The disorders represent a psychological disturbance due to transient or permanent dysfunction of the brain.
2. Selective areas of cognitive impairment may occur.
3. The disorders may resemble schizophrenia.
4. The disorders may resemble affective disorders.

**9.15.** Which of the following statements are true about the present classification of psychiatric disorders in the third edition of the *Diagnostic and Statistical Manual of Mental Disorders* (DSM-III):

1. It describes the manifestations of mental disorders.
2. It usually explains how the disturbances came about.
3. The definitions of the disorders consist of descriptions of the clinical features.
4. The mental disorders are not classified according to shared characteristics.

**DIRECTIONS:** Each group of questions below consists of five lettered headings followed by a list of numbered words or statements. For each numbered word or statement, select the *one* lettered heading that is most closely associated with it. Each lettered heading may be selected once, more than once, or not at all.

### Questions 9.16–9.20
A. Paranoid personality disorder
B. Passive-aggressive personality disorder
C. Dependent personality disorder
D. Borderline personality disorder
E. Schizotypal personality disorder

**9.16.** Ideas of reference and magical thinking

**9.17.** Stubborn and procrastinates

**9.18.** Suspicious and hypervigilant

**9.19.** Impulsive and self-destructive

**9.20.** Clinging and subordinates own needs to those of others

### Questions 9.21–9.25
A. Phobic disorders
B. Panic disorder
C. Obsessive-compulsive disorder
D. Posttraumatic stress disorder
E. Generalized anxiety disorder

**9.21.** Predominant experience of episodic anxiety

**9.22.** Predominant experience of chronic and persistent anxiety

**9.23.** Development of characteristic anxiety after experiencing events outside the range of normal human experience

**9.24.** Persistent avoidance behavior secondary to irrational anxieties attached to an object or situation

**9.25.** Characterized by disturbing, unwanted, anxiety-provoking thoughts and repetitive impulses to perform acts to counteract the thoughts

# Answers

# Classification in Psychiatry

**9.1. The answer is B** (*Synopsis*, ed. 4, page 184).

*Homosexuality* is not classified as a paraphilia, nor is it classified as a mental disorder in the current nomenclature of diseases as set forth in DSM-III. Whether or not homosexuality per se should be classified as a mental disorder has been and continues to be the focus of considerable controversy. In 1973, the Board of Trustees of the American Psychiatric Association voted to eliminate homosexuality per se as a mental disorder. A new category, ego-dystonic homosexuality, reserved for those persons who are disturbed by, in conflict with, or wish to change their sexual orientation was defined in DSM-III. The removal of homosexuality as a paraphilia was supported by the following rationale: The crucial issue in determining whether or not homosexuality per se should be regarded as a mental disorder is not the cause of the condition but its consequences and the definition of mental disorder. A significant proportion of homosexuals are apparently satisfied with their sexual orientation, show no significant signs of manifest psychopathology (unless homosexuality by itself is considered psychopathology), and are able to function socially and occupationally with no impairment. If one uses the criteria of distress or disability, homosexuality per se is not a mental disorder. If one uses the criterion of inherent disadvantage, it is not clear that homosexuality is a disadvantage in all cultures or subcultures.

Paraphilias are limited to conditions that are associated with (1) preference for the use of a nonhuman object for sexual arousal, (2) repetitive sexual activity with humans involving real or simulated suffering or humiliation, or (3) repetitive sexual activity with nonconsenting or inappropriate partners. The following are some common paraphilias: *fetishism*, pedophilia, *transvestism, exhibitionism*, voyeurism, *sexual sadism*, sexual masochism, and zoophilia.

**9.2. The answer is B** (*Synopsis*, ed. 4, pages 183, 184, and 185).

Korsakoff's psychosis is the out-dated term used for what is now known as *alcohol amnestic disorder*. It is characterized by a profound memory impairment, particularly for recent events, for which the patient attempts to compensate by confabulation. It is an organic mental disorder seen in long-standing alcoholics.

Other terms were changed by DSM-III; for example, delirium tremens is now known as *alcohol withdrawal delirium*. Alcohol withdrawal delirium is an acute, sometimes fatal, reaction to withdrawal from alcohol, usually occurring 72 to 96 hours after the cessation of heavy drinking. Its distinctive characteristic is autonomic hyperactivity (tachycardia, fever, hyperhidrosis, dilated pupils), which is usually accompanied by tremulousness, hallucinations, illusions, and delusions.

*Alcohol intoxication* results from the recent ingestion of alcohol. It is marked by maladaptive behavior, such as fighting or impaired judgment, slurred speech, nystagmus, irritability, or loquacity. A blood level of 100 to 200 mg percent will cause intoxication in most persons. *Alcohol idiosyncratic intoxication*, by contrast, is a marked behavioral change after a small amount of alcohol is taken. The person can become markedly belligerent and assaultive in that state.

*Alcohol dependence* is associated with the repetitious daily ingestion of alcohol, usually over a long period of time, in amounts that the drinker is unable to handle physiologically, emotionally, or socially. Eventually, tolerance to alcohol develops, and withdrawal reactions may appear.

**9.3. The answer is E** (*Synopsis*, ed. 4, page 191).

There are four classes of psychosexual disorders: *gender-identity disorders*, characterized by the person's feelings of discomfort and inappropriateness about his or her anatomical sex and by persistent behaviors generally associated with the other sex; *paraphilias*, characterized by arousal in response to sexual objects or situations that are not part of normative arousal-activity patterns; psychosexual dysfunctions, characterized by *inhibition in sexual desire* or the psychophysiological changes that characterize the sexual response cycle; and other psychosexual disorders, which include *ego-dystonic homosexuality*.

*Hysteria* (known in DSM-III as conversion disorder or dissociative disorder) is characterized by either a functional impairment in one of the special senses or in the voluntary nervous system (conversion disorder) or by an alteration in state of consciousness, such as amnesia (dissociative disorder). Freud's early theory was that hysteria was a symbolic representation of a repressed sexual trauma. He believed that the strong affect associated with the traumatic memory is diverted into the wrong somatic channels (conversion), and the hysterical symptom results. The symptom may be motor, sensory, visceral, or mental, i.e. dissociative, amnesia, fugue, or dream state. Freud later revised his theory when he came to believe that the sexual traumata uncovered in hysterical patients were really fictitious memories designed to mask the autoerotic activities or fantasies of childhood.

**9.4.   The answer is B** (*Synopsis,* ed. 4, page 192).

The essential features of personality disorders are deeply ingrained, inflexible, maladaptive patterns of relating to, perceiving, and thinking about the environment and one's self that are of sufficient severity to cause either a significant impairment in adaptive functioning or subjective distress. Persons with *paranoid, schizoid,* and schizotypal disorders often seem odd or eccentric. Persons with histrionic, narcissistic, antisocial, and borderline personality disorders often seem dramatic, emotional, or erratic. Persons with *avoidant,* dependent, compulsive, and passive-aggressive personality disorders often seem anxious or fearful.

There is no personality disorder classified as *explosive* in DSM-III. The characteristic of explosiveness may be seen in several different personality disorders, such as histrionic, antisocial, or *borderline.*

**9.5.   The answer is D** (*Synopsis,* ed. 4, page 191).

All the somatoform disorders involve physical symptoms suggesting physical disorder for which no demonstrable organic findings are adequate to explain the symptoms and for which positive evidence or a strong presumption indicates that the symptoms are linked to psychological factors or conflicts. The first disorder in this category is *somatization disorder,* a chronic polysymptomatic disorder that begins early in life. The second disorder is *conversion disorder,* in which the predominant disturbance is conversion symptoms that are not symptomatic of another disorder. *Psychogenic pain disorder* refers to psychologically induced pain not attributable to any other mental or physical disorder. *Hypochondriasis* involves an unrealistic and persistent interpretation of physical symptoms or

sensations as abnormal, leading to the preoccupation with the fear or belief of having a serious disease.

In contrast, *dissociative disorders* are characterized by a sudden, temporary alteration in the normally integrated functions of consciousness, identity, or motor behavior. This class includes psychogenic amnesia, psychogenic fugue, multiple personality, and depersonalization disorder.

**9.6.   The answer is A (1, 2, 3)** (*Synopsis,* ed. 4, pages 190 and 191).

*The essential feature of affective disorders is a disturbance of mood* accompanied by related symptoms. This major class contains two specific minor classes. The first, *major affective disorders, includes bipolar disorder* and major depression. Bipolar disorder is subdivided according to the current episode as mixed, manic, or depressed. Major *depression is subdivided according to whether the disturbance is a single episode or recurrent.* There is also provision for further characterizing the current episode as in remission, with psychotic features, with or without melancholia (for a major depressive episode), and without psychotic features (for manic episodes). The second minor class, other specific affective disorders, includes cyclothymic disorder and dysthymic disorder (chronic mild depression).

Major affective disorders, both manic and depressed, may be accompanied during their acute phases by *psychotic features,* such as delusions and hallucinations.

**9.7.   The answer is C (2, 4)** (*Synopsis,* ed. 4, page 181).

Reliability is the extent to which users of a system will achieve the *same diagnosis when applied to a series of cases.* It reflects the *extent to which subjects can be discriminated from each other* and for that reason *is not the same as agreement among physicians in classifying a single case.* The extent to which the classification of a disorder enables the user to communicate to colleagues, to understand a mental disorder, and to treat or control the illness is a measure of validity, rather than reliability. Validity and reliability are both important criteria for judging the value of a classification.

**9.8.   The answer is A (1, 2, 3)** (*Synopsis,* ed. 4, page 182).

DSM-III *is generally atheoretical with regard to the causes of disorders,* with the exception of those disorders in which the pathophysiological processes are known, such as the organic mental disorders. The general approach is descriptive, in that the definitions of the disorders *describe the manifestations of the disorders, rather than how the disorders come about.* Specified diagnostic criteria are provided for each mental disorder (the only exception being for schizoaffective disorder), and there are *essential criteria* for each disorder that must be met to make the diagnosis.

DSM-III *is a multiaxial system* because it includes five axes. Axis I is the major clinical syndromes, Axis II is personality and developmental disorders, Axis III is physical disorders, Axis IV is the severity of psychosocial stressors, and Axis V is the highest level of adaptive functioning during the past year.

**9.9.   The answer is E (all)** (*Synopsis,* ed. 4, page 181).

Validity is the degree to which a test measures what it claims to measure and the degree to which an experimental design yields data truly applicable to the phenomenon under investigation.

Predictive validity is one type of validity used to judge the classification of a mental disorder. The validity of mental disorder classification is the extent to which the entire classification and each of its specific diagnostic categories achieve the purposes of communication, control, and comprehension. Predictive validity is also *the extent to which knowledge that a person has a particular mental disorder is useful in predicting such factors as the future course of the illness,* complications, and response to treatment. Clearly, predictive validity *is directly related to the major practical purposes of management and treatment.* For example, it is possible to distinguish unipolar from bipolar depression on the basis that *bipolar patients will improve when treated with lithium, whereas unipolar patients will not. Emil Kraepelin was also able to differentiate manic-depressive illness from schizophrenia* because, in the latter illness, deterioration occurred, whereas in manic-depressive illness, the patient did not ultimately deteriorate.

**9.10.   The answer is E (all)** (*Synopsis,* ed. 4, page 191).

In anxiety disorders, some form of anxiety is the most predominant disturbance. This anxiety is experienced *if the person tries to resist* giving in to his or her symptoms. *Anxiety disorders differ from phobic disorders in that only the phobic disorder is characterized by fear of a specific object,* activity, or situation. In anxiety states, the *predominant experience is of the anxiety itself,* which is not necessarily attached to a specific stimulus. *If anxiety is episodic, it is classified as a panic disorder*; if it is chronic and

persistent, it is classified as a generalized anxiety disorder.

**9.11.   The answer is C (2, 4)** (*Synopsis,* ed. 4, page 186).

Tobacco dependence is defined in DSM-III as having the essential features of either unsuccessful attempts to stop or reduce the amount of tobacco use on a permanent basis, *the development of tobacco withdrawal,* or the presence of a serious physical disorder that the person knows is exacerbated by tobacco use. People with this disorder are often distressed by *their inability to stop tobacco use,* especially when they have physical symptoms that are made worse by continued use. DSM-III stipulates that the diagnosis will only be made when either the person is seeking help to stop smoking or when, in the judgment of the diagnostician, the use of tobacco is seriously affecting the person's physical health.

Clearly, there are potentially *many serious medical complications of long-term tobacco dependence.* The list of medical complications associated with long-term use include lung cancer, heart disease, premature birth, and emphysema, among others. If the person with a serious case of one of the tobacco-related physical disorders continues to use tobacco, despite knowing about its serious effects, the assumption can be made that the person is tobacco dependent. Also, because tobacco use rarely causes an intoxicated state, such as with alcohol, there is *no impairment of social or occupational functioning* as an immediate consequence of tobacco use. Of course, some tobacco dependent people may have difficulty remaining in social or occupational situations that prohibit smoking.

**9.12.   The answer is E (all)** (*Synopsis,* ed. 4, page 190).

The classification of substance use disorders includes disorders in which behavioral changes are caused by taking substances that affect the central nervous system. The categories of substance abuse are defined by (1) *minimal duration* (1 month); (2) *social complication of use,* such as impairment in social or occupational functioning; and (3) *pathological pattern of use,* such as the inability to cut down or stop use. Dependence is generally defined by *the presence of either tolerance or withdrawal* and is also considered an essential feature necessary to make a diagnosis of substance use disorder.

**9.13.   The answer is B (1, 3)** (*Synopsis,* ed. 4, pages 182 and 188).

In DSM-III, *stress is coded on a seven-point*

scale on Axis IV, not on Axis III. Axis III is used for associated medical illness. The over-all severity of *stress can be a significant contributor to the development or exacerbation of a mental disorder. A person's prognosis may be better if a disorder develops after severe stress than if it develops after minor stress or none at all.*

*The rating of severity of stress should be based on the clinician's assessment of the stress that an average person with similar sociocultural values and circumstances would experience* from the psychosocial stressors. That judgment involves a consideration of the amount of change in the person's life due to the stressor, the degree to which the event is desired and under the person's control, and the number of stressors. In addition, in certain settings it may be useful to note the specific psychosocial stressors. This information may be important in formulating a treatment plan that includes attempts to remove the psychosocial stressors or to help the person cope with them.

**9.14.   The answer is E (all)** (*Synopsis*, ed. 4, pages 189 and 190).

The essential feature of all organic mental disorders is *a psychological or behavioral disturbance that is due to transient or permanent dysfunction of the brain.* DSM-III recognizes the following organic brain syndromes: (1) delirium and dementia, with relatively global cognitive impairment; (2) amnestic syndrome and organic hallucinosis, with *relatively selective areas of cognitive impairment;* (3) organic delusional syndrome and organic affective syndrome, with features resembling schizophrenic or affective disorders; (4) organic personality syndrome, with features affecting the personality; (5) intoxication and withdrawal associated with drug ingestion or cessation and not meeting the criteria for any of the previous syndromes; strictly speaking, these two categories are defined by etiology, rather than by syndrome; and (6) other organic brain syndrome, a residual category for any other organic brain syndrome not classifiable as any of the previous syndromes. *Organic mental disorders may resemble schizophrenia* in that distortions of perception, such as hallucinations, may occur. *Major affective disorders may also mimic an organic mental disorder,* in which case the term "pseudodementia" is applied.

**9.15.   The answer is B (1, 3)** (*Synopsis*, ed. 4, pages 181 and 182).

The present classification of psychiatric disorders in DSM-III attempts to *describe comprehensively the manifestations of mental disorders* and only *rarely attempts to account for how the*

*disturbances come about,* unless the mechanism is included in the definition of the disorder. This general approach can be said to be descriptive in that the *definitions consist of descriptions of the clinical features of the disorders.*

Classification is the process by which the complexity of phenomena is reduced by arranging them for one or more purposes into categories according to some established criteria. A classification of mental disorders consists of a list of categories of specific mental disorders *grouped into various classes on the basis of some shared characteristics.*

**9.16–9.20.   The   answers   are   9.16–E, 9.17–B, 9.18–A, 9.19–D, and 9.20–C** (*Synopsis*, ed. 4, page 192).

Paranoid personality disorder is characterized by *suspiciousness* and mistrust. These people are *hypervigilant*, secretive, and hypersensitive and have a generally restricted affect. Schizotypal personality disorder is characterized by *ideas of reference* and *magical thinking.* People with this disorder may manifest an odd sense of speech, may have recurrent depersonalization experiences or illusions, and may be quite isolated and withdrawn. Borderline personalities are *impulsive* and unpredictable. They show patterns of unstable interpersonal relationships and may engage in *self-destructive* acts, including suicidal gestures. Dependent personalities are *clinging*, with a tendency to *subordinate their needs to the needs of others.* They are generally passive and find it very difficult to assume responsibility for major life duties. Passive-aggressive personalities are characterized by *stubbornness* and *procrastination.* There is long-standing social and occupational ineffectiveness, referred to in DSM-III as intentional inefficiency.

**9.21–9.25.   The   answers   are   9.21–B, 9.22–E, 9.23–D, 9.24–A, and 9.25–C** (*Synopsis*, ed. 4, page 184).

Panic disorder is characterized by the *experience of episodic anxiety,* whereas the generalized anxiety disorder is experienced as a *chronic and persistent anxiety level.* In posttraumatic stress disorder, *the anxiety is experienced after a specific event that is outside the range of normal experience.* In phobic disorders, *the anxiety is attached to a specific object or situation and leads to avoidance behavior.* In obsessive-compulsive disorder, the anxiety is attached to *disturbing, unwanted, anxiety-provoking thoughts.* All the above disorders are subsumed in DSM-III under the heading of anxiety disorders.

The following table lists the full classification of anxiety disorders as described in DSM-III.

**Anxiety Disorders***

---

Phobic disorders (or phobic neuroses)
  Agoraphobia with panic attacks
  Agoraphobia without panic attacks
  Social phobia
  Simple phobia

Anxiety states (or anxiety neuroses)
  Panic disorder
  Generalized anxiety disorder
  Obsessive-compulsive disorder (or obses-
    sive-compulsive neurosis)

Posttraumatic stress disorder
  acute
  chronic or delayed

Atypical anxiety disorder

---

* From American Psychiatric Association: *Diagnostic and Statistical Manual of Mental Disorders*, ed 3. American Psychiatric Association, Washington, DC, 1980. Used with permission.

## References

Berner P, Gabriel E, Hatschnig H, Kieffer W, Koeher K, Lenz G, Simhandl C: *Diagnostic Criteria for Schizophrenic and Affective Psychoses*. World Psychiatric Association, Geneva, 1983.

Feighner J P, Robins E, Guze S B, Woodruf R A, Winokur G, Munoz R: Diagnostic criteria for use in psychiatric research. Arch Gen Psychiatry *26:* 57, 1972.

Skodol A E: Identifying common errors in the use of the DSM-III through diagnostic supervision. Hosp Comm Psychiatry *35:* 251, 1984.

Spitzer R L, Williams J B W: Classification of mental disorders. In *Comprehensive Textbook of Psychiatry*, ed 4, H I Kaplan, B J Sadock, editors, p 591. Williams & Wilkins, Baltimore, 1985.

Spitzer R L, Williams J B W, Skodol A E: *International Perspectives on DSM-III*. American Psychiatric Press, Washington, DC, 1983.

World Health Organization: *International Classification of Diseases*, rev 9. World Health Organization, Geneva, 1977.

# 10

# Schizophrenic Disorders

Schizophrenia is a psychotic mental disorder characterized by disturbances in thinking, mood, and behavior. The thinking disturbance is manifested by a distortion of reality, sometimes with delusions and hallucinations, accompanied by a fragmentation of associations that results in characteristic disturbances of speech. The mood disturbance includes ambivalence and inappropriate or constricted affective responses. The behavior disturbance may be manifested by apathetic withdrawal or bizarre activity. Formerly known as dementia precox, the term schizophrenia was introduced by Eugen Bleuler.

The psychiatric importance of the schizophrenic disorders hardly requires documentation. About 1 percent of the population is diagnosed as having a schizophrenic illness, and many of those so afflicted run a chronic course. Obviously, the incidence and prevalence rates of any psychiatric disorder are a function of diagnostic criteria. The prevalence rate reported above was based on the diagnostic criteria of the past. The use of criteria from the third edition of the *Diagnostic and Statistical Manual of Mental Disorders* (DSM-III) for the diagnosis of schizophrenia has confirmed this figure, according to the study of the National Institute of Mental Health Epidemiologic Catchment Area (ECA) Program.

The illness frequently involves young adults and can produce severe psychological, social, and vocational disability during the potentially most creative and productive years of a person's life. Not only is the suicide rate in schizophrenia higher than that found in most psychiatric disorders, but the deaths tend to occur relatively early in life. This results in a greater loss of total years of expected life than is found in other psychiatric disorders.

The economic cost of schizophrenia in the United States has been estimated to be between $10 billion and $20 billion a year. About two-thirds of this cost is a consequence of the relative lack of productive employment. The social and psychological costs in human suffering cannot be expressed monetarily.

The etiology of schizophrenia is not yet clearly understood; consequently, treatment is largely empirical. The treatment of schizophrenia has been approached from two viewpoints, the organic and the psychological. Clinical experience, however, has shown that the most effective regimen for the treatment of schizophrenia is an integrated effort, combining organic, psychological, and environmental modalities in a unified therapeutic approach, which is carefully individualized for each patient.

For example, the value of antipsychotic medication has been confirmed by many clinical studies. These drugs have been found to be effective in relieving symptoms of acute psychosis and in enabling patients to maintain therapeutic gains; studies have shown that such medication may also prevent further psychiatric deterioration of the chronic patient. Yet, the prognosis in acute as well as chronic cases is stated by some to be even more favorable when the therapeutic program includes psychological, as well as pharmacological, treatment. Such psychotherapeutic techniques as the establishment of a supportive relationship, strengthening of patients' psychological defenses, and help with reality testing may facilitate recovery by helping the patients improve their tenuous adaptation and overcome their emotional isolation. Psychotherapy has been advocated by certain clinicians for protection against subsequent psychotic episodes. During hospitalization, the organization of a specially structured therapeutic environment may expedite recovery and limit the deterioration of schizophrenic patients. After discharge from the hospital, the use of such resources as the sheltered workshop often facilitates the patients' return to the community. Schizophrenia is as yet not curable; however, the judicious use of these different, but complementary, treatment methods offers many patients a good prognosis for social remission.

The reader should refer to Chapter 10 of *Modern Synopsis-IV*, which discusses the schizophrenic disorders. After reading that chapter, the reader can test his or her knowledge by studying the questions and answers that follow.

# Questions

**DIRECTIONS:** Each of the statements or questions below is followed by five suggested responses or completions. Select the *one* that is *best* in each case.

**10.1.** If both parents are schizophrenic, the children's risk of developing schizophrenia is

A. 0.1 percent
B. 5 percent
C. 10 percent
D. 50 percent
E. same as in the general population

**10.2.** Relapse in schizophrenia is most closely related to

A. the natural course of the illness
B. compliance in taking medicine
C. whether or not the patient is working
D. physical therapy
E. individual psychotherapy

**10.3.** Which of the following symptoms must be present to make a diagnosis of schizophrenia:

A. Thought broadcasting
B. Auditory hallucinations
C. Blunted affect
D. Disorganized behavior
E. All of the above

**10.4.** Which of the following is the factor that accounts for the diagnostic difference between schizophrenic and schizophreniform disorder:

A. Level of premorbid functioning
B. Age of first psychotic episode
C. Type of symptomatology
D. Duration of the illness
E. Presence of precipitating factors

**10.5.** Studies by the World Health Organization have shown that certain schizophrenic symptoms are found throughout the world and can be confirmed by independent examiners. Among the following, which symptom shows the highest reliability:

A. Elated thoughts
B. Lability of mood
C. Perplexity
D. Negativism
E. Body hallucinations

**10.6.** In order to make a diagnosis of schizophrenia, there must be continuous signs of the illness for at least

A. 2 months
B. 4 months
C. 6 months
D. 8 months
E. 1 year

**10.7.** A 20-year-old man was brought to the hospital lying in a rigid position on a stretcher. He did not respond to outside stimuli and had mask-like facies. His eyes were open, and he appeared to be aware of his surroundings. He did not answer questions, but would shut his eyes tightly for a few moments and refuse to open them when asked to do so by the examining physician. This patient is showing signs of which type of schizophrenia:

A. Paranoid
B. Catatonic
C. Hebephrenic
D. Residual
E. Latent

**10.8.** All of the following are considered prodromal symptoms of schizophrenia *except*

A. social isolation
B. peculiar behavior
C. delusions
D. change in affect
E. circumstantial speech

**10.9.** A patient who has a first episode of a schizophrenic illness that is present more or less continuously for 1 year is considered to be in which stage of the illness:

A. Chronic
B. Subchronic
C. Subchronic with acute exacerbation
D. Chronic with acute exacerbation
E. In remission

**10.10.** In general, pooled studies show expectancy rates for schizophrenia in monozygotic twins of

A. 0.1 percent
B. 5 percent
C. 25 percent
D. 40 percent
E. over 75 percent

**10.11.** Latent schizophrenia

A. is diagnosed in patients who have a
schizotypal personality make-up
B. is characterized by disturbances in
thinking
C. does not show clear psychotic pathology
D. is sometimes known as borderline
schizophrenia
E. all of the above

**10.12.** Paraphrenia is a synonym for

A. latent schizophrenia
B. catatonic schizophrenia
C. hebephrenia
D. simple schizophrenia
E. paranoid schizophrenia

**10.13.** All the following are characteristics of pseudoneurotic schizophrenia *except*

A. predominantly neurotic symptoms
B. pananxiety
C. schizophrenic thinking
D. sexual preoccupation
E. good response to psychoanalysis

**10.14.** The type of schizophrenia associated with the patient's changing levels of positive or negative nitrogen balance is known as

A. chronic catatonia
B. stuporous catatonia
C. excited catatonia
D. periodic catatonia
E. all of the above

**10.15.** A sloppy 23-year-old male patient on a psychiatric ward is aimlessly wandering around, bursting into unprovoked laughter, posturing, incongruously grimacing, and constantly gazing in a mirror. This behavior is characteristic of

A. paranoid schizophrenia
B. catatonic schizophrenia
C. conversion disorder
D. disorganized (hebephrenic) schizophrenia
E. dissociative disorder

**10.16.** A schizophrenic who cuts his penis off is said to be suffering from

A. penis envy
B. castration complex
C. the Van Gogh syndrome
D. *bouffée délirante*
E. homosexual panic

**10.17.** Group therapy is most likely to help schizophrenic patients when

A. it is combined with individual therapy
B. it is used without individual therapy
C. it is combined with drug therapy
D. it is insight-oriented
E. it focuses on psychoanalytic principles

**10.18.** A 22-year-old woman is brought to a psychiatrist by her mother within the first 6 months following her first schizophrenic episode. During this time, she is treated with neuroleptics. Which of the following problems is the physician *not* likely to encounter:

A. Relapse of psychosis
B. Depression
C. Tardive dyskinesia
D. A relative decrease in the level of
functioning
E. A flat affect

**10.19.** The most common type of schizophrenic hallucination is

A. visual
B. auditory
C. tactile
D. olfactory
E. gustatory

**10.20.** In general, pooled studies show an incidence of schizophrenia of

A. 1 per 1,000
B. 3 per 1,000
C. 5 per 1,000
D. 7 per 1,000
E. 10 per 1,000

**10.21.** The percentage of the total population likely to receive psychiatric treatment for a schizophrenic illness during any particular year is

A. less than 0.5 percent
B. 1 percent
C. 2.5 percent
D. 3 percent
E. 5 percent

**10.22.** A 34-year-old stuporous man has been in the hospital for 3 days and has not spoken to anyone or left his bed. After being given an intravenous injection of sodium amytal, the patient dramatically becomes lucid. The most likely diagnosis of the patient is

A. organic mental disorder
B. dysthymic disorder
C. catatonic schizophrenia
D. disorganized (hebephrenic) schizophrenia
E. meningioma

**10.23.** The mortality rate among schizophrenic patients

A. is higher than that for normal persons
B. is lower than that for normal persons
C. is the same as that for normal persons
D. has never been studied
E. is the same as that for phobics

**10.24.** A 33-year-old male psychiatric inpatient puts on his dark sunglasses whenever he meets with his doctor. He coherently states that doing so makes it impossible for the doctor to control his thoughts. This patient is exhibiting

A. social withdrawal
B. hypervigilance
C. fragmentation of thinking
D. delusional thinking
E. magical thinking

**10.25.** The patient illustrated below demonstrates the characteristic posture known as

A. catalepsy
B. mannerism
C. perseveration
D. cataplexy
E. none of the above

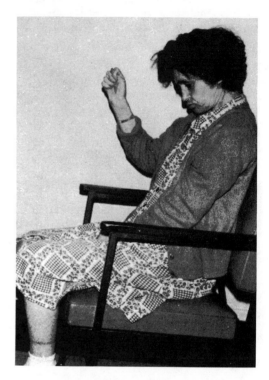

**(Courtesy of Heinz E Lehmann, MD.)**

**10.26.** The patient shown below is noted to be posturing, grimacing, and mirror gazing for long periods of time. These symptoms are most characteristic of

A. paranoid schizophrenia
B. catatonic schizophrenia
C. disorganized schizophrenia
D. schizotaxia
E. schizoaffective disorder

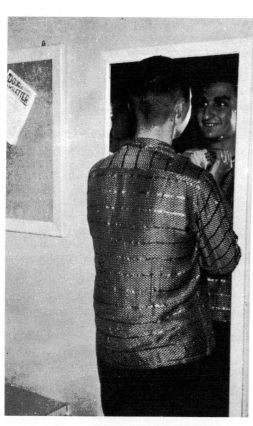

(Courtesy of Heinz E Lehmann, MD.)

**10.27.** A 15-year-old girl began developing severe temper tantrums in high school. She became easily angry with her friends and her family, whom she accused of not caring about her. After 6 months of exhibiting this kind of behavior, she thought people were following her, and she was afraid of being poisoned. She was admitted to a hospital, and shortly thereafter her behavior began to deteriorate further. She talked like a child, smiled in a silly fashion, began to wet her bed, and threw food at visitors. The most likely type of schizophrenia shown by this patient is

A. paranoid
B. disorganized
C. catatonic
D. residual
E. simple

**DIRECTIONS:** For each of the incomplete statements below, *one* or *more* of the completions given is correct. Choose answer:

A. if only **1**, **2**, and **3** are correct
B. if only **1** and **3** are correct
C. if only **2** and **4** are correct
D. if only **4** is correct
E. if all are correct

**10.28.** Relapse rates in schizophrenia have been found to be related significantly to expressed emotionality in the patients' homes that is characterized by

1. critical comments
2. hostility
3. emotional overinvolvement
4. psychosomatic illness

**10.29.** In the last 20 years, the use of mental hospital beds by schizophrenics has been characterized by

1. shorter hospital stays
2. increased readmissions
3. more frequent hospitalizations
4. approximately a 10 percent probability of patients being readmitted within a 2-year period after discharge from a hospital

**10.30.** The features associated with a good prognosis in schizophrenic disorders are

1. older age of onset
2. being married
3. more acute onset
4. a precipitating event

**10.31.** Which of the following are true regarding genetic theories of concordance rates in schizophrenia:

1. If both parents are schizophrenic, the risk for the children is between 15 and 55 percent.
2. For second-degree relatives, the risk is 2.5 percent.
3. For siblings, the risk is approximately 9 percent.
4. There is a risk of 40 percent to the unaffected twin of a dizygotic twin with schizophrenia.

**10.32.** The psychedelic model of schizophrenia is supported by the fact that

1. indolamines play a role in etiology
2. bufotenin produces a schizophrenic-like syndrome
3. dimethyltryptamine (DMT) has hallucinogenic properties
4. methionine reduces the symptoms of schizophrenia

**10.33.** Children found to be predisposed to schizophrenia were found to have

1. vasomotor instability
2. disturbed sleep patterns
3. poor temperature control
4. poor muscle tone

**10.34.** Catatonic schizophrenia

1. occurs in two forms
2. is not a common diagnosis in Third World countries
3. may be marked by stupor
4. is the most common diagnosis in hospitalized schizophrenic patients in the United States

**10.35.** A 25-year-old woman was arrested for shoplifting baby clothes. She stated to the arresting officer that she needed the stolen items to "dress the Holy Child" and laughed in what appeared to be a silly way. When seen by a psychiatrist in the local hospital, she further stated that she was pregnant and about to give birth to a "new Messiah." On further examination it was revealed that the patient had a history of previous shoplifting offenses during the preceding year. She had been fired from her job during that time and was noted by friends and co-workers to appear disorganized, confused, and hard to get along with. On physical examination, no evidence of pregnancy was noted.
This patient is showing which of the following schizophrenic signs:

1. Delusions of grandeur
2. Somatic delusions
3. Inappropriate affect
4. Pseudocyesis

**10.36.** Computed tomography (CT) scans of the brain of schizophrenic patients have shown

1. small lateral ventricles
2. reduced sulcal fluid volume
3. hypertrophy of the anterior vermis of the cerebellum
4. reversal of the normal asymmetrics of the brain

**10.37.** Thinking in schizophrenia is characterized by

1. autistic qualities
2. conclusions that are based on accepted rules of logic
3. concretization of thought
4. the maintenance of abstract attitudes

**10.38.** Paranoid schizophrenia may present with

1. persecutory delusions
2. grandiose delusions
3. delusional jealousy
4. grandiose hallucinations

**10.39.** Evidence supporting the dopamine hypothesis of schizophrenia includes which of the following:

1. Chlorpromazine causes a blockade of dopamine receptors.
2. Antipsychotic drugs decrease dopamine metabolism levels.
3. Dopamine agonists produce symptoms resembling schizophrenia.
4. The effects of amphetamine are exaggerated when the dopamine tracts are severed.

**10.40.** Which of the following are considered initiating factors in the development of a schizophrenic episode of illness:

1. Lysergic acid diethylamide (LSD) use
2. Death of a parent
3. Cannabis use
4. Rejection

**10.41.** Disorganized (or hebephrenic) schizophrenia is characterized by

1. frequent incoherence
2. absence of systematized delusions
3. silly affect
4. catalepsy

**10.42.** Etiological hypotheses about schizophrenia presume which of the following:

1. A low mean activity of monoamine oxidase (MAO) in blood platelets of chronic schizophrenic patients
2. Low calcium levels in patients with catatonia
3. β-Endorphins that may exacerbate symptoms in some schizophrenic patients
4. Electrolyte changes in the serum of schizophrenic patients

**10.43.** Eye movements of schizophrenic patients are characterized by

1. nystagmus
2. difficulty in fixating moving objects
3. defective oculomotor tracts
4. increased saccadic movements

**10.44.** A brief reactive psychosis is characterized by the essential features of

1. a recognizable stressful event that precedes symptoms
2. disorientation
3. duration of more than a few hours but less than 2 weeks
4. inappropriate, volatile affect

**10.45.** Which of the following statements have been applied to the rate of schizophrenia in the general population:

1. Social stresses experienced by the lower socioeconomic classes are causatively related to schizophrenia.
2. Schizophrenic patients tend to be downwardly mobile.
3. The prevalence of schizophrenia is rising among Third World populations.
4. Some cultures may be schizophrenogenic.

**10.46.** Undifferentiated schizophrenia refers to

1. patients who cannot easily be fitted into one of the other subtypes
2. patients who may meet the criteria for more than one subtype
3. some acute, excited schizophrenics
4. some inert, chronic patients

**10.47.** Residual schizophrenia is defined as a type of schizophrenia characterized by

1. continuing evidence of the illness but without any prominent psychotic symptoms
2. persecutory and grandiose delusions
3. a history of at least one previous episode of schizophrenia with prominent psychotic symptoms
4. frequent incoherence

**10.48.** Negativism in schizophrenia is characterized by

1. the patient appearing to be fatigued
2. the patient's failure to cooperate
3. the patient being incapable of physical movement
4. the patient doing the opposite of what is being asked

**10.49.** First-rank symptoms of schizophrenia, as described by Kurt Schneider, include

1. audible thoughts
2. thought withdrawal
3. delusional perception
4. voices heard arguing

| **Directions Summarized** | | | | |
| A | B | C | D | E |
| 1, 2, 3 | 1, 3 | 2, 4 | 4 | All are |
| only | only | only | only | correct |

**10.50.**   Which of the following statements about delusions are accurate:

1. The most frequent type of delusion in schizophrenia is the persecutory type.
2. The key symptom in paranoid schizophrenia is one or more delusions of persecution.
3. Delusions are idiosyncratic for a particular patient.
4. Delusions can be corrected by appropriate reasoning.

**10.51.**   Which of the following statements about the relationship of suicide and schizophrenia are true:

1. More schizophrenics than manic-depressives commit suicide.
2. The immediate risk of suicide is relatively greater among manic-depressives than among schizophrenics.
3. One of the incipient signs of schizophrenia may be a suicidal impulse.
4. Schizophrenics committing suicide have usually given clear warnings of their intentions.

**10.52.**   Symptoms seen in schizophrenics in a frequency of over 70 percent include

1. thoughts spoken aloud
2. auditory hallucinations
3. delusions of persecution
4. lack of insight

**10.53.**   Catatonic schizophrenia is characterized by

1. mutism
2. negativism
3. posturing
4. fatuous affect

**10.54.**   A 34-year-old woman is brought to the psychiatric emergency room after she was discovered trying to kill her 13-month-old son by putting him in a preheated broiler. The woman is seen by an attending psychiatrist who obtains the following history:

In the past 10 years the patient has had six psychiatric hospitalizations. The first admission, when she was 24 years old, lasted 1½ years; subsequent admissions have been for shorter periods. Each hospitalization was preceded by a period in which she had auditory hallucinations. She "heard the radiator speak to me and my brain answering back." This time, the voice from the radiator told her that her son was making sexual advances toward her and ordered her to "burn the little devil." The patient states that if she does not kill the child, her husband will, because the boy is "trying to steal his manhood." A diagnosis of paranoid schizophrenia was made.

Which of the following statements support the above diagnosis:

1. Persecutory delusions
2. The presence of hallucinations with persecutory or grandiose content
3. Delusional jealousy
4. Duration of illness

**DIRECTIONS:** Each group of questions below consists of five lettered headings followed by a list of numbered words or statements. For each numbered word or statement, select the *one* lettered heading that is most closely associated with it. Each lettered heading may be selected once, more than once, or not at all.

**Questions 10.55–10.59**
A. Incoherence
B. Neologism
C. Mutism
D. Echolalia
E. Verbigeration

**10.55.** Functional inhibition of speech

**10.56.** New expression or word

**10.57.** Empty or obscure language

**10.58.** Repeating the same words the examiner uses

**10.59.** Senseless repetition of words or phrases

# Answers

# Schizophrenic Disorders

**10.1.   The answer is D** (*Synopsis*, ed. 4, page 197).

If both parents are schizophrenic, the risk for the children is between 15 and 55 percent, according to various studies. In general, pooled results show about a *50 percent risk in the children of two schizophrenic parents.*

**10.2.   The answer is B** (*Synopsis*, ed. 4, page 221).

*Compliance in taking medication* after the first episode of a schizophrenic disorder is related to subsequent relapse. Those patients who do not take medication as prescribed have a higher relapse rate.

The risk of personality deterioration increases with each schizophrenic relapse. Schizophrenic recoveries are often called remissions because many of the patients later relapse. Although they may remit again, there is, with each schizophrenic attack, a greater probability of some permanent personality damage. *The natural course of the illness, however, does not inevitably lead to intellectual deterioration or relapse. Work, psychotherapy, or physical therapy* does not influence relapse as much as does medication.

**10.3.   The answer is E** (*Synopsis*, ed. 4, page 204).

To make a diagnosis of schizophrenia, at least one of the following symptoms must be present: delusions (e.g. *thought broadcasting*), *auditory hallucinations*, incoherence or loosening of associations, *blunted affect, and catatonic or grossly disorganized behavior.*

See the table on the facing page for the DSM-III diagnostic criteria for a schizophrenic disorder.

**10.4.   The answer is D** (*Synopsis*, ed. 4, page 204).

According to the DSM-III classification, the only difference between schizophreniform and schizophrenic disorders is the *duration of time the illness is present.* Symptoms that last less than 2 weeks are diagnosed as either atypical psychosis or brief reactive psychosis. If the symptomatology is present for more than 2 weeks or less than 6 months, the diagnosis of schizophreniform disorder may be made. For symptoms that persist for 6 months or longer, the diagnosis of schizophrenic disorder is then made.

**10.5.   The answer is A** (*Synopsis*, ed. 4, page 220).

*Elated thoughts* and delusions of grandeur are among the symptoms that show a high reliability across various international centers. *Perplexity* and *lability of mood* are in the medium range of reliability, and *negativism* and *body hallucinations* are in the low range.

The table on page 112 lists an analysis of schizophrenic symptoms, with high, medium, and low reliability scores, across nine international centers.

**10.6.   The answer is C** (*Synopsis*, ed. 4, page 204).

In order to diagnose schizophrenia, there must be continuous signs of the illness for at least *6 months* at some time during the person's life, with some signs of the illness at the time of diagnosis. The 6-month period must include an active phase during which symptoms of schizophrenia were present.

**10.7.   The answer is B** (*Synopsis*, ed. 4, page 214).

This patient was in a *catatonic stupor* in which he was rigid and uncommunicative. Mutism is characteristic of this state. These patients refuse to answer questions and seem oblivious to the environment, but they are usually aware of what is going on around them. The catatonic patient often resists the passive movement of a body part; but they do show catalepsy in which they will maintain a posture into which they are placed, often for long periods of time. A patient may come out of a catatonic stupor spontaneously or after a variable period of time, or the stupor may end in a state of extreme agitation or with violent behavior known as catatonic excitement. The patient is dangerous during this period, and physical restraint and neuroleptic medication are indicated to prevent harm from being done.

*Paranoid schizophrenia* is characterized by the presence of persecutory or grandiose delusions, often accompanied by hallucinations. *Re-*

## Diagnostic Criteria for a Schizophrenic Disorder*

A. At least one of the following during a phase of the illness:

1. Bizarre delusions (content is patently absurd and has *no* possible basis in fact), such as delusions of being controlled, thought broadcasting, thought insertion, or thought withdrawal;

2. Somatic, grandiose, religious, nihilistic, or other delusions without persecutory or jealous content;

3. Delusions with persecutory or jealous content if accompanied by hallucinations of any type;

4. Auditory hallucinations in which either a voice keeps up a running commentary on the individual's behavior or thoughts, or two or more voices converse with each other;

5. Auditory hallucinations on several occasions with content of more than one or two words, having no apparent relation to depression or elation; and

6. Incoherence, marked loosening of associations, markedly illogical thinking, or marked poverty of content of speech if associated with at least one of the following:

   a. Blunted, flat, or inappropriate affect
   b. Delusions or hallucinations
   c. Catatonic or other grossly disorganized behavior

B. Deterioration from a previous level of functioning in such areas as work, social relations, and self-care.

C. Duration: Continuous signs of the illness for at least 6 months at some time during the person's life, with some signs of the illness at present. The 6-month period must include an active phase during which there were symptoms from A, with or without a prodromal or residual phase, as defined below.

*Prodromal phase:* A clear deterioration in functioning before the active phase of the illness not due to a disturbance in mood or to a substance use disorder and involving at least *two* of the symptoms noted below.

*Residual phase:* Persistence, following the active phase of the illness, of at least *two* of the symptoms noted below, not due to a disturbance in mood or to a substance use disorder.

*Prodromal or Residual Symptoms*

1. Social isolation or withdrawal;

2. Marked impairment in role functioning as wage-earner, student, or homemaker;

3. Markedly peculiar behavior (e.g. collecting garbage, talking to self in public, or hoarding food);

4. Marked impairment in personal hygiene and grooming;

5. Blunted, flat, or inappropriate affect;

6. Digressive, vague, overelaborate, circumstantial, or metaphorical speech;

7. Odd or bizarre ideation, or magical thinking, e.g. superstitiousness, clairvoyance, telepathy, "sixth sense," "others can feel my feelings," overvalued ideas, ideas of reference;

8. Unusual perceptual experiences, e.g. recurrent illusions, sensing the presence of a force or person not actually present

*Examples:* Six months of prodromal symptoms with 1 week of symptoms from A; no prodromal symptoms with 6 months of symptoms from A; no prodromal symptoms with 2 weeks of symptoms from A and 6 months of residual symptoms; 6 months of symptoms from A, apparently followed by several years of complete remission, with 1 week of symptoms in A in current episode.

D. The full depressive or manic syndrome (criteria A and B of major depressive or manic episode), if present, developed after any psychotic symptoms, or was brief in duration relative to the duration of the psychotic symptoms in A.

E. Onset of prodromal or active phase of the illness before age 45.

F. Not due to any organic mental disorder or mental retardation.

*From American Psychiatric Association: *Diagnostic and Statistical Manual of Mental Disorders*, ed 3. American Psychiatric Association, Washington, DC, 1980. Used with permission.

*sidual schizophrenia* is that type in which the patient no longer is acutely psychotic, but has some remaining signs of the illness. *Latent schizophrenia* is a condition characterized by some schizophrenic symptoms without a history of prior overtly psychotic schizophrenic episodes. In DSM-III the condition is called schizotypal personality disorder and is not considered one of the schizophrenic subtypes. *Hebephrenia* is a complex of symptoms considered a form of schizophrenia. It is characterized by wild or silly behavior or mannerisms, inappropriate affect, frequent hypochondriacal complaints, and delusions and hallucinations that are transient and unsystematized. Hebephrenic schizophrenia is listed in DSM-III as disorganized schizophrenia.

**Reliability of Units of Schizophrenic Symptom Analysis Across Nine International Centers***

| Units of Analysis | | |
|---|---|---|
| 0.93: High | 0.62–0.60: Medium | 0.59–0.47: Low |
| Suicidal | Change of interest | Stereotyped behavior |
| Elated thoughts | Dissociation of speech | Increased libido |
| Ideas of reference | Perplexity | Negativism |
| Delusions of grandeur | Lability | Perseveration |
| Thought hearing | | Body hallucinations |
| Derealization | | Morose mood |
| Lack of concentration | | |
| Hopelessness | | |
| Delusions of persecution | | |
| Delusions of reference | | |

* Adapted from World Health Organization: *Report of the International Pilot Study of Schizophrenia.* World Health Organization, Geneva, 1973.

**10.8.   The answer is C** (*Synopsis*, ed. 4, page 204).

The prodromal phase of schizophrenia is marked by a clear deterioration in functioning before the active phase—characterized by delusions and hallucinations—begins. Prodromal symptoms consist of *social isolation,* impaired vocational or school functioning, markedly *peculiar behavior, change in affect, circumstantial speech,* odd or bizarre ideation, and unusual perceptual experiences.

*Delusions* are part of the active phase of the illness. Both the prodromal and active phases of the illness should be present for at least 6 months before a diagnosis of schizophrenia is made.

**10.9.   The answer is B** (*Synopsis*, ed. 4, page 222).

The *subchronic* form of schizophrenia shows a course of illness during which the patient shows signs of schizophrenia more or less continuously for a period lasting from 6 months to 2 years. During that time, if prominent signs of psychosis occur, the patient would be considered to be *subchronic with an acute exacerbation.*

The table in column 2 lists the DSM-III classification of the various courses of schizophrenia.

**10.10.   The answer is E** (*Synopsis*, ed. 4, page 197).

In general, pooled studies show expectancy rates of about *80 percent for monozygotic twins.*

**10.11.   The answer is E** (*Synopsis*, ed. 4, pages 216 and 217).

Latent schizophrenia is not listed as a classification in DSM-III; it is now subsumed under the classification of *schizotypal personality disorder.* The syndrome is diagnosed in those patients who show occasional *behavioral peculiar-*

**Classification of Course***

The course of the illness is coded in the fifth digit:

1. *Subchronic.* The time from the beginning of the illness, during which the individual began to show signs of the illness (including prodromal, active, and residual phases) more or less continuously, is less than 2 years but at least 6 months;

2. *Chronic.* Same as above, but greater than 2 years;

3. *Subchronic with Acute Exacerbation.* Reemergence of prominent psychotic symptoms in an individual with a subchronic course who has been in the residual phase of the illness;

4. *Chronic with Acute Exacerbation.* Reemergence of prominent psychotic symptoms in an individual with a chronic course who has been in the residual phase of the illness;

5. *In Remission.* This should be used when an individual with a history of schizophrenia, now is free of all signs of the illness (whether or not on medication). The differentiation of schizophrenia in remission from no mental disorder requires consideration of the period of time since the last period of disturbance, the total duration of the disturbance and the need for continued evaluation of prophylactic treatment.

* From American Psychiatric Association: *Diagnostic and Statistical Manual of Mental Disorders,* ed 3. American Psychiatric Association, Washington, DC, 1980. Used with permission.

*ities or thought disorders, without consistently manifesting any clearly psychotic pathology.* The syndrome is *sometimes known as borderline schizophrenia.*

The table on the facing page describes the DSM-III diagnostic criteria for schizotypal personality disorder.

**10.12.   The answer is E** (*Synopsis*, ed. 4, pages 215 and 216).

## Diagnostic Criteria for Schizotypal Personality*

A. At least four of the following must be present:

1. Magical thinking, e.g., superstitiousness, clairvoyance, telepathy, "6th sense," "others can feel my feelings" (in children and adolescents, bizarre fantasies or preoccupations);

2. Ideas of reference;

3. Social isolation, e.g. no close friends or confidants, social contacts limited to essential everyday tasks;

4. Recurrent illusions, sensing the presence of a force or person not actually present (e.g. "I felt as if my dead mother were in the room with me"), depersonalization, or derealization not associated with panic attacks;

5. Odd speech (without loosening of associations or incoherence), e.g. speech that is digressive, vague, overelaborate, circumstantial, metaphorical

6. Inadequate rapport in face-to-face interaction due to constricted or inappropriate affect, e.g. aloof, cold;

7. Suspiciousness or paranoid ideation;

8. Undue social anxiety or hypersensitivity to real or imagined criticism.

B. Does not meet the criteria for schizophrenia

* From American Psychiatric Association: *Diagnostic and Statistical Manual of Mental Disorders*, ed 3. American Psychiatric Association, Washington, DC, 1980. Used with permission.

Paraphrenia is not included in DSM-III as a diagnostic entity; however, it appears in the ninth revision of the *International Classification of Diseases* (ICD-9) as a synonym for *paranoid schizophrenia*. It is a chronic condition characterized by fantastic and absurd delusions without significant personality deterioration and without the primary disturbances of thought and affect that characterize schizophrenia. The personalities of paraphrenic patients are usually well-preserved, and they quite often live happily with their life situations. Some paraphrenics seem to derive satisfaction from delusions, which appear to be more often of a grandiose nature, rather than of a persecutory one.

In *paranoid schizophrenia* there is a deterioration and splitting off of many of the psychic functions, whereas in paraphrenia the delusions are so logical, at least on the surface, as to appear to be little more than an extension of the premorbid personality. *Latent schizophrenia* is a form of schizophrenia in which, despite the existence of fundamental symptoms, no clear-cut psychotic episode or gross break with reality has occurred. It is not a term used in DSM-III, but is subsumed under schizotypal personality disorder. In *simple schizophrenia* there is an insid-

ious psychic impoverishment that affects the emotions, the intellect, and the will. Chronic dissatisfaction or complete indifference to reality is characteristic, and the simple schizophrenic is isolated, estranged, and asocial. *Catatonic schizophrenia* is a state characterized by muscular rigidity and immobility. *Hebephrenia* is a complex of symptoms considered to be a form of schizophrenia. It is characterized by wild or silly behavior or mannerisms, inappropriate affect, frequent hypochondriacal complaints, and delusions and hallucinations that are transient and unsystematized.

**10.13.    The answer is E** (*Synopsis*, ed. 4, page 217).

In 1949, Hoch and Polatin described a clinical variety of schizophrenia to which they gave the name pseudoneurotic schizophrenia. Pseudoneurotic schizophrenics are, as the name implies, patients who present *predominantly neurotic symptoms* and who are usually treated for years as neurotics. On close and careful examination, however, they may reveal *abnormalities of thinking* and emotional reaction that resemble schizophrenia. Sometimes these abnormalities are so well compensated that it is all but impossible to demonstrate schizophrenic symptoms in clinical examinations, in psychological tests, or even in the history.

The pseudoneurotic schizophrenic is characterized by a *lack of response to years of psychiatric treatment* that would have produced improvement in most neurotics, by a strange, all-pervading anxiety, and by a constant *preoccupation with sexual problems*. The diffuse *pananxiety* is probably the most specific diagnostic criterion. They have been described as having a triad of pananxiety, panneurosis, and chaotic sexuality.

Pseudoneurotic schizophrenics may have phobias, but these phobias are not fixed and may amorphously affect all areas of life over a period of time. Unlike patients suffering from anxiety neurosis, the pseudoneurotic schizophrenic has anxiety that is always free-floating and that hardly ever subsides, even temporarily. The existence of this diagnostic category of schizophrenia has been contested. In DSM-III, this diagnosis is replaced by schizotypal personality disorder. Its use may have the practical value of reorienting the therapeutic strategy in certain patients from unsuccessful psychotherapy to physical treatment methods—in particular, pharmacotherapy.

**10.14.    The answer is D** (*Synopsis*, ed. 4, page 215).

A rare but intriguing form of catatonia is *periodic catatonia*, also known as Gjessing's disease. Motor functions, ideation, and perception in periodic catatonia are closely linked to the patient's changing levels of positive or negative nitrogen balance. Patients affected with the disease have periodic recurrences of stuporous or excited catatonic states. Each recurrence of catatonic behavior is associated with an extreme shift in the patient's metabolic nitrogen balance. Relapses in such patients can be prevented by regulating their nitrogen balance through the continuous administration of thyroxin. These metabolic and therapeutic observations, however, apply only to patients suffering from periodic catatonia, and most schizophrenic patients who present catatonic symptoms do not fall into this category. Most of the rare cases of periodic catatonia seen in recent years responded well to neuroleptic medication, and relapses were usually prevented by neuroleptic maintenance medication.

The illness is not included in DSM-III, and when it occurs, it is diagnosed as schizophrenia, catatonic type. Catatonic patients may also be classified as chronic—having an illness of more than 2 years' duration; stuporous—characterized by a loss of contact with the immediate environment; and excited—characterized by outbursts of agitated or violent behavior.

**10.15.   The answer is D** (*Synopsis*, ed. 4, page 215).

The *disorganized* (DSM-III) *or hebephrenic subtype of schizophrenia* is characterized by a marked regression to primitive, disinhibited, and unorganized behavior. Hebephrenic patients are usually active but in an aimless, nonconstructive manner. Their thought disorder is pronounced, and their contact with reality is extremely poor. Their personal appearance and their social behavior are dilapidated. Their emotional responses are inappropriate, and they often burst out laughing without any apparent reason. Incongruous grinning and grimacing are common in these patients, whose behavior is best described as silly or fatuous.

*Paranoid schizophrenia* is characterized by persecutory delusions and *catatonic schizophrenia* by stupor or catalepsy. *Conversion disorder* and *dissociative disorder* are types of hysterical neuroses.

**10.16.   The answer is C** (*Synopsis*, ed. 4, page 214).

Dramatic self-mutilation in schizophrenic patients—for example, the gouging out of an eye or the cutting off of the penis—occurs in probably less than 1 percent of all cases. It has been referred to as *the Van Gogh syndrome* (not a DSM-III classification) and may sometimes be the expression of dysmorphophobic delusions,

the irrational conviction that a serious bodily defect exists, or reflect other complex, unconscious mechanisms. The syndrome is named after the painter Vincent Van Gogh, who cut off a part of his ear during a psychotic episode.

*Penis envy* is a concept developed by Freud that maintains that the woman envies the man for his possession of a penis. It is sometimes used to refer to a woman's generalized envy of men. In psychoanalytic theory, the *castration complex* is a group of unconscious thoughts and motives that are referable to the fear of losing the genitals, usually as punishment for forbidden sexual desires. *Homosexual panic* is the sudden, acute onset of severe anxiety, precipitated by the unconscious fear or conflict that one may be a homosexual or act out homosexual impulses. *Bouffée délirante* is an acute delusional psychosis diagnosed in France; about 40 percent of patients with this diagnosis are later reclassified as suffering from schizophrenia.

**10.17.   The answer is C** (*Synopsis*, ed. 4, page 224).

In general, the balance of experimental evidence indicates that *group therapy, combined with drugs*, produces somewhat better results than drug treatment alone, particularly with outpatients. Positive results are more likely to be obtained when treatment focuses on real-life plans, problems, and relationships; on social and work roles and interaction; on cooperation with drug therapy and discussion of its side effects; or on some practical recreational or work activity.

There is considerable doubt whether dynamic interpretation and insight therapy have much value for the usual schizophrenic patient. Accordingly, *insight-oriented therapy* based on *psychoanalytic principles* is not indicated in the treatment of schizophrenics. *Individual therapy* is of use, but should be combined with neuroleptics and be supportive in nature. There is no evidence that *combined individual and group therapy* is superior to group therapy plus drug therapy.

**10.18.   The answer is C** (*Synopsis*, ed. 4, pages 220 and 221).

*Tardive dyskinesia*, an extrapyramidal syndrome, emerges relatively late during the course of neuroleptic treatment, especially when these drugs have been used in high doses over several years. This late-occurrence syndrome may appear several days or weeks after the drug has been discontinued and can be present for years. There is no specific treatment, and symptoms can be suppressed by putting the patient on high-dose phenothiazines or butyrophenones.

A *relapse of psychotic symptoms* within the

first 6 months of a primary schizophrenic episode is extremely common. Also seen with regularity is postschizophrenic *depression*, which is estimated by some researchers to be present in 50 percent of all initial schizophrenic episodes. A *flat affect* and a *relative deterioration in functioning* are both pathognomonic of the clinical picture seen in schizophrenic disorders. These findings are listed in DSM-III as diagnostic criteria.

**10.19. The answer is B** (*Synopsis*, ed. 4, page 206).

In schizophrenia, the *auditory hallucination*, the hearing of voices, is most common. Characteristically, two or more voices talk about the patient, discussing him or her in the third person. Frequently, the voices address the patient, comment on the patient's activities and what is going on around that person, or are threatening or obscene and very disturbing to the patient. Many schizophrenic patients experience the hearing of their own thoughts. When they are reading silently, for example, they may be quite disturbed by hearing every word they are reading clearly spoken to them.

*Visual hallucinations* occur less frequently than auditory hallucinations in schizophrenic patients, but they are not rare. Patients suffering from organic or affective psychoses experience visual hallucinations primarily at night or during limited periods of the day, but schizophrenic patients hallucinate as much during the day as they do during the night, sometimes almost continuously. They get relief only in sleep. When visual hallucinations occur in schizophrenia, they are usually seen nearby, clearly defined, in color, life-size, in three dimensions, and moving. Visual hallucinations almost never occur by themselves but always in combination with hallucinations in one of the other sensory modalities. *Tactile, olfactory,* and *gustatory* hallucinations are less common than visual hallucinations.

**10.20. The answer is A** (*Synopsis*, ed. 4, page 194).

The prevalence rates for schizophrenia from studies that considered all ages varied from a low of 0.43 per 1,000 population to a high of 0.68 per 1,000. For the age group 15 and over, the rates ranged from a low of 0.30 per 1,000 to a high of 1.20 per 1,000. In general, pooled studies show a prevalence of *1 per 1,000*. The 1 percent prevalence figure has recently been confirmed by the NIMH Epidemiologic Catchment Area (ECA) Program conducted by Darell Regier.

**10.21. The answer is A** (*Synopsis*, ed. 4, page 195).

Summarizing the prevalence data available in

the United States, one can state that *between 0.23 percent and 0.47 percent* of the total population are likely to receive psychiatric treatment for a schizophrenic illness during any particular year, provided adequate mental health care facilities are available in all communities. This means that a minimum of 500,000 and a maximum of 1 million persons annually will need treatment for the illness. For 62 percent of each group, treatment will involve at least one hospitalization during the year. With a lifetime prevalence of about 1 percent, about 2 million Americans may be suffering from a mental disorder that would be classified today as schizophrenia. Of that figure, 50 percent have some kind of treatment or mental health contact within a 6-month period.

**10.22. The answer is C** (*Synopsis*, ed. 4, page 214).

Stuporous catatonic patients may be in a state of complete stupor or may show a pronounced decrease of spontaneous movements and activity. They may be mute or nearly so, or they may show distinct negativism, stereotypies, echopraxia, or automatic obedience. Occasionally, *catatonic schizophrenics* exhibit the phenomenon of catalepsy or waxy flexibility. Patients in a state of complete catatonic stupor usually can be roused from it in a dramatic manner by the intravenous injection of a short-acting barbiturate, such as sodium amytal. In many instances they become, for an hour or two, relatively lucid.

*Organic mental disorder* is a disturbance caused by transient or permanent brain dysfunction attributable to specific organic factors. *Meningioma* is a brain tumor and is an example of an organic condition that may produce psychiatric symptoms. The symptoms characteristically worsen under the influence of sodium amytal. *Disorganized (hebephrenic) schizophrenia* is characterized by wild or silly behavior or mannerisms, inappropriate affect, frequent hypochondriacal complaints, and delusions and hallucinations that are transient and unsystematized. *Dysthymic disorder* is the DSM-III term for depressive neurosis. It is considered a relatively mild, but chronic, form of mood disturbance, not of sufficient severity to meet the criteria for a major depressive episode. A patient with this disorder would not present, as part of the clinical picture, a state of stupor or mutism.

**10.23. The answer is A** (*Synopsis*, ed. 4, page 195).

The mortality rate for schizophrenic patients *is higher than that for normal persons*. There is not, at present, any explanation for this phenomenon. In the past, institutional care was considered one of the major contributors to the high mortality rate of schizophrenics, but presently it does not appear to be a major factor in the death rate of this population. *Phobics have a mortality rate similar to that of the general population.*

**10.24.    The answer is D** (*Synopsis*, ed. 4, page 213).

This male psychiatric inpatient is exhibiting symptoms of *delusional thinking*. He believes that the doctor can control his thoughts. A characteristic feature of most schizophrenic conditions is the so-called loss of ego boundaries. It renders patients extremely vulnerable to any kind of external stimulation. Their identity may fuse with that of any object in the universe around them, and they may suffer personally when they become aware that some object in their environment is being attacked. The loss of contact with reality is the core symptom of any psychosis.

*Social withdrawal* is a pathological retreat from interpersonal contact and social involvement. It is an extreme decrease of intellectual and emotional interest in the environment. It may be seen in schizophrenia and depression. *Hypervigilance* is the continual scanning of the environment for signs of threat. It is most often seen in paranoid disorders. *Fragmentation of thinking* is a disturbance in association, characterized by loosening, in which basic concepts become vague and incoherent and the thinking processes become so confused that they cannot result in a complete idea or action. It is a form of thinking often associated with schizophrenia. *Magical thinking* is a notion that thinking something is either the same thing as doing it or that it might cause it to happen. It is commonly experienced in dreams, in certain mental disorders, and by children.

**10.25.    The answer is A** (*Synopsis*, ed. 4, page 211).

*Catalepsy* is a condition in which a person maintains the body position in which it has been placed. The position can be maintained for long periods of time, even though it may appear to be uncomfortable. This condition is also known as waxy flexibility and cerea flexibility.

A *mannerism* is a stereotyped gesture or expression that is peculiar to a given person. *Cataplexy* is the temporary sudden loss of muscle tone, causing weakness and immobilization. It can be precipitated by a variety of emotional states, and it is often followed by sleep. *Perseveration* refers to speech, rather than motor, behavior and consists of the patient giving the same verbal response to different questions.

**10.26.    The answer is C** (*Synopsis*, ed. 4, page 215).

Hebephrenic or *disorganized schizophrenia* is characterized by primitive, unorganized behavior. Posturing, grimacing, and such aimless behavior as mirror gazing are common. Emotional responses are inappropriate, and silly laughter is often noted.

*Catatonic schizophrenics* are noted for their immobile positions and waxy flexibility; *paranoid schizophrenics* are noted for their delusional systems; and *schizoaffective* patients are noted for a strong element of either depressive or manic affect added to otherwise schizophrenic symptoms. *Schizotaxia* is a concept that proposes the existence of a genetic defect in the nervous system of persons predisposed to develop schizophrenia.

**10.27.    The answer is B** (*Synopsis*, ed. 4, page 215).

*Disorganized schizophrenia* begins earlier than the other types of schizophrenia and may be ushered in with acute behavioral changes and delusional thinking. Eventually, the patient acts in an inappropriate and silly manner and exhibits prominent regressive features, such as fecal soiling, bed wetting, food throwing, and a generalized inability to function. There is a complete disintegration of the total personality.

**10.28.    The answer is A (1, 2, 3)** (*Synopsis*, ed. 4, page 221).

Relapse rates among certain schizophrenic patients have been found to be related significantly to three measures of expressed emotionality in the home: *critical comments, hostility, and emotional overinvolvement*. Separation of the patients from the family members in homes where expressed emotionality was high improved their relapse rates. Drugs only reduce the relapse rate of schizophrenics living in homes where these conditions are found. Thus, familial stress can play a critical role in the relapse rates of certain schizophrenic patients.

The presence or absence of *psychosomatic illness* is not related either to the incidence or relapse rates of schizophrenia.

**10.29.    The answer is A (1, 2, 3)** (*Synopsis*, ed. 4, page 196).

Patterns of hospitalization for schizophrenic patients have changed over the past two decades. *The duration of each hospital experience has diminished, and the number of readmissions has increased. Patients are now hospitalized more often for shorter periods of time.*

*The probability of patients being readmitted within a 2-year period after discharge from the first hospitalization varies between 40 and 60 percent*, depending on the study. Between 15 and 25 percent of discharged schizophrenics will eventually be readmitted and receive continued care for a prolonged period of time.

**10.30. The answer is E (all)** (*Synopsis*, ed. 4, pages 220 and 221).

The *more acute the onset* of a schizophrenic attack, the better are the chances for a good remission or complete recovery. If a *precipitating event* has clearly triggered the breakdown, the chances for a favorable outcome are also relatively better.

The *younger patients* are at the onset of their schizophrenic psychosis, the worse is their prognosis, as a rule. Patients who break down in childhood or early puberty seldom recover completely.

A history of good adjustment in the important areas of social, sexual, and occupational functioning before the breakdown also indicates a favorable prognosis. *Married* schizophrenics have a better prognosis than do single, divorced, or widowed patients; the fact that they are married is evidence that interpersonal bonds may serve as a bridge for a return to the community. The presence of depression as a feature of the schizophrenic syndrome also makes for a better prognosis. Conversely, sustained emotional withdrawal and aloofness or shallow and inappropriate affective responses are ominous prognostic signs.

**10.31. The answer is A (1, 2, 3)** (*Synopsis*, ed. 4, page 197).

According to studies of concordance rates for schizophrenia done on the basis of hospital records, *if both parents are schizophrenic, the risk for the children is between 15 and 55 percent. For second-degree relatives, the median risk value is 2.5 percent.* Pooled results of family studies show about a *9 percent risk in siblings* and a 12 percent risk in children of one schizophrenic parent.

In studies of genetic theories regarding dizygotic twins, the percentage rates for an *unaffected twin of an affected twin would be approximately 9 to 10 percent*, not 40 percent.

**10.32. The answer is A (1, 2, 3)** (*Synopsis*, ed. 4, page 199).

The psychedelic model of schizophrenia is based on the observation that two substances, *bufotenin and dimethyltryptamine (DMT)—the N-methylated derivatives of serotonin and tryptamine, respectively—both have hallucinogenic properties.* Early investigations demonstrated increased blood and urine levels of methylated *indolamines* in schizophrenic patients and showed that an enzyme that mediates the methylation of tryptamine to DMT—indolamine-*N*-methyltransferase—is present in the human brain. The feasibility of the hypothesis was enhanced by clinical studies that demonstrated that normal persons, given large doses of the two amino acids, tryptophan and *methionine*, or a combination of the two, experience an excited state. The same regimen in *schizophrenics produces a recurrence and exacerbation of psychosis*, with the disorder being more severe if there is concurrent administration of a monoamine oxidase inhibitor (MAOI).

**10.33. The answer is E (all)** (*Synopsis*, ed. 4, page 200).

When predictions are made, on the basis of a physical examination, that a child will become psychotic and the prediction is borne out to a significant degree, support is found for the idea that a physical alteration of the brain—due either to genetic, intrauterine, or perinatal factors—impairs neural and psychological development. Infants who from the age of 1 month manifested disturbed regulation of physiological patterns—such as *vasomotor instability, disturbed sleep patterns, poor temperature control, poor muscle tone*—and of alertness and uneven patterns of growth, with retardation or precocity in motor, perceptual, and language skills and in the social sphere, were found to be predisposed to schizophrenia in later childhood.

**10.34. The answer is B (1, 3)** (*Synopsis*, ed. 4, page 214).

Catatonic schizophrenia *occurs in two forms*: inhibited or *stuporous* catatonia and excited catatonia. The essential feature of both forms is the marked abnormality of motor behavior.

Paranoid schizophrenia *is the most commonly diagnosed type of schizophrenia in the United States. In Africa and South America, however, catatonic schizophrenia is still the most common diagnosis* among the institutionalized population.

**10.35. The answer is A (1, 2, 3)** (*Synopsis*, ed. 4, page 215).

This patient is demonstrating *delusions of grandeur* manifested by the false, fixed belief that she is going to give birth to a "Messiah." Her belief that she is pregnant is a *somatic delusion*. Laughing in a silly way when arrested is a sign of an *inappropriate affect* because the emotional tone is not consonant with the seriousness of her situation.

The history of repeated antisocial acts, inappropriate affect, disorganized speech, confusion, and interpersonal and vocational deterioration are prodomal signs of schizophrenia. When prodromal signs have been present for 6 months and have been followed by the active signs of delusional thinking, a diagnosis of schizophrenia disorder can be made. Delusions of grandeur are seen in the paranoid type of schizophrenia. The absence of symptoms, such as pressured speech, flight of ideas, or a disorder of moods, points against an affective disorder being present.

In order for *pseudocyesis* (false pregnancy) to be diagnosed, signs and symptoms of pregnancy, such as missed menstrual periods, uterine or breast swelling, and morning sickness, must be present. Pregnancy tests are negative in that disorder, even though the patient shows presumptive signs of pregnancy. Pseudocyesis is not a sign of schizophrenia.

**10.36.   The answer is C (2, 4)** (*Synopsis*, ed. 4, page 200).

As determined by computed tomography (CT) scans, some schizophrenic patients have *enlarged (not small) lateral ventricles* of the brain, *reduced sulcal fluid volumes, reversal of the normal asymmetries of the brain,* or *atrophy (not hypertrophy) of the anterior vermis of the cerebellum.* Studies supporting these findings, however, are not consistent, and there is much controversy about the validity of these findings.

**10.37.   The answer is B (1, 3)** (*Synopsis*, ed. 4, page 207).

The schizophrenic disturbance of thinking and conceptualization is one of the most characteristic features of the disease. The one feature common to all manifestations of schizophrenic thought disorder is that schizophrenic patients think and reason on their *autistic terms,* according to their own intricate *private rules of logic.* Schizophrenics may be highly intelligent, certainly not confused, and they may be very painstaking in their abstractions and deductions; but their thought processes are strange and do not lead to conclusions based on reality or universal logic.

A schizophrenic patient may reason: "John is Peter's father; therefore, Peter is John's father." Such symmetrical reasoning is sometimes justified. For instance, John is Peter's brother; therefore, Peter is John's brother. At other times such symmetrical conclusions are not justified, and the schizophrenic does not seem to know when or when not to apply them.

A *concretization of thought* and a *loss of the abstract attitude* are typical of schizophrenic thinking. Patients lose their ability to generalize correctly, and they exhibit, in the ordering of their concepts, a defect similar to a loss of the figure-ground relation in perceptual performance. This defect is often brought out by the simple clinical test of asking patients to interpret a well-known proverb. One schizophrenic interpreted the saying "A stitch in time saves nine" as "I should sew nine buttons on my coat"—an overly personalized and concrete explanation.

**10.38.   The answer is E (all)** (*Synopsis*, ed. 4, page 215).

*Persecutory delusions* and hallucinations, *grandiose delusions and hallucinations,* and *delusional jealousy* may present in paranoid schizophrenia.

The following table lists the DSM-III diagnostic criteria.

**Diagnostic Criteria for Paranoid Type***

A type of schizophrenia dominated by one or more of the following:

1. Persecutory delusions;
2. Grandiose delusions;
3. Delusional jealousy;
4. Hallucinations with persecutory or grandiose content.

* From American Psychiatric Association: *Diagnostic and Statistical Manual of Mental Disorders,* ed 3. American Psychiatric Association, Washington, DC, 1980. Used with permission.

**10.39.   The answer is B (1, 3)** (*Synopsis*, ed. 4, pages 198 and 199).

The dopamine hypothesis of schizophrenia relates the specific behavioral symptoms of the disorder to an increased amount of dopamine available at synapses or to hyperactivity of the dopamine pathways. Clinical and laboratory evidence supporting this concept is abundant.

The idea that schizophrenia is associated with dysfunction in the dopamine system was based on the observation that all clinically effective *antipsychotic drugs increase (not decrease) dopamine metabolite levels* and thus, it was inferred, cause a central elevation of dopamine activity. The mechanism responsible for the phenomenon, it was speculated, is a drug-induced blockade of dopamine receptors, which triggers an increased production of the transmitter. Further evidence for the dopamine hypothesis is that *chlorpromazine and other antipsychotic drugs block both norepinephrine and dopamine receptors* and allow for a build-up of dopamine at nerve endings.

Studies repeatedly demonstrated an acceleration of dopamine turnover and dopamine neuron firing rate after the administration of phenothiazines or other neuroleptics. It was further demonstrated that these drugs inhibit dopamine-sensitive adenylate cyclase in certain receptor membranes. Normally, cyclase activity increases when dopamine stimulation provokes biological activity.

Antipsychotic agents have been shown, through the use of X-ray crystallography, to assume molecular configurations similar to that of dopamine. It has also been shown that these drugs do, in fact, compete with dopamine and exhibit an affinity for stereospecific dopamine-binding sites. This ability has been correlated with their clinical potency.

Other evidence supporting the dopamine hypothesis is that agents that increase amounts of catecholamines in the brain increase psychotic symptoms.

The long-known ability of amphetamines to induce clinical symptoms similar to those seen in schizophrenia supports that observation, as does the fact that amphetamine worsens the symptoms of schizophrenia. Dopamine and *dopamine agonists, such as apomorphine, produce symptoms that resemble the amphetamine-induced psychosis.* When the *dopamine tracts are lesioned, however, high doses of both amphetamines and dopamine-like drugs fail to produce stereotyped behavior.*

**10.40. The answer is E (all)** (*Synopsis*, ed. 4, page 198).

Although a person must be predisposed to schizophrenic illness for some stress or event to initiate the illness, one cannot disregard such initiating factors in any etiological theory.

Many other factors, including drugs—such as alcohol, *LSD*, the amphetamines, and *cannabis*—may initiate the schizophrenia. In addition, many schizophrenic patients become ill after being *rebuffed*, brutalized, or raped. The loss or rebuff has a portentous meaning to these patients. Divorce or *death of a parent*, child, or spouse often precipitates the illness. Many of the schizophrenic symptoms can be understood as a way of expressing this loss and of compensating for it in highly personal metaphors. Clearly, however, the patients cannot cope with the loss or rebuff in the manner that most people do—by grieving or by finding a surrogate for the lost person. Their manner of dealing with the loss or rebuff is by denial, projection, total identification with the lost person, or some other primitive means.

**10.41. The answer is A (1, 2, 3)** (*Synopsis*, ed. 4, page 215).

*Incoherence, absence of a clear delusional system,* and *silly affect* are characteristic of the disorganized type of schizophrenia. *Catalepsy* is seen in the catatonic type of schizophrenia.

The table in column 2 lists the DSM-III diagnostic criteria for the disorganized type of schizophrenia.

**10.42. The answer is B (1, 3)** (*Synopsis*, ed. 4, page 200).

Researchers have reported a *somewhat lower mean activity of monoamine oxidase (MAO)* in

**Diagnostic Criteria for Disorganized Type\***

A type of schizophrenia in which there are the following:

A. Frequent incoherence;

B. Absence of systematized delusions;

C. Blunted, inappropriate, or silly affect.

\* From American Psychiatric Association: *Diagnostic and Statistical Manual of Mental Disorders*, ed 3. American Psychiatric Association, Washington, DC, 1980. Used with permission.

*blood platelets of chronic schizophrenic patients* than in normal control subjects. Subsequent attempts to replicate the original observations have produced conflicting results. Indeed, some investigations have suggested higher values of platelet MAO values in certain groups of schizophrenic patients. At present, low MAO activity does not seem to be a specific feature of schizophrenic disorders or of vulnerability to the development of schizophrenia.

Some neurotransmitters, such as *β-endorphins have exacerbated symptoms of schizophrenia in certain patients,* and increased amounts of endorphins have been found in the spinal fluid of some patients. The meaning of the role of endorphins, however, is not yet clear.

Researchers have also reported a *relationship between malignant catatonia and high calcium levels.* During the clinical course of one patient over a 25-year period, concurrent hyperthermia was noted during catatonic episodes, a phenomenon linked to increased muscle calcium levels. Calcium affects neurotransmitter activity and competes with neuroleptic drugs at the neuronal membrane site. Calcium and magnesium levels are decreased by antipsychotic treatment. It was found that serum calcium levels increased markedly at the onset of catatonic episodes, and it has been hypothesized that elevations of serum calcium levels are temporarily involved in the switch process of affective state changes.

*No electrolyte changes in the serum of schizophrenics have been demonstrated.*

**10.43. The answer is D (4)** (*Synopsis*, ed. 4, page 202).

Smooth-pursuit movements are used to follow moving targets. Saccadic (jerky) movements are mobilized to place this target on the fovea quickly and accurately; they correct the point of gaze and interrupt pursuit movements or replace them if inaccurately carried out. *The saccadic movements are qualitatively intact in schizophrenic patients, but are increased in number.* Eye-tracking movements in schizophrenic patients who are ill or in remission show more back and forth saccades.

Schizophrenics do not show *nystagmus, can fixate on moving objects*, and have *intact oculomotor nerve tracts.*

### 10.44. The answer is B (1, 3) (*Synopsis*, ed. 4, page 218).

A brief reactive psychosis is characterized by a number of essential and associated features. Essential features are those that must be present to make the diagnosis. These include the presence of *a recognizable stressful event preceding the appearance of symptoms*, and *a duration of more than a few hours but less than 2 weeks.*

Associated features are those that may be present but are not necessary to making the diagnosis. These include *disorientation* and *inappropriate, volatile affect.*

The table below describes the DSM-III diagnostic features in detail.

### 10.45. The answer is E (all) (*Synopsis*, ed. 4, page 196).

Two major hypotheses have been proposed to explain the relationship of social class to schizophrenia. The first hypothesis is generally known as the social causation hypothesis, which assumes that *the social and economic stresses experienced by the lower classes are causatively related to schizophrenic illness.* The second hypothesis is generally known as the social selection or drift hypothesis, which claims that low social class membership rates in schizophrenia are more a function of schizophrenic illness and that *schizophrenic patients tend to be down-wardly mobile.* Neither of these hypotheses has been definitely proved, nor has the extent of the contribution of either hypothesis been demonstrated.

Several other factors have been proposed as having some influence on the rates of schizophrenia; however, the results from different investigations have not substantiated the influence of these factors conclusively. The first of these factors is migration. Some studies suggested that immigrants have higher rates of first hospital admissions for schizophrenia than their counterparts who remained at home. The second factor considered is industrialization, because higher rates of schizophrenia are attributed to highly industrialized societies. *The prevalence of schizophrenia has also been found to rise among Third-World populations* as contact with technologically advanced cultures increases. A third related factor is the influence of sociocultural factors and of culture change on the rates of schizophrenia. It has been argued that *cultures may be more or less schizophrenogenic*, depending on how mental illness is perceived, the content of the patient role, the system of social supports, and the complexity of social communication.

### 10.46. The answer is E (all) (*Synopsis*, ed. 4, pages 216 and 217).

Undifferentiated schizophrenics are those *patients who cannot easily be fitted into one of the other subtypes*, usually because *they meet the criteria for more than one subtype. Some acute,*

### Diagnostic Features of Brief Reactive Psychosis*

| Essential Features | Associated Features | Other Features† |
|---|---|---|
| Recognizable stressful event preceding the appearance of symptoms | Perplexity | Disorder is often unofficially called hysterical psychosis |
| Emotional turmoil and at least one of the following: | Bizarre behavior | |
| | Inappropriate, volatile affect | |
| 1. Incoherence; markedly illogical thinking | Disorientation; clouding of consciousness | |
| 2. Delusions | Poor insight | |
| 3. Hallucinations | Patient is usually incapacitated and dependent on the close assistance of others | |
| 4. Grossly disorganized behavior | | |
| Duration of disorder more than a few hours but less than 2 weeks | | |
| Disorder may be superimposed on other disorders, such as personality disorder | Sometimes followed by mild depression | |
| Rule out organic mental disorder, manic episode, and factitious illness with psychological symptoms (Ganser's syndrome) | | |

\* Adapted from American Psychiatric Association: *Diagnostic and Statistical Manual of Mental Disorders*, ed 3. American Psychiatric Association, Washington, DC, 1980.

† Not cited as a clinical feature in DSM-III but may be present in this disorder.

excited schizophrenics, and *some very chronic patients* fall into this category. DSM-III adds the criteria of the presence of prominent delusions, hallucinations, incoherence, or grossly disorganized behavior.

The table below lists the DSM-III criteria for undifferentiated schizophrenia.

#### Diagnostic Criteria for Undifferentiated Type*

A. A type of schizophrenia in which there are prominent delusions, hallucinations, incoherence, or grossly disorganized behavior.

B. Does not meet the criteria for any of the other listed types or meets the criteria for more than one.

* From American Psychiatric Association: *Diagnostic and Statistical Manual of Mental Disorders*, ed 3. American Psychiatric Association, Washington, DC, 1980. Used with permission.

**10.47.   The answer is B (1, 3)** (*Synopsis*, ed. 4, page 217).

Residual schizophrenia is that type of schizophrenia characterized by a clinical picture *without prominent psychotic symptoms, but with continuing evidence of the illness,* such as inappropriate affect or loosening of associations. There must be a *history of at least one previous episode of schizophrenia associated with prominent psychotic symptoms.*

*Persecutory and grandiose delusions* are seen primarily in paranoid schizophrenia, whereas *frequent incoherence* is seen in disorganized (hebephrenic) schizophrenia.

The DSM-III table of diagnostic criteria for residual schizophrenia is shown below.

#### Diagnostic Criteria for Residual Type*

A. A history of at least one previous episode of schizophrenia with prominent psychotic symptoms.

B. A clinical picture without any prominent psychotic symptoms that occasioned evaluation or admission to clinical care.

C. Continuing evidence of the illness, such as blunted or inappropriate affect, social withdrawal, eccentric behavior, illogical thinking, or loosening of associations.

* From American Psychiatric Association: *Diagnostic and Statistical Manual of Mental Disorders*, ed 3. American Psychiatric Association, Washington, DC, 1980. Used with permission.

**10.48.   The answer is C (2, 4)** (*Synopsis*, ed. 4, page 212).

Negativism refers to a patient's *failure to cooperate,* without any apparent reason for that failure. The patient *does not appear to be fatigued,* depressed, suspicious, or angry. *Although obviously capable of physical movement,* the patient fails to carry out even the simplest requests. Sometimes the patient may even *do the opposite of what is asked;* for instance, lowering a hand when asked to raise it.

**10.49.   The answer is E (all)** (*Synopsis*, ed. 4, page 203).

Kurt Schneider identified the most common signs and symptoms in schizophrenic patients and referred to them as symptoms of the first rank. These symptoms include *audible thoughts, voices heard arguing,* voices commenting on one's actions; the experience of influences playing on the body (somatic passivity experiences); *thought withdrawal* and other interferences with thought; diffusion of thought; *delusional perception* and all feelings, impulses (drives), and volitional acts that are experienced as being caused by or done under the influence of others. Second-rank symptoms were also described by Schneider and included other disorders of perception, perplexity, sudden delusional ideas, and mood changes.

Schneider did not mean these symptoms to be rigidly applied, and he warned the clinician that the diagnosis of schizophrenia could even be made in certain patients who failed to show first-rank symptoms. Unfortunately, this warning is frequently ignored, and the absence of such symptoms in a single interview is taken as evidence that the person is free of a schizophrenic disorder.

**10.50.   The answer is A (1, 2, 3)** (*Synopsis*, ed. 4, page 207).

By definition, delusions are false ideas that *cannot be corrected by reasoning* and that are *idiosyncratic for the patient*—that is, not part of the patient's cultural environment. They are among the most common symptoms of schizophrenia.

*Most frequent are delusions of persecution,* which are the *key symptom in the paranoid type of schizophrenia.* The conviction of being controlled by some unseen mysterious power that exercises its influence from a distance is a common delusion. It occurs in most, if not all, schizophrenics at one time or another, and for many it is a daily experience. Modern schizophrenics whose delusions have kept up with the scientific times may be preoccupied with atomic power, X-rays, or spaceships that take control over their minds and bodies. Also typical for many schizophrenics are delusional fantasies about the destruction of the world.

**10.51.   The answer is A (1, 2, 3)** (*Synopsis*, ed. 4, page 214).

Suicide is a danger for schizophrenics that must never be forgotten. *More schizophrenics than manic-depressives commit suicide*, although *the immediate risk of suicide is relatively greater among manic-depressives*. Schizophrenics may commit suicide because they are deeply depressed—for instance, during a psychotic depressive disorder. Or they may kill themselves in response to the relentless commands they are receiving from hallucinatory voices.

Some chronic schizophrenics have unpredictable suicidal impulses during brief spells of dejection. Suicide rates were reported to be as high as 4 percent in a group of schizophrenics followed for several years.

In many cases, the psychiatrist and the nurses who knew the suicidal patient or the patient's family for a long time are unable, in retrospect, to recognize any change in condition that might have been considered a warning signal from the patient of the impending tragedy.

Probably the greatest number of schizophrenic suicides occurs among those suffering from *the beginning stages of schizophrenia*. Sometimes, when the disease is in an early stage of development, even the victim's family and best friends have virtually no inkling of the terrible problem with which the patient is grappling.

Many of the unexplained suicides among students on a university campus are probably committed by young persons who have become aware of a malignant, insidious process that threatens to destroy their minds. Rather than seek psychiatric treatment or confide their feelings of uncontrollable disintegration to their friends, they choose to end their lives. *They do not give clear warnings of their intentions.*

**10.52.   The answer is C (2, 4)** (*Synopsis*, ed. 4, page 219).

In a pooled sample of schizophrenics examined in nine international centers, *lack of insight* was seen in a frequency of 97 percent, *auditory hallucinations* in 74 percent, and verbal hallucinations in 70 percent. *Delusions of persecution* were seen in 64 percent, and *thoughts spoken aloud* were seen in 50 percent.

The table at the top of column 2 lists the 12 most common schizophrenic symptoms.

**10.53.   The answer is A (1, 2, 3)** (*Synopsis*, ed. 4, page 214).

Catatonic schizophrenia may have a variety of signs and symptoms, including catatonic stupor, *mutism, negativism*, rigidity, excitement and *posturing*. A *fatuous or silly affect* is most often associated with disorganized (hebephrenic) schizophrenia.

**Frequency of Symptoms in a Pooled Sample of Core Schizophrenic Patients Examined in Nine International Centers***

| Symptom | Frequency (%) |
| --- | --- |
| Lack of insight | 97 |
| Auditory hallucinations | 74 |
| Verbal hallucinations | 70 |
| Ideas of reference | 67 |
| Suspiciousness | 66 |
| Flatness of affect | 66 |
| Voices speaking to patient | 65 |
| Delusional mood | 64 |
| Delusions of persecution | 64 |
| Inadequate description of problems | 64 |
| Thought alienation | 52 |
| Thoughts spoken aloud | 50 |

* Adapted from Sartorius N, Shapiro R, Jablensky A: The international pilot study of schizophrenia. Schizophr Bull *1:* 21, 1974.

**Diagnostic Criteria for Catatonic Type***

A type of Schizophrenia dominated by any of the following:

1. Catatonic stupor (marked decrease in reactivity to environment and/or reduction of spontaneous movements and activity) or mutism;

2. Catatonic negativism (an apparently motiveless resistance to all instructions or attempts to be moved);

3. Catatonic rigidity (maintenance of a rigid posture against efforts to be moved);

4. Catatonic excitement (excited motor activity, apparently purposeless and not influenced by external stimuli);

5. Catatonic posturing (voluntary assumption of inappropriate or bizarre posture).

* From American Psychiatric Association: *Diagnostic and Statistical Manual of Mental Disorders*, ed 3. American Psychiatric Association, Washington, DC, 1980. Used with permission.

The DSM-III table above lists and further describes the diagnostic criteria for catatonic schizophrenia.

**10.54.   The answer is E (all)** (*Synopsis*, ed. 4, page 215).

The paranoid type of schizophrenia is characterized primarily by the presence of *delusions of persecution* or grandeur. Paranoid schizophrenics are usually older than catatonics or hebephrenics when they break down; that is, they are usually in their late twenties or in their thirties. Patients who have been well up to that age have usually established a place and an identity for themselves in the community. Their ego resources are greater than those of catatonic and hebephrenic patients. Paranoid schizophrenics show less regression of mental faculties, emotional response, and behavior than do other subtypes of schizophrenia.

For further information concerning the diagnosis of the paranoid type of schizophrenia, see the table on page 118.

**10.55–10.59. The answers are 10.55–C, 10.56–B, 10.57–A, 10.58–D, and 10.59– E** (*Synopsis*, ed. 4, pages 207, 210, and 211).

The schizophrenic's characteristic bizarre speech results from the interaction of various factors on cognitive processes, such as the following:

1. **Incoherence.** For schizophrenics, language is primarily a means of self-expression, rather than a means of communication. Their *verbal and graphic productions are often either empty or obscure.* Schizophrenic speech uses a larger number of words that do not belong, and schizophrenics tend to repeat words more frequently than do normals in long speech samples.

2. **Neologisms.** Occasionally, schizophrenics create a completely *new expression*, a neologism, when they need to express a concept for which no ordinary word exists.

3. **Mutism.** This *functional inhibition of speech* and vocalization may last for hours or

days, but before the days of modern treatment methods, it often used to last for years in chronic schizophrenics of the catatonic type. Many schizophrenics tend to be monosyllabic and to answer questions as briefly as possible. They attempt to restrict contact with the interviewer as much as possible without being altogether uncooperative.

4. **Echolalia.** Occasionally, the schizophrenic patient exhibits echolalia, *repeating in answers to the interviewer's questions many of the same words the questioner has used.* For instance, Examiner: "How did you sleep last night?" Patient: "I slept well last night." Examiner: "Can you tell me the name of your head nurse?" Patient: "The name of my head nurse? The name of my head nurse is Miss Brown."

Echolalia seems to signal two facts—that patients are aware of some shortcomings in their ideation, and that they are striving to maintain an active rapport with the interviewer. They act much like somebody who is learning a new language and who, in answering the teacher's questions, uses as many of the teacher's words in the strange language as can possibly be managed.

5. **Verbigeration.** This rare symptom is found almost exclusively in chronic and very regressed schizophrenics. It consists of the *senseless repetition of the same words or phrases,* and it may, at times, go on for days.

## References

Babigian H N: Schizophrenia: Epidemiology. In *Comprehensive Textbook of Psychiatry*, ed 4, H I Kaplan, B J Sadock, editors, p 643. Williams & Wilkins, Baltimore, 1985.

Bellack A S, editor: *Treatment and Care of Schizophrenia.* Grune & Stratton, New York, 1984.

Bleuler M: What is schizophrenia? Schizo Bull *10:* 8, 1984.

Cancro R: Schizophrenia: Overview. In *Comprehensive Textbook of Psychiatry*, ed 4, H I Kaplan, B J Sadock, editors, p 631. Williams & Wilkins, Baltimore, 1985.

Lehmann H E, Cancro R: Schizophrenia: Clinical features. In *Comprehensive Textbook of Psychiatry*, ed 4, H I Kaplan, B J Sadock, editors, p 680. Williams & Wilkins, Baltimore, 1985.

Liberman R: Schizophrenia: Psychosocial treatment. In *Comprehensive Textbook of Psychiatry*, ed 4, H I

Kaplan, B J Sadock, editors, p 724. Williams & Wilkins, Baltimore, 1985.

Regier D A, Myers J K, Kramer M, Robins L N, Blazer D G, Hough R L, Eaton W W, Locke B Z: The NIMH Epidemiologic Catchment Area Program. Arch Gen Psychiatry *41:* 934, 1984.

Schultz C G: Schizophrenia: Individual psychotherapy. In *Comprehensive Textbook of Psychiatry*, ed 4, H I Kaplan, B J Sadock, editors, p 734. Williams & Wilkins, Baltimore, 1985.

Simpson G, May P R A: Schizophrenia: Somatic treatment. In *Comprehensive Textbook of Psychiatry*, ed 4, H I Kaplan, B J Sadock, editors, p 713. Williams & Wilkins, Baltimore, 1985.

Weiner H: Schizophrenia: Etiology. In *Comprehensive Textbook of Psychiatry*, ed 4, H I Kaplan, B J Sadock, editors, p 650. Williams & Wilkins, Baltimore, 1985.

# 11

# Paranoid Disorders

Paranoia is one of the oldest terms used in medical literature, dating back at least 2,000 years to the time of the ancient Greeks. This disorder has fascinated both the lay public and the medical profession, and over the years such psychiatrists as Kahlbaum, Kraepelin, Freud, and Cameron, among others, have turned their attention to attempting an understanding of this illness.

Today, paranoia is classified in the third edition of the *Diagnostic and Statistical Manual of Mental Disorders* (DSM-III) as one of a group of three paranoid disorders, the other two being the acute paranoid state and shared paranoid disorders, which was previously known as *folie à deux*. As a group, the paranoid disorders constitute about 10 percent of all psychiatric admissions to mental hospitals.

The reader is referred to Chapter 11 of *Modern Synopsis*-IV, "Paranoid Disorders," and should then read the following questions and answers to test his or her knowledge in this area.

# Questions

**DIRECTIONS:** Each of the statements or questions below is followed by five suggested responses or completions. Select the *one* that is *best* in each case.

**11.1.** A 43-year-old white male has been brought to the psychiatric emergency room by his wife. For the past 2 years he has become increasingly convinced that the Russian KGB is planning to kidnap and torture him. At first, he was mildly suspicious of certain men in the neighborhood, but this suspicion has now progressed to global suspiciousness, fearfulness, and angry outbursts. He does not experience auditory hallucinations, nor does he manifest a formal thought disorder. His wife says that there is no possibility that her husband's fears are factually grounded. Despite these problems, the patient has been functioning well in his job. He has had a full medical work-up with negative results. The most likely diagnosis is

A. paranoid personality disorder
B. paranoid schizophrenia
C. paranoia
D. conjugal paranoia
E. hypochondriacal paranoid psychosis

**11.2.** A 62-year-old unmarried man was brought to the hospital because he refused to leave the office of a lawyer he was consulting. The man was attempting to obtain redress from a large corporation that he believed was trying to influence his mind by beaming special rays into his home. He claimed that this harassment had been going on for the past 10 years, but he had warded off the rays with special invisible shields, which were no longer working, around his house. The patient had been successful in business, he was intelligent, and, on examining his mental status, he showed no abnormalities other than the belief that he was being irradiated. Physical examination was normal. The most likely diagnosis in this case is

A. acute paranoid state
B. paranoia
C. paranoid schizophrenia
D. paranoid personality
E. schizotypal personality

**11.3.** All of the following diagnostic criteria are characteristic of paranoid disorder *except*

A. persistent delusions of persecution
B. delusional jealousy
C. symptoms present for at least 1 week
D. behavior that is appropriate to the delusion
E. hallucinations

**11.4.** The characteristic feature of conjugal paranoia is a(n)

A. delusion of persecution
B. delusion of grandeur
C. somatic delusion
D. delusion of infidelity
E. idea of reference

**11.5.** A 45-year-old man, who had recently arrived in this country from his native Italy, was brought to the emergency room by his family because of changes in behavior that had occurred during the previous few weeks. He had developed the feeling that people on the street were following him and laughing at him, and he had become unwilling to leave his apartment. The patient was assigned to a therapist and, after 5 months of psychotherapy, is now freely walking the streets without fear or suspicion. His family states he is back to "his old self." The most likely diagnosis is

A. paranoia
B. paranoid personality disorder
C. organic mental disorder
D. acute paranoid disorder
E. schizophrenia

**11.6.** The percentage of patients with various diagnoses who exhibit paranoid symptoms is

A. 5 percent
B. 10 percent
C. 15 percent
D. 20 percent
E. 25 percent

**DIRECTIONS:** For each of the incomplete statements below, *one* or *more* of the completions given is correct. Choose answer:

A. if only **1, 2,** and **3** are correct
B. if only **1** and **3** are correct
C. if only **2** and **4** are correct
D. if only **4** is correct
E. if all are correct

**11.7.**  Shared paranoid disorder is
1. also known as *folie à deux*
2. seen between two persons, one of whom is dominant and the other more dependent and suggestible
3. seen only in pairs who have lived a very close existence for a long time
4. most commonly seen between a brother and a sister

**11.8.**  Which of the following statements are correct with regard to differential diagnosis of paranoid disorders:
1. The delusions of paranoid schizophrenia tend to be bizarre and fragmented, in contrast to the better-organized delusions of the paranoid disorder.
2. In the few patients who have hallucinations in conjunction with a paranoid disorder, the hallucinations are associated with the delusions, whereas hallucinations in schizophrenics are not necessarily connected with delusions.
3. In paranoid patients with a depressed affect, the affect is secondary to the delusional system, whereas in depressed patients the delusions are secondary to the depression.
4. Paranoid states seen in organic mental disorders are characterized by forgetfulness and disorientation, whereas paranoid states not associated with an organic etiology are characterized by intact orientation and memory.

**11.9.**  Which of the following major defense mechanisms is primarily used by paranoiacs:
1. Denial
2. Reaction formation
3. Undoing
4. Projection

**DIRECTIONS:** Each group of questions below consists of five lettered headings followed by a list of numbered words or statements. For each numbered word or statement, select the *one* lettered heading that is most closely associated with it. Each lettered heading may be selected once, more than once, or not at all.

**Questions 11.10–11.14**
A. Delusions of guilt and somatic delusions
B. Delusions secondary to perceptual
    disturbances
C. Grandiose delusions
D. Bizarre delusions of being controlled
E. Delusions of jealousy and persecution

**11.10.** Schizophrenia

**11.11.** Paranoid disorders

**11.12.** Mania

**11.13.** Organic mental disorders

**11.14.** Depression

**Questions 11.15–11.19**
A. Paranoid personality disorder
B. Paranoid disorder
C. Schizophrenia
D. Manic episode
E. Depressive episode

**11.15.** Psychomotor retardation

**11.16.** Thought broadcasting

**11.17.** Easily distracted with elevated mood

**11.18.** Persecutory delusions

**11.19.** Suspiciousness and mistrust of people

# Answers

## Paranoid Disorders

**11.1. The answer is C** (*Synopsis*, ed 4, page 228).

The patient described is suffering from *paranoia*. He presents an insidious 2-year development of a persistent persecutory delusional system, with the preservation of clear and orderly thinking. He does not manifest bizarre delusions, loosening of associations, or hallucinations that characterize *paranoid schizophrenia*. His presentation also differs from that of a *paranoid personality disorder*, which has as its essential feature a long-standing mistrust of people. Patients with this personality disorder have, for most of their lives, been sullen, withdrawn, humorless, haughty, and arrogant, often exaggerating insignificant slights into hidden motives and meanings; delusions are absent.

*Conjugal paranoia* is another form of paranoid disorder and is characterized by delusions that involve only the spouse. Initial minor criticism of the marital partner slowly progresses through suspiciousness to frank delusions revolving around thoughts of the spouse's infidelity. *Hypochondriacal paranoid psychosis* is a term reserved for somatic delusions that constitute the sole or primary delusions of underlying paranoia or paranoid schizophrenia. Hypochondriacal delusions are the main symptom.

The following table shows the DSM-III diagnostic criteria for paranoia.

### Diagnostic Criteria for Paranoia*

A.  Meets the criteria for paranoid disorder.

B.  A chronic and stable persecutory delusional system of at least 6 months' duration.

C.  Does not meet the criteria for shared paranoid disorder.

\* From American Psychiatric Association: *Diagnostic and Statistical Manual of Mental Disorders*, ed 3. American Psychiatric Association, Washington, DC, 1980. Used with permission.

**11.2. The answer is B** (*Synopsis*, ed. 4, page 228).

In classical *paranoia*, the personality remains organized except for the delusional idea, which is usually clearly formed and well systematized, as in the case described. The disorder evolves over a long period of time and often goes unnoticed. The patients are generally personable, intelligent, and do not get into difficulties with the authorities unless something happens to impinge on their delusional system. For example, if they decide to use the courts—as they often do—to redress an imagined wrong, the delusional system may be uncovered.

In the *acute paranoid state*, the delusion develops within a 6-month period and is less well organized than in paranoia. In *paranoid schizophrenia*, the disorder starts before age 45, the delusions are bizarre, thinking is fragmented, and social or vocational deterioration is often present. By contrast, neither the *paranoid personality* nor *schizotypal personality disorder* shows evidence of delusional thinking.

**11.3. The answer is E** (*Synopsis*, ed 4, page 228).

The table below lists the DSM-III criteria for diagnosing paranoid disorder. *Hallucinations* and *nonpersecutory delusional symptoms are not present in paranoid disorders, and their presence precludes making this diagnosis.* If these symptoms are present, the most likely differential diagnosis would include schizophrenia or major affective disorder.

### Diagnostic Criteria for Paranoid Disorder*

A.  *Persistent persecutory delusions or delusional jealousy.*

B.  Emotion and *behavior appropriate to the content of the delusional system.*

C.  *Duration of illness of at least 1 week.*

D.  None of the symptoms of criterion A of schizophrenia, such as bizarre delusions, incoherence, or marked loosening of associations.

E.  No prominent hallucinations.

F.  The full depressive or manic syndrome (criteria A and B of major depressive or manic episode) is either not present, developed after any psychotic symptoms, or was brief in duration relative to the duration of the psychotic symptoms.

G.  Not due to an organic mental disorder.

\* From American Psychiatric Association: *Diagnostic and Statistical Manual of Mental Disorders*, ed 3. American Psychiatric Association, Washington, DC, 1980. Used with permission.

**11.4.  The answer is D** (*Synopsis,* ed. 4, page 228).

The characteristic feature of conjugal paranoia is a *delusion of infidelity,* in which one spouse believes that the other is being sexually unfaithful. Initial minor criticism of one partner by the other slowly progresses through suspiciousness to frank delusions revolving around thoughts of the spouse's infidelity. Conjugal paranoia is unlike pathological jealousy, which is a symptom that occurs in such illnesses as alcoholism, schizophrenia, affective psychosis, and the organic mental disorders. According to DSM-III, conjugal paranoia is a variant of paranoia.

The characteristic feature of a *somatic delusion* is that the body is perceived or felt to be disturbed or disordered in all, or in individual, organs or parts. An *idea of reference* is a morbid preoccupation with the idea that actions of other persons relate to oneself. The characteristic feature of a *delusion of grandeur* is an exaggerated concept of one's importance, power, knowledge, or identity. A *delusion of persecution* involves the pathological belief that one is being attacked, harassed, cheated, or conspired against.

**11.5.  The answer is D** (*Synopsis,* ed. 4, page 230).

*Acute paranoid disorder* is defined as a paranoid disorder of less than 6 months' duration. This disorder is characterized by an acute onset and a complete clearing within 6 months. One of the most common examples of acute paranoid disorder occurs in immigrants who become suspicious and develop paranoid ideas. The immigrants' appearance, way of speaking, and mannerisms often are seen by those around them as ridiculous or contemptuous, and uncertainty in the new environment can easily increase isolation. The incidence of acute paranoid disorder in foreign-born patients is 16.5 percent.

**Diagnostic Criteria for Acute Paranoid Disorder***

A.  Meets the criteria for paranoid disorder.

B.  Duration of less than 6 months.

C.  Does not meet the criteria for shared paranoid disorder.

---

\* From American Psychiatric Association: *Diagnostic and Statistical Manual of Mental Disorders,* ed 3. American Psychiatric Association, Washington, DC, 1980. Used with permission.

*Paranoia* is diagnosed if the duration of a persecutory delusional system is more than 6 months. *Paranoid personality disorder* is characterized by pervasive and long-lasting mistrust of others. No delusions are present. *Organic mental disorder* is diagnosed when disorientation, rapidly fluctuating clinical features, perceptual disturbances, and impaired impulse control are present. *Schizophrenia* is characterized by bizarre delusions, auditory hallucinations, and loosening of associations.

The table shown in column 1 lists the DSM-III diagnostic criteria for acute paranoid disorder.

**11.6.  The answer is B** (*Synopsis,* ed. 4, page 226).

A study of patients with various diagnoses who exhibited paranoid symptoms found that *10 percent* of the patients had paranoid disorders. It is difficult to make accurate estimates of the incidence of paranoid disorders. Everyone uses denial, projection, and paranoid ideation to a certain extent in daily living. The reason for the lack of valid statistics on the syndrome of the paranoid disorders lies in poor definition, imprecise instruments, and haphazard investigation.

**11.7.  The answer is A (1, 2, 3)** (*Synopsis,* ed. 4, pages 229 and 230).

Shared paranoid disorder, *folie à deux,* develops as a result of a close relationship with another person who already has an established paranoid psychosis. *One of the two persons is generally a dominant paranoid person* with fixed delusions; *the other person is likely to be dependent and suggestible.* The latter person takes on the dominant one's delusions when they are together, but gives them up relatively easily when there is separation and therapy.

The most common pairs are two sisters. There are other more unusual pairings, such as a husband and wife, a parent and child, or a *brother and sister.* The condition is very uncommon. It is seen only when the two persons involved have *lived a very close existence for a long time* in the same environment, isolated from the outside world. It is seen more commonly in women than in men.

The following table lists the DSM-III diagnostic criteria for shared paranoid disorder.

**Diagnostic Criteria for Shared Paranoid Disorder***

A.  Meets the criteria for paranoid disorder.

B.  Delusional system develops as a result of a close relationship with another person or persons who have an established disorder with persecutory delusions.

---

\* From American Psychiatric Association: *Diagnostic and Statistical Manual of Mental Disorders,* ed 3. American Psychiatric Association, Washington, DC, 1980. Used with permission.

**11.8.   The answer is E (all)** (*Synopsis*, ed. 4, page 231).

All of the examples given concerning potential differential diagnosis of paranoid disorders are correct. Further elaboration on the differential diagnosis of paranoid disorders is seen in the table shown in column 2.

**11.9.   The answer is D (4)** (*Synopsis*, ed. 4, page 227).

Primarily, paranoiacs use the defense of *projection,* in which they attribute to other people the thoughts, feelings, or impulses that are unacceptable in themselves. Consumed with anger and hostility and unable to face responsibility for this rage, the paranoiacs' resentment and anger are projected onto others.

Hypersensitivity causes other people to avoid paranoiacs, and this reaction tends to amplify their hostile and suspicious attitudes. Intolerant of criticism, paranoiacs readily criticize others. Being overaggressive, paranoiacs see an aggressor in everyone around them; thus, they treat others as projections of their own unconscious hostilities. Such alienating behavior incurs the hostility of others, resulting in an increase in psychopathology. A psychotic delusional system results as a defense against feelings of rejection and inadequacy. Feelings of inferiority are replaced by delusions of superiority, grandiosity, and omnipotence, and delusional erotic ideas replace feelings of rejection.

Secondarily, paranoiacs may sometimes use the defense mechanisms of reaction formation and denial. *Reaction formation* is used as a defense against aggression, dependency needs, and feelings of affection. The need for dependency is transformed into staunch independence. *Denial* is used to avoid awareness of painful reality.

*Undoing* is the defense mechanism by which a person symbolically acts out in reverse something that is unacceptable. Undoing is a form of magical expiatory action. Repetitive in nature, it is commonly observed in patients with obsessive-compulsive disorder.

**11.10–11.14.   The answers are 11.10–D, 11.11–E, 11.12–C, 11.13–B, and 11.14–A** (*Synopsis*, ed. 4, page 232).

There are significant differences in the types of delusions found in various mental disorders. In *paranoid disorders*, delusions of jealousy and persecution are mostly found. In *schizophrenia*, delusions of being controlled, bizarre delusions, and delusions of persecution can occur. In *mania*, grandiose delusions are seen. In *depression*, delusions of guilt and somatic delusions may occur. In *organic mental disorders*, delusions are seen secondary to perceptual disturbances.

Of all the delusions, the most common is the persecutory type, regardless of the particular psychiatric illness involved.

**Differential Diagnosis\***

| | |
|---|---|
| Paranoid personality disorder | Pervasive and long-standing suspiciousness of other people |
| Paranoid disorder | Delusions of jealousy or persecution |
| Schizophrenia | One symptom from the following:<br>Delusions of being controlled<br>Thought broadcasting<br>Thought insertion<br>Thought withdrawal<br>Fantastic or implausible delusions<br>Other delusions without persecutory or jealous content<br>Auditory hallucination—a voice keeps up a running commentary on the patient's thoughts or behavior<br>Auditory hallucination not associated with depression or elation or limited to two words<br>Delusions of any type accompanied by hallucination of any type<br>Loosening of association combined with inappropriate affect |
| Manic episode | Elevated, expansive, or irritable mood with pressured speech and hyperactivity |
| Depressive episode | Pervasive loss of interest or pleasure combined with at least four of the following:<br>Change in weight when not dieting<br>Sleep difficulty<br>Psychomotor agitation or retardation<br>Loss of energy<br>Decrease in sex drive<br>Feelings of self-reproach or excessive guilt, either of which may be delusional<br>Indecisiveness<br>Suicidal thoughts |
| Organic mental disorder | Disordered memory and orientation<br>Impairment in judgment and impulse control<br>Perceptual disturbance—simple misinterpretations, illusions, and hallucinations<br>Clinical features that may fluctuate rapidly |

\* Adapted from American Psychiatric Association: *Diagnostic and Statistical Manual of Mental Disorders,* ed 3. American Psychiatric Association, Washington, DC, 1980.

**11.15–11.19.   The answers are 11.15–E, 11.16–C, 11.17–D, 11.18–B, and 11.19–A.** (*Synopsis,* ed. 4, page 231).

*Psychomotor retardation* is a general slowing of mental and physical activity. It is often a sign of depression, which is a mental state characterized by feelings of sadness, loneliness, despair, low self-esteem, and self-reproach. The term refers either to a mood that is so characterized or to an affective disorder. Accompanying signs include psychomotor retardation or at times agitation, withdrawal from interpersonal contact, and vegetative symptoms, such as insomnia and anorexia.

*Thought broadcasting* is the feeling that one's thoughts are being broadcast or projected into the environment. Such feelings are encountered in schizophrenia, but not in paranoid disorders. The delusions of paranoid schizophrenia are bizarre and fragmented, in contrast to the better-organized delusions of the paranoid disorders. In those few patients who have hallucinations in conjunction with a paranoid disorder, the hallucinations are associated with the delusions; hallucinations in the schizophrenic are not necessarily connected with delusions.

Manic patients who present with hostile aggression may be mistaken for patients with acute paranoid reactions. The angry mood of the manic patient quickly passes; in the paranoid disorder, the haughty, complaining, and hostile behavior remains. Often, the manic patient is *easily distracted*, whereas the paranoiac is adamant. In the manic episode, there is an *elevated, expansive, or irritable mood* with pressured speech and hyperactivity.

Paranoid disorders are characterized by *persecutory or grandiose delusions* and related disturbances in mood, thought, and behavior. In DSM-III the paranoid disorders include paranoia, shared paranoid disorder, acute paranoid disorder, and atypical paranoid disorder. Paranoid disorders should be distinguished from psychotic depressions. Although patients with psychotic depressions may have delusions, with somatic delusions predominating, they also exhibit the biological signs of depression, which are not present in paranoid disorders. If a paranoid patient has a depressed affect, the affect is secondary to the delusional system. In a depressed patient, however, the converse is true; that is, the delusions are secondary to the depression.

The essential feature of paranoid personality disorder is a long-standing *mistrust of people*. Patients with this disorder are hypersensitive and continually alert for environmental clues that will validate their original prejudicial ideas. Often sullen, withdrawn, humorless, haughty, arrogant, cold, and calculating, they tend to view life negatively and exaggerate insignificant slights into hidden motives and special meanings; but delusions are absent. Although occupational difficulties are common and the patients have grossly impaired interpersonal relationships, with special difficulty in relating to authority figures, patients with paranoid personality disorder rarely seek psychiatric help. Under stress, these patients can easily develop a full-blown paranoid delusion, at which point they are classified under the paranoid disorder.

# References

Cameron N: *Personality Development and Psychopathology.* Houghton Mifflin, Boston, 1963.

Freud S: Some neurotic mechanisms in jealousy, paranoia, and homosexuality. In *Standard Edition of The Complete Psychological Works of Sigmund Freud,* vol 18, p 221. Hogarth Press, London, 1955.

Kaplan H I, Sadock B J: The status of the paranoid today: Diagnosis, prognosis, treatment. Psychiatr Q 45: 520, 1971.

Kendler K S: The nosologic validity of paranoia (simple delusional disorder), a review. Arch Gen Psychiatry 37: 669, 1980.

Walker J I, Brodie K H: Paranoid disorders, In *Comprehensive Textbook of Psychiatry,* ed 4, H I Kaplan, B J Sadock, editors, p 747. Williams & Wilkins, Baltimore, 1985.

Walker J I, Cavenar J O, Jr: Paranoid symptoms and conditions. In *Signs and Symptoms in Psychiatry,* p 483. J B Lippincott, Philadelphia, 1983.

Winokur G: Delusional disorder (paranoia). Compr Psychiatry 18: 511, 1977.

# 12
# Schizoaffective Disorders

Schizoaffective disorder is not included in the third edition of the *Diagnostic and Statistical Manual of Mental Disorders* (DSM-III) as a distinct diagnostic entity. Instead, it is listed in the category of psychotic disorders not elsewhere classified. Many patients with schizophrenia experience alteration of mood, and many patients who are either manic or depressed show disorganized thinking characteristic of schizophrenia. For that reason, it is often difficult to distinguish which patients fall into which diagnostic category.

Cases that in the past were diagnosed as schizoaffective disorder are now classified under the DSM-III diagnostic category as either schizophrenia, major affective disorder (unipolar or bipolar), schizophreniform disorder, or brief reactive psychosis. The student must deal with the current confusion about schizoaffective disorder. Where possible, an attempt should be made to distinguish between schizophrenia and affective disorders. In those cases where it is impossible to make a differential diagnosis between the two, a schizoaffective disorder should be appropriately diagnosed.

The reader should read Chapter 12 of *Modern Synopsis-IV*, "Schizoaffective Disorders," and should then refer to the following questions and answers to assess his or her knowledge of the above concepts.

# Questions

**DIRECTIONS:** Each of the statements or questions below is followed by five suggested responses or completions. Select the *one* that is *best* in each case.

**12.1.** Which of the following statements applies to schizoaffective disorders:

A. The patients present with a mixture of affective and psychotic features.
B. Delusions of control and auditory hallucinations are common features of this disorder.
C. Mood-incongruent delusions and hallucinations are part of the expected clinical picture.
D. The diagnosis cannot be made if the patient is suffering from any organic mental disorder.
E. All of the above

**12.2.** The major treatment methods used in schizoaffective disorders are all of the following *except*

A. psychoanalysis
B. antipsychotic agents
C. tricyclic antidepressants
D. antimanic drugs
E. electroconvulsive therapy

**12.3.** All of the following are associated with schizoaffective disorders *except*

A. delusions of control
B. thought insertion
C. organic brain disorder
D. manic symptoms
E. auditory hallucination

**12.4.** Which of the following combinations best characterizes the occurrence of mental illness among relatives of schizoaffective patients:

A. Frequency of schizophrenia comparable to that seen among relatives of schizophrenics; frequency of affective illness greater than that expected for the general population

B. Frequency of schizophrenia less than that seen in the general population; frequency of affective illnesses greater than that expected for relatives of patients with affective disorders

C. Frequency of schizoaffective disorder greater than that seen in the general population; frequency of affective disorders less than that seen among relatives of patients with affective disorders

D. Frequency of schizophrenia less than that seen in relatives of schizophrenics; frequency of affective disorders comparable to that seen in relatives of patients with affective disorders

E. Frequency of schizoaffective disorder comparable to that of the general population; frequency of schizophrenia greater than that of the general population

**12.5.** Which of the following statements does *not* apply to the diagnosis of schizoaffective disorder:

A. It is a condition that does not fit the DSM-III diagnostic criteria for any of the affective, schizophreniform, or schizophrenic disorders.

B. It is a mixture of depressive or manic symptoms with hallucinations or delusions that are atypical in uncomplicated affective disorders.

C. Substance use disorder has been ruled out before making the diagnosis.

D. Neuroleptic agents are of little help in treating this disorder.

E. Electroconvulsive therapy can be of help in some schizoaffective cases.

**12.6.** If a schizoaffective patient has a monozygotic twin, which of the following would be expected:

A. A concordance rate twice as high as that found in monozygotic schizophrenic twins

B. Less than a 12 percent chance that the other twin would be affected

C. A different rate of concordance than would be found if the patient was suffering from a bipolar disorder

D. No possibility that the twin would be affected

E. An almost 100 percent certainty that the twin would be affected.

**12.7.** A reasonable estimate of the prevalence of schizoaffective disorders is

A. 0.5 percent
B. 1 percent
C. 1.5 percent
D. 2 percent
E. 5 percent

**DIRECTIONS:** For each of the incomplete statements below, *one* or *more* of the completions given is correct. Choose answer:

A. if only **1, 2,** and **3** are correct
B. if only **1** and **3** are correct
C. if only **2** and **4** are correct
D. if only **4** is correct
E. if all are correct

**12.8.** The validity of schizoaffective disorders as being distinct from schizophrenia has been suggested because
1. close relatives of patients with schizoaffective disorders show a lower prevalence of schizophrenia than is seen in relatives of schizophrenics
2. no sex differences have been reported
3. relatives of patients with schizoaffective disorders show an increased frequency of affective illness
4. hallucinations and delusions are present

**12.9.** Which of the following factors would tend to indicate that schizoaffective disorders are really atypical cases of depression or mania, rather than cases more similar to schizophrenia:
1. DSM-III definition of schizoaffective disorder
2. Suicide rate among schizoaffective patients
3. Auditory hallucinations
4. Patterns of mental illness among relatives of schizoaffectives

# Answers
# Schizoaffective Disorders

**12.1.** **The answer is E** (*Synopsis,* ed. 4, page 235).

Schizoaffective disorder is a syndrome of depressive or manic features that develop before or concurrently with certain psychotic symptoms, such as *mood-incongruent delusions or hallucinations,* that are not consistent with the person's mood. The diagnosis of schizoaffective illness is not made if the illness is due to any *organic mental disorder.*

Two kinds of psychotic symptoms define schizoaffective disorders. The first kind includes the symptoms that are part of the criterion list for schizophrenia, such as *delusions of control* and certain types of *auditory hallucinations* that would suggest schizophrenia if there were no accompanying affective syndrome. The second kind includes the symptoms that arise in the context of an affective syndrome without an apparent relationship to depression or elation. Otherwise, the clinical features consist of various *mixtures of affective and schizophrenia-like symptoms.*

**12.2.** **The answer is A** (*Synopsis,* ed. 4, page 237).

Most patients with schizoaffective disorders require hospitalization because of their psychotic features, affective disturbances, or risk of suicide. *Antipsychotic agents* (such as the phenothiazines and butyrophenones), *tricyclic antidepressants, antimanic drugs* (such as lithium), and *electroconvulsive therapy* (ECT) are the major treatment methods used.

Most patients are helped by the available treatments. For many, drugs or ECT or both result in prompt recovery and the ability to return to work or school. To what extent the continuation of an antipsychotic or antimood drug prevents relapse is not clear, but some evidence indicates that such a prophylactic effort is helpful, at least in some cases. Unfortunately, some patients relapse after only a brief remission and must be treated vigorously to achieve a more lasting remission. A minority of patients show very little improvement, despite the application of all available treatments, and such patients progress to a chronic state of illness.

As schizoaffective disorders are defined as a syndrome that includes psychotic symptoms that are part of the criterion list for schizophrenia and affective illness, it would follow that

*psychoanalysis* would not be the treatment of choice. Rather, psychopharmacologic or biological treatments are indicated, perhaps ideally in conjunction with some form of supportive psychotherapy.

**12.3.** **The answer is C** (*Synopsis,* ed. 4, page 236).

Schizoaffective disorders are not considered to be caused by organic illnesses, such as *organic brain disorder;* nor are they accompanied by signs of an organic mental disorder. Thus organic etiology or symptomatology excludes the diagnosis of schizoaffective disorder.

*Delusions of control, thought insertion,* and *auditory hallucination* are among the various features of the schizophrenic component of schizoaffective illness, and *manic symptoms* are consistent with its affective component.

**12.4.** **The answer is D** (*Synopsis,* ed. 4, page 235).

The occurrence of mental illness among relatives of schizoaffective patients includes an increased risk of schizoaffective disorders, a frequency of *schizophrenia that is less than that seen in relatives of schizophrenics,* and a *frequency of affective disorders similar to that seen in relatives of patients with affective disorder,* but greater than that expected of the general population. In fact, most of the ill relatives of schizoaffective patients suffer from uncomplicated affective illnesses.

**12.5.** **The answer is D** (*Synopsis,* ed. 4, pages 235 and 236).

DSM-III does not define or give diagnostic criteria for schizoaffective disorder; however, schizoaffective disorder is defined as a syndrome of *depressive or manic features* that develops before or concurrently with certain psychotic symptoms that are considered unusual in an uncomplicated affective disorder. The diagnosis is not made if the illness is due to *substance use disorder* or any organic mental disorder.

*Neuroleptics are of considerable help in the treatment of this syndrome.* Antipsychotic agents, tricyclic antidepressants, and antimanic drugs are the mainstays of treatment; however, *electroconvulsive therapy may be of help in some cases.* Hospitalization may also be indicated for symptoms of severe depression of mania.

**Diagnostic Features of Schizoaffective Disorders***

| Essential Features | Associated Features |
|---|---|
| Depressive or manic syndrome | Course of illness; episodic, chronic, or in remission |
| One of more of these symptoms: | |

1. Delusions of control
2. Thought broadcasting
3. Thought insertion
4. Thought withdrawal
5. Auditory hallucinations: voices commenting on patient or conversing with each other
6. Auditory hallucinations: not related to depression or elation, more than one or two words
7. Preoccupation with delusion or hallucination that is not related to depression or elation
8. Delusions for at least 1 month after resolution of affective disturbance
9. Repeated incoherence, unless concurrent with manic syndrome

Depressive or manic symptoms simultaneous with above symptoms
Duration of illness at least 1 week
Not due to organic mental disorder

* Adapted from American Psychiatric Association: *Diagnostic and Statistical Manual of Mental Disorders,* ed 3. American Psychiatric Association, Washington, DC, 1980. Used with permission.

For further diagnostic features of schizoaffective disorder, see the table above.

**12.6.  The answer is A** (*Synopsis,* ed. 4, pages 197 and 235).

It has been found that the monozygotic concordance rate for schizoaffective disorders is greater than 80 percent; that is, *twice as high* as that of schizophrenia. This high rate of genetic transmission is the same as that seen in manic-depressive illness. It is this fact that leads some workers to believe that schizoaffective disorder is really a variant of affective illness.

**12.7.  The answer is B** (*Synopsis,* ed. 4, page 235).

A reasonable estimate of the prevalence of schizoaffective disorders may be no more than *1 percent.*

**12.8.  The answer is B (1, 3)** (*Synopsis,* ed. 4, page 235).

Two kinds of psychotic symptoms define schizoaffective disorders. The first kind includes those symptoms that are part of the criterion list for schizophrenia, such as *delusions of control and certain types of auditory hallucinations,* and that would suggest schizophrenia if there were no accompanying affective syndrome. The second kind includes those symptoms that arise in the context of an affective syndrome without an apparent relationship to depression or elation. Otherwise, the clinical features consist of various mixtures of affective and schizophrenia-like symptoms.

*Close relatives of patients with schizoaffective disorders show a lower prevalence of schizophrenia than is seen in relatives of schizophrenics;* instead, *the relatives of patients with schizoaffective disorders show an increased frequency of affective illness,* a frequency similar to that seen in the relatives of patients with affective disorders. Most of the ill relatives of schizoaffective patients suffer from uncomplicated, straightforward affective illnesses. At the same time, an increased frequency of schizoaffective conditions may be seen among the relatives.

*No striking sex differences* in the frequency of schizoaffective disorders have been reported.

**12.9.  The answer is C (2, 4)** (*Synopsis,* ed. 4, page 236).

Schizoaffective patients present a significant risk for completed *suicide,* with suicidal ideation also being very common. This risk is closer to that seen in the depressed phase of bipolar disorder than to that seen in schizophrenia. In addition, the schizoaffective *familial occurrence of manic and depressive disorders* closely parallels that seen for uncomplicated affective disorders.

*DSM-III does not include schizoaffective disorders among the affective or schizophrenic disorders,* and its listing among psychotic disorders not elsewhere classified indicates strong reservations about its validity as a separate disorder.

*Auditory hallucinations* may be present in both affective and schizophrenic disorders and thus cannot be used as a specific criterion for placing schizoaffective disorders closer to either schizophrenia or affective disorder.

# References

Clayton P J: Schizoaffective disorders. J Nerv Ment Dis *170:* 646, 1982.

Goodnick P J: Treatment of schizoaffective disorders. Schizophr Bull *10:* 30, 1984.

Goodwin D W, Guze S B: Psychiatric Diagnosis, ed 3. Oxford University Press, New York, 1984.

Guze S B: Schizoaffective disorder. In *Comprehensive Textbook of Psychiatry*, ed 4, H I Kaplan, B J Sadock, editors, p 756. Williams & Wilkins, Baltimore, 1985.

Pope H G, Jr, Lipinski J F, Conen B M, Axelrod D T: "Schizoaffective disorder": An invalid diagnosis? A comparison of schizoaffective disorder, schizophrenia, and affective disorder. Am J Psychiatry *137:* 921, 1980.

van Praag H M, Nijo L: About the course of schizoaffective psychoses. Compr Psychiatry *25:* 8, 1984.

# 13

# Major Affective Disorders

The term affective disorders groups together a number of clinical conditions whose common and essential feature is a disturbance of mood accompanied by related cognitive, psychomotor, psychophysiological, and interpersonal difficulties.

Mood usually refers to sustained emotional states that color the whole personality and psychic life. Affect sometimes refers to the subjective aspect of emotion, apart from its bodily component; mood refers to the pervasive or prevailing emotion. Therefore, some authorities have suggested that the term mood disorders would be the more precise designation. In the clinical disorders under consideration, the emotional changes are pervasive and sustained, meeting the definition of mood. Because historical continuity and clinical usage have preferred affective disorders, however, that term is used in the third edition of the *Diagnostic and Statistical Manual of Mental Disorders* (DSM-III) and here. Although human experience includes a variety of emotions—such as fear, anger, pleasure, and surprise—the clinical conditions considered under the affective disorders involve depression and mania.

Grouping the affective disorders according to the patient's predominant symptoms represents less than the ideal basis for nosology. An ideal nosology would base classification on causes—genetic, psychodynamic, and biological factors. Those and other factors have been proposed as causal for the affective disorders, and investigations are under way to establish their precise roles. It is probable that the conditions grouped together as affective disorders are heterogeneous as to cause; some or most are probably multifactorial in causation, involving complex interactions of genetic, biochemical, developmental, and environmental factors. In view of the limited extent of the current knowledge about the causes of most mental disorders, however, classification by type of psychological impairment has had great heuristic value. Since the late 19th century, mental disorders have been classified by the psychological faculty manifestly most impaired: intelligence (mental retardation), thinking and cognition (the dementias, the deliriums, the schizophrenias), social behavior (character and personality disorders), and mood (affective disorders). That approach to the classification of mental disorders parallels the classification of internal medicine disorders by organ (heart, kidney, and so on), the faculties of the mind assuming the place of mental structures equivalent to body organs in providing a basis for classification when a causal classification is not yet sufficiently substantiated by research or clinical experience.

The prevalence of depressive symptoms in adults is between 9 and 20 percent. According to the 1984 Epidemiologic Catchment Area (ECA) Program, major depression was among the four most frequent DSM-III psychiatric disorders in both men and women. There have been major advances in the treatment of depression, particularly with the use of the newer antidepressant medications. Those advances, coupled with psychotherapy, offer depressed patients a better prognosis than ever before.

The reader should refer to Chapter 13 of *Modern Synopsis-IV*, "Major Affective Disorders," for an overview of this subject and should then study the questions and answers that follow.

# Questions

**DIRECTIONS:** Each of the statements or questions below is followed by five suggested responses or completions. Select the *one* that is *best* in each case.

**13.1.** In the dexamethasone suppression test (DST), when a serum cortisol is greater than 4.5 to 5.0 μg/dl, it may be associated with all of the following *except*

A. use of barbiturates
B. use of indomethacin
C. major (endogenous) depression
D. alcohol abuse
E. dehydration

**13.2.** Among patients with depressive disorders, what percentage will show evidence of impaired reality testing, such as delusions:

A. 5 percent
B. 10 percent
C. 15 percent
D. 20 percent
E. 25 percent

**13.3.** Major depression (unipolar)

A. is more common in men
B. peaks in women after age 55
C. shows no conclusive data regarding prevalence for blacks and whites
D. is higher among the poor
E. all of the above

**13.4.** The number of patients who are in remission from bipolar or unipolar disorders and who will have another attack is about

A. 5 percent
B. 10 percent
C. 25 percent
D. 50 percent
E. 90 percent

**13.5.** The affective disorders are a group of conditions with a common and essential feature best described as a disturbance of

A. thinking
B. mood
C. attention
D. conation
E. association

**13.6.** A patient who has a single episode of mania is best diagnosed as suffering from

A. unipolar disorder
B. bipolar disorder
C. cyclothymic disorder
D. dysthymic disorder
E. schizoaffective disorder

**13.7.** Which of the following conditions may be associated with symptoms of depression:

A. Schizophrenia
B. Cyclothymia
C. Alcoholism
D. Anxiety disorders
E. All of the above

**13.8.** Of the patients hospitalized for cardiac disease, the percentage of patients who develop a depression is

A. less than 5 percent
B. 10 percent
C. 20 percent
D. 30 percent
E. more than 60 percent

**13.9.** A patient treated with reserpine for hypertension may develop which of the following disorders:

A. Schizophreniform psychosis
B. Depression
C. Conversion disorder
D. Hysteria
E. Mania

**13.10.** A 59-year-old white married attorney, with a promising practice, two daughters, and a good marriage, is noticed by his wife to be "not functioning properly" during the previous 2 months. He calls the office frequently, telling his partners that he is ill, while actually he cannot get out of bed in the mornings. His colleagues are concerned about his frequent cancellation of appointments and his change in behavior. He has stopped taking pride in his appearance, has lost his appetite for food and his interest in sex, and is sleeping many hours each day. He has told his wife that he is unsure if he wants to go on living. There is no history of drug or alcohol use. He had a thorough physical examination 3 months earlier and was told that he was in good health.

With the information provided above, which of the following is the most likely diagnosis:

A. Major affective disorder, bipolar
B. Major affective disorder, unipolar
C. Undifferentiated schizophrenia
D. Anxiety disorder
E. None of the above

**13.11.** Which of the following would be of help in the differential diagnosis and formulation of a treatment plan for a patient with major depression:

A. Previous family history of psychiatric illness
B. Knowledge of type of psychiatric medication used in the past
C. Medical problems
D. Past or present substance abuse
E. All of the above

**13.12.** In the diagnosis of unipolar major affective disorder, which medication would be the best to try first:

A. Imipramine
B. Fluphenazine
C. Tranylcypromine
D. Pargyline
E. Phenothiazine

**13.13.** A few days after a 27-year-old housewife's father had been killed in a car accident, she showed profound behavioral changes. Suddenly, she told her husband that she did not love him, she went on spending sprees, and she was arrested by the police for driving at excessive speeds. Her speech became disorganized, her mood became elated, and she showed psychomotor agitation. The woman was brought to a local psychiatric emergency room, where she revealed to the examining psychiatrist that she had no appetite, had not been able to sleep for days, and, in the past, she had had periods of severe depression.

On the basis of the information given, the most likely diagnosis is

A. schizoaffective disorder
B. major affective disorder, depressed
C. bipolar disorder, mixed
D. undifferentiated schizophrenia
E. none of the above

**13.14.** The drug treatment indicated for the acute management of mania is

A. lithium carbonate
B. nortriptyline
C. haloperidol and lithium
D. phenelzine
E. chlordiazepoxide and lithium

**13.15.** The animal experimental model of learned helplessness has been applied to

A. schizophrenia
B. affective disorders
C. anxiety state
D. phobic disorder
E. mental retardation

**13.16.** Affective disorders include all of the following diagnoses *except*

A. bipolar disorder, mixed
B. atypical depression
C. cyclothymic disorder
D. schizoaffective disorder
E. dysthymic disorder

**13.17.** The defense mechanism most commonly used in depression is

A. projection
B. introjection
C. sublimation
D. altruism
E. undoing

**DIRECTIONS:** For each of the incomplete statements below, *one* or *more* of the completions given is correct. Choose answer:

A. if only **1, 2,** and **3** are correct
B. if only **1** and **3** are correct
C. if only **2** and **4** are correct
D. if only **4** is correct
E. if all are correct

**13.18.** Age-associated features of major depression include
1. separation anxiety
2. antisocial behavior
3. running away
4. pseudodementia

**13.19.** Cortisol escapes the suppressive action of dexamethasone in the dexamethasone suppression test (DST) in
1. schizophrenia
2. dysthymia
3. cyclothymia
4. unipolar depression

**13.20.** Monoideatic delusions of control are inconsistent with which of the following diagnoses:
1. Schizophrenia
2. Paranoia
3. Toxic psychosis
4. Mania

**13.21.** Bipolar disorder
1. shows no difference in incidence between men and women
2. usually has an onset before age 30
3. is more frequent in the upper socioeconomic groups
4. is more common among divorced persons

**13.22.** Melancholia is associated with
1. a positive response to both tricyclics and electroconvulsive therapy (ECT) and a negative response to psychotherapy
2. a central group of symptoms occurring together
3. a difficulty in eliciting a recent history of external stress
4. elderly patients more often than young patients

**13.23.** The hypothesis that circadian rhythm activities are delayed in mania is based on
1. increased total sleep time
2. decreased percentage of dream time
3. decreased dream latency
4. increased activity of the intrinsic pacemaker

**13.24.** Factors supporting a strong genetic component in affective disorders include which of the following:
1. Relatives of bipolar patients have a higher risk for bipolar illness than for unipolar illness.
2. Relatives of unipolar patients are more at risk for unipolar illness than for bipolar illness.
3. Twin studies indicate greater risk in monozygotic twins than in dizygotic twins for similar affective disorders.
4. Monozygotic twins reared apart show about a 10 percent concordance rate for affective disorder.

**13.25.** In the families of late-onset (after age 40) unipolar depression in males, one finds
1. more depression in males than in females
2. a low incidence of alcoholism in male relatives
3. a high incidence of schizophrenia
4. a low incidence of sociopathy in male relatives

**13.26.** To diagnose a major depressive episode, which of the following criteria may be present:
1. Dysphoric mood
2. Insomnia
3. Suicidal ideation
4. Symptoms present for at least 2 weeks

**13.27.** Serotonin
1. is a biogenic amine
2. is metabolized to 5-hydroxyindoleacetic acid (5-HIAA)
3. is partially synthesized from tryptophan
4. is increased in the brain by reserpine

**13.28.** Persons prone to depression are characterized by which of the following:
1. Paranoid personality
2. Strong superego
3. Enduring object relations
4. Low self-esteem

**13.29.** A test for growth hormone (GH) activity involves measuring the expected rise in plasma levels of GH after the administration of insulin. In depressed patients, it has been found that

1. there is a decreased response in GH to such insulin-induced hypoglycemia
2. in bipolar depression the response of GH rise may be enhanced
3. GH release is impaired in postmenopausal women with major depression
4. infants with failure-to-thrive (FTT) syndrome show enhanced GH secretion

**13.30.** Depressed patients exhibit
1. an increased luteinizing hormone (LH) secretion in depressed postmenopausal women
2. a decreased thyroid-stimulating hormone (TSH) response to thyrotropin-releasing hormone (TRH) challenge
3. increased REM latency
4. decreased REM sleep

**13.31.** The lifetime expectancy of developing an affective disorder of any type is
1. about 10 percent for males
2. no higher in first-degree relatives of the patient than in the general population
3. higher in females than in males
4. higher for blacks than for whites

**13.32.** The biogenic amine hypothesis of depression is supported by the observation that
1. monoamine oxidase inhibitors (MAOI's) increase brain catecholamines
2. lithium decreases the release of norepinephrine
3. 3-Methoxy-4-hydroxyphenylglycol (MHPG) is decreased in the urine of some depressed patients
4. amphetamine elevates mood

**13.33.** Electroconvulsive therapy is considered a specific treatment for depression
1. with severe psychomotor retardation
2. associated with somatic delusions
3. resistant to antidepressant drugs
4. with suicidal ideation

**13.34.** Which of the following drugs can produce depressive symptoms:
1. Cortisone
2. Levodopa
3. Propranolol
4. Estradiol

**13.35.** Which of the following somatic disorders are causally related to depressive syndromes:
1. Infectious diseases, such as mononucleosis
2. Rheumatoid arthritis
3. Malnutrition
4. Addison's disease

**13.36.** Which of the following drugs may produce a manic response:
1. Steroids
2. Amphetamines
3. Amitriptyline
4. Imipramine

**13.37.** In the elderly, which of the following disorders may mimic affective illness:
1. Pseudodementia
2. Multi-infarct dementia
3. Presenile dementia
4. Pervasive developmental disorder

**13.38.** Which of the following statements concerning the epidemiology of affective disorders are true?
1. The female to male sex ratio in major (unipolar) depression is 2:1, whereas there is no apparent sex difference seen in bipolar disorder.
2. The of onset in unipolar depression peaks in women between ages 35 to 45 and in men after age 55, whereas in bipolar disorder, the onset is usually before age 30.
3. The lifetime expectancy for unipolar depression is 10 percent for men and 20 percent for women, whereas for bipolar disorder, it is approximately 1 percent for both men and women.
4. Unipolar depression is more frequently seen in upper socioeconomic classes, whereas there is no pattern seen in bipolar disorder.

**13.39.** Veraguth's fold may be associated with
1. a major depressive episode
2. persons who are not clinically depressed
3. electromyographic changes in the tone of the corrugator and zygomatic facial muscles
4. the temporomandibular joint

**13.40.** Major depression with psychotic features is characterized by
1. delusions
2. hallucinations
3. stupor
4. posturing

| Directions Summarized | | | | |
|---|---|---|---|---|
| A | B | C | D | E |
| 1, 2, 3, only | 1, 3 only | 2, 4 only | 4 only | All are correct |

**13.41.** A 40-year-old man is brought to the psychiatric emergency room after becoming involved in a fistfight at a bar. He is speaking very rapidly, jumping from one thought to another in response to simple, specific questions (e.g. "When did you come to New York?" "I came to New York, the Big Apple, it's rotten to the core, no matter how you slice it, I sliced a bagel this morning for breakfast ....."). The patient describes experiencing his thoughts as "racing." He is unable to explain how he got into the fight other than to say that the other person was jealous of the patient's obvious sexual prowess, the patient having declared that he had slept with at least 100 women. He makes allusions to his father being God, and he states that he has not slept in 3 days. "I don't need it," he says. The patient's speech is full of amusing puns, jokes, and plays on words.

Associated findings consistent with this patient's probable diagnosis might be

1. nocturnal electroencephalographic (EEG) findings of a decreased total sleep time and a decreased percentage of dream time
2. emotional lability with rapid shifts to brief depression
3. hallucinations, frank delusions, and ideas of reference
4. an episode of less than 1 week's duration

**DIRECTIONS:** Each group of questions below consists of five lettered headings followed by a list of numbered words or statements. For each numbered word or statement, select the *one* lettered heading that is most closely associated with it. Each lettered heading may be selected once, more than once, or not at all.

### Questions 13.42–13.46
A. Mood-incongruent delusion
B. Mood-congruent delusion
C. Both
D. Neither

**13.42.** A 52-year-old suicidal man believes that he is the new Messiah.

**13.43.** A 25-year-old depressed woman believes that she has committed terrible crimes.

**13.44.** A 12-year-old boy thinks he hears voices telling him to jump out of the window.

**13.45.** A 45-year-old man is elated because he believes that he has been reincarnated as a millionaire.

**13.46.** A 30-year-old woman who is negativistic and stuporous believes that she is the Virgin Mary.

# Answers

# Major Affective Disorders

**13.1. The answer is B** (*Synopsis*, ed. 4, page 243).

The dexamethasone suppression test (DST) is a test used to determine the presence of a *major (endogenous) depression* by measuring serum cortisol levels. After administering 1 mg of dexamethasone, serum samples are taken the next day, with approximately 98 percent of patients without major depression showing a suppressed level of cortisol. This suppression is considered a negative finding. If suppression

**Medical Conditions and Pharmacological Agents That May Interfere with Results of the Dexamethasone Suppression Test\***

False-positive results are associated with
  Phenytoin
  Barbiturates
  Meprobamate
  Glutethimide
  Methyprylon
  Methaqualone
  Carbamazepine
  Cardiac failure
  Hypertension
  Renal failure
  Disseminated cancer and serious infections
  Recent major trauma or surgery
  Fever
  Nausea
  Dehydration
  Temporal lobe disease
  High-dosage estrogen treatment
  Pregnancy
  Cushing's disease
  Unstable diabetes mellitus
  Extreme weight loss (malnutrition, anorexia nervosa)
  Alcohol abuse
False-negative results are associated with
  Hypopituitarism
  Addison's disease
  Long-term synthetic steroid therapy
  Indomethacin
  High-dosage cyproheptadine treatment
  High-dosage benzodiazepine treatment

\* From Young M, Stanford J: The dexamethasone suppression test for the detection, diagnosis, and management of depression. Arch Int Med *100:* 309, 1984. Used with permission.

does not occur, as it does not in 50 percent of patients with *major depression*, it is considered a positive finding. This positive finding is associated with serum cortisol levels greater than 4.5 to 5.0 $\mu$g/dl.

False-positive results are associated with a variety of conditions, including the *use of barbiturates, alcohol abuse,* and *dehydration.* False-negative results may be seen in various conditions, including hypopituitarism and Addison's disease, as well as with *the use of indomethacin* and with high dosages of benzodiazepines. The DST is believed to reflect changed activity in the hypothalamic-pituitary-adrenal axis in certain depressed patients. The table in column 1 details conditions and agents that may interfere with DST.

**13.2. The answer is B** (*Synopsis*, ed. 4, page 247).

Depressions with psychotic features are relatively infrequent in current clinical practice. *Only 10 percent* of large samples show delusions, hallucinations, confusion, and other manifestations of impaired reality testing.

For clinical description, however, the term "psychotic" does have some limited clinical usefulness. The description of a psychotic depression implies severe impairment, high suicidal risk, and possible need for hospitalization. Patients with psychotic depressions are difficult to treat and are often refractory to antidepressants, neuroleptics, and electroconvulsive therapy.

**13.3. The answer is C** (*Synopsis*, ed. 4, page 240).

Major depression (unipolar) *shows no conclusive evidence for any difference between blacks and whites,* even though more blacks than whites are hospitalized for affective disorder. The illness is *twice as common in women* than in men, and it *peaks in women between the ages of 35 and 45.* There is *no pattern of depression and social class.*

**13.4. The answer is D** (*Synopsis*, ed. 4, page 241).

*Fifty to sixty percent* of patients who are in remission from bipolar or unipolar depression will have another attack. Episodes usually recur every 3 to 9 years.

**13.5.   The answer is B** (*Synopsis*, ed. 4, pages 238 and 239).

The affective disorders are a group of clinical conditions with a common and essential feature that is described as a disturbance of *mood* accompanied by related cognitive, psychomotor, psychophysiological, and interpersonal difficulties.

*Mood* usually refers to sustained emotional states that color the whole personality and psychic life. It is a pervasive or prevailing emotion that affects the total personality.

*Disturbances of thinking* and *association* are most commonly found in schizophrenia. *Conation* is that part of a person's mental life concerned with strivings, motivations, drives, and wishes as expressed through that person's behavior. *Attention* is the ability to focus one's concentration on a particular task.

**13.6.   The answer is B** (*Synopsis*, ed. 4, page 239).

The student needs to be aware that confusion exists in the field of the nosology of depression. It is best to think of depression as falling into two major categories: *bipolar disorder* (defined by one or more manic episodes) and major or unipolar depression (defined by one or more depressions without manic episodes).

The DSM-III category of affective disorders groups all the affective disorders together. Within that group, the subcategory "major affective disorders" includes bipolar disorder (mixed, manic, or depressed) and major depression (single episode or recurrent). There are two additional categories of affective disorder: other specific affective disorders (*cyclothymic disorder* and *dysthymic disorder*) and atypical affective disorder (atypical bipolar disorder and atypical depression).

*Unipolar* disorder is an affective disorder characterized by recurrent episodes of depression without manic episodes at any time. *Schizoaffective disorder* is a psychotic disorder with signs and symptoms compatible with both an affective disorder and a schizophrenic disorder.

**13.7.   The answer is E** (*Synopsis*, ed. 4, page 251).

Depressive symptoms may be associated with or superimposed on any other psychological disorder. Of particular relevance are *cyclothymic* personality *disorder*—which, by definition, is a syndrome of depressive and manic syndromes not severe enough to be classified as depressive or manic episodes—and *schizophrenia.* That situation may also be true of patients with *alcoholism*—especially when there is a family history of both depression and alcoholism—somatization disorder; and *anxiety disorders*, including

children with separation anxiety disorders who develop the full-blown clinical picture.

**13.8.   The answer is E** (*Synopsis*, ed. 4, page 250).

*Over 60 percent* of the patients hospitalized for cardiac disease are depressed during the course of their hospital stay. After a myocardial infarction, about one-third of the patients develop a depression within 18 months.

**13.9.   The answer is B** (*Synopsis*, ed. 4, page 251).

Depressive syndromes are known to occur after substance use—for example, *reserpine-induced depression*—and in organic illnesses, such as cancers of all types and infectious diseases. In both cases, the disorder is considered an organic affective syndrome secondary to the known causative agent. If a full-blown affective syndrome develops in reaction to a functional impairment secondary to a physical illness, the syndrome is a full-blown affective disorder, and the physical disorder is also diagnosed.

**13.10.   The answer is B** (*Synopsis*, ed. 4, page 245).

The most likely diagnosis for this patient is one of *unipolar major affective disorder.* The patient has had symptoms for 2 months and according to DSM-III, the minimal criterion for length of depression is 2 weeks. Other symptoms illustrated by this case are loss of appetite, hypersomnia, loss of interest or pleasure in usual activities, decreased libido, loss of energy, and recurrent thoughts of death, suicidal ideation, and wishes to kill oneself.

*Bipolar disorders*, by definition, must involve an episode of mania—not seen in this case— either currently or in the past. *Anxiety disorder* is ruled out by the absence of any prominent symptoms of anxiety. *Schizophrenia* is also ruled out because there are no indications of psychotic symptoms, such as hallucinations, delusions, or disorganized thinking.

**13.11.   The answer is E** (*Synopsis*, ed. 4, pages 141, 251, and 652).

A *past psychiatric history* and family history can provide invaluable information as to the patient's clinical picture. Suicide in a parent, for example, increases the risk of suicide in the patient. If a patient has been depressed before, knowing which *medications* have or have not worked can provide the physician with a head start. Knowing if the patient has ever had a period of mania or if the patient has had a recent severe emotional trauma is essential in making the correct diagnosis and formulating an effective treatment plan. For example, a history of a manic episode would be indicative of a bipolar disorder rather than a unipolar one.

*Medical problems,* such as cancer of the pancreas, multiple sclerosis, or a space-occupying lesion of the brain, can all produce depression. Also, certain *substances,* such as alcohol and amphetamines, can mimic the clinical picture of depression.

**13.12.   The answer is A** (*Synopsis,* ed. 4, page 245).

The classical tricyclic antidepressant, namely, *imipramine,* has been shown to be effective in the treatment of depression. The tricyclic antidepressants should be given a careful and adequate trial, being the primary drug of choice for the treatment of depression.

Monoamine oxidase inhibitors, such as *tranylcypromine* and *pargyline,* are indicated only after tricyclic antidepressants have been tried and failed. This precaution is taken because of the serious side effects that are seen with the use of these agents. They are also indicated for certain specific types of depression and in those patients who are refractory or have a suboptimal response to tricyclic antidepressants. Neuroleptics, such as *fluphenazine,* and *phenothiazine,* are useful in schizophrenic disorders.

**13.13.   The answer is C** (*Synopsis,* ed. 4, pages 235 and 248).

The most probable diagnosis for this patient is one of *bipolar disorder, mixed.* The diagnostic criteria, according to DSM-III, indicate the patient is in a manic state, with the presence of mood swings and with a history of depressive episode.

This patient presents with the essential feature of a manic episode, which is a distinct period of intense psychophysiological activation. In that state, the predominant mood is either elevated or irritable, accompanied by one or more of the following symptoms: hyperactivity, the undertaking of too many activities, lack of judgment of the consequences of actions, pressure of speech, flight of ideas, distractibility, inflated self-esteem, hypersexuality, and a feeling of decreased need for sleep.

In *schizoaffective disorders,* as described by DSM-III, there are depressive and manic features that develop with atypical psychotic symptoms. These psychotic symptoms are considered unusual in an uncomplicated affective disorder and are not present in the above case, which illustrates a classical clinical picture of a manic episode.

In *major affective disorder, depressed,* the criteria in DSM-III state that the patient must have experienced one or more depressive episodes and must never have had a previous manic or hypomanic episode.

Patients with *undifferentiated schizophrenia* show classical DSM-III symptomatology of a schizophrenic disorder, with a specific component of disorganization of thoughts and function. This condition must also be present for more than 6 months.

**13.14.   The answer is C** (*Synopsis,* ed. 4, pages 651, 659, 663, and 675).

Most experts favor treating these cases with a combination of *lithium* and *haloperidol* until the desirable behavioral control is accomplished and the patient can be safely managed on lithium alone.

*Lithium carbonate* is the treatment of choice for manic-depressive illness. It has several advantages over neuroleptics, including a greater degree of specificity, as well as ease of monitoring through plasma levels. In addition, lithium lacks the stigma associated with the antischizophrenic drugs and does not produce tardive dyskinesia or sedation. From the patient's perspective, therefore, it is a much more acceptable drug. It should be noted, however, that lithium has a slower onset of action—a 7- to 12-day lag period—which may be a disadvantage in the treatment of highly disturbed manics.

Monoamine oxidase inhibitors (MAOI's), such as *phenelzine,* are not indicated for the treatment of mania for a number of reasons, including poor clinical response and the fact that they tend to agitate and can occasionally cause hypomania or an acute schizophrenic psychosis. MAOI's can also produce an acute confusional reaction, with disorientation, mental clouding, and illusions.

Tricyclic antidepressants, such as *nortriptyline,* are not indicated for the treatment of mania. In particular, the desmethyl derivatives—desipramine and *nortriptyline*—are similar in many pharmacological parameters to their parent compounds, but appear to be more stimulating and may aggravate anxiety, tension, and mania.

Minor tranquilizers, such as the benzodiazepines (*chlordiazepoxide*), are used for the treatment of anxiety and are not indicated for the control of manic symptoms.

**13.15.   The answer is B** (*Synopsis,* ed. 4, page 245).

In some animal experiments in which dogs were exposed to electric shocks from which they could not escape, the dogs reacted with helplessness and made no attempt to escape future shocks. They learned to give up and appeared to be helpless. In humans with *affective disorders* who are depressed, one can find a similar state of helplessness. If the psychiatrist can instill in a depressed patient a sense of control and mastery of the environment, the depression frequently lifts. Similarly, reward and positive re-inforcement from one's environment can often help the patient overcome depression. Those behavioral techniques are used in individual and group therapy.

Other important factors in learned helplessness are reduced voluntary response initiation, a hopeless attitude about the potential effectiveness of one's own responses, decreased aggressive response, diminution of appetite and sex drive, and physiological decrease in norepinephrine.

**13.16.   The answer is D** (*Synopsis*, ed. 4, page 216).

*Schizoaffective disorder* is not classified in DSM-III under affective disorders but is listed separately under "Psychotic Disorders Not Elsewhere Classified." The following table gives the DSM-III classification of Affective Disorders.

**Affective Disorders\***

Major affective disorders
  Bipolar disorder
    mixed
    manic
    depressed
  Major depression
    single episode
    recurrent

Other specific affective disorders
  Cyclothymic disorder
  Dysthymic disorder (Depressive neurosis)

Atypical affective disorders
  Atypical bipolar disorder
  Atypical depression

\* From American Psychiatric Association: *Diagnostic and Statistical Manual of Mental Disorders*, ed 3, American Psychiatric Association, Washington, DC, 1980. Used with permission.

**13.17.   The answer is B** (*Synopsis*, ed. 4, page 244).

In Freud's structural theory, the *introjection* of the lost object into the ego leads to the typical depressive symptoms diagnostic of a lack of energy available to the ego. The superego, unable to retaliate against the lost object externally, flails out at the psychic representation of the lost object, now internalized in the ego as an introject. When the ego overcomes or merges with the superego, there is a release of energy that was previously bound in the depressive symptoms, and a mania supervenes with the typical symptoms of excess.

Later analytic writers have elaborated the basic Abraham-Freud conceptualization in various ways. Although most analytic writers pay lip service to the concept that the disease has an underlying neurophysiological substrate, few attempt to conceptualize that state in any but psychological terms.

Heinz Kohut made significant contributions to the psychology of the self and the treatment of narcissistic personality disorders. Narcissistic personality disorder is one of the frequent differential diagnostic considerations in manic-depressive patients, because patients with narcissistic personality disorder frequently demonstrate transient periods of elation and depression, often with grandiosity and euphoria in one phase and self-depreciation in a succeeding phase, just as is seen in classic manic-depressive disorder.

*Projection* is the unconscious defense mechanism in which a person attributes to another those generally unconscious ideas, thoughts, feelings, and impulses that are personally undesirable or unacceptable. *Sublimation* is an unconscious defense mechanism in which the energy associated with unacceptable impulses or drives is diverted into personally and socially acceptable channels. *Undoing* is an unconscious defense mechanism by which a person symbolically acts out in reverse something unacceptable that has already been done or against which the ego must defend itself. *Altruism* is the regard for and dedication to the welfare of others.

**13.18.   The answer is E (all)** (*Synopsis*, ed. 4, page 246).

There are certain age-associated features of major depression. In early childhood, *separation anxiety* may lead to clinging behavior and school phobia. In latency, and in early-adolescent boys especially, negative and *antisocial behavior* may occur (depressive equivalents). Sexual acting out, truancy, and *running away* are seen in older boys and girls. In the elderly, *pseudodementia*—that is, depression presenting primarily as a loss of intellectual functioning—must be carefully differentiated from true dementia caused by organic mental disorder.

When the depression is mild, environmental changes may lead to some amelioration of the condition; but when the depression is severe, no such effect is found.

**13.19.   The answer is D (4)** (*Synopsis*, ed. 4, page 243).

The dexamethasone suppression test (DST) is a laboratory test used to determine the endogenous depressive state (*major depression with melancholia*). The test consists of administering at bedtime 1 mg of oral dexamethasone and collecting several serial plasma samples on the following day, usually at 8 A.M., 4 P.M., and 11 P.M. Approximately 98 percent of normal patients show a suppressed level of cortisol. That is considered a negative finding. In 50 percent of endogenous depressed patients, however, that suppression does not occur. In those patients, cortisol escapes the suppressive action of dexamethasone, and the finding is considered positive. A serum cortisol level greater than 4.5 to 5.0 μg/dl for any of the blood samples is abnormal. The test is believed to reflect changed activity in the hypothalamic-pituitary-adrenal axis in certain depressed patients.

**13.20. The answer is D (4)** (*Synopsis*, ed. 4, pages 250 and 251).

*Mania* is excluded if any of the following symptoms of schizophrenia are present: (1) delusions of control from outside; (2) delusions of broadcasting thoughts; (3) delusions of insertion of thoughts into the patient's mind; (4) experience of withdrawal of thoughts from the patient's mind; (5) auditory hallucination of a commentary on the patient's behavior or thoughts or of a conversation between voices; (6) auditory hallucination not related to levels of depression or elation; (7) monoideatic delusions or hallucination other than those related to delusions of poverty, guilt, and self-depreciation; (8) persistence of delusions or hallucinations 1 month after the resolution of the affective state within which they were experienced.

*Schizophrenia* is a psychotic mental disorder characterized by disturbances in thinking, mood, and behavior. *Paranoia* is a rare psychiatric syndrome marked by the gradual development of a highly elaborate and complex delusional system, generally involving persecutory or grandiose delusions, with few other signs of personality disorganization or thought disorder. *Toxic psychosis* is a psychosis caused by toxic substances produced by the body or introduced into it in the form of chemicals or drugs.

**13.21. The answer is E (all)** (*Synopsis*, ed. 4, page 241).

Bipolar disorder has an *onset usually before age 30*. There is *no difference in incidence* between men and women. It is *more frequent* among persons in the *upper socioeconomic groups* and among *divorced persons*.

**13.22. The answer is E (all)** (*Synopsis*, ed. 4, pages 246 and 247).

About 50 percent of the inpatients who have a major depressive episode have melancholic symptom features. These features include a *positive response to tricyclics and electroconvulsive therapy (ECT) and a negative response to psychotherapy; a central group of symptoms*—such as retardation, early morning awakening, weight loss, guilt, and unreactivity—*occurring together; a difficulty in eliciting a history of recent stressful life* or precipitating events; a correlation with age—*old patients are affected more frequently;* and a correlation with personality. That is, patients suffering from melancholia are more likely to have had a more stable, nonneurotic form of premorbid personality. The table below lists the DSM-III criteria for melancholia.

**13.23. The answer is C (2, 4)** (*Synopsis*, ed. 4, page 248).

Nocturnal electroencephalographic findings in mania are of a *decreased total sleep time* and a *decreased percentage of dream time*, as well as an *increased dream latency*. Those findings may be interpreted as supportive of the hypothesis that circadian rhythm activities are delayed in mania because of an *increase in the activity of the intrinsic pacemaker*.

**13.24. The answer is A (1, 2, 3,)** (*Synopsis*, ed. 4, page 241).

Family studies found relatives of bipolar patients to have a significantly *higher risk for bipolar illness than for unipolar illness*, but *relatives of unipolar patients were more at risk for unipolar illness* than bipolar illness. *Twin studies indicate significantly greater risk in monozygotic twins than in dizygotic twins* for similar affective disease processes.

Monozygotic twins reared apart show about a

---

### Diagnostic Criteria for Melancholia*

Loss of pleasure in all or almost all activities, lack of reactivity to usually pleasurable stimuli (doesn't feel much better, even temporarily, when something good happens), and at least three of the following:

1. Distinct quality of depressed mood; that is, the depressed mood is perceived as distinctly different from the kind of feeling experienced after the death of a loved one;
2. The depression is regularly worse in the morning;
3. Early-morning awakening (at least two hours before usual time of awakening);
4. Marked psychomotor retardation or agitation;
5. Significant anorexia or weight loss;
6. Excessive or inappropriate guilt.

---

* From American Psychiatric Association: *Diagnostic and Statistical Manual of Mental Disorders*, ed 3. American Psychiatric Association, Washington, DC, 1980. Used with permission.

*65 percent concordance rate* for affective disorder.

**13.25.    The answer is C (2, 4)** (*Synopsis,* ed. 4, page 241).

Two subgroups of major depression patients—early-onset females (onset before age 40) and late-onset males (onset after age 40)—have been described. Those subgroups demonstrate family members with very different illnesses. In the families of late-onset male probands, one finds *depression as often in the males as in the females,* and one finds *little alcoholism or sociopathy in male relatives.* In the families of early-onset female probands, however, one finds more depression in female relatives than in male relatives, and one finds more alcoholism and sociopathy in male relatives than in the other families. Those findings have been generalized to form two prototype subgroups: depression spectrum disease (early-onset females) and pure depressive disease (late-onset males). The findings require further confirmation.

There is *no greater incidence of schizophrenia* in relatives of unipolar depression patients than in the general population.

**13.26.    The answer is E (all)** (*Synopsis,* ed. 4, page 246).

A major depressive episode is characterized by *dysphoric mood* and such symptoms as poor appetite, *insomnia,* feelings of worthlessness, and *suicidal ideation.* The symptoms must be present nearly every day for a period of *at least 2 weeks.* For a complete summary of the DSM-III diagnostic criteria for major depressive episode, see the table below.

**13.27.    The answer is A (1, 2, 3)** (*Synopsis,* ed. 4, page 242).

Serotonin is a *biogenic amine* distributed in the central nervous system, and some depressed patients have been found to have a decreased serotonin metabolite, 5-hydroxyindoleacetic acid (*5-HIAA*), in their cerebrospinal fluid. The findings are not consistent, however, in that the amount of 5-HIAA derived from brain tissue or from noncentral nervous system sites has not been determined.

Another piece of evidence that suggests the involvement of serotonin in depression is the observation that *tryptophan,* a serotonin precursor, relieves depression in some patients. Also,

---

### Diagnostic Criteria for Major Depressive Episode*

A. Dysphoric mood or loss of interest or pleasure in all or almost all usual activities and pastimes. The dysphoric mood is characterized by symptoms such as the following: depressed, sad, blue, hopeless, low, down in the dumps, irritable. The mood disturbance must be prominent and relatively persistent, but not necessarily the most dominant symptom, and does not include momentary shifts from one dysphoric mood to another, e.g. anxiety to depression to anger, such as are seen in states of acute psychotic turmoil. (For children under 6, dysphoric mood may have to be inferred from a persistently sad facial expression.)

B. At least four of the following symptoms have each been present nearly every day for a period of at least 2 weeks (in children under 6, at least three of the first four symptoms):

1. Poor appetite or significant weight loss (when not dieting) or increased appetite or significant weight gain (in children under 6, consider failure to make expected weight gains);
2. Insomnia or hypersomnia;
3. Psychomotor agitation or retardation (but not merely subjective feelings of restlessness or being slowed down) (in children under 6, hypoactivity);
4. Loss of interest or pleasure in usual activities, or decrease in sexual drive not limited to a period when delusional or hallucinating (in children under 6, signs of apathy);
5. Loss of energy, fatigue;
6. Feelings of worthlessness, self-reproach, or excessive or inappropriate guilt (either may be delusional);
7. Complaints or evidence of diminished ability to think or concentrate, such as slowed thinking, or indecisiveness not associated with marked loosening of associations or incoherence;
8. Recurrent thoughts of death, suicidal ideation, wishes to be dead, or suicidal attempt.

C. Neither of the following dominates the clinical picture when an affective syndrome (i.e., criteria A and B above) is not present; that is, before it developed or after it has remitted:

1. Preoccupation with a mood-incongruent delusion or hallucination
2. Bizarre behavior

D. Not superimposed on either schizophrenia, schizophreniform disorder, or a paranoid disorder.

E. Not due to any organic mental disorder or uncomplicated bereavement.

\* From American Psychiatric Association: *Diagnostic and Statistical Manual of Mental Disorders,* ed 3. American Psychiatric Association, Washington, DC, 1980. Used with permission.

*reserpine depletes brain serotonin*, and antidepressants increase brain serotonin activity.

Studies have shown a possible altered serotonin rhythmicity, rather than an absolute deficiency, in particular subgroups of depression. It has been reported that platelet serotonin, which shows a normal diurnal rhythmicity, was desynchronized in unipolar depressives, especially among postmenopausal women.

**13.28. The answer is C (2, 4)** (*Synopsis,* ed. 4, page 244).

It is widely believed that persons prone to depression are characterized by *low self-esteem, strong superego*, clinging and dependent interpersonal relations, and limited capacity for mature and enduring object relations. Although those traits are common among depressives, no single personality trait, constellation, or type has been established as uniquely predisposed to depression. All humans, of whatever personality pattern, can and do become depressed under appropriate circumstances, although certain personality types—the oral-dependent, the obsessive-compulsive, and the hysterical—may be at greater risk for depression than the antisocial, the paranoid, and certain other types who use projection and other externalizing modes of defense.

The essential feature of the *paranoid personality* is the long-standing suspiciousness and mistrust of people in general. Paranoid personalities are further distinguished by the fact that they refuse responsibility for their own feelings and assign responsibility to others.

*Object relations* is the emotional attachment that one person forms with another, as opposed to interest in and love for oneself.

**13.29. The answer is A (1, 2, 3)** (*Synopsis,* ed. 4, pages 242 and 243).

Basal secretions of growth hormone (GH) by the pituitary gland are normally augmented in response to a drop in blood sugar, starvation, stress, exercise, and estrogens. A conventional test of GH activity involves the administration of insulin, followed by the measurement of the expected rise in plasma GH levels. Using this method, investigators have repeatedly demonstrated that, in many instances of depression, there is a *diminished response to such insulininduced hypoglycemia*. The phenomenon is noted most often in unipolar depressions. In *biopolar depressions the response is normal or enhanced. GH release is impaired in a significant percentage of postmenopausal women with diagnosed unipolar depression.*

A number of clinical and laboratory investigations have demonstrated an association between maternal deprivation and inhibition of

GH secretion. It is noted among human infants with the *failure-to-thrive (FTT) syndrome*. Similar findings have been noted in rat pups who are removed from their mothers soon after birth. When the pups are returned to their mothers, there is a rapid reversal of the deprivationinduced GH abnormality.

Control of GH release seems to reside in catecholinergic neurons. GH release is increased by dopaminergic stimulation.

**13.30. The answer is C (2, 4)** (*Synopsis,* ed. 4, pages 243 and 244).

A significant proportion of depressed patients exhibit an absent or *diminished thyroid-stimulating hormone (TSH) response to thyrotropinreleasing hormone (TRH) challenge*.

Additional changes in neuroendocrine activity have been discerned. Prolactin levels may exhibit irregular circadian rhythm, and *luteinizing hormone (LH) secretion is often diminished* in depressed postmenopausal women.

Periodic variations in physiological and psychological functions occur. Circadian rhythm shows a periodicity of about 24 hours. Sleep is one such periodic state, divided into REM and non-REM periods.

Polysomnograph studies show that in a major depression there is decreased total sleep time, an increased percentage of dream time, and a *decreased REM latency* (the time between falling asleep and the first REM period). There is also a very long first REM period.

In mania there is a *decreased percentage of dream (REM) time*. That finding has led to the idea of depriving depressed patients of dream time (REM sleep) to see if their mood improves. When depressed patients are deprived of sleep for one or two nights (and thus of dreaming), mood does appear to improve somewhat.

**13.31. The answer is B (1, 3)** (*Synopsis,* ed. 4, pages 240 and 241).

The lifetime expectancy of developing an affective disorder of any type is about *20 percent for females* and *10 percent for males*. For Western nations, if attention is limited to bipolar disorder, lifetime expectancy is about 1 percent for both sexes. If broadly defined depressions of all types are included, however, lifetime expectancy rates increase markedly, going as high as 30 percent in some estimates.

A considerable proportion of persons with depression never see a physician. In all categories of depression, only 20 to 25 percent of depressed people receive treatment. Reported prevalence and incidence figures must be viewed as minimum estimates.

There is no conclusive evidence for any differences between *blacks and whites*; however, more blacks than whites are hospitalized for affective disorders.

The *first-degree relatives* of unipolar depressives show a lifetime risk of 20 percent for affective disorder. The first-degree relatives of bipolar patients show a lifetime risk of 25 percent for an affective disorder.

**13.32.   The answer is E (all)** (*Synopsis*, ed. 4, page 242).

The biogenic amines include three catecholamines: dopamine, norepinephrine, and epinephrine. Indolamine is another biogenic amine represented by serotonin, and acetylcholine is also a biogenic amine. The catecholamine hypothesis is based, in part, on the observations that such drugs as the monoamine oxidase inhibitors (MAOI's) and tricyclic antidepressants, which potentiate or *increase brain catecholamines*, cause behavior stimulation and excitement and have an antidepressant effect. Conversely, drugs that deplete or inactivate central amines produce sedation or depression. *Lithium carbonate, effective in the treatment of mania, decreases the release and increases the reuptake of norepinephrine.*

Some studies have shown that there may be a shortage of brain norepinephrine in depression. A metabolite 3-methoxy-4-hydroxyphenyl glycol (*MHPG*) *has been found to be decreased in the cerebrospinal fluid and urine of depressed patients.* Drugs that reduce norepinephrine levels, such as methyldopapropranolol and reserpine, may cause depression, and *amphetamine, which causes synaptic release of norepinephrine, causes elevated mood.*

**13.33.   The answer is E (all)** (*Synopsis*, ed. 4, page 253).

Electroconvulsive therapy (ECT) is regarded by many as a specific therapy for those *retarded depressions* characterized by *somatic delusions* and delusional guilt, accompanied by a lack of interest in the world, *suicidal ideation*, and weight loss. It is also used in less severe depression that is *resistant to antidepressant drugs.* Historically, the emergence of antidepressant drugs lessened the use of ECT in depression. In many respects that was unfortunate, for although ECT has the reputation among some persons of being brutal, morbidity and mortality after its use have been reported to be lower than that seen after the use of antidepressants. In addition, ECT is used to terminate a mania when all other measures fail.

**13.34.   The answer is E (all)** (*Synopsis*, ed. 4, page 251).

The table below lists some of the pharmacological agents that can produce depression.

**13.35.   The answer is E (all)** (*Synopsis*, ed. 4, page 250).

The table on the facing page lists some of the somatic disorders that may be causally related to depression.

**Pharmacological Agents**

| Product Category | Chemical Name | Product Company Name and Pharmaceutical |
|---|---|---|
| Antineoplastics | *Mitotane* | Lysodren (Bristol) |
| | Asparaginase, MDS | Elspar (Merck, Sharp, & Dohme) |
| Antiparkinsonism drugs | *Levodopa*-carbidopa | Sinemet (Merck, Sharp, & Dohme) |
| | Amantadine hydrochloride | Symmetrel (Endo) |
| Adrenal cortical steroids | *Cortisone* acetate | Cortisone Acetate Tablets (Upjohn) |
| Antibacterials | Cycloserine | Seromycin (Lilly) |
| Cardiovascular preparations | *Propranolol* | Inderal (Ayerst) |
| | Metoprolol tartrate | Lopressor (Geigy) |
| | Prazosin hydrochloride | Minipress (Pfizer) |
| | Rescinnamine | Moderil (Pfizer) |
| | Pindolol | Visken (Sandoz) |
| | Atenolol | Tenormin (Stuart) |
| | Quanabenz acetate | Wytensin (Wyeth) |
| Progestational agents | Norethindrone acetate | Norlutate (Parke-Davis) |
| | Norgestrel | Ovrette (Wyeth) |
| Estrogen Agents | *Estradiol* | Estrace (Mead Johnson) |

## Somatic Disorders

| | |
|---|---|
| *Addison's* or Cushing's disease | A deficiency or excess of adrenocortico steroids has a variable effect on mood. |
| *Rheumatoid arthritis* | Between 40 and 50 percent of patients show depressive features. |
| *Infectious diseases* | Particularly virus diseases, e.g. *mononucleosis.* |
| *Various neoplasms* | Depression is sometimes the first manifestation. More than 40 percent of cancer patients, especially those receiving chemotherapy, show depressive symptoms. |
| *Malnutrition* | Elderly people, because of poor eating habits and impaired absorption, are highly susceptible to protein and vitamin (B) deficiencies and resulting depression. |

**13.36.   The answer is E (all)** (*Synopsis*, ed. 4, page 250).

Certain substances used to treat somatic illnesses may trigger a manic response. The most commonly encountered manic response is to *steroids.* Cases exist in which spontaneous manic and depressive episodes originated some years later in patients whose first illness episode seemed to be triggered by the steroids used to treat an organic illness. Other drugs are also known to have the potential for initiating a manic syndrome, e.g. *amphetamines* and tricyclic antidepressants, such as *imipramine* and *amitriptyline.*

**13.37.   The answer is A (1, 2, 3)** (*Synopsis*, ed. 4, page 251).

Senile, *presenile*, and *multi-infarct dementia* must be differentiated from depressive episodes in the elderly. In the case of *pseudodementia*, the depression presents with symptoms mimicking an organic state that clears with appropriate treatment of the depression. In the dementias, treatment of the depression is not rewarding.

*Pervasive developmental disorder* is a disorder characterized by severe distortions in the development of social skills, language, and contact with reality. It occurs in children.

**13.38.   The answer is A (1, 2, 3)** (*Synopsis*, ed. 4, page 240).

Bipolar disorder is more frequently seen in people of upper socioeconomic class, whereas unipolar or major depression does not appear to correlate with socioeconomic class. The table on page 154 outlines in more detail the specific epidemiology of affective disorders.

**13.39.   The answer is A (1, 2, 3)** (*Synopsis*, ed. 4, page 247).

The Swiss neuropsychiatrist, Veraguth, first described a particular triangular-shaped fold in the *nasal corner of the upper eyelid.* Veraguth felt this fold was often associated with depression, either in patients with a *major depressive episode* or in *individuals who were not clinically depressed* but were displaying a mild depressive affect. In fact, distinct *changes in the tone of the corrugator and zygomatic facial muscles* have been electromyographically shown to accompany depression, and they may be responsible for Veraguth's fold. The figure that follows on page 154 illustrates the fold.

**13.40.   The answer is E (all)** (*Synopsis*, ed. 4, page 248).

Major depression with psychotic thinking shows a loss of reality testing with *hallucinations* and *delusions.* Catatonic symptoms, such as *stupor, posturing*, or negativism, may be present. The disorder is distinguished from schizophrenia by the absence of fragmented thinking and other signs of schizophrenia. Mood-incongruent delusions usually point toward a schizophrenic diagnosis. (See table at the top of page 155).

**13.41.   The answer is A (1, 2, 3)** (*Synopsis*, ed. 4, page 249).

The patient is experiencing a manic episode, characterized by a change from his normal mood to a predominantly elevated, expansive, or irritable mood. The *mood may be labile, with rapid shifts to brief depression.* The essential feature is a distinct period of intense psychophysiological activation with a number of accompanying symptoms, including lack of judgment of the consequence of actions, pressure of speech, flight of ideas, inflated self-esteem, and hypersexuality. *Delusional grandiosity, hallucinations* of any type, and *ideas of reference* may be present. *Nocturnal electroencephalography (EEG) findings in mania have shown a decreased total sleep*

**Epidemiology of Affective Disorders in Western Industrialized Nations**

|  | Major Depression (Unipolar) | Bipolar Disorder |
|---|---|---|
| Prevalence (No. of cases at a point in time) | 2–3 cases/100 men (2–3%)<br>5–9 cases/100 women (5–9%) | 0.6–0.9 cases/100 men and women combined |
| Incidence (No. of new cases per year) | 82–201 new cases/100,000 per year for men<br>247–598 new cases/100,000 per year for women (Only 20–25% of people receive treatment for depression) | 9–15.2 cases/100,000 per year for men (0.009–0.015%)<br>7.4–30 cases/100,000 per year for women (0.007–0.030%) |
| Sex | *2:1, women:men* | *No apparent difference* |
| Age | *Peaks in women at ages 35–45, peaks in men after 55,* and then increases with age | *Onset usually before age 30* |
| Social class | *No pattern* | *More frequent in upper socioeconomic class* |
| Race | No conclusive data for blacks and whites | No relationship |
| Family history | Increased risk with family history of depression or alcoholism | Increased risk with family history of bipolar illness |
| Childhood experiences | Increased risk with parental loss before age 11 | Inconclusive |
| Marital status | Increased risk in those who lack close relationship with another person | More common among divorced persons |
| Lifetime expectancy | *10 % for men*<br>*20 % for women* | *0.9–1.1 % for men*<br>*0.6–1.3 % for women* |

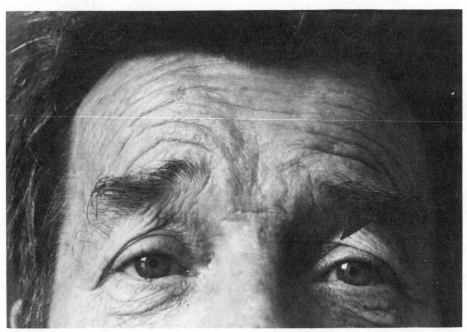

**This illustration shows the physiognomic feature in a 50-year-old man during a major depressive episode. (Courtesy of Heinz E Lehmann, MD.)**

*time and a decreased percentage of dream time,* as well as an increased dream latency. These findings have been interpreted as indicating that circadian rhythm activities are delayed in mania because the activity of the intrinsic pacemaker is increased. The diagnosis of manic episode requires a *disturbance of affect lasting at least 1 week.*

## Major Depression with Psychotic Features*

This category should be used when there apparently is gross impairment in reality testing, as when there are delusions or hallucinations or grossly bizarre behavior. When possible, specify whether the psychotic features are mood-incongruent. (The non-ICD-9-CM fifth-digit 7 may be used instead to indicate that the psychotic features are mood-incongruent; otherwise, mood-congruence may be assumed.)

*Mood-congruent Psychotic Features:* Delusions or hallucinations whose content is entirely consistent with the themes of inflated worth, power, knowledge, identity, or special relationship to a deity or famous person; flight of ideas without apparent awareness by the individual that the speech is not understandable.

*Mood-incongruent Psychotic Features:* Either (a) or (b):
(a) Delusions or hallucinations whose content does not involve themes of either inflated worth, power, knowledge, identity, or special relationship to a deity or famous person. Included are such symptoms as persecutory delusions, thought insertion, and delusions of being controlled, whose content has no apparent relationship to any of the themes noted above.
(b) Any of the following catatonic symptoms: stupor, mutism, negativism, posturing.

* From American Psychiatric Association: *Diagnostic and Statistical Manual of Mental Disorders*, ed 3. American Psychiatric Association, Washington, DC, 1980. Used with permission.

The table below lists the DSM-III diagnostic criteria for manic episode.

**13.42–13.46. The answers are 13.42–A, 13.43–B, 13.44–D, 13.45–B, and 13.46–A** (*Synopsis*, ed. 4, page 248).

A mood-incongruent delusion is characterized by content that is not consistent with the patient's mood. Thus, a depressed patient who has delusions of inflated worth, power, identity or a special relationship to a deity or famous person would have a mood-incongruent delusion, as in the case of a *suicidal man who believes that he is the Messiah* or a *30-year-old depressed woman who believes she is the Virgin Mary.* Mood-congruent delusions are those that are consistent with the patient's mood. An *elated man who believes himself to be a millionaire* or a *depressed woman who thinks she has committed terrible crimes* is suffering from a mood-congruent delusion. The *patient who hears voices* is experiencing a hallucination, and hallucinations can also be described as either mood-congruent or mood-incongruent.

### Diagnostic Criteria for Manic Episode*

A. One or more distinct periods with a predominantly elevated, expansive, or irritable mood. The elevated or irritable mood must be a prominent part of the illness and relatively persistent, although it may alternate or intermingle with depressive mood.

B. Duration of at least 1 week (or any duration if hospitalization is necessary), during which, for most of the time, at least three of the following symptoms have persisted (four if the mood is only irritable) and have been present to a significant degree:

1. Increase in activity (either socially, at work, or sexually) or physical restlessness;
2. More talkative than usual or pressure to keep talking;
3. Flight of ideas or subjective experience that thoughts are racing;
4. Inflated self-esteem (grandiosity, which may be delusional);
5. Decreased need for sleep;
6. Distractibility, i.e. attention is too easily drawn to unimportant or irrelevant external stimuli;
7. Excessive involvement in activities that have a high potential for painful consequences, which is not recognized, e.g. buying sprees, sexual indiscretions, foolish business investments, reckless driving.

C. Neither of the following dominates the clinical picture when an affective syndrome, i.e. criteria A and B above, is not present; that is, before it developed or after it has remitted:

1. Preoccupation with a mood-incongruent delusion or hallucination;
2. Bizarre behavior.

D. Not superimposed on either schizophrenia, schizophreniform disorder, or a paranoid disorder.

E. Not due to any organic mental disorder, such as substance intoxication.

* From American Psychiatric Association: *Diagnostic and Statistical Manual of Mental Disorders*, ed 3. American Psychiatric Association, Washington, DC, 1980. Used with permission.

# References

Cancro R: Affective disorders: Overview. In *Comprehensive Textbook of Psychiatry*, ed 4, H I Kaplan, B J Sadock, editors, p 760. Williams & Wilkins, Baltimore, 1985.

Davidson J: Comparative diagnostic criteria for melancholia and endogenous depression. Arch Gen Psychiatry *41:* 506, 1984.

Georgotas A: Affective disorders: Pharmacotherapy. In *Comprehensive Textbook of Psychiatry*, ed 4, H I Kaplan, B J Sadock, editors, p 821. Williams & Wilkins, Baltimore, 1985.

Georgotas A, Cooper T, Kim M, Hapworth W: The treatment of affective disorders in the elderly. Psychopharmacol Bull *19:* 226, 1983.

Gershon E S, Hamovit J, Guroff J J, Dibble E, Leckman J F, Sceery W, Targum S D, Nurnberger J I, Jr, Goldin L R, Bunney W E, Jr: A family study of schizoaffective, bipolar I, bipolar II, unipolar, and normal control probands. Arch Gen Psychiatry *39:* 1157, 1982.

Gershon E S, Nurnberger J I, Jr, Goldin L R, Berrettini W H: Affective disorders: Genetics. In *Comprehensive Textbook of Psychiatry*, ed 4, H I Kaplan, B J Sadock, editors, p 778. Williams & Wilkins, Baltimore, 1985.

Hirshfeld R M, Shea M T: Affective disorders: Psychosocial treatment. In *Comprehensive Textbook of Psychiatry*, ed 4, H I Kaplan, B J Sadock, editors, p 811. Williams & Wilkins, Baltimore, 1985.

Lehman H E: Affective disorders: Clinical features. In *Comprehensive Textbook of Psychiatry*, ed 4, H I Kaplan, B J Sadock, editors, p 786. Williams & Wilkins, Baltimore, 1985.

Nurnberger J I, Jr, Gershon E S: Genetics of affective disorders. In *Neurobiology of Mood Disorders*, R M Post, J C Ballenger, editors, p 76. Williams & Wilkins, Baltimore, 1984.

Schildkraut J J, Green A I, Mooney J J: Affective disorders: Biochemical aspects. In *Comprehensive Textbook of Psychiatry*, ed 4, H I Kaplan, B J Sadock, editors, p 769. Williams & Wilkins, Baltimore, 1985.

Weissman M M, Boyd J H: Affective disorders: Epidemiology. In *Comprehensive Textbook of Psychiatry*, ed 4, H I Kaplan, B J Sadock, editors, p 764. Williams & Wilkins, Baltimore, 1985.

# 14

# Other Specific Affective Disorders: Dysthymic and Cyclothymic Disorders

The essential features characterizing both dysthymia and cyclothymia are long-standing disturbances of mood. The symptoms are usually not severe enough to meet the criteria for a major affective disorder, hence their classification in DSM-III under the rubric of other specific affective disorders.

To a large extent, the differentiation between a major depressive episode and a dysthymic disorder is based on the degree of severity of the illness. Dysthymia is a more mild form of major depression and has fewer symptoms. In addition, dysthymia is a chronic condition that, on completion of a careful history, can be noted to have been present for years; whereas major depression is characterized by a more precipitous change from the person's previous behavior. In a similar fashion, cyclothymia is a less severe version of manic-depressive illness and has fewer symptoms.

The prevalence of these disorders, using the DSM-III diagnostic criteria, is currently undergoing extensive investigations. Preliminary data indicate that dysthymia is one of the four categories of mental illness most frequently diagnosed in both men and women.

Students should review Chapter 14 of *Modern Synopsis-IV*, "Other Specific Affective Disorders," and should then assess their knowledge of these disorders by studying the questions and answers that follow.

# Questions

**DIRECTIONS:** Each of the statements or questions below is followed by five suggested responses or completions. Select the *one* that is *best* in each case.

**14.1.** Which of the following symptoms is incompatible with dysthymic disorder:

A. Weight change
B. Suicidal ideas
C. Delusions of guilt
D. Decreased sexual performance
E. Sleep difficulty

**14.2.** The reported lifetime prevalence of cyclothymia is

A. less than 1 percent
B. 2 percent
C. 5 percent
D. 10 percent
E. 15 percent

**14.3.** A 25-year-old junior executive is referred to the health service because he has been drinking excessively over the past 2 weeks. The patient reports that he has been "down" for about a month, cries frequently, and has no interest in sex or work. The history reveals that he has suffered these down periods for several years; but he also describes himself as having experienced periods of elation during which he was gregarious, productive, and optimistic. During these latter times, he says he does not drink at all.

The young man also states that this type of behavior has been present "on and off" since he was about 15 years old.

The patient is suffering from

A. manic-depressive illness (bipolar disorder)
B. alcohol dependence
C. cyclothymia
D. dysthymia
E. major depression (unipolar disorder)

**14.4.** The lifetime prevalence for dysthymic disorder is

A. 5 cases per 1,000 persons
B. 10 cases per 1,000 persons
C. 20 cases per 1,000 persons
D. 35 cases per 1,000 persons
E. 45 cases per 1,000 persons

**DIRECTIONS:** For each of the incomplete statements below, *one* or *more* of the completions given is correct. Choose answer:

A. if only **1, 2,** and **3** are correct
B. if only **1** and **3** are correct
C. if only **2** and **4** are correct
D. if only **4** is correct
E. if all are correct

**14.5.** In cyclothymia

1. the mood cycles alternate biphasically
2. there may be episodes of normal mood for long periods of time
3. the patient may be irritable during the elated phase
4. nihilistic delusions may appear during the depressed phase

**14.6.** Drugs useful in the treatment of dysthymic disorder include

1. monoamine oxidase inhibitors (MAOI's)
2. tricyclic antidepressants
3. alprazolam
4. amphetamine

**14.7.** Cyclothymia is considered an attenuated form of bipolar disorder because

1. there is a similarity of symptoms in the two disorders
2. a significant number of cyclothymic patients eventually develop a bipolar disorder
3. both disorders respond to lithium
4. there may be a hypomanic response to tricyclic drugs among cyclothymic patients

**14.8.** Dysthymic disorder is characterized by

1. depressed mood
2. long duration (more than 2 years)
3. onset in young adulthood
4. hallucinations

**DIRECTIONS:** Each set of lettered headings below is followed by a list of numbered words or phrases. For each numbered word or phrase, select

    A. if the item is associated with **A** *only*
    B. if the item is associated with **B** *only*
    C. if the item is associated with *both* **A** *and* **B**
    D. if the item is associated with *neither* **A** *nor* **B**

**Questions 14.9–14.14**
    A. Dysthymic disorder
    B. Cyclothymic disorder
    C. Both
    D. Neither

**14.9.** Treatment with antidepressants, possibly leading to hypomanic symptoms

**14.10.** Delusions and hallucinations

**14.11.** Response to lithium

**14.12.** Alcohol abuse

**14.13.** Sexual promiscuity

**14.14.** Often confused with drug abuse

# Answers

# Other Specific Affective Disorders: Dysthymic and Cyclothymic Disorders

**14.1.  The answer is C** (*Synopsis*, ed. 4, pages 256 and 257).

The presence of delusions and hallucinations is by definition inconsistent with the diagnosis of dysthymic disorder. Among the associated symptoms are those commonly associated with depressive episodes, including poor appetite, *weight change, sleep difficulty* (particularly early-morning wakening), loss of energy, fatigability, psychomotor retardation, loss of interest or pleasure in activities, decreased sexual drive, *decreased sexual performance*, feelings of guilt (*not delusions of guilt*) and self-reproach, obsessive preoccupation with health, complaints of difficulty in thinking, indecisiveness, *thoughts of suicide*, feelings of helplessness and hopelessness, and pessimism.

Among the signs of decreased sexual performance in male patients is impotence, the inability to achieve a penile erection. In DSM-III, impotence is classified as a psychosexual dysfunction with inhibited sexual excitement.

Weight change in dysthymia is usually decreased, but at times, depressed patients may gain weight.

**14.2.  The answer is A** (*Synopsis*, ed. 4, page 259).

The reported lifetime prevalence of cyclothymia is *less than 1 percent*. This figure was reported by investigators from an epidemiologic study known as the New Haven Community Study. It is likely, however, that this figure is underestimated because of the variability of the diagnostic criteria and the reluctance of persons with cyclothymic disorder to identify themselves as patients.

**14.3.  The answer is C** (*Synopsis*, ed. 4, page 260).

The patient is suffering from a *cyclothymic disorder* in that he has symptoms of both depression and hypomania. His "down" or depressed periods are marked by crying and loss of interest in sex and work, and his excessive use of alcohol during these times is a defense against depression and not the primary illness from which he suffers. When elated, the patient is gregarious, optimistic, and productive. It is

rare for such patients to come to the attention of psychiatrists at such times of elation. If, however, the manic episodes become more severe, with specific symptoms, such as physical recklessness or buying sprees, medical intervention may occur.

The essential feature of a major depressive (unipolar) episode is a severe dysphoric mood and persistent loss of interest or pleasure in all usual activities. Because of the hypomanic episodes and the mild depressive symptoms, a *unipolar disorder* is ruled out.

*Alcohol dependence* is a pattern of alcohol use, characterized by tolerance or withdrawal, that causes impairment in social or occupational functioning. For this diagnosis to be made, the pattern of use must continue for a month, rather than for 2 weeks as in this case.

*Manic-depressive illness* (bipolar disorder) is characterized by severe alterations in mood that are usually episodic and recurrent. The depressed type is characterized by severe episodes of depression; the manic type, by severe episodes of mania; and the mixed type, by both mania and depression intermixed, or rapidly alternating every few days. The patient in this case has affective changes similar to those seen in manic-depressive illness, but the mildness of his symptoms preclude the full diagnosis of bipolar disorder.

A diagnosis of *dysthymia* is excluded because the patient shows episodes of elated moods. In dysthymia, the patient's mood is one of chronic depression; in adult patients, a 2-year history of such depression is required before this diagnosis can be ascertained.

**14.4.  The answer is E** (*Synopsis*, ed. 4, page 255).

The lifetime prevalence for dysthymic disorder has been reported by a number of studies to be *45 cases per 1,000 persons*. It is a fairly common illness.

**14.5.  The answer is A (1, 2, 3)** (*Synopsis*, ed. 4, page 260).

The essential features of cyclothymic disorder are chronic disturbances involving frequent periods during which there are nonpsychotic symptoms characteristic of both depressive and manic syndromes. There is an absence of psychotic features, such as delusions, during both the depressive and manic phases. Thus, *nihilistic delusions*—the delusion that the world has ceased to exist—*during the depressive phase* would preclude the diagnosis of cyclothymia.

In this disorder, the patient's symptoms are usually not of sufficient severity or duration to meet the criteria for a full-blown manic or depressive episode. Usually, the manifestations of the *mood cycles alternate biphasically*, or they may be intermixed. In other cases there may be *periods as long as several months of relatively normal mood*. During the periods of affective change, the symptoms related to either depression or mania are present in a mild form. *During the elated phase, the patient may be irritable* or have an elevated or expansive mood. There may

also be decreased sleep need, increased productivity, unusual self-imposed working habits, a sense of increased capacity for attention and concentration, and sharpened or unusual creative thinking. Characteristic of the hypomanic or elated phase are episodes of buying sprees, with financial extravagance, gift-giving, and excessive indulgence. The sprees may be severe enough to produce business failure and bankruptcy. There may be frequent job changes, periods of sexual promiscuity, or religious or political changes.

The table below lists in detail the DSM-III criteria for cyclothymia.

**14.6.   The answer is E (all)** (*Synopsis*, ed. 4, page 259).

Many dysthymic patients respond to *tricyclic antidepressants*, and *monoamine oxidase inhibi-*

---

### Diagnostic Criteria for Cyclothymic Disorder*

A. During the past 2 years, numerous periods during which some symptoms characteristic of both the depressive and the manic syndromes were present but were not of sufficient severity and duration to meet the criteria for a major depressive or manic episode.

B. The depressive periods and hypomanic periods may be separated by periods of normal mood lasting as long as months at a time; they may be intermixed, or they may alternate.

C. During depressive periods there is depressed mood or loss of interest or pleasure in all, or almost all, usual activities and pastimes, and there are at least three of the following:

During hypomanic periods there is an elevated, expansive, or irritable mood and at least three of the following:

| | |
|---|---|
| 1. Insomnia or hypersomnia; | 1. Decreased need for sleep; |
| 2. Low energy or chronic fatigue; | 2. More energy than usual; |
| 3. Feelings of inadequacy; | 3. Inflated self-esteem; |
| 4. Decreased effectiveness or productivity at school, work, or home; | 4. Increased productivity, often associated with unusual and self-imposed working hours; |
| 5. Decreased attention, concentration, or ability to think clearly; | 5. Sharpened and unusually creative thinking; |
| 6. Social withdrawal; | 6. Uninhibited people-seeking (extreme gregariousness); |
| 7. Loss of interest in or enjoyment of sex; | 7. Hypersexuality without recognition of possibility of painful consequences; |
| 8. Restriction of involvement in pleasurable activities; guilt over past activities; | 8. Excessive involvement in pleasurable activities with lack of concern for the high potential for painful consequences, e.g. buying sprees, foolish business investments, reckless driving; |
| 9. Feeling slowed down; | 9. Physical restlessness; |
| 10. Less talkative than usual; | 10. More talkative than usual; |
| 11. Pessimistic attitude toward the future, or brooding about past events; | 11. Overoptimism or exaggeration of past achievements; |
| 12. Tearfulness or crying. | 12. Inappropriate laughing, joking, punning. |

D. Absence of psychotic features, such as delusions, hallucinations, incoherence, or loosening of associations.

E. Not due to any other mental disorder, such as partial remission of bipolar disorder; however, cyclothymic disorder may precede bipolar disorder.

---

* From American Psychiatric Association: *Diagnostic and Statistical Manual of Mental Disorders*, ed 3. American Psychiatric Association, Washington, DC, 1980. Used with permission.

tors (MAOI's) may be of particular value for a subgroup of depressed patients who do not show response to tricyclics, especially patients with atypical features marked by anxiety, hysterical, and depersonalization symptoms. *Alprazolam* has also been found to be of use in this subgroup and has the advantage of having less side effects than MAOI's.

Although there is controversey about the use of *amphetamines* and amphetamine-like drugs for depression, some clinicians have found that, in selected cases, the judicious use of these drugs is of value, although this use is not recommended by the United States Food and Drug Administration (USFDA).

Amphetamine can be used to gauge the potential effectiveness of certain tricyclics in depressed patients. A positive response, as measured by improved mood, to a 2 or 3 day trial of amphetamine usually means that a tricyclic is likely to be effective.

In addition, amphetamine has been found to be useful in some patients with involutional depression and to be of value in medically ill depressed patients. A beneficial synergistic effect using desipramine and methylphenidate in combination for the treatment of depression has been reported, and methylphenidate has been found to be of value in a selected group of patients experiencing depression after cardiac surgery.

**14.7.   The answer is E (all)** (*Synopsis*, ed. 4, page 259).

Although the manifestations of cyclothymia are usually of insufficient severity to meet the diagnostic criteria for bipolar disorders, certain similarities have led to a consensus that cyclothymia is an attenuated form of bipolar disorder.

These similarities include the following: *similarities in symptoms* and behavior of affected persons; the *tendency for cyclothymia to eventually develop into a bipolar disorder;* and pharmacological similarities (notably, a *favorable response to lithium* and, frequently, a *hypomanic response to tricyclic drugs.*

In addition, cyclothymia occurs with increased frequency in the biological relations of patients with bipolar disorders.

**14.8.   The answer is A (1, 2, 3)** (*Synopsis*, ed. 4, pages 255 and 256).

The essential feature of dysthymic disorder is a chronic nonpsychotic disturbance, involving *depressed mood* or a loss of interest or pleasure in all or almost all usual activities and pastimes. Usually, associated symptoms are not of sufficient severity to meet the criteria for major depression. (See the table in column 2.)

Dysthymic disorder is defined as a longstanding illness of *at least 2 years' duration*, with either sustained or intermittent disturbances in depressed mood and associated symptoms. The disorder *may begin in early adult life*, often without a clear onset. In the past, patients with this disorder included those with depressive neu-

**Diagnostic Criteria for Dysthymic Disorder***

A. During the past 2 years (or 1 year for children and adolescents), the individual has been bothered most or all of the time by symptoms characteristic of the depressive syndrome but that are not of sufficient severity and duration to meet the criteria for a major depressive episode (although a major depressive episode may be superimposed on dysthymic disorder).

B. The manifestations of the depressive syndrome may be relatively persistent or separated by periods of normal mood lasting a few days to a few weeks, but no more than a few months at a time.

C. During the depressive periods, there is either prominent depressed mood—e.g. sad, blue, down in the dumps, low—or marked loss of interest or pleasure in all, or almost all, usual activities and pastimes.

D. During the depressive periods at least three of the following symptoms are present:
  1. Insomnia or hypersomnia;
  2. Low energy level or chronic tiredness;
  3. Feelings of inadequacy, loss of self-esteem, or self-deprecation;
  4. Decreased effectiveness or productivity at school, work, or home;
  5. Decreased attention, concentration, or ability to think clearly;
  6. Social withdrawal;
  7. Loss of interest in or enjoyment of pleasurable activities;
  8. Irritability or excessive anger (in children, expressed toward parents or caretakers);
  9. Inability to respond with apparent pleasure to praise or rewards;
  10. Less active or talkative than usual, or feels slowed down or restless;
  11. Pessimistic attitude toward the future, brooding about past events, or feeling sorry for self;
  12. Tearfulness or crying;
  13. Recurrent thoughts of death or suicide.

E. Absence of psychotic features, such as delusions, hallucinations, or incoherence, or loosening of associations.

F. If the disturbance is superimposed on a preexisting mental disorder, such as obsessive-compulsive disorder or alcohol dependence, the depressed mood, by virtue of its intensity or effect on functioning, can be clearly distinguished from the individual's usual mood.

* From American Psychiatric Association: *Diagnostic and Statistical Manual of Mental Disorders*, ed 3. American Psychiatric Association, Washington, DC, 1980. Used with persmission.

rosis. Subgroups include patients with masked depression or depressive equivalents, such as alcoholism, antisocial behavior, and psychosomatic illnesses.

*Hallucinations* are false sensory perceptions occurring in the absence of external stimuli and do not occur in dysthymia. They are common in schizophrenia and toxic psychoses.

**14.9–14.14. The answers are 14.9–B, 14.10–D, 14.11–B, 14.12–C, 14.13–B, and 14.14–C** (*Synopsis*, ed. 4, pages 256 and 260).

The essential feature of dysthymic disorder is a nonpsychotic depressive symptom complex of at least 2 years' duration. *Delusions and hallucinations* are, by definition, inconsistent with the diagnosis of both dysthymic and cyclothymic disorder. It is generally believed that cyclothymia is a mild or attenuated form of bipolar disorder. Evidence supporting this supposition includes observations that a significant proportion of cyclothymic disorders evolve into bipolar disorders, that there is a *tendency for hypomanic symptoms to appear in response to antidepres-*

*sants*, and that there is a *favorable response to lithium*. During the hypomanic phase of cyclothymia, *hypersexuality with promiscuity may be seen*. In dysthymia, however, there may be a favorable response, particularly to a combined use of psychotherapy and tricyclic antidepressants; there also may be an associated diminished interest in or enjoyment of sex. With regard to *alcohol abuse*, 25 to 50 percent of chronic alcoholics develop secondary dysthymic depressions, while mood swings, such as those seen in cyclothymia, have also been described as part of the secondary affective disorder related to chronic alcoholism. Both dysthymia and cyclothymia may be confused with *drug abuse*. Steroids, amphetamines, barbiturates, and CNS depressants produce depression after periods of heavy use, while mood swings may also be associated with the ingestion of steroids, cocaine, amphetamines, and hallucinogens.

The table listing DSM-III criteria for dysthymic disorder is shown in the answer to 14.8, and the table listing criteria for cyclothymic disorder is shown in the answer to 14.5.

## References

Cancro R: Affective disorders: Overview. In *Comprehensive Textbook of Psychiatry*, ed 4, H I Kaplan, B J Sadock, editors, p 760. Williams & Wilkins, Baltimore, 1985.

Davidson, J: Comparative diagnostic criteria for melancholia and endogenous depression. Arch Gen Psychiatry 41: 506, 1984.

Georgotas A: Affective disorders: Pharmacotherapy. In *Comprehensive Textbook of Psychiatry*, ed 4, H I Kaplan, B J Sadock, editors, p 821. Williams & Wilkins, Baltimore, 1985.

Georgotas A, Cooper T, Kim M, Hapworth W: The treatment of affective disorders in the elderly. Psychopharmacol. Bull 19: 226, 1983.

Gershon E S, Hamovit J, Guroff J J, Dibble E, Leckman J F, Sceery W, Targum S D, Nurnberger J I, Jr, Goldin L R, Bunney W E, Jr: A family study of schizoaffective, bipolar I, bipolar II, unipolar, and normal control probands. Arch Gen Psychiatry 39: 1157, 1982.

Gershon E S, Nurnberger J I, Jr, Berrettini W H, Goldin L R: Affective disorders: Genetics. In *Comprehensive Textbook of Psychiatry*, ed 4, H I Kaplan,

B J Sadock, editors, p 786. Williams & Wilkins, Baltimore, 1985.

Hirshfeld R, Shea T: Affective disorders: Psychosocial treatment. In *Comprehensive Textbook of Psychiatry*, ed 4, H I Kaplan, B J Sadock, editors, p 811. Williams & Wilkins, Baltimore, 1985.

Lehman H E: Affective disorders: Clinical features. In *Comprehensive Textbook of Psychiatry*, ed 4, H I Kaplan, B J Sadock, editors, p 786. Williams & Wilkins, Baltimore, 1985.

Nurnberger J I, Jr, Gershon E S: Genetics of affective disorders. In *Neurobiology of Mood Disorders*, R Post, J Ballenger, editors, p 76. Williams & Wilkins, Baltimore, 1984.

Schildkraut J, Green A I, Mooney J J: Affective disorders: Biochemical aspects. In *Comprehensive Textbook of Psychiatry*, ed 4, H I Kaplan, B J Sadock, editors, p 769. Williams & Wilkins, Baltimore, 1985.

Weissman M M, Boyd J H: Affective disorders: Epidemiology. In *Comprehensive Textbook of Psychiatry*, ed 4, H I Kaplan, B J Sadock, editors, p 764. Williams & Wilkins, Baltimore, 1985.

# 15

# Other Affective Disorders: Atypical Affective Disorders, Grief, Mourning, Bereavement, and Thanatology

This section on other affective disorders includes the atypical depressive and atypical bipolar disorders, as well as discussions on grief, mourning, bereavement, and thanatology. Grief and mourning are normal phenomena that all persons experience as part of the life cycle; however, some do not spontaneously return to their normal state as expected. Instead, they pass into a pathological state of depression that requires psychiatric intervention. The student, therefore, needs to be aware of the differences between the normal signs of grief and bereavement and the abnormal signs of major depression.

Thanatology is the comprehensive study of death and dying. Although not every preterminal or terminal patient requires psychiatric intervention, many of them can be helped by contributions from psychiatry. The psychosocial diagnosis and management of patients who are dying and of their families is a growing field of practice.

The reader should refer to Chapter 15, "Other Affective Disorders," in *Modern Synposis-IV* and should then study the questions and answers below to assess his or her knowledge of the subject.

# Questions

**DIRECTIONS:** Each of the statements or questions below is followed by five suggested responses or completions. Select the *one* that is *best* in each case.

**15.1.** Atypical depression is characterized by all of the following *except*

A. it is not a reaction to a psychosocial stressor
B. there are periods of normal mood existing more than 2 months
C. no familial patterns are reported
D. overeating, excessive sleeping, and lethargy may occur
E. it does not occur in the residual type of schizophrenia

**15.2.** Which of the following drugs can be used in patients with atypical bipolar disorder:

A. Amphetamine
B. Imipramine
C. Amitriptyline
D. Methylphenidate
E. None of the above

**15.3.** The most effective approach for the physician to take with the person experiencing an acute grief reaction is to

A. prescribe antianxiety drugs
B. prescribe antidepressants
C. encourage ventilation of feelings
D. recommend electroconvulsive therapy
E. support the defense of denial

**15.4.** Kübler-Ross has described dying as being typified by five stages that occur most often in which of the following orders:

A. Denial, bargaining, anger, depression, acceptance
B. Bargaining, anger, denial, acceptance, depression
C. Denial, anger, bargaining, depression, acceptance
D. Depression, denial, acceptance, bargaining, anger
E. Acceptance, anger, bargaining, depression, denial

**15.5.** The *identification phenomena* in a grief reaction refer to

A. personality characteristics of the bereaved becoming more fixed
B. the bereaved taking on the qualities and mannerisms of the deceased person
C. the spouse who commits suicide to be with the deceased loved one
D. becoming angry at the deceased person for having died
E. not wanting to leave the side of the deceased loved one

**15.6.** Bowlby described four stages of mourning that occur in sequence during childhood. They are

A. despair, protest, detachment, reorganization
B. protest, detachment, despair, yearning
C. protest, yearning, despair, reorganization
D. despair, protest, reorganization, detachment
E. detachment, protest, despair, yearning

**DIRECTIONS:** For each of the incomplete statements below, *one* or *more* of the completions given is correct. Choose answer:

A. if only **1, 2,** and **3** are correct
B. if only **1** and **3** are correct
C. if only **2** and **4** are correct
D. if only **4** is correct
E. if all are correct

**15.7.** Which of the following personality disorders may predispose the patient toward developing an affective disorder:

1. Compulsive personality
2. Histrionic personality
3. Narcissistic personality
4. Borderline personality

**15.8.** Freud's theories on mourning and melancholia include which of the following concepts:

1. A diminished capacity to love occurs in both states.
2. An **exaggerated** loss of self-esteem is not part of normal grief.
3. Mourning can result from the giving up of an ideal or abstraction.
4. Profound dejection occurs while mourning.

**15.9.** Anticipatory grief occurs in persons who are

1. facing the death of a loved one
2. anticipating their own death
3. facing declining health
4. facing the loss of a body part

**15.10.** Grief that is inhibited from being expressed may

1. evolve into a false euphoria
2. be displaced onto another lost object
3. cause an overreaction to another person's trouble
4. cause physical symptoms

**15.11.** Management of a terminally ill patient in a hospice involves

1. less cost to the patient and family than is experienced with traditional hospitalization
2. nonuse of narcotics for pain relief
3. prevention of morbid grief reaction
4. less supervision of the patient

**15.12.** Initial grief is characterized by

1. a sense of being stunned
2. sleep disturbances
3. dreams of the deceased
4. withdrawal of interest in the outside world

**15.13.** In normal grief

1. illusions of the dead person may occur
2. the bereaved may deny that the loss actually occurred
3. objects belonging to the deceased may be overvalued
4. a false, fixed belief that the person is still alive may occur

**15.14.** According to Freud, pathological grief or depression results from

1. mobility of the libido
2. fixation of the libido
3. the use of projection as the major mechanism
4. introjection of an object toward which there was ambivalence

# Answers

# Other Affective Disorders: Atypical Affective Disorders, Grief, Mourning, Bereavement, and Thanatology

**15.1.   The answer is E** (*Synopsis*, ed. 4, page 262).

Atypical depression is a residual category for classifying patients with depressive features that cannot be classified as a major affective disorder or dysthymic disorder, or as an adjustment disorder. Examples of atypical depression include (1) a disorder that does not satisfy the symptomatic criteria for a major affective disorder, and that is *apparently not reactive to psychosocial stress*, so that it cannot be classified as an adjustment disorder; (2) a disorder that fulfills the criteria for dysthymic disorder with the exception that there have been *intermittent periods of normal mood lasting more than 2 months*; (3) a pattern of recurrent short-lived depressive reactions after personal rejection or some other loss of romantic attachment; during one form of the condition, the person is likely to show such symptoms as *overeating, excessive sleeping, and lethargy* in the absence of significant endogenous features; the syndrome, when seen in a person with histrionic personality disorder, has been referred to by some as hysteroid dysphoria; and (4) a distinct and sustained episode of *depression in a patient with schizophrenia, residual type*, that develops without an activation of the psychotic symptoms, and is not an apparent reaction to a psychosocial stressor.

Because atypical depression is a new category, defined mainly by its residual quality, it is not possible to generate specific information about its epidemiology, prevalence, sex ratio, and *familial patterns*.

**15.2.   The answer is E** (*Synopsis*, ed. 4, page 264).

A number of drugs should not be used with these patients, most notably *amphetamine, methylphenidate, tricyclic antidepressants*, and MAO inhibitors, which are likely to aggravate the manic predisposition and intensify latent psychotic features. The treatment of choice is lithium, either alone or in combination with psychotherapy.

**15.3.   The answer is C** (*Synopsis*, ed. 4, page 268).

With the recognition that grief cannot be permanently postponed and is going to reach expression in some way, however circuitous, *ventilation of feelings is to be encouraged*, rather than to be "narcotized," because the more sustained the inhibition of feelings the more intense they are likely to be when finally expressed.

Whether requested by the grief-stricken person or not, *medications of any kind should probably be used cautiously*. Most authorities do not recommend the use of *antidepressants* when the person is experiencing an appropriate expression of grief, for example, nor are *antianxiety agents* generally considered necessary. At most, a mild sedative to facilitate sleep is probably all that is warranted. It can be held that the person should not be deprived of an opportunity to experience a process that ultimately can be rewarding and maturing in its effect.

*Ventilation* is the expression of conflict-laden ideas, thoughts, or feelings to a listener. It does *not support the defense of denial* in which the existence of unpleasant realities is disavowed.

*Electroconvulsive therapy* (ECT) is used only in major depressions of great severity—usually suicidal—that are intractable to other therapies. It is not indicated in acute grief reactions, but should a major depression follow a grief reaction, then ECT may play a role.

**15.4.   The answer is C** (*Synopsis*, ed. 4, pages 268 and 269).

Elizabeth Kübler-Ross has described dying as being typified by five stages: *denial, anger, bargaining, depression, and acceptance*.

*Denial* is accompanied by shock; the patient may refuse to believe that he or she is going to die or has a fatal illness. *Anger* is characterized by the patient venting personal frustrations about death on family, friends, or physicians. In the *bargaining* stage, the patient promises something—such as giving to charity—in exchange for a respite from death or a change in the diagnosis of the illness. *Depression* ranges from feelings of sadness about events to acute suicidal impulses or attempts. With *acceptance*, the patient is able to deal with impending death and often requests to be left alone or to be with one or two loved ones.

The trajectory of death, however, is hardly smooth. There are many fluctuations due to impersonal, intrapersonal, and interpersonal factors related to disease, personality, and social supports. Stages, phases, and dimensions of a chronic fatal illness represent a confluence of psychosocial factors, rather than distinct stages.

**15.5. The answer is B** (*Synopsis*, ed. 4, page 265).

As part of what has been labeled "identification phenomena," *the person may take on the qualities, mannerisms, or characteristics of the deceased person*, as if to perpetuate that person in some concrete way. This maneuver can reach potentially pathological expression, with the development of physical symptoms similar to those experienced by the deceased or to those suggestive of the illness from which the deceased died.

**15.6. The answer is C** (*Synopsis*, ed. 4, page 265).

In 1970, John Bowlby hypothesized four stages of mourning that occur in children after separation from the parent. They include an early phase of numbness or *protest* (stage 1), which may be interrupted by outbursts of distress, fear, or anger, being soon followed by a phase of *yearning* and searching for the lost figure (stage 2), which may last for several months or even years. This second phase is characterized by preoccupations with the lost person, a physical restlessness, and a perceptual set that leads the grieving child to interpret these personal experiences as reflections of the presence of the deceased. Weeping and anger are characteristic expressions of this search. Gradual recognition and integration of the reality lead to a subsequent phase of disorganization and *despair* (stage 3). Restlessness and aimlessness may now characterize inefficient and ineffective efforts to initiate and perpetuate productive patterns of behavior, interpersonal or otherwise. Finally, with the establishment of new patterns, objects, and goals, the bereaved child reaches a phase of greater or lesser degree of *reorganization* (stage 4), during which grief recedes into cherished memories.

**15.7. The answer is E (all)** (*Synopsis*, ed. 4, page 264).

Patients with affective disorders may also have a variety of personality disorders. These personality features may be extensions of normal personality functioning, or they may be of sufficient intensity or duration, or have enough maladaptive consequences, to warrant being called disorders. Certain types of personality disorders may predispose the patients toward developing affective disorders. They include *compulsive personality, histrionic personality*, and *narcissistic and borderline personalities*.

*Compulsive personality disorder* is characterized by rigidity, overconscientiousness, extreme inhibition, inability to relax, and performance of repetitive patterns of behavior.

*Histrionic personality disorder* is a condition in which the patient—usually an immature and dependent person—exhibits unstable, overreactive, and excitable self-dramatizing behavior that is aimed at gaining attention and is at times seductive, although the person may not be aware of that fact.

*Narcissistic personality disorder* is marked by a grandiose sense of self-importance, preoccupation with fantasies of unlimited success, exhibitionistic need for attention and admiration, exaggerated responses to criticism or other perceived threats to self-esteem, and disturbance in interpersonal relationships.

*Borderline personality disorder* is characterized by identity disturbances, impulsiveness, inappropriate emotions, unstable interpersonal relationships, and physically self-damaging acts, such as suicidal acts.

**15.8. The answer is E (all)** (*Synopsis*, ed. 4, pages 265 and 266).

An enduring differentiation of normal grief (mourning) and abnormal reactions to loss (melancholia) was provided by Freud in 1917. In his definition of mourning is the recognition that it is a reaction resulting not only from the death of a loved person but also may arise from less obvious losses, even from *some abstraction, such as an ideal* that has taken the place of a loved person. It was obviously the idea of loss per se of which Freud wrote, although still maintaining it within an interpersonal context.

According to Freud, the distinguishing features of mourning include profound dejection, a lack of interest in the outside world, a *diminished capacity to love*, and an inhibition of activity, all of which are viewed as normal in spite of their departure from usual attitudes. Melancholia, however, involves all of these features and one other—a lowering of self-esteem—that is viewed as valid today; that is, *an exaggerated loss of self-esteem is not a prominent aspect of normal grief, however profound the dejection and sense of loss*.

**15.9.  The answer is E (all)** (*Synopsis*, ed. 4, page 266).

Anticipatory grief can occur in a variety of situations in which loss is expected. *Facing the death of a loved one, anticipating one's own death, facing declining health, or facing the loss of a body part*, such as a mastectomy, can all cause such a reaction.

The concept of anticipatory grief has been applied to grief expressed in advance of a loss that is perceived as inevitable, as distinguished from grief that occurs at or after the loss. By definition, anticipatory grief ends with the occurrence of the anticipated loss, regardless of what reactions follow. Unlike conventional grief, which diminishes in intensity with the passage of time, anticipatory grief may increase in intensity as the expected loss becomes more imminent. In some instances, however, particularly when the occurrence of the loss is delayed, anticipatory grief may be expended, leaving the individual showing fewer of the manifestations of acute grief when the actual loss occurs. Once anticipatory grief has been expended, it may be difficult to reestablish the prior relationship, as has been demonstrated with the return from combat or concentration camps of persons previously thought to be dead.

**15.10.  The answer is E (all)** (*Synopsis*, ed. 4, page 266).

Grief that is inhibited or denied expression because the person is unable to deal with the reality of the loss can result in pathological states. A *false euphoria* may prevail, suggesting that bereavement is on a pathological course. Inhibited or denied grief reactions contain the seeds of such unfortunate consequences as the person's experiencing persisting *physical symptoms* similar to those of the deceased, or unaccountable reactions on the anniversary of the loss or on occasions of significance to the deceased. Denied or inhibited grief may also reach expression by being *displaced to some other loss* that, although seemingly insignificant in its own right, may symbolize the original loss. *Overreaction to another person's trouble* may be one manifestation of displacement.

**15.11.  The answer is B (1, 3)** (*Synopsis*, ed. 4, page 269).

Among the advantages of the hospice are (1) better care for both the family and the patient through an established, *supervised program*; (2) an effective *alternative to unnecessary, expensive hospitalization* or consignment to a substandard custodial facility; (3) *consistent control over pain medication;* (4) prevention of social isolation and neglect; (5) *possible prevention of morbid grief reactions* among the survivors.

**15.12.  The answer is E (all)** (*Synopsis*, ed. 4, pages 264 and 265).

Initial grief is often manifested as a state of shock that may be expressed in a feeling of numbness and a sense of bewilderment or a *sense of being stunned.* This apparent inability to comprehend what has happened may be short-lived, followed by expressions of suffering and distress most usually indicated by sighing and crying, although in Western culture this expected feature of grief is less common among men than among women. Other physical expressions of grief may include the following: feeling of weakness; decreased appetite; weight loss; and difficulty in concentrating, breathing, and talking. *Sleep disturbances* may include difficulty going to sleep, waking up during the night, or awakening early. *Dreams of the deceased* often occur, with the dreamer awakening with a sense of disappointment in finding that the experience was only a dream. Preoccupation with thoughts of the deceased are a specific identifying feature of grief, as the person relives experiences shared with the deceased or tries instead to avoid all thoughts of the deceased. Simultaneously, a *withdrawal of interest in the outside world* may include decreased interest in eating, manner of dress, and usual social activities.

**15.13.  The answer is A (1, 2, 3)** (*Synopsis*, ed. 4, page 265).

Forms of denial occur throughout the entire period of bereavement, with the bereaved person becoming aware of inadvertently thinking or acting as if the *loss had not occurred*. Efforts to perpetuate the lost relationship are evidenced by an *investment in objects* that may have been treasured by the deceased or that remind the grief-stricken person of the deceased (linkage objects). A sense of the presence of the deceased may be so intense as to constitute an *illusion* or a hallucination, although in normal grief the person recognizes that it is a false impression. In normal grief, *the false fixed belief that the person is still alive does not occur.*

**15.14.  The answer is D (4)** (*Synopsis*, ed. 4, page 268).

The *introjection of an object toward which there was intense ambivalence* gives rise to depression, self-accusations, and feelings of worthlessness that reflect the previously unacceptable aspects of the original relationship. That is, the ambivalence, originally directed to the introjected or incorporated object, is now expressed against the self because the object and the self are not distinguished. The self-accusation of a depressed person can thus be the unconscious accusations the person is directing at someone else (the incorporated object). In a cry for attention, love, and service, the person may also be acting out an unconscious desire to punish someone else. Further guilt and depression ensue.

Introjection and incorporation are generally used synonymously; however, some workers see incorporation as a more primitive defense mechanism than introjection. To them, incorporation is the symbolic swallowing of the object, whereas introjection is the creation of a mental image of the introjected object.

*Projection is a defense mechanism* in which ideas unacceptable to the self are attributed to others. It is seen most often in paranoid states.

According to psychoanalytic theory, *mobility of the libido* refers to the transfer of libido or mental energy from one object to another. Some persons can do that with ease. For others, the *libido is fixed* and is attached to a particular object for life.

## References

Bowlby J: Process of mourning. Int J Psychoanal *42:* 317, 1961.

Carr A C: Grief, mourning, and bereavement. In *Comprehensive Textbook of Psychiatry*, ed 4, H I Kaplan, B J Sadock, editors, p 1286. Williams & Wilkins, Baltimore, 1985.

Enzell K: Mortality among persons with depressive symptoms and among responders and non-responders in a health check-up. Acta Psychiatr Scand *69:* 89, 1984.

Freud S: Mourning and melancholia (1917). In *The Standard Edition of the Complete Psychological Works of Sigmund Freud*, vol 14. Hogarth Press and the Institute of Psychoanalysis, London, 1957.

Gonda T A, Ruark J E: *Dying Dignified: The Health Professionals Guide to Care*. Addison-Wesley, Menlo Park, CA, 1984.

Hansen L, McAleer C: Terminal cancer and suicide: The health care professional's dilemma. Omega *14:* 241, 1984.

Hirschfeld R M A, Klerman G L: Personality attributes and affective disorders. Am J Psychiatry *136:* 67, 1979.

Kaltreider N B: Relationship testing after loss of a parent. Am J Psychiatry *141:* 243, 1984.

Weisman A D: Thanatology. In *Comprehensive Textbook of Psychiatry*, ed 4, H I Kaplan, B J Sadock, editors, p 1277. Williams & Wilkins, Baltimore, 1985.

# 16

# Organic Mental Disorders

It is an odd paradox that, despite their increasing frequency and importance, organic mental disorders (OMD) constitute one of the most neglected areas of clinical psychiatry in this country. In the past few years psychiatrists have started to pay increased attention to this area. They have been compelled to do so by the growing frequency of organic mental disorders that are related to the aging of the population (some 23 million Americans are currently aged 65 years or over), to the abuse of alcohol and other substances, to the advances in critical care medicine that allow the survival of many brain-damaged persons, and to the so-called diseases of medical progress; that is, cerebral complications of modern drugs and surgical treatments for cardiovascular, renal, and other diseases.

Organic mental disorders are characterized by temporary or permanent brain tissue functional impairment. Previously the term was used synonymously with organic brain syndrome, but according to the third edition of the *Diagnostic and Statistical Manual of Mental Disorders* (DSM-III), the term organic mental disorders is used only when a causative agent, such as an infectious agent or toxin, can be demonstrated. Diagnostically, organic mental disorders are placed on Axis I of DSM-III. The term organic brain syndrome is used to refer to a cluster of signs and symptoms without reference to etiology, e.g. delirium, dementia.

The reader should refer to Chapter 16 of *Modern Synopsis-IV*, "Organic Mental Disorders," and should then study the questions and answers that follow.

# Questions

**DIRECTIONS:** Each of the statements or questions below is followed by five suggested responses or completions. Select the *one* that is *best* in each case.

**16.1.** Organic affective syndrome

A. is characterized solely by a depressive mood disorder
B. has not been attributed to a clearly defined organic factor
C. shows no clouding of consciousness
D. antedates the onset of a defined causative organic factor
E. always has an insidious onset

**16.2.** On psychological testing, which function is often impaired in organic mental disorders:

A. Calculation
B. Memory
C. Abstraction
D. Judgment
E. All of the above

**16.3.** Impairment in memory as the predominant cognitive defect is seen in

A. barbiturate intoxication
B. hypnotic withdrawal delirium
C. hypnotic intoxication
D. barbiturate amnestic disorder
E. barbiturate withdrawal

**16.4.** For a typical grand mal seizure, which of the following most accurately describes the sequence of symptoms:

A. Preseizure aura, clonic movements, tonic movements
B. Trembling, loss of consciousness, clonic movements, tonic movements
C. Epileptic cry, generalized tonic-clonic movements, diffuse trembling
D. Loss of consciousness, tonic stiffening, clonic movements, postictal stupor
E. Loss of consciousness, tonic movements, clonic movements, epileptic cry

**16.5.** As a general rule, the most effective medication for an agitated, restless, or belligerent delirious patient is

A. barbiturates
B. haloperidol
C. paraldehyde
D. imipramine
E. phenytoin

**16.6.** The electroencephalogram (EEG) shown below is an example of

A. Jacksonian seizure
B. grand mal seizures
C. petit mal (absence) seizures
D. psychomotor epilepsy
E. none of the above

**16.7.** The drug of choice for the treatment of anticholinergic delirium is

A. haloperidol
B. benztropine
C. diphenhydramine
D. physostigmine
E. diazepam

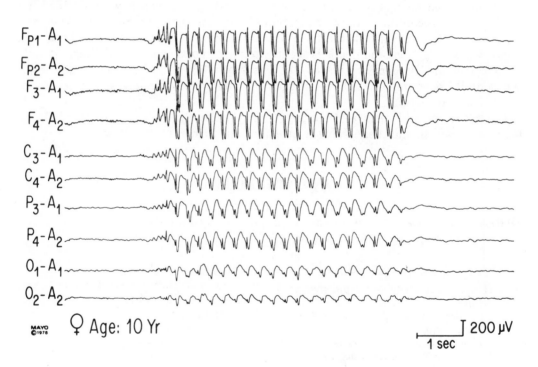

$F_{P1}-A_1$
$F_{P2}-A_2$
$F_3-A_1$
$F_4-A_2$
$C_3-A_1$
$C_4-A_2$
$P_3-A_1$
$P_4-A_2$
$O_1-A_1$
$O_2-A_2$

MAYO ©1978   ♀ Age: 10 Yr

200 µV
1 sec

**16.8.** The computed tomography (CT) scan of the brain illustrated below shows grade 3 dilation of the lateral ventricles and severe cerebral atrophy. These findings are consistent with

A. multi-infarct dementia
B. Alzheimer's disease
C. Wernicke's encephalopathy
D. meningitis
E. multiple sclerosis

**16.9.** All of the following statements about the clinical differentiation of delirium and dementia are true *except*

A. awareness in delirium is always reduced and tends to fluctuate—being worse at night—whereas in dementia, it is usually intact
B. the sleep-wakefulness cycle is always disrupted in delirium and is usually normal for age in dementia
C. the onset of delirium is acute, whereas in dementia, it is usually insidious
D. the duration of delirium is usually less than 1 month, whereas dementia lasts at least 1 month and usually much longer
E. hallucinations, especially visual ones, and transient delusions are more common in dementia than in delirium

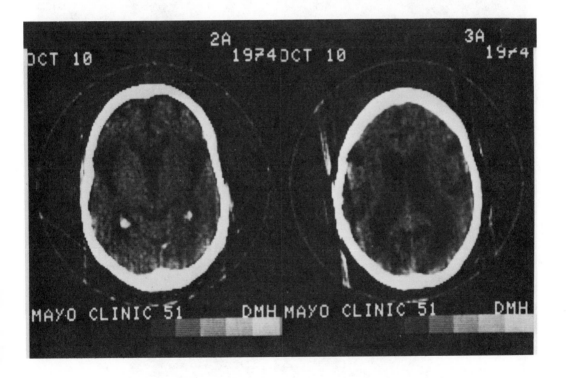

**16.10.** The illustration below demonstrates severe atrophy of the frontal and temporal lobe of the brain. These findings are consistent with

A. Alzheimer's disease
B. multiple sclerosis
C. chronic subdural hematoma
D. Pick's disease
E. none of the above

**16.11.** The neurofibrillary degenerations and senile plaques of a section of the cerebral cortex in the bottom figure are indicative of

A. multi-infarct dementia
B. Alzheimer's disease
C. meningioma
D. Pick's disease
E. none of the above

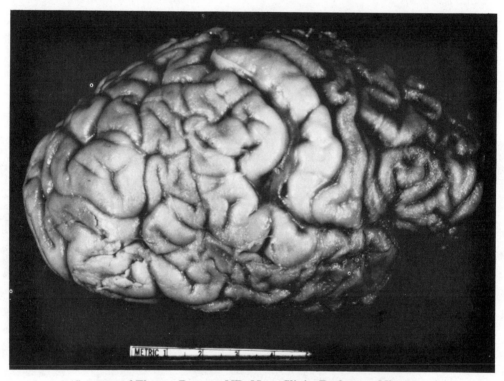

(Courtesy of Thomas Reagan, MD, Mayo Clinic, Rochester, Minnesota.)

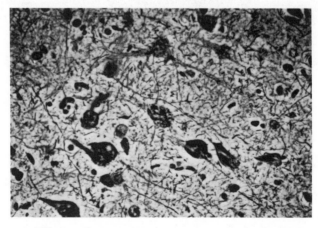

(Courtesy of Thomas Reagan, MD, Mayo Clinic, Rochester, Minnesota.)

**16.12.** All of the following statements about delirium are true *except*

A. delirium may be chronic
B. history of the sudden onset of essential features is highly suggestive
C. diurnal fluctuations and nocturnal exacerbation of symptoms are quite characteristic
D. an onset at night is very suggestive
E. diagnosis requires the presence of multiple cognitive deficits on the mental status examination

**16.13.** The incidence of delirium after open-heart and coronary-bypass surgery is about

A. 10 percent
B. 20 percent
C. 30 percent
D. 40 percent
E. 50 percent

**16.14.** The incidence of delirium in surgical intensive care units is

A. less than 5 percent
B. 10 to 15 percent
C. 18 to 30 percent
D. 50 percent
E. over 50 percent

**16.15.** The incidence of delirium on general medical and surgical wards is

A. less than 5 percent
B. 5 to 15 percent
C. 20 percent
D. 25 to 40 percent
E. 50 percent

**16.16.** The most common mental disorder diagnosed by liaison psychiatrists in general hospitals is

A. schizophrenia
B. paranoid disorder
C. depressive disorder
D. delirium
E. mania

**16.17.** After emerging from a delirium, the patient usually

A. remembers the delirious events clearly
B. has impaired memory of events before the onset of delirium
C. develops schizophrenia
D. refers to the delirium as a nightmare that is clearly remembered
E. all of the above

**16.18.** The fatal dose of barbiturates is usually in the range of

A. 200 mg to 500 mg
B. 500 mg to 1,000 mg
C. 1,000 mg to 1,500 mg
D. 1,500 mg to 2,000 mg
E. 2,000 mg to 3,000 mg

**16.19.** The number of Americans over age 65 with the degree of impairment to justify a diagnosis of dementia is

A. 250,000
B. 500,000
C. 1 million
D. 2.5 million
E. 5 million

**16.20.** All of the following statements concerning organic hallucinosis are true *except*

A. presence of recurrent or persistent hallucinosis as the predominant or only symptom
B. a state of full wakefulness without clouding of consciousness
C. significant loss of intellectual abilities
D. most often encountered in a setting of chronic alcoholism
E. usually an acute onset and an average duration of days to weeks

**16.21.** All of the following are considered organic brain syndromes *except*

A. organic hallucinosis
B. Tourette's disorder
C. organic affective syndrome
D. organic personality syndrome
E. organic delusional syndrome

**DIRECTIONS:** For each of the incomplete statements below, *one* or *more* of the completions given is correct. Choose answer:

    A.  if only **1, 2,** and **3** are correct
    B.  if only **1** and **3** are correct
    C.  if only **2** and **4** are correct
    D.  if only **4** is correct
    E.  if all are correct

**16.22.**  True statements about multi-infarct dementia include which of the following:

1. The DSM-III diagnosis corresponds to what has been termed the lacunar state.
2. It is found in hypertensive patients.
3. There is a stepwise progression of bilateral, sometimes fluctuating, motor symptoms.
4. It may present with such personality changes as emotional lability and hypochondriasis.

**16.23.**  Important causes of organic personality syndrome include

1. chronic poisoning
2. brain tumor
3. head trauma
4. vascular disease

**16.24.**  Conditions associated with organic affective syndrome include

1. systematic lupus erythematosus
2. parkinsonism
3. infectious mononucleosis
4. use of reserpine

**16.25.**  The outcome of delirium may be

1. death
2. full recovery
3. dementia
4. paranoia

**16.26.**  Susceptibility to organic mental disorder is increased by

1. age more than 60
2. preexisting brain damage
3. reduced ability to metabolize drugs
4. familiar environment

**16.27.**  Potentially reversible causes of dementia include

1. head trauma
2. Addison's disease
3. encephalitis
4. Alzheimer's disease

**16.28.**  Dementia

1. is characterized by a severe acquired decrement of intellectual abilities
2. when fully developed, features either an accentuation or an alteration of the patient's habitual character traits
3. is affected by psychosocial factors, in that they are involved in determining the degree of severity of the dementia and possibly its onset
4. may be reversible

**16.29.**  Amnestic syndrome is characterized by

1. an impairment of memory as the single or predominant cognitive defect
2. retrograde and anterograde amnesia
3. preservation of the ability for immediate recall
4. evidence of a specific organic factor that is etiologically related to the memory disturbance

**16.30.**  In differentiating dementia from depressive pseudodementia, one would see which of the following:

1. In dementia, intellectual deficits antedate depression, whereas in pseudodementia, depressive symptoms antedate cognitive deficits.
2. In dementia, the patient is very disturbed by memory impairment and poor intellectual performance and verbalizes this disturbance, whereas in pseudodementia, the patient denies, minimizes, or conceals cognitive deficits by a variety of means.
3. The patient with dementia is usually globally impaired with consistently poor intellectual performance, whereas in pseudodementia, the deficit is often confined to memory impairment and is inconsistently poor.
4. In a sodium amobarbital interview, the performance is improved in dementia, whereas the cognitive deficits are accentuated in pseudodementia.

**16.31.**   Atypical or mixed organic brain syndrome

1. may occur during sleep
2. may fulfill the criteria for one of the organic brain syndromes described in DSM-III
3. is not itself a DSM-III diagnostic category
4. requires a specific organic factor that is judged to be etiologically related

**16.32.**   Delirium may be caused by

1. hypoglycemia
2. hypokalemia
3. migraine headaches
4. infectious mononucleosis

**16.33.**   Conditions associated with organic hallucinosis include

1. focal cerebral lesion
2. migraine
3. temporal arteritis
4. epilepsy

**16.34.**   Intoxication

1. is a substance-specific syndrome
2. has maladaptive behavior as one of its essential diagnostic criteria
3. follows the recent ingestion of a substance
4. may result from use of amphetamines

**16.35.**   In organic personality syndrome

1. many patients exhibit low drive and initiative
2. true sadness and depression are common
3. emotions are characteristically labile and shallow
4. the expression of impulses is characteristically inhibited

**16.36.**   Amnestic syndrome may be

1. transient
2. persistent
3. permanent
4. slowly progressive

**16.37.**   True statements about organic delusional syndrome include which of the following:

1. The syndrome often lifts after whatever has induced it is resolved.
2. Schizophreniform-like psychosis can be produced by lesions involving the limbic system.
3. The delusions may or may not be systematized.
4. A specific etiological organic factor need not be found to make the diagnosis.

**16.38.**   Features present in the amnestic syndrome include

1. impairment of short-term memory
2. impairment of long-term memory
3. clear consciousness
4. evidence of an etiological organic factor

**16.39.**   Acute intoxication with a barbiturate may produce

1. stupor
2. disinhibition of sexual and aggressive impulses
3. general depression of the central nervous system (CNS)
4. excitement

**16.40.**   Transient global amnesia is characterized by

1. the abrupt inability to recall recent events
2. the confusion of events of the distant past
3. the patient's ability to still perform highly complex mental and physical acts
4. irreversibility

**DIRECTIONS:** Each group of questions below consists of five lettered headings followed by a list of numbered words or statements. For each numbered word or statement, select the *one* lettered heading that is most closely associated with it. Each lettered heading may be used once, more than once, or not at all.

**Questions 16.41–16.45**
A. Mercury poisoning
B. Manganese madness
C. Thallium intoxication
D. Lead poisoning
E. Arsenic poisoning

**16.41.** Alopecia

**16.42.** Calcium disodium edetate

**16.43.** Mad Hatter's disease

**16.44.** Masked facies

**16.45.** Increased pigmentation of the neck, eyelids, nipples, and axillae

**DIRECTIONS:** Each set of lettered headings below is followed by a list of numbered words or phrases. For each numbered word or phrase, select

A. if the item is associated with **A** only
B. if the item is associated with **B** only
C. if the item is associated with *both* **A** *and* **B**
D. if the item is associated with *neither* **A** *nor* **B**

**Questions 16.46–16.50**
A. Withdrawal
B. Intoxication
C. Both
D. Neither

**16.46.** Is a substance-specific syndrome

**16.47.** Requires maladaptive behavior as an essential diagnostic criteria

**16.48.** Follows the cessation or reduction of intake of a substance

**16.49.** Follows the recent ingestion and presence in the body of a substance

**16.50.** Clinical picture may correspond to one of the specific organic brain syndromes

**Questions 16.51–16.55**
A. Barbiturate delirium
B. Barbiturate withdrawal
C. Both
D. Neither

**16.51.** Tachycardia

**16.52.** Occur after cessation of prolonged use

**16.53.** Coarse tremor of hands, tongue, and eyelids

**16.54.** Elevated blood pressure

**16.55.** Produces schizophrenia

# Answers

## Organic Mental Disorders

**16.1.** **The answer is C** (*Synopsis*, ed. 4, pages 283 and 285).

Organic affective syndrome is characterized by *either a depressive or a manic mood disorder* that is *clearly attributable to a defined organic factor. There is no clouding of consciousness.* Often, a depression will accompany a physical illness and can be viewed as a psychological response to the meaning of the illness to the patient. In those disorders classified under organic affective syndrome, however, an affective syndrome may be induced by some form of direct organic interference with processes regulating normal mood. In these cases, the affective disturbance may arise quite separately from the meaning of the illness to the patient. The onset of the syndrome may be *acute* or *insidious,* and the disturbances are attributed to a clearly defined *organic factor, the onset of which must antedate the affective syndrome.*

The table at the bottom of this page summarizes the DSM-III diagnostic criteria for this syndrome.

**16.2.** **The answer is E** (*Synopsis*, ed. 4, page 272).

The loss of abstraction, of reasoning ability, and of capacity to understand the nature of a problem constitutes the most common manifestation of impaired brain function found on psychological testing. The deterioration of efficiency in performance on intellectual and cognitive tasks is another such manifestation.

The impairment of abstraction, memory, and efficiency in intellectual and cognitive performance is the hallmark of relatively widespread brain pathology, reversible or not. The presence of these cognitive abnormalities in a given patient constitutes presumptive evidence of cerebral damage or dysfunction and should lead to appropriate investigations of the presumed brain disorder by nonpsychological techniques—radiographic, electroencephalographic, and so on.

*Memory* is a process whereby what is experienced or learned is established as a record in the central nervous system, where it persists and can be retrieved. *Abstraction* is the ability to see the whole from the sum of its parts, and *judgment* is the ability to recognize the true relationship of ideas and of comparing choices. *Calculation* is the ability to perform mathematical operations.

**16.3.** **The answer is D** (*Synopsis*, ed. 4, page 291).

*Barbiturate amnestic disorder* has as one of its essential diagnostic criteria the amnestic syndrome, of which memory impairment is the single or predominant defect. Impairment of memory and attention may also be seen in *barbiturate or other hypnotic intoxication* and in *barbiturate or other hypnotic withdrawal delirium,* but it is not the predominant cognitive defect.

The table below gives the DSM-III diagnostic criteria for the amnestic disorder.

### Diagnostic Criteria for Barbiturate or Similarly Acting Sedative or Hypnotic Amnestic Disorder*

A. Prolonged, heavy use of a barbiturate or similarly acting sedative or hypnotic.

B. Amnestic syndrome.

C. Not due to any other physical or mental disorder.

\* From American Psychiatric Association: *Diagnostic and Statistical Manual of Mental Disorders,* ed 3. American Psychiatric Association, Washington, DC, 1980. Used with permission.

### Diagnostic Criteria for Organic Affective Syndrome*

A. The predominant disturbance is a disturbance in mood, with at least two of the associated symptoms listed in criterion for manic or major depressive episode.

B. No clouding of consciousness, as in delirium; no significant loss of intellectual abilities, as in dementia; no predominant delusions or hallucinations, as in organic delusional syndrome or organic hallucinosis.

C. Evidence, from the history, physical examination, or laboratory tests, of a specific organic factor that is judged to be etiologically related to the disturbance.

\* From American Psychiatric Association: *Diagnostic and Statistical Manual of Mental Disorders,* ed 3. American Psychiatric Association, Washington, DC, 1980. Used with permission.

**16.4.  The answer is D** (*Synopsis*, ed. 4, pages 301, 302, and 303).

The typical grand mal seizure begins with *loss of consciousness*, *tonic stiffening* (brought about by continuous contraction of body muscles) *and the epileptic cry* (as air is forcefully expelled through closed vocal cords). Cyanosis, pupillary dilation, urinary and fecal incontinence, and biting of the tongue may also occur. Following this tonic stage are several seconds of *diffuse body trembling* and then rhythmic *clonic movements* (bilaterally synchronous contraction and relaxation of body and limb muscles). After a minute or so of seizure activity, the patient enters a *postictal stupor*, characterized by limpness and unresponsiveness. Later, the patient may exhibit confused or aggressive behavior.

An *aura* occurs in the beginning of a secondarily generalized seizure, and its symptoms reflect the function of the focal origin. In this situation, the patient is usually forewarned of the onset of the generalized seizure by the appearance of lights, parasthesia—e.g. tingling sensation—and other bodily sensations, such as nausea.

For an outline of the classification of epileptic seizures, see the table below.

**16.5.  The answer is B** (*Synopsis*, ed. 4, page 276).

An agitated, restless, and fearful or belligerent delirious patient needs to be sedated to prevent complications and accidents. No single psychotropic drug available today is recommended for all cases of delirium. As a general rule, *haloperidol* is the drug of choice in most cases. Depending on the patient's age, weight, and physical condition, the initial dose may range from 2 to 10 mg intramuscularly, to be repeated hourly if the patient continues to be agitated. The effective total daily dose may range between 10 and 60 mg for most delirious patients. As soon as the patient is calm, oral medication in the form of tablets or liquid concentrate should begin. Two daily oral doses should suffice, with two-thirds of the dose being given at bedtime. The oral dose should be about 1.5 times higher than the parenteral dose to achieve the same therapeutic effect. A mildly to moderately agitated patient may be given oral haloperidol from the start in two daily doses of 2 to 10 mg.

*Barbiturates* and *paraldehydes* are sedatives of use with younger agitated patients. *Imipramine* is an antidepressant, and *phenytoin* is an anticonvulsant.

### Outline of the International Classifications of Epileptic Seizures*

I. Partial seizures (seizures beginning locally)
   A. Partial seizures with elementary symptoms (generally without impairment of consciousness)
      1. With motor symptoms
      2. With sensory symptoms
      3. With autonomic symptoms
      4. Compound forms
   B. Partial seizures with complex symptoms (generally with impairment of consciousness) (temporal lobe or psychomotor seizures)
      1. With impairment of consciousness only
      2. With cognitive symptoms
      3. With affective symptoms
      4. With psychosensory symptoms
      5. With psychomotor symptoms (automatisms)
      6. Compound forms
   C. Partial seizures secondarily generalized

II. Generalized seizures (bilaterally symmetric and without local onset)
   A. Absences (petit mal)
   B. Myoclonus
   C. Infantile spasms
   D. Clonic seizures
   E. Tonic seizures
   F. Tonic clonic seizures (grand mal)
   G. Atonic seizures
   H. Akinetic seizures

III. Unilateral seizures

IV. Unclassified seizures (because of incomplete data)

*Modified from Gastaut H: Clinical and electroencephalographical classification of epileptic seizures. Epilepsia *11:* 102, 1970.

**16.6.    The answer is C** (*Synopsis*, ed. 4, pages 301 and 302).

*Petit mal or absence seizures* occur predominantly in children. They usually consist of simple absence attacks lasting 5 to 10 seconds, during which there is an abrupt alteration in awareness and responsiveness and an interruption in motor activity. The child often has a blank stare, associated with an upward deviation of the eyes, and some mild twitching movements of the eyes, eyelids, face, or extremities. The petit mal absence siezure is associated with a characteristic generalized, bilaterally synchronous, 3-Hz spike-and-wave pattern in the electroencephalogram (EEG) and is often easily induced by hyperventilation. Petit mal is usually a fairly benign siezure disorder, often resolving after adolescence.

A *Jacksonian seizure* is a type of epilepsy characterized by recurrent episodes of focal motor seizures. It begins with localized tonic or clonic contraction, increases in severity and spreads progressively through the entire body, and terminates in a generalized convulsion with loss of consciousness. *Grand mal epilepsy* is the major form of epilepsy. Gross tonic-clonic convulsive siezures are accompanied by loss of consciousness and, often, incontinence of stool or urine. *Psychomotor epilepsy* is a type of epilepsy characterized by recurrent behavioral disturbances. Complex hallucinations or illusions, frequently gustatory or olfactory, often herald the onset of the seizure, which typically involves a state of impaired consciousness resembling a dream (dreamy state) during which paramnestic phenomena, such as *déjà vu* and *jamais vu*, are experienced and the patient exhibits repetitive, automatic, or semipurposeful behaviors. In rare instances, violent behavior may be prominent. Electroencephalography reveals a localized seizure focus in the temporal lobe.

**16.7.    The answer is D** (*Synopsis*, ed. 4, page 295).

Treatment of the anticholinergic delirium involves evacuation of the stomach and sedation, if necessary, with a minor tranquilizer or barbiturate. Sedation with one of the major tranquilizers, such as chlorpromazine, should be avoided, as it may aggravate the anticholinergic delirium. Intramuscular injection of *physostigmine* salicylate in a dose of 1 mg, followed in 15 to 20 minutes by an additional dose if necessary, is indicated. The dose may have to be repeated after an hour.

**16.8.    The answer is B** (*Synopsis*, ed. 4, page 289).

The diagnosis of *Alzheimer's disease* is made on the basis of a clinical history of progressive and insidious dementia in middle or late life. A work-up is indicated to exclude other treatable causes of dementia. In many patients, computer-assisted tomography of the head may be helpful in demonstrating cortical atrophy by visualizing fluid over the surface of the brain and in the dilated ventricles.

The differential diagnosis must include such reversible metabolic diseases as myxedema and pernicious anemia, such infectious diseases as syphilis, and such tumors as frontal lobe meningiomas.

**16.9.    The answer is E** (*Synopsis*, ed. 4, page 279).

The distinction between delirium and dementia may be quite difficult and, at times, impossible to make, particularly at the transition time between delirium and dementia. *Delirium is characterized by rapid onset, generally brief duration, fluctuation of the cognitive impairment during the course of the day, nocturnal worsening of symptoms, and marked disturbance of the sleep-wakefulness cycle. Visual hallucinations and transient delusions are seen more commonly in delirium than in dementia, and intellectual deterioration of more than 1 month is more likely to be dementia than delirium.*

The table on page 184 lists in more detail some of the differences between delirium and dementia.

**16.10.    The answer is D** (*Synopsis*, ed. 4, pages 286, 287, and 289).

*Pick's disease* shows clinical manifestations similar to Alzheimer's disease; however, the brain pathology differs. In Pick's disease, there is marked localized asymmetrical atrophy of all or part of the frontal lobe or temporal lobe, as can be seen in the figure on page 184. Under the microscope, severe neuronal loss is seen, with destruction of normal cortical layers. *Alzheimer's disease* is characterized by generalized cortical atrophy and microscopically neurofibrillary tangles, and senile plaques are present.

Gross examination of the brain in *multiple sclerosis* reveals scattered gray, sharply demarcated plaques of demyelination that are variable in size and shape and are most numerous in the areas adjacent to the ventricles. *Chronic subdural hematoma* shows a marked displacement of the brain toward the opposite side of the lesion.

**16.11.    The answer is B** (*Synopsis*, ed. 4, pages 287 and 289).

*Alzheimer's disease* is most common in later life. It is characterized by neurofibrillary degeneration and senile plaques that are distinctive. The illness begins insidiously. Usually, the patient presents with an impairment of recent memory and then an impairment of judgment. These symptoms are generally associated with

### Clinical Differentiation of Delirium and Dementia*

| | Delirium | Dementia |
| --- | --- | --- |
| Onset | Acute | Usually insidious; if acute, preceded by coma or delirium |
| Duration | Usually less than 1 month | At least 1 month, usually much longer |
| Orientation | Faulty, at least for a time; tendency to mistake unfamiliar for familiar place, person | May be correct in mild cases |
| Thinking | Disorganized | Impoverished |
| Memory | Recent impaired | Both recent and remote impaired |
| Attention | Invariably disturbed, hard to direct or sustain | May be intact |
| Awareness | Always reduced, tends to fluctuate during daytime and be worse at night | Usually intact |
| Alertness | Increased or decreased | Normal or decreased |
| Perception | Misperceptions often present | Misperceptions often absent |
| Sleep-wakefulness cycle | Always disrupted | Usually normal for age |

* From Lipowski Z J: *Delirium: Acute Brain Failure in Man.* Charles C Thomas, Springfield, IL, 1979.

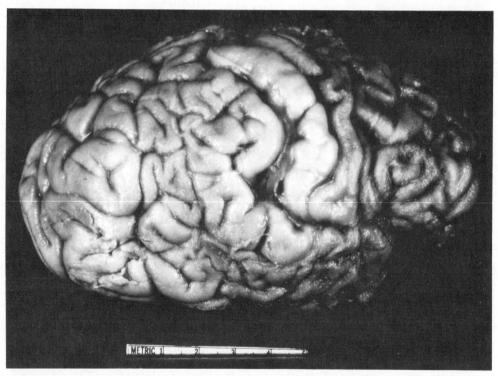

**(Courtesy of Thomas Reagan, MD, Mayo Clinic, Rochester, Minnesota.)**

some slowing and rigidity of movement and often with a slow and shuffling gait. The illness is progressive and commonly lasts for 1 to 10 years. As it progresses, no one feature is characteristic of the dementia. Later, it may be associated with specific intellectual changes, such as aphasia, apraxia, and agnosia. Late in the illness, myoclonic or generalized seizures may develop, and the patient often becomes helpless. Death is usually from intercurrent illness.

During the disease, the patient's attempts to adapt to the dementia may lead to an exaggeration of any prior psychopathology. The symptoms then often include depression or paranoid responses. These symptoms are often the ones that bring the patient to the attention of the physician.

*Multi-infarct dementia* is a disorder affecting small-size and medium-size cerebral vessels and generally produces multiple parenchymal lesions, spread over wide areas of the brain. The resultant clinical expression represents a summation of the effects of these multiple lesions and consists of a combination of neurological and psychiatric symptoms. *Meningioma*, an intracranial neoplasm, accounts for 15 percent of all intracranial tumors in adults. The clinical signs and symptoms depend on the specific site or origin of the tumor. *Pick's disease* is a dementia characterized by atrophy of the temporal and frontal lobe.

**16.12.   The answer is A** (*Synopsis*, ed. 4, pages 274 and 275).

Delirium is, by definition, a *transient disorder*, which implies that the syndrome is *never chronic*. The outcome, however, is not always one of the return of premorbid mental functioning. On an average, delirium lasts 1 week, less often several weeks, and quite rarely a few months. Delirium may recur at varying intervals, and if the underlying cerebral disorder persists, delirium becomes dementia or a more chronic brain syndrome in which there is a relatively stable cognitive impairment. *Delirium may first become apparent at night*, when the patient experiences confusion about his or her whereabouts, situation, and the dividing line between dreams and hallucinations. The essential features of delirium include *a rapid onset; multiple disturbances of attention, memory, orientation, and thinking; and a disorder of the sleep-wakefulness cycle.*

The table in column 2 outlines the DSM-III diagnostic criteria for delirium.

**16.13.   The answer is C** (*Synopsis*, ed. 4, page 273).

The incidence of delirium after open-heart and coronary-bypass surgery is about *30 percent*. Of severely burned patients, about 20 to 30 percent become delirious.

**16.14.   The answer is C** (*Synopsis*, ed. 4, page 273).

The incidence of delirium in surgical intensive care units has been reported to range from *18 to 30 percent.*

**16.15.   The answer is B** (*Synopsis*, ed. 4, page 273).

Some *5 to 15 percent* of the patients on general medical and surgical wards are likely to manifest delirium of some degree of severity.

**Diagnostic Criteria for Delirium***

A. Clouding of consciousness (reduced clarity of awareness of the environment), with reduced capacity to shift, focus, and sustain attention to environmental stimuli.

B. At least two of the following:

1. Perceptual disturbance: misinterpretations, illusions, or hallucinations
2. Speech that is at times incoherent
3. Disturbance of sleep-wakefulness cycle, with insomnia or daytime drowsiness
4. Increased or decreased psychomotor activity

C. Disorientation and memory impairment (if testable).

D. Clinical features that develop over a short period of time (usually hours to days) and tend to fluctuate over the course of a day.

E. Evidence, from the history, physical examination, or laboratory tests, of a specific organic factor judged to be etiologically related to the disturbance.

* From American Psychiatric Association: *Diagnostic and Statistical Manual of Mental Disorders*, ed 3. American Psychiatric Association, Washington, DC, 1980. Used with permission.

**16.16.   The answer is D** (*Synopsis*, ed. 4, page 273).

*Delirium* is one of the most common mental disorders diagnosed by liaison psychiatrists in general hospitals. At least 20 percent of patients seen by them in psychiatric consultation exhibit an organic brain syndrome, most often delirium.

**16.17.   The answer is B** (*Synopsis*, ed. 4, page 275).

After emerging from delirium, there is *impaired recall of memories formed before the onset of the delirium*, and defective registration and probably retention of current percepts. After resolution of the delirium, *recall of the experiences during delirium is characteristically spotty*, and the patient may refer to it as a bad dream or a *nightmare that is only vaguely remembered*. *Schizophrenia does not develop after emergence from delirium*, i.e. delirium does not produce schizophrenia. Schizophrenia, however, can be exacerbated by an episode of delirium.

**16.18.   The answer is C** (*Synopsis*, ed. 4, pages 291 and 292).

Classified by duration of action, the barbiturates comprise the long-acting types, such as phenobarbital; the short-acting types, such as secobarbital and pentobarbital; and the ultra short-acting types most commonly used in general anesthesia, such as thiopental. Acute intoxication produces general depression of the central nervous system, with dizziness, ataxia, confusion, slurred speech, stupor, and coma. Initial excitation may be seen in early intoxication because of the disinhibiting effects on the cortex.

In general, severe intoxication is produced by the ingestion of 200 to 1,000 mg orally; the fatal dose is only slightly higher, about *1,000 to 1,500 mg*. In patients with already compromised brain function or those who have ingested other sedative substances, such as alcohol, much smaller doses may produce severe acute intoxication or death.

**16.19.   The answer is C** (*Synopsis*, ed. 4, page 276).

About *1 million Americans over age 65* have a significant degree of intellectual impairment justifying the diagnosis of dementia. About 65 percent of them suffer from Alzheimer's type of dementia. These estimates do not take into account dementia of various causes occurring in people less than 65 years old. Each year, approximately 10 million Americans sustain head injuries of sufficient severity to require medical attention, and 633,000 persons have cerebral lacerations, contusions, or subdural or epidural hematomas. Thus, head trauma alone is likely to contribute significantly to the incidence and the prevalence of dementia. Alcoholism is another cause, of an unknown, but probably considerable, magnitude.

**16.20.   The answer is C** (*Synopsis*, ed. 4, pages 282 and 283).

Organic hallucinosis is a mental disorder in which *recurrent or persistent hallucinations in a state of no clouding of consciousness (such as in delirium) are the predominant or only symptom*, and are attributed to some clearly defined organic factor. As a rule, the patient is fully oriented, but may display a *mild intellectual deficit*. A significant loss of intellectual abilities, as in dementia, is not seen. Organic hallucinosis is *most often seen in the context of chronic alcoholism* or hallucinogen abuse, or as a toxic side effect of a drug, such as levodopa. The course

and the prognosis depend on whatever is the underlying pathology. *The onset is usually acute, with an average duration of days to weeks.*

Below is a table summarizing the DSM-III diagnostic criteria for organic hallucinosis.

**16.21.   The answer is B** (*Synopsis*, ed. 4, pages 271, 272, and 273).

*Tourette's disorder* is not considered an organic brain syndrome. It is a rare illness having its onset in childhood and is characterized by involuntary muscular movements, motor incoordination, echolalia, and coprolalia.

According to DSM-III, a distinction is made between organic brain syndrome and organic mental disorder. Organic brain syndrome refers to a constellation of psychological or behavioral signs and symptoms without reference to etiology, e.g. delirium, dementia. Organic mental disorder designates a particular brain syndrome in which the etiology is known or presumed.

Organic brain syndromes represent clusters of psychological or behavioral abnormalities or symptoms that show a tendency to occur together; these constitute the class of mental disorders designated organic. These syndromes share a common feature in that a cerebral disorder constitutes a necessary condition for their occurrence. Their essential clinical characteristics, however, differ widely and reflect such variables as the degree of spread, the localization, the rate of onset and progression, and the nature of the underlying pathological process in the brain. Further, the clinical picture displayed by any given patient is modified to some extent by his or her personality structure, intelligence, education, emotional state, interpersonal relationships, and other psychological and social factors.

The whole class of conditions caused by or associated with cerebral disease or dysfunction is designated organic mental disorders. The disorders encompass nine purely descriptive clusters of psychopathological symptoms referred to as organic brain syndromes. The nine syndromes include four groups: (1) those with relatively global cognitive impairment—delirium

---

**Diagnostic Criteria for Organic Hallucinosis***

A. Persistent or recurrent hallucinations are the predominant clinical feature.

B. No clouding of consciousness, as in delirium; no significant loss of intellectual abilities, as in dementia; no predominant disturbance of mood, as in organic affective syndrome; no predominant delusions, as in organic delusional syndrome.

C. Evidence, from the history, physical examination, or laboratory tests, of a specific organic factor that is judged to be etiologically related to the disturbance.

---

* From American Psychiatric Association: *Diagnostic and Statistical Manual of Mental Disorders*, ed 3. American Psychiatric Association, Washington, DC, 1980. Used with permission.

and dementia; (2) those characterized by relatively circumscribed cognitive impairment or abnormality—amnestic syndrome and *organic hallucinosis*; (3) those that are predominantly manifested by personality disturbances or that closely resemble some of the functional mental disorders—*organic personality syndrome, affective syndrome, and delusional syndrome*; and (4) those that are associated with ingestion (intoxication) or reduction (withdrawal) in the use of a substance.

No single set of psychological abnormalities may be regarded as characteristic or pathognomonic of the class of organic mental disorders as a whole. Only those symptoms that are most commonly and predictably associated with demonstrable cerebral disease are discussed here. The most common and, hence, clinically the most important psychopathological manifestations of brain pathology involve the impairment of one or more cognitive functions, including memory, thinking, perception, and attention. The following list includes the most common manifestations of impaired cognitive functions and information processing.

1. Memory impairment, especially that manifested by the impaired recall of relatively recent events and by the inadequate formulation of new memories and, thus, by impaired ability to learn;

2. Impairment of abstract thinking, manifested by the reduced ability to generalize, synthesize, differentiate, reason logically, form concepts, solve problems, and plan action;

3. Impairment of ability to perform novel tasks and to sustain cognitive performance, especially under time pressure and in the face of irrelevant stimuli or distraction;

4. Decrement of over-all intellectual functioning;

5. Impairment of judgment; that is, reduced ability to anticipate and appreciate likely adverse consequences of one's action, especially in a social context;

6. Attention disturbance, such as impaired ability to mobilize, focus, sustain, or shift attention;

7. Impaired spatiotemporal orientation;

8. Impaired ability to calculate;

9. Impaired ability to grasp the meaning of information inputs;

10. Impaired or distorted perception of one's body and one's environment, and of the self-environment boundary, with consequent perplexity and tendency to misperceptions or body image disorders or both.

Verbal and nonverbal expression of emotions, drives, and impulses are often changed and inappropriate in patients with cerebral disease. Apathy, euphoria, and irritability are common emotional concomitants of cognitive impairment and of organic personality disorder. The patient with brain damage tends to exhibit emotional lability—that is, undue readiness to cry, laugh, or show anger—and a tendency to shift rapidly from one form of emotional expression to another. Such reduced capacity for the control and fine modulation of emotional expression is the most common form of emotional pathology in the patient with an organic mental disorder.

Disturbances of alertness and wakefulness (vigilance) also occur. A typical feature of an acute or transient and widespread cerebral disorder is a disturbance of awareness of self and the environment. Basic to this disturbance is a disorder of wakefulness and of alertness; that is, readiness to respond to stimuli. This type of psychopathology is often referred to in the literature as disturbances of consciousness. Terms such as clouding, reduction, alteration, and narrowing of consciousness are commonly used in this context.

Patients with cerebral damage or dysfunction tend to exhibit characteristic behavior patterns aimed at maintaining adequate performance and avoiding distress engendered by its failure. These compensatory and protective coping strategies are referred to here as symptoms, whether they are adaptive or maladaptive.

A person suffering from an organic mental disorder tends to react to it cognitively, emotionally, and behaviorally. These reactions reflect the subjective meaning of the disorder for the patient and his or her personality, value system, social and economic situation, and other psychosocial variables. Specifically, psychotic symptoms represent the most severe form of reactive pathology. For example, a habitually suspicious and mistrustful person may develop frank paranoid delusions of persecution, jealousy, or somatic change. Another patient may display delusions of grandeur or of poverty accompanied by appropriate affect. As a general rule, reactive psychopathology is most likely to accompany relatively mild or moderate cognitive impairment or abnormality. It may be difficult or even impossible to distinguish reactive symptoms from those more directly related to cerebral damage or dysfunction.

**16.22.    The answer is E (all)** (*Synopsis*, ed. 4, page 290).

Multi-infarct dementia is the *DSM-III diagnosis for the disorder also known as the lacunar state.* This disorder affects small- and medium-sized cerebral vessels, producing multiple, widely spread cerebral lesions that result in a combination of neurological and psychiatric symptoms. Multi-infarct dementia *is found in hypertensive patients* and manifests with a *stepwise progression of bilateral, sometimes fluctuat-*

### Diagnostic Criteria for Multi-infarct Dementia*

A. Dementia.

B. Stepwise deteriorating course (i.e. not uniformly progressive) with "patchy" distribution of deficits (i.e. affecting some functions, but not others) early in the course.

C. Focal neurological signs and symptoms (e.g. exaggeration of deep tendon reflexes, extensor plantar response, pseudobulbar palsy, gait abnormalities, weakness of an extremity, etc.).

D. Evidence, from the history, physical examination, or laboratory tests, of significant cerebrovascular disease that is judged to be etiologically related to the disturbance.

* From American Psychiatric Association: *Diagnostic and Statistical Manual of Mental Disorders*, ed 3. American Psychiatric Association, Washington, DC, 1980. Used with permission.

*ing, motor symptoms.* These symptoms are accompained by dementia. The clinical description of this disorder includes a variety of symptoms, ranging from headaches, dizziness, and transient focal neurological symptoms to *personality changes, such as emotional lability and hypochondriasis.*

The above table gives the DSM-III diagnostic criteria for multi-infarct dementia.

**16.23.   The answer is E (all)** (*Synopsis*, ed. 4, page 285).

Organic personality syndrome is characterized by a marked change in personality that is due to a specific organic factor. *Head trauma* is among the most important causes of organic personality syndrome. Conditions most often associated with the syndrome are listed in the table below.

### Conditions Associated with Organic Personality Syndrome

*Head trauma*
Subarachnoid hemorrhage and other *vascular accidents*
*Space-occupying lesions of the brain:* neoplasm, aneurysm, abscess, granuloma
Temporal lobe epilepsy
Postencephalitic parkinsonism
Huntington's chorea
Multiple sclerosis
Endocrine disorders
*Chronic poisoning:* manganese, mercury
Drugs: cannabis, LSD, steroids, etc.
Neurosyphilis
Arteritis, such as in systemic lupus erythematosus

**16.24.   The answer is E (all)** (*Synopsis*, ed. 4, pages 283 and 284).

The organic affective syndrome may be caused by a number of organic factors, and in fact its diagnosis is dependent on the finding of a clearly defined causative organic condition. Many somatic disorders, such as *infectious mononucleosis* and *systemic lupus erythemato-*

*sus,* and drugs, such as *reserpine,* have been implicated in the causes of depressive and, to a lesser degree, manic disorders.

*Parkinsonism* is an extrapyramidal dyskinesia characterized by resting tremor, rigidity, bradykinesia, and postural abnormalities. Primary parkinsonism—also called paralysis agitans, Parkinson's disease, and idiopathic parkinsonism—is a disorder of middle or late life, typically with a gradual progression and a prolonged course. Its cause is unknown. A parkinsonian syndrome may develop during the course of therapy with antipsychotic phenothiazine or butyrophenone drugs. Such drug-induced parkinsonism is reversible when the causative drug is withdrawn or its dosage reduced.

Conditions reported to be associated with depressive or manic symptoms are listed in the following table.

### Conditions Associated with Organic Affective Syndrome

Drugs: *reserpine,* corticosteroids, methyldopa, levodopa, cycloserine, ethionamide, oral contraceptives, amphetamines, hallucinogens
Endocrine diseases: hypothyroidism, Cushing's syndrome, Addison's disease, hyperparathyroidism
Infectious diseases: influenza, *infectious mononucleosis,* infectious hepatitis, viral pneumonia
Pernicious anemia
Carcinoma of the pancreas
Brain tumor
*Systemic lupus erythematosus*
*Parkinsonism*
Carcinoid syndrome
Neurosyphilis

**16.25.   The answer is E (all)** (*Synopsis*, ed. 4, page 275).

Delirium may have one of four outcomes: (1) *full recovery* of premorbid functioning, the most common outcome; (2) *death*; (3) transition to *dementia* or another organic brain syndrome; or (4) transition to a nonorganic mental disorder, such as *paranoia* or schizophrenia—a rare event.

**16.26.  The answer is A (1, 2, 3)** (*Synopsis*, ed. 4, page 272).

*An age of 60 years or more* increases suceptibility to organic mental disorders. Both delirium and dementia are particularly frequent in the elderly, and *preexisting brain damage* of any origin enhances susceptiblity to delirium. *Reduced ability to metabolize drugs* is a factor predisposing elderly patients to the development of delirium in response to even therapeutic doses of medical drugs.

Certain features of the environment may facilitate the occurrence of an organic mental disorder, especially delirium or dementia. Social isolation, interpersonal conflicts and losses, unfamiliarity of the environment, and deficient or excessive sensory inputs may have such an influence. A *familiar environment* is helpful in decreasing a patient's vulnerability to an organic mental disorder.

**16.27.  The answer is A (1, 2, 3)** (*Synopsis*, ed. 4, page 277).

Dementia represents the result of relatively widespread brain pathology caused by any one of a large number of cerebral and systemic diseases. The term has come to mean a progressive and irreversible intellectual deterioration; however, this progression and irreversibility are not necessarily the course in all cases of dementia. Probably the connotation of irreversibility came about through the erroneous equation of dementia—a syndrome—with presenile and senile dementia, such as *Alzheimer's*—a group of typically progressive and irreversible cerebral dysfunctions. Of the 1 million Americans over age 65 who carry the diagnosis of dementia, about 65 percent suffer from Alzheimer's type of dementia. There are also other dementias of various causes occurring in people younger than 65 years old, which are reversible. Head trauma alone contributes significantly to the incidence and prevalence of dementia.

The table below lists a number of diseases and conditions causing dementia.

#### Diseases and Conditions Causing Dementia

Degenerative diseases of the central nervous system
  *Alzheimer's disease*
  Senile dementia
  Simple cortical atrophy
  Pick's disease
  Huntington's chorea
  Parkinson's disease
  Progressive supranuclear palsy
Vascular disorders
  Multi-infarct dementia
  Carotid artery occlusive disease
  Cranial arteritis
  Subarachnoid hemorrhage
  Arteriovenous malformation
  Cerebral embolism
  Binswanger's disease
Metabolic, endocrine, and nutritional disorders
  Hepatic, renal, or pulmonary failure
  Dialysis dementia
  Endocrinopathies: hypothyroidism, hypopituitarism, hypoparathyroidism, hyperparathyroidism, *Addison's disease*, Cushing's syndrome, hyperinsulinism
  Chronic disorders of electrolyte metabolism: hypercalcemia, hypocalcemia, hyponatremia, hypernatremia, hypokalemia
  Hypoxia or anoxia of any origin, such as secondary to cardiac arrest or congestive heart failure
  Hepatolenticular degeneration (Wilson's disease)
  Paget's disease
  Porphyria
  Avitaminosis: cyanocobalamine, folate, nicotinic acid, thiamine
  Vitamin intoxication: vitamins A and D
  Remote effects of carcinoma and lymphomas

Intracranial space-occupying lesions
  Neoplasm, benign or malignant
  Aneurysm
  Colloid cyst
  Chronic subdural hematoma
  Chronic abscess
  Parasitic cyst
  Tuberculoma
  Lymphoma and leukemia
*Head trauma*
Epilepsy
Infections
  Meningitis of any cause
  *Encephalitis of any cause*
  Brucellosis
  Syphilis
  Subacute sclerosing panencephalitis
  Creutzfeldt-Jakob disease
  Kuru
  Multifocal leukoencephalopathy
Intoxication
  Alcohol
  Heavy metals: mercury, lead, arsenic, thallium
  Carbon monoxide
  Medical drugs, such as barbiturates
Normal-pressure hydrocephalus
Heat stroke
Electric injury
Disorders of the hematopoietic system
  Erythremia
  Thrombotic thrombocytopenic purpura
Miscellaneous diseases of unknown origin
  Sarcoidosis
  Histiocytosis X
  Multiple sclerosis

**16.28.   The answer is E (all)** (*Synopsis*, ed. 4, pages 276, 277, and 279).

Below is a table summarizing the DSM-III criteria for the diagnosis of dementia.

### Diagnostic Criteria for Dementia*

A.  A loss of intellectual abilities of sufficient severity to interfere with social or occupational functioning.

B.  Memory impairment.

C.  At least one of the following:
1.  Impairment of abstract thinking, as manifested by concrete interpretation of proverbs, inability to find similarities and differences between related words, difficulty in defining words and concepts, and other similar tasks;
2.  Impaired judgment;
3.  Other disturbances of higher cortical function, such as aphasia (disorder of language due to brain dysfunction), apraxia (inability to carry out motor activities despite intact comprehension and motor function), agonosia (failure to recognize or identify objects despite intact sensory function), "constructional difficulty" (e.g. inability to copy three-dimensional figures, assemble blocks, or arrange sticks in specific designs);
4.  Personality change, i.e. alteration or accentuation of premorbid traits.

D.  State of consciousness not clouded (i.e. does not meet the criteria for delirium or intoxication, although these may be superimposed).

E.  Either (1) or (2):
1.  Evidence, from the history, physical examination, or laboratory tests, of a specific organic factor that is judged to be etiologically related to the disturbance;
2.  In the absence of such evidence, an organic factor necessary for the development of the syndrome can be presumed if conditions other than organic mental disorders have been reasonably excluded and if the behavioral change represents cognitive impairment in a variety of areas.

* From American Psychiatric Association: *Diagnostic and Statistical Manual of Mental Disorders*, ed 3. American Psychiatric Association, Washington, DC, 1980. Used with permission.

Dementia is an organic brain syndrome, characterized by a manifestation of relatively widespread cerebral pathology, *an acquired decrement of intellect* severe enough to impair social or occupational performance, or both. A fully developed case features impairment of memory, abstract thinking, and judgment; defective control of impulses and emotions; and personality change in the direction of either *an accentuation or alteration of the patient's usual character traits.* To make the diagnosis, evidence of change

in the patient's accustomed performance and behavior in ordinary life situations is sought, especially if the patient is over 40 years old and has a negative psychiatric history. The cause of dementia is multifactorial in that *psychosocial factors influence its occurrence, severity, and cause.* Premorbid personality, intelligence, and education seem to influence the patient's motivation and capacity to compensate for the intellectual deficits. The patient's current emotional state may influence the degree of severity of impairment, especially when the patient is anxious or depressed. The disorder may be progressive, static, or *reversible.* The syndrome may recede over a period of time in response to treatment or as a result of a natural healing process. Treatment should be directed at the dementia's cause, but in more than 50 percent of the cases of dementia in the elderly, no effective treatment of the underlying cerebral disorder is available.

**16.29.   The answer is E (all)** (*Synopsis*, ed. 4, page 280).

The core feature of the amnestic syndrome is the impairment of memory. It is an organic mental disorder characterized by *an impairment of memory as the single or predominant cognitive defect.* The memory pathology is of two types, *retrograde and anterograde.* Retrograde is a loss of memories based before the onset of the illness, and anterograde is the reduced ability to recall current events. Although recent memory is impaired, there is *preservation of the ability for immediate recall*, such as is tested by digit span. A number of organic pathological factors and conditions can give rise to the amnestic syndrome, and in fact, *evidence of a specific etiological organic factor* is required for the diagnosis.

The following table lists the DSM-III diagnostic criteria for amnestic syndrome.

### Diagnostic Criteria for Amnestic Syndrome*

A.  Both short-term memory impairment (inability to learn new information) and long-term memory impairment (inability to remember information that was known in the past) are the predominant clinical features.

B.  No clouding of consciousness, as in delirium and intoxication, or general loss of major intellectual abilities, as in dementia.

C.  Evidence, from the history, physical examination, or laboratory tests, of a specific organic factor that is judged to be etiologically related to the disturbance.

* From American Psychiatric Association: *Diagnostic and Statistical Manual of Mental Disorders*, ed 3. American Psychiatric Association, Washington, DC, 1980. Used with permission.

**16.30. The answer is B (1, 3)** (*Synopsis,* ed. 4, page 280).

A very important clinical diagnostic problem concerns the differentiation of dementia from a depressive disorder with cognitive impairment—pseudodementia. There are a number of factors that are helpful in making the differentiation, including *onset of depressive symptoms, presentation of cognitive deficits, intellectual performance,* and *sodium amobarbital interviews.*

The following table lists these factors, and others, in detail.

### Differentiation of Dementia from Depressive Pseudodementia

| | Dementia | Pseudodementia |
| --- | --- | --- |
| Onset | Intellectual deficits antedate depression | Depressive symptoms antedate cognitive deficits |
| Presentation of symptoms | Patient minimizes or denies cognitive deficits, tries to conceal them by circumstantiality, perseveration, changing topic of conversation | Patient complains vocally of memory impairment and poor intellectual performance, exaggerates and dwells on these deficits |
| Appearance and behavior | Often neglected, sloppy; manner facetious or apathetic and indifferent; catastrophic reaction may be evoked; emotional expression often labile and superficial | Facial expression sad, worried; manner retarded or agitated, never facetious or euphoric; bemoans or ridicules own impaired performance but no true catastrophic reaction |
| Response to questions | Often evasive, angry, or sarcastic when pressed for answers, or tries hard to answer correctly but just misses | Often slow, "I don't know" type of answer |
| Intellectual performance | Usually globally impaired and consistently poor | Often confined to memory impairment; inconsistent; if globally impaired, it is so because patient refuses to make effort |
| Sodium amobarbital interview | All cognitive deficits accentuated | Performance improved |

**16.31. The answer is D (4)** (*Synopsis,* ed. 4, page 287).

Atypical or mixed organic brain syndrome is *a DSM-III category* describing a disturbance that *occurs in the waking state* and that *does not meet the criteria for any of the other organic brain syndromes described in DSM-III.* Like the other syndromes, however, it also *requires evidence of a specific organic factor judged to be causally related to the disturbance.*

The following table summarizes the DSM-III diagnostic criteria for this syndrome.

### Diagnostic Criteria for Atypical or Mixed Organic Brain Syndrome*

A. The disturbance occurs during the waking state and does not fulfill the criteria for any of the previously described organic brain syndromes.

B. Evidence, from the history, physical examination, or laboratory tests, of a specific organic factor that is judged to be etiologically related to the disturbance.

* From American Psychiatric Association: *Diagnostic and Statistical Manual of Mental Disorders,* ed 3. American Psychiatric Association, Washington, DC, 1980. Used with permission.

**16.32. The answer is E (all)** (*Synopsis,* ed. 4, pages 273 and 274).

Delirium has a multitude of organic causes. In fact, the term delirium denotes a transient organic mental disturbance characterized by a global impairment of cognitive functions and a widespread disturbance of cerebral metabolism. Delirium has been known in the past as acute confusional state, acute brain syndrome, or toxic psychosis. A large number of diseases, both cerebral and systemic, and toxic agents introduced into the body from outside can lead to delirium.

The table at the top of page 192 lists in detail many of the organic causes of delirium.

**16.33. The answer is A (1, 2, 3)** (*Synopsis,* ed. 4, page 282).

The appearance of hallucinosis should prompt the search for organic etiological factors. Visual hallucinosis should alert one to the possibility of a *focal cerebral lesion,* hallucinogen abuse, side effects of medical drugs, *migraine,* or *temporal arteritis.* Auditory hallucinosis should raise a question about alcohol abuse. Organic

## Organic Cause of Delirium*

1. Introduction
   A. Drugs: anticholinergic agents, sedative-hypnotics, digitalis derivatives, cimetidine, methyldopa, levodopa, opiates, salicylates, anticonvulsants, antiarrhythmic agents, phencyclidine, etc.
   B. Alcohol
   C. Addictive inhalants: gasoline, glue, ether, nitrous oxide
   D. Industrial poisons: carbon monoxide and disulfide, organic solvents, methyl chlorides, heavy metals
2. Alcohol and drug withdrawal
   A. Alcohol—delirium tremens
   B. Sedatives and hypnotics: barbiturates, chloral hydrate, benzodiazepines, ethchlorvynol, methyprylon, glutethimide, meprobamate, paraldehyde
   C. Amphetamines—occasionally
3. Metabolic encephalopathies
   A. Hepatic, renal, pulmonary, pancreatic insufficiency or failure
   B. Hypoxia
   C. *Hypoglycemia*
   D. Vitamin deficiency: nicotinic acid, thiamine, cyanocobalamine, folate
   E. Endocrinopathies: hyperinsulinism, hyperthyroidism, hypothyroidism, hypopituitarism, Addison's disease, Cushing's syndrome, hypoparathyroidism, hyperparathyroidism
   F. Disorders of fluid, electrolyte, and acid-base balance: hypernatremia, hyponatremia, hyperkalemia, *hypokalemia*, hypercalcemia, hypocalcemia, hypermagnesemia, hypomagnesemia, alkalosis, acidosis, dehydration, water intoxication
   G. Errors of metabolism: porphyria, carcinoid syndrome
4. Infections
   A. Systemic: pneumonia, typhoid, typhus, acute rheumatic fever, malaria, influenza, mumps, diphtheria, brucellosis, Rocky Mountain spotted fever, *infectious mononucleosis*, infectious hepatitis, Legionnaires' disease
   B. Intracranial: viral, bacterial, fungal, protozoal encephalitis and meningitis, postvaccinial and postinfectious encephalomyelitis, trichinosis
5. Epilepsy
6. Head injury
7. Vascular diseases
   A. Cerebrovascular: hypertensive encephalopathy; arteritis—systemic lupus erythematosus, rheumatoid vasculitis, polyarteritis nodosa; temporal arteritis; thrombosis, embolism, subarachnoid hemorrhage
   B. Cardiovascular: myocardial infarction, congestive heart failure, cardiac arrhythmias
   C. *Migraine*
8. Intracranial tumor
   A. Neoplasm
   B. Abscess
   C. Subdural hematoma
   D. Aneurysm
   E. Parasitic cyst
9. Cerebral degenerative diseases
   A. Multiple sclerosis
   B. Alzheimer's disease—senile dementia
10. Injury by physical agents
    A. Hyperthermia
    B. Hypothermia
    C. Electric injury
11. Diseases due to hypersensitivity
    A. Serum sickness
    B. Food allergy

\* Modified from Lipowski Z J: *Delirium: Acute Brain Failure in Man.* Charles C Thomas, Springfield, IL. 1979.

### Causative Factors in Organic Hallucinosis

Space-occupying lesions of the brain:
  Neoplasm: craniopharyngioma, chromophobe adenoma, meningioma of the olfactory groove, temporal lobe tumors
  Aneurysm
  Abscess
Temporal arteritis
Migraine
Hypothyroidism
Neurosyphilis
Huntington's chorea
Cerebrovascular disease
Disease of sense organs: bilateral cataracts, glaucoma, otosclerosis
Substance abuse
  Alcohol (acute alcoholic hallucinosis)
  Hallucinogens: LSD, psilocybin, mescaline, morning glory seed
  Cocaine
Drug toxicity: levodopa, bromocriptine, amantadine, ephedrine, pentazocine, propranolol, methylphenidate

hallucinosis must be distinguished from delirium, which may be accompanied by hallucinations.

*Epilepsy* may feature auditory or visual hallucinations or both; however, such hallucinations usually occur in a setting of reduced, not clear, awareness, such as part of an ictal state. As a rule, the patient with organic hallucinosis is fully oriented without an impairment of attention or cognitive functions.

The table above outlines a number of causative factors for organic hallucinosis.

**16.34.  The answer is E (all)** (*Synopsis*, ed. 4, page 287).

In DSM-III, intoxication is listed as a residual category for a clinical picture not fitting any specific organic brain syndrome. Common ex-amples of intoxication might be *maladaptive behavior* caused by the use of marijuana, *amphetamines*, or alcohol.

The following table lists the DSM-III diagnostic criteria for intoxication.

### Diagnostic Criteria for Intoxication*

A. Development of a *substance-specific syndrome that follows the recent ingestion and presence in the body of a substance.*

B. Maladaptive behavior during the waking state due to the effect of the substance on the central nervous system, e.g. impaired judgment, belligerence.

C. The clinical picture does not correspond to any of the specific organic brain syndromes, such as delirium, organic delusional syndrome, organic hallucinosis, or organic affective syndrome.

* From American Psychiatric Association: *Diagnostic and Statistical Manual of Mental Disorders*, ed 3. American Psychiatric Association, Washington, DC, 1980. Used with permission.

**16.35.  The answer is B (1, 3)** (*Synopsis*, ed. 4, pages 285 and 286).

Organic personality syndrome is character-ized by a change in personality style manifested by *reduced desire* and by an impaired control of behavioral expressions of emotions and im-pulses. There must be evidence of some causa-tive organic factors antedating the onset of the syndrome. *Emotions are typically labile and shallow*, with euphoria or apathy predominating. Apathy may lead one to assume the presence of a depressed mood, but *true sadness and depression are uncommon*. Temper outbursts with little or no provocation may occur, resulting in violent behavior, and *expression of impulses is characteristically disinhibited*, resulting in inappro-priate jokes, a crude manner, improper sexual advances, or outright antisocial behavior.

The following table summarizes the DSM-III criteria for diagnosing organic personality syn-drome.

### Diagnostic Criteria for Organic Personality Syndrome*

A. A marked change in behavior or personality involving at least one of the following:

1. Emotional lability, e.g. explosive temper outbursts, sudden crying;
2. Impairment in impulse control, e.g. poor social judgment, sexual indiscretions, shoplifting;
3. Marked apathy and indifference, e.g. no interest in usual hobbies;
4. Suspiciousness or paranoid ideation.

B. No clouding of consciousness, as in delirium; no significant loss of intellectual abilities, as in dementia; no predominant disturbance of mood, as in organic affective syndrome; no predominant delusions or hallucinations, as in organic delusional syndrome or organic hallucinosis.

C. Evidence, from the history, physical examination, or laboratory tests, of a specific organic factor that is judged to be etiologically related to the disturbance.

D. This diagnosis is not given to a child or adolescent if the clinical picture is limited to the features that characterize attention deficit disorder.

* From American Psychiatric Association: *Diagnostic and Statistical Manual of Mental Disorders*, ed 3. American Psychiatric Association, Washington, DC, 1980. Used with permission.

**16.36.  The answer is E (all)** (*Synopsis*, ed. 4, pages 280 and 281).

The mode of onset, the course, and the prog-nosis of the amnestic syndrome depend on its cause. The syndrome may be *transient, persistent, or permanent*, and its outcome may be complete or partial recovery of memory function or an irreversible or even progressive memory defect. The transient syndrome may result from such conditions as head injury, carbon monoxide poisoning, temporal lobe epilepsy, migraine, car-diac arrest, or electroconvulsive therapy. Per-sistent memory impairment may result from subarachnoid hemorrhage, cerebral infarction, or herpes simplex encephalitis. The *slowly progressive* syndrome suggests a brain tumor, Alz-heimer's disease, or senile dementia.

The table at the top of page 194 lists a number of causes of amnestic syndrome.

### Causes of Amnestic Syndrome

Thiamine deficiency (Wernicke-Korsakoff's syndrome) usually due to alcoholism

Head trauma with damage of the diencephalic or temporal regions; postconcussive states; whiplash injury

Brain tumor involving the floor and the walls of the third ventricle or both hippocampal formations

Subarachnoid hemorrhage

Intoxication: carbon monoxide, isoniazid, arsenic, lead

Vascular disorders: bilateral hippocampal infarction due to thrombosis or embolism occluding posterior cerebral arteries or their inferior temporal branches

Intracranial infections: herpes simplex encephalitis, tuberculous meningitis

Cerebral anoxia: after unsuccessful hanging attempt, cardiac arrest, inadequate aeration or prolonged hypotension during general anesthesia

Degenerative cerebral diseases: Alzheimer's disease, senile dementia

Bilateral temporal lobectomy with bilateral hippocampal lesions

Surgery for ruptured aneurysm of the anterior communicating artery

Electroshock treatment

Epilepsy

Transient global amnesia

---

**16.37.   The answer is A (1, 2, 3)** (*Synopsis*, ed. 4, page 283).

Organic delusional syndrome is characterized by the predominance of delusions in a state of full orientation and attention, which are attributed to some clearly defined organic factor. These *delusions may or may not be systematized*, and their content may vary. The syndrome needs to be distinguished from schizophrenic, schizophreniform, and paranoid disorders, with which it may share various features. The basis for distinguishing the disorders is that, for the diagnosis of organic delusional syndrome to be made, evidence of a *specific organic factor judged to be etiologically significant must be found*. A variety of chemical substances and cerebral or systemic diseases may induce the syndrome, and the syndrome often, but not always, *lifts after the toxic agent is removed or the physical illness is resolved*. For instance, amphetamine intoxication appears to be limited to a paranoid-type

psychosis, whereas *lesions of the limbic system appear to be linked to a schizophreniform-like psychosis.*

The table below summarizes the DSM-III diagnostic criteria for organic delusional syndrome.

**16.38.   The answer is E (all)** (*Synopsis*, ed. 4, pages 280 and 281).

The core feature of the amnestic syndrome is the impairment of memory. Regardless of the cause, there is an impairment of recent memory, with preservation of the ability for immediate recall, as tested by digit span, for example. Remote memories are preserved. *The ability to learn new material is defective*, the patient is unable to learn and remember such information as the name of the hospital or of his or her physician, and the *recall of events of the past decade or longer is defective*. The *sensorium and consciousness are clear.*

*Short-term memory impairment* is defined as the inability to learn new information, and *long-term memory impairment* is defined as the inability to remember information that was known in the past.

A number of organic pathological factors and conditions can give rise to the amnestic syndrome. Probably the most common cause in this country is thiamine deficiency associated with chronic alcoholism.

In the absence of epidemiological data, no definite statement about the frequency of the various causative associations can be given. *Most factors and disorders known to be associated with the amnestic syndrome can be seen in the table in column 1, above.*

**16.39.   The answer is E (all)** (*Synopsis*, ed. 4, pages 291 and 292).

The barbiturates are classified by duration of action, from long-acting types such as phenobarbital, to short-acting types such as secobarbital, to ultra short-acting types most commonly used in general anesthesia, such as thiopental. Acute intoxication produces *a general depression of the CNS*, although initial *excitement* may be seen in early intoxication due to the disinhibiting effects on the cortex. Signs and symptoms

---

### Diagnostic Criteria for Organic Delusional Syndrome*

A. Delusions are the predominant clinical feature.

B. There is no clouding of consciousness, as in delirium; there is no significant loss of intellectual abilities, as in dementia; there are no prominent hallucinations, as in organic hallucinosis.

C. There is evidence, from the history, physical examination, or laboratory tests, of a specific organic factor that is judged to be etiologically related to the disturbance.

---

*From American Psychiatric Association: *Diagnostic and Statistical Manual of Mental Disorders*, ed 3. American Psychiatric Association, Washington, DC, 1980. Used with permission.

may include dizziness, ataxia, confusion, irritability, *stupor*, and slurred speech.

The following table lists the DSM-III diagnostic criteria for barbiturate intoxication.

### Diagnostic Criteria for Barbiturate or Similarly Acting Sedative or Hypnotic Intoxication*

A. Recent use of a barbiturate or similarly acting sedative or hypnotic.

B. At least one of the following psychological signs:
   1. Mood lability;
   2. *Disinhibition of sexual and aggressive impulses*;
   3. Irritability;
   4. Loquacity.

C. At least one of the following neurological signs:
   1. Slurred speech;
   2. Incoordination;
   3. Unsteady gait;
   4. Impairment in attention or memory.

D. Maladaptive behavioral effects, e.g. impaired judgment, interference with social or occupational functioning, failure to meet responsibilities.

E. Not due to any other physical or mental disorder.

---

\* From American Psychiatric Association: *Diagnostic and Statistical Manual of Mental Disorders*, ed 3. American Psychiatric Association, Washington, DC, 1980. Used with permission.

**16.40.   The answer is B (1, 3)** (*Synopsis*, ed. 4, page 307).

Transient global amnesia is thought to result from a temporary physiological alteration of the brain. The precise cause of this disorder is unknown. Most clinicians now believe it to be an organic, rather than psychogenic, disturbance, but whether its cause is epileptiform or vascular, or neither, is unclear.

The patient with this syndrome *abruptly loses the ability to recall recent events* or to record new memories. *Events of the distant past are readily recalled.* Although often aware of some disturbance in function during the episode, the patient *may still perform highly complex mental and physical acts.*

*The syndrome is reversible*, but tends to recur.

**16.41–16.45.   The answers are 16.41–C, 16.42–D, 16.43–A, 16.44–B, and 16.45–E** (*Synopsis*, ed. 4, pages 298 and 299).

Chronic lead intoxication occurs when the amount of lead ingested exceeds the ability to eliminate it. It takes several months for toxic symptoms to appear. The signs and symptoms of lead intoxication depend on the level of lead in the blood. When lead reaches levels above 200 $\mu$g per 100 ml, symptoms of severe lead

encephalopathy occur, with dizziness, clumsiness, ataxia, irritability, restlessness, headache, and insomnia. Later, an excited delirium, with associated vomiting and visual disturbances, occurs, progressing to convulsions, lethargy, and coma. Treatment of lead encephalopathy should be instituted as rapidly as possible, even without laboratory confirmation, because of the high mortality. The treatment of choice to facilitate lead excretion is the intravenous administration of *calcium disodium edetate* daily for 5 days. One gram is given in each dose.

In acute mercury intoxication, central nervous system symptoms of lethargy and restlessness may occur, but the primary symptoms are secondary to severe gastrointestinal irritation, with bloody stools, diarrhea, and vomiting leading to circulatory collapse because of dehydration. Chronic mercury intoxication, resulting from the exposure to small amounts of mercury compounds over extended periods, is more important in the production of central nervous system syndromes. The *Mad Hatter* in Alice's Adventures in Wonderland was a parody of the madness resulting from the inhalation of mercury nitrate vapors, for mercury nitrate was used in the past in the processing of hair for felt hats. Central nervous system symptoms include mental depression, insomnia, fatigue, irritability, lethargy, and hallucinosis. Behavioral changes include excessive ease of embarrassment, timidity, withdrawal, and despondency. Mercury poisoning is best treated as soon as it is recognized with the use of a metal chelating agent, such as penicillamine or dimercaprol.

Early intoxication with manganese produces manganese madness, with symptoms of headache, irritability, joint pains, and somnolence. An eventual picture appears of emotional lability, pathological laughter, nightmares, hallucinations, and compulsive and impulsive acts associated with periods of confusion and aggressiveness. Lesions involving the basal ganglia and pyramidal system result in gait impairment, rigidity, monotonous or whispering speech, tremors of the extremities and tongue, *masked facies* (manganese mask), micrographia, dystonia, dysarthria, and loss of equilibrium.

Thallium intoxication initially causes severe pains in the legs, diarrhea, and vomiting. Within a week, delirium, convulsions, cranial nerve palsies, blindness, choreiform movements, and coma may occur. Behavioral changes include paranoid thinking and depression, with suicidal tendencies. *Alopecia* is a common and important diagnostic clue. Treatment is generally symptomatic.

Severe acute arsenic poisoning results in marked vomiting and diarrhea, followed by dryness of the mucous membranes and severe thirst. Death is the result of shock from fluid loss.

Chronic arsenic intoxication has a more insidious onset, with weakness, lethargy, anorexia, diarrhea, nausea, inflammation of the nose and upper respiratory tract, coughing, soreness of the mouth, and dermatitis, with *increased pigmentation of the neck, eyelids, nipples, and axillae.*

**16.46–16.50.   The answers are 16.46–C, 16.47–B, 16.48–A, 16.49–B, and 16.50–D** (*Synopsis*, ed. 4, pages 286 and 287).

Intoxication is defined as a substance-specific syndrome that develops *following the recent* *ingestion and presence in the body of a substance,* whereas withdrawal is that state that *follows the cessation or reduction of intake of a substance.* As with intoxication, the withdrawal syndrome that develops varies according to the substance involved; *both are substance-specific.* The clinical picture in withdrawal and intoxication *does not correspond to any specific organic brain syndrome,* and *maladaptive behavior* is listed only as an essential feature for intoxication.

The DSM-III diagnostic criteria for withdrawal are listed below.

---

### Diagnostic Criteria for Withdrawal*

A. Development of a substance-specific syndrome that follows the cessation of or reduction in intake of a substance that was previously regularly used by the individual to induce a state of intoxication.

B. The clinical picture does not correspond to any of the specific brain syndromes, such as delirium, organic delusional syndrome, organic hallucinosis, or organic affective syndrome.

---

* From American Psychiatric Association: *Diagnostic and Statistical Manual of Mental Disorders*, ed 3. American Psychiatric Association, Washington, DC, 1980. Used with permission.

**16.51–16.55.   The answers are 16.51–C, 16.52–B, 16.53–B, 16.54–C, and 16.55–D** (*Synopsis*, ed. 4, page 292).

Barbiturate withdrawal results after the *cessation of prolonged, heavy use* of a barbiturate, or more prolonged use of smaller doses of a minor tranquilizer, such as benzodiazepine. The withdrawal syndrome may produce a number of

### Diagnostic Criteria for Barbiturate or Similarly Acting Sedative or Hypnotic Withdrawal*

A. Prolonged, heavy use of barbiturate or similarly acting sedative or hypnotic, or more prolonged use of smaller doses of a benzodiazepine.

B. At least three of the following due to recent cessation of or reduction in substance use:

  1. Nausea and vomiting;
  2. Malaise or weakness;
  3. Autonomic hyperactivity, e.g. tachycardia, sweating, elevated blood pressure;
  4. Anxiety;
  5. Depressed mood or irritability;
  6. Orthostatic hypotension;
  7. Coarse tremor of hands, tongue, and eyelids.

C. Not due to any other physical or mental disorder, such as barbiturate or similarly acting sedative or hypnotic withdrawal delirium.

---

* From American Psychiatric Association: *Diagnostic and Statistical Manual of Mental Disorders*, ed 3. American Psychiatric Association, Washington, DC, 1980. Used with permission.

signs and symptoms, including gastrointestinal disturbances, autonomic hyperactivity, and *coarse tremor of hands, tongue, and eyelids.* Acute delirium may be caused by both high doses of barbiturates and by withdrawal of barbiturates. The withdrawal delirium is classified separately in DSM-III and is defined as delirium within 1 week following cessation of or reduction in heavy use of a barbiturate, associated with autonomic hyperactivity. *Tachycardia and elevated blood pressure* may clearly be seen in both intoxication and withdrawal, and incoordination with unsteady gait is seen during the intoxicated state. *Schizophrenia is not caused by either condition,* but may be aggravated by them.

The two DSM-III tables shown here summarize the diagnostic criteria for barbiturate withdrawal and withdrawal delirium.

### Diagnostic Criteria for Barbiturate or Similarly Acting Sedative or Hypnotic Withdrawal Delirium*

A. Delirium within 1 week after cessation of or reduction in heavy use of a barbiturate or similarly acting sedative or hypnotic.

B. Autonomic hyperactivity, e.g. tachycardia, sweating, elevated blood pressure.

C. Not due to any other physical or mental disorder.

---

* From American Psychiatric Association: *Diagnostic and Statistical Manual of Mental Disorders*, ed 3. American Psychiatric Association, Washington, DC, 1980. Used with permission.

# References

Alexander M P: Traumatic brain injury. In *Psychiatric Aspects of Neurologic Disease*, D F Benson, D Blumer, editors, vol 2, p 219. Grune & Stratton, New York, 1982.

Blass J P, Plum F: Metabolic encephalopathies in older adults. In *The Neurology of Aging*, R Katzman, R Terry, editors, p 189. F A Davis Co, Philadelphia, 1983.

Hill J: Disorders of memory, language, and beliefs, following closed head injury. Psychol Med *14:* 193, 1984.

Liston E H: Diagnosis and management of delirium in the elderly patient. Psychiatric Ann *14:* 109, 1984.

Reisberg B, Ferris S H, Gershon S: An overview of pharmacologic treatment of cognitive decline in the aged. Am J Psychiatry *138:* 593, 1981.

Wells C E: Diagnosis of dementia. Psychosom *25:* 183, 1984.

Wells C E: Organic mental disorders. In *Comprehensive Textbook of Psychiatry*, ed 4, H I Kaplan, B J Sadock, editors, p 834. Williams & Wilkins, Baltimore, 1985.

# 17

# Neurotic Disorders

The term neurosis has had differing connotations over the years. At one time, it implied a very severe mental disorder; but at the present time, it suggests a less serious syndrome with a mild to mildly moderate level of psychological pain, anxiety, hyperalertness, and withdrawal. The term implies a kind of maladaptation that restricts to some extent the person's over-all judgment, ability to make good contact with reality, and capacity to relate effectively with others in the environment.

The etiology of the neurotic disorders is not clearly understood, and several approaches—psychological and biological—to their etiology have been postulated. Freud, whose psychological approach is most noteworthy, believed that neuroses originated in childhood as a result of unconscious conflicts. He believed that both the libido (sexual instinct) and the aggressive instinct are in conflict with the ego, which attempts to defend itself against those impulses. Normally, repression and the use of other defense mechanisms allow for the healthy expression of instincts. If repression is weakened or if the defensive system is ineffective, however, the impulse breaks through in such a way that a neurotic symptom is produced. Neurotic disorders also may result from adverse life experiences, such as the loss of a loved one early in life or from parental neglect or abuse, which lead to a sense of mistrust as described by Erik Erikson, a follower of Freud. According to learning theorists, neurotic disorders are maladaptive behavior patterns that are learned either by faulty role modeling or as a result of a distorted reward-punishment paradigm.

Finally, biological models have been hypothesized to explain neuroses. For example, catecholamine levels have been found to decrease in some depressive states, and anxiety levels can be changed using various pharmacological agents, such as lactate infusions, carbon dioxide inhalation, $\beta$-noradrenergic agonists to increase anxiety, and diazepam to block anxiety. Other findings strongly indicate various distinct genetic, biological, and behavioral factors associated with the etiology of specific syndromes.

According to the third edition of the *Diagnostic and Statistical Manual of Mental Disorders* (DSM-III), a neurotic disorder is defined as "a mental disorder in which the predominant disturbance is a symptom or group of symptoms that is distressing to the individual and is recognized by him or her as unacceptable and alien (ego-dystonic); reality testing is grossly intact. Behavior does not actively violate gross social norms (though it may be quite disabling). The disturbance is relatively enduring or recurrent without treatment and is not limited to a transitory reaction to stressors. There is no demonstrable organic etiology or factor."

In this chapter, the authors have included under neurotic disorders the following: anxiety state, which is subdivided into panic disorder, generalized anxiety disorder, and obsessive-compulsive disorder; phobic disorder; posttraumatic stress disorder; somatoform disorder; and dissociative disorder. Dysthymic disorder and psychosexual disorder are also classified as neuroses, but are discussed separately. This organization is consistent with the DSM-III classification of neurotic disorders.

The student should read Chapter 17 of *Modern Synopsis-IV* on the neurotic disorders and should then study the questions and answers below to assess his or her knowledge of this area. Dysthymic disorder or depressive disorder may be found in Chapter 14 and psychosexual disorder in Chapter 20.

# Questions

**DIRECTIONS:** Each of the statements or questions below is followed by five suggested responses or completions. Select the *one* that is *best* in each case.

**17.1.** Which of the following symptoms are found in depersonalization disorder:

A. Change in body image
B. Anxiety
C. Fear of going insane
D. Loss of feelings of reality
E. All of the above

**17.2.** Panic attacks associated with agoraphobia are treated most effectively with

A. chlordiazepoxide
B. diazepam
C. meprobamate
D. propranolol
E. imipramine

**17.3.** A man of 39 developed a low back pain following a back injury and underwent a laminectomy for the removal of an L–4–5 disk. After surgery, he continued to have moderate pain, diagnosed as arachnoiditis. Despite this, he managed to keep on with a full life of work and activities. Finally, at his family's urging, he agreed to have further surgery. After the operation, he became totally bedridden and incapacitated—not because of pain but because of an extensive weakness of his entire spinal and neck musculature that prevented him from walking or even sitting. When given sodium amytal, his weakness disappeared, and he was able to sit without support.

The most likely diagnosis in this case is

A. somatization disorder
B. conversion disorder (hysterical neurosis, conversion type)
C. psychogenic pain disorder
D. hypochondriasis (hypochondriacal neurosis)
E. atypical somatoform disorder

**17.4.** Indecisiveness, procrastination, and stereotyped behavior most likely to be associated with patients who have

A. obsessive-compulsive personality
B. somatization disorder
C. conversion disorder
D. psychogenic fugue
E. histrionic personality

**17.5.** The most common form of phobia is

A. photophobia
B. thanatophobia
C. acrophobia
D. agoraphobia
E. nyctophobia

**17.6.** A chronically anxious 29-year-old woman has experienced increasing difficulty in leaving her house without a companion. As soon as she opens the door, she feels panicky and breaks out in a sweat. Once on the street, she experiences repeated similar attacks, and her surroundings take on an unreal and unfamiliar quality. She now rarely leaves home at all. The disorder most likely to account for the clinical picture is

A. generalized anxiety disorder
B. panic disorder
C. simple phobia
D. agoraphobia
E. social phobia

**17.7.** A 37-year-old male business executive experiences almost incapacitating anxiety whenever he is about to make a public speech. "I'm afraid I'll make a fool of myself," he states. There is no comparable anxiety associated with any of his other activities. The executive is most likely to have which of the following disorders:

A. Agoraphobia
B. Simple phobia
C. Social phobia
D. Panic disorder
E. Obsessive-compulsive disorder

**17.8.** A third-year medical student returns to the student health services for the third time with a complaint of ulcerative colitis. After a thorough medical work-up, he is told that there is no organic disease present. Despite that reassurance, the student continues to test his stool for blood and continues to believe that his doctors have missed the correct diagnosis. The student is exhibiting which of the following:

A. Depersonalization
B. Phobia
C. Bulimia
D. Conversion
E. Hypochondriasis

**17.9.** The anxiety of a phobia may have its origin in all the following *except*

A. fear of castration
B. thought disorder
C. the superego
D. separation
E. shame

**17.10.** An 11-year-old boy frequently leaves his bed and goes to the living room late at night. On several occasions, his parents have talked to the child at that time and found him acting as if he were in a dream and staring into space with his eyes open. The next morning the child denies having left his room. The child is most likely exhibiting the symptoms of

A. multiple personality
B. pervasive developmental disorder
C. insomnia
D. nocturnal enuresis
E. somnambulism

**17.11.** A 35-year-old man comes to a psychiatrist because, he says, "It often seems to me that I am not a part of the world. My voice sounds strange to me, and other people seem like figures in a dream." Those feelings have been present intermittently for about 10 years. There is no history of hallucinations and no current indications of disorganized thinking. The disorder this patient is describing is most probably

A. schizophrenia
B. affective disorder
C. depersonalization disorder
D. toxic psychosis
E. somatoform disorder

**17.12.** A 23-year-old woman visits a physician because of multiple physical complaints that, after a thorough examination, are found not to be due to physical illness. She presents the complaints in a dramatic and exaggerated way, and her history reveals numerous medical visits to various physicians. She complains coyly that her last doctor described her as "a real hysteric." According to the DSM-III classification system, the patient is most likely suffering from

A. psychogenic pain disorder
B. psychosomatic illness
C. hysterical neurosis, dissociative type
D. malingering
E. somatization disorder

**17.13.** The most characteristic behavioral feature in patients with conversion disorders is

A. somatic compliance
B. *la belle indifférence*
C. autonomic dysfunction
D. sensory disturbance
E. sexual problems

**17.14.** A 23-year-old female stockbroker complains of "anxiety attacks" with fear, apprehension, severe headaches, trembling, and an inability to function during these attacks. She reports that, after her "spells" have passed, all these symptoms disappear. These attacks last a number of minutes and occur approximately every other week. Physical examination is unremarkable, except for an elevated blood pressure and excessive sweating. Which of the following is the most likely cause:

A. Ménière's disease
B. Pheochromocytoma
C. Panic disorder
D. Systemic lupus erythematosus
E. Generalized anxiety disorder

**17.15.** A patient experiencing posttraumatic stress disorder is most likely to reexperience the traumatic event through

A. dissociative-like states
B. intrusive recollections
C. recurrent dreams or nightmares
D. hallucinations
E. repetition compulsions

**17.16.** The obsessive-compulsive patient who tries to resist carrying out the compulsion generally experiences

A. anxiety
B. hypochondriasis
C. somatization
D. dissociation
E. ambivalence

**17.17.** In DSM-III, the three types of phobic disorders are subdivided into social phobia, simple phobia, and

A. photophobia
B. mysophobia
C. acrophobia
D. hydrophobia
E. agoraphobia

**17.18.** The epidemiology of obsessive-compulsive disorder indicates that the disorder is

A. most frequent in lower-class persons
B. most frequent in those with low intelligence levels
C. more frequent in women than in men
D. more frequent in family members of patients with the disorder than in the general population
E. rare in the unmarried

**17.19.** Freud postulated that the following defense mechanisms are necessary in phobic disorder:

A. Repression, avoidance, and displacement
B. Regression, condensation, and projection
C. Regression, repression, and isolation
D. Repression, projection, and displacement
E. Regression, condensation, and dissociation

**17.20.** All the following may be used effectively in the treatment of phobias *except*

A. chlordiazepoxide
B. diazepam
C. imipramine
D. hypnosis
E. chlorpromazine

**DIRECTIONS:** For each of the incomplete statements below, *one* or *more* of the completions given is correct. Choose answer:

A. if only **1, 2,** and **3** are correct
B. if only **1** and **3** are correct
C. if only **2** and **4** are correct
D. if only **4** is correct
E. if all are correct

**17.21.** Current psychodynamic theories about anxiety disorders suggest that the

1. anxiety is used as a signal to the ego
2. defense mechanism of repression should prevent symptom formation
3. anxiety represents an unacceptable drive that is pressing for conscious representation and discharge
4. anxiety may produce a variety of neurotic symptoms

**17.22.** The primary gain in a neurotic disorder includes

1. satisfaction of dependency needs
2. increased attention or sympathy
3. monetary compensation
4. reduction of tension and conflict

**17.23.** Conversion disorders begin in

1. adolescence
2. early adulthood
3. middle age
4. old age

**17.24.** During hysterical seizures, patients

1. react to stimuli
2. resist forced movements of the extremities
3. show eyelid flutter
4. are amnesic for the events surrounding the seizure

**17.25.** A simple phobia is characterized by

1. persistent fear and avoidance of a specific object
2. a recognition by the patient that the fear is irrational
3. the frequent involvement of animals
4. humiliation in social situations

**17.26.** The prognosis in obsessive-compulsive disorders is observed to be better than average if there is a

1. short duration of symptoms before the time the patient is first treated
2. great element of environmental stress associated with the onset of the disorder
3. good environment to which the patient returns after treatment
4. good general social adjustment and quality of relationships

**17.27.** Conversion symptoms include which of the following:

1. Blindness
2. Vomiting
3. Anosmia
4. Pseudocyesis

**17.28.** Psychogenic amnesia

1. is the most common dissociative disorder
2. occurs suddenly
3. may follow physical trauma
4. is associated with a sense of indifference

**17.29.** Panic disorder

1. may manifest with chronic anxiety between attacks
2. manifests with sudden periods of apprehension and fear
3. is the diagnostic category given to an acute anxiety state as opposed to a chronic one
4. begins slowly and insidiously with general feelings of tension and nervous discomfort

**17.30.** A 42-year-old man gets into an angry shouting match with a fellow worker and experiences a strong urge to throw a punch. He then attempts to raise his right arm and finds that it is paralyzed. Examination by the company doctor shows no neurological findings except for paralysis. The most likely diagnosis of the man's symptom is

1. factitious disorder
2. phobic disorder
3. posttraumatic stress disorder
4. conversion disorder

**17.31.** In patients suffering from multiple personality,

1. the transition from one personality to another is gradual
2. there is generally amnesia for the existence of the other personalities
3. there may be a blurring of one personality with the others
4. one personality is uppermost in consciousness at any given time

**17.32.** The concept of somatic compliance refers to

1. the patient's not complaining of his or her disorder
2. the susceptibility of the symptom to treatment and rehabilitation
3. the affected organ's representation of symbolic conflict
4. the fact that symptoms tend to occur in organs that have previously been the site of symptom-producing lesions

**17.33.** In obsessive-compulsive disorder, the obsession or compulsion is

1. ego-syntonic
2. ego-alien
3. recognized as being essentially rational
4. an impulse that persistently compels itself into consciousness

**17.34.** In phobic disorder, anxiety is

1. attached to an object
2. free-floating
3. out of proportion to the situation
4. justified by the stimulus that provokes it

**17.35.** In hysterical aphonia,

1. the patient is unable to whisper
2. the patient can make no vocalized sounds
3. there are abnormal movements of the pharynx during respiration
4. the muscles of the vocal cords are affected

**17.36.** Which of the following statements apply to conversion disorders:

1. Certain symptoms may be mediated by the autonomic nervous system.
2. Symptoms represent symbolic communications.
3. The disorder develops when drives are rendered unconscious by repression.
4. If the dysfunction continues long enough, actual lesions may occur.

**17.37.** Which of the following concepts are involved in behavioral therapy:

1. Desensitization
2. Hierarchy
3. Flooding
4. Modeling

**17.38.** Astasia abasia is

1. a disturbance of gait
2. characterized by frequent falls
3. characterized by pseudoataxic movements
4. accompanied by rhythmical clonic movements

| Directions Summarized | | | | |
|---|---|---|---|---|
| A | B | C | D | E |
| 1, 2, 3 | 1, 3 | 2, 4 | 4 | All are |
| only | only | only | only | correct |

**17.39.** Factors that make for a good prognosis in the treatment of conversion disorders are

1. stable interpersonal relationships
2. a capacity for introspection
3. an absence of anxiety or depression
4. conflicts that center on oedipal sexuality

**17.40.** When patients have a conversion disorder that results in pain,

1. the symptoms may be motivated by strong, unconscious dependency needs
2. they may allow themselves to become incapacitated invalids
3. they view the symptom of pain as ego-alien
4. they generally have a conscious image of themselves as strong and independent

**17.41.** Symptoms associated with posttraumatic stress disorder include

1. hyperalertness
2. memory impairment
3. insomnia
4. phobic avoidance of situation

**17.42.** Epidemiological studies of somatization disorder reveal that

1. it occurs in 15 percent of the female population
2. it is more common in women than in men
3. there is usually no familial history
4. it is associated with sociopathy and alcoholism in relatives

**17.43.** A 52-year-old man was one of the last to be rescued from a hotel fire in which 60 people died. The psychiatrist is asked to see the patient in the hospital to prepare him for some of the emotional symptoms that may occur in the future. Which symptoms listed below are likely to occur:

1. Feelings of guilt
2. Memory impairment
3. Insomnia
4. Hallucinations

**17.44.** Hypochondriasis serves to

1. enable the patient to gratify dependency needs
2. prevent the patient from dealing with low self-esteem
3. protect the patient from guilt
4. provide the patient with various secondary gains

**17.45.** Psychogenic pain disorder is characterized by the pain

1. being unrelated to a psychological conflict
2. not interfering with a specific activity
3. being consistent with anatomical distribution of the nervous system
4. enabling the person to gain support from the environment

**17.46.** Typical features of psychogenic fugue include

1. the wandering of the patient, usually far from home and often for days at a time
2. complete forgetting of a past life, but without the patient's awareness that anything is forgotten
3. no evidence of acting out any specific memory of a traumatic event
4. behavior that is out of the ordinary, often drawing attention to the patient

**DIRECTIONS:** Each set of lettered headings below is followed by a list of numbered words or phrases. For each numbered word or phrase, select

> A. if the item is associated with **A** *only*
> B. if the item is associated with **B** *only*
> C. if the item is associated with *both* **A** *and* **B**
> D. if the item is associated with *neither* **A** *nor* **B**

**Questions 17.47–17.50**
A. Generalized anxiety disorder
B. Panic disorder
C. Both
D. Neither

**17.47.** Chronic and persistent

**17.48.** Thought disorder

**17.49.** Usually episodic in nature

**17.50.** Feelings of fear

**Questions 17.51–17.55**
A. Panic disorder
B. Generalized anxiety disorder
C. Both
D. Neither

**17.51.** Discrete and episodic

**17.52.** Chronic and persistent

**17.53.** Dizziness and paresthesias

**17.54.** Psychiatric symptoms other than anxiety symptoms

**17.55.** Obvious physical evidence of respiratory alkalosis

# Answers

# Neurotic Disorders

**17.1. The answer is E** (*Synopsis*, ed. 4, page 358).

The central characteristic of depersonalization is the *quality of unreality* and estrangement that is attached to conscious experiences. Inner mental processes and external events go on seemingly exactly as before, yet everything is different and seems no longer to have any personal relation or meaning to the person who is aware of them. The feeling of unreality affects persons' perceptions of their physical and psychological self and of the world around them. *Parts of one's body or one's entire physical being may appear foreign.* All of a person's mental operations and behavior may feel alien. *There is anxiety and, sometimes, a fear of going insane.*

The essential and associated features of depersonalization disorder and the DSM-III diagnostic criteria are listed in the tables below.

### Clinical Features of Depersonalization Disorder*

| Essential Features | Associated Features |
|---|---|
| Alteration of the perception or experience of the self, with *loss of sense of one's own reality* and associated *change in body image* | Dizziness, *anxiety*, hypochondriasis, *fear of going insane*, disturbance in sense of time often associated |
| Onset and disappearance rapid | Derealization—loss of feeling of reality of the world—and perceived changes in size and shape of external objects may be present |
| Feeling of loss of control of one's actions and speech may be present | |
| Episodes last for many minutes to hours and recur frequently | |

\* Adapted from American Psychiatric Association: *Diagnostic and Statistical Manual of Mental Disorders*, ed 3. American Psychiatric Association, Washington, DC, 1980.

**17.2. The answer is E** (*Synopsis*, ed. 4, page 320).

*Imipramine* has been used to block panic attacks successfully. When the patient complains of phobias and anxiety, antidepressant medication, including monoamine oxidase inhibitors (MAOI's), have been useful. Most patients respond adequately to therapeutic doses of the minor tranquilizers, such as *chlordiazepoxide, diazepam*, and *meprobamate*. The adrenergic blocking agents, such as *propranolol*, are not yet in regular clinical use, but reports indicate that they may be effective in selected patients.

Findings have shown that panic attacks can be caused by a variety of pharmacological agents, such as carbon dioxide inhalation, $\beta$-noradrenergic agonists (such as isoproterenol), and $\alpha_2$-noradrenergic compounds, which increase locus ceruleus discharge.

**17.3. The answer is B** (*Synopsis*, ed. 4, page 342).

*Conversion disorder* is, along with the other disorders mentioned, one of the somatoform disorders. The essential features of somatoform disorders are that there are no organic findings to account for the symptoms and there is strong evidence for their being psychological in origin. In this case, there is evidence that psychological factors are involved because the symptoms disappear under the influence of sodium amytal. In conversion disorders, the symptom is not under voluntary control. Conversion symptoms frequently mimic neurological disease, and paralysis, seizures, dyskinesias, and paresthesias are common. The autonomic nervous system may also be affected. A predisposing factor in the development of a conversion disorder is often an antecedent physical disorder or accident that provides the substrate for the conversion symptoms.

The disorder often masks deep-seated con-

### Psychogenic Criteria for Depersonalization Disorder*

A. One or more episodes of depersonalization sufficient to produce significant impairment in social or occupational functioning.

B. The symptom is not due to any other disorder, such as schizophrenia, affective disorder, organic mental disorder, anxiety disorder, or epilepsy.

\* From American Psychiatric Association: *Diagnostic and Statistical Manual of Mental Disorders*, ed 3. American Psychiatric Association, Washington, DC, 1980. Used with permission.

flicts, impulses, or emotions. In the case given, study under sodium amytal narcosis uncovered the fact that the patient had been utterly opposed to further surgery and had deeply resented his family's pressure, to which he had finally felt he must submit. As he described all this under narcosis, he began to express bitter anger at his family. Speaking of at last agreeing to the operation, he said, "So I finally decided if I had to cut my throat, I *would* cut my throat—and here I am; the family needed a lesson." When fully conscious both before and after the amytal interview, the patient consciously felt and exhibited no anger whatsoever toward those who had forced him into surgery. This had been translated by conversion into the physical symptom of muscular weakness, which, without his being aware of its meaning or the feelings it expressed, gave him the means for revenge against his family.

In *somatization disorder*, one or more conversion symptoms may occur, but to make the diagnosis, there must be a history of many different physical symptoms of several years' duration beginning before the age of 30. These patients believe that they have been sickly for most of their lives. *Psychogenic pain disorder* is diagnosed when severe and prolonged pain is the major symptom. In these cases the pain present is inconsistent with the autonomic distribution of the nervous system. In *hypochondriasis* there is the constant fear or belief that a serious disease is present. The diagnosis of *atypical somatoform disorders* is made only when the criteria of the other somatoform disorders described above cannot be made.

The DSM-III diagnostic criteria for conversion disorder are described in the table shown below.

**17.4. The answer is A** (*Synopsis*, ed. 4, pages 332 and 333).

According to DSM-III, an *obsessive-compulsive disorder* is a neurotic disorder characterized by obsessions, which are recurrent, persistent ideas, thoughts, and images, and by compulsions, which are repetitive patterns of behavior. Both the obsessions and compulsions are egodystonic; that is, they are experienced as unwanted.

Patients with obsessive-compulsive disorder are often neatly dressed and groomed, sometimes with almost fussy tidiness. Reserved and formal in manner, they sit before the examiner stiff and prim, showing little in the way of gestures or facial expression, and their movements are careful and precise, without spontaneity or easy grace. The controlled quality of their posture and movement is matched in their speech. Their sentences may be long and involved, and full of stilted phraseology or stereotyped expressions. They characteristically balance one clause against another—"whereas ..., yet ..." "on the one hand ... on the other ...." They say the same thing several times in succession, introducing each paraphrase with "Again" or "In other words" or "To put it in another way." They qualify any direct statement with words like "maybe," "perhaps," or "possibly," to avoid sounding dogmatic or to escape being caught in an error. They rely heavily on rational argument and talk in highly intellectual and intellectualized terms about the simplest matters, interlarding their pronouncements with the copious and needless interjection of words or phrases like "indeed," "to be sure," "be that as it may." They recount events in infinite detail, with a painful attention to accuracy and completeness, sometimes referring to written

---

**Diagnostic Criteria for Conversion Disorder***

A. The predominant disturbance is a loss of or alteration in physical functioning suggesting a physical disorder.

B. Psychological factors are judged to be etiologically involved in the symptom, as evidenced by one of the following:

    1. There is a temporal relationship between an environmental stimulus that is apparently related to a psychological conflict or need and the initiation or exacerbation of the symptom;

    2. The symptom enables the individual to avoid some activity that is noxious to him or her;

    3. The symptom enables the individual to get support from the environment that otherwise might not be forthcoming.

C. It has been determined that the symptom is not under voluntary control.

D. The symptom cannot, after appropriate investigation, be explained by a known physical disorder or pathophysiological mechanism.

E. The symptom is not limited to pain or a disturbance in sexual functioning.

F. Not due to somatization disorder or schizophrenia.

* From American Psychiatric Association: *Diagnostic and Statistical Manual of Mental Disorders*, ed 3. American Psychiatric Association, Washington, DC, 1980. Used with permission.

notes they have brought with them. It often turns out that they have rehearsed what they plan to say in the interview for hours before it takes place, and have tried to anticipate every move and question the interviewer may introduce. Any attempt to hurry them along, to cut them short, or to switch to another topic is met by patients' resistance and rigid adherence to their preconceived program of action. Evidence or expression of emotion, save possibly controlled anxiety, is at a minimum or entirely absent. If they are sophisticated about psychiatric theory, and such patients often are, they discourse at length about their "conflicts," their "defenses," their "aggression," or their "libido." In answer to direct questioning, however, they deny having any of the feelings related to these words. Their self-awareness and self-knowledge, however extensive, are entirely intellectual in nature and quite without emotional correlates.

A *somatization disorder* is a somatoform disorder characterized by recurrent and multiple physical complaints with no apparent physical cause. It is also known as Briquet's syndrome. *Conversion disorder* is a somatoform disorder in which the patient experiences an involuntary limitation or alteration of physical function that is an expression of psychological conflict or need, not physical disorder. According to DSM-III, *psychogenic fugue* is a classification of dissociative disorder characterized by periods of total amnesia in which one travels and assumes a new identity. *Histrionic personality disorder* is a condition in which the patient, usually an immature and dependent person, exhibits unstable, overreactive, and excitable self-dramatizing behavior that is aimed at gaining attention and is at times seductive, although the person may

not be aware of that aim. It was previously termed hysterical personality.

The DSM-III diagnostic criteria for obsessive-compulsive disorder are listed in the table below.

**17.5.    The answer is D** (*Synopsis*, ed. 4, page 321).

As is so often the case with the less severe emotional disorders, accurate information about the incidence, distribution, and natural history of phobic disorders is not readily available. *Agoraphobia*, which is a dread of open spaces, seems to be the most common form, constituting some 60 percent of all phobic disorders and having its onset in the patient's late teens or early twenties, although it may first be manifested much later in life. Social phobias are characteristically associated with adolescence. Simple phobia, especially of animals, is a common if transitory phenomenon during the early oedipal phases of growth and development; it may persist into adulthood, or, after a long period of freedom from phobic manifestations, an adult may develop a simple phobia that is often idiosyncratic and determined by inner psychological processes.

Taken as a group, phobic disorders seem to affect less than 1 percent of a given population, and estimates derived from outpatient clinic figures suggest that they constitute less than 5 percent of all neurotic disorders seen in patients over 18.

*Photophobia* is most commonly used to refer to an organically determined hypersensitivity to light (as in many acute infectious diseases with conjunctivitis) that results in severe pain and marked tearing when the patient is exposed to

---

### Diagnostic Criteria for Obsessive-Compulsive Disorder*

A. Either obsessions or compulsions:

*Obsessions:* recurrent, persistent ideas, thoughts, images, or impulses that are ego-dystonic, i.e. they are not experienced as voluntarily produced, but rather as thoughts that invade consciousness and are experienced as senseless or repugnant. Attempts are made to ignore or suppress them.

*Compulsions:* repetitive and seemingly purposeful behaviors that are performed according to certain rules or in a stereotyped fashion. The behavior is not an end in itself, but is designed to produce or prevent some future event or situation. However, either the activity is not connected in a realistic way with what it is designed to produce or prevent, or may be clearly excessive. The act is performed with a sense of subjective compulsion coupled with a desire to resist the compulsion (at least initially). The individual generally recognizes the senselessness of the behavior (this may not be true for young children) and does not derive pleasure from carrying out the activity, although it provides a release of tension.

B. The obsessions or compulsions are a significant source of distress to the individual or interfere with social or role functioning.

C. Not due to another mental disorder, such as Tourette's disorder, schizophrenia, major depression, or organic mental disorder.

---

* From American Psychiatric Association: *Diagnostic and Statistical Manual of Mental Disorders*, ed 3. American Psychiatric Association, Washington, DC, 1980. Used with permission.

light. It can also be defined as a neurotic fear or avoidance of light. *Thanatophobia* refers to the fear of death. *Acrophobia* refers to the fear of high places. *Nyctophobia* refers to fear of night or darkness.

**17.6. The answer is D** (*Synopsis*, ed. 4, pages 323 and 324).

*Agoraphobia* is popularly interpreted as being a fear of open spaces, but it has wider implications. Agoraphobic patients are generally thrown into a state of trepidation when they are forced into a situation in which they may be subjected to the sense of helplessness or humiliation that results from the eruption of the panic attacks to which they are subject. They are threatened not only by open, public places but by those situations—such as crowded stores, public transportation, elevators, and theaters—from which they can find no ready escape from public view. Although they may feel more comfortable when accompanied by a friend or a relative, they tend to avoid the dangerous situations by restricting their activities and excursions to an increasingly smaller area, and in extreme cases they may be totally confined to their house.

*Generalized anxiety disorder* is a DSM-III classification of anxiety disorder characterized by severe generalized anxiety not attached to any particular idea, object, or event. A *panic attack* is an episode of acute intense anxiety occurring in panic disorder, schizophrenia, major depression, and somatization disorder. It is the key symptom in *panic disorder*, which is a DSM-III classification of anxiety disorder characterized by attacks of acute intense anxiety. *Simple phobia* is a phobic disorder characterized by fear and avoidance of an object or situation not included in agoraphobia or social phobia. *Social phobia* is a phobic disorder characterized by a fear of being observed by others. The social phobias include fears of public speaking, blushing, eating in public, writing in front of others, and using public lavatories.

The DSM-III diagnostic criteria for agoraphobia are listed in the table below.

**17.7. The answer is C** (*Synopsis*, ed. 4, page 324).

Central to *social phobia* is the concern over appearing shameful, stupid, or inept in the presence of others. In particular, persons with social phobia fear that their behavior—talking or writing in public, for example—or one of their bodily functions, such as eating, urinating, or blushing, will be the focus of scornful scrutiny by those around them, a fact that often further impairs their performance. Two particular varieties of this class should be noted: erythrophobia and fear of eating. They are quite common; the fear of public speaking is one of the most commonly reported phobias in the general population.

*Agoraphobia*, a fear of open places, is a phobic disorder characterized by a fear of leaving one's home. It may present with or without panic attacks. *Simple phobia* is a phobic disorder characterized by fear and avoidance of an object or situation not included in agoraphobia or social phobia. *Panic disorder* is a DSM-III classification of anxiety disorder characterized by attacks of acute intense anxiety. *Obsessive-compulsive disorder* is a neurotic disorder characterized by the persistent recurrence of obsessions and compulsions.

The DSM-III diagnostic criteria for social phobia are listed on the following page.

**17.8. The answer is E** (*Synopsis*, ed. 4, pages 349 and 350).

In DSM-III, the diagnostic term *hypochondriasis* refers to those patients in whom the predominant disturbance is an unrealistic interpretation of physical signs or sensations as abnormal, leading to the preoccupation with the fear or belief of having a disease.

Salient features of the manifestations of hypochondriasis are as follows: (1) The symptoms are diffuse and variegated, involving many areas of the body—the most common sites are the abdominal viscera, the chest, and the head and neck—but they may be related to any part of the anatomy or may consist of a generalized bodily sense of fatigue or malaise. Less often, patients complain of disturbances in mental

---

### Diagnostic Criteria for Agoraphobia*

A. The individual has marked fear of and thus avoids being alone or in public places from which escape might be difficult or help not available in case of sudden incapacitation, e.g. crowds, tunnels, bridges, public transportation.

B. There is increasing constriction of normal activities until the fears or avoidance behavior dominate the individual's life.

C. Not due to a major depressive episode, obsessive-compulsive disorder, paranoid personality disorder, or schizophrenia.

---

* From American Psychiatric Association: *Diagnostic and Statistical Manual of Mental Disroders*, ed 3. American Psychiatric Association, Washington, DC, 1980. Used with permission.

### Diagnostic Criteria for Social Phobia*

A. A persistent, irrational fear of, and compelling desire to avoid, a situation in which the individual is exposed to possible scrutiny by others and fears that he or she may act in a way that will be humiliating or embarrassing.

B. Significant distress because of the disturbance and recognition by the individual that his or her fear is excessive or unreasonable.

C. Not due to another mental disorder, such as major depression or avoidant personality disorder.

* From American Psychiatric Association: *Diagnostic and Statistical Manual of Mental Disorders*, ed 3. American Psychiatric Association, Washington, DC, 1980. Used with permission.

functioning that lead them to believe they are losing their minds or going crazy. (2) There is often a curious mixture of the minutely specific and the diffusely vague in the quality of the patient's complaints. (3) The symptoms often arise from the patient's heightened awareness of a bodily sensation (a mild ache, pain, or discomfort), of a normal bodily function (bowel movements, heart beats, peristaltic action, for example), or of a minor somatic abnormality (occasional mucus in the stools, nasal discharge, or a slightly enlarged lymph node). (4) To the trained medical observer, the symptoms have little pathological significance. Individually, they usually suggest no known or specific malfunction or pathological process in an organ system; taken collectively, they form no pattern that is recognizable as being characteristic of physical disease.

*Depersonalization* is a nonspecific syndrome in which patients feel that they have lost their personal identity. As a result, they experience themselves as strange or unreal. It can be seen in schizophrenia, depersonalization disorder, and schizotypal disorder. A *phobia* is a persistent, pathological, unrealistic, intense fear of an object or situation. The phobic person may realize that the fear is irrational but is, nonetheless, unable to dispel it. *Conversion* is an unconscious defense mechanism by which the anxiety that stems from an intrapsychic conflict is converted and expressed in a symbolic somatic symptom. *Bulimia* refers to a morbidly increased appetite, in which a large amount of food is ingested in a short period of time, usually less than 2 hours.

**17.9. The answer is B** (*Synopsis*, ed. 4, page 324).

*Thought disorder* is any disturbance of thinking that affects language, communication, or thought content. Its manifestations range from simple blocking to loosening of associations, and it is one of the hallmarks of schizophrenia. It is not present in phobic disorders.

It was originally thought, particularly by psychoanalytic investigators, that the fear manifested by phobic patients was a form of castration anxiety. On more careful observation, how-

ever, it becomes evident that many fears do not fall exclusively into this category. In agoraphobia, for example, separation anxiety clearly plays a leading role, and in erythrophobia the element of shame implies the involvement of superego anxiety. It is perhaps closer to clinical observation to view the anxiety associated with phobias as having a variety of sources and colorings.

In psychoanalytic theory, *fear of castration* involves a group of unconscious thoughts and motives that are referable to the fear of losing the genitals, usually as punishment for forbidden sexual desires. In psychoanalysis, the *superego* is part of the personality structure that represents the internalized values, ideals, and moral attitudes of society. Its psychic functions are expressed in guilt, self-criticism, and conscience. It develops through children's identification with their parents, and the severity of its prohibitions or demands is said to be related to the intensity and extent of resolution of the Oedipus complex. It has a rewarding function, referred to as the ego ideal, and a critical and punishing function, which evokes the sense of guilt.

*Separation* refers to the infant's or child's fear and apprehension on being removed from the parent figure. In DSM-III, this anxiety is known as a separation anxiety disorder.

*Shame* is an affect that develops from the revelation of one's previously hidden shortcomings. In psychoanalysis, shame is believed to be founded in the anal and urethral stages of psychosexual development. It is considered to be the specific force directed against urethral eroticism.

**17.10. The answer is E** (*Synopsis*, ed. 4, page 356).

The term *somnambulism* is used to refer both to the dissociative disorders and to episodes of activity during sleep that have a different character and significance. Very often in childhood, and less frequently when adulthood has been reached, a person may, during actual sleep, get out of bed and wander around. Such behavior is not necessarily pathological, especially in children, and it differs from dissociative somnambulism in that the nondissociative somnambulism occurs during deep sleep unassociated with dreams, is poorly integrated and nonpurposive in nature, and is characterized by actions that are awkward and fumbling and show a lack of dexterity. Dissociative somnambulistic episodes may occur at night, but they are as different from normal sleepwalking as hypnosis is from true sleep.

*Multiple personality* is a disorder in which an individual maintains two distinct personalities. *Pervasive developmental disorder* is characterized by severe distortions in the development of social skills, language, and contact with reality. A child with pervasive developmental disorder develops abnormalities that are not normal for any stage of development. Pervasive developmental disorder was previously known as childhood schizophrenia. *Insomnia* is a sleep disorder in which an individual has difficulties in falling asleep or difficulties in staying asleep. *Nocturnal enuresis* is a condition in which urinary incontinence develops at night.

**17.11. The answer is C** (*Synopsis*, ed. 4, pages 357 and 358).

In DSM-III, *depersonalization disorder* is considered one of the dissociative disorders and is characterized by "an alteration in the perception of the self so that the feeling of one's own reality is temporarily lost." The central characteristic of depersonalization is the quality of unreality and estrangement that is attached to conscious experience. Inner mental processes and external events go on seemingly exactly as before, yet everything is different and seems no longer to have any personal relation or meaning to the person who is aware of them. The feeling of unreality affects the persons' perceptions of their physical and psychological self and of the world around them. Parts of one's body or one's entire physical being may appear foreign. All of a person's mental operations and behavior may feel alien. These episodes can last for many minutes to hours and recur frequently. Dizziness, anxiety, hypochondriasis, and fears of going insane are associated features.

*Schizophrenia* is classified as a psychotic mental disorder in which a disturbance in thinking, mood, and behavior occurs. The thinking disturbance is manifested by a distortion of reality, sometimes with delusions and hallucinations, accompanied by a fragmentation of associations that results in characteristic disturbances of speech. The mood disturbance includes ambivalence and inappropriate or constricted affective responses. The behavior disturbance may be manifested by apathetic withdrawal or bizarre activity.

An *affective disorder* is a mental disorder characterized by a primary disturbance of mood,

such as depression or elation. This mood disturbance is the disorder's primary characteristic; disturbances in thinking and behavior are secondary characteristics. *Toxic psychosis* is a psychosis that is caused by toxic substances produced by the body or introduced into it in the form of chemicals or drugs. *Somatoform disorder* is a mental disorder characterized by physical symptoms but no organic cause. The production of the symptoms is linked to psychological factors or conflicts, but is not under voluntary control.

**17.12. The answer is E** (*Synopsis*, ed. 4, pages 340 and 341).

The most striking behavioral aspect of the psychiatric examination of patients with *somatization disorder* is the dramatic, exaggerated, and emotional way in which they present themselves and their symptoms, as did the female patient in this case. Careful analysis of the behavior pattern reveals a number of elements to which specific adjectives may be applied:

**Dramatic.** The patient tells her history and describes symptoms, especially pain, in vivid, colorful language. The patient is often discursive and circumstantial in her account, recounting how her symptoms have affected her life and her relationships with people, rather than giving a description of their nature, character, location, onset, and duration—all of which tend to be overlooked. Her description of previous encounters with doctors is interlarded with recitations of what she said to the doctor and what he said to her.

**Exhibitionistic.** The patient is often overly made-up and overdressed for the occasion, whether it is a visit to the doctor's office or a stay in a hospital bed. She tends to be revealing of her body and, during physical examinations, exposes more of herself than is necessary for the part being examined.

**Narcissistic.** The patient shows a predominant preoccupation with herself and her own concerns and interests, to the exclusion of those of others. She requires and seeks open and direct admiration and praise from other people.

**Emotional.** In tone and intensity of voice, by gestures, and in language, the patient freely expresses the whole gamut of emotions in an often bewildering array, and at times in such a histrionic fashion that she gives the impression of play-acting and of not really being capable of experiencing any lasting, real, or profound emotions.

**Seductive.** The patient is often coy, flirtatious, and seductive. The impression is gained partly from the quality of exhibitionism mentioned earlier and is reinforced by the patient's facial expression, movements, gestures, verbal innuendos, and even openly seductive invitations to sexual activity.

**Dependent.** Although it may not always be evident in one's initial observation of the patient, it frequently becomes apparent as the doctor-patient relationship develops that the patient is overly dependent, needing not only the gifts of praise and admiration, mentioned as a part of narcissism, but more direct evidence of help, such as advice and medications, which the patient demands with increasing insistence; moreover, she is capable of anger, which at times reaches the proportion of violent temper tantrums, if her needs are not being properly satisfied.

**Manipulative.** The patient is skilled in getting what she wants from other people by using a variety of artful maneuvers, such as threats to produce a fit of temper; attempts at suicide that are aimed at influencing others, rather than being basically self-destructive; and behavior that otherwise plays on the guilt of others.

*Malingering* consists of feigning disease in order to achieve a specific goal—for example, to avoid an unpleasant responsibility. *Psychogenic pain disorder* is a disorder in which the predominant feature is the complaint of pain in the absence of adequate physical findings and in which there is evidence that psychological factors play a causal role. It is also known as psychalgia.

A *psychosomatic disorder* is a disorder characterized by physical symptoms caused by psychological factors. It usually involves a single organ system innervated by the autonomic nervous system. The physiological and organic changes stem from a sustained emotional disturbance. It was previously known as psychophysiological disorder. In DSM-III, it is called psychological factor affecting physical condition.

*Hysterical neurosis* is a diagnostic category for a neurosis involving a sudden impairment of function in response to emotional stress. In the conversion type, there is functional impairment in one of the special senses or in the voluntary nervous system; the dissociative type is manifested by an alteration in state of consciousness or by such symptoms as amnesia, disorientation, fugue, somnambulism, or multiple personality. In DSM-III these neuroses are also called conversion disorder and dissociative disorder.

**17.13.   The answer is B** (*Synopsis*, ed. 4, page 347).

The most characteristic behavioral feature in patients with conversion disorder is what the French authors of the 19th century called *la belle indifférence*. Despite what appear to be the most extensive and crippling disturbances in func-

tion, the patient is completely unconcerned and, indeed, may not spontaneously mention such disturbances, which often results in their being overlooked unless specifically searched for. *La belle indifférence* is an extremely calm mental attitude of acquiescence and complacency directed specifically at the physical symptom.

*Somatic compliance* is the degree to which persons' organic structures coincide with their psychological mechanisms in the symptomatic expression of their pathological defenses. In conversion symptoms, for instance, the entire cathexis of the objectionable impulses is condensed onto a definite physical function. The ability of the affected function to adsorb this cathexis is its somatic compliance.

*Autonomic dysfunctions* may be reflected in various visceral symptoms, such as anorexia, vomiting, hiccoughs, and other abdominal complaints, which are considered a part of the classical syndrome of conversion disorders. *Sensory disturbances*—anesthesias, in particular—are also quite typical of the physical symptoms of hysterical neurosis.

A history of *sexual disturbances*, especially impotence, anorgasmia, and a lack of desire, is frequently seen along with conversion symptoms. According to psychoanalytic theory, conversion disorder has been linked to a psychosexual conflict arising from failure to relinquish oedipal ties and to rid the normal adult libido of its incestuous ties.

**17.14.   The answer is B** (*Synopsis*, ed. 4, pages 314, 316, 140, and 141).

The possibility of a *pheochromocytoma* must be kept in mind when patients complain of several anxiety-like symptoms. It is, however, a rare disorder, occurring in only 0.1 percent of patients with hypertension, and can usually be differentiated from panic disorder.

Pheochromocytoma is seen in adults, with an equal distribution between males and females. The patient commonly complains of cephalgia and sweating, which occur during transient increases in blood pressure. Symptoms of anxiety, such as panic, trembling, apprehension, and an inability to do any activity, also occur during these transient attacks. The classic symptoms of anxiety attacks coupled with intermittent normal blood pressure readings may discourage further diagnostic studies.

For a diagnosis of *panic disorder*, the anxiety attacks must occur at least 3 times within a 3-week period in circumstances other than marked physical exertion or a life-threatening situation. The attacks are not precipitated by exposure to a phobic stimulus. In the case presented, the anxiety occurred less often—every other week.

*Systemic lupus erythematosus* (SLE), which

is a collagen vascular disease, generally has a chronic course that may last many years. The psychiatric picture in this disorder is variable over time and may present as a toxic-like psychosis unrelated to the steroids used in its treatment. The patient may present with variable symptoms, such as depression, confusion, and, eventually, a thought disorder resembling schizophrenia.

In *generalized anxiety disorders*, persistent anxiety is manifested by motor tension, autonomic hyperactivity, apprehensive expectation, and vigilance and scanning. This anxious mood must be continuous for at least 1 month and must not be due to another mental disorder.

The sudden attacks of dizziness in *Ménière's disease* may occasionally be confused with acute anxiety. Characteristically, the dizziness of Ménière's disease is a true vertigo and is associated with nystagmus, deafness, and other signs of middle-ear disease that are not found in panic disorder.

**17.15. The answer is C** (*Synopsis*, ed. 4, page 337).

A patient experiencing posttraumatic stress disorder is always troubled by unwelcome reexperiencing of the traumatic event in a variety of ways. *Recurrent dreams or nightmares*, from which the patient often awakes in a state of terror, are perhaps the most common mode of reexperiencing the event. Other patients complain of repeated and *intrusive recollections* of the event; these recollections persist in spite of attempts to forget and to focus attention and energy on other aspects of life. Some complain of *dissociative-like states*, during which patients react behaviorally to the experience they are reliving; the reaction may last from a few minutes to several hours or even days.

Dissociative-like states are characterized by a sudden, temporary alteration in the normally integrated functions of consciousness, identity, or motor behavior. *Hallucinations* are false sensory perceptions occurring in the absence of any relevant external stimulation of the sensory modality involved. The theory of *repetition compulsion*, as propounded by Freud, is that there is a tendency for persons to repeat earlier experiences and situations in their current life situation.

**17.16. The answer is A** (*Synopsis*, ed. 4, page 329).

The anxiety-allaying function of compulsive acts can readily be noted in the clinical manifestations of obsessive-compulsive disorders. What should be observed here is that the compulsive act constitutes the surface manifestation of a further defensive operation, aimed at reduc-

ing anxiety and at controlling the underlying impulse that has not been sufficiently contained by isolation.

*Anxiety* is an unpleasurable emotional state associated with psychophysiological changes in response to an intrapsychic conflict. In contrast to fear, the danger or threat in anxiety is unreal. Physiological changes consist of increased heart rate, disturbed breathing, trembling, sweating, and vasomotor changes. Psychological changes consist of an uncomfortable feeling of impending danger, an overwhelming awareness of being powerless, the inability to perceive the unreality of the threat, prolonged feeling of tension, and exhaustive readiness for the expected danger.

*Hypochondriasis* is a somatoform disorder characterized by excessive, morbid anxiety about one's health. Hypochondriacal patients exhibit a predominant disturbance in which the physical symptoms or complaints are not explainable on the basis of demonstrable organic findings and are apparently linked to psychological factors. *Somatization disorder* is a somatoform disorder characterized by recurrent and multiple physical complaints with no apparent physical cause. *Dissociation* is an unconscious defense mechanism involving the segregation of any group of mental or behavioral processes from the rest of the person's psychic activity. It may entail the separation of an idea from its accompanying emotional tone, as seen in dissociative disorders. When a patient experiences *ambivalence*, strong and often overwhelming simultaneous contrasting attitudes, ideas, feelings, and drives toward an object, person, or goal are present. The term was coined by Eugen Bleuler, who differentiated three types of ambivalence: affective ambivalence, intellectual ambivalence, and ambivalence of the will.

**17.17. The answer is E** (*Synopsis*, ed. 4, page 321).

The phobic disorders are subdivided into three types: *agoraphobia*, the most common and severest form; *social phobia*; and *simple phobia*. *Agoraphobia* is a fear of open places, a phobic disorder characterized by a fear of leaving one's home. It may present with or without panic attacks. *Social phobias* are characterized by a fear of being observed by others. The social phobias include fears of public speaking, blushing, eating in public, writing in front of others, and using public lavatories. *Simple phobias* are characterized by fear and avoidance of an object or situation not included in agoraphobia or social phobia.

Other examples of phobias are the following: *photophobia*, a fear of light or a sensitivity to it; *mysophobia*, a fear of contamination mostly observed in incessant hand washing; *acrophobia*, a fear of high places; and *hydrophobia*, a fear of water.

**17.18.  The answer is D** (*Synopsis*, ed. 4, page 328).

The exact incidence of obsessive-compulsive disorder is hard to determine. Scattered anecdotal evidence indicates that it has occurred throughout history. Those who have studied the natural history of the disorder have found an incidence that is never higher than 5 percent of all neurotic patients, and its prevalence in the population at large has been estimated at 0.05 percent. The data on familial patterns are meager, but *suggest that parents and siblings of patients with obsessive-compulsive disorder have a significantly higher incidence of the condition, as compared with a control population*, and that the presence of obsessional traits is similarly increased.

There seems to be *no significant sexual difference* in the disorder. *A large proportion of obsessive-compulsive patients remain unmarried*, up to 50 percent in some surveys. Recent studies indicate that the frequency of the disorder is *higher in upper-class persons, and in those with higher intelligence levels*, than in the general population.

**17.19.  The answer is A** (*Synopsis*, ed. 4, pages 321 and 322).

Freud presented a formulation of the phobic neurosis, which has remained in its essentials the analytic explanation of the disorder. Freud took a view that anxiety could be the ego's reactions to danger and proposed that the quality of being a response was its primary attribute, the response being to a danger arising not only from perilous external situations but also from inner drives and affects that were unacceptable and threatening to the ego. Anxiety had as its major function the task of signaling to the ego the fact that a forbidden unconscious drive was pushing for conscious expression, thus alerting the ego to strengthen and marshal its defenses against the threatening instinctual force.

Freud viewed the phobic disorder—or anxiety hysteria, as he continued to call it—as resulting from conflicts centered on an unresolved childhood oedipal situation. In the adult, because the sexual drive continued to have a strong incestuous coloring, its arousal tended to arouse anxiety that was characteristically a fear of castration. The anxiety then alerted the ego to exert *repression* to keep the drive away from conscious representation and discharge, but repression failing to be entirely successful in its function, it was necessary for the ego to call on auxiliary defenses. In phobic patients, the defenses, arising genetically from an earlier phobic

response during the initial childhood period of the oedipal conflict, involved primarily the use of *displacement*—that is, the sexual conflict was transposed or displaced from the person who evoked the conflict to a seemingly unimportant, irrelevant object or situation, which then had the power to arouse the entire constellation of affects, including signal anxiety. On examination, it can usually be determined that the phobic object or situation thus selected has a direct associative connection with the primary source of the conflict and has thus come naturally to symbolize it. Furthermore, the situation or object is usually such that the patient is able to keep out of its way and, by the additional defense mechanism of *avoidance*, can escape suffering from serious anxiety. This theoretical formulation of phobia formation, which attributes the phobia to the use of the ego defense mechanisms of displacement and avoidance against incestuous oedipal genital drives and castration anxiety, was first discussed by Freud in his famous case of Little Hans, a 5-year-old boy who had a fear of horses.

*Regression* is an unconscious defense mechanism in which a person undergoes a partial or total return to earlier patterns of adaptation. *Condensation* is a mental process in which one symbol stands for a number of components. In psychoanalysis, *isolation* refers to a defense mechanism involving the separation of an idea or memory from its attached feeling tone. Unacceptable ideational content is thereby rendered free of its disturbing or unpleasant emotional charge. *Dissociation* is an unconscious defense mechanism involving the segregation of any group of mental or behavioral processes from the rest of the person's psychic activity. *Projection* refers to an unconscious defense mechanism in which persons attribute to another those generally unconscious ideas, thoughts, feelings, and impulses that are undesirable or unacceptable themselves. Projection protects persons from anxiety arising from an inner conflict. By externalizing whatever is unacceptable, persons deal with it as a situation apart from themselves.

**17.20.  The answer is E** (*Synopsis*, ed. 4, pages 320 and 327).

*Chlorpromazine* is a phenothiazine derivative used primarily as an antipsychotic agent and in the treatment of nausea and vomiting. The drug was synthesized in 1950 and was used in psychiatry for the first time in 1952. It is not used in phobias.

*Hypnosis*, however, is useful not only in enhancing the suggestion that is a part of the therapist's generally supportive approach but in directly combating the anxiety arising from the phobic situation. The psychiatrist can teach patients the techniques of autohypnosis, through which they can achieve a degree of relaxation when they are facing the phobic situation that will enable them to tolerate it. Those patients who cannot be hypnotized may be taught techniques of muscle relaxation.

Minor tranquilizers, such as *diazepam* and *chlordiazepoxide*, may be useful in decreasing symptoms of anxiety. They should be prescribed with caution, however, for those patients who have a history suggesting a tendency to develop psychological or physical dependency on drugs. *Imipramine* may be useful in decreasing phobic or depressive symptoms. These drugs should be used with considerable caution in patients suffering from acute posttraumatic stress disorder after accidents that have led to serious physical illness. Imipramine in particular may precipitate symptoms of delirium in patients suffering from serious medical illness.

**17.21. The answer is E (all)** (*Synopsis*, ed. 4, pages 316 and 317).

When anxiety occurs, it is a sign of movement within; it is an indication that something is disturbing the internal psychological equilibrium.

*Anxiety is a signal to the ego that an unacceptable drive is pressing for conscious representation and discharge;* as a signal, it arouses the ego to take defensive action against the pressures from within. If the defenses are successful, the anxiety is dispelled or safely contained, but depending on the nature of the defenses used, *the person may develop a variety of neurotic symptoms.* Ideally, the *use of repression alone should result in a restoration of psychological equilibrium without symptom formation,* because effective repression completely contains the drives and their associated affects and fantasies by rendering them unconscious. More often than not, however, repression is not entirely effective, and it is necessary to call into play auxiliary defenses. Such defenses include conversion, displacement, regression, and others, through which the drives achieve a partial, although disguised, expression in the symptoms of hysteria, phobic disorder, or obsessive-compulsive disorder, depending on the defense that predominates.

If repression fails to function adequately and if other defenses are not called into play, anxiety is found as the only symptom; when it rises above the low level of intensity characteristic of its function as a signal, it may emerge with all the fury of a panic attack.

**17.22. The answer is D (4)** (*Synopsis*, ed. 4, page 336).

Psychoanalytic theory has stressed the distinction between primary gain and secondary gain in the discussion of neurotic disorders. The primary gain is the *reduction of tension and conflict* through such neurotic defense mechanisms as regression, repression, and denial. In addition to this internal primary gain, the victim may also receive a secondary gain from the external world. Common forms of secondary gain include *monetary compensation, increased attention or sympathy, and the satisfaction of dependency needs.* These various forms of secondary gain may further reinforce the patient's disorder and contribute to its persistence.

**17.23. The answer is E (all)** (*Synopsis*, ed. 4, page 346).

Conversion disorder frequently begins in *adolescence* or *early adulthood,* but the symptoms may appear for the first time during *middle age* or even in the *later decades of life.*

**17.24. The answer is A (1, 2, 3)** (*Synopsis*, ed. 4, page 345).

Convulsive movements of the entire body are sometimes found; unlike true neurogenic epilepsy, hysterical seizures are characterized not by rhythmical clonic movements of the extremities, but by a wild, disorganized, seemingly unpatterned thrashing and writing of the body. Patients appear to be completely out of control, their bedclothes are thrown into complete disarray, their arms and legs wave about with abandon, but they rarely hurt themselves, bite their tongues, or void. Such seizures may last many minutes and are accompanied by what appears to be complete unresponsiveness. Careful observation, however, reveals that, in fact *patients do react to stimuli; they often resist movements of their limbs forced by the examiner;* although their eyes are closed, *the lids often flutter,* and they vigorously resist attempts to open them. *When patients recover from the seizure and become responsive, they can often remember or can be made to remember what was going on around them during the convulsion.* This is quite different from the complete amnesia of the patient with neurogenic epilepsy for the events occurring during the period of true physiological unconsciousness. The hysterical patient exhibits an altered state of consciousness, but it is a dissociative state, rather than the unconsciousness accompanying gross disturbances of brain function.

**17.25. The answer is A (1, 2, 3)** (*Synopsis*, ed. 4, page 323).

Simple phobia must be distinguished from social phobia, which involves *social situations,* such as public speaking or being away from home. The DSM-III clinical features and diagnostic criteria for simple phobia are listed below.

**17.26.  The answer is E (all)** (*Synopsis*, ed. 4, page 332).

Obsessive-compulsive disorder is a neurotic disorder characterized by a persistent recurrence of obsessions and compulsions. In general, this disorder is chronic, often following a remitting course. The prognosis is better than average (1) *the shorter the duration of symptoms before the time the patient is first seen*, (2) *the greater the element of environmental stress associated with the onset of the disorder*, (3) *the better the environment to which the patient must return after treatment*, and (4) *the better the patient's general social adjustment and relationship*.

**17.27.  The answer is E (all)** (*Synopsis*, ed. 4, page 344).

Conversion symptoms are not under voluntary control, and many symptoms suggest neurological disease. More rarely, conversion symptoms can affect the autonomic nervous system, as in *vomiting*, or the endocrine system, as in *pseudocyesis* (false pregnancy). Hysterical *blindness*, in which the pupils continue to react to light, usually begins suddenly. The onset is usually related to an event involving the act of seeing that has symbolic significance. *Anosmia* is the loss of smell that may occur on a functional basis.

**17.28.  The answer is E (all)** (*Synopsis*, ed. 4, pages 354 and 355).

Patients suffering from psychogenic amnesia, *the most common dissociative disorder*, are often brought to general hospital emergency wards by police who have found them wandering confusedly around the streets.

The clinical features and the DSM-III diagnostic criteria of psychogenic amnesia are outlined in the tables at the top of the facing page.

**17.29.  The answer is A (1, 2, 3)** (*Synopsis*, ed. 4, page 318).

The essential feature in panic disorder is recurrent anxiety attacks, characterized by *acute and episodic periods of intense apprehension or terror, that have a sudden onset. The acute panic attacks are often seen in conjunction with less intense, more chronic anxiety persisting in the periods between acute attacks.*

Panic disorders peak in patients between 15 and 35 years of age. There is a prevalence of 2.5 to 5 percent. Females are affected twice as often as males. The risk of panic disorder among first-degree relatives of patients is 18 percent, as compared to 2 percent in first-degree kin of control groups.

The classification of *generalized anxiety disorder is reserved for anxiety that is chronic, of insidious onset, and characterized by general feelings of tension and nervous discomfort.*

The table at the bottom of the facing page summarizes the DSM-III criteria for the diagnosis of panic disorder.

**17.30.  The answer is D (4)** (*Synopsis*, ed. 4, pages 342 and 346).

According to DSM-III, *conversion disorder* is considered a subtype of the somatoform disor-

### Clinical Features of Simple Phobia*

| Essential Features | Associated Features |
| --- | --- |
| Phobic object is discrete object or situation other than those seen in agoraphobia and social phobia | Anticipatory anxiety may lead patient to seek detailed information before entering situation in which phobic stimulus may be present |
| Anticipatory anxiety leads to avoidance of situation felt to be dangerous | |
| Sudden exposure to phobic stimulus may produce panic attack | |

* Adapted from American Psychiatric Association: *Diagnostic and Statistical Manual of Mental Disorders*, ed 3. American Psychiatric Association, Washington, DC, 1980.

### Diagnostic Criteria for Simple Phobia*

A. *A persistent, irrational fear of, and compelling desire to avoid, an object* or a situation other than being alone, or in public places away from home (agoraphobia), or of *humiliation or embarrassment in certain social situations* (social phobia). *Phobic objects are often animals*, and phobic situations frequently involve heights or closed spaces.

B. Significant distress from the disturbance and *recognition by the individual that his or her fear is excessive or unreasonable*.

C. Not due to another mental disorder, such as schizophrenia or obsessive-compulsive disorder.

* From American Psychiatric Association: *Diagnostic and Statistical Manual of Mental Disorders*, ed 3. American Psychiatric Association, Washington, DC, 1980. Used with permission.

## Clinical Features or Psychogenic Amnesia*

| Essential Features | Associated Features |
|---|---|
| Temporary disturbance in the ability to recall important personal information already registered and stored in the memory without evidence or underlying brain disease | Conflict over sexual or aggressive drives common |
| | *May follow physical trauma* |
| *Sudden onset* | *Indifference to presence of amnesia frequently present* |
| Amnesia generally of localized or systematized form: generalized and continuous amnesias less common | |
| Awareness of disturbance of recall is present | |

\* Adapted from American Psychiatric Association: *Diagnostic and Statistical Manual of Mental Disorders*, ed 3. American Psychiatric Association, Washington, DC, 1980. Used with permission.

ders, a group of disorders in which the essential features are physical symptoms suggesting physical illness for which there are no demonstrable organic findings to explain the symptoms.

For example, paralysis in conversion disorder does not conform to the pattern resulting from damage to the peripheral or central nervous system; rather, it follows a distribution conforming to the conventional idea of the part affected. The hand is paralyzed from the wrist down, the forearm from the elbow down, and the whole arm from the shoulder down. If the problem is one of paresis, the weakness may be most severe at the proximal portion of the limb, rather than distally—the opposite of what occurs in central nervous system disease. For example, in hysterical hemiplegia, the patient, when walking, drags the affected leg along limp behind, rather than swinging it through at the hip, as in neurogenic hemiplegia. When the paralyzed or paretic part is examined carefully, it becomes apparent that there is no genuine deficit in muscle function. If the patient is asked to move the afflicted member, one may note a spasm of the antagonist

### Diagnostic Criteria for Psychogenic Amnesia*

A. Sudden inability to recall important personal information that is too extensive to be explained by ordinary forgetfulness.

B. The disturbance is not due to an organic mental disorder (e.g. blackouts during alcohol intoxication).

\* From American Psychiatric Association: *Diagnostic and Statistical Manual of Mental Disorders*, ed 3. American Psychiatric Association, Washington, DC, 1980. Used with permission.

### Diagnostic Criteria for Panic Disorder*

A. At least three panic attacks within a 3-week period in circumstances other than during marked physical exertion or in a life-threatening situation. The attacks are not precipitated only by exposure to a circumscribed phobic stimulus.

B. Panic attacks are manifested by discrete periods of apprehension or fear, and at least four of the following symptoms appear during each attack:

1. Dyspnea;
2. Palpitations;
3. Chest pain or discomfort;
4. Choking or smothering sensations;
5. Dizziness, vertigo, or unsteady feelings;
6. Feelings of unreality;
7. Paresthesias (tingling in hands or feet);
8. Hot and cold flashes;
9. Sweating;
10. Faintness;
11. Trembling or shaking;
12. Fear of dying, going crazy, or doing something uncontrolled during an attack.

C. Not due to a physical disorder or another mental disorder, such as major depression, somatization disorder, or schizophrenia.

D. The disorder is not associated with agoraphobia.

\* From American Psychiatric Association: *Diagnostic and Statistical Manual of Mental Disorders*, ed 3. American Psychiatric Association, Washington, DC, 1980. Used with permission.

muscles, and this spasm prevents motion. On passively flexing the paralyzed limb, the observer may find a contracture of the muscle groups opposing the movement. Reflexes remain within the range of normal, the plantar response is always flexor, and there is no reaction of degeneration on electrical stimulation.

*Factitious disorder* is a mental disorder in which the subject voluntarily produces physical or psychological symptoms. *Phobic disorder* is an anxiety disorder characterized by an intense specific fear of a situation or object. The most common form of phobia is agoraphobia, which is a fear of open spaces. *Posttraumatic stress disorder* is an anxiety disorder with characteristic symptoms that develop after the patient experiences a stressful situation or a series of events outside the range of normal experience.

**17.31.  The answer is C (2, 4)** (*Synopsis*, ed. 4, page 355).

The characteristics of multiple personality disorder may be summarized as follows: (1) At any given time, *patients are dominated by one of two or more distinct personalities, each of which determines the nature of their behavior and attitudes during the period that it is uppermost in consciousness.* (2) *The transition from one personality to another is sudden*, often dramatic in occurrence. (3) *There is generally amnesia during each state for the existence of the others* and for the events that took place when another personality was in the ascendancy. Often, however, one personality state is not bound by such amnesia and retains complete awareness of the existence, qualities, and activities of the other personalities. (4) *Each personality has a fully integrated, highly complex set of associated memories with characteristic attitudes, personal relationships, and behavior patterns.* On examination, patients generally show nothing unusual in their mental status, other than a possible amnesia for periods of time of varying duration, and one is unable to tell from a single, casual encounter that the patients lead other lives at other times. Only prolonged contact that enables one to observe the sudden discontinuities in mental functioning discloses this information.

The first appearance of the secondary person-

ality or personalities may be spontaneous, or it may emerge in relation to what seems to be a precipitant. In some patients, the change occurs after an emotional shock or physical trauma, and the initial phase may take the form of a typical episode of amnesia that leads to the development of a secondary personality.

The DSM-III diagnostic criteria for multiple personality are listed in the table below.

**17.32.  The answer is D (4)** (*Synopsis*, ed. 4, page 346).

The concept of somatic compliance refers to *conversion symptoms that tend to appear in locations and organ systems that are or have previously been the site of symptom-producing lesions.* The existence of the physical disorder apparently facilitates the subsequent appearance of the conversion symptoms in the same location. Hysterical disturbances of sensation, especially anesthesias, may go unnoticed unless they are specifically looked for, because *patients do not often complain of them.* This is because of both the complexity of the clinical ingredients and *the refractoriness of such patients to programs of treatment and rehabilitation.* Somatic compliance *does not refer to the phenomenon of the affected organ's representation of a symbolic conflict.*

**17.33.  The answer is C (2, 4)** (*Synopsis*, ed. 4, page 328).

Obsessions and compulsions have certain features in common: (1) An idea or *an impulse obtrudes itself insistently, persistently, and impellingly into the person's conscious awareness.* (2) A feeling of anxious dread accompanies the central manifestation and frequently leads the person to take countermeasures against the initial idea or impulse. (3) *The obsession or compulsion is ego-alien*—that is, it is experienced as being foreign to and not a usual part of one's experience of oneself as a psychological being; it is undesired, unacceptable, and uncontrollable. (4) No matter how vivid and compelling the obsession or compulsion, *the person recognizes it as absurd and irrational;* insight is retained. (5) Finally, the person suffering from the manifestations feels a strong need to resist them.

---

### Diagnostic Criteria for Multiple Personality*

A. The existence within the individual of two or more distinct personalities, each of which is dominant at a particular time.

B. The personality that is dominant at any particular time determines the individual's behavior.

C. Each individual personality is complex and integrated with its own unique behavior patterns and social relationships.

---

\* From American Psychiatric Association: *Diagnostic and Statistical Manual of Mental Disorders*, ed 3. American Psychiatric Association, Washington, DC, 1980. Used with permission.

The term *ego-syntonic* refers to features of a person's personality that are perceived as acceptable and consistent with his or her total personality. In contrast, ego-alien aspects of a person's personality are viewed as repugnant, unacceptable, or inconsistent with the rest of his or her personality.

**17.34. The answer is B (1, 3)** (*Synopsis*, ed. 4, page 321).

In phobic disorder, anxiety is a central component—*no longer free floating*, as in anxiety state disorder, but *attached to a specific object*, activity, or situation; the anxiety either is *not justified by the stimulus that provokes it*, or is *out of proportion to the real situation;* and sufferers are completely aware of the irrationality of their reaction.

Anxiety is an unpleasurable emotional state associated with psychophysiological changes in response to an intrapsychic conflict. In contrast to fear, the danger or threat in anxiety is unreal. Physiological changes consist of increased heart rate, disturbed breathing, trembling, sweating, and vasomotor changes. Psychological changes consist of an uncomfortable feeling of impending danger, an overwhelming awareness of being powerless, the inability to perceive the unreality of the threat, prolonged feeling of tension, and exhaustive readiness for the expected danger.

**17.35. The answer is C (2, 4)** (*Synopsis*, ed. 4, page 346).

Hysterical aphonia is a special and localized form of paralysis that occurs in the *muscles affecting the vocal cords*. In this condition, *the patient is usually able to whisper with no difficulty but can make no vocalized sound* whatsoever. *Examination reveals normal movement of the lips, tongue, pharynx, and vocal cords during respiration.*

**17.36. The answer is E (all)** (*Synopsis*, ed. 4, pages 344 and 345).

Certain symptoms, such as nausea, vomiting, and fainting, that have always been considered part of the classical syndrome of conversion disorder are *mediated in part, at least, by the autonomic nervous system.* Psychophysiological disorders may, like conversion disorder, represent nonverbal, *symbolic communications* expressed in body language. In psychophysiological disorders, as well as in hysterical symptoms, an affect or *drive that is rendered unconscious by repression* seems to be converted into a somatic symptom.

There is little to be said about the pathology of conversion disorder. No known neuropathological lesions underlie the symptoms, and the pathology that is associated with the condition is purely secondary to the hysterical paralyses and contractures. *If they are of long duration,*

*muscle atrophy, stiffening, and limitation of motion of the joints of the affected limb or limbs may occur* as a result of prolonged disuse.

**17.37. The answer is E (all)** (*Synopsis*, ed. 4, page 326).

A variety of behavioral treatment techniques have been employed, the most common being *desensitization*, a method pioneered by Joseph Wolpe. In desensitization, the patient is exposed serially to a predetermined list of anxiety-provoking stimuli graded in a *hierarchy* from the least to the most frightening. Each of the anxiety-provoking stimuli is paired with the arousal of another affect of an opposite quality that is strong enough to suppress the anxiety. Specifically, through the use of tranquilizing drugs, hypnosis, and instruction in the art of muscle relaxation, patients are taught how to induce in themselves both mental and physical repose. Once they have mastered these techniques, patients are instructed to employ them in the face of each anxiety-provoking stimulus in the hierarchy as the stimuli are presented to them seriatim from the least to the most potent. As they become desensitized to each stimulus in the scale, the patients move up to the next stimulus until, ultimately, what previously produced the most anxiety is no longer capable of eliciting the painful affect.

Other behavioral techniques that have more recently been employed involve intensive exposure to the phobic stimulus either through imagery or in vivo. In *flooding* (implosion therapy), patients are exposed to phobic anxiety produced by images of the phobic stimulus for as long as they can tolerate the fear until they reach a point at which they can no longer feel the fear. In vivo flooding requires patients to experience similar anxiety through an exposure to the actual phobic stimulus itself. *Modeling* is a form of behavior therapy based on the principles of imitative learning; it obviates the need for the patient to discover effective responses through trial-and-error emulation of the therapist.

Varying degrees of success have been reported in treating phobic disorders by behavioral techniques, although it is not always clear how much the effects are to be attributed to the measures specifically characteristic of behavior therapy and how much to other factors that accompany the effects, such as suggestion or the supportive relationship with an enthusiastic therapist. In general, the simple and social phobias respond best to behavioral methods, whereas patients with agoraphobia, especially when panic attacks are a prominent and continuous feature, fare less well and often run a long and fluctuating course of continuing symptoms and disability. Even in the agoraphobic group, nearly half the patients report sufficient improvement with behavior therapy to enable them to lead reasonably active lives, despite a persistence of their anxiety. It is clear that behavioral therapeutic techniques have added an important dimension to the psychiatrist's therapeutic armamentarium and should be considered for every patient with a phobic disorder.

**17.38.   The answer is B (1, 3)** (*Synopsis,* ed. 4, page 345).

Astasia abasia is a form of hysterical ataxia in which a *disturbance of gait* is maintained. It is characterized by gross, irregular, *pseudoataxic,* jerky movements of the trunk and by dancing, staggering, drunken steps. In addition, as patients try to maintain balance or clutch for the support of walls, furniture, or people, they wildly thrash and wave their hands and arms. *They rarely fall,* but if they do, they avoid injury.

**17.39.   The answer is E (all)** (*Synopsis,* ed. 4, page 346).

The most important factors that make for a good prognosis in the treatment of conversion disorders are psychological *conflicts that center on oedipal sexuality and evidence of stability in relationships,* such as with family, friends, or coworkers. The ability to relate to the physician is an important factor in developing a good therapeutic alliance. The patient's capacity to feel and to express emotions *without developing incapacitating anxiety or depression* is important, as well as the ability to have psychological distance from consciously experienced emotion and the *capacity for introspection.* According to psychoanalysis theory, conflicts that center on oedipal sexuality have a better chance of being resolved than those that are considered to be centered on oral or anal fixations.

**17.40.   The answer is E (all)** (*Synopsis,* ed. 4, pages 343 and 344).

For patients with conversion disorders involving pain or the prolongation or exacerbation of an existing lesion, the existence of a bodily illness serves not only to gratify *strong but unconscious dependency needs* but also to resolve the conflict between these needs and *their self-image as a strong, self-sufficient individual.* The conversion symptoms are viewed as *ego-alien* accidental events over which the patients have no control. As such, the sickness and any ensuing disability are viewed as perfectly permissible. The *patients may thus allow themselves to become incapacitated invalids,* dependent on others for care, but still able to maintain the image of independence.

**17.41.   The answer is E (all)** (*Synopsis,* ed. 4, page 337).

In addition to painful reexperiencing of the traumatic event and psychic numbing, patients usually experience a number of other symptoms characteristic of posttraumatic stress disorder. Excessive autonomic arousal is very common and includes such symptoms as *hyperalertness,* an exaggerated startle response, and *difficulty in falling asleep* (these sleep disturbances may involve recurrent nightmares of the traumatic event). Cognitive symptoms also occur, particularly in those patients who have experienced both severe physical and psychic trauma, as in the survivors of death camps. These symptoms include *impaired memory* and difficulty in concentrating or completing tasks.

For some patients, symptoms of posttraumatic stress are intensified by situations that resemble or arouse recollection of the original trauma. These situations will often elicit a reaction of *phobic avoidance.*

**17.42.   The answer is C (2, 4)** (*Synopsis,* ed. 4, page 340).

Somatization disorder is a mental disorder in which recurrent and multiple physical complaints exist with no apparent physical cause. Studies show that it is *more common in women than men* and *tends to run in families.* In addition, it seems to be significantly *associated with sociopathy and alcoholism in first-degree male relatives of somatization patients.*

The DSM-III diagnostic criteria for somatization disorder are listed in the table on the facing page.

**17.43.   The answer is A (1, 2, 3)** (*Synopsis,* ed. 4, page 335).

The single classic posttraumatic syndrome—involving recurrent nightmares, anxiety, numbing of responsiveness, insomnia, impaired concentration, irritability, hypersensitivity, and depressive symptoms—has been described in response to an enormous variety of overwhelmingly stressful situations—prisoner-of-war camps, death camps, combat, auto accidents, industrial accidents, such mass catastrophes as Hiroshima, as well as rape, and severe accidents in the home. These various stressors all tend to produce a single syndrome that appears to be the final common pathway in response to severe stress. This syndrome may occur acutely after the disaster, or it may become chronic. Not all victims of disaster are necessarily normal personalities, although the stressor must be of sufficient severity to invoke the syndrome in most normal people. Consequently, the disorder may be diagnosed in persons who have a prior psychiatric diagnosis but who develop the classic posttraumatic syndrome in response to a severe stressor. Some persons who experience the

**Diagnostic Criteria for Somatization Disorder***

A. A history of physical symptoms of several years duration beginning before the age of 30.

B. Complaints of at least 14 symptoms for women and 12 for men, from the 37 symptoms listed below. To count a symptom as present the individual must report that the symptom caused him or her to take medicine (other than aspirin), alter his or her life pattern, or see a physician. The symptoms, in the judgment of the clinician, are not adequately explained by physical disorder or physical injury and are not side effects of medication, drugs or alcohol. The clinician need not be convinced that the symptom was actually present, e.g. that the individual actually vomited throughout her entire pregnancy; report of the symptom by the individual is sufficient.

*Sickly:* Believes that he or she has been sickly for a good part of his or her life.

*Conversion or pseudoneurological symptoms:* Difficulty swallowing, loss of voice, deafness, double vision, blurred vision, blindness, fainting or loss of consciousness, memory loss, seizures or convulsions, trouble walking, paralysis or muscle weakness, urinary retention or difficulty urinating.

*Gastrointestinal symptoms:* Abdominal pain, nausea, vomiting spells (other than during pregnancy), bloating (gassy), intolerance (e.g. gets sick) of a variety of foods, diarrhea.

*Female reproductive symptoms:* Judged by the individual as occurring more frequently or severely than in most women: painful menstruation, menstrual irregularity, excessive bleeding, severe vomiting throughout pregnancy or causing hospitalization during pregnancy.

*Psychosexual symptoms:* For the major part of the individual's life after opportunities for sexual activity: sexual indifference, lack of pleasure during intercourse, pain during intercourse.

*Pain:* Pain in back, joints, extremities, genital area (other than during intercourse); pain on urination; other pain (other than headaches).

*Cardiopulmonary symptoms:* Shortness of breath, palpitations, chest pain, dizziness.

* From American Psychiatric Association: *Diagnostic and Statistical Manual of Mental Disorders*, ed 3. American Psychiatric Association, Washington, DC, 1980. Used with permission.

symptoms of posttraumatic stress disorder may also display symptoms of another disorder, such as an organic mental disorder or major depressive disorder.

The patient is likely to experience emotional symptoms in the future that are characteristic of posttraumatic stress disorder, which is defined in DSM-III as a reaction to "a psychologically traumatic event or events outside the range of human experience usually considered normal." The characteristic symptoms include exaggerated startle response, *memory impairment*, difficulty in concentrating, *guilt feelings*, and *insomnia*. In DSM-III, these symptoms are classified as autonomic, dysphoric, and cognitive.

*Memory impairment* involves difficulties in registration, retention, or recall of what is experienced or learned in everyday life, due to disorders or diseases of the central nervous system. *Guilt feelings* are characterized by an emotional state associated with self-reproach and the need for punishment. Guilt has normal psychological and social functions, but special intensity or absence of guilt characterizes many mental disorders, such as depression and antisocial personality. *Insomnia* is characterized by difficulty in falling asleep or in staying asleep.

A *hallucination* is a false sensory perception occurring in the absence of any relevant external stimulation of the sensory modality involved. It

is not a feature of a posttraumatic stress disorder.

The DSM-III diagnostic criteria for posttraumatic stress disorder are listed in the table at the top of the following page.

**17.44.   The answer is E (all)** (*Synopsis*, ed. 4, page 350).

Investigators see hypochondriacal symptoms as playing primarily a defensive role in the psychic economy. For Harry Stack Sullivan, they represented protective substitutive activity that prevents the person from experiencing the pain of directly facing a dangerously *low self-esteem*. In other words, persons can substitute an image of themselves as physically ill or deficient for the far more devastating view of themselves as a worthless human being.

Hypochondriasis also serves to *enable patients to gratify dependency needs, protect them from guilt*, and *provide them with various secondary gains*. Secondary gain is the obvious advantage that persons gain from their illness, such as gifts, attention, and release from responsibility.

One must view all the theoretical explanations of hypochondriasis with cautious reservation. They have been constructed from observations made on a small number of patients who are generally limited in their ability to reveal the kind of psychological introspections on which psychodynamic formulations must be

## Diagnostic Criteria for Posttraumatic Stress Disorder*

A. Existence of a recognizable stressor that would evoke significant symptoms of distress in almost everyone.

B. Reexperiencing of the trauma as evidenced by at least one of the following:

1. Recurrent and intrusive recollections of the event;
2. Recurrent dreams of the event;
3. Sudden acting or feeling as if the traumatic event were reoccurring, because of an association with an environmental or ideational stimulus.

C. Numbing of responsiveness to or reduced involvement with the external world, beginning some time after the trauma, as shown by at least one of the following:

1. Markedly diminished interest in one or more significant activities;
2. Feeling of detachment or estrangement from others;
3. Constricted affect.

D. At least two of the following symptoms that were not present before the trauma:

1. Hyperalertness or exaggerated startle response;
2. Sleep disturbance;
3. Guilt about surviving when others have not, or about behavior required for survival;
4. Memory impairment or trouble concentrating;
5. Avoidance of activities that arouse recollection of the traumatic event;
6. Intensification of symptoms by exposure to events that symbolize or resemble the traumatic event.

*From American Psychiatric Association: *Diagnostic and Statistical Manual of Mental Disorders*, ed 3. American Psychiatric Association, Washington, DC, 1980. Used with permission.

based and tested. Perhaps their major value lies in the fact that they focus attention on the important and still poorly understood problem of narcissism. As most investigators have recognized, hypochondriasis is grounded on a narcissistic personality organization, and the continued investigation of hypochondriacal disorders is essential to a deeper understanding of narcissistic phenomena.

The DSM-III diagnostic criteria for hypochondriasis are listed below.

**17.45.  The answer is D (4)** (*Synopsis*, ed. 4, page 349).

Psychogenic pain disorder is seen more frequently by internists than by psychiatrists, partly because the somatic nature of the complaint leads patients to a medical physician and partly because their obtuse, often adamant un-

awareness of even obvious emotional causative factors causes them more often than not to reject psychiatric consultation. The mechanisms involved in the production of psychogenic pain are not clearly understood. Researchers who investigated patients suffering from the syndrome found that many of them exhibit alexithymic (i.e. the inability to express feelings) characteristics. Psychological factors are etiologically involved in the pain, and *the pain enables the patient to get support from the environment* that might not otherwise be forthcoming.

See the table on page 223 for DSM-III diagnostic criteria for psychogenic pain disorder.

**17.46.  The answer is A (1, 2, 3)** (*Synopsis*, ed. 4, page 313).

Psychogenic fugue is a disorder with several typical features, including the *sudden and un-*

## Diagnostic Criteria for Hypochondriasis*

A. The predominant disturbance is an unrealistic interpretation of physical signs or sensations as abnormal, leading to preoccupation with the fear or belief of having a serious disease.

B. Thorough physical evaluation does not support the diagnosis of any physical disorder that can account for the physical signs or sensations or for the individual's unrealistic interpretation of them.

C. The unrealistic fear or belief of having a disease persists despite medical reassurance and causes impairment in social or occupational fuctioning.

D. Not due to any other mental disorder such as schizophrenia, affective disorder, or somatization disorder.

*From American Psychiatric Association: *Diagnostic and Statistical Manual of Mental Disorders*, ed 3. American Psychiatric Association, Washington, DC, 1980. Used with permission.

**Diagnostic Criteria for Psychogenic Pain Disorders***

A. Severe and prolonged pain is the predominant disturbance.

B. *The pain presented as a symptom is inconsistent with the anatomic distribution of the nervous system*; after extensive evaluation, no organic pathology or pathophysiological mechanism can be found to account for the pain; or, when there is some related organic pathology, the complaint of pain is grossly in excess of what would be expected from the physical findings.

C. *Psychological factors are judged to be etiologically involved in the pain*, as evidenced by at least one of the following:

1. A temporal relationship between an environmental stimulus that is apparently related to a psychological conflict or need and the initiation or exacerbation of the pain;
2. *the pain's enabling the individual to avoid some activity* that is noxious to him or her;
3. *the pain's enabling the individual to get support from the environment* that otherwise might not be forthcoming.

D. Not due to another mental disorder.

* From American Psychiatric Association: *Diagnostic and Statistical Manual of Mental Disorders*, ed 3. American Psychiatric Association, Washington, DC, 1980. Used with permission.

---

expected traveling of the patients away from their home, with an inability to recall their past. Unlike the patient with psychogenic amnesia, *patients in a psychogenic fugue are unaware that anything is forgotten. They do not appear to others to be acting in any way out of the ordinary, nor do they appear to be acting out any specific traumatic event.* Usually, in fact, these patients lead a quiet, isolated life, doing nothing to elicit suspicion or attention.

The table below lists the DSM-III criteria for this diagnosis.

**17.47–17.50.   The answers are 17.47–A, 17.48–D, 17.49–B, and 17.50–C** (*Synopsis*, ed. 4, pages 315 and 316).

There are two classifications in DSM-III associated with anxiety neurosis in which anxiety is the main disturbance. If anxiety is *episodic in nature*, it is known as a panic disorder; if it is *chronic and persistent*, it is known as generalized anxiety disorder. DSM-III states that, in panic disorder, recurrent anxiety (panic) attacks and nervousness are manifested by discrete periods of sudden onset of intensive apprehension, fearfulness, or terror often associated with feelings of impending doom; whereas in the generalized

anxiety disorder, the anxiety is persistent for at least 1 month and tends to be chronic in nature.

The essential features of both panic disorders and generalized anxiety disorders are *feelings of fear*, dizziness, trembling, hot and cold flashes, and paresthesias (tingling in the hands or feet). Neither one of these disorders is due to another mental disorder, such as major depression or schizophrenia. Because *thought disorders* are a feature of schizophrenia, they are not considered a feature of panic disorder or generalized anxiety disorder.

Symptoms of panic attacks differ from those of generalized anxiety disorder in that at least four of the following appear during each attack: dyspnea; palpitations; chest pain and discomfort; choking or smothering sensations; vertigo or unsteady feelings; feelings of unreality; sweating; fainting; or fear of dying, going crazy, or doing something uncontrolled during an attack. This disorder is not associated with the phobic disorder, agoraphobia.

Generalized anxiety disorder is manifested by symptoms from three of the following four categories, which are not seen in panic disorders: motor tension, including jitteriness, jumpiness, tension, muscle aches, fatigability, inability to relax, eyelid twitch, furrowed brow, strained

---

**Diagnostic Criteria for Psychogenic Fugue***

A. Sudden unexpected travel away from one's home or customary place of work, with inability to recall one's past.

B. Assumption of new identity (partial or complete).

C. The disturbance is not due to an organic mental disorder.

* Adapted from American Psychiatric Association: *Diagnostic and Statistical Manual of Mental Disoders*, ed 3. American Psychiatric Association, Washington, DC, 1980. Used with permission.

face, fidgeting, restlessness, and easy startle; autonomic hyperactivity, including upset stomach, heart pounding or racing, cold clammy hands, dry mouth, light-headedness, frequent urination, diarrhea, discomfort in the pit of the stomach, lump in the throat, flushing, pallor, and high resting pulse and respiration rate; apprehensive expectation, including anxiety, worry, rumination, and anticipation of misfortune to self or others; and symptoms of vigilance and scanning, including hyperattentiveness resulting in distractability, difficulty in concentrating, insomnia, feeling "on edge," irritability, and impatience.

**17.51–17.55.   The answers are 17.51–A, 17.52–B, 17.53–C, 17.54–D, and 17.55– A** (*Synopsis*, ed. 4, pages 316, 317, and 318).

The classifications of panic disorder and generalized anxiety disorder are reserved for those syndromes in which *characteristic anxiety symptoms are present without other psychiatric symptoms*, such as obsessions and phobias. Panic disorder is characterized by *discrete and episodic* attacks of anxiety, whereas generalized anxiety disorder is characterized by anxiety that is *chronic and persistent*. Patients with chronic and lesser degrees of anxiety show many of the same features as those with more acute anxiety, but the features are less intense. Such symptoms as *dizziness*, *paresthesia*, restlessness, and palpitations are seen in both types of anxiety. Hyperventilation may be seen in both types of anxiety, but only in the more acute, intense form would sufficient carbon dioxide be blown off to bring on severe enough *respiratory alkalosis* to cause such symptoms as muscle twitching and even tetany.

The table below lists the DSM-III diagnostic criteria for generalized anxiety disorder.

---

### Diagnostic Criteria for Generalized Anxiety Disorder*

A. Generalized, persistent anxiety is manifested by symptoms from three of the following four categories:

1. *Motor tension:* shakiness, jitteriness, jumpiness, trembling, tension, muscle aches, fatigability, inability to relax, eyelid twitch, furrowed brow, strained face, fidgeting, restlessness, easy startle;

2. *Autonomic hyperactivity:* sweating, heart pounding or racing, cold, clammy hands, dry mouth, dizziness, light-headedness, paresthesias (tingling in hands or feet), upset stomach, hot or cold spells, frequent urination, diarrhea, discomfort in the pit of the stomach, lump in the throat, flushing, pallor, high resting pulse and respiration rate;

3. *Apprehensive expectation:* anxiety, worry, fear, rumination, and anticipation of misfortune to self or others;

4. *Vigilance and scanning:* hyperattentiveness resulting in distractibility, difficulty in concentrating, insomnia, feeling "on edge," irritability, impatience.

B. The anxious mood has been continuous for at least one month.

C. Not due to another mental disorder, such as a depressive disorder or schizophrenia.

D. At least 18 years of age.

---

* From American Psychiatric Association: *Diagnostic and Statistical Manual of Mental Disorders*, ed 3. American Psychiatric Association, Washington, DC, 1980. Used with permission.

## References

Anderson D J: A Comparison of panic disorder and generalized anxiety disorder. Am J Psychiatry *141:* 572, 1984.

Andreasen N C: Posttraumatic stress disorders. In *Comprehensive Textbook of Psychiatry*, ed 4, H I Kaplan, B J Sadock, editors, p 918. Williams & Wilkins, Baltimore, 1985.

Bliss E L: Hysteria and hypnosis. J Nerv Ment Dis *172:* 203, 1984.

Curtis G C: Anxiety disorders. In *The Psychiatric Clinics of North America*, F E F Larocca, editor, p 376. W B Saunders, Philadelphia, 1985.

Goodwin D W, Guze S B: Hysterical (somatization disorder). In *Psychiatric Diagnosis*, ed 3, p 89. Oxford University Press, New York, 1984.

Hoover C F: Families of origin in obsessive-compulsive disorder. J Nerv Ment Dis *172:* 207, 1984.

Nemiah J C: Neurotic disorders. In *Comprehensive Textbook of Psychiatry*, ed 4, H I Kaplan, B J Sadock, editors, p 883. Williams & Wilkins, Baltimore, 1985.

Noyes R, Anderson J, Clancey J, Crouse R, Slymen D, Ghoneim M, Hinrichs V: Diazepam and propranolol in panic disorder and agoraphobia. Arch Gen Psychiatry 41: 287, 1984.

Pasnau R, editor: *Diagnosis and Treatment of Anxiety Disorders*. American Psychiatric Press, Washington, DC, 1983.

# 18

# Personality Disorders

Personality has generally been used as a global descriptive label for the totality of a person's objectively observable behavior and subjectively reportable inner experience. The wholeness of an individual described in this way represents both the public and the private aspects of that person's life.

Personality diagnosis is based on a concept of behavioral categorization that takes into account the interplay of currently active psychological tendencies and that depends for its typology on varieties of formative developmental experiences. Such a concept must be concerned with the learning of environmentally useful responses. Personality reflects a person's techniques for getting along with people and things. It represents a person's usual behavior in the process of establishing and maintaining a stable, reciprocal relationship with the surrounding human and nonhuman environment. It also reflects the nature of the person's psychological defense system, the mechanisms of defense that are automatically and customarily employed in order to maintain his or her intrapsychic stability.

According to psychoanalytic theory, these defensive and adaptive techniques are to an important degree a function of the level of psychosexual development an individual has achieved.

The importance of early development may also be described in other terms, most of which deal with the influence of society and culture, mediated through child-rearing patterns, on adult behavior. A wide range of investigations have suggested the presence of basic personality patterns that emerge in certain cultures. These are determined, at least in part, by the universality within the culture of parental methods of dealing with the child's basic needs, such as eating, excreting, sleeping, and moving; with the child's expression of thought and, especially, of feeling; and with the crises that accompany the maturational sequences and the societally determined shifts in context, such as the shift from the family to the school. Such personality organizations are also determined by patterns of sanctioned and prohibited adult behavior and by related factors that prevail within the culture.

In the multiaxial system of the third edition of the *Diagnostic and Statistical Manual of Mental Disorders* (DSM-III), the personality disorders are coded on Axis II. A person may have a psychotic or neurotic disorder that would be coded on Axis I, but that does not preclude the presence of a current or preexisting personality disorder from also being diagnosed on Axis II. Some personality disorders may be associated with an increased vulnerability toward one of the neurotic or psychotic disorders. For example, there is evidence that schizotypal personality disorders may predispose to later schizophrenia and that dependent or avoidant personality may be associated with depressive neurosis.

DSM-III groups personality disorders into three clusters. The first cluster of odd or eccentric behavior consists of paranoid, schizoid, or schizotypal personalities. The second cluster of dramatic, emotional, or erratic behavior consists of histrionic, narcissistic, antisocial, and borderline personality disorders. The third cluster of anxious or fearful behavioral patterns includes avoidant, dependent, compulsive, and passive-aggressive personality disorders.

The reader should refer to Chapter 18, "Personality Disorders," in *Modern Synopsis-IV* and should then study the questions and answers that follow to assess his or her knowledge of the field.

# Questions

**DIRECTIONS:** Each of the statements or questions below is followed by five suggested responses or completions. Select the *one* that is *best* in each case.

**18.1.** Adult borderline patients who pigeonhole people into all-good or all-bad categories are demonstrating which of the following mechanisms:

A. Undoing
B. Intellectualization
C. Projection
D. Splitting
E. Displacement

**18.2.** Borderline personality disorders manifest all of the following characteristics *except*

A. unpredictability
B. identity diffusion
C. intense hostility
D. below-average intelligence
E. manipulative behavior

**18.3.** All of the following statements about antisocial personality disorder are true *except*

A. it is infrequently seen in most clinical, traditional psychiatric settings
B. it should be thought of as synonymous with criminality
C. the onset occurs before the age of 15
D. it is most common in highly mobile residents of impoverished urban areas
E. often the opposite-sex clinician will emphasize the colorful, seductive aspects of the patient's personality, whereas the same-sex clinician will see manipulation and entitlement in the patient

**18.4.** Schizoid personality disorder is found in what percentage of the population:

A. 2 percent
B. 3.5 percent
C. 4 percent
D. 5 percent
E. 7.5 percent

**18.5.** All the following criteria apply to the diagnosis of schizotypal personality disorder *except*

A. magical thinking
B. ideas of reference
C. social isolation
D. paranoid ideation
E. early schizophrenia

**18.6.** All the following characteristics of histrionic personality disorder apply *except*

A. self-dramatization
B. craving for excitement
C. irrational outbursts
D. suicidal threats
E. psychotic episodes

**18.7.** All the following characteristics of the dependent personality disorder apply *except*

A. it is more often diagnosed in men than in women
B. it is more common in the youngest children of a sibship than in the older children
C. pessimism
D. the patient has a marked lack of self-confidence
E. the patient gets others to assume responsibility for major areas of his or her life

**18.8.** All the following criteria are required to make the diagnosis of compulsive personality disorder *except*

A. emotional constriction
B. orderliness
C. indecisiveness
D. suspiciousness
E. perseverance

**18.9.** A pattern of unstable but intense interpersonal relationships, impulsivity, inappropriately intense anger, identity disturbance, affective instability, and problems with being alone suggest a diagnosis of

A. antisocial personality disorder
B. narcissistic personality disorder
C. histrionic personality disorder
D. schizoid personality disorder
E. borderline personality disorder

**18.10.** Clinical experience suggests that too little consistent discipline results in

A. avoidant personality
B. dependent personality
C. histrionic personality
D. compulsive personality
E. antisocial personality

**18.11.** In prison populations, the prevalence of antisocial personality may be as high as

A. 35 percent
B. 45 percent
C. 55 percent
D. 65 percent
E. 75 percent

**18.12.** In the paranoid personality disorder, all the following criteria exist *except*

A. hypervigilance
B. offense being easily taken
C. hallucinations
D. doubting of others
E. litigiousnous

**18.13.** A person who characteristically procrastinates, resists demands for adequate performance, and finds fault with those on whom he or she depends can be said to have which personality disorder:

A. Borderline
B. Passive-aggressive
C. Narcissistic
D. Schizotypal
E. Paranoid

**18.14.** A grandiose sense of self-importance, preoccupation with fantasies of unlimited success, and demands for constant attention suggest the diagnosis of

A. schizotypal personality disorder
B. passive-aggressive personality disorder
C. borderline personality disorder
D. narcissistic personality disorder
E. paranoid personality disorder

**18.15.** The symptoms of patients with personality disorder are characterized as

A. autoplastic
B. ego-dystonic
C. ego-syntonic
D. flexible
E. adaptive

**DIRECTIONS:** For each of the incomplete statements below, *one* or *more* of the completions given is correct. Choose answer:

A. if only **1, 2**, and **3** are correct
B. if only **1** and **3** are correct
C. if only **2** and **4** are correct
D. if only **4** is correct
E. if all are correct

**18.16.** Paranoid personality disorder consists of

1. pervasive, unwarranted mistrust
2. hypersensitivity
3. restricted affectivity
4. fixed delusions

**18.17.** Schizoid personality disorder is diagnosed in patients

1. who display a lifelong pattern of social withdrawal
2. with eccentricities of communication, behavior, and thought
3. who display a cold, aloof, distant nature with an absence of tender feelings for others
4. who make up the less healthy end of the schizophrenic spectrum

| Directions Summarized | | | | |
|---|---|---|---|---|
| A | B | C | D | E |
| 1, 2, 3 | 1, 3 | 2, 4 | 4 | All are |
| only | only | only | only | correct |

**18.18.** True statements about histrionic personality disorder include behavior that

1. is overly reactive and intensely expressed
2. may appear dependent and helpless
3. is viewed by others as superficially warm and charming with an underlying shallowness
4. is quite different when seen in men than when seen in women

**18.19.** Which of the following criteria are required to make the diagnosis of narcissistic personality disorder:

1. A grandiose sense of self-importance and uniqueness
2. A preoccupation with fantasies of unlimited success and beauty
3. Demands for constant attention and admiration
4. Depressed mood

**18.20.** The passive-aggressive personality is characterized by

1. impulsiveness
2. compliance
3. hypermnesia
4. intentional inefficiency

**18.21.** Sadomasochistic personality disorder

1. is not included in the current DSM-III classification
2. has unconscious castration anxiety as one of its dynamics
3. is characterized by severe guilt about sex
4. is best treated with insight-oriented psychotherapy

**18.22.** A patient with a compulsive personality disorder shows

1. emotional constriction
2. stubbornness
3. impaired capacity for tenderness
4. autoplastic behavior

**18.23.** Patients with avoidant personality disorders

1. are hypersensitive to rejection
2. lack self-confidence
3. are withdrawn
4. have no friends

**DIRECTIONS:** Each set of lettered headings below is followed by a list of numbered words or phrases. For each numbered word or phrase, select

    A. if the item is associated with **A** *only*
    B. if the item is associated with **B** *only*
    C. if the item is associated with *both* **A** *and* **B**
    D. if the item is associated with *neither* **A** *nor* **B**

### Questions 18.24–18.28
    A. Schizoid personality disorder
    B. Schizotypal personality disorder
    C. Both
    D. Neither

**18.24.** Strikingly odd or strange behavior

**18.25.** Ideas of reference

**18.26.** Social isolation

**18.27.** Loose associations

**18.28.** Formerly called simple or latent schizophrenia

# Answers

# Personality Disorders

**18.1. The answer is D** (*Synopsis*, ed. 4, page 376).

Functionally, adult borderline patients distort their present relationships by pigeonholing people into all-good and all-bad categories, a defense mechanism known as *splitting*. People are seen as either nurturant and attachment figures or hateful and sadistic persons who deprive the patients of security needs and threaten them with abandonment whenever they feel dependent.

As a result of this splitting, the good person is idealized, and the bad person is devalued. Patients experience good feelings only by a flight into omnipotence that requires a defensive denial of past and present feelings and of facts that may contradict their present feelings. At times, however, this vacillation between polar-opposite feeling states is recognized by patients and is felt as a source of insecurity and self-hatred.

*Undoing* is an unconscious defense mechanism by which a person symbolically acts out in reverse something unacceptable that has already been done or against which the ego must defend itself. A primitive defense mechanism, undoing is a form of magical expiatory action. Repetitive in nature, it is commonly observed in obsessive-compulsive disorder. *Intellectualization* is an unconscious defense mechanism in which reasoning or logic is used in an attempt to avoid confrontation with an objectionable impulse and thus defend against anxiety. It is also known as brooding compulsion and thinking compulsion. *Projection* is an unconscious defense mechanism in which persons attribute to another those generally unconscious ideas, thoughts, feelings, and impulses that are personally undesirable or unacceptable. Projection protects persons from anxiety arising from an inner conflict. By externalizing whatever is unacceptable, persons deal with it as a situation apart from themselves. *Displacement* is an unconscious defense mechanism by which the emotional component of an unacceptable idea or object is transferred to a more acceptable one.

**18.2. The answer is D** (*Synopsis*, ed. 4, pages 375 and 376).

Borderline patients demonstrate *ordinary reasoning and intellectual abilities* on structural tests, such as the Wechsler Adult Intelligence Scale.

The behavior of borderline personalities, however, is highly *unpredictable*; as a consequence, they rarely achieve up to the level of their abilities. The painful nature of their lives is reflected in repetitive self-destructive acts; wrist slashing and other such self-mutilations are performed to elicit help from others, to express anger, and to numb themselves to overwhelming affect.

Because both dependence and *hostility are intensely felt*, the interpersonal relationships of borderline personalities are tumultuous. They can be clinging—sometimes literally so—and very dependent on those to whom they are close. In contrast to dependent personalities, borderline personalities can express enormous anger at their intimate friends when frustrated. In their capacity to *manipulate groups of people*, borderline personalities have no peer among the personality disordered. Borderline patients tolerate being alone very poorly and prefer a frantic search for companionship, no matter how unsatisfactory, to sitting with feelings of loneliness and emptiness. This facet of behavior excludes borderline personalities from inclusion in the schizophrenic spectrum. They often complain about the lack of a consistent sense of identity (*identity diffusion*) and, when pressed, described how depressed they feel most of the time, despite the flurry of other affects. In therapy, borderline patients frequently regress and become demanding, difficult, and suicidal.

See the table on the following page for the DSM-III diagnostic criteria for borderline personality disorder.

**18.3. The answer is B** (*Synopsis*, ed. 4, pages 372 and 373).

Antisocial personality *should not be thought of as synonymous with criminality*, as the disorder reflects a chronic antisocial mode of behavior involving many aspects of the patient's personality. This disorder is *rarely seen in most traditional psychiatric settings*; rather, it is more frequently apparent in courts and prisons. Antisocial personality disorder begins in childhood or early adolescence with *symptoms appearing before the age of 15* and with the child becoming seriously delinquent by the age of 18. The dis-

### Diagnostic Criteria for Borderline Personality Disorder*

The following are characteristics of the individual's current and long-term functioning, are not limited to episodes of illness, and cause either significant impairment in social or occupational functioning or subjective distress.

A. At least five of the following are required:

1. Impulsivity or unpredictability in at least two areas that are potentially self-damaging, e.g. spending, sex, gambling, substance use, shoplifting, overeating, physically self-damaging acts;

2. A pattern of unstable and intense interpersonal relationships, e.g. marked shifts of attitude, idealization, devaluation, manipulation (consistently using others for one's own ends);

3. Inappropriate, intense anger or lack of control of anger, e.g. frequent displays of temper, constant anger;

4. Identity disturbance manifested by uncertainty about several issues relating to identity, such as self-image, gender identity, long-term goals or career choice, friendship patterns, values, and loyalities, e.g. "Who am I?", "I feel like I am my sister when I am good";

5. Affective instability: marked shifts from normal mood to depression, irritability, or anxiety, usually lasting a few hours and only rarely more than a few days, with a return to normal mood;

6. Intolerance of being alone, e.g. frantic efforts to avoid being alone, depressed when alone;

7. Physically self-damaging acts, e.g. suicidal gestures, self-mutilation, recurrent accidents or physical fights;

8. Chronic feelings of emptiness or boredom.

B. If under 18, does not meet the criteria for identity disorder.

* From American Psychiatric Association: *Diagnostic and Statistical Manual of Mental Disorders,* ed 3. American Psychiatric Association, Washington, DC, 1980. Used with permission.

---

order appears to be *most common in highly mobile residents of poor inner-city neighborhoods.* This personality may often present a normal and even a charming facade. Often, *the patient's antisocial personality impresses the opposite-sex clinician with the seductive aspects of his or her personality, whereas the same-sex clinician may see the patient's manipulative aspects.*

The table on the facing page describes in detail the DSM-III diagnostic criteria for antisocial personality disorder.

**18.4. The answer is E** (*Synopsis*, ed. 4, pages 367 and 368).

Primarily because of the inconsistent diagnostic criteria used in various studies, the prevalence of schizoid personality is not clearly established. In one major study, it was found that schizoid disorders may encompass *7.5 percent of* the population. The sex ratio of the disorder is unknown.

**18.5. The answer is E** (*Synopsis*, ed. 4, page 369).

Largely as a result of family studies in schizophrenia, the term schizotypal was introduced into DSM-III. Schizotypal personality disorder has been postulated to include patients who exhibit some traits of schizophrenia but not enough to warrant that diagnosis. The term schizotypal personality disorder is applied to many patients whom DSM-II would have called simple or latent schizophrenics or schizoid. It encompasses many patients who in the past were labeled ambulatory or pseudoneurotic schizo-

phrenics. *According to DSM-III, however, it is incorrect to view schizotypal personalities as having an early schizophrenia.*

In DSM-III at least four of the following criteria characteristic of the patient's long-term functioning and not limited to episodes of illness are required to make the diagnosis of schizotypal personality disorder: (1) *magical thinking,* such as superstitiousness, clairvoyance, telepathy, a sixth sense; (2) *ideas of reference* and self-referential thinking; (3) *social isolation,* such as no close friends or confidants; (4) recurrent illusions, sensing the presence of a force or person not actually present, depersonalization or derealization not associated with panic attacks; (5) odd communications not clearly due to derailment, loose association, or incoherence, such as speech that is tangential, digressive, overelaborate, or circumstantial; (6) cold, aloof, inadequate rapport in face-to-face interaction; (7) *paranoid ideation*; (8) undue social anxiety or hypersensitivity to criticism.

**18.6. The answer is E** (*Synopsis*, ed. 4, page 370).

In DSM-III, the following criteria are required to make the diagnosis of histrionic personality disorder, and they should characterize the patient's long-term functioning. There is behavior that is overly reactive and expressed intensely without reserve, as indicated by at least three of the following: (1) *self-dramatization* and exaggerated expression of emotions; (2) incessantly drawing attention to oneself; (3) *craving for activity and excitement*; (4) emotional

## Diagnostic Criteria for Antisocial Personality Disorder*

A. Current age at least 18.

B. Onset before age 15 as indicated by a history of three or more of the following before that age:

1. Truancy (positive if it amounted to at least 5 days per year for at least 2 years, not including the last year of school);
2. Expulsion or suspension from school for misbehavior;
3. Delinquency (arrested or referred to juvenile court because of behavior);
4. Running away from home overnight at least twice while living in parental or parental surrogate home;
5. Persistent lying;
6. Repeated sexual intercourse in a casual relationship;
7. Repeated drunkenness or substance abuse;
8. Thefts;
9. Vandalism;
10. School grades markedly below expectation in relation to estimated or known I.Q. (may have resulted in repeating a year);
11. Chronic violations of rules at home and or at school(other than truancy);
12. Initiation of fights.

C. At least four of the following manifestations of the disorder since age 18:

1. Inability to sustain consistent work behavior, as indicated by any of the following: (a) too frequent job changes (e.g. three or more jobs in 5 years not accounted for by nature of job or economic or seasonal fluctuation), (b) significant unemployment (e.g. 6 months or more in 5 years when expected to work), (c) serious absenteeism from work (e.g. average 3 days or more of lateness or absence per month, (d) walking off several jobs without other jobs in sight (Note: similar behavior in an academic setting during the last few years of school may substitute for this criterion in individuals who by reason of their age or circumstances have not had an opportunity to demonstrate occupational adjustment);
2. Lack of ability to function as a responsible parent as evidenced by one or more of the following: (a) child's malnutrition, (b) child's illness resulting from lack of minimal hygiene standards, (c) failure to obtain medical care for a seriously ill child, (d) child's dependence on neighbors or nonresident relatives for food or shelter, (e) failure to arrange for a caretaker for a child under 6 when parent is away from home. (f) repeated
3. Failure to accept social norms with respect to lawful behavior, as indicated by any of the following: repeated thefts, illegal occupation (pimping, prostitution, fencing, selling drugs), multiple arrests, a felony conviction;
4. Inability to maintain enduring attachment to a sexual partner as indicated by two or more divorces and/ or separations (whether legally married or not), desertion of spouse, promiscuity (ten or more sexual partners within 1 year);
5. Irritability and aggressiveness, as indicated by repeated physical fights or assault (not required by one's job or to defend someone or oneself), including spouse or child beating;
6. Failure to honor financial obligations, as indicated by repeated defaulting on debts, failure to provide child support, failure to support other dependents on a regular basis;
7. Failure to plan ahead, or impulsivity, as indicated by traveling from place to place without a prearranged job or clear goal for the period of travel or clear idea about when the travel would terminate, or lack of a fixed address for a month or more;
8. Disregard for the truth as indicated by repeated lying, use of aliases, "conning" others for personal profit;
9. Recklessness, as indicated by driving while intoxicated or recurrent speeding.

D. A pattern of continuous antisocial behavior in which the rights of others are violated, with no intervening period of at least 5 years without antisocial behavior between age 15 and the present time (except when the individual was bedridden or confined in a hospital or penal institution).

E. Antisocial behavior is not due to either severe mental retardation, schizophrenia, or manic episodes.

* From American Psychiatric Association: *Diagnostic and Statistical Manual of Mental Disorders*, ed 3. American Psychiatric Association, Washington, DC, 1980. Used with permission.

excitability in response to minor stimuli; (5) *irrational, angry outbursts* or tantrums; (6) *manipulative suicide threats*, gestures, or attempts. There are also characteristic disturbances in interpersonal relationships, as indicated by at least two of the following: (1) seen by others as shallow even if the person has superficial warmth, charm and appeal; (2) demands and lack of consideration for the wishes of others; (3) vanity, egocentricity, and self-absorption; (4)

dependence, helplessness, constant seeking of assurance.

*Histrionic personalities do not show the loss of reality testing characteristic of the psychoses.*

**18.7.    The answer is A** (*Synopsis*, ed. 4, pages 378 and 379).

Dependent personality is *more often diagnosed in women than in men*. It is *more common in the youngest children of a sibship than in the older children*. In the Midtown Manhattan study, 9.8 percent of their sample showed a personality disorder, and a fourth of them—2.5 percent of the entire sample—were diagnosed as passive-dependent.

*Pessimism, self-doubt*, passivity, and fears about expressing sexual and aggressive feelings characterize the behavior of patients with dependent personality disorder. They have learned to externalize many of their problems in such a fashion that in any relationship they become the passive member. *They avoid positions of responsibility* and become anxious when forced into them. They may express their helplessness and need for companionship in artful and effective ways. When on their own, they find it difficult to persevere at tasks for their own benefit, but may find it easy to perform those tasks for someone else, e.g. in food preparation, hospitals, and beauty and child care professions. The dependent personality may be seen as storing up credits for the good things done, in order to feel entitled to be attached to another person. Intimate relationships are often distorted by the need to maintain the attachment bond. The dependent person can tolerate more unpleasant feelings in intimate relationships than can most other people. An abusive, unfaithful, or alcoholic spouse may be borne as long as the sense of attachment is not disturbed too greatly or for too long.

The table shown below lists the DSM-III diagnostic criteria for dependent personality disorder.

**18.8.    The answer is D** (*Synopsis*, ed. 4, page 380).

In DSM-III, the following criteria are required to make the diagnosis of compulsive personality disorder: (1) There is *emotional constriction*, such as undue conventionality, seriousness, formality, and stinginess with warm and tender emotions. (2) Patients show *orderliness* and preoccupation with rules, order, organization, schedules, and lists; they are stubborn, inflexible, and insist that others submit to their way of doing things. (3) They show *perseverance* and excessive devotion to work and productivity to the exclusion of pleasure and interpersonal relationships. (4) They are *indecisive* to the point that decision making is either avoided or postponed because of rumination and fears of making mistakes.

Patients with compulsive personality disorder are not *suspicious*, a trait seen in the paranoid personality.

**18.9.    The answer is E** (*Synopsis*, ed. 4, pages 375 and 376).

According to DSM-III, at least five of the following eight criteria are required to make the diagnosis of *borderline personality disorder*.

1. Self-detrimental impulsivity in at least two areas, such as extravagance, promiscuity, gambling, overeating, substance abuse, and shoplifting.

2. A pattern of unstable but intense interpersonal relationships, with marked shifts in idealization, devaluation, and manipulation.

3. Inappropriately intense anger or lack of control of anger.

4. Identity disturbance, including uncertainty about self-image, gender identity, friendship patterns and values—for example, "I feel like I am my sister when I am good."

5. Affective instability, as indicated by marked shifts from normal mood to depression, irritability, or anxiety, usually lasting only

---

### Diagnostic Criteria for Dependent Personality Disorder*

The following are characteristic of the individual's current and long-term functioning, are not limited to episodes of illness, and cause either significant impairment in social or occupational functioning or subjective distress.

A. *Passively allows others to assume responsibility for major areas of life* because of inability to function independently, e.g. lets spouse decide what kind of job he or she should have.

B. Subordinates own needs to those of persons on whom he or she depends in order to avoid any possibility of having to rely on self, e.g. tolerates abusive spouse.

C. Lacks self-confidence, e.g. sees self as helpless, stupid.

---

* From American Psychiatric Association: *Diagnostic and Statistical Manual of Mental Disorders*, ed 3. American Psychiatric Association, Washington, DC, 1980. Used with permission.

hours, with a return to the patient's normal mood.

6. Problems with being alone.

7. Self-mutilation, recurrent accidents, suicidal gestures, polysurgery, or physical fights.

8. Chronic feelings of emptiness or boredom.

*Antisocial personality disorder* is a disorder characterized by the inability to get along with other members of society and by repeated conflicts with individual persons and groups. Common attributes include impulsiveness, egocentricity, hedonism, low frustration tolerance, irresponsibility, inadequate conscience development, exploitation of others, and rejection of authority and discipline. *Narcissistic personality disorder* is a personality disorder characterized by a grandiose sense of self-importance, preoccupation with fantasies of unlimited success, exhibitionistic need for attention and admiration, exaggerated responses to criticism or other perceived threats to self-esteem, and disturbance in interpersonal relationships. This diagnostic category was introduced in DSM-III. *Histrionic personality disorder* is a condition in which the patient, usually an immature and dependent person, exhibits unstable, overreactive, and excitable self-dramatizing behavior that is aimed at gaining attention and is at times seductive, although the person may not be aware of that aim. It was termed hysterical personality in DSM-II. *Schizoid personality disorder* is a diagnostic category in DSM-III for persons with defects in the capacity to form social relationships but without other striking communicative or behavioral eccentricities.

**18.10. The answer is E** (*Synopsis*, ed. 4, page 373).

Clinical experience suggests that, whereas *the antisocial personality* has encountered too little consistent discipline from parental figures, *the compulsive personality* has often encountered too much discipline. There is no evidence that punishment is involved in the evolution of the *avoidant, dependent,* or *histrionic personality*.

*Antisocial personality disorder* is a disorder characterized by the inability to get along with other members of society and by repeated conflicts with individual persons and groups. Common attributes include impulsiveness, egocentricity, hedonism, low frustration tolerance, irresponsibility, inadequate conscience development, exploitation of others, and rejection of authority and discipline. The *compulsive personality disorder* is characterized by rigidity, overconscientiousness, extreme inhibition, inability to relax, and the performance of repetitive patterns of behavior. The *avoidant personality disorder* is characterized by low self-esteem, hyper-

sensitivity to rejection, and social withdrawal but a desire for affection and acceptance. *Dependent personality disorder* is a personality disorder characterized by lack of self-confidence, a tendency to have others assume responsibility for significant areas of one's life, and a subordination of one's own needs and wishes to those of others on whom one is dependent. Solitude is extremely discomforting to a person with this disorder. *Histrionic personality disorder* is a condition in which the patient, usually an immature and dependent person, exhibits unstable, overreactive, and excitable self-dramatizing behavior that is aimed at gaining attention and is at times seductive, although the person may not be aware of that aim. It was termed hysterical personality in DSM-II.

**18.11. The answer is E** (*Synopsis*, ed. 4, pages 373 and 374).

In prison populations, the prevalence of antisocial personality may be as high as 75 *percent.*

Prevalence estimates for antisocial personality disorder in the general population range from 0.05 percent to 15 percent. Some recent estimates set the prevalence as high as 3 percent in American men and less than 1 percent in American women. The disorder is most common in highly mobile residents of impoverished urban areas.

**18.12. The answer is C** (*Synopsis*, ed. 4, pages 365 and 366).

In DSM-III the following criteria are required to make the diagnosis of paranoid personality disorder, and they should characterize the patient's long-term functioning. At least four of the following criteria of pervasive and unwarranted mistrust of others must be present: (1) the expectation of harm or trickery; (2) *hypervigilance* (i.e. increased awareness of the environment), injustice collecting, and continual searching for signs of external threat; (3) guardedness; (4) refusal of warranted blame; (5) *chronic doubting of the fidelity of others*; (6) ideas of reference—narrow, focused searching for confirmation of bias; (7) overconcern with hidden motives and special meanings. There is evidence of hypersensitivity, as indicated by at least two of the following: (1) chip on shoulder, *easily taking offense*; (2) making mountains out of molehills; (3) *litigiousness* (i.e. quick to take legal action), readiness to counterattack any threat; (4) inability to relax. There is also limited affect, as reflected by at least two of the following; (1) apparently cold, unemotional nature; (2) pride in self as being rational and unemotional; (3) inability to laugh at self; (4) apparent absence of passive, soft, tender, and sentimental feelings.

Schizophrenia is absent, and *hallucinations* and delusions are not present.

**18.13.   The answer is B** (*Synopsis*, ed. 4, page 382).

*Passive-aggressive persons* characteristically procrastinate, resist demands for adequate performance, find excuses for delays, and find fault with those they depend on, yet refuse to extricate themselves from the dependent relationship. They usually lack assertiveness and are not direct about their own needs or wishes. They fail to ask needed questions about what is expected of them, and may become anxious when forced to succeed or when their usual defense of turning anger against the self is removed.

*Borderline personality disorder* is a personality disorder classified in DSM-III that is marked by instability in various areas. *Narcissistic personality disorder* is a personality disorder characterized by a grandiose sense of self-importance, preoccupation with fantasies of unlimited success, exhibitionistic need for attention and admiration, exaggerated responses to criticism or other perceived threats to self-esteem, and disturbance in interpersonal relationships. This is a diagnostic category introduced in DSM-III. *Schizotypal personality disorder* is a diagnostic category in DSM-III for persons who exhibit various eccentricities in communication or behavior, coupled with defects in the capacity to form social relationships. The term emphasizes a possible relationship with schizophrenia. *Paranoid personality disorder* is a personality disorder characterized by rigidity, hypersensitivity, unwarranted suspicion, jealousy, envy, an exaggerated sense of self-importance, and a tendency to blame and ascribe evil motives to others.

**18.14.   The answer is D** (*Synopsis*, ed. 4, pages 371 and 372).

According to DSM-III, the following criteria are required to make the diagnosis of *narcissistic personality disorder*. The patient shows a grandiose sense of self-importance and uniqueness. There is a preoccupation with fantasies of unlimited success, power, brilliance, beauty, and ideal love, as well as demands for constant attention and admiration. Indifference to criticism or responses to criticism marked by feelings of rage, humiliation, or emptiness are present. Finally, at least two of the following characteristics must be present in interpersonal relationships: (1) inability to empathize; (2) entitlement, surprise, and anger that people do not do what the patient wants; (3) interpersonal exploitiveness; (4) relationships that vacillate between the extremes of overidealization and devaluation.

*Schizotypal personality disorder* is a diagnos-

tic category in DSM-III for persons who exhibit various eccentricities in communication or behavior, coupled with defects in the capacity to form social relationships. The term emphasizes a possible relationship with schizophrenia. *Passive-aggressive personality disorder* is a personality disorder in which the patient manifests aggressive behavior in passive ways, such as obstructionism, pouting, stubbornness, and intentional inefficiency. *Borderline personality disorder* is a personality disorder classified in DSM-III that is marked by instability in various areas. *Paranoid personality disorder* is a personality disorder characterized by rigidity, hypersensitivity, unwarranted suspicion, jealousy, envy, an exaggerated sense of self-importance, and a tendency to blame and ascribe evil motives to others.

**18.15.   The answer is C** (*Synopsis*, ed. 4, page 361).

The symptoms of personality disorder, in contrast to those of neurotic disorders, are *egosyntonic*; that is, they are perfectly acceptable to the ego, and the patient, as a consequence, will often refuse psychiatric help.

Whereas the symptoms of neurotic disorders exhibit *autoplasty* (adaptation by changing the self) and are experienced as *ego-dystonic* (unacceptable to the ego), those of personality disorders are alloplastic (adaptation by altering the external environment) and are characterized by an *inflexible* and *maladaptive* response to stress.

**18.16.   The answer is A (1, 2, 3)** (*Synopsis*, ed. 4, page 366).

Paranoid personality disorder manifests with a number of clinical features, subsumed under the general categories of *pervasive mistrust, hypersensitivity*, and *restricted affectivity*. Included among these features are hypervigilance, inability to relax, and lack of a true sense of humor. This personality disorder can be differentiated from the paranoid disorders because *fixed delusions are absent* in the personality disorder.

The table at the top of the facing page describes the DSM-III diagnostic criteria for paranoid personality disorder.

**18.17.   The answer is B (1, 3)** (*Synopsis*, ed. 4, page 367).

Schizoid personality disorder is diagnosed in patients with current and *long-term functioning characterized by discomfort with human interaction*, introversion, and a bland, constricted affect. These *personalities are often viewed as isolated, cold, and aloof with an insensitivity to feelings of others*. By definition, there is *no eccentricity of communication, behavior, or thought*, and the diagnosis is therefore consid-

### Diagnostic Criteria for Paranoid Personality Disorder*

The following are characteristic of the individual's current and long-term functioning, are not limited to episodes of illness, and cause either significant impairment in social or occupational functioning or subjective distress.

A. Pervasive, unwarranted suspiciousness and mistrust of people as indicated by at least three of the following:

1. Expectation of trickery or harm;
2. Hypervigilance, manifested by continual scanning of the environment for signs of threat, or taking unneeded precautions;
3. Guardedness or secretiveness;
4. Avoidance of accepting blame when warranted;
5. Questioning the loyalty of others;
6. Intense, narrowly focused searching for confirmation of bias, with loss of appreciation of total context;
7. Overconcern with hidden motives and special meanings;
8. Pathological jealousy.

B. Hypersensitivity as indicated by at least two of the following.

1. Tendency to be easily slighted and quick to take offense;
2. Exaggeration of difficulties, e.g. "making mountains out of molehills";
3. Readiness to counterattack when any threat is perceived;
4. Inability to relax.

C. Restricted affectivity as indicated by at least two of the following:

1. Appearance of being "cold" and unemotional;
2. Pride taken in always being objective, rational, and unemotional;
3. Lack of a true sense of humor;
4. Absence of passive, soft, tender, and sentimental feelings.

D. Not due to another mental disorder such as schizophrenia or a paranoid disorder.

* From American Psychiatric Association: *Diagnostic and Statistical Manual of Mental Disorders*, ed 3. American Psychiatric Association, Washington, DC, 1980. Used with permission.

### Diagnostic Criteria for Schizoid Personality Disorder*

The following are characteristic of the individual's current and long-term functioning, are not limited to epsiodes of illness, and cause either significant impairment in social or occupational functioning or subjective distress.

A. Emotional coldness and aloofness, and absence of warm, tender feelings for others.

B. Indifference to praise or criticism or to feelings of others.

C. Close friendships with no more than one or two persons, including family members.

D. No eccentricities of speech, behavior, or thought characteristic of schizotypal personality disorder.

E. Not due to a psychotic disorder such as schizophrenia or paranoid disorder.

F. If under 18, does not meet the criteria of schizoid disorder of childhood or adolescence.

* From American Psychiatric Association: *Diagnostic and Statistical Manual of Mental Disorders*, ed 3. American Psychiatric Association, Washington, DC, 1980. Used with permission.

ered as *belonging on the healthier end of the schizophrenic spectrum.*

The table above lists in more detail the DSM-III diagnostic criteria for schizoid personality disorder.

**18.18. The answer is A (1, 2, 3)** (*Synopsis*, ed. 4, page 370).

Histrionic personality disorder is characterized by *overly dramatic* and extroverted behavior

in excitable people. Associated with this feature are characteristic disturbances in interpersonal relationships that manifest as a disturbed ability to maintain deep, long-lasting attachments. A *superficial quality of warmth and charm is also present, but there is a perception by others of the patient's underlying shallowness* and insensitivity. The diagnosis is reported as exceedingly more common in women than men, but this outcome appears to be at least partly due to sex bias in its description. *When it is diagnosed in men, the clinical picture is very similar to that seen in women.*

The table below provides the DSM-III diagnostic criteria for histrionic personality disorder.

---

### Diagnostic Criteria for Histrionic Personality Disorder*

The following are characteristic of the individual's current and long-term functioning, are not limited to episodes of illiness, and cause either significant impairment in social or occupational functioning or subjective distress.

A. Behavior that is overly dramatic, reactive, and intensely expressed, as indicated by at least three of the following:

    1. Self-dramatization, e.g. exaggerated expression of emotions;
    2. Incessant drawing of attention to oneself;
    3. Craving for activity and excitement;
    4. Overreaction to minor events;
    5. Irrational, angry outbursts or tantrums.

B. Characteristic disturbances in interpersonal relationships as indicated by at least two of the following:

    1. Perceived by others as shallow and lacking genuineness, even if superficially warm and charming;
    2. Egocentric, self-indulgent, and inconsiderate of others;
    3. Vain and demanding;
    4. *Depende•.t, helpless,* constantly seeking reassurance;
    5. Prone to manipulative suicidal theats, gestures, or attempts.

---

* From American Psychiatric Association: *Diagnostic and Statistical Manual of Mental Disorders*, ed 3. American Psychiatric Association, Washington, DC, 1980. Used with permission.

---

**18.19.   The answer is A (1, 2, 3)** (*Synopsis,* ed. 4, pages 371 and 372).

Certain characteristics of narcissistic personality disorder must be present to make the diagnosis. As DSM-III states, however, individuals diagnosed with this disorder may also meet criteria for other personality disorders, such as histrionic, borderline or antisocial. The required criteria include *a grandiose sense of self-importance, preoccupation with fantasies of unlimited power and success,* and an exhibitionism that *demands constant attention and admiration.*

*Depressed mood* is extremely common in a narcissistic personality, as the person's self-esteem is invariably low; however, *it is not a required criteria for the diagnosis.*

The table below lists in further detail the DSM-III diagnostic criteria for this disorder.

---

### Diagnostic Criteria for Narcissistic Personality Disorder*

The following are characteristic of the individual's current and long-term functioning, are not limited to episodes of illness, and cause either significant impairment in social or occupational functioning or subjective distress:

A. Grandiose sense of self-importance or uniqueness, e.g. exaggeration of achievements and talents, focus on the special nature of one's problems.

B. Preoccupation with fantasies of unlimited success, power, brillance, beauty, or ideal love.

C. Exhibitionism: The person requires constant attention and admiration.

D. Cool indifference or marked feelings of rage, inferiority, shame, humiliation, or emptiness in response to criticism, indifference of others, or defeat.

E. At least two of the following characteristics of disturbances in interpersonal relationships:

    1. Entitlement: expectation of special favors without assuming reciprocal responsibilities, e.g. surprise and anger that people will not do what is wanted;
    2. Interpersonal exploitativeness: taking advantage of others to indulge own desires or for self-aggrandizement; disregard for the personal integrity and rights of others;
    3. Relationships that characteristically alternate between the extremes of overidealization and devaluation;
    4. Lack of empathy: inability to recognize how others feel, e.g. unable to appreciate the distress of someone who is seriously ill.

---

* From American Psychiatric Association: *Diagnostic and Statistical Manual of Mental Disorders*, ed 3. American Psychiatric Association, Washington, DC, 1980. Used with permission.

**18.20.    The answer is D (4)** (*Synopsis*, ed. 4, page 382).

Passive-aggressive personalities are *not impulsive*; rather they tend to procrastinate and dawdle. They are stubborn, *noncompliant,* and appear forgetful. *Intentional inefficiency* is common. *Hypermnesia* is an exaggerated degree of retention and recall that is more common in obsessive-compulsive disorders.

The table below lists the DSM-III diagnostic criteria for passive-aggressive personality disorder.

### Diagnostic Criteria for Passive-Aggressive Personality Disorder*

The following are characteristic of the individual's current and long-term functioning, and are not limited to episodes of illness.

A. Resistance to demands for adequate performance in both occupational and social functioning.

B. Resistance expressed indirectly through at least two of the following:

1. Procrastination;
2. Dawdling;
3. Stubbornness;
4. Intentional inefficiency;
5. "Forgetfulness."

C. As a consequence of A and B, pervasive and long-standing social and occupational ineffectiveness (including in roles of housewife or student), e.g. intentional inefficiency that has prevented job promotion.

D. Persistence of the behavior pattern even under circumstances in which more self-assertive and effective behavior is possible.

E. Does not meet the criteria for any other personality disorder, and if under age 18, does not meet the criteria for oppositional disorder.

* From American Psychiatric Association: *Diagnostic and Statistical Manual of Mental Disorders*, ed 3. American Psychiatric Association, Washington, DC, 1980. Used with permission.

**18.21.    The answer is E (all)** (*Synopsis*, ed. 4, page 383).

Sadomasochistic personalities are characterized by elements of sadism, masochism, or a combination of the two. Although *not part of the official DSM-III nosology*, these personality disorders are of clinical interest.

Sadism (named after the Marquis de Sade, who wrote of people experiencing sexual pleasure when inflicting pain on others) consists of the desire to cause others pain, either through sexual abuse or by being more generally abusive.

Freud believed that sadists warded off *castration anxiety* and were able to achieve sexual pleasure only when they were able to do to others what they feared would be done to them.

Masochism (named after Leopold Von Sacher-Masoch, a 19th-century Austrian novelist) is characterized by achieving sexual gratification by inflicting pain on the self. More generally, the so-called moral masochist seeks humiliation and failure, rather than physical pain.

Freud believed that masochists' ability to achieve orgasm is disturbed by anxiety and *guilt feelings about sex* that are alleviated by their own suffering and punishment.

Clinical observations indicate that elements of both sadistic and masochistic behavior are usually present in the same person. *Treatment with insight-oriented psychotherapy, including psychoanalysis, has been effective* in some cases. As a result of therapy, the patient becomes aware of the need for self-punishment secondary to excessive unconscious guilt and also comes to recognize repressed aggressive impulses that have their origins in early childhood.

**18.22.    The answer is E (all)** (*Synopsis*, ed. 4, page 380).

The essential features of compulsive personality disorder are *emotional constriction*, orderliness, perseverance, *stubbornness*, and indecisiveness. Although compulsive personalities lack the fear of people that characterizes schizoid personalities, they show a *restricted ability to express warm and tender feelings*. Through their stubborn insistence on doing things their own way, and by their preoccupation with order and detail, compulsive personalities often alienate others. Of all the personality disorders, compulsiveness is the most occupationally adaptive, and because its symptoms are more often *autoplastic* than alloplastic, it is the personality disorder least often confused with misbehavior. Alloplasty refers to adaptation to stress by attempting to change the environment. Autoplasty refers to adaptation to stress by changing intrapsychic processes.

For an outline of the DSM-III diagnostic criteria for compulsive personality, see the table at the top of page 238.

## Diagnostic Criteria for Compulsive Personality Disorder*

At least four of the following are characteristic of the individual's current and long-term functioning, are not limited to episodes of illness, and cause either significant impairment in social or occupational functioning or subjective distress.

1. Restricted ability to express warm and tender emotions, e.g. the individual is unduly conventional, serious and formal, and stingy;
2. Perfectionism that interferes with the ability to grasp "the big picture," e.g. preoccupation with trivial details, rules, order, organization, schedules, and lists;
3. Insistence that others submit to his or her way of doing things, and lack of awareness of the feelings elicited by this behavior, e.g. a husband stubbornly insists his wife complete errands for him regardless of her plans;
4. Excessive devotion to work and productivity to the exclusion of pleasure and the value of interpersonal relationships;
5. Indecisiveness: decision-making is either avoided, postponed, or protracted, perhaps because of an inordinate fear of making a mistake, e.g. the individual cannot get assignments done on time because of ruminating about priorities.

* From American Psychiatric Association: *Diagnostic and Statistical Manual of Mental Disorders*, ed 3. American Psychiatric Association, Washington, DC, 1980. Used with permission.

**18.23.   The answer is A (1, 2, 3)** (*Synopsis,* ed. 4, pages 377 and 378).

*Hypersensitivity to rejection* by others is the central clinical feature of the avoidant personality. Persons with this disorder desire the warmth and security of human companionship, but justify their avoidance of forming relationships by their alleged fear of rejection. When talking with someone, persons express uncertainty and a *lack of self-confidence*, and may speak in a self-effacing manner. They are afraid to speak up in public or to make requests of others, because they are hypervigilant about re-

jection. They are apt to misinterpret other people's comments as derogatory or ridiculing. The refusal of any request leads persons to *withdraw from others* and to feel hurt.

Avoidant personalities may display an appealing waif-like quality; they *may have friends* or a spouse who also tends to be introverted but loyal. Often, such friends offer unconditional acceptance of the patients and attempt to bolster them up or mollify their self-denigrating attitude.

See the table below for the DSM-III diagnostic criteria for avoidant personality disorder.

## Diagnostic Criteria for Avoidant Personality Disorder*

The following are characteristic of the individual's current and long-term functioning, are not limited to episodes of illness, and cause either significant impairment in social or occupational functioning or subjective distress.

A. Hypersensitivity to rejection, e.g. apprehensively alert to signs of social derogation, interprets innocuous events as ridicule.

B. Unwillingness to enter into relationships unless given unusually strong guarantees of uncritical acceptance.

C. Social withdrawal, e.g. distances self from close personal attachments, engages in peripheral social and vocational roles.

D. Desire for affection and acceptance.

E. Low self-esteem, e.g. devalues self-achievements and is overly dismayed by personal shortcomings.

F. If under 18, does not meet the criteria for avoidant disorder of childhood or adolescence.

* From American Psychiatric Association: *Diagnostic and Statistical Manual of Mental Disorders*, ed 3. American Psychiatric Association, Washington, DC, 1980. Used with permission.

**18.24–18.28.   The answers are 18.24–B, 18.25–B, 18.26–C, 18.27–D, and 18.28–B** (*Synopsis,* ed. 4, page 369).

As opposed to schizoid personality disorder, schizotypal personality disorder manifests with *strikingly odd or eccentric behavior.* Magical

thinking, *ideas of references,* illusions, and derealization are common, and their presence formerly led to defining this disorder as borderline, *simple, or latent schizophrenia.* Odd communication, which is not due to derailment, *loose associations,* or incoherence, is present and is characterized by tangentiality, circumstantiality, and digressiveness; however, odd communication is not present in schizoid personality disorder.

*Social isolation*, along with a cold and aloof manner, is seen in both schizoid and schizotypal personality disorders.

The table below details the DSM-III diagnostic criteria for the diagnosis of schizotypal personality disorder.

### Diagnostic Criteria for Schizotypal Personality Disorder*

The following are characteristic of the individual's current and long-term functioning, are not limited to episodes of illness, and cause either significant impairment in social or occupational functioning or subjective distress.

A. At least four of the following:

1. Magical thinking, e.g. superstitiousness, clairvoyance, telepathy, "sixth sense," "others can feel my feelings," (in children and adolescents, bizarre fantasies or preoccupations);

2. Ideas of reference;

3. Social isolation, e.g. no close friends or confidants, social contacts limited to essential everyday tasks;

4. Recurrent illusions, sensing the presence of a force or person not actually present (e.g. "I felt as if my dead mother were in the room with me"), depersonalization, or derealization not associated with panic attacks;

5. Odd speech (without loosening of associations or incoherence), e.g. speech that is digressive, vague, overelaborate, circumstantial, metaphorical;

6. Inadequate rapport in face-to-face interaction due to constricted or inappropriate affect, e.g. aloof, cold;

7. Suspiciousness or paranoid ideation;

8. Undue social anxiety or hypersensitivity to real or imagined criticism.

B. Does not meet the criteria for schizophrenia.

* From American Psychiatric Association: *Diagnostic and Statistical Manual of Mental Disorders* ed 3. American Psychiatric Association, Washington, DC, 1980. Used with permission.

# References

Cleckley H: *The Mask of Sanity*, ed 4. C V Mosby, St. Louis, 1964.

Endell W S: The borderline syndrome index. J Nerv Ment Dis *172:* 254, 1984.

Kernberg O F: *Borderline Conditions and Pathological Narcissism.* Jason Aronson, New York, 1975.

Lion J R, editor: *Personality Disorders Diagnosis and Management*, ed 2. Williams & Wilkins, Baltimore, 1981.

Millon T: *Disorders of Personality: DSM-III Axis II.* John Wiley & Sons, New York, 1981.

Slavney P R: Histrionic personality and antisocial personality. Compr Psychiatry *25:* 129, 1984.

Soloff P H, Millward J W: Psychiatric disorders in the families of borderline patients. Arch Gen Psychiatry *40:* 37, 1983.

Thomas A, Chess S: *Temperament and Development.* Bruner/Mazel, New York, 1977.

Vaillant G E: *Adaptation to Life.* Little Brown and Co, Boston, 1977.

Vaillant G E, Perry J C: Personality disorders. In *Comprehensive Textbook of Psychiatry*, ed 4, H I Kaplan, B J Sadock, editors, p 958. Williams & Wilkins, Baltimore, 1985.

# 19

# Substance Use Disorders
# (Drug Dependence)

Substance use disorders—also known as drug dependence—are divided into substance abuse and substance dependence according to the third edition of the *Diagnostic and Statistical Manual of Mental Disorders* (DSM-III). Substance abuse is characterized by a pattern of repeated pathological use of a drug over a long period of time, with such usage causing impairment in social or occupational functioning. Substance dependence is more severe than substance abuse in that both tolerance and withdrawal symptoms to the drug develop. The classes of substances associated with use disorders include alcohol, barbiturates and other sedatives and hypnotics, opioids, amphetamines, marijuana, cocaine, hallucinogens, tobacco, and caffeine.

DSM-III makes a careful distinction between these two classifications of abuse and dependence, but the general literature is not so clear. For example, some workers use the term "drug abuse" to refer to the self-administration of any drug in a manner that deviates from the approved medical or social patterns of a given culture. The term is not used, as in DSM-III, to describe any particular pattern of drug use or its potential adverse consequences. Similarly, the term "addiction" has been defined as the compulsive use of a drug—including the behavioral patterns involved in securing its supply—that causes a withdrawal syndrome to develop when the drug is not used. This term is not included in DSM-III.

The problem of substance use disorders has been recorded throughout history and has been present in every society in which drugs have been used to affect thinking, feeling, and behavior. Currently, in the United States, the problems associated with drugs are a major mental health concern. For example, there are approximately 500,000 heroin addicts in this country, and about 5 percent of the population are suffering from alcoholism.

Readers should refer to Chapter 19, "Substance Use Disorders," in *Modern Synopsis-IV* and should study the questions and answers below to test their knowledge of this area.

# Questions

**DIRECTIONS:** Each of the statements or questions below is followed by five suggested responses or completions. Select the *one* that is *best* in each case.

**19.1.** All of the following are associated with caffeine withdrawal symptoms *except*

A. nervousness
B. depression
C. hallucinations
D. headache
E. insomnia

**19.2.** Diazepam abuse is diagnosed when the use of the drug exceeds

A. 20 mg/day
B. 40 mg/day
C. 60 mg/day
D. 80 mg/day
E. 120 mg/day

**19.3.** The most important objective in treating the alcoholic patient is to achieve

A. a return to social drinking
B. improved interpersonal relations
C. total abstinence from alcohol
D. intensive insight-oriented psychotherapy
E. a trial period of disulfiram

**19.4.** For a diagnosis of opioid abuse, there must be continuous or episodic use of an opioid for at least

A. 1 day
B. 1 week
C. 1 month
D. 2 months
E. 3 months

**19.5.** Of the following drugs, which is considered the least conducive to aggression:

A. Alcohol
B. Secobarbital
C. Pentobarbital
D. Amphetamines
E. Cocaine

**19.6.** The most widely used method of detoxification from heroin dependence is

A. narcotic antagonists
B. drug-free detoxification
C. psychotherapy
D. methadone substitution
E. none of the above

**19.7.** Withdrawal signs from heroin use include all of the following *except*

A. agitation
B. rhinorrhea
C. muscular cramps
D. miosis
E. rise in temperature

**19.8.** Alcohol dependence is characterized by all the following *except*

A. absence of withdrawal symptoms
B. compelling desire to use alcohol
C. amnesic periods for events occurring while intoxicated
D. violence while intoxicated
E. continuous or episodic use of alcohol for at least 1 month

**19.9.** A 29-year-old school teacher who lives alone is brought to the emergency room because she has become increasingly suspicious, hyperactive, and anorexic over the past 2 days. She believes that "people in the neighborhood are out to get me." The patient rarely sleeps at night. She reports seeing snakes crawling on the wall. Based on this information, the most likely diagnosis of the woman's problem is

A. anorexia nervosa
B. paranoia
C. paranoid personality
D. psychostimulant abuse
E. shared paranoid disorder

**19.10.** Amphetamines have accepted therapeutic applications in treating all the following *except*

A. narcolepsy
B. attention-deficit disorders of childhood
C. long-term adjunct to tricyclic antidepressants
D. short-term therapy for weight reduction
E. Alzheimer's disease

**19.11.** "Mandrakes" and "soaps" or "soapers" contain as their active drug of abuse

A. amphetamine
B. barbiturate
C. methaqualone
D. meprobamate
E. benzodiazepine

**19.12.** The street term "crystallized" is used to describe long-term users of

A. amphetamine
B. methaqualone
C. barbiturate
D. cocaine
E. phencyclidine (PCP)

**19.13.** LSD and marijuana are similar in that they may produce all the following effects *except*

A. depersonalization
B. dilation of pupils
C. increased sensitivity to sound
D. anxiety
E. paranoid reactions

**19.14.** Among the effects of cyclazocine are all the following *except*

A. analgesia
B. dysphoria
C. anxiety
D. sedation
E. delusions

**19.15.** A 55-year-old man with a long history of alcoholism is admitted to a medical ward. At the time of admission, he is noted to have alcohol on his breath. Two days after admission he becomes acutely agitated and reports hearing other patients calling him homosexual. He appears to be alert and well-oriented. It is likely that the patient is exhibiting symptoms of

A. schizophrenia
B. delirium tremens
C. alcoholic hallucinosis
D. pathological intoxication
E. methanol ("wood alcohol") intoxication

**19.16.** Amphetamine delirium occurs within which of the following time periods:

A. 5 to 24 hours
B. 24 to 36 hours
C. 36 to 48 hours
D. 36 to 72 hours
E. 36 hours to 1 week of use of amphetamine

**DIRECTIONS:** For each of the incomplete statements below, *one* or *more* of the completions given is correct. Choose answer:

A. if only **1, 2,** and **3** are correct
B. if only **1** and **3** are correct
C. if only **2** and **4** are correct
D. if only **4** is correct
E. if all are correct

**19.17.** Which of the following statements apply to alcoholism in women:

1. Women tend to become alcoholic at a later age than men do.
2. Women show an increased incidence after age 60.
3. Alcoholism among women is increasing.
4. Women generally enter treatment more quickly than men do.

**19.18.** Cannabis abuse is characterized by

1. intoxication throughout the day
2. episodic use, such as once a week
3. loss of interest in activities
4. no or few legal problems

**19.19.** Amphetamine withdrawal may present with

1. disturbed sleep
2. increased dreaming
3. suicidal ideation
4. severe fatigue

**19.20.** Cocaine abuse, at times with severe intoxication, may be marked by

1. inability to stop use
2. hallucinations
3. legal problems
4. delusions

| **Directions Summarized** | | | | |
|:---:|:---:|:---:|:---:|:---:|
| A | B | C | D | E |
| 1, 2, 3 | 1, 3 | 2, 4 | 4 | All are |
| only | only | only | only | correct |

**19.21.** Tobacco dependence is characterized by

1. the presence of tobacco-related physical disease
2. unsuccessful attempts to stop smoking
3. the need for repeated tobacco use
4. withdrawal symptoms

**19.22.** Methadone

1. is used to treat heroin addiction
2. blocks opioid withdrawal symptoms
3. is an analgesic
4. does not cause addiction

**19.23.** The delirium associated with amphetamine use

1. usually occurs within 1 hour
2. is over in about 6 hours
3. disappears completely after disuse
4. is not produced by intravenous use

**19.24.** A 20-year-old man is seen in the emergency room in a severely agitated state. He is labile emotionally, appears frightened and markedly anxious, and shows slurred speech and dysarthria. According to a friend, the patient took "angel dust" about 1 hour previous to being seen in the emergency room. The reaction the patient is having

1. is probably caused by phencyclidine (PCP)
2. will clear spontaneously within 48 hours
3. can be diagnosed by urine testing for PCP
4. may be accompanied by violent acts

**19.25.** The characteristic symptoms associated with amphetamine delusional disorder include

1. passivity
2. persecutory delusions
3. euthymia
4. ideas of reference

**19.26.** Signs and symptoms of acute amphetamine poisoning include

1. tetany
2. ataxia
3. convulsions
4. orthostatic hypotension

**19.27.** Which of the following drugs are narcotic antagonists:

1. Naloxone
2. Nalorphine
3. Naltrexone
4. Cyclazocine

**19.28.** The heroin-behavior syndrome includes which of the following:

1. Depression
2. Fear of failure
3. Low self-esteem
4. Need for immediate gratification

**19.29.** The DSM-III diagnostic criteria for amphetamine intoxication includes which of the following symptoms:

1. Grandiosity
2. Elevated blood pressure
3. Elation
4. Maladaptive behavior

**DIRECTIONS:** Each set of lettered headings below is followed by a list of numbered words or phrases. For each numbered word or phrase, select

    A. if the item is associated with **A** *only*
    B. if the item is associated with **B** *only*
    C. if the item is associated with *both* **A** *and* **B**
    D. if the item is associated with *neither* **A** *nor* **B**

**Questions 19.30–19.33**
A. Delirium tremens
B. Alcohol hallucinosis
C. Both
D. Neither

**19.30.** Grand mal seizures

**19.31.** Auditory hallucinations

**19.32.** Clear sensorium

**19.33.** Chlordiazepoxide

# Answers

## Substance Use Disorders (Drug Dependence)

**19.1.   The answer is C** (*Synopsis*, ed. 4, page 429).

A *hallucination* is a false sensory perception occurring in the absence of any relevant external stimulation of the sensory modality involved. Hallucinations do not occur during caffeine withdrawal.

According to laboratory experiments, the symptom of caffeine withdrawal most often reported is *headaches*. In nonlaboratory settings, it is reported that as many as one-third of the moderate and high caffeine consumers suffer this symptom if their daily caffeine intake is interrupted. This headache, which seems to be remarkably consistent in different persons, is described as generalized and throbbing, proceeding from lethargy to a sense of cerebral fullness to a full-blown headache. It occurs about 18 hours after the discontinuation of habitual caffeine intake and responds best to a renewed elevation of caffeine plasma levels, perhaps explaining why many tension headache-prone persons prefer over-the-counter analgesics that contain caffeine.

Other withdrawal symptoms include *nervousness*, a vague feeling of *depression*, drowsiness and lethargy, rhinorrhea, a disinclination to work, occasional yawning, nausea, and *insomnia* or sleep disturbances. Few recent reports have emphasized depression as a central feature of caffeinism. Surveys of psychiatric patients, however, revealed that the highest caffeine consumers (ingesting more than 750 mg daily) reported significantly greater scores on the Beck Depression Scale. Caffeine toxicity may induce psychosis in susceptible persons, or exacerbate thinking disruptions in patients previously diagnosed as having schizophrenia.

The symptoms of caffeinism are listed in the table shown in column 2.

**19.2.   The answer is C** (*Synopsis*, ed. 4, page 407).

Abuse of sedative and hypnotics is a major national problem. Diazepam abuse is diagnosed when the use of the drug exceeds *60 mg* per day. Dependence is diagnosed when tolerance or withdrawal occurs. See the following tables for

**246**

---

### Caffeinism*

Confirmed history of recent caffeine consumption, usually exceeding 250 mg a day, more often exceeding 500 mg a day

Presence of at least five of the following signs and symptoms at a time when caffeine is being consumed:

Restlessness, nervousness, irritability, agitation, tremulousness, muscle twitching, or fasciculation

*Insomnia* or sleep disruption

Headache

Sensory disturbances (hyperesthesia, ringing in ears, lightheadedness, flashing of light, ocular dyskinesias)

Diuresis

Cardiovascular symptoms (palpitations, extrasystoles, arrhythmias, flushing, tachycardia, increased cardiac awareness)

Gastrointestinal complaints (epigastric pain, nausea, vomiting, diarrhea)

Rambling flow of thoughts and speech, periods of inexhaustability

Persistence of symptoms daily or sporadically for at least 2 weeks in conjunction with caffeine consumption, or consistent development of such symptoms each time higher caffeine consumption occurs

Absence of any disorder that otherwise accounts for the symptoms of caffeinism, such as anxiety, hyperthyroidism, pheochromocytoma, mania, hypomania, and electrolyte disturbances; caffeinism may contribute to and aggravate these conditions

Onset of caffeine withdrawal symptoms following cessation of caffeine consumption after a prolonged period with at least three (probable) or four (definite) of the following signs and symptoms present:

*Headache*, being relieved by further caffeine intake

Irritability

Inability to work effectively

*Nervousness*

Lethargy

---

\* Adapted from American Psychiatric Association: *Diagnostic and Statistical Manual of Mental Disorders*, ed 3. American Psychiatric Association, Washington, DC, 1980. Used with permission.

the DSM-III diagnostic criteria for sedative and hypnotic abuse and dependence.

**19.3. The answer is C** (*Synopsis*, ed. 4, page 425).

The most important objective in treating the alcoholic patient is to achieve *total abstinence from alcohol*, because it is impossible to determine which alcoholic will be able to *return to drinking in a controlled fashion*.

*Intensive psychotherapy* designed to expose and interpret unconscious material is usually more deleterious than helpful to the alcoholic. Most alcoholics have a rather frail ego structure, and the interpretation of previously unconscious material may prove extremely anxiety producing, frustrating, or depressing for them, often to the extent that they have to be reassured at great length after the interpretations. Their intolerance of anxiety may result in a premature abandonment of treatment.

*Disulfiram* is a drug that, when combined with alcohol, produces unpleasant side-effects or even severe symptoms, such as respiratory distress and copious vomiting. The drug is given to alcoholics to deter them from using alcohol.

---

**Diagnostic Criteria for Barbiturate or Similarly Acting Sedative or Hypnotic Dependence***

---

Either tolerance or withdrawal:

*Tolerance:* need for markedly increased amounts of the substance to achieve the desired effect, or markedly diminished effect with regular use of the same amount.

*Withdrawal:* development of barbiturate or similarly acting sedative or hypnotic withdrawal after cessation of or reduction in substance use.

---

* From American Psychiatric Association: *Diagnostic and Statistical Manual of Mental Disorders*, ed 3. American Psychiatric Association, Washington, DC, 1980. Used with permission.

**19.4. The answer is C** (*Synopsis*, ed. 4, pages 385 and 386).

For a diagnosis of opioid abuse according to DSM-III criteria, there must be continuous or episodic use of an opioid for at least *1 month*. A pattern of pathological use also includes the inability to reduce or stop use, intoxication throughout the day, and episodes of opioid overdose; that is, intoxication so severe that respiration and consciousness are impaired.

Examples of criteria of abuse involving impairment in social or occupational functioning include fights, loss of friends, absence from work, loss of job, or legal difficulties. The duration of disturbance to meet the diagnostic criteria for abuse is at least 1 month.

Diagnostic criteria for opioid dependence require only the presence of either tolerance (the need for increased amount of drug to achieve desired effect), or opioid withdrawal after cessation or reduction in use. Generally, opioid dependence occurs after a period of opioid abuse. As defined in DSM-III, however, opioid dependence does not require antecedent abuse and is synonymous with what has been designated as physical dependence in standard pharmacological textbooks. Technically, to note the presence of both a pattern of pathological use and physical dependence, two diagnoses are required. Current DSM-III criteria make no provision for indicating differences in severity of the dependence syndrome.

The diagnostic criteria for opioid abuse and dependence are listed in the table on page 248.

**19.5. The answer is E** (*Synopsis*, ed. 4, page 405).

*Cocaine* is not as conducive to aggression as are other drugs, such as *alcohol, barbiturates,* and *amphetamines*. Because cocaine increases energy and confidence and can produce irritability and paranoia, it has often been said to cause physical aggression and crime. Although it clearly can do so in some circumstances, there is no evidence of any consistent association.

---

**Diagnostic Criteria for Barbiturate or Similarly Acting Sedative or Hypnotic Abuse***

---

A. *Pattern of pathological use:* inability to cut down or stop use; intoxication throughout the day; frequent use of the equivalent of 600 mg or more of secobarbital or 60 mg or more of diazepam; amnesic periods for events that occurred while intoxicated.

B. *Impairment in social or occupational functioning due to substance use:* e.g. fights, loss of friends, absence from work, loss of job, or legal difficulties (other than a single arrest due to possession, purchase, or sale of the substance).

C. Duration of disturbance of at least 1 month.

---

* From American Psychiatric Association: *Diagnostic and Statistical Manual of Mental Disorders*, ed 3. American Psychiatric Association, Washington, DC, 1980. Used with permission.

## Diagnostic Criteria for Opioid Abuse and Dependence*

*Diagnostic criteria for opioid abuse*

A. *Pattern of pathological use:* inability to reduce or stop use; intoxication throughout the day; use of opioids nearly every day for at least 1 month; episodes of opioid overdose (intoxication so severe that respiration and consciousness are impaired).

B. *Impairment in social or occupational functioning due to opioid use:* e.g. fights, loss of friends, absence from work, loss of job, or legal difficulties (other than due to a single arrest for possession, purchase, or sale of the substance).

C. Duration of disturbance of at least 1 month.

*Diagnostic criteria for opioid dependence*

Either tolerance or withdrawal:

   *Tolerance:* need for markedly increased amounts of opioid to achieve the desired effect, or markedly diminished effect with regular use of the same amount.

   *Withdrawal:* development of opioid withdrawal after cessation of or reduction in substance use.

* From American Psychiatric Association: *Diagnostic and Statistical Manual of Mental Disorders*, ed 3. American Psychiatric Association, Washington, DC, 1980. Used with permission.

**19.6.   The answer is D** (*Synopsis*, ed. 4, pages 394 and 395).

The most widely used method of detoxification is that of *methadone substitution*, now most often managed on an ambulatory basis. The necessary prerequisites are a complete medical and psychiatric history and a thorough physical examination.

An initial dose of methadone, large enough to suppress the abstinence syndrome, is administered orally in an orange juice solution. Various methods may be used to make a rough estimate of the amount of heroin being taken—the amount of money spent a day or the number of bags bought, for instance. Generally, an initial dose of 30 to 40 mg is sufficient. In calculations, 1 mg of methadone can be considered equivalent in its ability to suppress the abstinence syndrome to 1 mg of heroin, and 3 mg of methadone can be considered equivalent to 4 mg of morphine or 0.5 mg of hydromorphone.

After the satisfactory initial suppression of the abstinence syndrome, the methadone is withdrawn progressively over a period of 3 to 7 days. Generally, the rate of withdrawal is 5 mg a day. In this manner, the withdrawal is generally smooth and without complications, except for complaints of weakness, disturbed sleep, or vague pains when the dose of methadone gets low or shortly after its total withdrawal. The judicious use of sedatives or tranquilizers can be beneficial.

There are various modifications of the methadone-withdrawal schedule. For example, in some instances, addicts have been allowed to set their own schedules for the gradual reduction of the methadone dose. Alternatively, rapid or precipitated withdrawal has been recommended. Patients on low-dosage methadone can begin

a *narcotic antagonist* in 48 hours, but the procedure is limited because its implementation requires inpatient care. Clonidine has been used with reported success in withdrawal from methadone. Clonidine is given orally (0.1 to 0.3 mg, 3 to 4 times per day). The therapy is based on the hypothesis that opiate withdrawal is mediated through a noradrenergic mechanism that is blocked by clonidine.

Propoxyphene and dextropropoxyphene have been tried as detoxification agents with some success.

The therapeutic community—whatever its set-up, program, or degree of isolation—adheres to the concept that the abuse of drugs is symptomatic of underlying antisocial personality problems and behavior patterns. The nation's largest therapeutic community for *drug-free treatment* and rehabilitation of former heroin addicts is Phoenix House.

Therapeutic communities often use *group psychotherapy* and encounter groups, as well as milieu therapy, in which the addict lives and works within a certain social structure. Through peer influence, behavior modification is encouraged. In a study, it was concluded that "addiction is an aspect of a general sickness dimension which undergoes a positive therapeutic change with time spent in the Phoenix House Program."

The problem with therapeutic communities as a treatment method is that they seem to be suitable for very few people. Often as many as three-quarters of those who enter drop out within the first month.

**19.7.   The answer is D** (*Synopsis*, ed. 4, page 389).

Tolerance to heroin occurs fairly rapidly, within days during periodic administration of the drug. If the tolerant person is challenged with an antagonist, such as naloxone, a precipitated withdrawal syndrome follows. Withdrawal signs include restlessness, *agitation, rhinorrhea*, tearing, gooseflesh, abdominal and *muscular cramps*, tachycardia, and a *rise in temperature*, with dilation of the pupils. These signs and symptoms do not often appear after a short exposure to heroin, but they inevitably appear if drug use is continued. An abrupt cessation of drug intake is then followed by the characteristic signs of abstinence. These signs can be reversed by the administration of heroin or another opioid at lower doses than were previously used by the addict.

*Miosis* refers to the contraction of the pupil; it can also refer to the period of decline of a disease in which symptoms begin to abate.

One of the central concerns of modern biochemistry has been to discover what it is about relatively simple chemicals—the opioids—that makes them produce powerful pharmacological effects within the human system.

The two outstanding pharmacological effects are dependence and tolerance. Opinion is divided as to whether there is a single explanation for both phenomena. Some have held that tolerance and physical dependence seemed to be inextricably linked, but others have maintained that the linkage is not valid. Because studies of mechanisms apply to both dependence and tolerance, it is more convenient in the case of the opioids to discuss these two phenomena together.

Dependence has been variously defined. Dependence is a state induced by a drug that, when withdrawn, gives rise to physiological or psychological disturbance, or both, that can be removed by again administering the drug or a drug with which it is cross-dependent. This description allows for the possibility that dependence can arise from a single dose of the drug. If physiological disturbances follow withdrawal, the dependence may be called physical; if the disturbance is psychological, the dependence may be called psychic. In the case of morphine, both physical and psychic dependence occur.

Tolerance is a phenomenon characteristic of the opioids; that is, to continue to maintain the same effect from the opioid that was obtained initially, increasing amounts of opioid will be required. Tolerance to heroin can be increased to levels more than 100 times the initial effective dose. Tolerance can persist in animals for periods of many months without any behavioral signs of abstinence.

**19.8.   The answer is A** (*Synopsis*, ed. 4, page 415).

Alcoholism has been described as a chronic behavioral disorder, manifested by the repeated drinking of alcoholic beverages in excess of the dietary and social uses of the community, that interferes with the drinker's health or social and economic functioning.

According to DSM-III, there are two alcohol disorders: alcohol dependence (alcoholism) and alcohol abuse. This separation must be viewed as somewhat arbitrary, and it has little relevance from a treatment viewpoint. Clinically, patients probably shift back and forth between these two categories.

According to DSM-III, the essential features of alcohol abuse are (1) *continuous or episodic use of alcohol for at least 1 month*; (2) social complications of alcohol use including impairment in social or occupational functioning—such as arguments or difficulties with family or friends over excessive alcohol use, *violence while intoxicated*, missed work, being fired—or legal difficulties, such as being arrested for intoxicated behavior and traffic accidents while intoxicated; and (3) either psychological dependence—a *compelling desire to use alcohol*, an inability to cut down or stop drinking, repeated efforts to control or reduce excess drinking by going on the wagon (periods of temporary abstinence) or restricting drinking to certain times of the day—or a pathological pattern of use—drinking nonbeverage alcohol, going on binges (remaining intoxicated throughout the day for at least 2 days), occasionally drinking a fifth of spirits or its equivalent in wine or beer, or having two or more blackouts (*amnesic periods for events occurring while intoxicated*).

Alcohol dependence (alcoholism) is described in DSM-III as having these features plus either tolerance—that is, increasing amounts of alcohol are required to achieve the desired effect, or a diminished effect is achieved with regular use of the same dose—or *withdrawal symptoms*—for example, morning shakes and malaise that is relieved by drinking—after the cessation or reduction of drinking.

See the first two tables on page 250 for the DSM-III diagnostic criteria for alcohol dependence and abuse.

**19.9.   The answer is D** (*Synopsis*, ed. 4, pages 403 and 404).

Based on the information given, the most likely diagnosis of this woman's problem is *psychostimulant abuse*. The adverse psychological effects from which the patient was suffering—effects commonly seen with acute and chronic amphetamine use—are restlessness, dysphoria, logorrhea, insomnia, some degree of confusion, tension, anxiety, and fear to the point of acute panic have been reported by a large number of authors. Amphetamine psychosis, once consid-

## Diagnostic Criteria for Alcohol Dependence*

A. Either a pattern of pathological alcohol use or impairment in social or occupational functioning due to alcohol use:

*Pattern of pathological alcohol use:* need for daily use of alcohol for adequate functioning; inability to cut down or stop drinking; repeated efforts to control or reduce excess drinking by "going on the wagon" (periods of temporary abstinence) or restricting drinking to certain times of the day; binges (remaining intoxicated throughout the day for at least 2 days); occasional consumption of a fifth of spirits (or its equivalent in wine or beer); amnesic periods for events occurring while intoxicated (blackouts); continuation of drinking despite a serious physical disorder that the individual knows is exacerbated by alcohol use; drinking of nonbeverage alcohol.

*Impairment in social or occupational functioning due to alcohol use:* e.g. violence while intoxicated, absence from work, loss of job, legal difficulties–e.g. arrest for intoxicated behavior, traffic accidents while intoxicated—arguments or difficulties with family or friends because of excessive alcohol use.

B. Either tolerance or withdrawal:

*Tolerance:* need for markedly increased amounts of alcohol to achieve the desired effect, or markedly diminished effect with regular use of the same amount.

*Withdrawal:* development of alcohol withdrawal—e.g. morning "shakes" and malaise relieved by drinking—after cessation of or reduction in drinking.

* From American Psychiatric Association: *Diagnostic and Statistical Manual of Mental Disorders*, ed 3. American Psychiatric Association, Washington, DC, 1980. Used with permission.

## Diagnostic Criteria for Alcohol Abuse*

A. *Pattern of pathological alcohol use:* need for daily use of alcohol for adequate functioning; inability to cut down or stop drinking; repeated efforts to control or reduce excess drinking by "going on the wagon" (periods of temporary abstinence) or restricting drinking to certain times of the day; binges (remaining intoxicated throughout the day for at least 2 days); occasional consumption of a fifth of spirits (or its equivalent in wine or beer); amnesic periods for events occurring while intoxicated (blackouts); continuation of drinking despite a serious physical disorder that the individual knows is exacerbated by alcohol use; drinking of nonbeverage alcohol.

* From American Psychiatric Association: *Diagnostic and Statistical Manual of Mental Disorders*, ed 3. American Psychiatric Association, Washington, DC, 1980. Used with permission.

## Diagnostic Criteria for Amphetamine or Similarly Acting Sympathomimetic Abuse*

A. *Pattern of pathological use:* inability to reduce or stop use; intoxication throughout the day; use of substance nearly every day for at least 1 month; episodes of either amphetamine or similarly acting sympathomimetic delusional disorder or amphetamine or similarly acting sympathomimetic delirium.

B. *Impairment in social or occupational functioning due to amphetamine or similarly acting sympathomimetic use:* e.g. fights, loss of friends, absence from work, loss of job, or legal difficulties (other than due to a single arrest for possession, purchase, or sale of the substance).

C. Duration of disturbance of at least 1 month.

* From American Psychiatric Association: *Diagnostic and Statistical Manual of Mental Disorders*, ed 3. American Psychiatric Association, Washington, DC, 1980. Used with permission.

ered extremely rare, is another reported effect. Even short-term administration of dextroamphetamine to persons who are nonpsychotic can precipitate a paranoid psychosis. Other sympathomimetic drugs—such as phenylpronanoline, which is used in over-the-counter decongestant or anorectic agents—have been implicated in producing psychotic-like states.

With few exceptions, the symptoms disappear within days or, at the most, weeks after the drug has been withdrawn. Distinguishing amphetamine psychosis from paranoid schizophrenia depends heavily on this factor of duration of the symptoms. In some patients, suspiciousness and tendencies toward misinterpretation and ideas of reference may remain for months after the manifest, overt psychosis has disappeared.

The table directly above lists the DSM-III diagnostic criteria for amphetamine or similarly acting sympathomimetic abuse.

**19.10. The answer is E** (*Synopsis*, ed. 4, page 403).

Amphetamines are synthetic drugs that produce a sense of increased energy, an enhanced capacity for work, and a feeling of exhilaration.

Amphetamines have accepted therapeutic applications in treating *narcolepsy* and *attention deficit* (hyperkinetic) *disorders of childhood*, and they are used as a *short-term adjunct to tricyclic antidepressants* in the treatment of depression. They are also prescribed as a *short-term therapy for weight reduction*, as well as for mild depression and senile withdrawn behavior in the elderly. They are of *no use in Alzheimer's disease*.

*Narcolepsy* is a sleep disorder characterized by recurrent, brief, uncontrollable episodes of sleep. *Alzheimer's disease* is a chronic organic mental disorder of unknown cause characterized by progressive mental deterioration secondary to diffuse cerebral atrophy. In DSM-III, it is called primary degenerative dementia, presenile onset. *Attention deficit disorder* is a DSM-III category for a childhood mental disorder characterized by developmentally inappropriate short attention span and poor concentration. Hyperactivity (hyperkinesis) may or may not be present. The category subsumes abnormal behavior patterns that had been referred to by a variety of names, including hyperkinetic syndrome, hyperactive child syndrome, and minimal brain dysfunction.

**19.11. The answer is C** (*Synopsis*, ed. 4, page 409).

Street names for *methaqualone* include "mandrakes" (from the British preparation Mandrax, a combination of methaqualone and diphenhydramine) and "soaps" or "soapers" (from the Arnar-Stone brand name Soper). "Luding out" refers to the common practice of taking the drug with alcohol, usually wine.

Methaqualone is a nonbarbiturate sedative-hypnotic whose growth as a drug of abuse, particularly among young people, has accelerated rapidly over the past few years. The drug is no longer available as a prescription drug in this country because of its high abuse level. Abusers take large quantities, which they obtain from illegitimate sources.

**19.12. The answer is E** (*Synopsis*, ed. 4, page 412).

Little is known about chronic effects, but the street term "crystallized" is sometimes used to describe long-term users of *phencyclidine* (*PCP*) who suffer from dulled thinking and reflexes, confusion, lethargy, and difficulty in concentration. There is no evidence of permanent brain cell damage, but neurological and cognitive dysfunction have been reported to persist in chronic users, even after 2 to 3 weeks of abstinence. Tolerance seems to develop, but no withdrawal syndrome has been described.

**19.13. The answer is B** (*Synopsis*, ed. 4, page 401).

Marijuana, or cannabis, is commonly referred to as a hallucinogen. Many of the phenomena associated with lysergic acid diethylamide (LSD) and LSD-type substances can be produced by cannabis. As with LSD, the wave-like aspect of the experience is often reported, as is the distorted perception of various parts of the body, spatial and temporal distortion, and *depersonalization*. Other phenomena commonly associated with both types of drugs are *increased sensitivity to sound*, synesthesia, heightened suggestibility, and a sense of thinking more clearly and having a deeper awareness of the meaning of things. *Anxiety* and *paranoid reactions* sometimes are also seen as consequences of either drug; however, the agonizingly nightmarish reactions that even the experienced LSD user may endure are quite rare to the experienced marijuana smoker. This rarity is not simply due to the smoker using a far less potent drug but is also due to a much closer and continuing control by the smoker over the extent and the type of reaction that person wishes to induce. Furthermore, cannabis has a tendency to produce sedation, whereas LSD and the LSD-type drugs may induce long periods of wakefulness and

---

**Diagnostic Criteria for Cannabis Dependence***

A. Either a pattern of pathological use or impairment in social or occupational functioning due to cannabis use.

*Pattern of pathological use:* intoxication throughout the day; use of cannabis nearly every day for at least a month; episodes of cannabis delusional disorder.

*Impairment in social or occupational functioning due to cannabis use:* e.g. marked loss of interest in activities previously engaged in, loss of friends, absence from work, loss of job, or legal difficulties (other than a single arrest due to possession, purchase, or sale of an illegal substance).

B. *Tolerance:* need for markedly increased amounts of cannabis to achieve the desired effect or markedly diminished effect with regular use of the same amount.

---

* From American Psychiatric Association: *Diagnostic and Statistical Manual of Mental Disorders*, ed 3. American Psychiatric Association, Washington, DC, 1980. Used with permission.

even restlessness. Unlike LSD, *marijuana does not dilate the pupils* or materially heighten blood pressure, reflexes, and body temperature; but it does increase the pulse rate. It is questionable, however, whether marijuana in doses ordinarily used in this country can produce true hallucinations. An important difference is that tolerance rapidly develops with the LSD-type drugs, but develops very little, if at all, with cannabis. Finally, marijuana lacks the potent consciousness-altering qualities of LSD, peyote, mescaline, psilocybin, and so on. These differences, particularly the last, cast considerable doubt on marijuana's credentials for inclusion in this group of drugs.

The DSM-III table on the preceding page lists the diagnostic criteria for cannabis dependence. DSM-III also states that, "The existence and significance of tolerance and withdrawal with regular heavy use of cannabis (cannabis dependence) is controversial."

**19.14.   The answer is E** (*Synopsis*, ed. 4, pages 397 and 398).

Cyclazocine, an *N*-substitute benzomorphan derivative, which is chemically similar to nalorphine hydrochloride, is an effective opioid-blocking agent. In addition, cyclazocine is a powerful analgesic but has several side effects, including *dysphoria*, visual distortions, racing thoughts, *anxiety, sedation,* and *analgesia.*

A *delusion* is a false belief that is firmly held, despite objective and obvious contradictory proof or evidence and despite the fact that other members of the culture do not share the belief.

*Analgesia* is a state in which one feels little or no pain. *Dysphoria* is a feeling of unpleasantness or discomfort; a mood of general dissatisfaction, restlessness, depression, and anxiety. *Sedation* is a state of decreased responsivity to common stimuli that may proceed to sleepiness, but not to drowsiness. *Anxiety* is an unpleasurable emotional state associated with psychophysiological changes in response to an intrapsychic conflict. In contrast to fear, the danger or threat in anxiety is unreal. Physiological changes consist of increased heart rate, disturbed breathing, trembling, sweating, and vasomotor changes. Psychological changes consist of an uncomfortable feeling of impending danger, an overwhelming awareness of being powerless, the inability to perceive the unreality of the threat, prolonged feeling of tension, and exhaustive readiness for the expected danger.

**19.15.   The answer is C** (*Synopsis*, ed. 4, page 420).

The usual case of alcohol hallucinosis differs from schizophrenia by the temporal relation to alcohol withdrawal, the short-lived course, and the absence of a past history of schizophrenia.

*Alcohol hallucinosis* is usually described as a condition manifested primarily by auditory hallucinations, sometimes accompanied by delusions, in the absence of symptoms of an affective disorder or organic mental disorder. Hallucinosis is differentiated from delirium tremens by the absence of a clear sensorium in delirium tremens.

*Schizophrenia* refers to a psychotic mental disorder in which there exist disturbances in thinking, mood, and behavior.

*Delirium tremens* results from the cessation of drinking and in DSM-III is called alcohol withdrawal delirium, a condition that can be fatal. The following characteristics appear: autonomic hyperactivity—tachycardia, fever, hyperhidrosis, dilated pupils—accompanied by tremulousness, hallucinations, illusions, and delusions.

*Methanol (wood alcohol) intoxication* refers to the ingestion of methyl alcohol, a colorless flammable liquid used as industrial solvent and fuel, which upon ingestion causes severe acidosis and visual impairment due to its effects on the central nervous system.

The term *pathological intoxication* is presently classified in DSM-III as alcohol idiosyncratic intoxication. It is characterized by extreme excitement (alcoholic fury) with aggressive, dangerous, and even homicidal reactions. Persecutory ideas are common. The condition terminates with the patient falling into a deep sleep. There is usually complete amnesia for the episode.

**19.16.   The answer is A** (*Synopsis*, ed. 4, page 404).

Amphetamine delirium is, by definition, delirium *within 24 hours* of use of amphetamine.

**19.17.   The answer is B (1, 3)** (*Synopsis*, ed. 4, page 424).

*Women tend to become alcoholic at a later age than men do* (45, women; 30, men), but the women move rapidly from social drinking to alcoholism. *Both men and women show a decreased incidence after age 60.*

In general, attempts to establish a female alcoholic personality as a unique phenomenon have not materialized. Clinical observations have indicated an *increase in alcoholism in women.* The changing societal role of women has been suggested as a possible reason for the increase.

Women are twice as likely as men to associate their alcoholism with specific circumstances or situations.

*Women alcoholics are more apt than men to postpone treatment,* and their families are more reluctant to force them into treatment. They

### Diagnostic Criteria for Cannabis Abuse*

A. *Pattern of pathological use:* intoxication throughout the day; use of cannabis nearly every day for at least a month; episodes of cannabis delusional disorder.

B. *Impairment in social or occupational functioning due to cannabis use:* e.g. marked loss of interest in activities previously engaged in, loss of friends, absence from work, loss of job, or legal difficulties (other than due to a single arrest for possession, purchase, or sale of the substance).

C. Duration of disturbance of at least 1 month.

* From American Psychiatric Association: *Diagnostic and Statistical Manual of Mental Disorders*, ed 3. American Psychiatric Association, Washington, DC, 1980. Used with permission.

### Diagnostic Criteria for Hallucinogen Abuse*

A. *Pattern of pathological use:* inability to reduce or stop use; intoxication throughout the day (possible only with some hallucinogens); episodes of hallucinogen delusional disorder or hallucinogen affective disorder.

B. *Impairment in social or occupational functioning due to hallucinogen use:* e.g. fights, loss of friends, absence from work, loss of job, or legal difficulties (other than due to a single arrest for possession, purchase, or sale of the illegal substance).

C. Duration of disturbance of at least 1 month.

* From American Psychiatric Association: *Diagnostic and Statistical Manual of Mental Disorders*, ed 3. American Psychiatric Association, Washington, DC, 1980. Used with permission.

often have a greater opportunity for remaining closet alcoholics.

**19.18.   The answer is B (1, 3)** (*Synopsis*, ed. 4, page 402).

Cannabis abuse is marked by almost daily use and *intoxication throughout the day.* Patterns of *pathological use* include the abuse of marijuana nearly *every day for at least 1 month.* An example of impaired social functioning is a marked *loss of interest in activities* in which the person previously engaged. *Legal problems are common* among abusers. See the table above for the DSM-III diagnostic criteria for cannabis abuse.

Hallucinogens, such as marijuana, mescaline, and lysergic acid diethylamide, are chemical agents that produce hallucinations. Abuse patterns occur with this class of drugs, and an affective disorder may be produced. The tables directly above in columns 1 and 2 give the DSM-III diagnostic criteria for hallucinogen abuse and hallucinogen affective disorder.

**19.19.   The answer is E (all)** (*Synopsis*, ed. 4, page 403).

Prolonged, heavy use of amphetamines produces a marked tolerance and a withdrawal syndrome. Withdrawal is marked by mental depres-

### Diagnostic Criteria for Hallucinogen Affective Disorder*

A. Recent use of a hallucinogen.

B. Development of an organic affective syndrome that persists beyond 24 hours after cessation of hallucinogen use.

C. Absence of delusions.

D. Not due to any other physical or mental disorder, such as preexisting affective disorder.

* From American Psychiatric Association: *Diagnostic and Statistical Manual of Mental Disorders*, ed 3. American Psychiatric Association, Washington, DC, 1980. Used with permission.

### Diagnostic Criteria for Amphetamine or Similarly Acting Sympathomimetic Withdrawal*

A. Prolonged heavy use of amphetamine or a similarly acting sympathomimetic.

B. After cessation of or reduction in substance use, depressed mood and at least two of the following:
1. Fatigue;
2. Disturbed sleep;
3. Increased dreaming.

C. Not due to any other physical or mental disorder, such as amphetamine or similarly acting sympathomimetic delusional disorder.

* From American Psychiatric Association: *Diagnostic and Statistical Manual of Mental Disorders*, ed 3. American Psychiatric Association, Washington, DC, 1980. Used with permission.

sion—sometimes with *suicidal ideation—disturbed sleep* with *severe fatigue,* and *increased dreaming.* The above table lists the DSM-III diagnostic criteria for amphetamine withdrawal.

**19.20.   The answer is E (all)** (*Synopsis*, ed. 4, page 405).

Cocaine abuse is marked by *pathological use patterns,* which in severe cases of intoxication may include *hallucinations* and *delusions.* Because of the illegality of the drug and its high price, *legal problems* are common.

See the table directly below for the DSM-III diagnostic criteria for cocaine abuse.

**19.21.   The answer is E (all)** (*Synopsis*, ed. 4, page 430).

Tobacco dependence is defined as either persistent tobacco use, despite the person's psychological distress at the *need for repeated use*, or persistent tobacco use whenever a person has developed *serious tobacco-related physical disorders*—for example, emphysema, bronchitis, coronary artery disease, peripheral vascular diseases, various cancers, and tobacco amblyopia—but continues to be so dependent on the drug that he or she is *unable to discontinue its use.*

*Tobacco withdrawal* is defined as a physiological withdrawal syndrome that is precipitated by the cessation of chronic tobacco use and that is characterized by a strong craving for tobacco, anxiety, irritability, impaired attention, a cognitive preoccupation with actions associated with tobacco use, and mild physiological alterations. Withdrawal from the nicotine contained in tobacco is presumably responsible for most facets of this syndrome.

See the tables below for the DSM-III diagnostic criteria for tobacco dependence and withdrawal.

**19.22.   The answer is A (1, 2, 3)** (*Synopsis*, ed. 4, pages 395 and 396).

Methadone is a drug that *is used to treat*

---

**Diagnostic Criteria for Cocaine Abuse***

A. *Pattern of pathological use:* inability to reduce or stop use; intoxication throughout the day; episodes of cocaine overdose (intoxication so severe that hallucinations and delusions occur in a clear sensorium).

B. *Impairment in social or occupational functioning due to cocaine use:* e.g. fights, loss of friends, absence from work, loss of job, or legal difficulties (other than due to a single arrest for possession, purchase, or sale of the substance).

C. Duration of disturbance of at least 1 month.

* From American Psychiatric Association: *Diagnosis and Statistical Manual of Mental Disorders,* ed 3. American Psychiatric Association, Washington, DC, 1980. Used with permission.

---

**Diagnostic Criteria for Tobacco Dependence***

A. Continuous use of tobaccco for at least 1 month.

B. At least one of the following:

1. Serious attempts to stop or significantly reduce the amount of tobacco use on a permanent basis have been unsuccessful;
2. Attempts to stop smoking have led to the development of tobacco withdrawal;
3. The individual continues to use tobacco despite a serious physical disorder (e.g. respiratory or cardiovascular disease) that he or she knows is exacerbated by tobacco use.

* From American Psychiatric Association: *Diagnostic and Statistical Manual of Mental Disorders,* ed 3. American Psychiatric Association, Washington, DC, 1980. Used with permission.

---

**Diagnostic Criteria for Tobacco Withdrawal***

A. Use of tobacco for at least several weeks at a level equivalent to more than 10 cigarettes per day, with each cigarette containing at least 0.5 mg of nicotine.

B. Abrupt cessation of or reduction in tobacco use, followed within 24 hours by at least four of the following:

1. Craving for tobacco;
2. Irritability;
3. Anxiety;
4. Difficulty concentrating;
5. Restlessness;
6. Headache;
7. Drowsiness;
8. Gastrointestinal disturbances.

* From American Psychiatric Association: *Diagnostic and Statistical Manual of Mental Disorders,* ed 3. American Psychiatric Association, Washington, DC, 1980. Used with permission.

*heroin addiction.* It is given orally, usually in orange juice, and *is an analgesic* that interferes with pain perception. Long-term use of methadone *blocks opioid withdrawal,* and methadone itself *is an addicting drug.* The use of methadone for heroin addiction is sometimes known as substitution therapy.

**19.23.   The answer is A (1, 2, 3)** (*Synopsis, ed. 4, page 404*).

According to DSM-III, delirium *usually occurs within 1 hour* of substance use and *is over in about 6 hours.* When the substance is *taken intravenously, the onset is almost immediate.* More rarely the delirium follows a period of intoxication. When the other pharmacological effects of the substance have worn off, the delirium *disappears completely.* The DSM-III diagnostic criteria for amphetamine delirium refer to the time of onset of the disorder, as indicated in the following table.

**Diagnostic Criteria for Amphetamine or Similarly Acting Sympathomimetic Delirium***

A. Delirium within 24 hours of use of amphetamine or similarly acting sympathomimetic.

B. Not due to any other physical or mental disorder.

* From American Psychiatric Association: *Diagnostic and Statistical Manual of Mental Disorders,* ed 3. American Psychiatric Association, Washington, DC, 1980. Used with permission.

**19.24.   The answer is E (all)** (*Synopsis, ed. 4, page 411*).

The patient is having a reaction to *phencyclidine (PCP),* which is known as "angel dust." The reaction is related to the dose taken. Less than 5 mg of phencyclidine is considered a low dose, and doses above 10 mg are considered high. Experienced users report that the effects of 2 to 3 mg of smoked PCP begin within 5 minutes and plateau within ½ hour. In the early phases, users are frequently not communicative, appear oblivious, and report active fantasy production. They experience bodily warmth and tingling, peaceful floating sensations, and occasional feelings of depersonalization, isolation, and estrangement; sometimes there are auditory or visual hallucinations. There is often a striking alteration of body image; users may believe that their hands or feet are very small and very distant, and that their bodies are flattened like paper, shrunken in size or weightless. Distortions of space and time perception are prominent, and delusions may occur. There may also be an intensification of dependency feelings, as well as confusion and disorganization of

thought. The user may be sympathetic, sociable, and talkative at one moment and hostile and negative at another. Euphoria resembling alcohol intoxication is common, and the behavioral

**Diagnostic Criteria for Phencyclidine (PCP) or Similarly Acting Arylcyclohexylamine Intoxication***

A. Recent use of phencyclidine or a similarly acting arylcyclohexylamine.

B. Within 1 hour (less when smoked, insufflated, or used intravenously), at least two of the following physical symptoms:

1. Vertical or horizontal nystagmus;
2. Increased blood pressure and heart rate;
3. Numbness or diminished responsiveness to pain;
4. Ataxia;
5. Dysarthria.

C. Within 1 hour, at least two of the following psychological symptoms:

1. Euphoria;
2. Psychomotor agitation;
3. Marked anxiety;
4. Emotional lability;
5. Grandiosity;
6. Sensation of slowed time;
7. Synesthesias.

D. Maladaptive behavioral effects, e.g. belligerence, impulsivity, unpredictability, impaired judgment, assaultiveness.

E. Not due to any other physical or mental disorder, e.g. delirium.

* From American Psychiatric Association: *Diagnostic and Statistical Manual of Mental Disorders,* ed 3. American Psychiatric Association, Washington, DC, 1980. Used with permission.

**Diagnostic Criteria for Phencyclidine (PCP) or Similarly Acting Arylcyclohexylamine Abuse***

A. *Pattern of pathological use:* intoxication throughout the day; episodes of phencyclidine or similarly acting arylcyclohexylamine delirium or mixed organic mental disorder.

B. *Impairment in social or occupational functioning due to substance use:* e.g. fights, loss of friends, absence from work, loss of job, or legal difficulties (other than due to a single arrest for possession, purchase, or sale of the substance).

C. Duration of disturbance of at least 1 month.

* From American Psychiatric Association: *Diagnostic and Statistical Manual of Mental Disorders,* ed 3. American Psychiatric Association, Washington, DC, 1980. Used with permission.

toxicity resembles that of alcohol. Anxiety is also sometimes reported; it is often the most prominent presenting symptom in an adverse reaction. Sometimes observed are head-rolling movements, stroking, grimacing, and repetitive chanting speech. The high lasts for about 4 to 6 hours and gradually gives way to a state of mild depression, during which the user may become irritable, somewhat paranoid, and occasionally even belligerent and *irrationally assaultive*. Users sometimes find that it takes *from 24 to 48 hours to recover* completely from the high; laboratory tests show that PCP may remain in the blood and *urine* for more than a week.

See the tables on the preceding page for the DSM-III diagnostic criteria for abuse and intoxication with phencyclidine.

**19.25.   The answer is C (2, 4)** (*Synopsis*, ed. 4, page 403).

Amphetamine delusional disorder is a rapidly developing syndrome consisting of a paranoid psychosis, including *persecutory delusions* (false, fixed ideas of persecution) and *ideas of reference*, during a period of long-term use of moderate or high doses of amphetamine. The following table summarizes DSM-III's diagnostic criteria for this disorder.

An *idea of reference* is a misinterpretation of incidents and events in the outside world as having a direct personal reference to oneself. Occasionally observed in normal persons, ideas of reference are frequently seen in paranoid patients. If present with sufficient frequency or intensity or if organized and systematized, they constitute delusions of reference.

*Euthymia* means normal mood, which is not

#### Diagnostic Criteria for Amphetamine or Similarly Acting Sympathomimetic Delusional Disorder*

A. Recent use of amphetamine or similarly acting sympathomimetic during a period of long-term use of moderate or high doses.

B. A rapidly developing syndrome consisting of persecutory delusions as the predominant clinical feature and at least three of the following:

  1. Ideas of reference;
  2. Aggressiveness and hostility;
  3. Anxiety;
  4. Psychomotor agitation.

C. Not due to any other physical or mental disorder.

* From American Psychiatric Association: *Diagnostic and Statistical Manual of Mental Disorders*, ed 3. American Psychiatric Association, Washington, DC, 1980. Used with permission.

present with this disorder. These patients are generally aggressive and hostile, not passive. *Passivity* is a type of behavior characterized by compliance, submission to authority, and lack of initiative. See the table in column 1 for the DSM-III diagnostic criteria for amphetamine delusional disorder.

**19.26.   The answer is A (1, 2, 3)** (*Synopsis* ed. 4, page 403).

The signs and symptoms of acute amphetamine poisoning and poisoning from chronic use include flushing, pallor, cyanosis, fever, tachycardia, serious cardiac problems, markedly elevated blood pressure, hemorrhage or other vascular accidents, nausea, vomiting, difficulty in breathing, tremor, *ataxia*, loss of sensory abilities, twitching, *tetany*, *convulsions*, loss of consciousness, and coma. Death from overdose is usually associated with hyperpyrexia, convulsions, and cardiovascular shock. When intravenous abuse of amphetamines became increasingly popular in the early 1960's, several new spectra of serious physiological reactions were reported. Since then, severe serum hepatitis, lung abscess, endocarditis, and necrotizing angiitis resulting from intravenous abuse of amphetamines have been fairly common occurrences.

*Orthostatic hypotension* refers to a form of low blood pressure that occurs when the individual stands. It is a side effect seen in patients taking drugs that have anticholinergic actions, such as the neuroleptics and tricylic antidepressants.

Ataxia is a lack of coordination, either physical or mental. In neurology, it refers to loss of muscular coordination. In psychiatry, the term intrapsychic ataxia refers to lack of coordination between feelings and thoughts; the disturbance is found in schizophrenia.

Tetany is a tonic muscular contraction, usually painful, affecting various muscle groups, sometimes the laryngeal muscles.

**19.27.   The answer is E (all)** (*Synopsis*, ed. 4, page 397).

Since the 1960s, various antagonists have been used to treat opioid dependence. These agents are useful in heroin and other narcotic addictions, because they block or antagonize the opioids, preventing them from acting. Unlike methadone, the narcotic antagonists do not in themselves exert narcotic effects, nor are they addictive.

The conditioning hypothesis suggests that the extinction of drug-seeking behavior could provide a means to reverse the pathophysiology of addiction. If the relief afforded by narcotics during the period of conditioned abstinence were blocked, the extinction would be accomplished by a substance without narcotic effects that would block the ability of administered opioids to affect the central nervous system. Narcotic antagonists are such substances. Molecular alterations of narcotic analgesics have yielded compounds that antagonize the respiratory effects of narcotics. *N*-Allylnormorphine or *nalorphine* was extensively studied in 1950 and has been used in the treatment of opioid overdose. Similar chemical substitutions have yielded *cyclazocine, naloxone,* and *naltrexone*—three antagonists used for the treatment of opioid dependence.

**19.28.   The answer is E (all)** (*Synopsis,* ed. 4, page 386).

Certain consistent behavior patterns seem especially pronounced in adolescent addicts. These patterns have been called the heroin behavior syndrome: Underlying *depression,* often of an agitated type and frequently accompanied by anxiety symptoms; impulsiveness, expressed by a passive-aggressive orientation; *fear of failure*; use of heroin as an antianxiety agent to mask feelings of *low self-esteem*, hopelessness, and aggression; limited coping strategies and low frustration tolerance, accompanied by the *need for immediate gratification*; sensitivity to drug contingencies, with a keen awareness of the relation between good feelings and the act of drug taking; feelings of behavioral impotence, counteracted by momentary control over the life situation by means of drugs, with the injection ritual a valued life event; disturbances in social and interpersonal relations, with peer relations maintained by mutual drug experiences.

With authentic engagement not attractive or feasible for many adolescents, drug abuse becomes, for a small but growing minority, a form of identification and engagement—although with an undesirable subculture.

**19.29.   The answer is E (all)** (*Synopsis,* ed. 4, page 404).

Amphetamines, having marked euphoric and antifatigue properties, act primarily on the central nervous system. There are a number of psychological and physical symptoms associated with amphetamine intoxication. The table in column 2 lists the specific DSM-III diagnostic criteria.

**19.30–19.33.   The answers are 19.30–A, 19.31–C, 19.32–B, and 19.33–C** (*Synopsis,* ed. 4, pages 419 and 420).

Among alcoholics who are hospitalized, about 5 percent develop delirium tremens, which is the severest form of the withdrawal syndrome. Pre-

### Diagnostic Criteria for Amphetamine or Similarly Acting Sympathomimetic Intoxication*

A. Recent use of amphetamine or similarly acting sympathomimetic.

B. Within 1 hour of use, at least two of the following psychological symptoms:
   1. Psychomotor agitation;
   2. *Elation*;
   3. *Grandiosity*;
   4. Loquacity;
   5. Hypervigilance.

C. Within 1 hour of use, at least two of the following physical symptoms:
   1. Tachycardia;
   2. Pupillary dilation;
   3. *Elevated blood pressure*;
   4. Perspiration or chills;
   5. Nausea or vomiting.

D. *Maladaptive behavior* effects, e.g. fighting, impaired judgment, interference with social or occupational functioning.

E. Not due to any other physical or mental disorder.

* From American Psychiatric Association: *Diagnostic and Statistical Manual of Mental Disorders,* ed 3. American Psychiatric Association, Washington, DC, 1980. Used with permission.

disposing factors to delirium tremens are believed to be the presence of other illnesses, including those to which alcoholics are vulnerable—pneumonia, fractures, head injuries, and liver disease.

The essential feature is a delirium that occurs within 1 week of the cessation or reduction of heavy alcohol ingestion. Additional features include autonomic hyperactivity, such as tachycardia, sweating, and elevated blood pressure; a disturbance of attention, as manifested by an impairment in the ability to sustain attention to environmental stimuli, goal-directed thinking, or goal-directed behavior; disordered memory and orientation; at least two of the following: (1) reduced wakefulness or insomnia, (2) perceptual disturbance (simple misinterpretations, illusions, hallucinations), or (3) increased or decreased psychomotor activity; clinical features that develop over a short period of time and fluctuate rapidly; and the presence of no other physical or mental disorder to account for the disturbance.

Tremor is almost always present. Periods of calm and agitation may alternate. The hallucinations are most frequently visual, but may also be auditory or tactile. Fever is frequent.

This disorder usually begins in patients who are in their thirties or forties. In general, the first episode is preceded by 5 to 15 years of heavy drinking, typically of the binge type.

*Grand mal seizures* infrequently occur as a complication of alcohol withdrawal with or without delirium tremens. They usually appear within 48 hours of drinking cessation and are nonfocal and one or two in number. They cease without specific treatment. The emergence of focal neurological symptoms, lateralizing seizures, increased intracranial pressure, skull fracture, nonmidline pineal or other indications of central nervous system pathology obviously calls for further neurological investigation and treatment. It is now generally believed that anticonvulsant medication is ineffectual in preventing or treating alcohol withdrawal convulsions; the use of *chlordiazepoxide* or paraldehyde is generally effective.

The essential feature of alcohol hallucinosis is hallucinations, usually *auditory*, persisting after a person has recovered from the symptoms of alcohol withdrawal and is no longer drinking. The hallucinations are not part of alcohol withdrawal delirium.

Although first episodes have been reported in people in their early to mid-twenties, the more typical onset is about age 40, following 10 or more years of heavy drinking. The disorder has been found to be 4 times more common in males than in females. In some cases, the hallucinations last for several weeks; in other cases, they last for several months; and in still other cases, they seem to be permanent. The condition is very rare. Hallucinosis is differentiated from delirium tremens by the absence of a *clear sensorium* in delirium tremens.

The best way to deal with delirium tremens is to prevent its occurrence. Patients withdrawing from alcohol who exhibit any withdrawal phenomena should receive 25 to 50 mg of *chlordiazepoxide* hydrochloride every 2 to 4 hours, as necessary, until they seem to be out of danger.

## References

Goodwin D W: Alcoholism and alcoholic psychoses. In *Comprehensive Textbook of Psychiatry*, ed 4, H I Kaplan, B J Sadock, editors, p 1016. Williams & Wilkins, Baltimore, 1985.

Greden J F: Caffeine and tobacco dependence. In *Comprehensive Textbook of Psychiatry*, ed 4, H I Kaplan, B J Sadock, editors, p 1026. Williams & Wilkins, Baltimore, 1985.

Grinspoon L, Bakalar J B: Drug dependence: Nonnarcotic agents. In *Comprehensive Textbook of Psychiatry*, ed 4, H I Kaplan, B J Sadock, editors, p 1003. Williams & Wilkins, Baltimore, 1985.

Jaffe J H: Drug addiction and drug abuse. In *The Pharmacological Basis of Therapeutics*, A G Gilman, L S Goodman, A Gilman, editors, ed 6, p 535. Macmillan, New York, 1980.

Jaffe J H: Opioid dependence. In *Comprehensive Textbook of Psychiatry*, ed 4, H I Kaplan, B J Sadock, editors, p 987. Williams & Wilkins, Baltimore, 1985.

Jaffe J H, Kanzler M: Nicotine: Tobacco use, abuse and dependence. In *Substance Abuse: Clinical Problems and Perspectives*, J H Levinson, C Ruiz, editors, p 256. Williams & Wilkins, Baltimore, 1981.

Meyer R E, Mirin S M: *The Heroin Stimulus: Implications for a Theory of Addiction*. Plenum Publishing Corp, New York, 1979.

Petersen L C, Stillman R C, editors: *Phencyclidine (PCP) Abuse: An Appraisal*. NIDA Research Monograph 21. US Government Printing Office, Washington, DC, 1978.

United States Public Health Service. *Smoking and Health: Report of the Advisory Committee to the Surgeon General of the Public Health Service*. US Government Printing Office, Washington, DC, 1964.

Zinberg N E: *Drug, Set, and Setting: The Basis for Controlled Intoxicant Use*. Yale University Press, New Haven, CT, 1984.

# 20

# Psychosexual Disorders

The pioneering work of Masters and Johnson, the sex researchers, that began in the 1970s has had a profound impact on the American public. Sexual problems have been brought out in the open, and new and more effective treatments for sexual disorders have been developed.

In the course of a psychiatric interview, the clinician comes into contact with a great variety of sexual patterns and behavior, and for this reason it is necessary that he or she be knowledgeable about sexual disorders. Sir James Paget, who is best known for classifying the disease that bears his name, was a crusader for sexual education. In the 19th century, he stated, "Ignorance about sexual affairs seems to be a notable characteristic of the more civilized part of the human race." The psychiatrist must not only use clinical skills but also educational skills in dealing with patients.

According to the third edition of the *Diagnostic and Statistical Manual of Mental Disorders* (DSM-III), psychosexual disorders are caused by psychological factors and are divided into four major groups: gender identity disorders, distortions of a person's sense of masculinity and femininity; paraphilias, also referred to as perversions and sexual deviations; psychosexual dysfunctions, such as impotence in the male and anorgasmia in the female; and ego-dystonic homosexuality, a group of homosexuals who are dissatisfied with a homosexual orientation and wish to become heterosexual. In addition, this chapter covers special areas of interest, such as rape and incest. In DSM-III, disorders of sexual functioning caused by organic disorders are not listed in this classification of psychosexual disorders.

It is increasingly recognized that a relationship exists between medical illness, drug use, contraceptive use, mental illness, and sexual behavior and function. The student needs to be aware of the interaction between these various factors in order to counsel the patient more effectively.

The reader should refer to Chapter 20, "Psychosexual Disorders," of *Modern Synopsis-IV* and should then read the following questions and answers to assess his or her understanding of this area.

# Questions

**DIRECTIONS:** Each of the statements or questions below is followed by five suggested responses or complications. Select the *one* that is *best* in each case.

**20.1.** The illustration on page 260 is of a male with small testes and gynecomastia. He has positive Barr bodies and an XXY karyotype. The most likely diagnosis is

A. androgen insensitivity
B. Klinefelter's syndrome
C. Turner's syndrome
D. Cushing's syndrome
E. hermaphroditism

**20.2.** All the following may be associated with paraphilias *except*

A. sexual fantasies
B. masturbation
C. sexual props
D. homosexual orientation
E. voyeurism

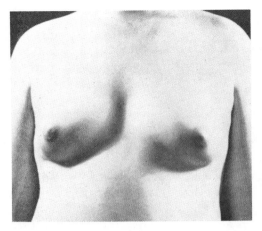 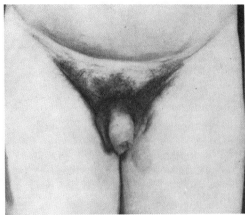

(Courtesy of Robert B Greenblatt, MD, and Virginia P McNamara, MD.)

**20.3.** The condition in which an anatomically normal male knows that he is anatomically normal but nonetheless has always considered himself to be a female is known as

A. secondary transsexualism
B. primary transsexualism
C. perversion
D. homosexuality
E. pseudohermaphroditism

**20.4.** Spouse abuse is estimated to occur in how many families in the United States:

A. 500,000
B. 1 million
C. 1.5 million
D. 2 million
E. over 3 million

**20.5.** A fetish is

A. a device with magical phallic qualities that is felt dynamically to be used as a bridge against castration anxiety
B. a nonliving inanimate object used as the preferred or necessary adjunct to arousal
C. a device that may function as a bridging object, serving as a hedge against separation anxiety
D. associated in actuality or in fantasy with the human environment, most often the human body
E. all of the above

**20.6.** All of the following statements about transvestism are true *except*

A. the basic preference is heterosexual
B. cross-dressing during at least the initial phase is for the purpose of sexual excitement
C. the overt clinical syndrome most often begins in early adulthood
D. cross-dressing often becomes increasingly frequent and may become habitual
E. the disorder may evolve into transsexualism

**20.7.** All of the following statements about sexual masochism are true *except*

A. the most common finding is that the masochist is unable to take the opposite role of sadist with arousal and pleasure
B. masochistic sexual fantasies are likely to have been present in childhood
C. the essential feature is sexual excitement produced in an individual by his or her own suffering
D. the disorder is usually chronic
E. self-mutilation, if engaged in, is likely to be repeated

**20.8.** The sequence of the DSM-III phases of the sexual response cycle is

A. appetitive, excitement, orgasm, resolution
B. excitement, appetitive, orgasm, resolution
C. resolution, appetitive, orgasm, excitement
D. excitement, orgasm, appetitive, resolution
E. none of the above

**20.9.** All of the following statements about transsexualism are true *except*

A. genetic abnormality is present
B. there is a sense of inappropriateness about one's anatomical sex
C. the disturbance has been continuous for at least 2 years
D. there is a wish to be rid of one's own genitals
E. physical intersex abnormality is absent

**20.10.** Which of the following conditions have been associated with erectile dysfunction in men:

A. Mumps
B. Atherosclerotic disease
C. Klinefelter's syndrome
D. Multiple sclerosis
E. All of the above

**20.11.** Orgasm is characterized by all the following *except*

A. involuntary contraction of the anal sphincter
B. blood pressure rise
C. absence of uterine contractions
D. slight clouding of consciousness
E. carpopedal spasm

**20.12.** Which of the following procedures is the most helpful to differentiate organically caused impotence from functional impotence:

A. Measuring nocturnal penile tumescence
B. Measuring the glucose tolerance curve
C. Measuring follicle-stimulating hormone levels
D. Cystometric examination
E. Plasma testosterone level

**DIRECTIONS:** For each of the incomplete statements below, *one* or *more* of the completions given is correct. Choose answer:

A. if only **1, 2,** and **3** are correct
B. if only **1** and **3** are correct
C. if only **2** and **4** are correct
D. if only **4** is correct
E. if all are correct

**20.13.** Female transsexuals

1. are anatomically normal females
2. prefer women as sex objects
3. desire to have their bodies changed to male
4. deny their anatomical sex

**20.14.** Which of the following statements about incest are true:

1. It is more common among families of low socioeconomic status than among other families.
2. Father-daughter incest is the most common form.
3. 15 million women have been the object of incestuous behavior.
4. One-third of incest cases occur before age 9.

**20.15.** Exhibitionists

1. repeatedly expose their genitals to an unsuspecting stranger
2. expose their genitals for the purpose of achieving sexual excitement
3. are usually aware of a wish to surprise or shock the observer
4. are usually physically dangerous to the victim

**20.16.** Inhibited sexual desire

1. is experienced only by women
2. does not affect frequency of coitus
3. is an uncommon complaint among married couples
4. protects against unconscious fear about sex

**20.17.** The squeeze technique

1. is used in the treatment of secondary impotence
2. involves the use of dilators
3. decreases the threshold of ejaculatory inevitability
4. is applied at the moment of impending ejaculation

| Directions Summarized | | | | |
|---|---|---|---|---|
| A | B | C | D | E |
| 1, 2, 3 | 1, 3 | 2, 4 | 4 | All are |
| only | only | only | only | correct |

**20.18.**  Dyspareunia

1. may lead to vaginismus
2. is caused by tension and anxiety
3. is associated with real pain
4. occurs in 15 percent of female surgical procedures on the genital area

**20.19.**  Zoophilia

1. is rarely chronic
2. may be an outgrowth of availability or convenience
3. is rarely practiced when other forms of sexual outlet are available
4. may include such activities as intercourse, masturbation, and oral-genital contact

**20.20.**  Which of the following statements apply to the effects of drugs on female sexual functioning:

1. Women are less vulnerable to drug effects than are men.
2. Phenelzine decreases libido in women.
3. Sexual dysfunction associated with the use of a drug disappears when the drug is stopped.
4. Drug effects in women have been less well studied than they have been in men.

**20.21.**  Which of the following statements are accurate about rape:

1. Over 60 percent of rapists are under age 25.
2. 90 percent of rapists are black.
3. Most rapists have a previous police record.
4. Black rapists tend to rape white women.

**20.22.**  Inhibited sexual excitement

1. in men is a failure to get an erection
2. in women is a failure to lubricate
3. is associated with orgasmic problems
4. is produced by alcohol

**20.23.**  Retarded ejaculation

1. is classified in DSM-III as inhibited male orgasm
2. is less common than premature ejaculation
3. can occur after prostate surgery
4. may be caused by antihypertensive drugs

**20.24.**  Ego-dystonic homosexuality

1. is characterized by a desire to acquire or increase heterosexual arousal
2. is characterized by a sustained pattern of overt homosexual arousal
3. is characterized by a persistently absent or weak heterosexual arousal
4. is not considered a psychosexual disorder in DSM-III

**20.25.**  Atypical paraphilias include

1. coprophilia
2. klismaphilia
3. urophilia
4. mysophilia

**20.26.**  Gender identity disorder of childhood manifests

1. in the girl by a persistent repudiation of female anatomical structures; for instance, by a belief that she has, or will grow, a penis
2. with a strong and persistently stated desire to be the opposite sex
3. in the boy by a possible preoccupation with female stereotypical activities as seen, for instance, in a preference for cross-dressing
4. in the girl with onset after puberty

**20.27.**  Voyeurism is

1. repetitive looking at unsuspecting people
2. observing while at the same time seeking sexual activity with the observed people
3. sexually exciting behavior wherein orgasm is brought about by masturbation during or after the event
4. is the same thing as watching pornography

**20.28.**  Cross-dressing (transvestism)

1. relieves anxiety or gender discomfort
2. may produce sexual arousal
3. usually begins in adolescence
4. occurs mainly in homosexuals

**20.29.** Sexual sadism is

1. sexual excitement that is linked to the active infliction of humiliation or abuse
2. not diagnosed when sexually sadistic acts are practiced on nonconsenting partners
3. associated with sadistic sexual fantasies that are likely to have been present in childhood
4. common in most rapists

**20.30.** Ego-dystonic homosexuals

1. show no or very weak heterosexual arousal
2. want to increase heterosexual arousal
3. have feelings of guilt or shame about their homosexual impulses
4. have not had homosexual relationships

**20.31.** Pedophilia

1. most frequently begins in middle age
2. involves dominance and power
3. may be exclusively homosexual or exclusively heterosexual
4. is more often seen among homosexuals toward children of the same sex

**20.32.** Dual-sex therapy as developed by Masters and Johnson is based on

1. the marital unit or dyad as the object of therapy
2. a male and female therapy team
3. the use of specific sexual exercises
4. heightening sensory awareness

**20.33.** The posttraumatic reaction after a rape

1. may last for more than a year
2. may cause the woman to become phobic of sex
3. is helped by the woman immediately being able to talk about the experience
4. is not helped if the rapist is arrested and convicted

**20.34.** Which of the following are common to all paraphilias:

1. Impairment in gender sense
2. A specific sexual fantasy
3. Protection against castration anxiety
4. Protection against separation anxiety

**DIRECTIONS:** Each group of questions below consists of five lettered headings followed by a list of numbered words or statements. For each numbered word or statement, select the *one* lettered heading that is most closely associated with it. Each lettered heading may be selected once, more than once, or not at all.

**Questions 20.35–20.39**
A. Turner's syndrome
B. Klinefelter's syndrome
C. Adrenogenital syndrome
D. Male pseudohermaphroditism
E. Androgen insensitivity syndrome

**20.35.** Androgenization of the external genitals

**20.36.** One sex chromosome missing (XO)

**20.37.** Two X chromosomes present (XXY)

**20.38.** Hermaphroditic external genitals

**20.39.** Fetal tissues remain in their female resting state

# Answers

# Psychosexual Disorders

**20.1. The answer is B** (*Synopsis*, ed. 4, page 438).

*Klinefelter's syndrome* is a chromosomal abnormality in which an extra sex chromosome exists; instead of the normal 46, the affected child is born with 47 chromosomes. For example, there is an XXY pattern, instead of the usual XX or XY pairs. The subjects affected are male in development, with small firm testes, eunuchoid habitus, variable gynecomastia and other signs of androgen deficiency, and elevated gonadotropin levels.

*Androgen insensitivity syndrome* is a congenital disorder resulting from an inability of target tissues to respond to androgen. *Turner's syndrome* is a chromosome disorder affecting females. Instead of an XX sex chromosome, a XO sex chromosome exists, and there is a total of 45 chromosomes, rather than the usual 46. *Hermaphroditism* is a state in which a person maintains both female and male gonads, usually with one sex dominating. *Cushing's syndrome* or hyperadrenocorticism is named for an American neurosurgeon, Harvey W. Cushing (1869–1939). The disorder is characterized by muscle wasting, obesity, osteoporosis, atrophy of the skin, and hypertension. Emotional lability is common, and frank psychoses are occasionally observed.

**20.2. The answer is D** (*Synopsis*, ed. 4, pages 445 and 446).

With the advent of DSM-III, the paraphilias have found their place in a new and major classification, psychosexual disorders. This classification also includes gender identity disorders, psychosexual dysfunctions, and ego-dystonic homosexuality. Subcategories of paraphilia recognized in DSM-III are fetishism, transvestism, zoophilia, pedophilia, exhibitionism, *voyeurism*, sexual masochism, sexual sadism, and atypical paraphilia.

Paraphilias are characterized by specialized *sexual fantasies, masturbatory practices, sexual props*, and requirements of the sexual partner. The special fantasy, with its unconscious and conscious components, is the pathognomonic element, arousal and orgasm being variously dependent on the active elaboration of that illusion. The influence of the fantasy and its elaborations in behavior extend beyond the sexual sphere to pervade the person's life.

*Homosexual orientation* is not associated with the paraphilias. It refers to a preferential sexual attraction or contact between same-sex persons. *Voyeurism* is classified as a paraphilia in which sexual excitement, frequently with orgasm, is derived from observing others naked, disrobing, or engaging in sexual activity. *Masturbation* is self-stimulation of the genitals for sexual pleasure. *Sexual props* include such objects as whips, chains, and vibrators. *Sexual fantasies* or daydreams are fabricated mental pictures of a situation or chain of events. A form of thinking dominated by unconscious material and primary processes, it seeks wish fulfillment and immediate solutions to conflicts. Fantasy may serve as the matrix for creativity or for neurotic distortions of reality.

**20.3. The answer is B** (*Synopsis*, ed. 4, page 434).

In male *primary transsexualism*, an anatomically normal male knows he is anatomically normal but nonetheless considers himself to be a female within and so makes every effort to arrange his body to conform with his gender identity.

The diagnosis is easily made clinically. This anatomically normal male is, at the time of evaluation—whether the patient is age 4, 14, 24, 44, or 84—the most feminine (by the cliches of his culture) of any male, has always been so without any episodes—for moments, months, or years—of living, with normal appearance, in roles typical for males of that culture (for example, heterosexual liaisons, marriage, employment in masculine professions, military service, fetishism, or other evidence of valuing one's penis), and has been feminine since the first behavior that can be distinguished as gender behavior (between 1 and 2 years of age). This history—which is confirmed by direct observation of transsexuals from childhood on, by interviews with parents and other members of the family, and by childhood photographs in family albums—has never been reported for anyone in the categories of gender disorders to be described later.

The word "primary" is used in this diagnosis because the condition starts in the patient's earliest years and remains constant throughout life. It can, therefore, be contrasted with *secondary transsexualism*, a later acquisition.

*Perversion* is classified as a deviation from

the correct, expected, or proper norm. In psychiatry, the term sexual deviation is used to refer to any sexual activity that deviates from the normal or to any abnormal means of reaching genital orgasm. *Secondary transsexualism* occurs later in life than the primary form of the disorder. It consists of the person wanting to be of the opposite sex. *Pseudohermaphroditism* is a state in which an individual has ambiguous external genitalia but is distinctly of one sex internally; for example, either having testes or ovaries, but not both. *Homosexuality* is a sexual attraction or contact between same-sex persons. Some authors distinguish two types: overt and latent.

**20.4.  The answer is E** (*Synopsis*, ed. 4, page 471).

Spouse abuse is estimated to occur in *from 3 to 6 million families in the United States*. This aspect of domestic violence has been recognized as a severe problem, largely as a result of the recent cultural emphasis on civil rights and the work of feminist groups, although the problem itself is one of long standing.

The major problem in spouse abuse is wife abuse, although some beatings of husbands are reported. In these cases, the husbands complain of fear of ridicule if they expose the problem, fear of charges of counterassault, and inability to leave the situation because of financial difficulties. Husband abuse has also been reported when a frail elderly man is married to a much younger woman.

Wife beating occurs in families of every racial and religious background, and crosses all socioeconomic lines. It is most frequent in families with problems of drug abuse, particularly when there is alcoholism.

Behavioral, cultural, intrapsychic, and interpersonal factors all contribute to the development of the problem. Abusive men are likely to have come from violent homes where they witnessed wife beating or were abused themselves as children. The act itself is reinforcing. Once a man has beaten his wife, he is likely to do so again. Abusive husbands tend to be immature, dependent, and nonassertive and to suffer from strong feelings of inadequacy.

**20.5.  The answer is E** (*Synopsis*, ed. 4, page 447).

The essential feature of fetishism is *the use of nonliving objects as a repeatedly preferred or exclusive method of becoming sexually aroused*. Sexual activity may involve the fetish alone, or *the fetish may be integrated into sexual activities with a human partner*. In the absence of the fetish, there may be impotence in the male. According to psychoanalytic theory, the fetish may *serve as a hedge against separation anxiety* from the love object and may also serve to *ward off castration anxiety*.

The table below gives the DSM-III diagnostic criteria for fetishism.

**20.6.  The answer is C** (*Synopsis*, ed. 4, page 437).

*The overt clinical syndrome of transvestism most typically begins in childhood or early adolescence*, although cross-dressing is usually not done in public until adulthood.

Transvestism is defined as recurrent and persistent cross-dressing by a male whose *basic preference is heterosexual. During at least the initial phase, the cross-dressing is for the purpose of sexual arousal*, although in some individuals, sexual arousal by the clothing tends to disappear. Cross-dressing usually begins as intermittent behavior, but *often it becomes more and more frequent and may become habitual*. Some individuals want to dress and live permanently as women, although this desire becomes rare as the transvestites grow older. When this evolution occurs, *the diagnosis is changed to transsexualism*.

The DSM-III diagnostic criteria for transvestism are listed in the table on the following page.

**20.7.  The answer is A** (*Synopsis*, ed. 4, page 449).

Sexual masochism is described as *sexual excitement produced by the individual's own suffering. Masochistic fantasies are likely to have been present in childhood*, although the age of onset of overt masochistic activities with partners is variable. The *disorder is usually chronic*, and *self-mutilation, if it occurs, is most likely to be*

---

**Diagnostic Criteria for Fetishism\***

A. The use of nonliving objects (fetishes) is a repeatedly preferred or exclusive method of achieving sexual excitement.

B. The fetishes are not limited to articles of female clothing used in cross-dressing (transvestism) or to objects designed to be used for the purpose of sexual stimulation, e.g. vibrator.

\* From American Psychiatric Association: *Diagnostic and Statistical Manual of Mental Disorders*, ed 3. American Psychiatric Association, Washington, DC, 1980. Used with permission.

### Diagnostic Criteria for Transvestism*

A. Recurrent and persistent cross-dressing by a heterosexual male.

B. Use of cross-dressing for the purpose of sexual excitement, at least initially in the course of the disorder.

C. Intense frustration when the cross-dressing is interfered with.

D. Does not meet the criteria for transsexualism.

* From American Psychiatric Association: *Diagnostic and Statistical Manual of Mental Disorders*, ed 3. American Psychiatric Association, Washington, DC, 1980. Used with permission.

*recurrent.* Masochistic practices tend to be more common in men.

Although relatively pure masochists do exist, the most common finding is that the perversion is preferred, but not exclusive. In other words, masochists also indulge in sadistic fantasies and practices and *are often quite able to take the opposite role with arousal and pleasure.*

The DSM-III diagnostic criteria for sexual masochism are listed in the table below.

**20.8.   The answer is A** (*Synopsis*, ed. 4, page 457).

DSM-III consolidates the Masters and Johnson excitement and plateau phases into a single excitement phase and precedes it with its unique appetitive phase. The orgasm and resolution phases remain the same as originally described by Masters and Johnson.

**DSM-III Phase I:** *Appetitive.* This phase is distinct from any identified solely through physiology and reflects the psychiatrist's fundamental concern with motivations, drives, and personality. The phase is characterized by sexual fantasies and the desire to have sexual activity.

**DSM-III Phase II:** *Excitement.* This phase consists of a subjective sense of sexual pleasure and accompanying physiological changes. All the physiological responses noted in Masters and Johnson's excitement and plateau phases are combined under this phase.

**DSM-III Phase III:** *Orgasm.* This phase consists of a peaking of sexual pleasure, with release of sexual tension and rhythmic contraction of the perineal muscles and pelvic reproductive organs. The phase is identical to Masters and Johnson's Phase III.

**DSM-III Phase IV:** *Resolution.* This phase entails a sense of general relaxation, well-being, and muscular relaxation. This phase as defined does not differ from the Masters and Johnson resolution phase.

See the tables on pages 267, 268, and 269 for a thorough survey of the male and female sexual response cycles.

**20.9.   The answer is A** (*Synopsis*, ed. 4, page 435).

Experts theorize that *transsexualism must be the result of genetic, hormonal, or central nervous system factors, but no such evidence has been found in humans.* The only biological contribution that appears to contribute to its etiology is the presence in boys of an exceptional beauty and grace; however, of course it is very rare for beautiful boys to become transsexuals. Transsexualism is defined as *a deep sense of discomfort about one's anatomical sex,* a belief that one is trapped inside the wrong sex body, and *a wish to be rid of one's own genitals* and live as a member of the opposite sex.

The table on page 270 lists the DSM-III diagnostic criteria for this disorder.

**20.10.   The answer is E** (*Synopsis*, ed. 4, page 459).

*Mumps* is an acute infectious and contagious disease caused by Paramyxovirus; it is characterized by inflammation and swelling of the parotid gland and sometimes of other glands, and occasionally there is inflammation of the testes, ovary, pancreas, and meninges.

*Atherosclerotic disease* is characterized by irregularly distributed lipid deposits in the intima of large and medium-sized arteries. These de-

### Diagnostic Criteria for Sexual Masochism*

Either (1) or (2):

1. A preferred or exclusive mode of producing sexual excitement is to be humiliated, bound, beaten, or otherwise made to suffer;

2. The individual has intentionally participated in an activity in which he or she was physically harmed or his or her life was threatened, in order to produce sexual excitement.

* From American Psychiatric Association: *Diagnostic and Statistical Manual of Mental Disorders*, ed 3. American Psychiatric Association, Washington, DC, 1980. Used with permission.

## The Male Sexual Response Cycle*†

| | I. Excitement Phase‡ (several minutes to hours) | II. Plateau Phase‡ (30 sec to 3 min) | III. Orgasmic Phase (3–15 sec) | IV. Resolution Phase (10–15 min.; if no orgasm, ½–1 day) |
|---|---|---|---|---|
| Skin | No change | Sexual flush: inconsistently appears; maculopapular rash originates on abdomen and spreads to anterior chest wall, face, and neck and can include shoulders and forearms | Well-developed flush | Flush disappears in reverse order of appearance; inconsistently appearing film of perspiration on soles of feet and palms of hands |
| Penis | Erection within 10–30 sec caused by vasocongestion of erectile bodies of corpus cavernosa of shaft; loss of erection may occur with introduction of asexual stimulus, loud noise | Increase in size of glans and diameter of penile shaft; inconsistent deepening of coronal and glans coloration | Ejaculation: marked by 3 to 4 contractions at 0.8 sec of vas, seminal vesicles, prostate, and urethra; followed by minor contraction with increasing intervals | Erection: partial involution in 5–10 sec with variable refractory period; full detumescence in 5–30 min |
| Scrotum and testes | Tightening and lifting of scrotal sac and partial elevation of testes toward perineum | 50 percent increase in size of testes over unstimulated state due to vasocongestion and flattening of testes against perineum signaling impending ejaculation | No change | Decrease to base line size due to loss of vasocongestion; testicular and scrotal descent within 5–30 min after orgasm; involution may take several hours if there is no orgasmic release |
| Cowper's glands | No change | 2–3 drops of mucoid fluid that contain viable sperm | No change | No change |
| Other | Breasts: inconsistent nipple erection | Myotonia: semispastic contraction of facial, abdominal, and intercostal muscles. Tachycardia: up to 175 per min Blood pressure: rise in systolic 20–80 mm; in diastolic 10–40 mm Respiration: increased | Loss of voluntary muscular control Rectum: rhythmical contractions of sphincter Up to 180 beats per min 40–100 systolic; 20–50 diastolic Up to 40 respirations per min Ejaculatory spurt: 12–20 inches at age 18 decreasing with age to seepage at 70 | Return to base line state in 5–10 min |

* Table prepared by Virginia A. Sadock, M.D., after Masters and Johnson data.

† The appetitive stage is not included in this table because it has no physiological component and consists only of fantasy. This also applies to the female sexual response cycle. The appetitive stage was not described by Masters and Johnson.

‡ In DSM-III, the excitement phase and the plateau phase are combined into one phase called the excitement phase.

### The Female Sexual Response Cycle*

| | I. Excitement Phase† (several minutes to hours) | II. Plateau Phase† (30 sec to 3 min) | III. Orgasmic Phase (3–15 sec) | IV. Resolution Phase (10–15 min; if no orgasm, ½–1 day) |
|---|---|---|---|---|
| Skin | No change | Sexual flush inconstant except in fair skinned; pink mottling on abdomen, spreads to breasts, neck, face, often to arms, thighs and buttocks—looks like measles rash | No change (flush at its peak) | Fine perspiration, mostly on flush areas; flush disappears in reverse order |
| Breasts | Nipple erection in two-thirds of subjects Venous congestion Areolar enlargement | Flush: mottling coalesces to form a red papillary rash Size: increase one-fourth over normal, especially in breasts that have not nursed Aerolae: enlarge; impinge on nipples so they seem to disappear | No change (venous tree pattern stands out sharply; breasts may become tremulous) | Return to normal in reverse order of appearance in ½ hour or more |
| Clitoris | Glans: half of subjects, no change visible, but with colposcope, enlargement always observed; half of subjects, glans diameter always increased 2-fold or more Shaft: variable increase in diameter; elongation occurs in only 10 percent of subjects | Retraction: shaft withdraws deep into swollen prepuce; just before orgasm, it is difficult to visualize; may relax and retract several times if phase II is unduly prolonged Intrapreputial movement with thrusting: movements synchronized with thrusting owing to traction on labia minor and prepuce | No change Shaft movements continue throughout if thrusting is maintained | Shaft returns to normal position in 5–10 sec; full detumescence in 5–30 min (if no orgasm, clitoris remains engorged for several hours) |
| Labia majora | Nullipara: thin down; elevated; flatten against perineum Multipara: rapid congestion and edema; increases to 2–3 times normal size | Nullipara: totally disappear (may reswell if phase II unduly prolonged) Multipara: become so enlarged and edematous, they hang like folds of a heavy curtain | No change | Nullipara: *increase* to normal size in 1–2 min or less Multipara: *decrease* to normal size in 10–15 min |
| Labia minora | Color change: to bright pink in nullipara and red in multipara Size: increase 2–3 times over normal; prepuce often much more; proximal portion firms, adding up to ¾ inch to functional vaginal sidewalls | Color change: suddenly turn bright red in nullipara, burgundy red in multipara, signifies onet of phase II; orgasm will then always follow within 3 min if stimulation is continued Size: enlarged labia gap widely to form a vestibular funnel into vaginal orifice | Firm proximal areas contract with contractions of lower third | Returns to pink blotchy color in 2 min or less; total resolution of color and size in 5 min (decoloration, clitoral return and detumescence of lower third all occur as rapidly as loss of the erection in men) |

## The Female Sexual Response Cycle (*continued*)*

| | I. Excitement Phase†<br>(several minutes to hours) | II. Plateau Phase†<br>(30 sec to 3 min) | III. Orgasmic Phase<br>(3–15 sec) | IV. Resolution Phase<br>(10–15 min; if no orgasm, ½–1 day) |
|---|---|---|---|---|
| Barthol-in's glands | No change | A few drops of mucoid secretion form; aid in lubricating vestibule (insufficient to lubricate vagina) | No change | No change |
| Vagina | Vaginal transudate: appears 10–30 sec after onset of arousal; drops of clear fluid coalesce to form a well-lubricated vaginal barrel (aids in buffering acidity of vagina to neutral pH required by sperm)<br>Color change: mucosa turns patchy purple | Copious transudate continues to form; quality of transudate generally increased only by prolonging preorgasm stimulation (increased flow occurs during premenstrual period)<br>Color change: uniform dark purple mucosa | No change (transudate provides maximum degree of lubrication) | Some transudate collects on floor of the upper two-thirds formed by its posterior wall (in supine position); ejaculate deposited in this area forming seminal pool |
| Upper two-thirds | Balloons: dilates convulsively as uterus moves up, pulling anterior vaginal wall with it; fornices lengthen; rugae flatten | Further ballooning creates diameter of 2½–3 inches; then wall relaxes in a slow, tensionless manner | No change: fully ballooned out and motionless | Cervical descent: descends to seminal pool in 3–4 min |
| Lower third | Dilation of vaginal lumen to 1–1¼ inches occurs; congestion of wall proceeds gradually, increasing in rate as phase II approaches | Maximum distension reached rapidly; contracts lumen of lower third and upper labia to ½ or more its diameter in phase I; contraction around penis allows thrusting traction on clitoral shaft via labia and prepuce | 3–15 contractions of lower third and proximal labia minora at ⅓-sec intervals | Congestion disappears in seconds (if no orgasm, congestion persists for 20–30 min) |
| Uterus | Ascent: moves into false pelvis late in phase I<br>Cervix: passively elevated with uterus (no evidence of any cervical secretions during entire cycle) | Contractions: strong sustained contractions begin late in phase II; have same rhythm as contractions late in labor, lasting 2+ min<br>Cervic: slight swelling; patchy purple (inconstant; related to chronic cervicitis) | Contractions throughout orgasm; strongest with pregnancy and masturbation | Descent: slowly returns to normal<br>Cervice: color and size return to normal in 4 min; patulous for 10 min |
| Others | Fourchette: color changes throughout cycle as in labia minora | Perineal body: spasmodic tightening with involuntary elevation of perineum<br>Hyperventilation and carpopedal spasms; both are usually present, the latter less frequently and only in female-supine position | Irregular spasms continue<br>Rectum: rhythmical contractions inconstant; more apt to occur with masturbation than coitus<br>External urethral sphincter: occasional contraction, no urine loss | All reactions cease abruptly or within a few seconds |

\* From *The Nature and Evolution of Female Sexuality*, by Mary Jane Sherfey, Copyright 1966, 1972 by Mary Jane Sherfey. Reprinted by permission of Random House, Inc.

† In DSM-III, the excitement phase and the plateau phase are combined into one phase called the excitement phase.

### Diagnostic Criteria for Transsexualism*

A. Sense of discomfort and inappropriateness about one's anatomic sex.

B. Wish to be rid of one's own genitals and to live as a member of the other sex.

C. The disturbance has been *continuous (not limited to periods of stress) for at least 2 years.*

D. *Absence of physical intersex or genetic abnormality.*

E. Not due to another mental disorder, such as schizophrenia.

---

\* From American Psychiatric Association: *Diagnostic and Statistical Manual of Mental Disorders,* ed 3. American Psychiatric Association, Washington, DC, 1980. Used with permission.

---

posits are associated with fibrosis and calcification and are almost always present to some degree in the middle-aged and elderly. In its severe form, atherosclerosis may lead to arterial narrowing, and the following disorders can occur: angina pectoris, myocardial infarction, strokes, intermittent claudication, and gangrene of the lower extremities.

*Klinefelter's syndrome* is a chromosomal anomaly in which there is an extra X chromosome (karyotype 47-XXY). Affected persons are male in development, with small firm testes, eunuchoid habitus, variable gynecomastia and other signs of androgen deficiency, and elevated gonadotropin levels. There is an increased frequency of mental retardation (about 25 percent) and other forms of psychopathology, particularly antisocial behavior and delinquency.

*Multiple sclerosis* is one of the demyelinating diseases of the central nervous system and, at least in temperate zones, one of the most common neurological disorders. It is characterized pathologically by swelling and then demyelination of the medullary sheath, which is followed by glial proliferation. The result is an irregular scattering of well-demarcated sclerotic plaques throughout the white and gray matter of the brain and spinal cord.

**20.11.   The answer is C** (*Synopsis,* ed. 4, pages 453, 456, and 457).

In the woman, orgasm is characterized by 3 to 15 involuntary contractions of the lower third of the vagina and by *strong sustained contractions of the uterus,* flowing from the fundus downward to the cervix. *Both men and women have involuntary contractions of the internal and external sphincter.* These and the other contractions during orgasm occur at intervals of 0.8 second. Other manifestations include voluntary and involuntary movements of the large muscle groups, including facial grimacing and *carpopedal spasm. Systolic blood pressure rises* 20 mm, diastolic blood pressure rises 40 mm, and the heart rate increases up to 160 beats a minute. Orgasm lasts from 3 to 15 seconds and is associated with a *slight clouding of consciousness.*

The parasympathetic nervous system activates the process of erection. The pelvic splanchnic nerves (S2, S3, and S4) stimulate the blood vessels of the area to dilate, causing the penis to become erect. In ejaculation, the sympathetic nervous system is involved. Through its hypogastric plexus, the sympathetic nervous system innervates the urethral crest and the muscles of the epididymis, vas deferens, seminal vesicles, and prostate. Stimulation of the plexus causes ejaculation of seminal fluid from those glands and ducts into the urethra. That passage of fluid into the urethra provides the man with a sensation of impending climax called the stage of ejaculatory inevitability. Indeed, once the prostate contracts, ejaculation is inevitable. The ejaculate is propelled through the penis by urethral contractions. The ejaculate consists of about 1 teaspoon (2.5 ml) of fluid and contains about 120 million sperm cells.

**20.12.   The answer is A** (*Synopsis,* ed. 4, page 459).

*Measuring nocturnal penile tumescence* is the simplest and most effective way of differentiating psychogenic from organic impotence. Normally, erections occur during sleep and are associated with rapid-eye-movement (REM) sleep. By the use of a simple strain gauge, the presence or absence of an erection can be determined. In cases where organic factors account for the impotence, there will be no nocturnal erections.

The *glucose tolerance curve* measures the metabolism of glucose over a specific period of time and is useful in diagnosing diabetes. *Follicle-stimulating hormone* is a hormone produced by the anterior pituitary that stimulates the secretion of estrogen in the female from the ovarian follicle and is also responsible for sperm production from the testes in men. A *cystometric examination* is a measure of bladder capacity, sensation, and residual urine. *Testosterone* is the male hormone produced by the interstitial cells of the testes. In the male, a low testosterone level produces a lack of desire as the chief complaint, which may be associated with impotence.

**20.13.   The answer is A (1, 2, 3)** (*Synopsis*, ed. 4, page 436).

Female transsexuals are the most masculine of females. These *anatomically normal females* have been masculine since early childhood and have not had episodes in their lives when they expressed femininity. Like the males, they are *exclusively homosexual if measured by the anatomy of their sex objects*, but heterosexual if measured by identity. They, like the males, *do not deny their anatomical sex* but are, nonetheless, unendingly preoccupied with the sense of really being men and with the *desire to have their bodies changed to male*. Although males can surgically receive a genital that can function in a female manner—even including, at times, capacity for orgasm—it is not yet possible to give a female functioning testes or a penis. With testosterone, mastectomy, and panhysterectomy, however, the patient can pass as a man.

**20.14.   The answer is E (all)** (*Synopsis*, ed. 4, page 472).

Accurate figures of the incidence of incest are difficult to obtain because of the general shame and embarrassment of the entire family that is involved. Females are victims more often than males. About *15 million women in the United States have been the object of incestuous attention*, and *one-third of sexually abused persons have been molested before the age of 9*.

Incestuous behavior is much *more frequently reported among families of low socioeconomic status* than among other families. This difference may be due to greater contact with reporting officials, such as welfare workers, public health personnel, and law enforcement agents, and is not a true reflection of higher incidence in that demographic group. Incest is more easily hidden by economically stable families than by the poor.

Social, cultural, physiological, and psychological factors all contribute to the breakdown of the incest taboo. Incestuous behavior has been associated with alcoholism, overcrowding and increased physical proximity, and rural isolation that prevents adequate extrafamilial contacts. Some communities may be more tolerant of incestuous behavior than is society in general. Major mental illnesses and intellectual deficiencies have been described in some cases of clinical incest. Some family therapists view incest as a defense designed to maintain a dysfunctional family unit. The older and stronger participant in incestuous behavior is usually male. Thus, incest may be viewed as a form of child abuse or as a variant of rape.

*Father-daughter incest is reported to be more common* than either sibling incest or mother-son incest. Many cases of sibling incest are denied by parents, or involve near-normal interaction if the activity is prepubertal sexual play and exploration.

**20.15.   The answer is A (1, 2, 3)** (*Synopsis*, ed. 4, page 449).

Exhibitionism is defined as repetitive acts of *exposing the genitals to an unsuspecting stranger*, with *the usual awareness of a wish to shock or surprise the victim*. The acts are for *the purpose of sexual excitement*, and at times the individual masturbates during the exposure. Exhibitionists are *usually not physically dangerous to the victim*. The condition apparently only occurs in males.

The table below gives the DSM-III diagnostic criteria for this disorder.

**20.16.   The answer is D (4)** (*Synopsis*, ed. 4, pages 457 and 458).

Desire disorders are not new, although they have recently become the focus of much attention. Patients with desire problems often have good ego strengths and use inhibition of desire in a defensive way to *protect against unconscious fears about sex*. Lack of desire can also be the result of chronic stress, anxiety, or depression.

Inhibited sexual desire is experienced by *both men and women*, who may not be hampered by any dysfunction once they are involved in the sex act. Lack of desire may be expressed by *decreased frequency of coitus*, perception of the partner as unattractive, or overt complaints of lack of desire.

The need for sexual contact and satisfaction varies among individuals, as well as in the same person over time. In a group of 100 couples with stable marriages, 8 percent reported having intercourse less than once a month. In another group of couples, one-third reported lack of sexual relations for periods of time averaging 8 weeks. Masters believes that lack of desire may be a *common complaint among married couples*; the true incidence, however, is not known.

The table on page 272 lists the DSM-III diagnostic criteria for inhibited sexual desire.

---

**Diagnostic Criteria for Exhibitionism***

Repetitive acts of exposing the genitals to an unsuspecting stranger for the purpose of achieving sexual excitement, with no attempt at further sexual activity with the stranger.

---

\* From American Psychiatric Association: *Diagnostic and Statistical Manual of Mental Disorders*, ed 3. American Psychiatric Association, Washington, DC, 1980. Used with permission.

## Diagnostic Criteria for Inhibited Sexual Desire*

A. Persistent and pervasive inhibition of sexual desire. The judgment of inhibition is made by the clinician taking into account factors that affect sexual desire, such as age, sex, health, intensity and frequency of sexual desire, and the context of the individual's life. In actual practice this diagnosis is rarely made unless the lack of desire is a source of distress to either the individual or his or her partner. Frequently, this category is used in conjunction with one or more of the other psychosexual dysfunction categories.

B. The disturbance is not caused exclusively by organic factors, e.g. physical disorder or medication, and is not due to another Axis I disorder.

* From American Psychiatric Association: *Diagnostic and Statistical Manual of Mental Disorders*, ed 3. American Psychiatric Association, Washington, DC, 1980. Used with permission.

**20.17.   The answer is D (4)** (*Synopsis*, ed. 4, page 466).

In cases of premature ejaculation, an exercise known as the squeeze technique is used *to raise the threshold of penile excitability*. In that exercise, the man or woman stimulates the erect penis *until the earliest sensations of impending ejaculation are felt*. At that point, the woman forcefully squeezes the coronal ridge of the glans, the erection is diminished, and ejaculation is inhibited. (See the figure below.) The exercise program eventually raises the threshold of the sensation of ejaculatory inevitability and allows the man to become more aware of his sexual sensations and confident about his sexual performance. A variant of the exercise is the stop-start technique, developed by J. H. Semans, in which the woman stops all stimulation of the penis when the man first senses an impending ejaculation. No squeeze is used. Research has shown that the presence or absence of circumcision has no bearing on a man's ejaculatory control. The glans is equally sensitive in either state.

**(Courtesy of Lyle Stuart, Inc.)**

In *secondary impotence*, the man has been potent and has developed his impotence subsequently. *Ejaculatory inevitability* was described by William Masters as that point at which the man cannot prevent his ejaculation from coming.

In cases of vaginismus the woman is advised to dilate her vaginal opening with her fingers or with *size-graduated dilators*.

The DSM-III diagnostic criteria for premature ejaculation are listed in the table on the facing page.

**20.18.   The answer is A (1, 2, 3)** (*Synopsis*, ed. 4, page 463).

Dyspareunia refers to recurrent and persistent pain during intercourse in either the man or the woman. The dysfunction *is related to and often coincides with vaginismus*. Repeated episodes of vaginismus may lead to dyspareunia and vice versa, but in either case somatic causes must be ruled out. Dyspareunia should not be diagnosed when an organic basis for the pain is found, or when, in a woman, it is associated with vaginismus or with lack of lubrication.

The true incidence of dyspareunia is unknown, but it has been estimated that *30 percent of surgical procedures on the female genital area result in temporary dyspareunia*. Additionally, of women with this complaint who are seen in sex therapy clinics, 30 to 40 percent have pelvic pathology.

Organic abnormalities leading to dyspareunia and vaginismus include irritated or infected hymenal remnants, episiotomy scars, Bartholin's gland infection, various forms of vaginitis and cervicitis, endometriosis, and other pelvic disorders. The postmenopausal woman may develop dyspareunia resulting from thinning of the vaginal mucosa and lessened lubrication. Dynamic factors are usually considered causative, although situational factors probably account more for secondary dysfunctions. Painful coitus may result from *tension and anxiety* about the sex act that causes the woman to involuntarily tense her vaginal muscles. The *pain is real* and makes intercourse unbearable or unpleasant. The anticipation of further pain may cause the woman to avoid coitus altogether.

The DSM-III diagnostic criteria for dyspareunia and vaginismus are listed in the tables that follow on the facing page.

**20.19.   The answer is C (2, 4)** (*Synopsis*, ed. 4, page 451).

Zoophilia is defined as the act or fantasy of engaging in sexual activity with animals as a repeatedly preferred or exclusive method of achieving sexual excitement. These activities

### Diagnostic Criteria for Premature Ejaculation*

A. Ejaculation occurs before the individual wishes it, because of recurrent and persistent absence of reasonable voluntary control of ejaculation and orgasm during sexual activity. The judgment of "reasonable control" is made by the clinician taking into account factors that affect duration of the excitement phase, such as age, novelty of the sexual partner, and the frequency and duration of coitus.

B. The disturbance is not due to another Axis I disorder.

* From American Psychiatric Association: *Diagnostic and Statistical Manual of Mental Disorders*, ed 3. American Psychiatric Association, Washington, DC, 1980. Used with permission.

### Diagnostic Criteria for Functional Dyspareunia*

A. Coitus is associated with recurrent and persistent genital pain, in either the male or the female.

B. The disturbance is not caused exclusively by a physical disorder and is not due to lack of lubrication, functional vaginismus, or another Axis I disorder.

* From American Psychiatric Association: *Diagnostic and Statistical Manual of Mental Disorders*, ed 3. American Psychiatric Association, Washington, DC, 1980. Used with permission.

### Diagnostic Criteria for Functional Vaginismus*

A. There is a history of recurrent and persistent involuntary spasm of the musculature of the outer third of the vagina that interferes with coitus.

B. The disturbance is not caused exclusively by a physical disorder and is not due to another Axis I disorder.

* From American Psychiatric Association: *Diagnostic and Statistical Manual of Mental Disorders*, ed 3. American Psychiatric Association, Washington, DC, 1980. Used with permission.

may include *intercourse*, licking, rubbing, *masturbation*, or *oral-genital contact*.

In this disorder, *the animal is preferred no matter what other forms of sexual outlet are available*, although at times, sexual relations with animals may be *an outgrowth of availability or convenience*. This act occurs most often in situations of enforced isolation with proximity to animals. Over a time, the animal becomes the most powerful sexual stimulus, even though initially there may also have been sexual arousal by humans. The preferred and exclusive use of animals occurs by early adulthood, and *the course then becomes chronic*.

The DSM-III diagnostic criteria for zoophilia are listed in the table below.

**20.20.   The answer is E (all)** (*Synopsis*, ed. 4, pages 460 and 461).

The *effects of various drugs on sexual functioning in women have not been studied as exten-* *sively as they have been in men*. In general, however, *women appear to be less vulnerable to pharmacologically induced sexual dysfunction than are men*. Oral contraceptives are reported to decrease libido in some women, and the monoamine oxidase inhibitor *phenelzine impairs the orgasmic response in some women*. Both an increase and decrease in libido have been reported with various psychoactive agents in women. *Sexual dysfunction associated with the use of a drug disappears when the drug is discontinued*.

The DSM-III diagnostic criteria for inhibited orgasm in women, which can occur with drugs, are described in the table on page 274.

**20.21.   The answer is B (1, 3)** (*Synopsis*, ed. 4, page 469).

Statistics show that *61 percent of rapists are under age 25*, 51 percent are white and tend to rape white victims, *47 percent are black and tend*

### Diagnostic Criteria for Zoophilia*

The act or fantasy of engaging in sexual activity with animals is a repeatedly preferred or exclusive method of achieving sexual excitement.

* From American Psychiatric Association: *Diagnostic and Statistical Manual of Mental Disorders*, ed 3. American Psychiatric Association, Washington, DC, 1980. Used with permission.

### Diagnostic Criteria for Inhibited Female Orgasm*

A. Recurrent and persistent inhibition of the female orgasm as manifested by a delay in or absence of orgasm following a normal sexual excitement phase during sexual activity that is judged by the clinician to be adequate in focus, intensity, and duration. The same individual may also meet the criteria for inhibited sexual excitement if at other times there is a problem with the excitement phase of sexual activity. In such cases, both categories of psychosexual dysfunction should be noted.

Some women are able to experience orgasm during noncoital clitoral stimulation, but are unable to experience it during coitus in the absence of manual clitoral stimulation. There is evidence to suggest that in some instances this represents a pathological inhibition that justifies this diagnosis, whereas in other instances it represents a normal variation of the female sexual response. This difficult judgment is assisted by a thorough sexual evaluation that may even require a trial of treatment.

B. The disturbance is not caused exclusively by organic factors, e.g. physical disorder or medication, and is not due to another Axis I disorder.

* From American Psychiatric Association: *Diagnostic and Statistical Manual of Mental Disorders*, ed 3. American Psychiatric Association, Washington, DC, 1980. Used with permission.

---

*to rape black victims*, and the remaining 2 percent come from all other races. A composite picture of a rapist drawn from police figures portrays a single, 19-year-old man from the lower socioeconomic classes *with a police record* of acquisitive offenses.

Studies of convicted rapists suggest that the crime is committed to relieve pent-up aggressive energies against persons toward whom the rapist is in some awe. Although these awesome (to the rapist) persons are usually men, the retaliatory violence is directed toward a woman. This finding dovetails with feminist theory, which proposes that the woman serves as an object for the displacement of aggression that the rapist cannot express directly toward other men. The woman is considered the property or vulnerable possession of men and is the rapist's instrument for revenge against other men.

Rape often occurs as an accompaniment to another crime. The rapist always threatens his victim with fists, gun, or knife and frequently harms her in nonsexual ways, as well as sexual ways. The victim may be beaten, wounded, and sometimes killed.

**20.22.   The answer is E (all)** (*Synopsis*, ed. 4, pages 458 and 459).

Psychosexual dysfunction with inhibited sexual excitement involves recurrent and persistent inhibition during sexual activity, manifested either by *the man's partial or complete failure to attain or maintain an erection* until the completion of the sex act or by *the woman's partial or complete failure to attain or maintain the lubrication-swelling response of sexual excitement* until the completion of the sexual act. The diagnosis is made in the light of clinical judgment that takes into account the focus, intensity, and the duration of the sexual activity in which the patient engages.

Women who have excitement-phase dysfunction often have *orgasmic problems* as well. In one series of relatively happily married couples, 33 percent of the women described difficulty in maintaining sexual excitement.

Numerous psychological factors are associated with female sexual inhibition. These conflicts may be expressed through inhibition of excitement or orgasm and are discussed under orgasmic phase dysfunctions. In some women, excitement-phase disorders are associated with dyspareunia or with lack of desire.

Less research has been done on physiological components of dysfunction in women than in men, but some recent work suggests a possible hormonal pattern contributing to responsiveness in women with desire and excitement phase dysfunction. Masters and Johnson found normally responsive women to be particularly desirous of sex premenstrually. In a recent study, dysfunctional women tended to be more responsive immediately following their periods. A third group of dysfunctional women felt the greatest sexual excitement at the time of ovulation.

Inhibited sexual excitement in the male is also called erectile dysfunction or impotence. In primary impotence, the man has never been able to obtain an erection sufficient for vaginal insertion. In secondary impotence, the man has successfully achieved vaginal penetration at some time in his sexual life, but is later unable to do so. In selective impotence, the man is able to have coitus in certain circumstances, but not in others; for example, a man may function effectively with a prostitute, but may be impotent with his wife.

It was estimated by Kinsey that a few men (2 to 4 percent) are impotent at age 35, but 77 percent are impotent at age 80. More recently, it has been found that the incidence of primary impotence in men 35 years old or under is about

1 percent. Masters and Johnson report a fear of impotence in all men over 40, which the researchers believe reflects the masculine fear of loss of virility with advancing age. (As it happens, however, impotence is not a regularly occurring phenomenon in the aged; having an available sexual partner is more closely related to continuing potency in the aging man than is age per se.) More than 50 percent of all men treated for sexual disorders have impotence as the chief complaint. The incidence of psychological as opposed to organic impotence has been the focus of many recent studies. Impotence may be physiologically due to a variety of organic causes. Some workers have reported an incidence of organic impotence in a medical clinic outpatient population as high as 75 percent. Other researchers believe that these same populations have not had adequate psychological screening and maintain that in more than 90 percent of cases the causes of impotence are psychological. In addition, the clinician should be aware of the possible pharmacological effects of medication and drugs, *especially alcohol*, on sexual functioning.

The DSM-III diagnostic criteria for inhibited sexual excitement are given in the table directly below.

**20.23.   The answer is E (all)** (*Synopsis*, ed. 4, page 462).

In *inhibited male orgasm*, also called retarded ejaculation, the man achieves climax during coitus with great difficulty, if at all. A man suffers from primary retarded ejaculation if he has never been able to ejaculate during coitus. The disorder is diagnosed as secondary if it develops after previous normal functioning.

Some workers suggest that a differentiation should be made between orgasm and ejaculation. Certainly, inhibited orgasm must be differentiated from retrograde ejaculation, in which ejaculation occurs but the seminal fluid passes backward into the bladder. The latter condition always has an organic cause. Retrograde ejaculation can develop after genitourinary surgery and is also associated with medications that have anticholinergic side effects, such as the phenothiazines.

*The incidence of inhibited male orgasm is much lower than that of premature ejaculation* and impotence. Masters and Johnson reported only 3.8 percent in one group of 447 sexual dysfunction cases. This problem is more common among men with obsessive-compulsive disorders than among others.

Inhibited male orgasm may have physiological causes and can occur *after surgery of the genitourinary tract, such as prostatectomy*. It may also be associated with Parkinson's disease and other neurological disorders involving the lumbar or sacral sections of the spinal cord. The *antihypertensive drugs* guanethidine and methyldopa, as well as the phenothiazines, have been implicated in retarded ejaculation.

The DSM-III diagnostic criteria for inhibited male orgasm are listed in the table below.

### Diagnostic Criteria for Inhibited Sexual Excitement*

A. Recurrent and persistent inhibition of sexual excitement during sexual activity, manifested by:

*In males*, partial or complete failure to attain or maintain erection until completion of the sexual act, or
*In females*, partial or complete failure to attain or maintain the lubrication-swelling response of sexual excitement until completion of the sexual act.

B. A clinical judgment that the individual engages in sexual activity that is adequate in focus, intensity, and duration.

C. The disturbance is not caused exclusively by organic factors, e.g. physical disorder or medication, and is not due to another Axis I disorder.

* From American Psychiatric Association: *Diagnostic and Statistical Manual of Mental Disorders*, ed 3. American Psychiatric Association, Washington, DC, 1980. Used with permission.

### Diagnostic Criteria for Inhibited Male Orgasm*

A. Recurrent and persistent inhibition of the male orgasm as manifested by a delay in or absence of ejaculation following an adequate phase of sexual excitement. The same individual may also meet the criteria for inhibited sexual excitement if at other times there is a problem with the excitement phase of sexual activity. In such cases, both categories of pychosexual dysfunction should be noted.

B. The disturbance is not caused exclusively by organic factors, e.g. physical disorder or medication, and is not due to another Axis I disorder.

* From American Psychiatric Association: *Diagnostic and Statistical Manual of Mental Disorders*, ed 3. American Psychiatric Association, Washington, DC, 1980. Used with permission.

**20.24.   The answer is A (1, 2, 3)** (*Synopsis*, ed. 4, page 443).

Ego-dystonic homosexuality *is classified as a psychosexual disorder in DSM-III.* Generally, individuals with this disorder have had homosexual relationships, but are persistently emotionally upset by them because of strong negative feelings associated with homosexuality. Typically, there is *a history of unsuccessfully initiated or sustained heterosexual relationships.* The *patterns of overt homosexual arousal are explicitly stated to be unwanted and a persistent source of distress.*

The table below gives the DSM-III diagnostic criteria for this disorder.

**20.25.   The answer is E (all)** (*Synopsis*, ed. 4, page 451).

Atypical paraphilias are those sexual perversions associated primarily with excretory functions. They include *coprophilia* (feces), *urophilia* (urine), *klismaphilia* (enemas), and *mysophilia* (filth). They are characterized by urination or defecation on or around sexual partners, the administration of enemas, and such derivative practices as obscenity during intercourse. Associated with these perversions is a fascination with dirtiness and soiling, the unifying feature being the incorporation of excretory processes or their close substitutes into sexual activity.

**20.26.   The answer is A (1, 2, 3)** (*Synopsis*, ed. 4, page 435).

Gender identity disorder of childhood is characterized by an *onset of the disturbance before puberty in both males and females.* This disorder is also characterized by the *persistently stated desire to be a member of the opposite sex.* Both the girl and boy *repudiate persistently their own anatomical structures* in preference for that of the opposite sex.

The table at the top of page 277 details the DSM-III diagnostic criteria for this disorder.

**20.27.   The answer is B (1, 3)** (*Synopsis*, ed. 4, page 449).

*Voyeurism is the repetitive looking at unsuspecting people* who are naked, undressing, or engaged in sexual activity. This act of looking is the repeatedly preferred or exclusive method of achieving sexual excitement, with *orgasm occurring with masturbation during or after the event.* The act of looking itself is what can lead to sexual arousal, and *no sexual activity with the observed person is sought or desired. Watching pornography is not the same thing as voyeurism,* although it is an act of looking that may cause sexual excitement. The difference is that, in pornography, the people being observed are willingly and knowingly being observed; they are not unsuspecting.

The DSM-III diagnostic criteria for voyeurism are listed in the table on the facing page.

**20.28.   The answer is A (1, 2, 3)** (*Synopsis*, ed. 4, page 437).

In DSM-III, transvestism is defined as "recurrent and persistent cross-dressing by a *heterosexual male* in the absence of the transsexual syndrome." It is diagnosed when the cross-dressing *relieves anxiety or gender discomfort.* When *sexual arousal is caused by the cross-dressing,* the diagnosis of fetishism is added.

Most transvestites are overtly heterosexual and marry. They work in professions requiring masculine interests and behavior; they dress, except when cross-dressed, in masculine clothes; and they have masculine interests and hobbies and engage in masculine sports. *Cross-dressing begins in childhood or early adolescence.*

**20.29.   The answer is B (1, 3)** (*Synopsis*, ed. 4, page 449).

*Sexual sadism is characterized by the achievement of sexual excitement through the infliction of physical or psychological suffering on another person. This behavior may occur with both consenting and nonconsenting partners. Sexually sadistic fantasies are likely to be present in childhood,* although overt sexually sadistic activities usually occur in early adulthood. Rape may be committed by people with this disorder; however, *it cannot be assumed that all or even many rapists are motivated by sexual sadism.* Often a rapist may even lose sexual desire as the result of inflicting suffering.

The DSM-III diagnostic criteria for sexual sadism are listed in the table on page 277.

---

**Diagnostic Criteria for Ego-Dystonic Homosexuality\***

A.  The individual complains that heterosexual arousal is persistently absent or weak and significantly interferes with initiating or maintaining wanted heterosexual relationships.

B.   There is a sustained pattern of homosexual arousal that the individual explicitly states has been unwanted and a persistent source of distress.

---

\* From American Psychiatric Association: *Diagnostic and Statistical Manual of Mental Disorders,* ed 3. American Psychiatric Association, Washington, DC, 1980. Used with permission.

## Diagnostic Criteria for Gender Identity Disorder of Childhood*

*For females:*

A. Strongly and persistently stated desire to be a boy or insistence that she is a boy (not merely a desire for any perceived cultural advantages from being a boy).

B. Persistent repudiation of female anatomic structures, as manifested by at least one of the following repeated assertions:

1. That she will grow up to become a man (not merely in role);
2. That she is biologically unable to become pregnant;
3. That she will not develop breasts;
4. That she has no vagina;
5. That she has, or will grow, a penis.

C. Onset of the disturbance before puberty. (For adults and adolescents, see atypical gender identity disorder.)

*For males:*

A. Strongly and persistently stated desire to be a girl or insistence that he is a girl.

B. Either (1) or (2):

1. Persistent repudiation of male anatomic structures, as manifested by at least one of the following repeated assertions:

a. That he will grow up to become a woman (not merely in role);
b. That his penis or testes are disgusting or will disappear;
c. That it would be better not to have a penis or testes.

2. *Preoccupation with female stereotypical activities as manifested by a preference for either cross-dressing* or simulating female attire or by a compelling desire to participate in the games and pastimes of girls.

C. Onset of the disturbance before puberty. (For adults and adolescents, see atypical gender identity disorder.)

* From American Psychiatric Association: *Diagnostic and Statistical Manual of Mental Disorders*, ed 3. American Psychiatric Association, Washington, DC, 1980. Used with permission.

## Diagnostic Criteria for Voyeurism*

A. The individual repeatedly observes unsuspecting people who are naked, in the act of disrobing, or engaging in sexual activity, and no sexual activity with the observed people is sought.

B. The observing is the repeatedly preferrred or exclusive method of achieving sexual excitement.

* From American Psychiatric Association: *Diagnostic and Statistical Manual of Mental Disorders*, ed 3. American Psychiatric Association, Washington, DC, 1980. Used with permission.

## Diagnostic Criteria for Sexual Sadism*

One of the following:

1. On a nonconsenting partner, the individual has repeatedly intentionally inflicted psychological or physical suffering in order to produce sexual excitement;
2. With a consenting partner, the repeatedly preferred or exclusive mode of achieving sexual excitement combines humiliation with simulated or mildly injurious bodily suffering;
3. On a consenting partner, bodily injury that is extensive, permanent, or possibly mortal is inflicted in order to achieve sexual excitement.

* From American Psychiatric Association: *Diagnostic and Statistical Manual of Mental Disorders*, ed 3. American Psychiatric Association, Washington, DC, 1980. Used with permission.

**20.30.  The answer is A (1, 2, 3)** (*Synopsis*, ed. 4, page 444).

In DSM-III, the diagnosis of ego-dystonic homosexuality is under the category of psychosexual disorders. Its features are the "desire to acquire or *increase heterosexual arousal* so that heterosexual relationships can be initiated or maintained, and a sustained pattern of overt homosexual arousal that the individual explicitly complains is unwanted and a source of distress. *Individuals with this disorder may either have no or very weak heterosexual arousal.* Typically, there is a history of unsuccessful attempts at initiating or sustaining heterosexual relationships. In some cases, no attempt has been made to initiate a heterosexual relationship because of the expectation of lack of sexual responsiveness. In other cases, the individual has been able to have short-lived heterosexual relationships, but complains that his heterosexual impulses are too weak to sustain such relationships. When the disorder is present in an adult, usually there is a strong desire to be able to have children and family life. *Usually individuals with this disorder have had homosexual relationships,* but often without satisfaction because of strong negative feelings regarding homosexuality. In some cases, the negative feelings are so strong that the homosexual arousal has been confined to fantasy." Associated features include loneliness, *guilt, shame,* anxiety, and depression in varying degrees.

**20.31.   The answer is A (1, 2, 3)** (*Synopsis,* ed. 4, page 450).

Pedophilia is defined as the preferential or exclusive mode of achieving arousal through fantasy or activity with prepubertal children. The disorder may begin at any time in adulthood but *most frequently occurs in middle age.* The adult activities or fantasies involving children *may be exclusively heterosexual or exclusively homosexual,* but *adults with this disorder are oriented toward opposite-sex children twice as often as toward children of the same sex.* Heterosexually oriented males tend to prefer 8–10-year-old girls, whereas homosexually oriented males tend to prefer slightly older boys. Apparently, only a small percentage of pedophilia encounters result in injury or death; however, aggression is an inherent component of pedophilia. The perversion *involves dominance and power* over the child and provides the adult with an opportunity to terrify, rather than be terrified.

The DSM-III diagnostic criteria for pedophilia are listed in the table below.

**20.32.   The answer is E (all)** (*Synopsis,* ed. 4, pages 465 and 466).

The theoretical basis of the dual-sex therapy approach is the concept of *the marital unit or dyad as the object of therapy.* The method of dual-sex therapy, the major advance in the diagnosis and treatment of sexual disorders in this century, was originated and developed by William Masters and Virginia Johnson. In dual-sex therapy, there is no acceptance of the idea of a sick half of a patient couple. Both members are involved in a relationship in which there is sexual distress, and both, therefore, must participate in the therapy program.

The sexual problem often reflects other areas of disharmony or misunderstanding in the marriage. The marital relationship as a whole is treated, with emphasis on sexual functioning as a part of that relationship. Psychological and physiological aspects of sexual functioning are discussed, and an educative attitude is used. Suggestions are made for specific sexual activity, and those suggestions are followed in the privacy of the couple's home.

The crux of the program is the roundtable session in which a *male and female therapy team* clarifies, discusses, and works through the problems with the couple. These four-way sessions require active participation on the part of the patients. The aim of the therapy is to establish or reestablish communication within the marital unit. Sex is emphasized as a natural function that flourishes in the appropriate domestic climate, and improved communication is encouraged toward that end.

Treatment is short-term and is behaviorally oriented. The therapists attempt to reflect the situation as they see it, rather than interpret underlying dynamics. An undistorted picture of the relationship presented by the psychiatrist often corrects the myopic, narrow view held individually by each marriage partner. The new perspective can interrupt the vicious cycle of relating in which the couple have been caught, and improved, more effective communication can be encouraged.

*Specific exercises are prescribed* for the couple to help them with their particular problem. Sexual inadequacy often involves lack of information, misinformation, and performance fear. The couples are, therefore, specifically prohibited

---

### Diagnostic Criteria for Pedophilia*

A. The act or fantasy of engaging in sexual activity with prepubertal children is a repeatedly preferred or exclusive method of achieving sexual excitement.

B. If the individual is an adult, the prepubertal children are at least 10 years younger than the individual. If the individual is a late adolescent, no precise age difference is required, and clinical judgment must take into account the age difference, as well as the sexual maturity of the child.

---

* From American Psychiatric Association: *Diagnostic and Statistical Manual of Mental Disoders,* ed 3. American Psychiatric Association, Washington, DC, 1980. Used with permission.

from any sexual play other than that prescribed by the therapists. Beginning exercises usually focus on *heightening sensory awareness* to touch, sight, sound, and smell. Initially, intercourse is interdicted, and couples learn to give and receive bodily pleasure without the pressure of performance. They are simultaneously learning how to communicate nonverbally in a mutually satisfactory way and learning that sexual foreplay is as important as intercourse and orgasm.

Roundtable sessions follow each new exercise period, and problems and satisfactions, both sexual and in other areas of the couple's lives, are discussed. Specific instructions and the introduction of new exercises geared to the individual couple's progress are reviewed in each session. Gradually, the couples gain confidence and learn or relearn to communicate, verbally and sexually. Dual-sex therapy is most effective when the sexual dysfunction exists apart from other psychopathology.

**20.33. The answer is A (1, 2, 3)** (*Synopsis*, ed. 4, page 470).

After the rape, the woman may experience shame, humiliation, confusion, fear, and rage. The type of reaction and the length of duration of the reaction are variable, but women report effects *lasting for 1 year or longer.* Many women experience the symptoms of a posttraumatic stress disorder. Some women are able to resume sexual relations with men, particularly if they have always felt sexually adequate. *Others be-* come *phobic of sexual interaction* or develop such symptoms as vaginismus. Few women emerge from the assault completely unscathed. The manifestations and the degree of damage depend on the violence of the attack itself, the vulnerability of the woman, and the support systems available to her immediately after the attack.

*The victim fares best when she receives immediate support and is able to ventilate her fear and rage* to loving family members and to believing physicians and law enforcement officials. *She is helped when she knows she has socially acceptable means of recourse at her disposal, such as the arrest and conviction of the rapist.* Therapy is usually supportive in approach, unless there is a severe underlying disorder, and focuses on restoring the victim's sense of adequacy and control over her life and relieving the feelings of helplessness, dependency, and obsession with the assault that frequently follow rape. Group therapy with homogeneous groups composed of rape victims is a particularly effective form of treatment.

**20.34. The answer is E (all)** (*Synopsis*, ed. 4, pages 447 and 448).

Common to paraphilia is the obligatory or nearly obligatory dependence of arousal and orgasm on a *sexual fantasy* featuring objects or acts that attenuate the linkages between sexual expression, genital congress, and human contact. Other features are described in the table below.

### Common Features in Paraphilias

| Essential Features | Associated Features | Other Features |
| --- | --- | --- |
| The nuclear perversion grows out of a blurring of sexual and generational differences and a poor infant-mother demarcation, particularly in the realm of the genitalia. | * There are persistent, repetitive, or intrusive sexual fantasies of an unusual nature. | * There may be preferential use of nonhuman objects for sexual arousal. |
| There is *impairment in gender and reality sense.* | The fantasies are for the most part ego-syntonic, although they are recognized as unusual. | * There may be repetitive sexual activity involving real or simulated suffering or humiliation. |
| The paraphilia serves to cover over flaws in the sense of bodily integrity and in the sense of reality. | * Sexual arousal and orgasm are dependent in an obligate way on the fantasies. | * There may be repetitive sexual activity with nonconsenting partners. |
| *The paraphilia protects against both castration anxiety and separation anxiety.* | The perverse fantasy is a powerful organizing motif in the patient's life. | * The sexual interest is focused on substitutive acts or objects or degraded or distanced objects. |
| The paraphilia provides an outlet for aggressive drives, as well as sexual drives. | There is general psychopathology characteristic of the spectrum of borderline disorders. | |
| The perverse fantasy and behavior are symptomatic compromise formations growing out of developmental conflict and distress. | | |

* Features considered essential in DSM-III.

**20.35.–20.39. The answers are 20.35–C, 20.36–A, 20.37–B, 20.38–D, and 20.39–E** (*Synopsis*, ed. 4, page 438).

In Turner's syndrome, *one sex chromosome is missing (XO)*. The result is an absence (agenesis) or minimal development (dysgenesis) of the gonads; no significant sex hormone, male or female, is produced in fetal life or postnatally. The sexual tissues thus retain a female resting state. Because the second X chromosome, which seems responsible for full femaleness, is missing, these girls are incomplete in their sexual anatomy and, lacking adequate estrogens, develop no secondary sex characteristics without treatment. They often suffer other stigmata, such as web neck.

In Klinefelter's syndrome, the person (usually XXY) has a male habitus, under the influence of the Y chromosome, but this effect is weakened by the presence of the *second X chromosome*. Although he is born with a penis and testes, the male has small and infertile testes, and the penis may also be small. In adolescence, some of these patients develop gynecomastia and other feminine-appearing contours.

In the andrenogenital syndrome in females, excessive adrenal fetal androgens cause *androgenization of the external genitals*, ranging from mild clitoral enlargement to external genitals that look like a normal scrotal sac, testes, and a penis; hidden behind these external genitals are a vagina and a uterus. These patients are otherwise normally female. At birth, if the genitals look male, the child is assigned to the male sex and is so reared.

In male pseudohermaphroditism, different conditions can lead to *hermaphroditic external genitals* in otherwise normal males. The genitals' appearance at birth, not the true biological maleness, determines the sex assignment, and the core gender identity is male, female, or hermaphroditic, depending on the family's conviction as to the child's sex.

The androgen insensitivity syndrome is a congenital (probably genetic but not chromosomal) disorder that results from an inability of target tissues to respond to androgens. Unable to respond, *the fetal tissues remain in their female resting state*, and the brain is not organized to masculinity. The infant at birth appears to be an unremarkable female, although she is later found to have cryptorchid testes, which produce the testosterone to which the tissues do not respond, and minimal or absent internal sexual organs and vagina.

## References

Freud S: Three essays on the theory of sexuality. In *Standard Edition of the Complete Psychological Works of Sigmund Freud*, vol 7, p 135. Hogarth Press, London, 1953.

Henderson D J: Incest. In *The Sexual Experience*, B J Sadock, H I Kaplan, A M Freedman, editors. p 415. Williams & Wilkins, Baltimore, 1976.

Kinsey A, Pomeroy W, Martin C, Gebhard P: *Sexual Behavior in the Human Female*. W B Saunders, Philadelphia, 1953.

Masters W H, Johnson V E: *Human Sexual Inadequacy*. Little Brown and Co, Boston, 1970.

Meyer J K: Ego-dystonic homosexuality. In *Comprehensive Textbook of Psychiatry*, ed 4, H I Kaplan, B J Sadock, editors, p 1056. Williams & Wilkins, Baltimore, 1985.

Meyer J K: Paraphilias. In *Comprehensive Textbook of Psychiatry*, ed 4, H I Kaplan, B J Sadock, editors, p 1065. Williams & Wilkins, Baltimore, 1985.

Nakdimen K A: The physiognomic basis of sexual stereotyping. Am J Psychiatry *141:* 499, 1984.

Sadock V A: The treatment of psychosexual dysfunctions: An overview. In *Psychiatry 1982, The American Psychiatric Association Annual Review*, L Grinspoon, editor. American Psychiatric Association, Washington, DC, 1982.

Sadock V A: Psychosexual dysfunctions and treatment. In *Comprehensive Textbook of Psychiatry*, ed 4, H I Kaplan, B J Sadock, editors, p 1977. Williams & Wilkins, Baltimore, 1985.

Stoller R J: Gender identity disorders in children and adults. In *Comprehensive Textbook of Psychiatry*, ed 4, H I Kaplan, B J Sadock, editors, p 1034. Williams & Wilkins, Baltimore, 1985.

# 21

# Adjustment and Impulse Control Disorders

Adjustment disorders represent a reaction to life crises or situational disturbances that can be treated efficiently and effectively. In most cases, these disturbances turn out to be transient, and the psychiatrist can play a very important role in helping these persons deal with the stresses that caused the disorder to occur in the first place.

Life stresses, such as marital problems, business problems, difficulties with children, physical illness, and natural disasters, are just a few of the events that may affect a person's life. The severity of the adjustment disorder produced by a stress is related not only to the duration and timing of the stress but also to a person's vulnerability to stress. Some persons seem to be immune to stress and are able to deal with the vicissitudes of life without any difficulty. Others, however, react with severe emotional upheaval and are unable to deal with even the most normal events, such as going to school, leaving the parental home, getting married, or becoming a parent. The psychiatrist has much to offer to that latter group.

This chapter also covers impulse control disorders, many of which are major national mental health problems. For example, pathological gambling, which results in severe disruption of the patient's personal, family, and vocational life, is becoming more frequent as gambling becomes legalized throughout the country. Pyromania, in which the person cannot resist the impulse to set fires, causes tremendous economic loss, as well as loss of life. In addition, many acts of violence are the result of a person not being able to control an aggressive or even murderous impulse.

The reader is referred to Chapter 21 of *Modern Synopsis-IV,* which covers both adjustment and impulse disorders, and should then study the questions and answers below to test his or her knowledge of these subjects.

# Questions

**DIRECTIONS:** Each of the statements or questions below is followed by five suggested responses or completions. Select the *one* that is *best* in each case.

**21.1.** Adjustment disorders may be associated with

A. beginning school
B. leaving home
C. getting married
D. becoming a parent
E. all the above

**21.2.** The number of pathological gamblers in the United States is about

A. 100,000
B. 250,000
C. 500,000
D. 750,000
E. over 1 million

**21.3.**  In an adjustment disorder
A. constitutional factors play a role
B. a premorbid personality disorder
   may increase vulnerability
C. the nature of early mothering experience
   affects the person's capacity to respond
   to stress
D. the severity of the stress is not always
   predictive of the severity of the disorder
E. all of the above are true

**DIRECTIONS:** For each of the incomplete statements below, *one* or *more* of the completions given is correct. Choose answer:

A. if only **1, 2**, and **3** are correct
B. if only **1** and **3** are correct
C. if only **2** and **4** are correct
D. if only **4** is correct
E. if all are correct

**21.4.**  An adjustment disorder is
1. an exacerbation of a preexisting psychiatric
   disorder
2. a normal response to a nonspecific stress
3. a normal response to a clearly identifiable
   event
4. a maladaptive reaction to adverse
   circumstances

**21.5.**  Pyromania is marked by
1. a sense of satisfaction in setting fires
2. a greater incidence of the disorder among
   men than among women
3. a failure to appreciate the consequence of the
   act
4. associated petty stealing

**21.6.**  Kleptomania is characterized by
1. an experience of pleasure, without guilt or
   remorse, at the time of stealing
2. an associated conduct disorder
3. the object not being stolen for its monetary
   value
4. planning before committing the act

**21.7.**  Adjustment disorders are characterized
by
1. impairment in social functioning
2. symptoms in excess of normal reaction to a
   stress
3. symptoms occurring within 3 months of the
   stress
4. spontaneous remission after the stress
   ceases

**21.8.**  An isolated explosive disorder
1. is also known as catathymic crisis
2. is caused by schizophrenia
3. is out of proportion to the precipitating
   stress
4. has consistent prodromal signs

**21.9.**  Which of the following biological
conditions have been implicated in impulse
disorders:
1. Mental deficiency
2. Minimal brain damage
3. Epilepsy
4. Cortical atrophy

**21.10.**  Patients with disorders of impulse
control
1. may consciously try to resist the impulse
2. experience pleasure gratification at the time
   of committing the act
3. experience the act as ego-syntonic
4. do not experience regret or guilt after the
   act

**21.11.**  Which of the following apply to
intermittent explosive disorder:
1. There is recurrent loss of control of
   aggressive impulses.
2. There is no regret or self-reproach after
   each episode.
3. The disorder is more common in males than
   in females.
4. It does not run in families.

# Answers

# Adjustment and Impulse Control Disorders

**21.1.   The answer is E** (*Synopsis*, ed. 4, page 476).

An adjustment disorder is defined as a maladaptive reaction to identifiable circumstances or life events that is expected to remit when the stress ceases. Specific developmental stages—such as *beginning school, leaving home, getting married, becoming a parent,* failing to achieve occupational goals, the last child leaving home, and retiring—are often associated with adjustment disorders.

The severity of a stressor is a complex function of degree, quantity, duration, reversibility, and the environment and personal context.

**21.2.   The answer is E** (*Synopsis*, ed. 4, pages 480 and 481).

Estimates place the number of pathological gamblers in the United States at *1 million or more.* The disorder is thought to be more common in men than in women. Males with fathers with the disorder and females with mothers with the disorder are more likely to have the disorder than is the population at large.

The DSM-III diagnostic criteria for pathological gambling are listed in the table below.

**21.3.   The answer is E** (*Synopsis*, ed. 4, page 477).

As adjustment disorders are currently defined, the existence of a prior personality disorder or organic mental disorder may increase the patient's vulnerability to stress. By definition, also, the *severity of the stressor or stressors is not always predictive of the severity of the adjustment disorder.* Personality organization and cultural or group norms and values play a role in the disproportionate responses to stressors.

Several psychoanalytic researchers have contributed to the understanding of the capacity of the same stress to produce a range of responses in various normal human beings. Throughout his life, Freud remained interested in why the stresses of ordinary life produced illness in some people and not in others, why an illness took a particular form, and why some experiences and not others predisposed to psychopathology. In contrast to a popular misconception, *Freud always laid considerable weight on the constitutional factor* and saw it as interacting with a person's life experiences to produce fixation.

Psychoanalytic research has emphasized the *role of the mother and the rearing environment in a person's later capacity to respond to stress.* Particularly important was Winnicott's concept of the "good-enough mother," a person who makes "active adaptation to the infant's needs, an active adaptation that gradually lessens, according to the infant's growing ability to account for failure of adaptation and to tolerate the results of frustration."

---

### Diagnostic Criteria for Pathological Gambling*

A. The individual is chronically and progressively unable to resist impulses to gamble.

B. Gambling compromises, disrupts, or damages family, personal, and vocational pursuits, as indicated by at least three of the following:

1. Arrest for forgery, fraud, embezzlement, or income tax evasion due to attempts to obtain money for gambling;
2. Default on debts or other financial responsibilities;
3. Disrupted family or spouse relationships due to gambling;
4. Borrowing of money from illegal sources (loan sharks);
5. Inability to account for loss of money or to produce evidence of winning money, if this is claimed;
6. Loss of work due to absenteeism in order to pursue gambling activity;
7. Necessity for another person to provide money to relieve a desperate financial situation.

C. The gambling is not due to antisocial personality disorder.

---

* From American Psychiatric Association: *Diagnostic and Statistical Manual of Mental Disorders,* ed 3. American Psychiatric Association, Washington, DC, 1980. Used with permission.

In the adjustment disorder, *a specific meaningful stress has found the point of vulnerability in a person of otherwise considerable ego strength.*

**21.4. The answer is D (4)** (*Synopsis*, ed. 4, page 476).

According to DSM-III, an adjustment disorder is a *maladaptive reaction to a clearly identifiable event or events or adverse circumstances.* It is a pathological response to what a layman might call bad luck or big change; *it is not an exacerbation of a psychiatric disorder meeting other criteria.* The disorder is expected to remit eventually after the stressor disappears or a new level of adaptation is attained. The response is maladaptive because of an impairment in social or occupational functioning, or because of symptoms or behaviors that are beyond the normal, usual, expectable response to such a stressor. Therefore, the diagnostic category should not be used if the patient meets the criteria for a more specific disorder. A concurrent personality disorder or organic impairment may render the patient more vulnerable to an adjustment disorder.

**21.5. The answer is A (1, 2, 3)** (*Synopsis*, ed. 4, pages 483 and 484).

Pyromania is characterized by the recurrent failure to resist impulses to set fires. The person gains *satisfaction* from giving into the impulse, and at times sexual pleasure may be experienced. The disorder *is more common in men than in women.* Unless there is a severe organic mental disorder, the pyromaniac is aware of the nature and consequences of the act; that is, that a fire is being set and that it can cause harm.

In addition to the essential features described above, DSM-III lists the following: Persons with the disorder are often recognized as regular watchers at fires in their neighborhoods, frequently set off false alarms, and show interest in fire-fighting paraphernalia. They *may be indifferent to the consequences* of the fire to life or property, or they may get satisfaction from the resulting destruction. Frequently the person

may leave obvious clues. Common associated features include alcohol intoxication, psychosexual dysfunctions, lower than average I.Q., chronic personal frustrations, and resentment toward authority figures. Some individuals are sexually aroused by the fire. *Petty stealing* is not associated with this disorder.

The DSM-III diagnostic criteria are listed in the table below.

**21.6. The answer is B (1, 3)** (*Synopsis*, ed. 4, page 482).

According to DSM-III, kleptomania's essential feature is "a recurrent failure to resist impulses to steal objects, *not for immediate use or for their monetary value.* The objects taken are either given away, returned surreptitiously, or are kept and hidden."

The person usually has the money to pay for the objects that are impulsively stolen. *There is the cycle found in other impulse disorders* of mounting tension followed by *gratification and of tension reduction with or without guilt, remorse, or depression.* Stealing is done *without long-term planning* and without the involvement of others. There can be guilt and anxiety afterward. When the object stolen is the goal, the diagnosis is not kleptomania; in kleptomania, the act of stealing itself is primary.

The DSM-III diagnostic criteria for kleptomania are listed in the table at the top of the facing page.

**21.7. The answer is E (all)** (*Synopsis*, ed. 4, page 477).

An adjustment disorder is a maladaptive reaction that produces symptoms that *impair social or occupational functioning.* The stressor produces *symptoms in the patient that are excessive.* The disturbance may be more or less severe depending on the patient's vulnerability. For example, the psychological reaction of going to school may produce a profound maladaptive reaction in one person but only mild homesickness in another person.

The table on the facing page lists the DSM-III diagnostic criteria for adjustment disorder.

---

### Diagnostic Criteria for Pyromania*

A. Recurrent failure to resist impulses to set fires.

B. Increasing sense of tension before setting the fire.

C. An experience of either intense pleasure, gratification, or release at the time of committing the act.

D. Lack of motivation, such as monetary gain or sociopolitical ideology, for setting fires.

E. Not due to an organic mental disorder, schizophrenia, antisocial personality disorder, or conduct disorder.

---

* From American Psychiatric Association: *Diagnostic and Statistical Manual of Mental Disorders*, ed 3. American Psychiatric Association, Washington, DC, 1980. Used with permission.

## Diagnostic Criteria for Kleptomania*

A. Recurrent failure to resist impulses to steal objects that are not for immediate use or their monetary value.

B. Increasing sense of tension before committing the act.

C. An experience of either pleasure or release at the time of committing the theft.

D. Stealing is done without long-term planning and assistance from, or collaboration with, others.

E. *Not due to conduct disorder* or antisocial personality disorder.

*From American Psychiatric Association: *Diagnostic and Statistical Manual of Mental Disorders*, ed 3. American Psychiatric Association, Washington, DC, 1980. Used with permission.

## Diagnostic Criteria for Adjustment Disorder*

A. A maladaptive reaction to an identifiable psychosocial stressor, that *occurs within 3 months of the onset of the stressor.*

B. The maladaptive nature of the reaction is indicated by either of the following:

1. *Impairment in social or occupational functioning;*
2. *Symptoms that are in excess of a normal and expectable reaction to the stressor.*

C. The disturbance is not merely one instance of a pattern of overreaction to stress or an exacerbation of one of the mental disorders previously described.

D. It is assumed that *the disturbance will eventually remit after the stressor ceases* or, if the stressor persists, when a new level of adaptation is achieved.

E. The disturbance does not meet the criteria for any of the specific disorders listed previously or for uncomplicated bereavement.

*From American Psychiatric Association: *Diagnostic and Statistical Manual of Mental Disorders*, ed 3. American Psychiatric Association, Washington, DC, 1980. Used with permission.

**21.8.   The answer is B (1, 3)** (*Synopsis,* ed. 4, page 486).

An isolated explosive disorder is usually manifested by a single episode of violence. The disorder was previously *known as a catathymic crisis.* The episode is usually *not due to any underlying psychiatric illness, such as schizophrenia,* and there are *no prodromal signs* of impulsive behavior or aggressivity in the patient. In general, the explosive episode is grossly *out of proportion to any stress.*

The DSM-III diagnostic criteria for this disorder are listed in the table below.

**21.9.   The answer is E (all)** (*Synopsis,* ed. 4, page 480).

Biological lesions of the nervous system may underly these disorders. For example, kleptomania has been reported as a presenting feature of *cortical atrophy.* Recent work has suggested the continuance of impulse disorder symptoms into adulthood in persons who were classified as suffering from childhood *minimal brain dysfunction* syndrome. Several studies reported evidence of brain disorders in a significant percentage of patients who exhibited episodic violence. Lifelong or acquired *mental deficiency,*

## Diagnostic Criteria for Isolated Explosive Disorder*

A. A single, discrete episode in which failure to resist an impulse led to a single, violent, externally directed act that had a catastrophic impact on others.

B. The degree of aggressivity expressed during the episode was grossly out of proportion to any precipitating psychosocial stressor.

C. Before the episode, there were no signs of generalized impulsivity or aggressiveness.

D. Not due to schizophrenia, antisocial personality disorder, or conduct disorder.

*From American Psychiatric Association: *Diagnostic and Statistical Manual of Mental Disorders*, ed 3. American Psychiatric Association, Washington, DC, 1980. Used with permission.

*epilepsy,* and even reversible acute brain syndromes have long been known to be implicated in lapses of impulse control.

*Mental deficiency* is a general term that refers to slower than and below normal mental development. *Minimal brain damage or dysfunction* refers to an abnormal childhood behavioral pattern characterized by learning problems, hyperactivity, irritability, and short attention span. *Epilepsy* is a chronic disorder due to excessive neuronal discharge and is usually associated with short-lived disturbances of consciousness and involuntary convulsive movements. *Cortical atrophy* is a loss of cortical tissue. It may be caused by head trauma or by one of the organic brain syndromes associated with diseases of unknown cause, e.g. Alzheimer's disease.

**21.10.   The answer is E (all)** (*Synopsis,* ed. 4, page 479).

According to DSM-III, a disorder of impulse control is characterized in the following way: (1) There is a failure to resist an impulse, drive, or temptation to perform some action that is harmful to the individual or others; *there may or may not be a conscious resistance to the impulse;* the act may or may not be premeditated or planned. (2) Prior to committing the act, there is an increasing sense of tension. (3) *At the time of committing the act, there is an experience of either pleasure gratification or release. The act is ego-syntonic* in that it is consonant with the immediate conscious wish and aim of the person. Immediately following the act, *there may or may not be feelings of genuine regret, self-reproach, or guilt.*

**21.11.   The answer is B (1, 3)** (*Synopsis,* ed. 4, pages 484 and 485).

According to DSM-III, this diagnostic category describes persons who have recurrent and paroxysmal episodes of significant *loss of control of aggressive impulses.* Behavior in these episodes results in serious assault or destruction of property and is grossly out of proportion to any psychosocial stressors that may have played a role in eliciting the episodes. The symptoms appear within minutes or hours and, regardless of duration, remit almost as quickly. *Each episode is followed by genuine regret or self-reproach.*

According to DSM-III, this disorder appears to be *more common in males than in females.* The males are likely to be seen in a correctional institution and the females in a psychiatric facility.

There is evidence that intermittent explosive disorder is *more common in family members* of persons with the disorder. A variety of factors could be contributory, however, and a simple genetic explanation seems unlikely.

The DSM-III diagnostic criteria for intermittent explosive disorder are listed in the table below.

---

**Diagnostic Criteria for Intermittent Explosive Disorder\***

A. Several discrete episodes of loss of control of aggressive impulses resulting in serious assault or destruction of property.

B. Behavior that is grossly out of proportion to any precipitating psychosocial stressor.

C. Absence of signs of generalized impulsivity or aggressiveness between episodes.

D. Not due to schizophrenia, antisocial personality disorder, or conduct disorder.

---

\* From American Psychiatric Association: *Diagnostic and Statistical Manual of Mental Disorders,* ed 3. American Psychiatric Association, Washington, DC, 1980. Used with permission.

# References

Andreasen N C, Warek P: Adjustment disorders in adolescents and adults. Arch Gen Psychiatry *37:* 1166, 1980.

Brown C L, Ebert M H, Goyer P F, Jimerson D C, Klein W T, Bunney W E, Goodwin F K: Aggression, suicide, and serotonin: Relationships of CFS amine metabolites. Am J Psychiatry *139:* 741, 1982.

Frosch J: The relation between acting out and disorders of impulse control. Psychiatry *40:* 295, 1977.

Ginsberg G L: Adjustment and impulse control disorders. In *Comprehensive Textbook of Psychiatry,* ed 4, H I Kaplan, B J Sadock, editors, p 1097. Williams & Wilkins, Baltimore, 1985.

Greenberg H R: Psychology of gambling. In *Comprehensive Textbook of Psychiatry,* ed 3, H I Kaplan, A M Freedman, B J Sadock, editors, p 3274. Williams & Wilkins, Baltimore, 1980.

McCormick R A: Affective disorders among pathological gamblers seeking treatment. Am J Psychiatry *141:* 215, 1984.

Yesavage J A: Plasma levels as predictors of clinical response and violent behavior. J Clin Psychiatry *2:* 13, 1984.

# 22

# Psychological Factors Affecting Physical Conditions (Psychosomatic Disorders)

Although psychosomatic (psychophysiological) medicine has only become a specific area of concern in the field of psychiatry within the past several decades, it is impossible to trace its history without considering the idea of mind-body unity, implied by the Greek words *psyche* (breath, to breathe) and *soma* (body). The problem of mind and body, and how they relate, has been considered throughout the ages. The controversy about their interrelationship can be seen currently in the third edition of the *Diagnostic and Statistical Manual of Mental Disorders* (DSM-III), which has deleted the nosological term psychophysiological disorder and replaced it with the classification of psychological factors affecting physical conditions.

The diagnostic criteria given in DSM-III for this category are as follows: (1) Psychologically meaningful environmental stimuli are temporally related to the initiation or exacerbation of a physical condition and (2) the physical condition has either demonstrable organic pathology, e.g. rheumatoid arthritis, or a known pathophysiological process, e.g. vomiting.

The concept of psychomedical treatment—that is, the approach that emphasizes the interrelation of mind and body in the genesis of symptom and disorder—calls for a greatly expanded sharing of responsibility among various professions. If one views disease from a multicausal point of view, every disease can be considered psychosomatic, because every disorder is affected in some fashion by emotional factors.

Hostility, depression, and anxiety, in varying proportions, are at the root of most psychosomatic disorders. Psychosomatic medicine is principally concerned with those illnesses that present primarily somatic manifestations. The presenting complaint is usually physical; the patient rarely complains of anxiety or depression or tension but, rather, of vomiting or diarrhea or anorexia.

An outgrowth of the renewed interest in psychosomatic medicine is the field of consultation-liaison psychiatry, which is the field of clinical psychiatry that includes diagnostic and therapeutic activities of the psychiatrist in the nonpsychiatric part of the hospital. In that setting, the psychiatrist identifies the psychological disorder causing the somatic complaints or interacting with the organic disease; he or she also describes the patient's defenses and coping strategies and the familial, social, economic, and environmental factors in the patient's situation that serve as potential assets or liabilities. Identifying psychosocial factors may be important in the development, modification, and potential chronicity of the physical illness.

Readers should review Chapter 22, "Psychological Factors Affecting Physical Conditions (Psychosomatic Disorders)," of *Modern Synopsis–IV* and should then study the questions and answers below to test their knowledge of the subject.

# Questions

**DIRECTIONS:** Each of the statements or questions below is followed by five suggested responses or completions. Select the *one* that is *best* in each case.

**22.1.** A psychosomatic disorder that occurs 7 times more frequently in women than in men, that is often precipitated by acute emotional stress or shock, sometimes developing only hours after a fright, and that has a personality pattern characterized by premature assumption of family responsibility is probably

A. peptic ulcer
B. rheumatoid arthritis
C. essential hypertension
D. bronchial asthma
E. thyrotoxicosis

**22.2.** Of the following, which is the most effective management of pain in the chronic cancer patient:

A. Antidepressants
B. Antidepressants plus phenothiazine
C. Thalamic ablation
D. Narcotic analgesia
E. Psychotherapy

**22.3.** The most common cause of time lost from work in this country is

A. hypochondriasis
B. low back pain
C. angina pectoris
D. gout
E. dental pain

**22.4.** The number of patients who came to a physician with headaches as their main complaint has been estimated to be

A. less than 10 percent
B. 10 to 20 percent
C. 20 to 30 percent
D. 30 to 40 percent
E. over 50 percent

**22.5.** Stressful life experiences, particularly experiences of separation and loss, have been implicated in the clinical onset of

A. cancer of the cervix
B. leukemia
C. lymphoma
D. benign prostatic hypertrophy
E. all of the above

**22.6.** During the acute active phase of a psychosomatic disorder, the psychiatric technique that is most valuable is

A. psychoanalysis
B. behavior therapy
C. support and reassurance
D. hypnotherapy
E. electroconvulsive therapy (ECT)

**22.7.** The personality type most often associated with vascular headaches is the

A. histrionic
B. dependent
C. borderline
D. schizoid
E. obsessional

**22.8.** All the following personality traits are frequently encountered in ulcerative colitis *except*

A. neatness
B. oversensitivity
C. compulsivity
D. compliance
E. exhibitionism

**22.9.** Anorexia nervosa is characterized by all of the following *except*

A. self-imposed dietary limitations
B. intense fear of gaining weight
C. normal menses
D. disturbed body image
E. profound weight loss

**22.10.** In hypothyroidism, a psychosis that occurs is called

A. hypothyroid crisis
B. paranoid schizophrenia
C. delirium
D. myxedema madness
E. bipolar disorder

**22.11.** In the treatment of delirium encountered 3 days after an acute myocardial infarction and in which the patient is markedly agitated, the most useful drug is

A. diazepam
B. morphine
C. codeine
D. chlorpromazine
E. haloperidol

**22.12.** The type A coronary-prone persons described by Friedman and Rosenman have all the following characteristics *except*

A. aggressiveness
B. competitiveness
C. ambition
D. drive for success
E. patience

**22.13.** Anorexia nervosa occurs most commonly in

A. females
B. lower socioeconomic groups
C. males
D. persons over 65 years of age
E. children under the age of 12

**22.14.** Most causes of urticaria have

A. a solely psychogenic basis
B. no psychogenic basis
C. only an allergic basis
D. both an allergic basis and a psychogenic basis
E. a chemical basis

**22.15.** The scratching of the skin in generalized pruritus is often said to represent

A. aggression turned against the self
B. poor body image
C. anal sadism
D. orality
E. orgasm

**22.16.** By convention, obesity is said to be present when body weight exceeds the standard weight listed in the usual height-weight tables by what percentage:

A. 10 percent
B. 15 percent
C. 20 percent
D. 25 percent
E. 30 percent

**22.17.** Evidence that stress predisposes patients to autoimmune disorders is

A. increased 19 S protein
B. decreased immunoglobins
C. breakdown of 19 S protein
D. variable immunoglobin levels
E. none of the above

**22.18.** Bulimia—which is characterized by the sudden, compulsive ingestion of large amounts of food in a very short time—is found in what percentage of obese persons:

A. Less than 5 percent
B. 10 percent
C. 15 percent
D. 20 percent
E. 25 percent

**22.19.** Hyperventilation is a physiological concomitant of all the following *except*

A. fear
B. lassitude
C. anxiety
D. pain
E. anger

**22.20.** All the following are traditionally considered psychosomatic disorders *except*

A. painful menstrual syndrome
B. migraine headache
C. hyperthyroidism
D. rheumatoid arthritis
E. cancer

**22.21.** Anorexia nervosa has a mortality rate up to

A. 3 percent
B. 25 percent
C. 30 percent
D. 40 percent
E. 50 percent

**22.22.** Biofeedback has been used therapeutically and with some benefits in all the following psychosomatic disorders *except*

A. essential hypertension
B. cardiac arrhythmia
C. epilepsy
D. tension headache
E. ulcerative colitis

**22.23.** "Parentectomy" in the treatment of asthmatic children refers to

A. treatment of the dominant parent
B. joint therapy of both parents
C. separation of the child from his or her family in a residential treatment center
D. separation of the child from his or her family for several hours a day
E. none of the above

**DIRECTIONS:** For each of the incomplete statements below, *one* or *more* of the completions given is correct. Choose answer:

A. if only **1, 2**, and **3** are correct
B. if only **1** and **3** are correct
C. if only **2** and **4** are correct
D. if only **4** is correct
E. if all are correct

**22.24.** A noticeably underweight 17-year-old female college freshman is brought to a physician by her mother because of an unexplained weight loss of 19 pounds in the past 3 months. On several occasions the mother thought she heard the daughter throwing up in the bathroom after a meal. The daughter, who was at one time overweight, does not think she is too thin. In taking a history of the patient, the physician may find that the patient has also

1. reduced the total intake of food
2. stopped menstruating
3. become involved in a vigorous exercise program
4. lost all interest in food

**22.25.** Correct statements about persons with asthma include which of the following:

1. They are overly dependent on their mothers.
2. Attacks follow episodes of frustration.
3. Poor impulse control may be seen.
4. Attacks follow separation from parents or parental figures.

**22.26.** The patient illustrated below has rejected all food and has lost over 30 percent of her original body weight. No physical illness has been found to account for the weight loss. One would also expect to find

1. an intense fear of becoming obese
2. a warm, seductive, and passive father
3. denial of emaciation by the patient
4. feelings of hunger

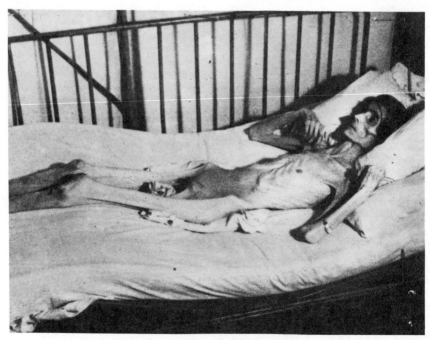

(Courtesy of Katherine Halmi, MD.)

**22.27.**   Chronic pain patients tend to

1. be young adults
2. come from upper socioeconomic groups
3. come from small families
4. have relatives with disabilities

**22.28.**   Which of the following may be associated with a complaint of chronic pain:

1. Depression
2. Grief and mourning
3. Psychosis
4. Delusions

**22.29.**   In evaluating patients with complaints of chronic pain of whatever cause, the physician must be alert to

1. the patient's use of an over-the-counter medication
2. addiction to alcohol
3. withdrawal symptoms during the evaluation period
4. an underlying medical disorder

**22.30.**   The premenstrual syndrome (PMS)

1. reaches a maximum of intensity about 5 days before the menstrual period
2. has a symptom-free time between menstruation and ovulation
3. occurs in women with intact ovaries after hysterectomy
4. is rare in teenage girls

**22.31.**   Factors associated with a risk of being obese include

1. age
2. sex
3. social mobility
4. socioeconomic status

**22.32.**   Neurocirculatory asthenia is characterized by

1. sighing respirations
2. dizziness
3. chest pain
4. ideas of reference

# Answers

# Psychological Factors Affecting Physical Conditions (Psychosomatic Disorders)

**22.1. The answer is E** (*Synopsis*, ed. 4, page 516).

The cause of endogenous *thyrotoxicosis* is not known. The disease may be precipitated by acute emotional stress or shock, sometimes even developing within hours after an extreme fright or emotional trauma. Several premorbid personality characteristics have been described and agreed on by independent investigators. One often-described personality pattern is characterized by premature assumption of responsibility and martyr-like reaction formation to and suppression of dependent wishes and needs, often combined with an exaggerated fear of death and injury.

*Peptic ulcer* is a psychophysiological disorder of the digestive tract consisting of circumscribed erosion of any of those areas exposed to acidic gastric juice, most commonly the lesser curvature of the stomach and the duodenal curvature.

*Rheumatoid arthritis* is a chronic proliferative inflammation of the synovial membrane, involving multiple joints but with a predilection for the smaller ones; it is characterized by wide variations in severity and a tendency to remissions and exacerbations. Some authorities have considered this condition to be primarily a psychophysiological or psychosomatic disturbance due, at least temporally, to emotional crises.

*Essential hypertension* is abnormally high blood pressure without known cause, although some investigators consider this to be a psychophysiological cardiovascular disorder. Psychologically, it is characterized by repression of all hostile, competitive tendencies, which are inhibited because of fears of retaliation and failure.

*Bronchial asthma* is a respiratory disorder characterized by recurrent attacks of bronchiolar spasm, which traps air in the lungs and results in inhibition of the expiratory muscles, assumption of the inspiratory position, and use of all the accessory muscles of respiration.

**22.2. The answer is D** (*Synopsis*, ed. 4, pages 537 and 538).

Patients with bona fide reasons for significant

chronic pain are often undermedicated with narcotics. Physicians hesitate to prescribe effective *analgesia* because of a lack of knowledge of the pharmacology of analgesics, an unrealistic fear of causing addiction (even in terminal patients), and the ethical judgment that only bad physicians prescribe large doses of narcotics. In this regard it is critical to differentiate patients with chronic benign pain (who tend to do much better with psychotherapy and psychotropic drugs) from those with chronic pain due to cancer or other chronic medical disorders. The former often respond to the combination of an antidepressant and a phenothiazine. The latter usually respond better to analgesics, nerve blocks, and neurodestructive procedures. Many cancer patients may be kept relatively active, alert, and comfortable with judicious use of morphine, avoiding costly and incompletely effective surgical procedures, such as peripheral nerve section, cordotomy, or stereotaxic *thalamic ablations* (the surgical destruction of the thalamic nuclei of the brain, specifically the area that deals with pain).

*Antidepressant drugs* are used in the treatment of pathological depression. The two main classes are the tricyclic antidepressant drugs and the monoamine oxidase inhibitors. Lithium carbonate also has antidepressant activity in certain patients. *Phenothiazine* is a class of psychotropic drugs, the prototype of which is chlorpromazine, that are effective in the treatment of psychoses. The efficacy of these agents in the treatment of schizophrenia has been demonstrated unequivocally. The drugs exert a favorable influence on the fundamental symptoms of schizophrenia—thought disorder, blunted affect, indifference, withdrawal, autistic behavior, and mannerisms—as well as the secondary or accessory symptoms—hallucinations, paranoid projection, belligerence, hostility, and resistiveness. They are currently among the most widely used drugs in medical practice.

*Psychotherapy* is a form of treatment for mental illness and behavioral disturbances in which a trained person establishes a professional contract with the patient and through definite therapeutic communication, both verbal and nonverbal, attempts to alleviate the emotional disturbance, reverse or change maladaptive patterns of behavior, and encourage personality growth and development. Psychotherapy is distinguished from such other forms of psychiatric treatment as the use of drugs and electroshock therapy.

**22.3.   The answer is B** (*Synopsis*, ed. 4, page 535).

Persistent pain is the most frequent complaint of patients, yet it is one of the most difficult symptoms to treat because of differing etiologies and individualized responses to pain. Chronic *low back pain* is the most common cause of time lost from work in this country.

*Hypochondriasis* is a somatoform disorder characterized by excessive, morbid anxiety about one's health. The term is derived from the belief that the state was caused by some dysfunction in the hypochondrium, especially the spleen. Hypochondriacal patients exhibit a predominant disturbance in which the physical symptoms or complaints are not explainable on the basis of demonstrable organic findings and are apparently linked to psychological factors. *Angina pectoris* refers to severe constricting pain in the chest that is usually caused by coronary artery disease. *Gout* is an inherited metabolic disorder most commonly occurring in males. It is characterized by an elevated blood uric acid level and recurrent acute arthritis of sudden onset, which then leads to progressive and chronic arthritis. *Dental pain* is a general term referring to any pain in the mouth, teeth, or gums caused by various oral disorders.

**22.4.   The answer is B** (*Synopsis*, ed. 4, page 530).

Headaches are the most common neurological symptom and one of the most common of all medical complaints. Every year about 80 percent of the population is estimated to suffer from at least one headache, and *10 to 20 percent* of the population presents to a physician with headaches as their primary complaint. Headaches also are a major cause or excuse given for absenteeism from work or avoidance of other undesired social or personal activities.

**22.5.   The answer is E** (*Synopsis*, ed. 4, pages 534 and 535).

A large literature has been accumulating on the relationship between psychosocial factors and cancer. It has been reported that stressful life experiences, particularly experiences of separation and loss, frequently precede the clinical onset of various neoplasms, including *cancer of the cervix*, *leukemia*, and *lymphoma*.

Several studies, in contrast, have found no association between life experience and the onset of cancer of the breast. In one of these studies, however, there was a relationship between life events and benign breast disease. A similar observation was reported in an investigation of benign prostatic hypertrophy, in which a relatively high rate of life change was found to precede the onset of *benign prostatic hypertrophy*, in contrast to a lower rate of life events before the onset of bladder cancer.

*Cancer of the cervix* refers to malignant changes of the cervix that may invade the surrounding tissue. *Leukemia* consists of a progressive proliferation of abnormal leukocytes found in hemopoietic tissues, other organs, and usually in the blood in increased numbers. *Lymphoma* is a general term referring to malignant neoplasms of lymph and reticuloendothelial tissues that present as apparently circumscribed solid tumors composed of cells that appear primitive or resemble lymphocytes, plasma cells, or histiocytes. *Benign prostatic hypertrophy* refers to an increase in the number of cells and absolute size of the prostate.

**22.6.   The answer is C** (*Synopsis*, ed. 4, page 540).

Supportive psychotherapy is a form of psychotherapy that seeks to strengthen the patient's defenses and to provide reassurance, rather than to probe deeply into the patient's conflicts. If during an initial attack of a psychosomatic disorder the patient responds to active medical therapy in association with the superficial *support*, ventilation, *reassurance*, and environmental manipulation provided by the internist, additional psychotherapy by a psychiatrist may not be required. Psychosomatic illness that does not respond to medical treatment, or that is in a chronic phase, should receive psychosomatic evaluation by a psychiatrist, and combined therapy, as indicated.

*Psychoanalysis* is a theory of human mental phenomena and behavior, a method of psychic investigation and research, and a form of psychotherapy originally formulated by Sigmund Freud. As a technique for exploring the mental processes, psychoanalysis includes the use of free association and the analysis and interpretation of dreams, resistances, and transferences. As a form of psychotherapy, it uses the investigative technique, guided by Freud's libido and instinct theories and by ego psychology, to gain insight into a person's unconscious motivations, conflicts, and symbols and thus to effect a change in maladaptive behavior. *Behavior therapy* is a psychiatric treatment modality that focuses on overt and objectively observable behavior and uses various conditioning techniques derived from learning theory to modify the patient's behavior directly. Behavior therapy aims exclusively at symptomatic improvement, without addressing psychodynamic causation. *Hypnotherapy* is a type of therapy that makes use of hypnosis. *Electroconvulsive therapy (ECT)* is a treatment, usually for depression, that involves the application of electric current to the brain for a fraction of a second through scalp electrodes, inducing a convulsive reaction and unconsciousness.

**22.7.   The answer is E** (*Synopsis*, ed. 4, page 531).

Vascular headaches often are precipitated by emotional conflicts or psychological stress. Some degree of vascular headaches may develop in about 15 to 20 percent of men and 20 to 30 percent of women in response to emotional stress. Two-thirds of those developing migraines have a family history of similar disorders. Although the presence of psychological triggers is universally accepted, evidence for specific personality types and unconscious conflict constellations is unconvincing. Persons with *obsessional personalities* who are overly controlled, perfectionistic, and who suppress anger may be at risk for numerous stress-related disorders, such as headache, colitis, and others.

*Histrionic personality disorder* is a condition in which the patient, usually an immature and dependent person, exhibits unstable, overreactive, and excitable self-dramatizing behavior that is aimed at gaining attention and is at times seductive, although the person may not be aware of that aim. It was termed hysterical personality in DSM-II. *Dependent personality disorder* is a personality disorder characterized by lack of self-confidence, a tendency to have others assume responsibility for significant areas of one's life, and a subordination of one's own needs and wishes to those of the others on whom one is dependent. Solitude is extremely discomforting to a person with this disorder. This category replaced the DSM-II term passive-aggressive personality, dependent type. *Borderline personality disorder* is a personality disorder classified in DSM-III that is marked by instability in various areas. *Schizoid personality disorder* is a diagnostic category in DSM-III for persons with defects in the capacity to form social relationships but without other striking communicative or behavioral eccentricities.

**22.8.   The answer is E** (*Synopsis*, ed. 4, pages 493 and 494).

There have been fairly uniform descriptions of the personalities of patients with ulcerative colitis. Attempts to identify these factors by standardized psychometric ratings and to validate findings with control or comparison groups have had mixed results.

The typical personality traits that have been described include *neatness*, carefulness, *oversensitivity*, and a seeming modesty that covers up a grandiose self-concept, egocentricity, passivity, lack of ambition, and a need for love, sympathy, and affection. Typical patients give little and have a naive infantile concept of love. They are deeply attached to their mothers.

The mixture of *compulsive* traits and underlying narcissistic vulnerability does not create a uniform ulcerative colitis personality but, rather, a range of psychological vulnerabilities and limitations in adaptation that manifest themselves in varying ways and intensities in different patients. Herbert Weiner stated that "ulcerative colitis patients . . . differ from each other in degree, but . . . demonstrate a spectrum of personal sensitivities and vulnerabilities that are brought to the fore in certain life settings or in the face of certain experiences."

In children, too, obsessional, fastidious, unemotional, rigid traits have been described, along with an intense need for approval. They tend to be either *compliant* and passive, or manipulative and petulant.

*Compulsion* is an uncontrollable, repetitive, and unwanted urge to perform an act. It serves as a defense against unacceptable ideas and desires, and failure to perform the act leads to overt anxiety. In clinical psychiatry, the term *compliance* implies a neurotic degree of oversubmissiveness. It is seen most commonly as part of the dependent personality disorder.

*Exhibitionism* is a paraphilia in which a man exposes his genitals to females in a socially inappropriate fashion. The condition rarely occurs in women. It has no relationship to ulcerative colitis.

**22.9.   The answer is C** (*Synopsis*, ed. 4, page 499).

Anorexia nervosa is an eating disorder characterized by *self-imposed dietary limitations*, behavior directed toward losing weight, peculiar patterns of handling food, *weight loss, intense fear of gaining weight, disturbance of body image*, and, in women, *amenorrhea*.

**22.10.   The answer is D** (*Synopsis*, ed. 4, page 516).

A high proportion of patients with an adult onset of hypothyroidism show evidence of mental disturbance as part of the syndrome. All mental processes, including speech, slow down. There is decreased initiative, slowness in comprehension, and impaired recent memory. The patient may complain of fatigue, lethargy, and drowsiness. An affective disturbance, predominantly depression, is common. Cognitive deficits may result in dementia. A frank organic mental disorder may develop and progress to stupor or coma. *Myxedema madness* is a psychosis in which a wide range of organicity, from minimal to marked, may be manifest. It is often characterized by paranoid suspicions and auditory hallucinations.

*Hypothyroid crisis* is marked by a sudden reduction in thyroid function. *Paranoid schizophrenia* is a schizophrenic disorder characterized by the presence of persecutory or grandiose delusions, often accompanied by hallucinations. *Bipolar affective disorder* is an affective disorder in which the patient exhibits both manic and depressive episodes. *Delirium* is an acute, reversible organic mental disorder characterized by confusion and some impairment of consciousness. It is generally associated with emotional lability, hallucinations or illusions, and inappropriate, impulsive, irrational, or violent behavior.

**22.11. The answer is E** (*Synopsis*, ed. 4, page 506).

Nocturnal sleep after a myocardial infarction is markedly disturbed. It is likely that the disruption contributes to the delirium observed in some patients, especially elderly ones, after a heart attack. Delirium is found in about 10 percent of elderly myocardial infarction patients. The delirium usually starts on the third to the fourth day after the infarction and lasts 2 to 5 days. The markedly agitated delirious patient may be given *haloperidol*, 2.5 to 10 mg orally or intramuscularly every 30 minutes until he or she is calm, followed by decreasing oral doses. The drug has proved to be remarkably safe in these acutely ill patients.

*Diazepam* is a skeletal muscle relaxant, sedative, and antianxiety agent. *Morphine* is a major alkaloid of opium and is most commonly used medically as an analgesic. *Codeine*, a less effective analgesic than morphine, is a demethylated form of morphine. *Chlorpromazine* is a major antipsychotic neuroleptic that in very low doses can prevent vomiting and nausea in certain disorders.

**22.12. The answer is E** (*Synopsis*, ed. 4, pages 504 and 505).

The most influential and widely tested hypothesis linking causal psychological variables and the occurrence of coronary heart disease is that formulated by Friedman and Rosenman. They asserted that a pattern of behavior, designated type A, distinguishes coronary-prone persons and has predictive value for the development of coronary heart disease and its complications. The type A behavior pattern features *aggressiveness, competitiveness, ambition, drive*

*for success*, restlessness, *impatience*, devotion to work, a subjective sense of time urgency, abruptness of speech and gesture, and a tendency to hostility. People relatively lacking these behavior characteristics have been designated as type B. Type A behavior is exhibited by persons who are constantly engaged in a struggle to achieve, to outdo others, and to meet deadlines. It is not synonymous with life stress, nor does it represent a response to life stress. Rather, it constitutes a habitual behavioral state the precursors of which have been observed in children. Parental attitudes characterized by escalating standards of performance may influence children to develop a chronic type A behavior pattern. Studies have shown that men exhibiting the pattern tend to have elevated plasma triglyceride and cholesterol values, a hyperinsulinemic response to a glucose challenge, and increased diurnal secretion of noradrenalin. Extreme type A persons have an increased serum level of corticotropin and a reduced serum level of growth hormone, and they show accelerated clotting. Preliminary reports indicate that young type A males show more marked heart rate and blood pressure responses to challenging perceptual-motor and cognitive tasks than do type B persons.

Data available at this time indicate that type A behavior pattern may be the final overt manifestation of different motives and that its role in the development of coronary heart disease may be co-determined by such factors as the degree to which it is at variance with the person's basic personality. Further, the extent to which striving is rewarded with success may also prove to be significant. One must avoid the temptation to oversimplify the results of the investigations carried out to date and mistake promising hypotheses for established facts. There is little doubt that the cause of coronary heart disease is multifactorial and that certain psychological and social factors represent no more than a set of contributory causal variables interacting in a still unknown but complex fashion with biological and biochemical factors.

**22.13. The answer is A** (*Synopsis*, ed. 4, pages 499 and 500).

Anorexia nervosa occurs predominantly *in females*. Various studies report that a *range of 4 to 6 percent of anorectic patients are males*. The morbidity risk for a sister of an anorectic patient is about 6.6 percent, which greatly exceeds normal expectation. Often, mothers or fathers had an explicit history of significantly low adolescent weight or weight phobia. At the present time, the evidence available does not permit any conclusions on the role of heredity in the development of this disorder because of possibly biased selection and the small numbers in the studies reported.

Recent prevalence studies have shown anorexia nervosa to be a common disorder in the age group at risk—*12 to 30 years*—and in the *higher socioeconomic classes*.

**22.14. The answer is D** (*Synopsis*, ed. 4, page 526).

Many physical, chemical, and biological factors have been incriminated as causative of urticarial eruptions. In acute cases, *an allergic basis* is often established with some degree of conviction, but in subacute, chronic, and recurrent cases, the most careful examination often fails to elicit an allergic cause. Most dermatologists agree that *emotional factors are of enormous relevance* to the cause of urticaria.

**22.15. The answer is A** (*Synopsis*, ed. 4, page 525).

In generalized pruritus, the rubbing of the skin provides a substitute gratification of the frustrated need, and the scratching represents *aggression turned against the self*. The emotions that most frequently lead to generalized psychogenic pruritus are repressed anger and repressed anxiety. An almost irresistible urge to scratch oneself results from the itching impulse. Whenever persons consciously or preconsciously experience anger or anxiety, they scratch themselves, often violently. An inordinate need for affection is a common characteristic of these patients. Frustrations of this need elicit aggressiveness that is then inhibited.

*Body image* is the conscious and unconscious perception of one's body at any particular time. One can perceive one's body image to be poor, good, or altered in some way. *Anal sadism* refers to the aggression, destructiveness, negativism, and externally directed rage that are typical components of the anal stage of development that occurs between the ages of 1 and 3. This concept derives from classical psychoanalytic theory. *Orality* or the oral phase refers to the earliest stage in psychosexual development, which lasts through the first 18 months of life. During this period the oral zone is the center of the infant's needs, expression, and pleasurable erotic experiences. An *orgasm* is a sexual climax or peak psychophysiological reaction to sexual stimulation.

**22.16. The answer is C** (*Synopsis*, ed. 4, page 495).

Obesity is a condition characterized by excessive accumulations of fat in the body. By convention, obesity is said to be present when body weight exceeds *by 20 percent* the standard weight listed in the usual height-weight tables.

**22.17. The answer is A** (*Synopsis*, ed. 4, page 528).

Some authors have suggested that stress predisposes patients to the so-called autoimmune disorders by leading to alterations in immunological reactivity. In support of this hypothesis is the finding of *increased 19 S protein* in stressed prison populations and reported *increased levels of certain types of immunoglobulins* in psychiatric patients.

An immunoglobin (Ig) is a polypeptide that functions as an antibody.

**22.18. The answer is A** (*Synopsis*, ed. 4, page 497).

Bulimia or binge eating, found in *fewer than 5 percent* of obese persons, is one of the rare exceptions to the pattern of impaired satiety. It is characterized by the sudden, compulsive ingestion of very large amounts of food in a very short time, usually with great subsequent agitation and self-condemnation. It appears to represent a reaction to stress. Bulimic episodes are followed by induced vomiting. These bouts of overeating are not periodic, and they are far more often linked to specific precipitating circumstances. Binge eaters can sometimes lose large amounts of weight by adhering to rigid and unrealistic diets, but such efforts are almost always interrupted by a resumption of eating binges.

**22.19. The answer is B** (*Synopsis*, ed. 4, page 511).

Hyperventilation refers to excessive breathing generally associated with anxiety. A reduction in blood carbon dioxide produces symptoms of lightheadedness, palpitations, numbness and tingling periorally and in the extremities, and occasionally syncope.

The hyperventilation syndrome may occur in a variety of different persons. Hyperventilation is a physiological concomitant of *fear, anxiety, pain,* and *anger*. Therefore, it may occur not only in the neurotic person, but on occasions in which anyone may become afraid or angry or have pain for any reason. In contrast, in certain hysterical persons, hyperventilation may have special meanings of which the patient is not aware; for instance, when such a patient becomes sexually aroused. Some hysterical patients hyperventilate because of a hysterical identification with a family member who suffered from dyspnea or asthmatic attacks. In the history of some hyperventilating patients, there is a family member who at some time in the past had difficulties in breathing that are analogous to or exactly like the patient's current symptoms.

*Fear* is an unpleasurable emotional state consisting of psychological and physiological changes in response to a realistic threat or danger. *Anxiety* is an unpleasurable emotional state associated with psychophysiological changes in response to an intrapsychic conflict. In contrast to fear, the danger or threat in anxiety is unreal. Physiological changes consist of increased heart rate, disturbed breathing, trembling, sweating, and vasomotor changes. Psychological changes consist of an uncomfortable feeling of impending danger, an overwhelming awareness of being powerless, the inability to perceive the unreality of the threat, prolonged feeling of tension, and exhaustive readiness for the expected danger. *Pain* is an unpleasant sensory and emotional experience associated with, or described in terms of, actual or potential tissue damage.

*Lassitude*, a state of incapacity or total exhaustion, is not a physiological concomitant of hyperventilation.

## 22.20. The answer is E (*Synopsis*, ed. 4, page 488).

A psychosomatic disorder is a disorder characterized by physical symptoms caused by psychological factors. It usually involves a single organ system innervated by the autonomic nervous system. The physiological and organic changes stem from a sustained emotional disturbance. It was previously known as psychophysiological disorder. In DSM-III, it is called psychological factors affecting physical conditions.

The cause of *cancer* is unknown. Although psychological factors have not traditionally been implicated in its etiology, recent research has investigated the relationship between the immune system and cancer and the relationship between the immune system and psychological stress. It has been found that chronic stress or depression can affect the immune system adversely.

*Premenstrual syndrome* occurs within 5 days of the woman's period and consists of pain, irritability, anxiety, depression, and fatigue. *Migraine headaches* are severe, unilateral, throbbing headaches that appear periodically, usually beginning during the teenage years and continuing to recur with diminishing frequency during advancing years. *Rheumatoid arthritis* is a chronic spreading or inflammation of the synovial membrane, involving many joints but with a predilection for the smaller ones. The etiology is unknown. Because many recurrences seem to be related to emotional crisis, however, rheumatoid arthritis is believed to be a psychosomatic disorder. *Hyperthyroidism* is an abnormality of the thyroid gland in which thyroxin secretion is usually increased and is no longer

under regulatory control of hypothalamic-pituitary centers.

A great variety of illnesses have traditionally been considered to be psychosomatic disorders. The student should be aware that psychological factors are not the sole etiological factor or even a major factor in many of these illnesses. Indeed, psychological factors may play only a minor role in some illnesses. Yet, the psychological factor should not be discounted. Some of the diseases traditionally considered to be psychosomatic disorders are listed in the table below.

**Some Psychosomatic Disorders***

| | |
|---|---|
| Acne | Nausea |
| Allergic reactions | Neurodermatitis |
| Angina pectoris | Obesity |
| Angioneurotic edema | *Painful menstruation* |
| Arrhythmia | Pruritis ani |
| Asthmatic wheezing | Pylorospasm |
| Bronchial asthma | Regional enteritis |
| Cardiospasm | *Rheumatoid arthritis* |
| Coronary heart disease | Sacroiliac pain |
| Diabetes mellitus | Skin diseases, such as |
| Duodenal ulcer | neurodermatitis |
| Essential hypertension | Spastic colitis |
| Gastric ulcer | Tachycardia |
| Headache | Tension headache |
| Hyperinsulinism | Tuberculosis |
| *Hyperthyroidism* | Ulcerative colitis |
| Hypoglycemia | Urticaria |
| Irritable colon | Vomiting |
| *Migraine headache* | Warts |
| Mucous colitis | |

\* Adapted, in part, with permission, from American Psychiatric Association: *Diagnostic and Statistical Manual of Mental Disorders*, ed 3. American Psychiatric Association, Washington, DC, 1980.

## 22.21. The answer is B (*Synopsis*, ed. 4, page 502).

The course of anorexia nervosa varies greatly—from spontaneous recovery without treatment, recovery after a variety of treatments, a fluctuating course of weight gains followed by relapses, to a gradually deteriorating course resulting in death due to complications of starvation. The short-term response of patients to almost all hospital treatment programs is good. Studies have shown a range of mortality rates from *5 percent to 21.5 percent*.

## 22.22. The answer is E (*Synopsis*, ed. 4, page 542).

Biofeedback has not been used therapeutically in *ulcerative colitis*, which is a chronic disease of unknown cause, characterized by ulceration of the colon and rectum (with bleeding) mucosal crypt abscesses, and inflammatory pseudopolyps. It frequently causes anemia, hypoproteinemia, and electrolyte imbalance.

The application of biofeedback treatment techniques to patients with *hypertension, cardiac arrhythmias, epilepsy,* and *tension headaches,* however, has provided encouraging but inconclusive therapeutic results. Controlled studies and outcome studies must still be carried out in the future.

*Essential hypertension* is considered by many to be a psychosomatic cardiovascular disorder. It is classified as an abnormally high blood pressure without a known cause. *Cardiac arrhythmias* consist of irregular, slow, or rapid heart beats. They are associated with both depression and anxiety, as well as with physical problems in the conduction system of the heart. *Epilepsy* is a neurological disorder resulting from a sudden, excessive, disorderly discharge of neurons in either a structurally normal or a diseased cerebral cortex. It is characterized by the paroxysmal recurrence of short-lived disturbances of consciousness, involuntary convulsive muscle movements, psychic or sensory disturbances, or some combination thereof. It is termed idiopathic epilepsy when there is no identifiable organic cause. *Tension headaches* are associated with nervous tension, anxiety, and chronic contraction of the scalp muscles.

**22.23.   The answer is C** (*Synopsis*, ed. 4, pages 513 and 514).

*Residential centers for asthmatic children* are located primarily in the western and southwestern parts of the United States, and it was originally assumed that their greatest benefit stemmed from the climate. Although climate may be important in certain cases, the concomitant "parentectomy" may be even more crucial in other cases in which separation of the child from his or her family psychopathology leads to marked improvement in the asthma, even without medication or other therapeutic measures. The children most apt to benefit by this environmental manipulation are those with neurotic features and few allergic problems.

**22.24.   The answer is A (1, 2, 3)** (*Synopsis*, ed. 4, page 501).

Anorexia nervosa is a serious and sometimes life-endangering condition characterized by self-imposed severe dietary limitation, usually resulting in serious malnutrition. Its onset typically occurs between the ages of 10 and 30, although there are cases reported of this illness developing before age 10; however, the onset is uncommon before age 10 and after age 30. Often those cases outside this age range are not typical and so their diagnoses are in question. From the

age of 13 years, the frequency of onset increases rapidly, with the maximum frequency at 17 to 18 years of age. About 85 percent of all anorectic patients develop the illness between the ages of 13 and 20 years.

Most of the aberrant behavior directed toward losing weight occurs in secret. The anorectic patients usually refuse to eat with their families or in public places. They lose weight by a drastic *reduction in the total food intake*, with a disproportionate decrease in high carbohydrate and fat-containing foods.

Unfortunately, the term anorexia is a misnomer, because the loss of appetite is usually rare until late in the illness. Evidence that *the patients are constantly thinking about food* is their passion for collecting recipes and engaging in elaborate meal preparations for others. Some patients cannot exert continuous control over their voluntary restriction of food intake, and they have eating binges. These binges usually occur secretly and often at night. Self-induced vomiting (bulimia) frequently follows the eating binge. Patients abuse laxatives and even diuretics in order to lose weight. *Ritualistic exercising,* extensive cycling, and walking are common activities.

Patients with this disorder exhibit peculiar behavior around food. They hide food, especially candies, all over the house and frequently carry large quantities of candies in their pockets and purses. While eating meals, they try to dispose of food in their napkins or hide it in their pockets. They cut their meat in very small pieces and spend a great deal of time rearranging the food items on their plate. If the patients are confronted about their peculiar behavior, they often deny that their behavior is unusual or flatly refuse to discuss it.

The patients' failure to recognize their starved bodies as too thin, or to regard them as normal or even overweight in the face of increasing cachexia, has been tested experimentally by several groups of investigators. The degree of body image disturbance appears to be related to the severity of the illness.

Many female anorectics come to medical attention because of *amenorrhea,* which often appears before noticeable weight loss has occurred.

**22.25.   The answer is E (all)** (*Synopsis*, ed. 4, page 513).

At the present time, clinical research on asthmatic patients, especially children, has been guided by these main principles: (1) No single or uniform personality type has bronchial asthma. (2) Many asthmatic patients (about one-half) have strong unconscious wishes for protection and for being encompassed by another person, *particularly the mother or her sur-*

*rogate, on whom they are very dependent.* These wishes sensitize some patients to separation from the mother. In other patients, the wish produces such an intense conflict that separation from the mother or her surrogate produces remission from asthmatic attacks. (3) The specific wishes for protection or envelopment are said to be caused by the mother's attitudes toward her asthmatic child. Studies of asthmatic children and their families, however, have shown that no single pattern of mother-child relationship obtains. The mother may be overprotective and oversolicitous of the child; perfectionistic and overambitious for the child; overtly domineering, punitive, or cruel to the child; or helpful and generative. Presumably, these attitudes both antecede the illness and are responsible for the child's conflicts and failure to develop psychologically. There is, however, no proof of these assumptions. In fact, the attitude of the mother is more likely related to the child's social adjustment—his or her truancy or invalidism—than to the asthmatic attacks. (4) The asthmatic attack occurs when these *wishes are frustrated by the mother* or some other person, or when they are activated and produce conflict. In both instances, strong emotions are aroused. (5) Some adult asthmatic patients have various psychological conflicts other than the ones already described.

Many asthmatic children demonstrate age-inappropriate behaviors and traits, and *poor impulse control.* Some of them are timid, babyish, and overly polite; others are tense, restless, rebellious, irritable, and explosive in their emotional outbursts. Asthmatic boys, in particular, tend to be passively dependent, timid, and immature, and at times they become irritable when frustrated. The asthmatic girls tend to depend on their fathers more than their mothers and try to be self-sufficient but are frequently chronically depressed. Asthmatic children are also dominated by a fear of losing parental support. They attempt to defend against this fear by a show of independence, maturity, and masculinity. The mothers of some of the children are seductive; others overemphasize achievement and self-control. Regardless of the quality of the parental attitudes, *whenever separation from their parents, particularly the mother, is threatened or actually occurs, the asthmatic children become anxious, lose control, become dependent, or have an asthmatic attack.*

**22.26. The answer is E (all)** (*Synopsis*, ed. 4, page 500).
This patient is suffering from anorexia nervosa, which is characterized by a weight loss of at least 25 percent of original body weight. There is an *intense fear of becoming obese*, a distur-

bance of body image, and amenorrhea. These patients *deny that they are emaciated*, and they *do not lose their appetite*, but steadfastly refuse to eat.

Psychodynamic theories in anorexia nervosa postulate that these patients reject, through starvation, a wish to be pregnant and have fantasies of oral impregnation. Other dynamic formulations have included a dependent, *seductive relationship with a warm but passive father* and guilt over aggression toward an ambivalently regarded mother.

Anorexia nervosa must be differentiated from bulimia, a disorder in which episodic binge eating, followed by depressive moods, self-deprecating thoughts, and often self-induced vomiting, occurs while the patients mantain their weight within a normal range. The table below lists the DSM-III diagnostic criteria for anorexia nervosa.

**Diagnostic Criteria for Anorexia Nervosa***

A. Intense fear of becoming obese, which does not diminish as weight loss progresses.

B. Disturbance of body image, e.g. claiming to "feel fat" even when emaciated.

C. Weight loss of at least 25 percent of original body weight or, if under 18 years of age, weight loss from original body weight plus projected weight gain expected from growth charts may be combined to make the 25 percent.

D. Refusal to maintain body weight over a minimal normal weight for age and height.

E. No known physical illness that would account for the weight loss.

* From American Psychiatric Association: *Diagnostic and Statistical Manual of Mental Disorders*, ed 3. American Psychiatric Association, Washington, DC, 1980. Used with permission.

**22.27. The answer is D (4)** (*Synopsis*, ed. 4, page 537).
*Chronic pain patients tend to be middle-aged or older, to come from a lower socioeconomic group and a larger family, to have more siblings, to have more relatives who have had painful illnesses and received disability compensation, and to have a history of more painful injuries and illnesses.* Some chronic pain patients previously were hard-working, independent persons who took care of others as a way of dealing with their strong underlying dependency needs and wishes to be taken care of themselves; chronic pain may make fulfillment of those wishes acceptable. The price paid, however, may be the threat or actual relinquishment of positions of authority in the family, social network, or at

work. Financial stresses may result from a decreased salary and the medical bills necessary to legitimize their sick role.

### 22.28. The answer is E (all) (*Synopsis*, ed. 4, pages 536 and 537).

A large number of emotional states and psychiatric disorders may lead to a chronic pain syndrome. Also, any type of ongoing pain is stressful and will cause some degree of disorganization of the personality because it indicates that the organism is failing to maintain or protect itself in some manner. Chronic, excessive pain may cause a psychological reaction termed pain shock, manifested by chronic irritability, anxiety, depression, fatigue, insomnia, and job and family problems. Ongoing pain results in decreased activity that may lead to atrophy, weakness, and further disability.

*Depressed patients* are especially prone to develop chronic pain, and if depression is severe, the patients may develop delusions of cancer, rotting, or other metaphors of decay and death to explain the chronic pain. The physician should assume masked depression is present until vigorous clinical trials of treatment for depression (possibly including antidepressants, monoamine oxidase inhibitors, and electroconvulsive treatment) have failed. Some chronic pain patients have been successfully treated in this manner without ever acknowledging that they felt depressed; their depression may have been entirely manifested through somatic equivalents.

The *mourning or grieving* person may develop pain similar to that experienced by the lost person as a means of identifying with and introjecting part of the person in an attempt to deny the loss. Patients with obsessive personalities often recount their history in seemingly endless detail and may develop compulsive rituals to alleviate their discomfort. Schizophrenic, demented, delirious, or psychotic patients develop bizarre forms of pain that are often attributed to some persecuting external force. *Psychotic* patients are also at risk for incorporating the pain of an organic illness, e.g. myocardial infarction, perforated ulcer, into a *delusion* and not seeking medical help.

*Depression* is a mental state characterized by feelings of sadness, loneliness, despair, low self-esteem, and self-reproach. The term refers either to a mood that is so characterized or to an affective disorder. Accompanying signs include psychomotor retardation or at times agitation, withdrawal from interpersonal contact, and vegetative symptoms, such as insomnia and anorexia. *Psychosis* is a mental disorder in which a person's thoughts, affective response, ability to recognize reality, and ability to communicate and relate to others are sufficiently impaired to grossly interfere with his or her capacity to deal with reality. *Delusions* refers to a false belief that is firmly held, despite objective and obvious contradictory proof or evidence and despite the fact that other members of the culture do not share the belief.

### 22.29. The answer is E (all) (*Synopsis*, ed. 4, page 536).

Most chronic pain patients attempt to treat themselves before seeking medical help. Billions of dollars are spent annually by people seeking relief through *over-the-counter preparations* or other nonmedical means. These persons often become *addicted to alcohol* and other drugs. Therefore, the physician should be alert for drug toxicity (especially overmedication) and *withdrawal symptoms during evaluation* and treatment of chronic pain patients. Explaining to the patient and family that sensitivity to pain may greatly increase during drug withdrawal may partially decrease anxiety and increase pain sensitivity caused by weaning.

A physician should always remember that a *psychiatric diagnosis does not preclude the existence of a concomitant medical illness*. It may be risky for a known chronic pain patient with a new organic illness to seek medical help because the physician may erroneously assume that the present symptoms are an exacerbation of the long-standing disorder. The medical evaluation should be repeated periodically, especially if chronic pain worsens or changes significantly. About 10 percent of patients (who have had thorough work-ups) referred to pain clinics eventually are found to have a neoplasm or other occult medical condition that slowly became manifest.

### 22.30. The answer is E (all) (*Synopsis*, ed. 4, pages 520 and 521).

The premenstrual syndrome (PMS) is composed of a variety of physical, psychological, and behavioral symptoms that may begin soon after ovulation, increase gradually, and *reach a maximum of intensity about 5 days before the menstrual period*. These symptoms also may intensify around the time of ovulation. The symptoms decline rapidly once menstruation starts, and a peak of well-being and positive feelings occurs during mid- and late-follicular phase. A *symptom-free time between menstruation and ovulation* helps to establish the diagnosis of PMS. The symptoms vary in severity from mild to incapacitating. Seventy to 90 percent of all women of childbearing age report at least some of these symptoms. Less than one-third of these women alter their daily routine in terms of work absence, bed rest, or seeing a doctor. The syndrome *is rare in teenage girls* and tends to increase in severity with age, particularly in the thirties and forties, ending after the menopause. The syndrome *continues in women with intact ovaries after hysterectomy.*

It has not been established firmly whether these changes are psychologically or hormonally determined or whether they are a variant of a normal pattern or manifestations of an abnormal process.

**22.31. The answer is E (all)** (*Synopsis*, ed. 4, page 496).

The most striking influence on obesity is that of *socioeconomic status.* Obesity is 6 times more common among women of low status than among those of high status. A similar, although weaker, relationship is found among men. Obesity is far more prevalent among lower-class children than it is among upper-class children; significant differences are already apparent by age 6. *Social mobility,* ethnic factors, and generation in the United States also influence the prevalence of obesity.

*Age* is the second major influence on obesity. There is a monotonic increase in the prevalence of obesity between childhood and age 50; a 3-fold increase occurs between ages 20 and 50. At age 50, prevalence falls sharply, presumably because of the very high mortality of the obese from cardiovascular disease in the older age groups.

*Women* show a higher prevalence of obesity than do men; this difference is particularly pronounced past age 50 because of the higher mortality rate among obese men after that age.

**22.32. The answer is A (1, 2, 3)** (*Synopsis*, ed. 4, page 510).

First described by DaCosta in 1871 and named irritable heart by him, neurocirculatory asthenia has some 20 synonyms, such as effort syndrome, DaCosta's syndrome, cardiac neurosis, vasoregulatory asthenia hyperkinetic heart syndrome, and hyperdynamic β-adrenergic circulatory state. Psychiatrists tend to view it as a clinical variant of anxiety disorder.

The diagnostic criteria for neurocirculatory asthenia used in the Framingham heart disease epidemiology study were (1) a respiratory complaint, such as *sighing respiration,* inability to get a deep breath, smothering and choking, or dyspnea and (2) one or more symptoms from at least two of the following groups: (a) palpitation, *chest pain,* or discomfort; (b) nervousness, *dizziness,* faintness, or discomfort in crowds; (c) undue fatigability or tiredness or limitation of activities. Breathlessness, palpitations, chest pain, fatigue, poor exercise tolerance, and nervousness constitute the core symptoms. In addition, the patient may complain of dizziness, tremulousness, easy startle response, paresthesias, faintness and syncopal attacks, excessive sweating, insomnia, and irritability. The symptoms usually start in adolescence or the patient's early twenties, but may have their onset in middle age. They are twice as common in women as in men and tend to be chronic, with recurrent acute exacerbations.

*Ideas of reference,* in which persons believe that events in the environment relate to them, are not present in this disorder. The management of neurocirculatory asthenia may be difficult, and prognosis is guarded if the condition is chronic, phobic elements are prominent, or the patient derives primary or secondary gains from his or her disability. Psychotherapy aimed at uncovering psychodynamic factors—usually issues relating to hostility, unacceptable sexual impulses, dependence, guilt, and death anxiety—may be effective in some cases, but most patients with the condition tend to shun psychiatric help. The use of propranolol may interrupt the vicious cycle of cardiac symptoms having a positive feedback effect on anxiety, which aggravates the symptoms. Physical training programs aimed at correcting faulty breathing habits and at gradually increasing the patient's effort tolerance may be helpful, especially if the programs are combined with group psychotherapy.

There is no DSM-III category for neurocirculatory asthenia. Depending on the symptom complex, the patient may be diagnosed as having dysthymic disorder or generalized anxiety disorder.

## References

Alexander F: *Psychosomatic Medicine: Its Principles and Application.* W W Norton, New York, 1950.

Drossman D A: The physician and the patient. In *Gastrointestinal Disease: Pathophysiology, Diagnosis, Management,* M H Sleisenger, J S Fordtran, editors, ed 3, p 3. W B Saunders, Philadelphia, 1983.

Hackett T P, Rosenbaum J F: Emotion, psychiatric disorders, and the heart. In *A Textbook of Cardiovascular Medicine,* E Braunwald, editor, ed 2, p 1826. W B Saunders, Philadelphia, 1984.

Halmi K A: Anorexia nervosa. In *Clinical Psychopharmacology,* D G Grahame-Smith, H Hippius, G Winokur, p 313. Excerpta Medica, Amsterdam, 1982.

Kaplan H I: Treatment of psychosomatic disorders.

In *Comprehensive Textbook of Psychiatry*, ed 4. H I Kaplan, B J Sadock, editors, p 1215. Williams & Wilkins, Baltimore, 1985.

Lipowski Z J, Lipsitt D R, Whybrow P C: *Psychosomatic Medicine: Current Trends and Clinical Applications.* Oxford University Press, New York, 1977.

Nemiah J C, Sifneos P C: Affect and fantasy in patients with psychosomatic disorders. In *Modern Trends in Psychosomatic Medicine*, O Hill, editor, p 126. Butterworth, London, 1970.

Rose R, Sachar E: Psychoendocrinology. In *Textbook of Endocrinology*, R H Williams, editor, ed 6, p 647. W B Saunders, Philadelphia, 1981.

Weiner H: *Psychobiology and Human Disease.* Elsevier, New York, 1977.

Whitlock F A. *Psychophysiological Aspects of Skin Disease.* W B Saunders, London, 1976.

# 23

# Other Psychiatric Disorders: Atypical Psychoses, Factitious Disorders, Postpartum Disorders

This chapter includes a diverse group of conditions, among which are a small group of unusual psychiatric disorders that are rare and exotic and do not easily fit into the current DSM-III classification.

Culture-bound syndromes—such as Amok and Latah, which occur in Malaya; Piblokto or Arctic hysteria, which occurs among the Eskimos; and Voodoo practice in certain African and West Indian cultures—fall within the category of unusual psychiatric disorders. Researchers have observed the gross distortions of reality testing, including the presence of hallucinations and delusions, that are common in these disorders but are qualitatively different from schizophrenia.

The postpartum disorders also fall within the category of atypical psychosis in that the symptoms of delusions, hallucinations, and disorganized behavior seen in a small percentage of puerperal women do not meet the DSM-III diagnostic criteria for another condition, such as an organic mental disorder, paranoid disorder, or affective disorders.

Brief reactive psychosis is included in this chapter. It is classified as a mental disorder in DSM-III and is characterized by sudden onset, a related severe psychosocial stressor—for example, the death of a loved one through an accident—a short duration, and a relatively good prognosis.

Finally, factitious disorders are also included in this chapter. These disorders are characterized by the repeated, knowing simulation of a physical or mental illness for no apparent purpose other than to obtain immediate medical or psychiatric treatment. To support their history, these patients may feign symptoms suggestive of a disorder, or they may initiate the production of symptoms through self-mutilation or interference with diagnostic procedures. For example, body temperature, routinely recorded and presumably an objective measure, may be made to appear elevated through either manipulation or substitution of one thermometer for another. Similarly, urine collected for laboratory examination may be contaminated with feces or blood, obtained by self-laceration, in order to suggest infection or renal disease.

The unique aspect of these disorders is that the sole objective is to assume the role of a patient. Without an acute emotional crisis or a recognizable motive—as would be evident in an act of malingering—and without a need for treatment, many of these patients make hospitalization itself a primary objective and, often, a way of life.

Factitious disorders must be differentiated from malingering, in which there is an obvious goal in feigning illness, such as avoiding jury duty or being drafted into military service. In factitious disorder, the person's goal is only to assume the role of a patient. It was previously known as Ganser's syndrome.

The reader should refer to Chapter 23 in *Modern Synopsis-IV*, which covers this diverse group of conditions, and should then study the following questions and answers to test his or her knowledge of the subject.

# Questions

**DIRECTIONS:** Each of the statements or questions below is followed by five suggested responses or completions. Select the *one* that is *best* in each case.

**23.1.** A key diagnostic feature of Ganser's syndrome is the phenomenon of

A. twilight state
B. hysteria
C. giving incorrect and ridiculous answers to questions
D. echolalia
E. waxy flexibility

**23.2.** In *folie à deux*, the psychological defense mechanism that plays a key role is

A. projection
B. regression
C. reaction formation
D. displacement
E. identification with the aggressor

**23.3.** Persons suffering from factitious disorders

A. simulate physical illness
B. practice self-mutilation
C. alter their body temperatures
D. try to assume the role of a patient
E. all of the above

**23.4.** The acute anxiety reaction characterized by the patient's desperate fear that his penis is shrinking and may disappear into his abdomen, thereby causing his death, is known as

A. amok
B. koro
C. piblokto
D. windigo
E. voodoo

**23.5.** Most patients with brief reactive psychosis recover, with treatment, in

A. several hours
B. less than 1 week
C. 2 weeks
D. 1 month
E. less than 2 months

**23.6.** A drug treatment especially useful in Tourette's disorder is

A. diazepam
B. amphetamine
C. haloperidol
D. barbiturate
E. propranalol

**23.7.** Chronic factitious illness with physical symptoms must be differentiated from all of the following *except*

A. somatoform disorders
B. hypochondriasis
C. antisocial personality disorders
D. schizophrenic disorders
E. Munchausen syndrome

**23.8.** According to DSM-III, postpartum disorders are best classified as

A. anxiety disorders
B. atypical psychoses
C. affective disorders
D. schizophrenic disorders
E. personality disorders

**23.9.** Most studies of normal pregnant women indicate that the percentage who report emotional disturbance in the early postpartum period ranges from

A. 10 to 20 percent
B. 20 to 40 percent
C. 60 to 70 percent
D. 80 to 90 percent
E. 90 to 100 percent

**DIRECTIONS:** For each of the incomplete statements below, *one* or *more* of the completions given is correct. Choose answer:

A. if only **1, 2,** and **3** are correct
B. if only **1** and **3** are correct
C. if only **2** and **4** are correct
D. if only **4** is correct
E. if all are correct

**23.10.** Factitious illness with psychological symptoms

1. is also known as Ganser's syndrome
2. is rare, but is seen relatively frequently among prisoners
3. frequently looks like a psychosis
4. is apparently not under the person's voluntary control

**23.11.** In brief reactive psychosis,

1. if the psychotic symptoms last more than 2 weeks, the diagnosis should be changed
2. the psychotic symptoms appear immediately following a recognizable psychosocial stressor
3. the clinical picture may involve delusions, hallucinations, and loosening of associations
4. a period of increasing psychopathology immediately precedes the psychosocial stressor

**23.12.** Chronic factitious illness with physical symptoms

1. is also known as Munchausen syndrome
2. is under voluntary control, but the patient often denies the voluntary production of the illness
3. is frequently seen in patients with a family history of serious illness or disability
4. is very frequently seen in persons with a history of previous or current employment in a health-related position

**23.13.** Tourette's disorder

1. has a duration of more than 1 year
2. has an age of onset in adulthood
3. presents with recurrent, repetitive, purposeless movements
4. is untreatable

**23.14.** Persons displaying a factitious illness usually

1. have a history of being exposed to a genuine illness in a family member
2. are commonly employed in a health-related field
3. view the physician as a loving parent
4. have a history of early parental rejection

# Answers

## Other Psychiatric Disorders: Atypical Psychoses, Factitious Disorders, Postpartum Disorders

**23.1. The answer is C** (*Synopsis*, ed. 4, pages 544 and 545).

The most remarkable and key feature of Ganser's syndrome is the phenomenon of the patient *giving an utterly incorrect and often ridiculous reply*, although it is quite clear that the sense of the question has been understood. Furthermore, although these patients often appear to be disoriented in time and place, their general behavior gives the distinct impression that they are alert. They are not confused in the usual sense.

Auditory and visual hallucinations, hysterical analgesia, true spatial and temporal disorientation, circumscribed amnesia, and lack of insight are often symptoms associated with the Ganser state. Thus, this syndrome frequently bears the marks of a psychosis.

Ganser's syndrome is a rare disease, but is observed relatively often in prisoners. The premorbid personality of the patient is often characterized by certain hysterical features. It has been pointed out that this condition has never been observed in persons of superior intelligence.

The condition was first described in 1898 by the German psychiatrist Sigbert J. M. Ganser, who published a report about patients who showed a peculiar hysterical twilight state whenever they were replying to a question, a state typified by what he called "passing by" or "passing beside the point" (*Vorbeireden*). A *twilight state* is characterized by a transitory disturbance of consciousness during which many acts—sometimes very complicated—may be performed without the subject's conscious volition and without retaining any remembrance of them.

*Hysteria* is a general term used in several ways: to describe a pattern of behavior, as in the hysterical personality; to refer to a conversion symptom, such as hysterical paralysis; to refer to a psychoneurotic disorder, such as conversion hysteria or anxiety hysteria; to refer to a specific psychopathological pattern in which repression is the major defense; and loosely, as a term of opprobrium. *Echolalia* is a repetition of another person's words or phrases. It is observed in certain cases of schizophrenia, particularly the catatonic types. The behavior is considered by some authors to be an attempt by the patient to maintain a continuity of thought processes. *Waxy flexibility* is characterized by a condition in which the muscular system permits the molding of the limbs into any position where they remain indefinitely.

**23.2. The answer is E** (*Synopsis*, ed. 4, page 546).

A virtually inevitable condition for the occurrence of *folie á deux* is the close physical association and the intimate emotional bond between the two affected people. The mechanism of *identification with the aggressor* (the dominant person) probably plays a key role. The initiator of induced or shared psychosis is usually a paranoid schizophrenic whose special adjustment to the world is characterized not only by his or her persecutory and grandiose delusions but also by a deeply rooted relationship with another, usually dependent, person. The recipient or passive partner in this psychotic relationship has much in common with the dominant partner because of many shared life experiences, common needs and hopes, and, most important, a deep emotional rapport with the partner.

Identification with the aggressor is an unconscious process by which persons incorporate within themselves the mental image of a person who represents a source of frustration from the outside world. A primitive defense, it operates in the interest and service of the developing ego. The classic example of this defense occurs toward the end of the oedipal stage, when a boy, whose main source of love and gratification is his mother, identifies with his father. The father represents the source of frustration, being the powerful rival for the mother; the child cannot master or run away from his father, so he is obliged to identify with him.

*Projection* is an unconscious defense mechanism in which a person attributes to another those generally unconscious ideas, thoughts, feelings, and impulses that are personally undesirable or unacceptable. Projection protects the person from anxiety arising from an inner conflict. By externalizing whatever is unacceptable, such persons deal with it as a situation apart from themselves. *Regression* is an unconscious defense mechanism in which a person undergoes a partial or total return to earlier patterns of adaptation. Regression is observed in many psychiatric conditions, particularly schizophrenia. *Reaction formation* is an unconscious defense mechanism in which a person develops a socialized attitude or interest that is the direct antithesis of some infantile wish or impulse that the person harbors either consciously or unconsciously. One of the earliest and most unstable defense mechanisms, it is closely related to repression; both are defenses against impulses or urges that are unacceptable to the ego. *Displacement* is an unconscious defense mechanism by which the emotional component of an unacceptable idea or object is transferred to a more acceptable one.

**23.3.  The answer is E** (*Synopsis*, ed. 4, page 551).

Factitious disorders are characterized by the repeated, knowing *simulation of a physical or mental illness* for no apparent purpose other than obtaining immediate medical or psychiatric treatment. To support their history, these patients may feign symptoms suggestive of a disorder, or they may initiate the production of symptoms through *self-mutilation* or interference with diagnostic procedures. For example, body temperature, routinely recorded and presumably an objective measure, may be made to appear elevated through either *manipulation or substitution of a thermometer*. Similarly, urine collected for laboratory examination may be contaminated with feces or blood, obtained by self-laceration, to suggest infection or renal disease.

The unique aspect of these disorders is that the sole objective is to *assume the role of a patient*. Without an acute emotional crisis or a recognizable motive, as would be evident in an act of malingering, and without a need for treatment, many of these patients make hospitalization itself a primary objective and, often, a way of life.

**23.4.  The answer is B** (*Synopsis*, ed. 4, page 549).

*Koro* is an acute anxiety reaction characterized by the patient's desperate fear that his penis is shrinking and may disappear into his abdomen, in which case he will die.

The koro syndrome occurs almost exclusively among the people of the Malay archipelago and among the south Chinese (Cantonese), by whom this reaction is referred to as *suk-yeong*. Corre-

sponding female cases have been described, the affected woman complaining of shrinkage of her vulva, labia, and breasts. Occasional cases of a koro syndrome among people belonging to the Western culture have also been reported. The typical syndrome is rather rare.

Koro is a psychogenic disorder resulting from the interaction of cultural, social, and psychodynamic factors in specially predisposed personalities. Culturally elaborated fears about nocturnal emission, masturbation, and sexual overindulgence seem to give rise to the condition. Probably all koro patients have been troubled by what they consider sexual excesses and by fears about their virility. The patients' insight into their own condition is usually quite impaired.

Koro patients have been treated with psychotherapy, neuroleptic drugs, and, in a few cases, electroshock treatment. As with other psychiatric disorders, the prognosis is related to the premorbid personality adjustment and the associated pathology.

*Amok* is a condition, usually associated with Malayan men, consisting of a sudden, unprovoked outburst of wild rage, usually resulting in homicide. *Piblokto* refers to a culture-specific syndrome seen in Eskimos, usually women. The affected person screams, cries, and runs naked through the snow, sometimes with suicidal or homicidal tendencies. *Windigo* is a culture-specific syndrome seen in Canadian Indians. It is characterized by a delusion of transformation into or possession by a windigo (*wihtigo*), a feared supernatural cannibalistic monster. *Voodoo* is a religious practice that is characterized by a belief in magic (witchcraft), fetishes, and rituals. The practice originated in Africa and is usually practiced in the Western Hemisphere, especially the West Indies.

**23.5.  The answer is B** (*Synopsis*, ed. 4, page 544).

Symptomatic treatment of brief reactive psychosis with antipsychotic drugs and careful observation and nursing assistance are usually effective. Brief hospitalization may be required. Most patients *recover within a few days*. Follow-up psychotherapy may be indicated to deal with the aftermath of the stressful events and underlying personality problems.

A group of brief psychotic disorders presents certain characteristic features that distinguish these disorders from other psychotic conditions. Most important, the symptoms of this type of psychotic breakdown are almost always preceded by stressful life events to which the patient reacts with strong dysphoric affect. In addition to a clear history of such precipitating events, the disorder is further characterized by its acute and florid symptoms, its short duration, and its good prognosis. The patient presents the picture of a severely disturbed person who has lost contact with reality and manifests at least one but frequently all the hallmarks of psychosis—specifically, hallucinations, delusions, formal thought disorder, and grossly aberrant behavior. These patients are often dangerous to themselves or to others in their environment.

DSM-III lists the condition under the name brief reactive psychosis. By definition, the main precipitating factor is a major stress experience, closely related in time to the emergence of symptoms. People with unstable personalities seem to be more susceptible than other persons to this kind of psychotic breakdown. No clear genetic links are known at this time, but it seems that the disorder is not one of the spectrum of schizophrenic disorders.

**23.6.    The answer is C** (*Synopsis*, ed. 4, pages 547 and 548).

Until recently, no reliable, effective treatment of Tourette's disorder was known. The outcome was almost always poor. Eventually, many patients had to be institutionalized or live as recluses. None of Gilles de la Tourette's original cases developed favorably.

*Haloperidol*, a butyrophenone derivative, is the standard treatment. Doses of 6 to 180 mg a day are being prescribed, and most patients show more than a 90 percent reduction of their symptoms after 1 year of treatment. There is the ever-present risk, however, that a patient receiving haloperidol may later develop tardive dyskinesia. It is possible that not only haloperidol but also other neuroleptic drugs will be effective in alleviating the symptoms of Tourette's disorder. In some cases, drug treatment has been reported to be more effective in combination with psychotherapy. Behavior therapy has also been reported to reduce behavioral tics.

*Diazepam* is a derivative of benzodiazepine and is presently used for the treatment of anxiety. *Amphetamine* is a central nervous system (CNS) stimulant. Its chemical structure and action are closely related to ephedrine and other sympathomimetic amines. *Barbiturate* is one of a class of sedative-hypnotic drugs derived from barbituric acid. The drug acts as a CNS depressant and readily produces psychic and physical dependence. Phenobarbital, secobarbital, and thiopental sodium are commonly used barbiturates. β-Adrenergic blocking agents are utilized in the management of cardiovascular disorders, including hypertension, angina pectoris, and cardiac arrythmias. *Propranalol* was the first β-adrenergic antagonist to come into wide clinical use.

**23.7.    The answer is E** (*Synopsis*, ed. 4, pages 553 and 554).

*Munchausen syndrome* refers to a condition characterized by the recurrent fabrication of clinically convincing simulations of disease. In DSM-III, it is known as factitious disorder. Factitious illness is differentiated from *somatization disorder* (Briquet's syndrome) by the voluntary production of factitious symptoms, the extreme course of multiple hospitalizations, and the seeming willingness of the patient to undergo an extraordinary number of mutilative procedures.

In *hypochondriasis*, the essential feature is the patients' fear that they have a disease, and their behavior, including doctor shopping and preoccupation with bodily functions, follows from that fear. Hypochondriasis differs from factitious illness in that the hypochondriacal patient does not voluntarily initiate the symptom production, and hypochondriasis typically has a later age of onset.

An *antisocial personality disorder* usually appears at an earlier age than does a factitious illness, and antisocial persons do not usually resort to a way of life marked by chronic hospitalizations and invasive procedures.

The diagnosis of *schizophrenia* is most likely made because of the patient's admittedly bizarre life-style, but the patient does not usually meet the specified criteria of schizophrenia. If these patients have the fixed delusion that they are actually ill and act on that belief by seeking chronic hospitalization, they may meet the criteria for a schizophrenic disorder. This diagnosis however, seems to be the exception, rather than the rule, for few of these patients show such evidence of thought disorder.

**23.8.    The answer is B** (*Synopsis*, ed. 4, page 555).

Postpartum disorders are a group of diverse conditions—affective disorders, functional psychoses, or organic-like mental disorders—that occur in the postpartum period. Depressive disorder is the most common of these conditions. Postpartum disorders are believed to result from the stresses undergone during pregnancy and the period from 3 days to approximately 30 days after childbirth. These stresses include (1) endocrine changes, (2) changes in body image, (3) activation of unconscious psychological conflicts pertaining to pregnancy, and (4) intrapsychic reorganization of becoming a mother. According to DSM-III, this disorder is classified as an *atypical psychosis*, a term that is used only when no other psychotic disorder can be diagnosed.

*Anxiety disorder* is a disorder in which anxiety is the most prominent disturbance or in which the patients experience anxiety if they resist giving in to their symptoms. In DSM-III, the anxiety disorders include phobic disorder, anxiety state, obsessive-compulsive disorder, posttraumatic stress disorder, and atypical anxiety disorder. *Affective disorder* is any mental disorder in which disturbance of mood is the primary characteristic; disturbances in thinking and behavior are secondary characteristics. In DSM-III, the affective disorders include bipolar affective disorder, major depression, cyclothymic disorder, dysthymic disorder, and atypical affective disorders. *Schizophrenia* is a psychotic mental disorder characterized by disturbances in thinking, mood, and behavior. *Personality disorder* is a mental disorder characterized by inflexible, deeply ingrained, maladaptive patterns of adjustment to life that cause either subjective distress or significant impairment of adaptive functioning. The manifestations are generally recognizable in adolescence or earlier. The types of personality disorders listed in DSM-III include paranoid, schizoid, schizotypal, histrionic, narcissistic, antisocial, borderline, avoidant, dependent, compulsive, passive-aggressive, and atypical.

**23.9.   The answer is B** (*Synopsis*, ed. 4, page 555).

Data from studies of normal pregnant women indicate that from *20 to 40 percent* of women report emotional disturbance or cognitive dysfunction, or both, in the early postpartum period, the so-called postpartum blues.

Questionnaires exploring psychiatric symptoms of a random sample of women up to 1 year after childbirth revealed that 25 percent had more than six symptoms that had apparently arisen postpartum. The most common symptoms were fatigue, irritability, tension, and anxiety. Disturbances of psychotic proportions occur with one to two patients per 1,000 deliveries.

**23.10.   The answer is A (1, 2, 3)** (*Synopsis*, ed. 4, pages 544 and 545).

*Ganser's syndrome*, or factitious illness with psychological symptoms, is defined as *the apparently voluntary production* of psychological symptoms that cannot be explained by any other mental disorder. These persons apparently are seeking to assume the patient role, and the secondary gain seems to be that they escape a threatening reality by conveying the impression of insanity. Such patients often seek admission to mental hospitals. This syndrome *is apparently rare, but it is observed relatively often in prisoners* and *frequently looks like a psychosis.*

The table below contains the essential DSM-III diagnostic criteria for this syndrome, along with other possible associated features.

**23.11.   The answer is A (1, 2, 3)** (*Synopsis*, ed. 4, page 545).

Brief reactive psychosis has a clear history of precipitating events and is characterized by its acute and florid psychotic symptoms and its short duration. Symptoms last more than a few hours but less than 2 weeks, and *if the symptoms last more than 2 weeks, the diagnosis should be changed.* Although the patient presents the *picture of a severely psychotic person, there is no period of increasing psychopathology immediately preceding the stressor.*

The table on page 310 gives the DSM-III diagnostic criteria for this disorder.

**23.12.   The answer is E (all)** (*Synopsis*, ed. 4, pages 552 and 553).

**Clinical Features of Factitious Illness with Psychological Symptoms (Ganser's Syndrome)***

| Essential Features | Associated Features | Other Features† |
|---|---|---|
| Production of psychological symptoms under the patient's voluntary control | Inconsistent mental symptoms, such as memory loss, hallucinations, dementia | May occur in adolescents |
| Symptoms do not fit any other mental disorder, but may be superimposed on one | Suggestibility or negativism and uncooperativeness | Feeling of being caught in an inescapable situation, such as jail or severe threat of disability |
| The patient's goals—in contrast to malingering—are not easily recognized and require careful knowledge of the patient's psychology to be understood | *Vorbeireden*—the giving of approximate answers, talking past the point | Has been observed under the stress of voluntary restraint, such as during disulfiram treatment of alcoholism |
|  | Substance use | Never observed in persons of superior intelligence |
|  | Manifestations may be present only when patient believes he or she is being watched |  |

* Adapted from American Psychiatric Association: *Diagnostic and Statistical Manual of Mental Disorders*, ed 3. American Psychiatric Association, Washington, DC, 1980.

† Not cited as a clinical feature in DSM-III, but may be present in this disorder.

---

**Diagnostic Criteria for Brief Reactive Psychosis***

---

A. *Psychotic symptoms appear immediately following a recognizable psychosocial stressor* that would evoke significant symptoms of distress in almost anyone.

B. The clinical picture involves emotional turmoil and at least one of the following psychotic symptoms:

1. Incoherence or *loosening of associations*;
2. *Delusions*;
3. *Hallucinations*;
4. Behavior that is grossly disorganized or catatonic.

C. The psychotic symptoms last more than a few hours but less than 2 weeks, and there is an eventual return to the premorbid level of functioning. (Note: The diagnosis can be made soon after the onset of the psychotic symptoms without waiting for the expected recovery. If the psychotic symptoms last more than 2 weeks, the diagnosis should be changed.)

D. No period of increasing psychopathology immediately preceded the psychosocial stressor.

E. The disturbance is not due to any other mental disorder, such as an organic mental disorder, manic episode, or factitious disorder with psychological symptoms.

---

* From American Psychiatric Association: *Diagnostic and Statistical Manual of Mental Disorders*, ed 3. American Psychiatric Association, Washington, DC, 1980. Used with permission.

---

The essential feature of factitious illness with physical symptoms, as detailed in DSM-III, is the patient's plausible presentation of physical symptoms that are apparently *under the person's voluntary control* and that lead to multiple hospitalizations. When confronted, however, *the patient most often denies the voluntary production of the illness*. This syndrome, which has also been known as *Munchausen syndrome*, is *frequently encountered in patients with a family history of serious illness, and in persons employed in health care jobs*. The disorder is felt to be a form of compulsive repetition, or the repeating of the basic conflict of needing and seeking acceptance and love while expecting that it will not be forthcoming. In this case, the hospital staff become the rejecting parents.

The following DSM-III table gives the diagnostic criteria for factitious disorders.

---

**Diagnostic Criteria for Chronic Factitious Disorders with Physical Symptoms***

---

A. Plausible presentation of physical symptoms that are apparently under the individual's voluntary control to such a degree that there are multiple hospitalizations.

B. The individual's goal is apparently to assume the "patient" role and is not otherwise understandable in light of the individual's environmental circumstances (as is the case of malingering).

---

* From American Psychiatric Association: *Diagnostic and Statistical Manual of Mental Disorders*, ed 3. American Psychiatric Association, Washington, DC, 1980. Used with permission.

**23.13.   The answer is B (1, 3)** (*Synopsis*, ed. 4, page 547).

Tourette's disorder is a syndrome with an *onset between the ages of 2 and 12*. It is manifested by *recurrent, involuntary, repetitive motor movements* and multiple vocal tics, in particular the uttering of obscenities. To make the diagnosis, *the disorder must have been present for more than 1 year. The disorder is now felt to be largely treatable*, with a 90 percent *reduction of symptoms in most patients after 1 year* of treatment. The treatment of choice is haloperidol in doses of 6 to 180 mg a day.

The table on the facing page contains the essential DSM-III features for this diagnosis, along with possible associated features.

**23.14.   The answer is E (all)** (*Synopsis*, ed. 4, page 552).

A frequent occurrence in the history of these patients is a personal history of serious illness, disability, or *exposure to genuine illness in a family member* or significant extrafamilial figure. A history of prior or current employment as a nurse, laboratory technician, ambulance driver, physician, or other *health-related position* is so common as to suggest inclusion as a clinical feature, as well as a causal factor. Consistent with the concept of poor identity formation is the observation that these patients oscillate between two separate roles—a health professional and a patient—with momentary confusion as to which role is being played at the time.

Psychological models of factitious illness generally emphasize the etiological *significance of childhood deprivation and rejection*. The usual history reveals that one or both parents are

Clinical Features of Tourette's Disorder (Gilles de la Tourette's Disease)*

| Essential Features | Associated Features | Other Features† |
|---|---|---|
| Presence of involuntary, rapid, repetitive, purposeless movements (tics) involving various muscle groups<br><br>Multiple vocal tics (coprolalia in 60 percent)<br><br>The movements can be voluntarily suppressed, vary in intensity over time, and disappear during sleep<br><br>Duration of more than 1 year<br><br>Age of onset usually before puberty | Symptoms are aggravated by stress<br><br>There may be echokinesia (imitation of movements of another person), palilalia (repetition of one's last words), obsessive thoughts, and compulsive impulses to touch<br><br>Nonspecific EEG abnormalities, soft neurological signs, and psychological test abnormalities occur in about 50 percent of those affected | Symptoms are exacerbated by amphetamine-like drugs and significantly reduced by neuroleptic drugs<br><br>Occasional onset in adulthood carries a poor prognosis |

* Adapted from American Psychiatric Associaton: *Diagnostic and Statistical Manual of Mental Disorders*, ed 3. American Psychiatric Association. Washington, DC, 1980.

† Not cited as a clinical feature in DSM-III but may be present in this disorder.

experienced as rejecting figures who are unable to form close relationships.

*The physician is perceived by these patients as a potential source of the sought-for love*, and as a person who will fulfill the unmet dependency needs. The physician serves as a substitute father figure and as the object of a father transference. The patient uses the facsimile of genuine illness to recreate the original parent-child interaction.

# References

Capgras J, Reboul-Lachaux J: L'illusion des "sosies" dans un délire systématisé chronique. Ann Méd Psychol *81:* 186, 1923.

De la Tourette G: Étude sur une affection nerveuse caractérisée par l'incoordination motrice accompagnée d'écholalie et de coprolalie. Arch Neurol (Paris) *9:* 158, 1885.

Evans D L: Munchausen syndrome, depression, and the dexamethasone suppression test. Amer J Psychiatry *141:* 570, 1984.

Ganser S J M: Uber einen eigenartigen hysterischen Dämmerzustand. Arch Psychiatr Nerven-kr *38:* 633, 1898.

Hyler S E, Sussman N: Chronic factitious disorder with physical symptoms (the Munchausen syndrome). Psychiatr Clin North Am *4:* 365, 1981.

Kane F J Jr: Postpartum disorders. In *Comprehensive Textbook of Psychiatry*, ed 4. H I Kaplan, B. J Sadock, editors, p 1238. Williams & Wilkins, Baltimore, 1985.

Lehmann H E: Unusual psychiatric disorders, atypical psychoses, and brief reactive psychoses. In *Comprehensive Textbook of Psychiatry*, ed 4, H I Kaplan, B J Sadock, editors, p 1224. Williams & Wilkins, Baltimore, 1985.

Melges F T: Postpartum psychiatric syndromes. In *Psychosomatic Medicine*, M F Reiser, editor, vol 30, no 1, p 59. Harper & Row, New York, 1968.

Metz A, Stump K, Cowen P J, Elliot J M, Gelder M G, Grahame-Smith L J: Changes in platelet $\alpha$-2-adrenoceptor binding postpartum: Possible relation to maternity blues. Lancet *1:* 495, 1983.

Sussman N, Hyler S E: Factitious disorders. In *Comprehensive Textbook of Psychiatry*, ed 4, H I Kaplan, B J Sadock, editors, p 1242. Williams & Wilkins, Baltimore, 1985.

# 24

# Sleep and Sleep Disorders

In 1953, Aserinsky and Kleitman discovered a phenomenon occurring during sleep that was characterized by rapid conjugate eye movement (REM). The REM periods were found to be associated with dreaming and other biological functions. Since that initial observation, the study of sleep has evolved, and sleep laboratories are common at most medical centers.

Although not part of the official nosology or the third edition of the *Diagnostic and Statistical Manual of Mental Disorders* (DSM-III), a complex classification of sleep disorders has been promulgated by the Association of Sleep Disorders Centers. The classification includes the following: disorders of initiating and maintaining sleep—the insomnias; disorders of excessive somnolence—the hypersomnias; disorder of the sleep-wake schedule; and dysfunctions associated with sleep, sleep stages, or partial arousals—the parasomnias.

Polysomnography is a method used to study the various stages of sleep by recording changes in brain waves with the electroencephalogram (EEG), changes in muscle tone with the electromyogram (EMG), and changes in eye movements, blood pressure, blood oxygen levels, and nocturnal penile tumescence, among other biological functions.

Readers should refer to Chapter 24, "Sleep and Sleep Disorders," of *Modern Synopsis-IV* and should then study the questions and answers below to test their knowledge of this area.

# Questions

**DIRECTIONS:** Each of the statements or questions below is followed by five suggested responses or completions. Select the *one* that is *best* in each case.

**24.1.** As one falls asleep, one's electroencephalogram (EEG) begins to show

A. a disappearance of $\alpha$-activity
B. spindle-shaped tracings
C. K-complexes
D. $\delta$-waves
E. high-voltage activity

**24.2.** Nocturnal myoclonus

A. is similar to narcolepsy
B. usually occurs only 1 time each night
C. is a generalized body twitch before falling asleep
D. is seen predominantly in middle-aged and older people
E. is associated with drug withdrawal

**24.3.** A 40-year-old man who snores loudly while sleeping and at times seems to stop breathing is likely to be suffering from which one of the following:

A. Narcolepsy syndrome
B. Catalepsy syndrome
C. Sleep apnea syndrome
D. Kleine-Levin syndrome
E. Hypersomnia disorder

**24.4.** The chief cause of insomnia in an otherwise medically healthy young adult is

A. depression
B. anxiety
C. bodily pain
D. hypochondriasis
E. drug use

**24.5.** In the course of a year, what percentage of the population suffers from and seeks help for insomnia:

A. 10 percent
B. 20 percent
C. 30 percent
D. 40 percent
E. 50 percent

**24.6.** The most widely used treatment for narcolepsy is

A. stimulant medication
B. dietary management
C. imipramine
D. phenothiazine
E. psychotherapy

**DIRECTIONS:** For each of the incomplete statements below, *one* or *more* of the completions given is correct. Choose answer:

A. if only **1, 2**, and **3** are correct
B. if only **1** and **3** are correct
C. if only **2** and **4** are correct
D. if only **4** is correct
E. if all are correct

**24.7.** Which of the following neurotransmitters are involved in sleep and waking mechanisms:

1. Dopamine
2. Norepinephrine
3. Acetylcholine
4. Serotonin

**24.8.** Hypersomnolence may be the result of

1. depression
2. withdrawal from amphetamines
3. sleep apnea
4. depressant medications

**24.9.** Restless legs syndrome is

1. possibly a genetically transmitted disorder
2. a painful disorder
3. exacerbated by sleep deprivation
4. made worse by fever

**24.10.** In sleepwalking disorder,

1. evidence indicates that the episodes occur during REM sleep
2. there are repeated episodes of arising from bed while asleep and walking about for a period of several minutes to a half hour
3. on awakening, the person can remember the route traversed and what occurred during the episode
4. the repeated episodes usually occur during sleep stages 3 and 4

**24.11.** Which of the following methods are useful in treating insomnia:

1. Psychotherapy
2. Minor tranquilizers
3. Change in environment
4. Antipsychotic drugs

**24.12.** The symptoms of narcolepsy include

1. cataplexy
2. sleep paralysis
3. daytime sleepiness
4. hallucinations

**24.13.** Nightmares

1. are different from night-terrors
2. occur during REM sleep
3. gradually decrease during adulthood
4. occur more frequently in females than in males

**24.14.** Bruxism

1. is associated with REM sleep only
2. occurs in about 15 percent of normal persons
3. does not produce damage to the teeth
4. is aggravated by alcohol intake

**24.15.** Sleep terror disorder

1. occurs during arousal from stage 3 or stage 4 sleep
2. involves definite physiological activation
3. is quite common between the ages of 3 and 5
4. usually involves the recall of a vivid nightmare

**24.16.** Hypersomnia is associated with which of the following conditions:
1. Kleine-Levin syndrome
2. Trypanosomiasis
3. Depression
4. Amphetamine withdrawal

**24.17.** Narcolepsy is associated with
1. episodic attacks of rapid eye movement (REM) sleep
2. hypnagogic hallucinations
3. cataplexy
4. excessive daytime sleepiness

**DIRECTIONS:** Each set of lettered headings below is followed by a list of numbered words or phrases. For each numbered word or phrase, select

    A. if the item is associated with **A** *only*
    B. if the item is associated with **B** *only*
    C. if the item is associated with *both* **A** *and* **B**
    D. if the item is associated with *neither* **A** *nor* **B**

**Questions 24.18–24.22**
    A. Nightmares
    B. Night-terrors
    C. Both
    D. Neither

**24.18.** REM sleep

**24.19.** NREM sleep

**24.20.** Usually followed by amnesia

**24.21.** Usually followed by relatively detailed recall

**24.22.** Perseverative movements

**Questions 24.23–24.27**
    A. REM sleep
    B. NREM sleep
    C. Both
    D. Neither

**24.23.** Sleepwalking (somnambulism)

**24.24.** Teeth grinding (bruxism)

**24.25.** Bed wetting (enuresis)

**24.26.** Cluster headaches

**24.27.** Erections

**Questions 24.28–24.33**
A. Predominantly associated with sleep-onset insomnia
B. Predominantly associated with sleep-maintenance insomnia
C. Both
D. Neither

**24.28.** Sleep apnea

**24.29.** Drug withdrawal

**24.30.** Jet lag

**24.31.** Work shift changes

**24.32.** Pain or discomfort

**24.33.** Aging

**Questions 24.34–24.39**
A. Nonrapid eye movement sleep (NREM)
B. Rapid eye movement sleep (REM)
C. Both
D. Neither

**24.34.** Orthodox sleep

**24.35.** Paradoxical sleep

**24.36.** Quiet sleep

**24.37.** Active sleep

**24.38.** D-sleep

**24.39.** S-sleep

**Questions 24.40–24.43**
A. 4 to 6 cycles per second
B. 0.5 to 2.5 cycles per second
C. Both
D. Neither

**24.40.** Lightest stage of sleep

**24.41.** Deepest stage of sleep

**24.42.** REM sleep

**24.43.** NREM sleep

# Answers

## Sleep and Sleep Disorders

**24.1.   The answer is A** (*Synopsis*, ed. 4, page 558).

As one falls asleep, one's electroencephalogram (EEG) begins to show *a disappearance of α-activity*. Stage 1, considered the lightest stage of sleep, is characterized by low-voltage, regular activity at 4 to 6 cycles per second. After a few seconds or minutes, this stage gives way to stage 2, a pattern showing frequent *spindle-shaped tracings* at 13 to 15 cycles per second (sleep spindles) and certain high-voltage spikes known as *K-complexes*. Soon thereafter, δ-*waves—high-voltage activity* at 0.5 to 2.5 cycles per second—make their appearance (stage 3). Eventually, in stage 4, these δ-waves occupy the major part of the record. The division of sleep into stages 1 through 4 is a somewhat arbitrary division of a continuous process. There is another division of sleep into two stages known as REM sleep (rapid eye movement sleep) and NREM sleep (non-rapid eye movement sleep).

**24.2.   The answer is D** (*Synopsis*, ed. 4, page 562).

Nocturnal myoclonus is seen *predominantly in middle-aged and older people*. It is extremely rare in children. Estimates of the incidence of nocturnal myoclonus among serious insomniacs range from 1 to 15 percent. There is some suggestion that the myoclonus worsens or appears in some patients at times of stress. A few studies suggest familial patterns for some types of nocturnal myoclonus, but the issue has not yet been explored in depth.

Nocturnal myoclonus is a neuromuscular abnormality that manifests itself in sudden, repeated contractions of one or more muscle groups—usually the leg muscle—during sleep. Each jerk lasts less than 10 seconds. Nocturnal myoclonus typically includes extension of the big toe and partial flexion of the ankles, the knee, and, less frequently, the hip. Myoclonus often occurs in both legs simultaneously, but it can occur in either leg alone, without any apparent pattern. Nocturnal myoclonic jerks usually occur in isolation, not as parts of generalized body movements. Partial arousal or a full awakening often follows the myoclonic jerk. *Myoclonic jerks usually occur every 20 to 40 seconds in episodes lasting from a few minutes to an hour or more*. Between the episodes of nocturnal myoclonus, sleep seems normal.

The patient is usually unaware of the myoclonus but complains either of frequent nocturnal awakenings and unrefreshing sleep or of excessive daytime sleepiness. Sometimes the patient is unaware of any problem, and only the bed partner complains.

Nocturnal myoclonus differs from the hypnic jerk, which is *a generalized body twitch that some people exhibit occasionally as they fall asleep*. *Narcolepsy* is a sleep disorder characterized by recurrent, brief, uncontrollable episodes of sleep. *Drug withdrawal* is associated with both sleep-onset insomnia and sleep-maintenance insomnia. Sleep-onset insomnia is defined as difficulty in falling asleep, and sleep-maintenance insomnia is associated with difficulty in staying asleep.

**24.3.   The answer is C** (*Synopsis*, ed. 4, page 562).

*Sleep apnea* is characterized by multiple apneas during sleep associated with loud snoring and daytime sleepiness. Although not a common cause of insomnia, it is important because it can be life threatening and is often treatable by nasopharyngeal surgery.

Sleep apnea is caused by an obstruction or occlusion of the airway by atonic or excessive tissue. The number and length of the apneic periods will determine the extent of cardiovascular involvement and change in oxygen saturation. In addition to disturbing sleep, apnea also produces chronic fatigue. Apnea is defined as the absence of breathing.

*Narcolepsy* syndrome is a sleep disorder characterized by recurrent, brief, uncontrollable episodes of sleep. *Catalepsy* syndrome is a condition in which a person maintains the body position in which the body is placed. It is a symptom observed in severe cases of catatonic schizophrenia. It is also known as waxy flexibility and cerea flexibilitas. *Kleine-Levin syndrome* is a condition characterized by periodic episodes of hypersomnia and bulimia; it is most often seen in adolescent boys and eventually disappears spontaneously. *Hypersomnia* disorder is characterized by excessive time spent sleeping. It is not related to narcolepsy.

**24.4.   The answer is B** (*Synopsis*, ed. 4, page 563).

*Anxiety* can sometimes produce insomnia. In a young, medically healthy person, some form of anxiety is probably the chief cause of insomnia.

Anxiety is an unpleasurable emotional state associated with psychophysiological changes in response to an intrapsychic conflict. In contrast to fear, the danger or threat in anxiety is unreal. Physiological changes consist of increased heart rate, disturbed breathing, trembling, sweating, and vasomotor changes. Psychological changes consist of an uncomfortable feeling of impending danger, an overwhelming awareness of being powerless, the inability to perceive the unreality of the threat, prolonged feeling of tension, and exhaustive readiness for the expected danger.

Simple or transient anxiety is a phenomenon all persons experience before an examination, a difficult meeting, or an interview. It can frequently produce one night or several nights of insomnia—almost always difficulty in falling asleep. *Depression* is a mental state characterized by feelings of sadness, loneliness, despair, low self-esteem, and self-reproach. The term refers either to a mood that is so characterized or to an affective disorder. Accompanying signs include psychomotor retardation or at times agitation, withdrawal from interpersonal contact, and vegetative symptoms, such as insomnia and anorexia. *Hypochondriasis* is a somatoform disorder characterized by excessive, morbid anxiety about one's health. The term is derived from the belief that the state was caused by some dysfunction in the hypochondrium, especially the spleen. Hypochondriacal patients exhibit a predominant disturbance in which the physical symptoms or complaints are not explainable on the basis of demonstrable organic findings and are apparently linked to psychological factors. It is also known as hypochondriacal neurosis. *Drug use* is the use of any drug, either under a physician's care or through self-administration.

**24.5.   The answer is C** (*Synopsis*, ed. 4, pages 561 and 562).

Insomnia is an extremely common complaint. In the course of a year, up to *30 percent* of the population suffers from insomnia and seeks help for it. In many cases, no treatment may be required; in many other cases, a careful diagnostic work-up reveals specific causes of the insomnia, and specific treatment aimed at the cause may be used. Psychological factors account for 50 percent of all insomnias evaluated in sleep laboratories. The prescription of a sleeping pill as a long-term remedy for insomnia should be a relatively rare occurrence.

**24.6.   The answer is A** (*Synopsis*, ed. 4, page 568).

The most widely used treatment for narcolepsy involves the use of *stimulant medication.*

This treatment controls sleep attacks and daytime sleepiness dramatically. Doses as high as 40 to 60 mg per day of amphetamine or methylphenidate may be required.

*Dietary management* refers to a prescribed course of eating and drinking in which the amount and kind of food, as well as the times at which it is to be eaten, are regulated by the physician for therapeutic purposes. *Imipramine* is a medication used in treatment for depression. *Phenothiazines* are used as antipsychotic drugs and include such compounds as promethiazine, chlorpromazine, and prochlorperazine. *Psychotherapy* is a form of treatment for mental illness and behavioral disturbances in which a trained person establishes a professional contract with the patient and, through definite therapeutic communication, both verbal and nonverbal, attempts to alleviate the emotional disturbance, reverse or change maladaptive patterns of behavior, and encourage personality growth and development. Psychotherapy is distinguished from such other forms of psychiatric treatment as the use of drugs and electroshock therapy.

**24.7.   The answer is E (all)** (*Synopsis*, ed. 4, page 561).

The neurohumor most clearly involved in sleep and waking mechanisms is brain *serotonin.* Studies demonstrated that the administration of the serotonin precursor *l*-tryptophan induces sleep (reduces sleep latency) and tends to increase total sleep and to increase D-sleep time in humans, as well as in animals, without altering the states and stages of sleep.

There is also good evidence that *dopamine* is involved in sleep-waking mechanisms. Pharmacological methods of increasing brain dopamine tend to produce arousal and wakefulness, whereas dopamine blockers, such as pimozide and the phenothiazines, tend to increase sleep time somewhat, without altering the cycles of sleep or the relative amounts of S-sleep and D-sleep.

*Norepinephrine* may also be involved in the control of sleep. There seems to be an inverse relationship between functional brain norepinephrine and D-sleep. Drugs and manipulations that increase the available brain norepinephrine produce a marked decrease in D-sleep, whereas reducing brain norepinephrine levels increases D-sleep. That action of norepinephrine almost certainly involves $\alpha$-adrenergic receptors, because an $\alpha$-blocker, such as phenoxybenzamine, increases D-time, but a $\beta$-blocker, such as propranolol, has no effect.

There is little question that *acetylcholine* is also involved in sleep. It has been demonstrated that physostigmine and similar cholinergic agents can trigger D-sleep in humans. Acetylcholine does not occur in well-delineated systems, as do the monoamines, but is extremely widespread in the brain.

Dopamine, norepinephrine, and epinephrine are catecholamines that are neurotransmitters, whereas acetylcholine is a parasympathetic agent that also serves as a neurotransmitter. Serotonin, also known as 5-hydroxytryptamine, is produced mainly in the midline (raphe) regions of the pons and upper brain stem and is the most studied brain neurotransmitter.

### 24.8.   The answer is E (all) (*Synopsis*, ed. 4, pages 565 and 566).

Hypersomnolence has as its principal symptom either excessive amounts of sleep (hypersomnia) or excessive daytime sleepiness. It may be due to medical or psychiatric and environmental causes.

The table below lists a variety of causes of hypersomnolence as divided into its two major symptom categories.

### 24.9.   The answer is B (1, 3) (*Synopsis*, ed. 4, page 562).

Restless legs syndrome, a condition closely related to nocturnal myoclonus, is characterized during waking by extremely disagreeable but *rarely painful* creeping sensations deep inside the calf, occasionally in the feet and the thighs, and, in rare instances, in the arms. The syndrome is *exacerbated by sleep deprivation*, often occurs with particular severity during pregnancy, and typically becomes more serious with age. Curiously, the syndrome often *disappears with fever.*

About one-third of patients with restless legs syndrome show a familial pattern. It has been suggested that the syndrome may be *transmitted as an autosomal, dominant trait* with reduced penetration. The cause of restless legs syndrome is currently unknown.

### 24.10.   The answer is C (2, 4) (*Synopsis*, ed. 4, pages 570 and 571).

DSM-III defines sleepwalking disorders as *repeated episodes of arising from bed during sleep and walking about for a period of several minutes to a half hour.* There is *no evidence that the episodes occur during REM sleep*, but rather they appear to *occur during the interval of sleep that usually contains EEG δ-activity, sleep stages 3 and 4.* During the episodes, persons are relatively unresponsive to the efforts of others to communicate with them, and *on awakening, they have amnesia for what occurred during the episode.*

The table on page 320 lists the DSM-III diagnostic criteria for this disorder.

### 24.11.   The answer is E (all) (*Synopsis*, ed. 4, page 564).

Insomnia that is secondary to psychiatric or environmental conditions usually responds to specific treatment. When anxiety of a psychotic or prepsychotic type is responsible for the insomnia, *antipsychotic medication* is indicated, and *psychotherapy* may also be useful. Anxiety related to particular conflicts—for instance, anxiety about letting go and losing control of one's aggressive or sexual impulses—is often treatable by psychotherapy. When the problem is chronic and closely related to the patient's character, long-term nondirective therapy—psychoanalysis—may occasionally be useful. In some cases of anxiety, antianxiety medications (*minor tranquilizers*) are helpful. When the anxiety is partly muscular such techniques as relaxation therapy, medication, and biofeedback can be effective. These techniques sometimes help other insomniacs as well. When environmental problems or schedules produce insomnia, a careful evaluation usually reveals some way in which the *environmental factors can be altered.*

### Causes of Hypersomnolence*

| Principal Symptom | Chiefly Medical | Chiefly Psychiatric or Environmental |
| --- | --- | --- |
| Excessive sleep (hypersomnia) | Kleine-Levin syndrome | *Depression (some)* |
| | Menstrual associated | Alcohol |
| | Metabolic or toxic conditions | *Other depressant medications* |
| | Trypanosomiasis or other encephalic conditions | *Withdrawal from amphetamines* and other stimulants |
| Excessive daytime sleepiness | Narcolepsy | Depression (some) |
| | *Sleep apnea* | Medication and medication |
| | Hypoventilation syndrome | withdrawal (as above) |
| | Hyperthyroidism | Phase shift |
| | Other metabolic and toxic conditions | Non-24-hour cycles |

Excessive daytime sleepiness is sometimes a secondary symptom of any of the causes of insomnia; in other words, insufficient sleep at night sometimes produces excessive daytime sleepiness.

* The items listed in the two columns are not entirely separable.

### Diagnostic Criteria for Sleepwalking Disorder*

A. There are repeated episodes of arising from bed during sleep and walking about for several minutes to a half hour, usually occurring between 30 and 200 minutes after onset of sleep (the interval of sleep that typically contains EEG δ-activity, sleep stages 3 and 4).

B. While sleepwalking, the individual has a blank, staring face; is relatively unresponsive to the efforts of others to influence the sleepwalking or to communicate with him or her; and can be wakened only with great difficulty.

C. Upon awakening (either from the sleeping episode or the next morning), the individual has amnesia for the route traversed and for what happened during the episode.

D. Within several minutes of awakening from the sleepwalking episode, there is no impairment of mental activity or behavior (although there may initially be a short period of confusion or disorientation).

E. There is no evidence that the episode occurred during REM sleep or that there is abnormal electrical brain activity during sleep.

* From American Psychiatric Association: *Diagnostic and Statistical Manual of Mental Disorders*, ed 3. American Psychiatric Association, Washington, DC, 1980. Used with permission.

In major depression, an antidepressant medication usually improves the insomnia, along with the depression. Amitriptyline is the medication of choice in a large number of cases.

**24.12.   The answer is E (all)** (*Synopsis*, ed. 4, page 567).

Excessive *daytime sleepiness* and naps, and the accessory symptoms of *cataplexy, sleep paralysis,* and hypnagogic *hallucinations,* are the classically recognized tetrad of narcolepsy. Patients generally first report the onset of daytime sleepiness before the accessory symptoms are noted.

The sleepiness may persist throughout the day, but more often it is periodic and may be relieved by a sleep attack or by a nap from which the patient characteristically awakens refreshed. Thus, there are often refractory periods of 2 or 3 hours of almost normal alertness. The sleep attacks are usually associated with characteristic times of the day, such as after meals, when some degree of sleepiness is quite normal. The attacks are typically irresistible and may even occur while eating, riding a bicycle, or actively conversing and also during sexual relations.

*Cataplexy,* which occurs in two-thirds to 95 percent of the cases, represents the paralysis or the paresis of the antigravity muscles in the awake state. A cataplectic attack often begins during expressions of emotion, such as laughter, anger, and exhilaration. The attacks vary in intensity and frequency; they can consist of a weakening of the knees, a jaw drop, a head drop, or a sudden paralysis of all the muscles of the body—except for the eyes and the diaphragm—leading to a complete collapse.

*Hypnagogic hallucinations* are vivid perceptual dream-like experiences occurring at sleep onset or on awakening. They occur in about 50 percent of the patients. The accompanying affect is usually fear or dread. The hallucinatory imagery is remembered best after a brief narcoleptic sleep attack, when it is often described as a dream.

*Sleep paralysis* is a neurological phenomenon that is most likely due to a temporary dysfunction of the reticular activating system. It consists of brief episodes of an inability to move or speak when awake or asleep.

**24.13.   The answer is A (1, 2, 3)** (*Synopsis*, ed. 4, page 573).

Nightmares, sometimes called "REM anxiety attacks," are simply long, frightening dreams that *are quite different from night-terrors.*

Nightmares usually awaken the sleeper during the second half of the sleep period, and there is long, vivid recall of a dream ending in a frightening episode; often, the dreamer is being chased or being attacked, or occasionally some catastrophe is threatening the entire world.

They *occur equally in males and females.* There is a high incidence of nightmares in children at ages 3 to 7, and generally they *gradually decrease during adulthood.* Although few adults report night-terror episodes, a number of adults—perhaps 10 percent of the population—do, however, report occasional nightmares.

**24.14.   The answer is C (2, 4)** (*Synopsis*, ed. 4, pages 573 and 574).

Bruxism is a grinding, gnashing, or clenching of the teeth during sleep. Some degree of bruxism is common and has been *reported in 13 to 15 percent of normal persons.* At times, it is a severe enough condition to *produce damage to the teeth,* and dentists claim that such damage is not at all rare.

Psychological factors are clearly involved in initiating or, at least, in exacerbating periods of bruxism in many persons. Bruxism patients are more anxious than are normal persons, and in patients who occasionally have bruxism, periods of tension and perhaps suppressed anger are related to increased bruxism. *Alcohol intake often aggravates bruxism.*

*Bruxism is not associated with REM sleep solely.*

**24.15.   The answer is A (1, 2, 3)** (*Synopsis*, ed. 4, page 572).

Sleep terror disorder (also known as *pavor nocturnus*) is defined as repeated episodes of abrupt awakening, *occurring during stage 3 or stage 4 sleep* and associated with a panicky scream and *definite physiological activation*, including tachycardia, tachypnea, sweating, and dilated pupils. When *the patient awakes, he or she has no dream recall or very little recall.* Very often, the person returns to sleep and has total amnesia for the event in the morning. This disorder is *quite common between the ages of 3 and 5*, with episodes usually lasting 10 to 20 minutes. Children are often quite unresponsive to the efforts of others to comfort or even wake them, and there is almost always associated confusion and disorientation during the episode.

The following table lists the DSM-III diagnostic criteria for this disorder.

**Diagnostic Criteria for Sleep Terror Disorder***

A.  Repeated episodes of abrupt awakening (lasting 1–10 minutes) from sleep, usually occurring between 30 and 200 minutes after onset of sleep (the interval of sleep that typically contains EEG δ-activity, sleep stages 3 and 4) and usually beginning with a panicky scream.

B.  Intense anxiety during the episode and at least three of the following signs of autonomic arousal:

   1.  Tachycardia;
   2.  Rapid breathing;
   3.  Dilated pupils;
   4.  Sweating;
   5.  Piloerection.

C.  Relative unresponsiveness to efforts of others to comfort the individual during the episode and, almost invariably, confusion, disorientation, and perseverative motor movements (e.g. picking at pillow).

D.  No evidence that the episode occurred during REM sleep or of abnormal electrical brain activity during sleep.

---

* From American Psychiatric Association: *Diagnostic and Statistical Manual of Mental Disorders*, ed 3. American Psychiatric Association, Washington, DC, 1980.

**24.16.   The answer is E (all)** (*Synopsis*, ed. 4, pages 565, 566, and 567).

Hypersomnolence includes two groups of symptoms: complaints about excessive amounts of sleep (hypersomnia) and complaints about excessive daytime sleepiness (somnolence). In some situations, the two symptoms are clearly separate, but many of the conditions responsible for hypersomnolence can, at times, produce both symptoms.

*Kleine-Levin syndrome* is characterized by recurrent periods of hypersomnia, usually associated with hyperphagia, and also by periodic episodes of bulimia. It is most often seen in adolescent boys and eventually disappears spontaneously. The hypersomnia is characterized by prolonged sleep from which the patient is incapable of being aroused.

Infectious causes of hypersomnolence as an isolated symptom are extremely rare or nonexistent at present in the United States, but they are common in Africa and have been seen at times in many parts of the world. The best-known such condition is *trypanosomiasis*, which produces sleeping sickness as classically described by von Economo.

Excessive sleep and *depression* are typical symptoms of *withdrawal from amphetamines*. Withdrawal from other stimulant drugs, including caffeine, can produce similar effects. Subgroups of depressed patients definitely show hypersomnia—excessive sleep—during their depressions. This finding may be quite typical in bipolar patients, and it occurs in some unipolar cases as well.

**24.17.   The answer is E (all)** (*Synopsis*, ed. 4, page 567).

The essential features of classical narcolepsy are an abnormal tendency to sleep during the day (*excessive daytime sleepiness*), often disturbed nocturnal sleep, and pathological, virtually undeniable, *episodic attacks of REM sleep.* D-Sleep abnormalities manifested in narcolepsy include sleep-onset REM periods, *hypnagogic hallucinations, cataplexy,* and sleep paralysis. The cataplexy and sleep paralysis are abnormally appearing and dissociated REM sleep motor inhibitory processes.

*Cataplexy* is a temporary sudden loss of muscle tone, causing weakness and immobilization. It can be precipitated by a variety of emotional states, and it is often followed by sleep. A *hypnagogic hallucination* is a hallucination occurring while falling asleep (ordinarily not considered pathological).

**24.18–24.22.   The answers are 24.18–A, 24.19–B, 24.20–B, 24.21–A, and 24.22–B** (*Synopsis*, ed. 4, pages 572 and 573).

Night-terrors need to be clearly distinguished from nightmares. *Nightmares occur during REM sleep* and manifest with less intense anxiety. They are usually not forgotten and, in fact, *can usually be recalled in some detail. Night-terrors occur during NREM sleep* and manifest with severe anxiety, being heralded by a panicky scream. They are accompanied by disorientation and *perseverative movements* and are generally overtaken by *complete amnesia* for the event.

**Episodic Nocturnal Events (Parasomnias)**

| Disorder | Associated Sleep Stage |
|---|---|
| *Sleepwalking (somnambulism)* | NREM sleep, stage 4 |
| Night-terrors (pavor nocturnus) | NREM sleep, in early stages 3 and 4 |
| *Bed wetting (enuresis)* | NREM sleep, stages 3 and 4 |
| Nightmares | REM sleep |
| *Teeth grinding (bruxism)* | NREM sleep, primarily in stage 2 and transitions |
| Sleeptalking | NREM sleep |
| Jactatio capitus nocturnus (head banging) | Pre-sleep period and sometimes early stage 1 of NREM sleep |
| *Painful erections* | REM sleep |
| Familial sleep paralysis | REM sleep, usually first episode of the night |
| Hyperactive gag reflex | Not determined |
| Paroxysmal nocturnal hemoglobinuria | Not determined |
| Nocturnal epileptic seizures | Most frequently occur in the first 2 hours and last 2 hours of sleep |
| *Cluster headaches* and chronic paroxysmal hemicrania | REM sleep |
| Nocturnal cardiovascular symptoms (angina and dyspnea) | REM sleep (association is inconsistent) |
| Nocturnal asthma | REM sleep most frequently; NREM sleep, stages 3 and 4 least frequently |
| Nocturnal gastroesophageal reflex | Not determined |

**24.23–24.27.   The answers are 24.23–B, 24.24–B, 24.25–B, 24.26–A, and 24.27–A** (*Synopsis*, ed. 4, page 570).

A variety of conditions may occur during the night, and most are clearly associated with a specific stage of sleep. The above table lists in more detail specific parasomnias and their associated sleep stage.

**24.28–24.33.   The answers are 24.28–B, 24.29–C, 24.30–A, 24.31–A, 24.32–C, and 24.33–B** (*Synopsis*, ed. 4, page 561).

Sleep-onset insomnia is defined as that insomnia which is associated with difficulty falling asleep, whereas sleep-maintenance insomnia is defined as that which is associated with difficulty staying asleep. The causes of both types of insomnia may be overlapping, but there are some causes that are predominantly seen in one or the other. Among the most common causes associated with both include environmental change, alcohol, and drug interactions. Anxiety or tension tends to lead to sleep-onset insomnia, whereas depression tends to lead to sleep-maintenance insomnia.

The table in column 2 lists in more detail a variety of causes of insomnia.

**24.34–24.39.   The answers are 24.34–A, 24.35–B, 24.36–A, 24.37–B, 24.38–B, and 24.39–A** (*Synopsis*, ed. 4, pages 558 and 560).

As one falls asleep, one's brain waves go through certain characteristic changes, classified as stages 1, 2, 3, and 4, with stage 1 being considered the lightest stage of sleep. There are 4 or 5 periods of emergence from the different stages; these periods are distinctly different from the basic stages. These distinct states of sleep (1, 2, 3 and 4) are characterized by rapid conjugate eye movements (REM) and a host of other

**Causes of Insomnia\***

| Sleep-onset Insomnia† | Sleep-maintenance Insomnia‡ |
|---|---|
| Anxiety or tension | Depression |
| Environmental change | Environmental change |
| Emotional arousal | *Sleep apnea* |
| Fear of insomnia | Nocturnal myoclonus |
| Phobia of sleep | Dietary factors |
| Disruptive environment | Parasomnias |
| *Pain or discomfort* | Drugs |
| Restless legs syndrome | Alcohol |
| Caffeine | Drug interactions |
| Alcohol | *Drug withdrawal* |
| Medications | Dream interruption |
| *Drug withdrawal* | *Pain or discomfort* |
| *Jet lag* | Disease |
| *Work-shift changes* | *Aging* |
| Delayed sleep phase | Advanced sleep phase |
| Akathisia | |

\* The boundaries between the columns are not entirely distinct.
  † Difficulty in falling asleep.
  ‡ Difficulty in staying asleep.

distinguishing factors, including pulse rate and blood pressure irregularity, the pressure of full or partial penile erections, and generalized muscle atony interrupted by sporadic movements. Persons awakened during these periods report

### Sleep Stage Terminology*

| Nonrapid Eye Movement Sleep | Rapid Eye Movement Sleep |
| --- | --- |
| Also known as | Also known as |
| NREM sleep | REM sleep |
| S-sleep | D-sleep |
| S-state | D-state |
| Orthodox sleep | Paradoxical sleep |
| Slow-wave sleep | Fast sleep |
| Quiet sleep | Active sleep |

* S = synchronized and D = desynchronized or dreaming.

that they have been dreaming. This is a separate state of sleep and is referred to as *D-sleep* (desynchronized or dreaming sleep), and the remainder of sleep is known as *S-sleep* (synchronized sleep). These two states are also known as REM sleep and NREM sleep, as *paradoxical* and *orthodox sleep*, and as *active* and *quiet sleep*. S-sleep can be organized according to depth. Stage 1 is the lightest and stage 4 is the deepest. Most D-sleep occurs in the last third of the night, whereas most stage 4 sleep occurs in the first third.

The table in column 1 lists sleep stage terminology.

**24.40–24.43.  The answers are 24.40–A, 24.41–B, 24.42–D, and 24.43–C** (*Synopsis,* ed. 4, pages 258 and 259).

The waking electroencephalogram (EEG) is

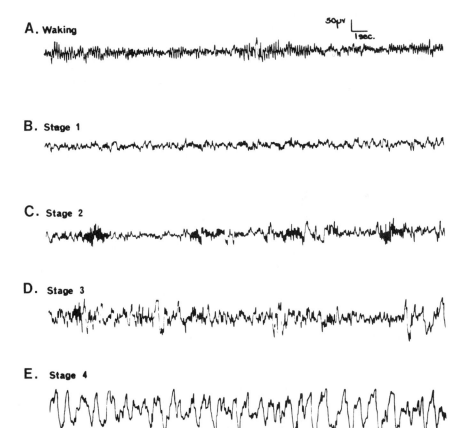

**A. Waking**

**B. Stage 1**

**C. Stage 2**

**D. Stage 3**

**E. Stage 4**

The electroencephalogram of sleep in a human adult. A single channel of recording—a monopolar recording from the left parietal area, referred to the ears as a neutral reference point—is shown for each stage. *A* (*waking*) is characterized by $\alpha$-waves at 8 to 12 cycles per second; *B* (*stage 1*) is characterized by the beginning disappearance of $\alpha$-waves and low-voltage, regular 4 to 6 cycles per second activity; *C* (*stage 2*) shows frequent spindle-shaped tracings at 13 to 15 cycles per second (sleep spindles) and certain high-voltage spikes known as K-complexes; *D* (*stage 3*) begins to show $\delta$-waves, high-voltage activity at 0.5 to 2.5 cycles per second; and *E* (*stage 4*) is characterized almost entirely by $\delta$-waves.

characterized by $\alpha$-waves of 8 to 12 cycles per second. Stage 1, which is considered *the lightest stage of sleep*, is characterized by low-voltage, regular activity at 4 to 6 cycles per second. Stage 4 sleep is the *deepest stage of sleep* and is characterized by high-voltage $\delta$-waves at 0.5 to 2.5 cycles per second. Stages 1 through 4 are considered *NREM sleep*, whereas *REM* sleep is considered a qualitatively different kind of sleep, which occurs as emergent periods from NREM sleep.

The EEG tracings on page 323 illustrate stages 1 through 4 NREM sleep.

## References

Berlin R M: Sleep disorders on a psychiatric consultation service. Am J Psychiatry *141:* 582, 1984.

Hartmann E L: Sleep disorders. In *Comprehensive Textbook of Psychiatry*, ed 4, H I Kaplan, B J Sadock, editors, p 1247. Williams & Wilkins, Baltimore, 1985.

Institute of Medicine: *Sleeping Pills, Insomnia, and Medical Practice.* National Academy of Sciences, Washington, DC, 1979.

Tan T L: Biopsychobehavioral correlates of insomnia. IV: Diagnosis based on DSM-III. Am J Psychiatry *141:* 357, 1984.

Williams R L, Karacon I: *Sleep Disorders: Diagnosis and Treatment.* John Wiley & Sons, New York, 1978.

Williams R L, Karacon I, Hursch C J: *Electroencephalography (EEG) of Human Sleep: Clinical Applications.* John Wiley & Sons, New York 1974.

# 25

# Psychiatric Emergencies

A psychiatric emergency is a disturbance in thoughts, feelings, or actions for which immediate treatment is deemed necessary. The physician may respond with condemnatory attitudes toward a patient whose psychiatric emergency has been precipitated by alcohol or drug abuse. Chronic mental illness may have led to social deterioration and lack of personal cleanliness. Many acutely disturbed patients are irritable, demanding, hostile, and provocative. For all these reasons, the physician may respond to the patient with negative feelings. Physicians must subject themselves constantly to self-criticism and self-appraisal and must alert themselves to feelings and attitudes that may adversely affect their relationship with their patients and thus impair their clinical judgment.

Crisis is manifested in many ways, most often through anger accompanied by varying degrees of aggressive behavior, severe anxiety accompanied by weeping, running, temporary states of confusion, and suicide attempts. Emergencies occur when individuals are faced with a situation beyond their particular adaptive capacity at a particular time. A person with considerable ego strength can cope with more stressful situations than someone with little ego reserve. Furthermore, a situation that is stressful for one person may not be so for another. The management of the suicidal patient is among the most challenging of the emergencies with which the psychiatrist must deal.

In the United States, suicide is the tenth major cause of death, with approximately 30,000 suicides recorded each year. It is estimated that each year there are about 10 times that number of attempted suicides. These figures do not fully reflect the magnitude of the problem. Some suicides are concealed. Other probable suicides are not recorded as such because of insufficient proof that a suicide, rather than an accident, was the cause of death. Because suicide (*sui* = self, *cide* = murder) is defined as the intentional taking of one's own life, the figures do not reflect unconsciously motivated fatal accidents or the many varieties of self-destructive behavior that are psychologically related to suicide.

The student is referred to Chapter 25 of *Modern Synopsis-IV*, which covers suicide and other psychiatric emergencies, and should then study the questions and answers that follow.

# Questions

**DIRECTIONS:** Each of the statements of questions below is followed by five suggested responses or completions. Select the *one* that is *best* in each case.

**25.1.** The best drug to be used in phencyclidine-induced psychosis is

A. trifluoperazine
B. diazepam
C. thioridazine
D. chlorpromazine
E. naloxone

**25.2.** Suicide rates among Protestants and Jews, as compared with Catholics, are

A. higher
B. lower
C. the same
D. not comparable
E. variable

**25.3.** A male patient who admits to abusing barbiturates refuses to tell the physician the amount of his customary daily dose. The physician prescribes a 200-mg test dose by mouth, and 1 hour later it is noted that the patient is awake, is able to speak, but is dysarthric. From that reaction, it is known that his average daily dose is

A. less than 200 mg/day
B. 500 mg/day
C. 700 mg/day
D. 900 mg/day
E. over 1 g/day

**25.4.** In neonates, the symptoms of heroin addiction generally appear

A. at birth
B. 6 to 48 hours after birth
C. 2 to 4 days after birth
D. 4 to 7 days after birth
E. 2 weeks after birth

**25.5.** The single most important psychiatric emergency is

A. paranoid schizophrenia
B. homosexual panic
C. suicidal depression
D. delirium
E. sedative-hypnotic withdrawal

**25.6.** A 40-year-old man, who is in a fearful and agitated state, is brought to the emergency room by a neighbor. His neighbor reports that there was a fire in the patient's apartment from which he was able to escape. Shortly thereafter the symptoms began. The disorder being described is

A. agoraphobia
B. anxiety disorder
C. isolated explosive disorder
D. posttraumatic stress disorder
E. panic disorder

**25.7.** Among men, suicide peaks after age 45; among women, it peaks after age

A. 35
B. 40
C. 45
D. 50
E. 55

**25.8.** The treatment for heroin overdose is

A. naloxone
B. diazepam
C. methadone
D. amphetamine
E. chlorpromazine

**25.9.** As a side effect, Rauwolfia alkaloids, such as reserpine, may produce

A. depression
B. akathisia
C. violence
D. catatonic schizophrenia
E. tardive dyskinesia

**25.10.** Which of the following variables has the highest correlation with high suicide risk:

A. Prior inpatient hospitalization
B. Loss of physical health
C. Age
D. Male sex
E. Alcoholism

**25.11.** In patients who are actively suicidal and are severe alcoholics, the best treatment is

A. immediate psychiatric hospitalization
B. exacting a promise from such patients not to kill themselves
C. daily psychotherapy sessions
D. daily group psychotherapy sessions
E. heavy doses of tranquilizers

**25.12.** A large percentage of persons who eventually commit suicide have had medical attention within what period of time before taking their own lives:

A. Within 6 months
B. Within 8 months
C. Within 1 year
D. Over 1 year
E. None of the above

**25.13.** In which of the following countries is the suicide rate the lowest:

A. Switzerland
B. West Germany
C. Austria
D. United States
E. Spain

**25.14.** The ratio of male to female suicides is

A. 1 to 3
B. 4 to 1
C. 3 to 1
D. 7 to 2
E. 1 to 2

**DIRECTIONS:** For each of the incomplete statements below, *one* or *more* of the completions given is correct. Choose answer:

    A. if only **1, 2,** and **3** are correct
    B. if only **1** and **3** are correct
    C. if only **2** and **4** are correct
    D. if only **4** is correct
    E. if all are correct

**25.15.** Increased risk of successful suicide attempts is associated with being

1. male
2. divorced
3. depressed
4. under age 45

**25.16.** Anomic suicide, according to Durkheim, explains the greater incidence of suicide among

1. Catholics
2. divorced persons
3. Protestants
4. unemployed persons

**25.17.** Which of the following groups are considered high suicidal risks, i.e. higher than the general population:

1. Physicians
2. Lawyers
3. Musicians
4. Insurance agents

**25.18.** Emergency treatment of the battered child includes

1. hospitalization
2. reporting the incident to the authorities
3. evaluating the safety of siblings
4. interviewing the parents separately

**25.19.** Encounter groups are reported to have caused which of the following adverse reactions:

1. Brief reactive psychosis
2. Suicidal behavior
3. Divorce
4. Violent behavior

**25.20.** In a hypertensive crisis associated with monoamine oxidase inhibitor (MAOI) use, the physician should

1. gradually decrease the type of prescribed MAOI
2. prescribe tyramine
3. use a sympathomimetic drug after the crisis has passed
4. prescribe phentolamine

**25.21.** Acute intermittent porphyria is associated with a genetically determined sensitivity to certain drugs that precipitate an attack when used. The known drugs include

1. barbiturates
2. tranquilizers
3. alcohol
4. oral contraceptives

**25.22.** In evaluating the possibilities of recurrent episodes of violence, one should inquire concerning

1. parental age at the time of the patient's birth
2. violent parental behavior during the patient's developmental years
3. the number of psychiatric hospitalizations
4. a history of previous acts of violence by the patient

**25.23.** The psychodynamics of persons who commit suicide include which of the following:

1. It is a means to a better life.
2. Someone is telling them to kill themselves.
3. It is a way to get revenge against someone.
4. It is a release from illness.

**25.24.** Treatment to control psychotic violent behavior includes

1. intravenous amobarbital
2. intravenous haloperidol
3. intravenous diazepam
4. mechanical restraint

# Answers

# Psychiatric Emergencies

**25.1. The answer is B** (*Synopsis*, ed. 4, page 589).

Phencyclidine (PCP, angel dust, hog) has become, next to alcohol, the most common cause of psychotic drug-related emergency hospital admissions. The presence of nystagmus (horizontal, vertical, rotary), muscular rigidity, and elevated blood pressure in a patient who is agitated, psychotic, or comatose and whose respirations are not depressed is diagnostic for PCP intoxication. Treatment of this condition with the major tranquilizers, such as the phenothiazines, is contraindicated. The so-called talking-down process does not help, because the patients are out of contact with reality. The following steps are recommended: (1) Sensory isolation is indicated in a darkened, quiet room with the patient on a floor pad; (2) gastric lavage may recover a significant amount of the drug; (3) *diazepam*, 10 to 20 mg orally (or 10 mg intramuscularly) should be given to quiet the patient and should be repeated at 3- to 4-hour intervals if necessary, 2 to 3 mg intravenously, if seizures intervene; (4) diazoxide should be given for serious hypertension, 300 mg intravenously, rapidly; (5) ammonium chloride, 0.5 to 1 g every 6 hours by mouth or nasogastric tube, should be administered, and the patient's urine pH (5.5 to 6) should be checked; (6) if the patient is comatose, the nasopharynx should be suctioned frequently, and the patient should be hydrated carefully and turned often; and (7) full recovery may require long-term treatment.

*Trifluoperazine, thioridazine,* and *chlorpromazine* are all phenothiazines and are used primarily as antipsychotic medications. *Naloxone* is an opiate antagonist. Unlike nalorphine, which it has largely replaced as a narcotic antagonist, naloxone is essentially devoid of agonist effects. In opioid-dependent persons, small doses of naloxone precipitate moderate to severe withdrawal symptoms, an effect that can be used to diagnose physical dependence on narcotic drugs. The most important use of naloxone, however, is in the treatment of narcotic overdosage.

**25.2. The answer is A** (*Synopsis*, ed. 4, page 575).

Historically, *suicide rates among Catholic populations have been recorded as lower than rates among Protestants and Jews.* It may be that the degree of orthodoxy and integration within a religion is a more accurate measure of risk within this category than is simple institutional religious affiliation.

**25.3. The answer is C** (*Synopsis*, ed. 4, page 588).

If it is not possible to learn from the patient the amount of his customary daily dose, it has been suggested that the patient receive by mouth a 200-mg test dose of amobarbital sodium and be observed 1 hour later. If the patient is clearly drowsy or asleep, it may be concluded that his intake is minimal, equivalent to 200 mg a day; if there is nystagmus, ataxia, and drooping eyelids without verbal responsiveness, that suggests moderate abuse in the range of 500 mg a day; if the patient is able to speak but is dysarthric, that suggests heavy use in the *600 to 700 mg daily dose range*; if the patient shows minimal effects, it may be concluded that there is extremely heavy use in the range of 900 mg or more a day. The withdrawal schedule can then be planned accordingly.

**25.4. The answer is B** (*Synopsis*, ed. 4, page 592).

Although appearing normal at birth, the heroin-addicted infant will present with symptoms of abstinence syndrome around *6 to 48 hours after birth.*

The infant develops a high-pitched, ear-piercing cry that is continuous and far louder than a normal cry. In its mildest form, the infant displays hypertonic muscles, with an exaggerated Moro reflex and tremulousness. In more severe forms there are, in addition, sweating, salivating, yawning, sneezing, and loose stools. In the most severe reaction, vomiting, diarrhea, and convulsions occur.

By contrast, the abstinence symptoms of barbiturate addiction do not appear until 4 to 7 days of birth. As with heroin addiction, the baby has a loud, shrill continuous cry. Otherwise, the symptoms differ in that there is vomiting (despite voracious appetite), as well as irritability and fitful sleep.

**25.5. The answer is C** (*Synopsis*, ed. 4, pages 581 and 582).

*Suicidal depression* is the single most important category in emergency psychiatry.

One must be alert to the danger signs; namely, a relatively abrupt onset in a previously competent person, early-morning insomnia and agitation, a loss of all appetites and interests, feelings of hopeless despair, inability to express one's thoughts or feelings, and progressive social withdrawal. The appearance of delusions, such as having committed an unpardonable sin, is a particularly ominous sign, calling for emergency inpatient care under constant nursing supervision, antidepressant medication, and possibly the emergency administration of electroconvulsive therapy.

*Paranoid schizophrenia* is a schizophrenic disorder characterized by the presence of persecutory or grandiose delusions, often accompanied by hallucinations. *Homosexual panic* is the sudden, acute onset of severe anxiety, precipitated by the unconscious fear or conflict that one may be a homosexual or act out homosexual impulses. *Delirium* is an acute, reversible organic mental disorder characterized by confusion and some impairment of consciousness. It is generally associated with emotional lability, hallucinations or illusions, and inappropriate, impulsive, irrational, or violent behavior.

Sedative-hypnotics refer to barbiturates, nonbarbiturates, and the so-called minor tranquilizers. The first symptoms of *sedative-hypnotic withdrawal* may start about 8 hours after the last pill has been taken, and may consist of anxiety, confusion, and ataxia. In time, gross tremors appear, with headache, nausea, and vomiting. Seizures, including status epilepticus, may occur sometime after the first 12 hours of withdrawal; seizures are a serious complication because head injuries may be incurred. Whenever seizures occur in a previously nonepileptic adult, withdrawal should be considered in the differential diagnosis.

**25.6.   The answer is D** (*Synopsis*, ed. 4, page 584).

*Posttraumatic stress disorder* is a term commonly used to designate the acute anxiety symptoms that start after a near escape from death in combat, an accident, or a natural catastrophe.

Usually, the patient retains self-control during the actual period of danger, although a panic reaction can occur, characterized by terror and ineffective efforts at flight, that may precipitate panic reactions in others. Such panic-stricken patients are extraordinarily suggestible and easily hypnotizable, so that reassurance and firm instructions concerning appropriate behavior are usually followed with child-like obedience by the patient.

Typically, gross neurotic symptoms appear only after removal of the patient from the stress that occurred. At such times, one may observe coarse tremors and a variety of symptoms involving sensory and motor abnormalities. Treatment should encourage an immediate return to previous responsibilities. Most of all, prolonged diagnostic and therapeutic inpatient procedures should be avoided, as these encourage regression and chronic invalidism.

*Agoraphobia* is a fear of open places, a phobic disorder characterized by a fear of leaving one's home. It may present with or without panic attacks. *Anxiety disorder* is a disorder in which anxiety is the most prominent disturbance or in which patients experience anxiety if they resist giving in to their symptoms. *Isolated explosive disorder* is a disorder of impulse control in which the person has a single episode characterized by failure to resist a violent impulse against others. *Panic disorder* is a DSM-III classification of anxiety disorder characterized by attacks of acute intense anxiety.

**25.7.   The answer is E** (*Synopsis*, ed. 4, page 575).

The significance of the mid-life crisis is underscored by suicide rates. Among men, suicides peak after age 45; among women, the greatest number of completed suicides *occurs after age 55*. Rates of 40 per 100,000 population are found in men age 65 and older; the elderly attempt suicide less often than younger people, but are successful more frequently, accounting for 25 percent of the suicides, although the elderly make up only 10 percent of the total population. A decline in suicide in men begins between the ages 75 to 85. A peak risk among males is found also in late adolescence, when suicide is the second leading cause of death, exceeded only by death attributed to accidents. It is also the second leading cause of death among college students.

**25.8.   The answer is A** (*Synopsis*, ed. 4, page 587).

Overdosed heroin patients are pale and cyanotic. They have pinpoint pupils and are areflexic. They may not be breathing at all, or they may take three or four shallow gasping breaths a minute. Without a moment's delay, their tongues should be pulled forward and out of the way, and the angles of their jaws should be strongly pushed forward and their mouths wiped free of blood and mucus. Vital signs should be noted; that is, level of consciousness, deep tendon reflexes, pupil size and reactivity, blood pressure, pulse rate, and respiration.

Blood should be drawn for a study of drug levels, and the patient given intravenous naloxone hydrochloride, 0.4 mg in a 1-ml dose. *Naloxone* is a narcotic antagonist that reverses the opiate effects, including respiratory depression, within 2 minutes of the injection. If the desired degree of counteraction and respiratory improvement is not obtained, the dose may be repeated after 2 or 3 minutes. Failure to obtain significant improvement after two or three such doses suggests that the condition may be due partly or completely to other disease processes or to nonnarcotic sedative drugs. If the veins are burned out, the naloxone should be injected into a lingual vein or the jugular vein. Patients who respond to naloxone should be carefully observed, lest they lapse into coma again.

If the overdose is due to methadone, breathing should be monitored for 24 hours because toxicity may last that long, and the naloxone action is quite brief. It may be necessary in methadone overdosage to provide naloxone in the form of a continuous intravenous drip overnight, 2.0 mg of naloxone in 500 ml of 0.45 normal saline, injected at a rate of 0.4 mg every 30 minutes.

*Diazepam* is a minor tranquilizer used as an antianxiety agent; *amphetamine* is a stimulant used primarily for children with attention deficit disorders; *chlorpromazine* is a phenothiazine used as an antipsychotic agent; and *methadone* is an opioid analogue used in the substitution therapy method for opioid dependence. None of these drugs are suitable for heroin overdose, and all may worsen the condition.

**25.9. The answer is A** (*Synopsis*, ed. 4, page 585).

Rauwolfia derivatives, such as reserpine, are particularly apt to precipitate an acute *depressive* action in a patient undergoing treatment for hypertension. If depression starts, Rauwolfia should be discontinued and another antihypertensive agent substituted. Once the depression has started, discontinuing the Rauwolfia by itself is usually not enough to relieve the condition. Antidepressant medications are ineffective for several weeks after Rauwolfia is discontinued, and electroconvulsive therapy (ECT) may be necessary in the presence of suicidal danger. If the depression is severe and there is danger of suicide, ECT is the procedure of choice. ECT should be withheld for at least 12 days after the last dose of Rauwolfia.

*Depression* is a mental state characterized by feelings of sadness, loneliness, despair, low self-esteem, and self-reproach. The term refers either to a mood that is so characterized or to an affective disorder. Accompanying signs include psychomotor retardation or at times agitation, withdrawal from interpersonal contact, and vegetative symptoms, such as insomnia and anorexia.

*Akathisia* is a state of motor restlessness manifested by the compelling need to be in constant movement. It may be seen as an extrapyramidal side effect of phenothiazine medication. *Violence* is physical aggression or willful physical harm inflicted by a person or group on itself or

**Discriminant Function Analyses***

| Variable in Rank Order | Content of Item | Direction for Suicide |
|---|---|---|
| 1 | Age | Older |
| 2 | Alcoholism | Yes |
| 3 | Irritation, rage, violence | No |
| 4 | Lethal prior behavior | Higher |
| 5 | Sex | Male |
| 6 | Accept help now | No |
| 7 | Duration of current episode | Longer |
| 8 | Prior inpatient psychiatric treatment | No |
| 9 | Recent loss or separation | No |
| 10 | Depression, somatic | Yes |
| 11 | *Loss of physical health* | Less |
| 12 | Occupational level | Higher |
| 13 | Depression, affective | No |
| 14 | Repeatedly discarded | No |
| 15 | Family available | Less |

\* From Litman R E, Farberow N L, Wold C I, Brown T R: Prediction models of suicidal behaviors. In *The Prediction of Suicide*, A T Beck, H L P Resnik, D J Lettieri, editors, p 141. Charles Press, Bowie, MD, 1974.

on another person or group. Violence represents the extreme pole of the aggressive spectrum of behavior, characterized by an explosive, sudden quality and the use of force to injure or destroy an object, a person, or an organization. *Catatonic schizophrenia* is a type of schizophrenia characterized by muscular rigidity, stupor, and negativism. *Tardive dyskinesia* is a late-appearing extrapyramidal syndrome associated with antipsychotic drug use. It is characterized by stereotyped involuntary movements of the lips, jaw, and tongue (tardive oral dyskinesia) and by other involuntary dyskinetic movements. Symptoms may persist indefinitely after discontinuation of the medication, and the condition does not respond to treatment with antiparkinsonism drugs.

**25.10. The answer is C** (*Synopsis*, ed. 4, page 577).

The most predictive items associated with high suicide risk are listed first in the table above. In descending order the first eight items are *age*; presence of *alcoholism* (the suicide rate is 50 times higher in alcoholics); no recent irritation, rage, or violence; high lethality of prior suicidal behavior; *male sex*; not accepting help at the time of evaluation; the longer the current suicidal episode the higher the risk; and *no prior psychiatric inpatient experience*.

**25.11. The answer is A** (*Synopsis*, ed. 4, pages 578 and 579).

Any patients who are suspected of being suicidal should be directly asked if they feel so bad that they would like to end it all. If the answer is yes and if a patient has a plan to end his or her life, then *immediate psychiatric hospitalization* is indicated. Fifty percent of patients who eventually kill themselves say that they want to die. No clinical evidence suggests that asking a patient this question inserts the thought or provides the psychic momentum needed to act it out. Rather, the contrary occurs. The patient is, by inference, usually relieved by the invitation to talk about such self-destructive feelings; this invitation can reassure the patient that the psychiatrist is comfortable with the subject and is experienced and competent in treating suicidal patients.

Once high suicidal risk is determined, patients must never be left alone until they are hospitalized. The alternatives to immediate hospitalization are limited in high risk cases. One approach is to ask any patients considered suicidal whether they will agree to call when they reach a point beyond which they are uncertain of controlling their suicidal impulses. If these patients can commit themselves to such an agreement, or *promise not to kill themselves*, they are reaffirming their belief tht they have sufficient strength to cry out for help. If patients who are considered seriously suicidal cannot make this commitment, immediate hospitalization may be indicated, and both the patients and their families should be apprised.

If outpatient management is undertaken, the clinician must be available 24 hours a day and be directly accessible during what patients understand to be usual consultation hours. *Daily sessions should be conducted, either individually or in groups.* Perhaps the only patients unable to honor such a commitment contract are those who are struggling with alcoholism or drug abuse at the time that they are actively suicidal. These patients should be hospitalized directly.

A therapist's anxiety and apprehension may result from fear that the patient will, indeed, commit suicide, despite the therapist's efforts. The therapist must remember that the state of suicide prediction and, indeed, of psychiatric care is such that the therapist cannot take full responsibility for any person's life for long periods of time without that person's eventually accepting a share of the responsibility. In a hospital, the responsibility is shared.

**25.12. The answer is A** (*Synopsis*, ed. 4, page 576).

The relationship of physical health and illness to suicide is significant. Prior medical care appears to be a positively correlated risk indicator of suicide; 42 percent of suicides have had medical attention *within 6 months* of death. Seventy percent of victims have been affected by one or more active—and, for the most part, chronic—illnesses at the time of death. Among the suicide attempts studied, more than one-third of the persons were actively ill at the time of the attempt, and more than 90 percent of the attempts were influenced by the illness. In both groups, psychosomatic illnesses constituted the majority of diagnoses.

**25.13. The answer is E** (*Synopsis*, ed. 4, page 575).

Suicide rates in the *United States* rank at or near the midpoint of national rates reported to the United Nations by industrialized countries. Internationally, suicide rates range from highs of more than 25 per 100,000 population in Scandinavia, *Switzerland*, *West Germany*, *Austria*, and eastern European countries (the suicide belt) and Japan to fewer than 10 per 100,000 in *Spain*, Italy, and the Netherlands.

About 20,000 to 35,000 suicides are recorded annually in the United States. This figure represents the lethal end of attempted suicides, which are estimated to exceed that number by 8 to 10 times. Lost in the reporting process are the purposeful misclassifications of cause of death, accidents of undetermined cause, and what are referred to as forms of chronic suicide: for example, alcoholism, drug abuse, and consciously poor adherence to medical regimens for diabetes, obesity, and hypertension.

Certified suicides constitute a rate of 12.5 deaths per 100,000 population, ranking suicide as the tenth over-all leading cause of death in the country. Out of every 20 attempted suicides, 1 succeeds.

**25.14. The answer is C** (*Synopsis*, ed. 4, page 575).

Men commit suicide *more than 3 times as often* as do women, a rate that is stable over all ages. Women, however, are 3 times as likely to attempt suicide as are men.

**25.15. The answer is A** (1, 2, 3) (*Synopsis*, ed. 4, pages 577 and 578).

Individuals at high-risk for successful suicide are likely to be *45 years of age and over*; *male*; *divorced*, widowed, or separated and living alone; and are likely to choose a highly lethal attempt.

Family disorganization is also a risk-related factor. Additional risk-related factors include occupation, precipitants of the attempt, elapsed time between the attempt and its discovery, motivation, and diagnosis of *depression*. Twenty-five percent of all suicides are alcoholics.

The table that follows on page 332 lists the high-risk and low-risk characteristics among attempted suicides.

**Suicide Rates\* Measured by High-Risk and Low-Risk Categories of Risk-Related Factors Among 1,112 Attempted Suicides†**

| Factor | High-risk Category | Suicide Rate | Low-risk Category | Suicide Rate |
|---|---|---|---|---|
| Age | 45 years and older | 40.5 | Under age 45 | 6.9 |
| Sex | Male | 33.8 | Female | 5.3 |
| Race | White | 16.7 | Nonwhite | 9.0 |
| Marital status | Separated, divorced, widowed | 41.9 | Single, married | 12.4 |
| Employment status‡ | Unemployed, retired | 24.8 | Employed§ | 16.3 |
| Living arrangements | Alone | 71.4 | With others | 11.1 |
| Health | Poor (acute or chronic condition in the 6-month period preceding the attempt) | 18.0 | Good§ | 13.8 |
| Mental Condition | Nervous or mental disorder, mood, or behavioral symptoms, including alcoholism | 17.6 | Presumably normal, including brief situational reactions§ | 11.7 |
| Method | Hanging, firearms, jumping, drowning | 45.5 | Cutting or piercing, gas or carbon monoxide, poison, combination of methods, other | 13.1 |
| Potential consequences of method | Likely to be fatal¶ | 31.5 | Harmless, illness producing | 6.0 |
| Police description of attempted suicide's condition | Unconscious, semiconscious | 16.3 | Presumably normal, disturbed, drinking, physically ill, other | 13.0 |
| Suicide note | Yes | 22.5 | No§ | 13.7 |
| Previous attempt or threat | Yes | 22.6 | No§ | 13.1 |
| Disposition | Admitted to psychiatric evaluation center | 21.0 | Discharged to self or relative, referred to family doctor, clergyman, or social agency, or other disposition | 11.6 |

\* Although mental health statistics generally use rates per 100,000 population, here it is more appropriate to use per 1,000 population because of the small size of the sample.

† From Tuckman Y, Youngman W F: Assessment of suicidal risk in attempted suicides. In *Suicidal Behaviors*, H L P Resnik, editor, p 190. Little Brown & Co, Boston, 1968.

‡ Does not include housewives and students.

§ Includes cases for which information on this factor was not given in the police report.

¶ Several criteria used in estimating whether the method used was likely to be fatal.

**25.16. The answer is C (2, 4)** (*Synopsis*, ed. 4, page 576).

Anomic suicide, according to Durkheim, occurs when a disturbance in the balance of the person's integration with society leaves him or her without the customary norms of behavior. Anomie could explain the greater incidence of suicide among the *divorced* as compared with the married, and the greater vulnerability of those who had undergone drastic changes in their economic situation, *especially unemployment*. Persons with strong religious affiliations generally have lower suicide rates than those who are not religious.

**25.17. The answer is E (all)** (*Synopsis*, ed. 4, page 576).

Among occupational rankings with respect to risk for suicide, physicians have traditionally been considered to stand out, and, among *phy-* sicians, psychiatrists are considered to be at greatest risk followed by ophthalmologists and anesthesiologists; but the trend is toward an equalization among all specialties. Special at-risk populations are *musicians*, dentists, law enforcement officers, *lawyers*, and *insurance agents*.

**25.18. The answer is E (all)** (*Synopsis*, ed. 4, page 591).

In all suspicious cases of child abuse, even when the injury is not serious, the child should be *hospitalized*. It is important to avoid accusations or premature confrontations, in order not to cause counterproductive defensive parental reactions. The first priority is to separate the child from a potentially dangerous environment.

The child's *parents should be interviewed separately*, starting with the mother. One should look for a history of violence in the parents' childhood backgrounds, including a history of parental alcoholism and broken marriage.

The maltreated child is usually different from his or her siblings in some way that makes the child more vulnerable than they to abuse. Precocious and hyperactive children, prematures, adopted children, and stepchildren are all abuse prone. In terms of the current crisis, one should inquire into the presence of a major setback in the child's family situation, stemming from parental loss of a job, physical or mental illness, death of a grandparent, and so on. In response to a family crisis, there may be an increased parental alcohol or drug intake that reduces judgment and control. The actual explosion of child battering may take place in a dissociative state for which the guilty parent is amnesic. Recent changes in the child are also important. A febrile condition, for example, causing fretfulness may provoke an already teetering parent to lose control.

*Most local governments require the reporting of child abuse.* This requirement should be followed and the parents so informed. In most cases, the reporting is all that is done, and the bureau of child welfare is not asked to take particular action.

*If the hospitalized child has siblings, their safety must be evaluated.* Sometimes one child is the exclusive family scapegoat. In other cases, however, removal of the abused child puts the other children in danger.

### 25.19. The answer is E (all) (*Synopsis*, ed. 4, page 593).

A variety of encounter groups are characterized by a lack of any screening procedures for admission to the group; a certain amount of coercion to participate in the group; a failure to obtain informed consent from persons entering the group; a failure to delineate clearly the rules and goals of the group, so that passive, frightened persons may feel unable to voluntarily disengage themselves from the group; a lack of available mental health professional consultation; a lack of follow-up concerning the subsequent clinical course of a group member; and, most important, a lack of proper training of the leaders—indeed, a lack of any screening procedure to eliminate persons incapable of providing responsible leadership.

With this spectrum of deficiencies as a background, it becomes understandable why there are increasing reports in the literature of *brief reactive psychotic episodes, suicidal acting out*, homosexual panic, depression, sexual and *aggressive acting out*, and ill-advised upheavals in personal life, including the breakup of families and *divorce*.

A careful psychiatric study of such cases may reveal that a precarious adaptational balance preceded the encounter experience and that drug use contributed to individual instances of breakdown. If these complications occur in settings away from home, such as a college campus or a vacation setting, it is advisable to have the patient return home at once—if possible, accompanied by parents or responsible relatives. Treatment of the individual case depends on the results of a careful diagnostic study. Perhaps the most urgent issue is to educate the public concerning the dangers of indiscriminate participation in nonprofessional groups led by incompetent leaders.

### 25.20. The answer is D (4) (*Synopsis*, ed. 4, page 590).

The hypertensive crisis can occur in a patient treated for depression with a monoamine oxidase (MAOI) inhibitor if he or she has eaten food with a high tyramine content—strong cheese, smoked or pickled fish, spiced meats, highly seasoned foods, wines and alcohol in general, chicken liver, yeast extract, excessive amounts of coffee, chocolate—or has taken sympathomimetic drugs, particularly by injection. The hypertensive crisis is characterized by a severe occipital headache that may radiate frontally, palpitation, neck stiffness and soreness, nausea, vomiting, sweating, photophobia, constricting chest pain, and dilated pupils. Intracranial bleeding, sometimes fatal, has been reported in association with hypertensive crisis.

If a hypertensive crisis occurs, *the MAOI should be discontinued at once (not gradually)*, and therapy should be instituted to reduce blood pressure. *Phentolamine*, 50-mg tablet, should be carried by the patient and taken by mouth if a severe headache occurs after a dietary infraction. If the crisis is severe and the patient is brought to a hospital emergency room, 5 mg of phentolamine should be administered intravenously, slowly, to avoid producing an excessive hypotensive effect.

*Tyramine or the use of a sympathemimetic drug is contraindicated* in patients who are using MAOI's.

### 25.21. The answer is E (all) (*Synopsis*, ed. 4, page 589).

Acute intermittent porphyria is a rare cause of an acute psychiatric emergency. A psychotic reaction associated with severe abdominal pain, grand mal seizures, and other evidences of central nervous system involvement characterize the disease. It is diagnosed by demonstrating the presence of specific abnormal porphyrins in the urine or abnormal blood enzymes characteristic of defective heme production. It is associated with a genetically determined sensitivity to *barbiturates, alcohol, tranquilizers, and oral contraceptives,* the use of which precipitates an attack. Treatment consists essentially of avoiding the precipitating substances.

**25.22. The answer is C (2, 4)** (*Synopsis,* ed. 4, page 583).

In evaluating the possibilities of recurrent episodes of violence, one should inquire concerning *a history of previous acts of violence by the patient*; of *violent parental behavior during the patient's developmental years*; of a childhood history of firesetting and cruelty to animals; the possession of weapons as a hobby or otherwise; and drug dependency states, involving, most of all, alcohol, but including the barbiturates, amphetamines, lysergic acid diethylamide (LSD) and phencylidine (PCP). Patients with schizoid personality disorders who harbor paranoid and vengeful obsessional thoughts about authority figures may be future candidates for assassination behavior.

These patients share in common a low frustration tolerance, and they react violently when crossed. Although violence is usually directed against family members, it may be expressed indiscriminately during periods of acute stress. Such people often come to the emergency room voluntarily, asking for help because of impending loss of control.

*There is no correlation between violence and parental age of the parent or the number of psychiatric hospitalizations of the patient.*

**25.23. The answer is E (all)** (*Synopsis,* ed. 4, page 577).

Edwin Schneidman and Neal Farberow have classified suicides into four groups: (1) patients who conceive of suicide as a *means to a better life*; (2) patients who commit suicide as a result of *psychosis with associated delusions or hallucinations*; (3) patients who commit suicide out of *revenge against a loved person*; and (4) patients *for whom suicide is a release from illness.*

**25.24. The answer is E** (*Synopsis,* ed. 4, page 582).

The violent struggling patient is most effectively subdued with an appropriate *intravenous* (IV) *sedative. Diazepam* may be given slowly IV, 5 to 10 mg, over 2 minutes. Sodium *amobarbital,* 0.5 g, may also be given slowly intravenously. It is most important to give intravenous medication with great care. It is essential that the IV not be injected too rapidly so that respiratory arrest does not occur. If the furor is due to alcohol or is part of a postseizure psychomotor disturbance, the sleep produced by a relative small amount of intravenous medication may go on for hours. On awakening, such patients are often entirely alert and rational, and typically they have a complete amnesia for the violent episode.

If the furor is part of an ongoing psychotic process and it returns as soon as the intravenous medication wears off, continuing parenteral medication may be given. The medication used should be one that the physician knows thoroughly. As a general principle, it is better to use small doses at ½- to 1-hour intervals—for example, *haloperidol,* 2 to 5 mg, or diazepam, 10 mg—until the patient is controlled, than to use larger doses initially and end up with an overmedicated patient. As the patient's disturbed behavior is brought under control, successively smaller and less frequent doses are used. During the preliminary period of treatment, the patient's blood pressure and other vital signs should be carefully monitored.

Violent psychotic patients are sometimes placed in *mechanical restraints.* The danger of that procedure should be noted. Not only does it create a vicious cycle by intensifying the patient's psychotic terror, but if prolonged, mechanical restraints can cause hyperthermia, and in some instances of catatonic excitement it can cause death. Mechanical restraints should be used with due regard to local laws; that is, with permission from the proper authorities and with careful monitoring of the patient's physical condition.

# References

Glick R A, Myerson A T, Robins E, Talbot J A, editors: *Psychiatric Emergencies.* Grune & Stratton, New York, 1976.

Linn L: Other psychiatric emergencies. In *Comprehensive Textbook of Psychiatry,* ed 4, H I Kaplan, B J Sadock, editors, p 1315. Williams & Wilkins, Baltimore, 1985.

Mezzich J E: Symptoms and hospitalization decisions. Am J Psychiatry *141:* 764, 1984.

Murphy G E: On suicide prediction and prevention. Arch Gen Psychiatry 40: 343, 1983.

Ninan P: CSF 5-hydroxyindoleacetic acid levels in suicidal schizophrenic patients. Am J Psychiatry *141:* 566, 1984.

Nurius P S: Stress: A pervasive dilemma in psychiatric emergency care. Compr Psychiatry 25: 345, 1984.

Robins E: Suicide. In *Comprehensive Textbook of Psychiatry,* ed 4, H I Kaplan, B J Sadock, editors, p 1311. Williams & Wilkins, Baltimore, 1985.

Roy A: Risk factors for suicide in psychiatric patients. Arch Gen Psychiatry *39:* 1089, 1981.

# 26

# Psychotherapies

The primary aim of psychiatric treatments is to alter pathological behavior. Although the dynamics of human behavior are not completely understood, it is clear that all behavior, whether normal or pathological, is the result of highly complex interactions involving biological, psychological, and environmental factors. Thus, the physiology of the individual's brain, the developmental history, store of cognitive information, interpersonal relations, sensory input, and affective experience, as well as the characteristics of the environment with which the individual interacts, are included among the variables that will determine his or her ultimate personality and behavior.

The psychological treatment methods in current use include, among others, the various forms of psychoanalysis and psychotherapy, behavior therapy, cognitive therapy, hypnosis, biofeedback, sex therapy, and group and family therapy. All these methods share one common feature: They all attempt to modify pathological behavior by intervening on a psychological level.

The goals of psychological treatment range from relief of a specific symptom, such as bed wetting, to attempts at effecting fundamental changes in a patient's basic character structure and pattern of adaptation to important areas of living, such as work, sex, and interaction with other people.

Theoretical assumptions and techniques of treatment also vary considerably. Thus, behavior therapy employs conditioning and extinction techniques that are derived from learning theory in order to relieve psychological symptoms. Other forms of psychotherapy and psychoanalysis rely heavily on the interactions between the doctor and patient to achieve the desired changes in behavior. This therapeutic transaction may involve the exchange of information, as well as a highly emotional component.

The emphasis in psychotherapy will depend on the diagnosis and the problems of the individual patient. Thus, the primary goal of treatment may be to provide a corrective emotional experience with the assumption that this will facilitate the development of more adequate adaptive responses. In other cases, treatment techniques will focus on fostering the patient's insight into the nature and source of fears, wishes, conflicts, and perceptual distortions, which may lie outside conscious awareness, but which are assumed to underlie the pathological behavior of the patient.

In contrast to the emphasis on the one-to-one doctor-patient relationship that is the hallmark of the individual psychotherapies, group therapy methods make use of the operation of multiple interactions among the members of the group, as well as between individual patients and the therapist. This procedure provides unique opportunities for the clarification and subsequent change of pathological interpersonal transactions, which are believed to contribute to many types of psychiatric disturbances.

The reader is referred to Chapter 26, "Psychotherapies," of *Modern Synopsis-IV* and should then study the questions and answers below to assess his or her knowledge of this area.

# Questions

**DIRECTIONS:** Each of the statements or questions below is followed by five suggested responses or completions. Select the *one* that is *best* in each case.

**26.1.** Obsessive-compulsive disorder is best treated by

A. pharmacotherapy
B. hypnotherapy
C. crisis intervention
D. brief dynamic psychotherapy
E. psychoanalytic psychotherapy

**26.2.** Of the following, which is the most effective method of treatment for patients with pathological gambling disorders:

A. Activity group therapy
B. Self-help group therapy
C. Family therapy
D. Psychodrama
E. Individual therapy

**26.3.** A patient with a fear of heights is brought to the top of a tall building and required to remain there as long as necessary for the anxiety to dissipate. This is an example of

A. graded exposure
B. participant modeling
C. positive reinforcement
D. flooding
E. relationship therapy

**26.4.** Dream interpretation is especially important in

A. behavior therapy
B. supportive psychotherapy
C. relationship psychotherapy
D. classical psychoanalysis
E. brief psychotherapy

**26.5.** The most important dynamic factor in group therapy is

A. universalization
B. cohesion
C. identification
D. intellectualization
E. ventilation

**26.6.** Cognitive therapy is best suited for patients suffering from

A. schizophrenia
B. substance abuse disorders
C. paranoid personality disorder
D. depression
E. organic mental disorders

**26.7.** In behavior therapy, most procedures are based on a method called

A. relaxation training
B. transference
C. reality testing
D. resistance
E. therapeutic alliance

**26.8.** The fundamental rule of orthodox psychoanalysis is

A. the patient agrees to be completely candid with the analyst
B. the patient agrees to attend four or five sessions a week
C. the patient agrees to use the couch
D. the patient agrees to keep the sessions confidential
E. the patient agrees to pay the fee on time

**26.9.** In psychodrama, the protagonist is

A. the director
B. the patient in conflict
C. the therapist
D. a member of the audience
E. the auxiliary ego

**26.10.** Hypnosis has been used successfully in all the following conditions *except*

A. pain
B. phobia
C. paranoia
D. anxiety
E. smoking

**26.11.** The most important concept in family therapy is

A. the patient is the family unit
B. sick persons produce family discord
C. families are usually cohesive units
D. there are rarely communication difficulties in families
E. family members cannot affect one another positively

**26.12.** All the following are necessary criteria for selecting patients who will benefit from brief dynamic psychotherapy *except*

A. a circumscribed chief complaint
B. the ability to express feelings
C. above-average intelligence
D. motivation only for symptom relief
E. a specific psychodynamic formulation

**26.13.** All the following are characteristic of orthodox Freudian psychoanalysis *except*

A. free association
B. four or more sessions a week
C. use of a couch
D. analyst out of sight of the patient
E. frequent use of many interpretations

**DIRECTIONS:** For each of the incomplete statements below, *one* or *more* of the completions given is correct. Choose answer:

A. if only **1**, **2**, and **3** are correct
B. if only **1** and **3** are correct
C. if only **2** and **4** are correct
D. if only **4** is correct
E. if all are correct

**26.14.** Patients who experience anxiety in group therapy include which of the following:

1. Patients who are fearful in the presence of authority
2. Patients who have had destructive relationships with peers
3. Children without siblings
4. Patients who were isolated from peers

**26.15.** Biofeedback has been applied to which of the following disorders:

1. Neuromuscular rehabilitation
2. Raynaud's syndrome
3. Migraine headaches
4. Essential hypertension

**26.16.** Which of the following methods are used in biofeedback:

1. Electromyography
2. Electroencephalography
3. Galvanic skin response
4. Strain gauge

**26.17.** While hypnotized, a patient is told that, when the hypnotist lights a cigarette after the trance, the patient will ask for it, take one or two puffs, and then put it out. After the trance, the patient will

1. be amnesic for the instruction
2. comply with the instruction
3. rationalize the act of putting out the cigarette
4. be influenced only if the signal was given during a light trance

**26.18.** In supportive therapy, the central techniques involve

1. strong leadership
2. gratification of dependency needs
3. warm and friendly atmosphere
4. support in development of legitimate independence

**26.19.** The cognitive therapy approach includes

1. eliciting automatic thoughts
2. testing automatic thoughts
3. identifying maladaptive underlying assumptions
4. testing the validity of maladaptive assumptions

**26.20.** Systematic desensitization has been shown to be most applicable in

1. obsessive-compulsive disorders
2. sexual problems
3. stuttering
4. bronchial asthma

**26.21.** Co-therapy in groups may be characterized by

1. neither therapist being in a position of greater authority than the other
2. replication of parental surrogates
3. having a male therapist and a female therapist
4. each therapist being as active as the other

| Directions Summarized | | | | |
|---|---|---|---|---|
| A | B | C | D | E |
| 1, 2, 3 | 1, 3 | 2, 4 | 4 | All are |
| only | only | only | only | correct |

**26.22.** Crisis theory postulates which of the following:
1. A crisis is a response to hazardous events and is experienced as a painful state.
2. Persons may be stronger psychologically after the crisis is resolved than they were before.
3. Consequences of crisis can be catastrophic and lead to suicide.
4. A crisis is self-limited.

**26.23.** Systematic desensitization
1. is a core procedure in behavior therapy
2. was developed by Wolpe
3. produces a psychophysiological state that inhibits anxiety
4. has the patient approach a feared situation quickly

**DIRECTIONS:** Each group of questions below consists of five lettered headings followed by a list of numbered words or statements. For each numbered word or statement, select the *one* lettered heading that is most closely associated with it. Each lettered heading may be selected once, more than once, or not at all.

### Questions 26.24–26.28
A. Relationship therapy
B. Psychoanalysis
C. Psychoanalytic therapy
D. Supportive therapy
E. None of the above

**26.24.** Transference neurosis is analyzed.

**26.25.** Real relationship and therapeutic alliance are emphasized.

**26.26.** Therapist actively intervenes and gives advice.

**26.27.** A limited number of interviews are used.

**26.28.** Transference to persons other than therapist is examined.

# Answers

# Psychotherapies

**26.1.** **The answer is E** (*Synopsis*, ed. 4, page 599).

An obsessive-compulsive disorder is characterized by the persistent recurrence of obsessions and by compulsions that are ego-alien and produce anxiety if not performed. These disorders are best treated with psychoanalysis or *psychoanalytic psychotherapy*. These methods use the investigative technique, guided by Freud's libido and instinct theories and by ego psychology, to gain insight into unconscious motivations, conflicts, and symbols and thus to effect a change in a person's obsessive-compulsive behavior.

The basic conflicts of an obsessive-compulsive disorder are, in general, primarily intrapsychic; that is, an opposition between segments or functions of the personality. The conflict usually rages over some force or drive, biological or psychological, that is called an instinctual striving. This drive is unacceptable to other segments of the personality—to other intrapsychic forces—and symptom formation arises from the conflict.

*Pharmacotherapy* involves the use of medication in the treatment of mental disorders. It is most effective when combined with psychotherapy. There have been some reports of the successful use of imipramine in the treatment of obsessive-compulsive disorder. *Hypnotherapy* is a type of therapy that makes use of hypnosis. *Crisis intervention* is a brief therapeutic approach used in emergency rooms of general or psychiatric hospitals that is ameliorative, rather than curative, of acute psychiatric emergencies. Often, treatment factors focus on environmental modification, although interpersonal and intrapsychic factors are also considered. Individual, group, family, or drug therapy is used within a time-limited structure of several days to several weeks. *Brief psychotherapy* is a form of psychotherapy in which the sessions are limited to 10 to 15 in number and during which time attempts to modify behavior occur. The approach is used in both individual and group settings.

**26.2.** **The answer is B** (*Synopsis*, ed. 4, pages 617 and 618).

*Self-help groups* are composed of persons who are concerned about coping with a specific problem or life crisis. Usually organized with a par-

ticular task in mind, the groups do not attempt to explore individual psychodynamics in great depth, nor do they attempt to change personality functioning significantly. Self-help groups have had a major impact on the emotional health and well-being of a great many people.

A distinguishing characteristic of the self-help group is its homogeneity. Members suffer from the same disorder, and they share their experiences—good and bad, successful and unsuccessful—with one another. By so doing, they educate each other, provide mutual support, and alleviate the sense of alienation that is usually felt by the person drawn to this type of group.

The dynamics involved in self-help groups emphasize the important role that identification plays in facilitating cohesion, which is exceptionally strong in these groups. Because of the shared problems and similar symptoms, a strong emotional bond develops, and the group is seen as possessing characteristics of its own to which magical qualities of healing may be attributed. Examples of self-help groups are Alcoholics Anonymous (AA), Gamblers Anonymous (GA), and Overeaters Anonymous.

The self-help group movement is in its ascendancy. The groups meet the needs of their members by providing acceptance, mutual support, and help in overcoming maladaptive patterns of behavior or states of feeling with which traditional mental health and medical professionals have not been generally successful. Increasingly, there is a convergence of the self-help and group therapy movements. The self-help groups have enabled their members to give up a pattern of unwanted behavior; the therapy groups have offered their members an in-depth understanding of why and how they got to be the way they were or are.

*Activity group therapy* is a type of group therapy introduced and developed by S. R. Slavson and designed for children and young adolescents, with emphasis on emotional and active interaction in a permissive, nonthreatening atmosphere. The therapist stresses reality testing, ego strengthening, and active interpretation. *Family therapy* is a treatment of more than one member of a family in the same session. Family relationships and processes are explored as potential causes of mental disorder in one or more of the family members. *Psychodrama* is a psychotherapy method originated by J. L. Moreno in which personality make-up, interpersonal relationships, conflicts, and emotional problems are expressed and explored through dramatization. The therapeutic dramatization of emotional problems includes (1) protagonist or patient, the person who presents and acts out his or her emotional problems with the help of (2) auxiliary egos, persons trained to act and dramatize the different aspects of the patient that are called for in a particular scene in order to help the patient express feelings, and (3) the director, leader, or therapist, the person who guides those involved in the drama for a fruitful and therapeutic session. *Individual therapy* is the traditional dyadic therapeutic technique in which a psychotherapist treats one patient during a given therapeutic session. Individual therapy techniques are useful with some impulse disorders, but in such disorders as pathological gambling, results are better when groups are composed of other gamblers who have mastered the problem.

**26.3.   The answer is D** (*Synopsis*, ed. 4, page 606).

*Flooding* is based on a model of the extinction of conditioned avoidance behavior by response prevention. In clinical situations, it consists of having the patient confront the anxiety-inducing object or situation at full intensity for prolonged periods of time, resulting in the patient being flooded with anxiety. The confrontation may be done in imagination, as in systematic desensitization, but results are better if real-life situations are used.

For example, the patient with a fear of heights may be brought to the top of a tall building and required to remain there as long as is necessary for the anxiety to dissipate. The groundless anxiety of the phobia tends to diminish to low levels after 5 to 25 minutes, depending on the patient's characteristics and the history of the disorder. In the next treatment session, preferably within a day or two, the initial anxiety is less, and less time is required to reach a state of calm. The process is repeated until there is little or no initial anxiety. Additional sessions are carried out at increasing intervals of time to avoid the spontaneous recovery of the conditioned anxiety, until the frequency with which the patient encounters heights in the natural environment is sufficient to prevent relapse. The success of the procedure depends on the patient remaining in the fear-generating situation on each trial until he or she is calm and feels a sense of mastery. Premature withdrawal from the situation or prematurely terminating the fantasized scene is tantamount to an escape, and both fear conditioning and avoidance (phobic) behavior are reinforced. Depending on some details of the particular case, as few as 5 and seldom more than 20 sessions are required.

Reinforcement is a process whereby any event or stimulus contingent on an operant response increases the probability of that response's recurring. *Positive reinforcement* refers to the process whereby a stimulus (the positive reinforcer) increases the frequency of performance of whatever response it follows. *Relationship therapy* is characterized by a warm and accepting therapeutic alliance between patient and doctor so that the patient feels supported and able to develop a sense of independence. *Graded exposure* is the process in which the patient is exposed, over a period of time, to objects that cause increasing levels of anxiety. *Participant modeling* is based on imitation, whereby patients learn to confront a fearful situation or object by modeling themselves after the therapist.

**26.4.   The answer is D** (*Synopsis*, ed. 4, page 598).

Dream interpretation is an important factor in *psychoanalysis*; in fact, the paradigm of psychoanalytic interpretation is the interpretation of the dream. Freud demonstrated that, contrary to the prevailing scientific opinion before 1900, dreams are meaningful and can be set into a context of happenings in which their nonsensical elements become sensible. A full exploration of the meaning of a dream reveals the various conflicts experienced by the patient. Freud referred to the dream as the royal road to the unconscious.

*Behavior therapy* is a psychiatric treatment modality that focuses on overt and objectively observable behavior and uses various conditioning techniques derived from learning theory to modify the patient's behavior directly. Behavior therapy aims exclusively at symptomatic improvement, without addressing psychodynamic causation. A major worker in the field was Joseph Wolpe, who developed and popularized the technique of systematic desensitization. *Supportive psychotherapy* is a form of psychotherapy that seeks to strengthen patient defenses and to provide them with reassurance, rather than to probe deeply into their conflicts. *Relationship psychotherapy* is based on the therapeutic alliance between the doctor and the patient that enables patients to realize their full potential in a warm and accepting atmosphere. *Brief psychotherapy* is a form of psychotherapy in which the sessions are limited to 10 to 15 in number, during which time attempts to modify behavior occur. The approach is used in both individual and group settings.

**26.5.   The answer is B** (*Synopsis*, ed. 4, page 615).

All groups, not only psychotherapy groups,

are marked by some amount of *cohesion*. Members feel a "we-ness," a sense of belonging. They value the group, which engenders loyalty and friendliness among them. They are willing to work together and to take responsibility for one another in achieving their common goals. They are also willing to endure a certain degree of frustration to maintain the group's integrity. A cohesive psychotherapy group is one in which members are accepting and supportive and have meaningful relationships with one another. Cohesion is the single most important factor in group therapy.

The more effectively the therapist can increase a member's cohesion in the group, the more probable is a successful outcome, for the patient will then be more receptive to the mechanisms that group therapy has to offer.

Although cohesion is the single most important dynamic factor in group therapy, other group dynamics, such as universalization, identification, intellectualization, and ventilation, also occur in the group. *Universalization* occurs when individuals in the group realize that the problems they are facing alone also concern other members of the group. *Identification* between members of the group and between members of the group and the therapist helps the patient learn new modes of adaptation and coping. *Intellectualization* is the process by which each member comes to evaluate personal defense mechanisms and ways of coping, as well as those of co-patients. *Ventilation* is the open expression of one's innermost thoughts and secrets. It is contrasted with another process called catharsis, which refers to the evocation of affect or feeling tones that may be attached to the ventilated thought or secret.

## 26.6. The answer is D (*Synopsis*, ed. 4, pages 626 and 627).

The cognitive theory of *depression* posits that cognitive dysfunctions are the core of depression and that affective and physical changes, and other associated features of depression, are consequences of the cognitive dysfunctions. For example, apathy and low energy are results of the individual's expectation of failure in all areas. Similarly, paralysis of will stems from the individual's pessimism and feelings of hopelessness. Cognitive therapy is best suited for patients suffering from depression.

The goal of therapy is to alleviate depression and to prevent its recurrence by helping the patient (1) identify and test negative cognitions; (2) develop alternative, more flexible schemas; and (3) rehearse both new cognitive and new behavioral responses. The goal is also to change the way an individual thinks and, subsequently, to alleviate the depressive syndrome.

The cognitive triad consists of negative cognitions regarding oneself, the world, and one's future. First is a negative self-percept involving seeing oneself as defective, inadequate, deprived, worthless, and undesirable. Second is a tendency to experience the world as a negative, demanding, and defeating place and to expect failure and punishment. Third is an expectation of continued hardship, suffering, deprivation, and failure.

Schemas are stable cognitive patterns through which one interprets experience. Schemas of depression are analogous to viewing the world through dark glasses. Depressogenic schemas may involve viewing experience as black or white without shades of gray, as categorical imperatives that allow no options, or as expectations that people are either all good or all bad.

Cognitive errors are systematic errors in thinking that lead to persistence of negative schemas despite contradictory evidence.

## 26.7. The answer is A (*Synopsis*, ed. 4, page 605).

In behavior therapy, most procedures are based on a method known as *relaxation training*. This method consists of having the patient relax the major muscle groups of the body. Relaxation begins with the upper portion of the body, with the patient using neck rolls, shoulder rolls, and so on until the whole body is in a relaxed state. At that point, the patient is instructed to imagine the anxiety-provoking stimulus for which he or she came for treatment. Sometimes the clinician will use hypnosis to help the patient achieve the relaxation response.

*Transference* is an unconscious tendency of a person to assign to others in the present and immediate environment those feelings and attitudes originally linked with significant figures in the person's early life. It is a crucial process in psychoanalytic psychotherapy, in which the patient usually identifies the therapist with a parent; the transference may be negative (hostile) or positive (affectionate). Analysis of transference phenomena is used as a major therapeutic tool in both individual therapy and group therapy to help patients better understand and gain insight into their behavior and its origins. *Reality testing* is a fundamental ego function consisting of tentative actions that test and objectively evaluate the nature and the limits of the environment. It includes the ability to differentiate between the external world and the internal world and to accurately judge the relation between the self and the environment. *Resistance* is a conscious or unconscious opposition to the uncovering of unconscious material. Resistance is linked to underlying psychological defense mechanisms against impulses from the id that are threatening to the ego. *Therapeutic alliance* is a conscious contractual relationship between therapist and patient in which each implicitly agrees that they need to work together to help the patient with personal problems. It involves a therapeutic splitting of the patient's ego into observing and experiencing parts. A good therapeutic alliance is especially necessary for the continuation of treatment during phases of strong negative transference.

**26.8.   The answer is A** (*Synopsis*, ed. 4, page 596).

The patients in psychoanalysis must adhere to the fundamental rule, which is that *the patient agrees to be completely candid with the analyst.* Implicit in the fundamental rule of psychoanalysis are two interrelated principles. First, in psychoanalysis there is a clear emphasis on the value of recognition and verbalization of psychic contents—of ideas, impulses, conflicts, and emotions. Second, psychoanalytic technique emphasizes the principle that action based on impulse without adequate prior consideration is to be avoided.

Some patients may take the fundamental rule so literally that they sabotage their treatment while giving an appearance of meticulously complying with its requirements. They may parody its spirit while obeying its letter. This is particularly likely to occur in some obsessional states, in which the fundamental rule may be used as a weapon against the analyst, rather than against the neurosis. Some analysts, therefore, do not always give their patients explicit statements about the fundamental rule, preferring, instead, to lead them to discover it for themselves through a study of the obstacles they place in the way of communication.

**26.9.   The answer is B** (*Synopsis*, ed. 4, pages 619 and 620).

Psychodrama is a method of group psychotherapy originated by Jacob Moreno, M. D., in which personality make-up, interpersonal relationships, conflicts, and emotional problems are explored by means of special dramatic methods. The therapeutic dramatization of emotional problems includes (1) protagonist or patient, the person who acts out personal problems with the help of (2) auxiliary egos, persons who enact different aspects of the patient, and (3) director, psychodramatist, or therapist, the person who guides those involved in the drama toward the acquistion of insight.

*The protagonist is the patient in conflict.* The patient chooses the situation to portray in the dramatic scene, or the therapist may choose it if the patient so desires.

*The director is the leader or therapist. Directors* must be active and participating. They encourage the members of their group to be spon-

taneous, and their function is catalytic. They must be available to meet the needs of the group and not superimpose their values on them. Of all the group psychotherapies, psychodrama requires the most participation and leadership abilities from the therapist.

*The auxiliary ego is another group member* who represents something or someone in the protagonist's experience. The use of the auxiliary ego helps account for the great range of therapeutic effects available in psychodrama.

*The members of the psychodrama scene and the audience make up the group.* Some are participants, and others are observers, but all benefit from the experience to the extent that they can identify with the ongoing events. The concept of spontaneity in psychodrama refers to the ability of each member of the group, especially the protagonist, to experience the thoughts and feelings of the moment fully and to communicate emotion in as authentic a manner as possible.

**26.10.   The answer is C** (*Synopsis*, ed. 4, page 610).

*Paranoia* is not amenable to hypnosis simply because paranoid patients are suspicious and usually avoid or resist efforts at hypnosis. A variety of other conditions, however, have been treated successfully using hypnosis. They include *smoking*, eating disorders, *anxiety*, *phobia*, and *pain*.

Patients who want to break the *smoking habit* are told to put themselves into the trance state. When they have done this on their own, the therapist presents these three points: (1) For my body smoking is a poison; (2) I need my body to live; and (3) I owe my body this respect and protection. While the patients are still in the trance, the therapist goes through these three points in greater detail, emphasizing the patients' learning to distinguish their desire for a cigarette from the need to act on the desire as long as they maintain the position that treating their bodies with respect and protection is of primary importance.

Eating disorders provide a more complex problem, because—unlike smoking, in which a habit change recedes as an issue—people are always faced with the problem of how much to eat. A variation of the three points listed above is taught to the patient, emphasizing that an excess of food is poison for the patient's body.

The sense of helplessness that accompanies *anxiety* is reinforced by the snowball effect of the psychological and somatic manifestations of anxiety. Patients can be taught to put themselves into the trance state and allow their bodies to float; floating, unlike the concept of relaxing, is in a sense body language. While maintaining this physical repose, patients are taught to picture and think through problems on an imaginary screen. Anxiety-provoking problems are thus addressed while using the dissociation of the trance state to minimize somatic distress.

*Phobias* are a complex problem. Rarely does a patient have only one phobia, and often some translating is needed to help the patient understand the message that the phobia is conveying. Hypnosis has been useful in reducing the anxiety associated with phobias.

Highly hypnotizable persons are capable of producing complete anesthesia, and major surgery has been performed in this country with hypnosis as the sole anesthetic. For most kinds of *acute and chronic pain*, however, hypnotic intervention is less dramatic, but can be quite effective.

**26.11.  The answer is A** (*Synopsis*, ed. 4, page 620).

Despite differences in specific models, what is unique to family therapy is its family orientation. All members of the family are interrelated, and one part of the family cannot be isolated from the rest. A family's structure and organization must be viewed as a unit and are important factors determining the behavior of the individual family members. Accordingly, the *patient is the family unit* as a whole, rather than one person in the family unit.

**26.12.  The answer is D** (*Synopsis*, ed. 4, pages 625 and 626).

The following criteria are used in selecting candidates for brief dynamic psychotherapy: *a circumscribed chief complaint* (this implies an ability to select one out of a variety of problems to which patients assign top priority and which they want to solve as a result of the treatment); one meaningful or give-and-take relationship during early childhood; the ability to interact flexibly with the evaluator and to *express feelings appropriately*; above-average psychological sophistication (this implies not only an *above-average intelligence* but also an ability to respond to interpretations); *a specific psychodynamic formulation*; a contract between the therapist and the patient to work on the specified focus and formulation of minimal expectations of outcome; and good to excellent motivation for change.

Those patients who are *motivated only for symptom relief* and who do not fulfill the above criteria are not suitable for brief dynamic psychotherapy. They may be better suited to one of the short-term behavioral approaches that treat a specific symptom, such as a phobia.

**26.13.  The answer is E** (*Synopsis*, ed. 4, pages 595 and 596).

The externals of the psychoanalysis situation—the setting—are little changed from Freud's day. The patient *lies on a couch* or sofa, and the analyst sits behind, *remaining for the most part outside the patient's field of vision* and intruding as little as possible into the patient's thought processes, except through interpretations. Sessions are usually *held four or more times a week* and have an average duration of 45 to 50 minutes. Innovators, such as Jacques Lacan from France, who has introduced decreases in session frequency and length, have caused much controversy; but some analyses are now being conducted in this country with session lengths varying from 20 to 30 minutes and frequency of one to two sessions per week. Patients are guided in their behavior by the so-called basic or fundamental rule—that they keep nothing back—and the analyst endeavors to maintain a kind of evenly suspended attention that is the counterpart to the patients' activity of *free association* in which patients verbalize without censorship the passing contents of their minds. For the most part, the analyst's activity is limited to timely interpretation of the patient's associations. Such interpretations are usually few in number.

Although the analyst tries not to impose his or her own personality and system of values on the patient, the analyst nevertheless must enter into some reality negotiations with the patient. There are schedules and fees to be arranged; and weekends, vacations, and illnesses will interrupt the course of treatment. Realistic aspects of the analyst's personality become apparent to the patient in many ways, and it is neither possible nor desirable for the analyst to maintain the much-misinterpreted blank screen. Thus, a real relationship underlies the analytic setting, and the handling of the real relationship may make the difference between success and failure in the treatment endeavor.

The reclining position of the patient on the couch, with the analyst seated nearby, attending to every word, reproduces symbolically an ancient parent-child situation, the nuances of which vary from patient to patient. This situation is not without the potential to generate anxiety in the patient, who is probably already in an anxious state because of his or her neurosis when analysis is begun. Preoedipal anxieties derived from the early mother-child dyad may be revived early in the analysis. The patient's difficulties in trusting the analyst—who is out of the patient's sight—to maintain this trust in the absence of immediate gratification and response, and to maintain an appreciation of the separateness of the patient from the analyst may occupy the center of the stage during the opening phases of analysis. The capacity of the patient to call on these ego functions through the analysis is indispensable for its ultimate success, and an estimate of this capacity is one of the important considerations in the assessment of analyzability.

Another aspect of the use of the couch is that it introduces an element of sensory deprivation because visual stimuli are limited. Also, an *analyst's interpretations and interventions tend to be rather sparse*, especially in the early phases of an analysis. A relative diminution of both visual and auditory stimuli tends to promote regression. In the analytic situation, however, regression must remain controlled and in the service of the treatment. Almost any verbal input from the analyst tends to counteract regression by its sensory impact.

**26.14.   The answer is E (all)** (*Synopsis*, ed. 4, pages 611 and 614).

Many patients experience anxiety when placed in a group or when group therapy is suggested. *That anxiety often relates to the patients' experiences with peers or with authority figures*—real or projected persons in a position of power, e.g. transferentially, a projected parent.

Relationship to peers and to authority figures, current and past, should be assessed.

Those patients whose primary problem centers on their relationship to authority, and who are extremely anxious in the presence of authority figures, often do better in the group setting than in the dyadic or one-to-one setting. Patients with a great deal of authority anxiety may be blocked, anxious, resistant, and unwilling to verbalize thoughts and feelings in the individual setting, generally for fear of censure or disapproval from the therapist. They may welcome the suggestion of group psychotherapy in order to avoid the scrutiny of the dyadic situation. Conversely, if the patient reacts negatively to the suggestion of group psychotherapy or is openly resistant to the idea, the therapist should consider the possibility of a high degree of peer anxiety.

*Patients who have destructive relationships with their peer group*, or who have *been extremely isolated from peer group* contact such as a schizoid personality, generally react negatively or with increased anxiety when placed in a group setting, as do patients—adults or *children—who have no siblings.*

In organizing the adult group, the therapist should be careful not to have only one member representative of the extreme age group. Both the child and the adolescent are best treated in groups composed of patients in their own age group. Some adolescent patients are quite capable of assimilating the material of the adult group, regardless of content, but they should not be deprived of a constructive peer experience that they might otherwise not have.

**26.15.   The answer is E (all)** (*Synopsis*, ed. 4, page 630).

Neal Miller gave credibility to biofeedback and its medical potentials by demonstrating that the normally involuntary autonomic nervous system could be operantly conditioned with appropriate feedback. Miller and his colleagues experimentally challenged a classical doctrine of psychology that instrumental conditioning principles operated only with the voluntary central nervous system and skeletal muscles. The implication seemed clear that instrumental conditioning via enhanced sensory awareness through biofeedback could be the scientific basis underlying a wide spectrum of poorly understood self-regulation techniques, including the placebo response (both positive and negative), hypnotic phenomena, meditation, autogenic therapy, relaxation, progressive relaxation, and other variants.

Biofeedback has been applied to the following conditions:

1. *Neuromuscular rehabilitation.* Mechanical devices or electromyographic (EMG) measurement of muscle activity displayed to a patient has increased the effectiveness of traditional therapies as documented by relatively long clinical histories in peripheral nerve-muscle damage, spasmodic torticollis, selected cases of tardive dyskinesia, cerebral palsy, and upper motor neuron hemiplegias.

2. *Raynaud's syndrome.* Cold hands and cold feet are frequent concomitants of anxiety and are given a formal diagnosis of primary idiopathic Raynaud's disease when vasospasm of arterial smooth muscle produces color changes in the digits or toes not associated with the physical stigmata of Raynaud's phenomenon, which frequently involves an autoimmune process. A number of studies report that thermal feedback from the hand, an inexpensive and benign procedure compared to surgical sympathectomy, is effective in about 70 percent of cases of primary Raynaud's syndrome.

3. *Migraine headaches.* The commonest biofeedback strategy with classic or common vascular headaches has been thermal biofeedback from a digit accompanied by autogenic self-suggestive phrases encouraging hand warming and head cooling. The mechanism is thought to be prophylactic in preventing excessive cerebral arterial vasoconstriction, often accompanied by an ischemic prodromal symptom, such as scin-

tillating scotomata, followed by rebound engorgement of arteries and stretching of vessel wall pain receptors.

4. *Essential hypertension.* A variety of specific (direct) and nonspecific biofeedback procedures, including blood pressure feedback, galvanic skin response, and foot-hand thermal feedback combined with relaxation procedures, have been used to teach patients to increase or decrease blood pressure. Some follow-up data indicate that these changes may persist for at least 2 years and often permit reduction or elimination of antihypertensive medications.

**26.16.   The answer is A (1, 2, 3)** (*Synopsis,* ed. 4, page 629).

Biofeedback is a word first coined in 1969, borrowing the feedback concept formalized by cybernetics during World War II. Biofeedback instrumentation signals persons about normally involuntary or subthreshold biological processes that they may be able to change by adjusting their behavior or mental processes within limitations set by homeostasis or pathology.

The methodology includes the following procedures:

1. *Electromyography (EMG).* Muscle fibers generate electrical potentials that can be measured on an electromyograph. Electrodes placed in or on a specific muscle groups—e.g. masseter, deltoid, temporalis—can be monitored for relaxation training.

2. *Electroencephalography (EEG).* The evoked potential of the EEG is monitored to determine relaxation. $\alpha$-Waves are generally indicative of meditative states, but wave frequency and amplitude are also measured.

3. *Galvanic skin response (GSR).* Skin conductance of electricity is measured as an indicator of autonomic nervous system activity. Stress increases electrical conduction and the GSR; conversely relaxation is associated with lowered autonomic activity and changes in skin response. Similarly, skin temperature as a measure of peripheral vasoconstriction is decreased under stress and can be measured with thermisters (thermal feedback).

A *strain gauge* is a device measuring nocturnal penile tumescence that is used to determine if erections occur during sleep. It has no biofeedback applications, but is of use in evaluating impotence in the male.

**26.17.   The answer is A (1, 2, 3)** (*Synopsis,* ed. 4, page 609).

Hypnosis is an artificially induced alteration of consciousness characterized by increased suggestibility and receptivity to direction.

While hypnotized, a patient may be told that,

when the hypnotist lights a cigarette after the trance, the patient will ask for one, puff at it once or twice, and then put it out. It can be predicted with confidence that after the trance the patient will (1) have an *amnesia, more or less, for the instruction,* technically called the signal; (2) *comply with the instruction* compulsively; and (3) *rationalize the act of snuffing out the cigarette* by saying, "This cigarette is stale" or something along those lines. *This triad is most clearly seen when the signal has been planted during a deep trance,* but it can also be observed in an attempted form when the signal has been implanted during a light trance.

**26.18.   The answer is E (all)** (*Synopsis,* ed. 4, page 600).

Supportive psychotherapy uses such techniques as *warm, friendly, strong leadership*; a *gratification of dependency needs,* if this can be done without evoking undue shame; *support in the development of legitimate independence*; help in the development of hobbies and of pleasurable but nondestructive sublimations, adequate rest and diversion; the removal of excessive external strain, if this is a productive step; hospitalization when it is indicated; medication that may alleviate symptoms and often does more; and guidance and advice in current issues. It uses these techniques that may make the patient feel more secure, accepted, protected, encouraged, safe, or less anxious and less alone.

**26.19.   The answer is E (all)** (*Synopsis,* ed. 4, pages 627 and 628).

The cognitive approach includes four processes: (1) *eliciting automatic thoughts,* (2) *testing automatic thoughts,* (3) *identifying maladaptive underlying assumptions,* and (4) *testing the validity of maladaptive assumptions.*

Automatic thoughts are cognitions that intervene between external events and the individuals' emotional reaction to the event. An example of an automatic thought is the belief that "everyone is going to laugh at me when they see how badly I bowl"—a thought that occurs to someone who has been asked to go bowling and responds negatively. Another example is a person's thought that "he doesn't like me," if someone passes that person in the hall without saying hello.

The therapist, acting as a teacher, helps the patient test the validity of automatic thought. The goal is to encourage patients to reject inaccurate or exaggerated automatic thoughts after careful examination. Patients often blame themselves for things that go wrong that may well have been outside their control. The therapist reviews with the patient the entire situation and helps to "reattribute" the blame or cause of the unpleasant events more accurately. Generating alternative explanations for events is another way of undermining inaccurate and distorted automatic thoughts.

**26.20.   The answer is E (all)** (*Synopsis*, ed. 4, page 605).

Joseph Wolpe first described systematic desensitization, in which the patient is trained in muscle relaxation and a hierarchy of anxiety-provoking thoughts or objects is paired with the relaxed state until the anxiety is systematically decreased and eliminated.

Generally, systematic desensitization is applicable when one can identify the stimulus antecedents that elicit anxiety, which, in turn, mediates maladaptive or disruptive behavior. Often, *obsessive-compulsive* behavior is mediated by the anxiety elicited by specific objects or situations.

Desensitization has been used effectively with some *stutterers* by deconditioning the anxiety associated with a range of speaking situations. Certain *sexual problems* are amenable to desensitization therapy. A number of psychophysiological disorders have been treated by desensitization, using a hierarchy of stimuli that elicit anxiety-related physiological reactions. The reactions include such diverse disorders as *bronchial asthma* and dysmenorrhea, a painful menstruation that is believed to have a psychogenic component.

*Obsessive-compulsive personality* is a personality disorder characterized by perfectionism, overconscientiousness, and excessive inhibition with regard to self-expression and relaxation. *Stuttering* is a speech disorder characterized by repetitions or prolongations of sounds, syllables, or words or by hesitations and pauses that disrupt the flow of speech. *Bronchial asthma* is a condition of the lungs in which there is widespread narrowing of the airways due to contraction of the smooth muscle and edema of the mucosa, the lumen of the bronchi, and bronchioles.

**26.21.   The answer is E (all)** (*Synopsis*, ed. 4, page 616).

Ideally, in groups conducted by co-therapists, *each therapist becomes actively involved, so that neither is in a position of greater authority or dominance. Co-therapists of different sexes* can stimulate the *replication of parental surrogates* in the group; if the two interact harmoniously, they can serve as a corrective emotional experience for the members. Even if the co-therapists are of the same sex, one often tends to be confrontative and interpretative and is seen as masculine, and the other tends to be evocative of

feelings and is seen as feminine. Styles of leadership and the personality characteristics of the co-therapists, regardless of their genders, also elicit transferential reactions.

**26.22.   The answer is E (all)** (*Synopsis*, ed. 4, page 623).

Crisis theory states that *a crisis is a response to hazardous events and is experienced as a painful state.* Because of this, it tends to mobilize powerful reactions to help persons alleviate the discomfort and return to the state of emotional equilibrium that existed before its onset. If this takes place, the crisis can be overcome, but in addition, persons learn how to use adaptive reactions that can serve them well at a future time. Furthermore, it is possible that by resolving the crisis *they may find themselves in a better state of mind, superior to the one that existed before the onset* of the psychological difficulties. If, however, they use maladaptive reactions, the painful state intensifies, the crisis deepens, and a regressive deterioration takes place, giving rise to psychiatric symptoms. These symptoms, in turn, may crystallize into a neurotic pattern of behavior that restricts their ability to function freely. At times, however, the situation cannot be stabilized, new maladaptive reactions are introduced, and the *consequences can be of catastrophic proportions, leading at times to death by suicide.* It is in this sense that psychological crises are painful and may be viewed as turning points for better or for worse.

*A crisis is self-limited* and can last anywhere from a few hours to about 6 weeks. The crisis as such is characterized by an initial phase in which anxiety and tension rise. This phase is followed by one in which problem-solving mechanisms are set in motion. These mechanisms may be successful or not, depending on whether they are adaptive or maladaptive.

**26.23.   The answer is A (1, 2, 3)** (*Synopsis*, ed. 4, page 605).

Systematic desensitization is a *core procedure in behavior therapy.* It is based on a general behavioral principle that may be stated as follows: A person can overcome maladaptive anxiety that is elicited by a class of situations or objects by *approaching the feared situations gradually* and *in a psychophysiological state that inhibits anxiety. Joseph Wolpe originated systematic desensitization.*

The patient is first trained in relaxation techniques. Then, a hierarchical list of anxiety-provoking images is established, and the patient moves from the least anxious to the most anxious image in the previously learned relaxed state. Eventually, the anxiety is completely inhibited. In vivo desensitization is similar, except instead of imagined events, real events are used. For example, for patients who are terrified of snakes, the therapist may bring a snake into the treatment room, and through a series of steps will eventually enable the patient to touch the snake. The patient has to fully complete each step before moving on, however, so that the maladaptive anxiety can be overcome.

**26.24–26.28.   The answers are 26.24–B, 26.25–A, 26.26–D, 26.27–E, and 26.28–C** (*Synopsis*, ed. 4, pages 600, 601, 602, and 603).

*Transference neurosis* is a phenomenon occurring in psychoanalysis in which the patient develops a strong emotional attachment to the therapist as a symbolized nuclear familial figure. The repetition and the depth of that misperception or symbolization characterize it as a trans-

ference neurosis. It is analyzed in psychoanalysis. The *transference to persons other than the analyst* is used in psychoanalytic therapy, which is also known as insight therapy or in-depth therapy. In relationship therapy, the therapist provides a warm atmosphere in which the patient feels accepted and a *real relationship and therapeutic alliance develops.* In supportive therapy the *therapist actively intervenes and gives advice* about the patient's current life problem.

All these therapies go on for an extended period, sometimes for years. In contrast, *a limited number of interviews* are used in the so-called brief therapies, which are used primarily in crisis intervention.

For a thorough overview of psychoanalysis and the various psychotherapies, see the table that follows.

### Psychoanalysis and Psychoanalytic Psychotherapy

|  | Psychoanalysis | Psychoanalytic Therapy | Relationship Therapy | Supportive Therapy |
|---|---|---|---|---|
| Basic theory | Psychoanalytic psychology. Reorganization of character structure, with diminution of pathological defenses, integration or ultimate rejection of warded-off strivings and ideation. Understanding rather than symptom relief the objective, but symptom relief usually results. Correction of developmental lags in otherwise relatively mature personalities | Psychoanalytic psychology. Resolution of selected conflicts and limited removal of pathological defenses. Understanding the primary goal, usually with secondary relief of symptoms | Psychoanalytic psychology. Growth of the relatively immature personality through catalytic relationship with therapist offsets the neurotogenic effects of prior significant relationships | Psychoanalytic psychology. Restoration of prior equilibrium, reduction of anxiety and fear in new situations. Help in tolerating unalterable situations |
| Activity of patient and therapist | Freely hovering attention by the analyst, free association by the patient. Interpretation of transference and resistance. Suggestion ultimately interpreted | Freely hovering attention by the therapist but with more focusing than in analysis. Less emphasis on free association, more on discussion by the patient. Suggestion usually eventually interpreted. | Therapist participates as a real person around current issues, becomes a helpful parental figure | Expressive techniques generally avoided except for some cathartic effects. Therapist actively intervenes, advises, fosters discussion, selects focus |

### Psychoanalysis and Psychoanalytic Psychotherapy (continued)

| | Psychoanalysis | Psychoanalytic Therapy | Relationship Therapy | Supportive Therapy |
|---|---|---|---|---|
| Interpretive emphasis | Focus on resistance and transference to the analyst | Greater emphasis on interpersonal events, less on transferences to the analyst than in analysis, but transference interpretation often effective. Transferences to persons other than the therapist often effectively interpreted | Discussion and clarification of interpersonal events. Transference may or may not be interpreted | Interpretations of transferences to therapist generally avoided unless significantly interfering with the therapeutic relationship. Strong focus on external events |
| Transference | Transference neurosis fostered on foundation of the therapeutic alliance and the real relationship | Transference neurosis discouraged; therapeutic alliance fostered | Transference neurosis discouraged. Real relationship and therapeutic alliance emphasized | Transference neurosis discouraged. Therapeutic alliance may be firm or weak |
| Confidentiality | Absolute. May be compromised by third-party payers | Absolute. May be compromised by third-party payers | Usually absolute but may be abrogated in some situations. May be compromised by third-party payers | Usually absolute but may be abrogated in some situations. May be compromised by third-party payers |
| Regression | Fostered in the form of the transference neurosis | Generally discouraged except as necessary to gain access to fantasy material and other derivatives of the unconscious | Regression generally discouraged | Generally discouraged but may occasionally be fostered for its own sake |
| Adjuncts | Couch | Couch less used. Psychotropic drugs used occasionally | Couch contraindicated. Group methods, family therapy, or family contacts on a planned basis. Other therapists and agencies may be involved | Couch usually contraindicated. Psychotropic drugs, occupational therapy, hospitalization (including day hospitalization). Family contact on planned basis. Other therapists and agencies may be involved |
| Frequency and duration | 4 to 5 times weekly, 2 to 5+ years. Sessions usually about 50 minutes. New modifications, shorter sessions | 1 to 3 times weekly, few sessions to several years. Sessions usually from ½ to 1 hour | 1 to 2 times weekly, 1 month to several years. Sessions usually ½ to 1 hour | Daily sessions to once every few months, one session to a lifelong process. Sessions may be brief, ranging from a few minutes to an hour |

## Psychoanalysis and Psychoanalytic Psychotherapy *(continued)*

|  | Psychoanalysis | Psychoanalytic Therapy | Relationship Therapy | Supportive Therapy |
|---|---|---|---|---|
| Prerequisites | Relatively mature personality, favorable life situation, motivation for long undertaking, capacity to tolerate frustration, capacity for stable therapeutic alliance, psychological mindedness | Relatively mature personality, capacity for therapeutic alliance, some capacity to tolerate frustration, adequate motivation, and some degree of psychological mindedness | Capacity for therapeutic alliance, personality capable of growth, reality situation not too unfavorable | Personality organization may range from psychotic to mature; at least some capacity to form a therapeutic alliance |

# References

APA Commission on Psychotherapies: *Psychotherapy Research: Methodological and Efficacy Issues.* American Psychiatric Association, Washington, DC, 1982.

Beck A T: Cognitive therapy. In *Comprehensive Textbook of Psychiatry*, ed 4, H I Kaplan, B J Sadock, editors, p 1432. Williams & Wilkins, Baltimore, 1985.

Brady J P: Behavior therapy, In *Comprehensive Textbook of Psychiatry*, ed 4, H I Kaplan, B J Sadock, editors, p 1365. Williams & Wilkins, Baltimore, 1985.

Buckley P: Psychodynamic variables as predictors of psychotherapy outcome. Am J Psychiatry *141:* 742, 1984.

Freud S: *The Standard Edition of the Complete Psychological Works of Sigmund Freud*, 24 vols. Hogarth Press, London, 1953–1974.

Sadock B J: Group psychotherapy. In *Comprehensive Textbook of Psychiatry*, ed 4, H I Kaplan, B J Sadock, editors, p 1403. Williams & Wilkins, Baltimore, 1985.

Simon R: Family therapy. In *Comprehensive Textbook of Psychiatry*, ed 4, H I Kaplan, B J Sadock, editors, p 1427. Williams & Wilkins, Baltimore, 1985.

Spiegel D, Spiegel H: Hypnosis. In *Comprehensive Textbook of Psychiatry*, ed 4, H I Kaplan, B J Sadock, editors, p 1389. Williams & Wilkins, Baltimore, 1985.

Stewart R L: Psychoanalysis and psychoanalytic psychotherapy. In *Comprehensive Textbook of Psychiatry*, ed 4, H I Kaplan, B J Sadock, editors, p 1331. Williams & Wilkins, Baltimore, 1985.

Stroebel C F: Biofeedback and behavioral medicine. In *Comprehensive Textbook of Psychiatry*, ed 4, H I Kaplan, B J Sadock, editors, p 1467. Williams & Wilkins, Baltimore, 1985.

# 27

# Organic Therapies

Organic therapy may be defined as an attempt to modify or correct pathological behavior by physical or chemical means. The relationship between the physical state of the brain and behavior is highly complex and imperfectly understood. It is clear, however, that the various parameters of normal, as well as deviant, behavior, such as perception, consciousness, affect, and the cognitive functions, may be profoundly affected by certain physical changes in the central nervous system.

Organic treatment of the psychiatric disorders is largely empirical. The underlying mechanisms through which a chemical or physical change in the brain produces an improvement of abnormal behavior have not as yet been completely delineated. Nevertheless, some of the organic therapy techniques have proved highly effective and may constitute the treatment of choice for certain psychopathological conditions. As such, they form an important part of the treatment armamentarium of the psychiatrist, and of practitioners in other medical specialties as well.

Important gains in organic therapy, particularly in pharmacological treatment, have been made in the last 5 years. A new generation of neuroleptics, antidepressants, and antianxiety agents has been produced during that time. Pharmacotherapy has been improved as a result of more precise methods of determining the blood level of medications in patients. Pharmacokinetics, which is the study of the absorption, metabolic pathways, and excretion patterns of drugs, is a major area of research that has ultimate practical value in patient care. For example, one drug may interact with another to negate therapeutic effects or even to produce dangerous side effects.

Electroconvulsive therapy (ECT) has withstood the test of time since its introduction in 1938 by Cerletti and Bini. The innovative use of unilateral ECT—placement of the electrodes over the nondominant hemisphere—has been shown to produce less memory loss than the traditional bilateral placement. Moreover, the antagonism toward the use of ECT both in and out of the profession appears to have lessened, contributing to renewed clinical interest in ECT. Despite this shift in opinion, strong anti-ECT groups exist in the United States that wish to ban its use entirely.

Similarly, psychosurgery, which is the alteration of brain tissue by surgical means to change behavior, is the subject of much controversy. In 1973, the last year for which statistics are available, only 321 procedures were performed. Currently, only a few are done in the United States, although the exact incidence is unknown. In general, psychosurgery is considered a treatment of last resort.

Finally, there are a variety of other organic therapies, ranging from nutritional supplementation to carbon dioxide inhalation. None have been proven to be of significant therapeutic value. The fact that so many miscellaneous forms of treatment exist indicates that the field of organic therapy of mental illness remains a frontier science with much still to be accomplished.

The reader is referred to Chapter 27, "Organic Therapies," in *Modern Synopsis-IV*. Studying the questions and answers below will test the student's knowledge of this area.

# Questions

**DIRECTIONS:** Each of the statements or questions below is followed by five suggested responses or completions. Select the *one* that is *best* in each case.

**27.1.** The treatment of choice for manic-depressive illness (bipolar disorder) is

A. lithium
B. amphetamine
C. methylphenidate
D. pemoline
E. all of the above

**27.2.** All of the following statements are true concerning lithium carbonate *except*

A. that it may abort mild manic attacks
B. that it is the treatment of choice for bipolar disorders
C. that it can be used as a prophylactic treatment to prevent manic episodes
D. that it is not always effective
E. that it can induce an exogenous depression

**27.3.** The following figure illustrates a

A. plasma level-clinical response curve
B. plasma level-toxicity curve
C. dose-response curve
D. therapeutic window curve
E. none of the above

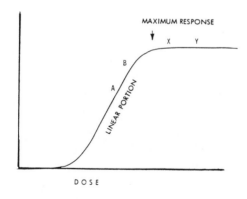

**27.4.** Which of the following statements concerning monoamine oxidase inhibitors (MAOI's) is true:

A. Phenelzine acts by inhibiting the enzyme monoamine oxidase, type A.
B. There is good evidence that the use of MAOI's and tricyclic antidepressants (TCA's) in combination does not pose a severe risk.
C. MAOI's generally work within 2 to 5 days.
D. Toxic reactions from overdoses of MAOI's do not usually appear until after several weeks of use.
E. Clinical improvement with MAOI treatment usually occurs within 1 week.

**27.5.** A patient who is being treated with haloperidol is noted to be constantly pacing back and forth and to be unable to sit down for any length of time. That behavior is an example of which of the following:

A. Akinesia
B. Tardive dyskinesia
C. Parkinsonian syndrome
D. Shuffling gait
E. Akathisia

**27.6.** A 68-year-old white man with a past medical history of a myocardial infarction and hypertension is admitted to a psychiatric unit for the treatment of paranoid symptoms. The most appropriate psychotropic agent to use in this case would be

A. haloperidol
B. thioridazine
C. chlorpromazine
D. alprazolam
E. none of the above

**27.7.** Which of the following neuroleptics is thought to have the fewest extrapyramidal symptoms associated with its use:

A. Haloperidol
B. Thioridazine
C. Fluphenazine
D. Butaperazine
E. Chlorpromazine

**27.8.** Risk of seizures occurring during neuroleptic treatment increases with

A. a premorbid history of seizures
B. withdrawal from alcohol
C. rapid increase in dosage of major tranquilizers
D. high daily dosage of antipsychotic agents
E. all of the above

**27.9.** A male patient who is taking phenelzine has eaten a half-pound of cheddar cheese against his doctor's orders. He subsequently develops an occipital headache, stiff neck, and nausea and on physical examination shows a highly elevated blood pressure. The treatment of choice for the complication is the

A. administration of epinephrine
B. administration of phentolamine
C. use of hemodialysis
D. use of electroshock treatment (ECT)
E. doing nothing until the crisis subsides

**27.10.** The lethal dose of tricyclic antidepressants is estimated to be

A. 5 to 10 times the daily dose level
B. 10 to 30 times the daily dose level
C. 30 to 50 times the daily dose level
D. 50 to 80 times the daily dose level
E. 70 to 100 times the daily dose level

**27.11.** The generally accepted therapeutic range of blood levels for lithium carbonate is

A. 0.5 to 1.2 meq/liter
B. 0.8 to 1.0 meq/liter
C. 0.8 to 1.5 meq/liter
D. 8.2 to 2.5 meq/liter
E. 8 to 15 meq/liter

**27.12.** Pigmentary retinopathy is associated with daily doses of thioridazine that exceed

A. 400 mg
B. 600 mg
C. 800 mg
D. 1,200 mg
E. 1,600 mg

**27.13.** All the following statements about phenothiazines and their derivatives are true *except*

A. about 70 percent of schizophrenic patients improve with phenothiazines
B. phenothiazines have little or no abuse potential
C. phenothiazines are classified as controlled substances
D. most of the therapeutic gains occur in the first 6 weeks of therapy
E. phenothiazines are more effective than placebos

**27.14.** The drug that most commonly causes orgasm without ejaculation is

A. cyclazocine
B. morphine
C. thioridazine
D. secobarbital
E. pentobarbital

**27.15.** Of the following, which would not be a side effect associated with the use of lithium:

A. Tremor of the hands
B. Thirst
C. Vermicular movements of the tongue
D. Abdominal cramps
E. Weight gain

**27.16.** A patient being treated with tranylcypromine who develops a severe occipital headache, stiff neck, sweating, nausea, vomiting, and sharply elevated blood pressure may have the prodromal symptoms of

A. hepatitis
B. agranulocytosis
C. hypertensive crisis
D. skin-eye syndrome
E. acute dystonic reaction

**27.17.** The first behavioral sign of a convulsion during ECT consists of

A. gooseflesh
B. movement of the big toe
C. movement of the fingers
D. apnea
E. slight plantar extension of the feet

**27.18.** All of the following are antipsychotic derivatives of the phenothiazines *except*

A. triflupromazine
B. perphenazine
C. haloperidol
D. thioridazine
E. fluphenazine

**27.19.** Sleep withdrawal therapy has been used successfully in the treatment of

A. hysteria
B. depression
C. schizophrenia
D. anxiety
E. none of the above

**DIRECTIONS:** For each of the incomplete statements below, *one* or *more* of the completions given is correct. Choose answer:

A. if only **1, 2,** and **3** are correct
B. if only **1** and **3** are correct
C. if only **2** and **4** are correct
D. if only **4** is correct
E. if all are correct

**27.20.** Succinylcholine, which is used in electroconvulsive therapy (ECT),

1. is a fast-acting depolarization agent
2. stops most major ictal body movements
3. may result in prolonged apnea
4. may have to be augmented by curare

**27.21.** Which of the following medications may cause depression following chronic use:

1. Levodopa
2. Estrogen
3. Cocaine
4. Lithium carbonate

**27.22.** Anticholinergic side effects of phenothiazine drugs include

1. paralytic ileus
2. excessive salivation
3. urinary retention
4. hypertension

**27.23.** A 72-year-old man with a long history of chlorpromazine treatment has his dosage of the medication markedly decreased. Within several days he is noted to make sucking and smacking movements of the lips and choreiform-like jerky movements of the arms. On the basis of that history, one can expect the patient's symptoms to decrease with

1. large doses of phenothiazines
2. choline
3. lecithin
4. levodopa

**27.24.** Mania that is refractory to lithium therapy

1. can occur in up to 40 percent of cases
2. is associated with the rapid cycling type of bipolar disorder
3. is associated with schizophreniform disorders
4. is not related to blood level

**27.25.** A patient receiving monoamine oxidase inhibitor (MAOI) antidepressant should be counseled by the prescribing psychiatrist to avoid entirely or limit the following foods from the diet:

1. Chocolate
2. Fava beans
3. Canned figs
4. Aged cheese

**27.26.** Pharmacokinetic studies of lithium show that

1. it is incompletely absorbed by the gastrointestinal tract
2. serum levels peak in 1.5 to 2.0 hours
3. it binds to plasma protein
4. it has an elimination half-life of about 24 hours

**27.27.** Which of the following statements apply to the interactions between drugs:

1. Antacids interfere with the absorption of antipsychotics.
2. Benzodiazepines elevate phenytoin levels.
3. Tricyclic antidepressants interfere with the effect of guanethidine.
4. Acid urine increases the excretion of amphetamine.

**27.28.** A 50-year-old woman has been receiving a phenothiazine medication for 7 weeks. She complains of a sudden onset of sore throat and fever. The psychiatrist should do which of the following:

1. Obtain a blood and throat culture
2. Discontinue the phenothiazine
3. Order an immediate blood count
4. Institute prophylactic antibiotic therapy

**27.29.** MAOI's potentiate the actions of

1. opioids
2. barbiturates
3. aspirin
4. ephedrine

**27.30.** Phenothiazines have an effect on which of the following symptoms of schizophrenia:

1. Thought disorder
2. Retardation
3. Hallucinations
4. Excitement

**27.31.** The unilateral placement of electrodes in ECT is

1. on the dominant side of the brain
2. not as effective as bilateral placement
3. associated with greater confusion than bilateral placement
4. associated with less amnesia than bilateral placement

**27.32.** Which of the following are classified as psychomotor stimulants:

1. Amphetamine
2. Deanol
3. Dextroamphetamine
4. Pemoline

**27.33.** Phenelzine

1. is a tricyclic antidepressant
2. has been found effective in treating depression, panic attacks, and agoraphobia
3. is metabolized to protryptiline
4. inhibits the reuptake of norepinephrine

**27.34.** Which of the following have associated physical dependence liability:

1. Chlordiazepoxide
2. Barbiturates
3. Diazepam
4. Phenothiazines

**27.35.** Ocular changes noted after long-term high-dose chlorpromazine therapy include

1. anterior lenticular opacities
2. brown pigmentation of the conjunctiva
3. posterior corneal opacities
4. retinitis pigmentosa

**27.36.** Electrocardiogram (EKG) changes characteristic or seen with tricyclic antidepressants include

1. bradycardia
2. prolonged Q-T interval
3. tall, spiked T-waves
4. S-T segment depression

**27.37.** Unwanted sedation due to chlorpromazine can generally be managed by

1. dose reduction
2. use of a sustained-release preparation
3. giving most of the drug at bedtime
4. concurrent administration of an anticholinergic compound

**27.38.** Acute side effects seen in lithium treatment include

1. renal failure
2. elevated serum TSH levels
3. polydipsia
4. polyuria

**27.39.** A 22-year-old man walks into the emergency room with his head tilted sideways, his tongue sticking out, and his eyes rolled up. With difficulty, he tells the doctor that he is stuck in this position and that it happened a few hours after getting a new medicine for his "nerves." At that point the physician should

1. hospitalize the patient
2. administer phenytoin
3. administer haloperidol intramuscularly
4. administer antiparkinsonian medication

**27.40.** Desipramine

1. is a metabolite of imipramine
2. has the weakest anticholinergic properties of the tricyclic antidepressants
3. is readily absorbed from the gastrointestinal tract
4. is useful for psychotic depression because of its marked antipsychotic properties

**27.41.** Neuroleptic-induced akathisia is

1. alleviated by a reduction in the dosage of the neuroleptic
2. alleviated by treatment with antiparkinsonian drugs
3. exacerbated by increasing the dosage of the neuroleptic
4. controlled by switching to a different phenothiazine

**27.42.** The side effects of phenothiazines include which one or more of the following:

1. Lactation
2. Abnormal glucose tolerance curve
3. Gynecomastia in male patients
4. False positive pregnancy test

| Directions Summarized | | | | |
|:---:|:---:|:---:|:---:|:---:|
| A | B | C | D | E |
| 1, 2, 3 | 1, 3 | 2, 4 | 4 | All are |
| only | only | only | only | correct |

**27.43.** Which of the following statements about psychosurgery are valid:
1. Results are attributed to sectioning the frontal cortex from the thalamus.
2. Lesions are produced in the limbic system.
3. Evaluation of results is hindered because of the multiplicity of procedures used.
4. The number of operations is on the increase.

**27.44.** A patient is being given physostigmine as treatment for an overdose of tricyclic antidepressants. The physician watches for signs of cholinergic toxicity and reduces the dosage of physostigmine when which one or more of the following develops:
1. Excess secretions
2. Tachycardia
3. Bradycardia
4. Hyperventilation

**27.45.** Which of the following statements about the tricyclic antidepressants are true:
1. Imipramine has mild sedative effects in normal persons.
2. Of depressed patients, about 75 percent benefit from tricyclics.
3. Improvement may be noted 3 to 10 days after the onset of treatment.
4. The tricyclic antidepressants are effective about twice as often as are placebos.

**27.46.** Which of the following statements about phenothiazine-induced orthostatic hypotension are true:
1. It occurs most frequently during the first few days of therapy.
2. Patients usually develop a tolerance to it.
3. It is most likely to occur with high-dose intramuscular administration.
4. Epinephrine is the drug of choice with severe phenothiazine-induced hypotension.

**27.47.** Phenobarbital
1. is an intermediate-acting barbiturate
2. has useful analgesic properties
3. can compete with coumarin-type drugs for metabolizing enzymes and thus increase their effective half-life
4. is an effective anticonvulsant

**27.48.** Drugs used in the treatment of serious tricyclic antidepressant overdose include
1. physostigmine
2. atropine
3. diazepam
4. trihexyphenidil

**27.49.** For which of the following is there increased risk to ECT:
1. Hypertension
2. Pregnancy
3. Osteoporosis
4. Brain tumor

**27.50.** Which of the following drugs are metabolized in the body to oxazepam:
1. Chlordiazepoxide
2. Lorazepam
3. Diazepam
4. Clorazepate

**27.51.** Characteristics of the central anticholinergic syndrome include
1. florid visual hallucinations
2. loss of immediate memory
3. confusion
4. disorientation

**27.52.** The following are advantages of flurazepam as a sedative hypnotic:
1. It produces hypnosis approximately equal in effectiveness to barbiturates.
2. It does not alter liver microsomal enzymes.
3. There is less abuse potential compared with barbiturates.
4. There is no evidence that it is dangerous in suicide attempts.

**27.53.** Which of the following are common electrocardiogram (EKG) changes seen with phenothiazine treatment:
1. Decreased P-R interval
2. Broad, flattened, or cloved T-waves
3. S-T segment elevation
4. Increased Q-R interval

**27.54.** Electroconvulsive therapy (ECT) may be effective in which of the following conditions:

1. Mania
2. Schizophrenia
3. Pseudodementia
4. Major depression

**27.55.** The following statements about MAOI's are true:

1. Tranylcypromine has a greater therapeutic effect than does a placebo.
2. Iproniazid is the MAOI most often used for treating depression.
3. Isocarboxazid appears to be the least effective of the MAOI's.
4. Tranylcypromine is the most effective of the MAOI's.

**DIRECTIONS:** Each group of questions below consists of five lettered headings followed by a list of numbered words or statements. For each numbered word or statement, select the *one* lettered heading that is most closely associated with it. Each lettered heading may be selected once, more than once, or not at all.

Match the lettered Drug Enforcement Adminstration (DEA) control levels with the characteristics of drugs at each control level or examples of drugs at each control level or both.

**Questions 27.56–27.61**
A. Schedule I
B. Schedule II
C. Schedule III
D. Schedule IV
E. Schedule V

**27.56.** Low abuse potential and limited psychological and physical dependence liability

**27.57.** Moderate physical dependence and high psychological dependence liability

**27.58.** No accepted medical treatment in United States

**27.59.** Amphetamine, morphine

**27.60.** Heroin, marijuana

**27.61.** Lowest abuse potential of all controlled substances

**DIRECTIONS:** Each set of lettered headings below is followed by a list of numbered words or phrases. For each numbered word or phrase, select

A. if the item is associated with **A** *only*
B. if the item is associated with **B** *only*
C. if the item is associated with *both* **A** *and* **B**
D. if the item is associated with *neither* **A** *nor* **B**

**Questions 27.62–27.66**
A. Side effect of tricyclic antidepressants
B. Side effect of phenothiazines
C. Both
D. Neither

**27.62.** Interferes with the antihypertensive effects of guanethidine

**27.63.** Can cause flattened T-waves on EKG

**27.64.** Hallucinations

**27.65.** Dry mouth and throat

**27.66.** Jaundice

# Answers

## Organic Therapies

**27.1. The answer is A** (*Synopsis*, ed. 4, pages 675 and 676).

*Lithium carbonate* should be considered the treatment of choice for manic-depressive illness. It has several advantages over neuroleptics, including a greater degree of specificity and ease of monitoring through plasma levels. In addition, lithium lacks the stigma associated with the antischizophrenic drugs and does not produce tardive dyskinesia or sedation. From the patient's perspective, therefore, it is a much more acceptable drug.

The stimulant drugs, such as *amphetamine*, *methylphenidate*, and *pemoline*, are effective in relieving fatigue and stimulating wakefulness. They have high abuse potential and can produce psychosis. They are not used in bipolar disorder.

**27.2. The answer is E** (*Synopsis*, ed. 4, pages 675 and 676).

*Lithium carbonate should be considered the treatment of choice for bipolar disorder (manic depressive illness). Its slow onset of action—i.e. a 7- to 12-day lag period—may be a disadvantage in the treatment of highly disturbed manics, but initial control can be achieved* with a combination of lithium and neuroleptics, and then the patient can be managed on lithium alone. Lithium has a number of side effects; however, the *production of depression is not seen* with the use of this agent. *Treatment failures with lithium carbonate usually range between 20 percent and 40 percent.* Nonresponders cannot be easily identified on clinical or biochemical grounds before beginning treatment with lithium.

**27.3. The answer is C** (*Synopsis*, ed. 4, pages 653 and 654).

The conceptually correct way to think about high and low dosage in psychiatry is in terms of *dose-response curves*, which is illustrated in the figure shown on page 352. When a very low dose is given, patients have no clinical response. Above a certain dosage range, there is the so-called linear portion of the curve in which an increase in dosage produces a proportionately increased therapeutic response. When all the responses that can occur do occur, a point of diminishing return ensues, and increasing the dose does not increase response; that is, there is a "ceiling effect." The inflection point at which

the linear portion changes to diminished returns is often referred to as the optimal part of the dose-response curve. The optimal point on the dose-response curve is the point that indicates the lowest dose necessary to achieve maximal clinical effects. A given dose-response curve applies to only one patient at a particular point in time, and a given patient may have different dose-response curves at different points in time. Although the basic pharmacologist often uses dose-response curves, they are rarely used in clinical studies. The dose is raised until the clinician is confident that the patient has achieved the best possible clinical response.

Most double-blind studies comparing doses used two doses: a higher dose and a lower (or standard) dose. Consider two doses (*A* and *B*), each producing at least some response; if *B* produces a better response than *A*, then *A* must be on the linear portion of the dose-response curve. Consider doses *X* and *Y*; if *X* and *Y* produce equal therapeutic improvement, then *X* and *Y* must be above the optimal point and well along on the flat curve of diminishing response. In reviewing paired comparisons, the location on the curve of the lower dose is particularly helpful in defining the dose-response curve.

The other curves relevant to an understanding of drug effects are illustrated on page 360.

The classic sigmoid curve shown in *A* illustrates a possible *plasma-level/clinical-response curve*. The first portion of the curve shows the relative lack of clinical response at low-drug plasma levels. The linear portion of the curve demonstrates a progressively better clinical response as more of the drug reaches the receptor site. Beyond the linear part of the curve, as large amounts of the drug are introduced, an area of diminishing returns appears.

*B* illustrates a *plasma level-toxicity curve*. A plasma-level/toxicity relationship exists with regard to various side effects. If one thinks in terms of the total clinical benefit for the patient and plots that benefit against plasma level, it might be expected that, as plasma levels rise, the patient will exhibit a better clinical response. As the curve begins to level off, the patient enters the area of optimal benefit. When plasma levels are markedly elevated, the resulting detrimental side effects may outweigh the beneficial therapeutic effects.

**359**

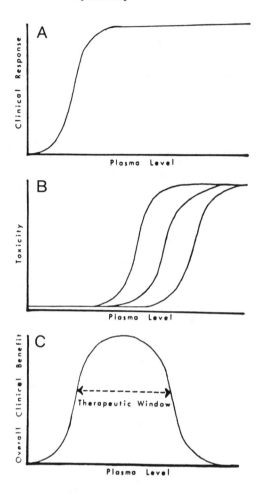

C illustrates the *therapeutic window curve.*
Combining the therapeutic curve and the side-
effects curve results in an inverted U-shaped
curve. With some drugs, when the plasma level
rises to a high level, there may be a loss of
therapeutic effect. A possible explanation is
that, at a given range of concentration, some
drugs may stimulate a receptor and, at a higher
range, inhibit the receptor. Most drugs show
increasing side effects as the plasma level increases. A drug that has neither of those high-
dose effects—loss of clinical efficacy or serious
toxicity—may not display a descending limb of
the inverted U-shaped curve. To state it another
way, the upper portion of the therapeutic window is absent. The inverted U-shaped curve is a
visual representation of the so-called therapeutic window. Below the therapeutic window, an
insufficient amount of the drug reaches the receptor site to produce the desired clinical response. The upper limit of the therapeutic window can be defined by either toxicity or a loss
of clinical response or both. Therefore, it is

important to describe clinically such information that may indicate whether either or both
effects are occurring. Because various investigators define the upper end of the therapeutic
window differently, one must be clear both conceptually and empirically so that disagreements
will not be merely definitional in nature.

**27.4. The answer is B** (*Synopsis*, ed. 4,
pages 657 and 658).

There are a number of large-scale studies in
the European literature that indicate that *there
are no serious risks in using a combination of
monoamine oxidase inhibitors (MAOI's) and tricyclic antidepressants (TCA's).* The combination
of TCA's and MAOI's is, however, not in standard use in the United States because of fears
of producing a hypertensive crisis.

The enzyme monoamine oxidase exists in at
least two forms: MAO-A, which is believed to be
found primarily in the gastrointestinal tract and
liver, and MAO-B, found primarily in the central nervous system and human platelets. Of
the four currently available FDA-approved
MAOI's—tranylcypromine, isocarboxazid, pargyline, and *phenelzine—none selectively inhibits
only one of these enzymes.* There are MAOI's
being used in Europe, however, that specifically
inhibit type A or type B monoamine oxidase.

*MAOI's may take 2 weeks or longer* before any
clinical improvement is seen. *The toxic reactions
seen in MAOI overdoses generally appear within
hours after ingestion.*

**27.5. The answer is E** (*Synopsis*, ed. 4, pages
643 and 644).

The most dramatic and, pharmacologically,
the most theoretically important group of side
effects shown by all the antipsychotic agents are
the extrapyramidal reactions. This family of side
effects is typically classified into three arbitrary
categories: parkinsonian syndrome, dystonias,
and *akathisia.*

*Akathisia* is a motor restlessness in which the
patient manifests a great urge to move about
and has considerable difficulty in sitting still.
Often, the symptom is of such intensity that it
becomes impossible for the patients to sit still
day or night, and it is often described as more
difficult to endure than any of the symptoms for
which the patient was originally treated. This
symptom may persist for some time after the
drug is withdrawn.

The *parkinsonian syndrome* consists of a
mask-like face, tremor at rest, rigidity, *shuffling
gait,* pill-rolling movement of the hand, and
motor retardation. In general, the syndrome is
quite similar to idiopathic parkinsonism in its
symptoms.

The dystonias consist of a broad range of

bizarre movements of the tongue, face, and neck, including buccofacial movements with salivation, torticollis, oculogyric crisis, and opisthotonos. Acute dystonia typically begins after only a few doses of the drug and occurs more frequently in males than in females.

*Tardive dyskinesia* (or late-appearing dyskinesia) consists of rhythmical, automatic stereotyped movements in a single muscle group or, more universally, especially in the tongue, lips, and mouth. It occurs as an undesirable side effect in some patients treated with the neuroleptics. Choreoathetoid movements of the trunk and limbs may also be part of the clinical picture.

*Akinesia* refers to the absence or diminution of voluntary motion, which may range from moderate inactivity to almost complete immobility. Usually, akinesia is accompanied by a parallel reduction in mental activity, as for example in the stuporous phase of catatonic schizophrenia.

**27.6.    The answer is A** (*Synopsis*, ed. 4, page 658).

The major clinical indication for the choice of a drug is its set of side effects. *Haloperidol* is the drug of choice because it has the fewest cardiovascular side effects.

*Thioridazine* and *chlorpromazine* cause hypotension, which may be dangerous in the elderly or in those with compromised circulation. *Alprazolam* is a benzodiazepine-type drug that has both anxiolytic and antidepressant properties. It is used in the management of anxiety disorders and the treatment of panic attacks. It is not used for the treatment of psychosis.

**27.7.    The answer is B** (*Synopsis*, ed. 4, page 642).

All neuroleptic medications produce extrapyramidal symptoms. Among the phenothiazines, *thioridazine* produces the fewest extrapyramidal effects; *haloperidol*, thiothixene, *butaperazine*, trifluoperazine, and *fluphenazine* produce the most extrapyramidal effects; and *chlorpromazine*, chlorprothixene, and acetophenazine occupy an intermediate position.

**27.8.    The answer is E** (*Synopsis*, ed. 4, page 646).

All neuroleptics can produce seizures by lowering the seizure threshold. The risk is increased when the patient has a *premorbid history of seizures* or is being *withdrawn from alcohol*, when *neuroleptics are given in high doses*, or when *the dose is increased rapidly*. Of the neuroleptics, molindone, which is a nonphenothiazine indolic compound, is the least epileptogenic.

When seizures do occur, they generally occur with high doses of the drug—that is, they are dose-related—and consist of a single isolated seizure. One can often treat the patient with a slightly lower dose of the drug. On occasion, one can add an anticonvulsant, such as phenytoin, to the treatment regimen and continue antipsychotic drugs with no seizures even at higher doses.

**27.9.    The answer is B** (*Synopsis*, ed. 4, pages 658 and 659).

The patient is having a hypertensive crisis, which consists of headache, nausea, elevated blood pressure, and possible intracranial bleeding. It occurs when a monoamine oxidase inhibitor (MAOI) is taken in conjunction with foods containing tyramine, such as cheddar cheese. The treatment is to *lower the blood pressure as quickly as possible.*

*Phentolamine*, an $\alpha$-adrenergic blocker that is a potent antihypertensive agent, is the drug of choice in the treatment of MAOI-induced hypertensive crisis. Chlorpromazine can also be used because of its hypotensive effects.

*Epinephrine*, as well as other sympathomimetic amines, is potentiated by MAOI's and raises blood pressure. For this reason, this class of substances is contraindicated in any patient on a MAOI. Electroshock treatment (*ECT*) is not a treatment of hypertensive crisis and, in fact, is contraindicated because of an increased mortality rate when used in conjunction with MAOI's. *Hemodialysis* has no clinical application in the treatment of hypertensive crisis.

**27.10.    The answer is B** (*Synopsis*, ed. 4, pages 656 and 657).

An adequate daily dose of tricyclic antidepressants varies with the particular drug and the individual patient, but generally the effective dose ranges from 50 to 300 mg per day, with some tricyclics, such as nortriptyline and protriptyline requiring doses in the lower ranges.

The lethal dose of these drugs has been estimated as being from *10 to 30 times the daily dose level.* Care should be taken so that the suicidal depressed patient does not have access to an excessive number of antidepressant tablets, because several grams—20 to 40 of the 50-mg tablets—can be fatal.

An overdose of an imipramine-type antidepressant produces a clinical picture known as the central anticholinergic syndrome or anticholinergic delerium. The syndrome is characterized by temporary agitation, delirium, convulsions, hyperreflexive tendons, bowel and bladder paralysis, orthostatic hypotension and hypertension disturbance of temperature regulation, and mydriasis. The patient then progresses to coma, with shock and respiratory depression. Disturbances of cardiac rhythm, such as tachycardia, atrial fibrillation, ventricular flutters, and atrioventricular or intraventricular block, can also occur. Coma is generally not protracted for more than 24 hours. All the above signs and symptoms may or may not be present to some degree.

**27.11. The answer is C** (*Synopsis*, ed. 4, page 676).

The precise amount of lithium required by an individual patient is determined by continuous periodic observations of the clinical state, achievement of a blood lithium level of *0.8 meq/ liter to 1.5 meq/liter*, and the avoidance of side effects. The amount of lithium in the blood is measured by atomic absorption photometry or flame emission photometry, using a few milliliters of venous blood drawn from the patient's arm.

**27.12. The answer is C** (*Synopsis*, ed. 4, page 649).

Thioridazine, in doses about 1600 mg a day, can cause retinitis pigmentosa with consequent visual impairment. The condition is sometimes said not to remit when the drug is stopped—or, at least, not to remit fully. Doses of thioridazine of more than *800 mg a day* are, therefore, to be assiduously avoided.

Pigmentary retinopathy, also known as retinitis pigmentosa, is a progressive atrophy of the retinal neuroepithelium. It is also seen with other phenothiazine drugs when they are used in high doses over long periods of time.

**27.13. The answer is C** (*Synopsis*, ed. pages 632 and 633).

Studies indicate that *antipsychotics are superior to a placebo* in the treatment of acute and chronic schizophrenic patients. The magnitude of the improvement produced by the drugs is considerable. *About 70 percent of patients significantly improve under phenothiazine* therapy, only one-tenth fail to be helped, and none show deterioration. Thus, worsening is prevented by phenothiazines. They prevent the emergence of new psychotic symptoms and suppress preexisting symptoms of schizophrenia.

In the case of the average patient, *most of the therapeutic gain occurs in the first 6 weeks of phenothiazine therapy*, although further treatment gains are made during the subsequent 12 or 18 weeks. Some patients show a rapid improvement in a single day or after a few weeks; other patients show a gradual rate of improvement over several months.

These agents have *little or no abuse potential* and *thus are not classified as controlled substances*.

**27.14. The answer is C** (*Synopsis*, ed. 4, page 650).

Delayed ejaculation, progressing to orgasm without ejaculation and ultimately ending in a loss of erectile ability, can occur with antipsychotic agents. The area of drug-induced impotence is one in which the psychiatrist may miss a disturbing drug side-effect because the patient is too embarrassed to speak of it.

*Thioridazine* is the phenothiazine drug most often implicated in orgasm without ejaculation, in which semen is forced backwards into the bladder.

Barbiturates, such as *secobarbital* and *pentobarbital*, are CNS depressants and are often associated with both abuse and dependence. Sexually related symptoms may range from disinhibition of sexual impulses to impotence. *Cyclazocine* prevents most of the effects of morphine-like opioids, but in the absence of opioids, it produces analgesia and constriction of the pupils, depresses respiration, and induces a type of physical dependence. *Morphine* is an opioid that generally produces sedation, analgesia, and a physical dependence.

**27.15. The answer is C** (*Synopsis*, ed. 4, pages 676 and 677).

Some patients, especially the elderly, with serum lithium levels over 1.2 meq/liter and occasionally patients with lower serum levels experience side effects associated with the use of lithium. The side effects include muscle weakness, *hand tremor, abdominal cramps*, nausea, vomiting, diarrhea, *thirst* and polyuria, fatigue, sleeplessness, and *weight gain*—sometimes 5 to 10 pounds in several weeks. During the first 2 to 4 weeks of lithium stabilization, mild side effects often occur, but they usually disappear spontaneously or with a lowering of the dosage. A slight tremor may persist, but it is of no particular significance.

*Vermicular movements of the tongue* are worm-like movements that are an early sign of tardive dyskinesia, a long-term side effect of high-dose phenothiazine medication.

**27.16. The answer is C** (*Synopsis*, ed. 4, page 658).

A side effect of special importance that may result from the use of MAOI's is the *hypertensive crisis*, which is occasionally accompanied by intracranial bleeding. Severe occipital headache, stiff neck, sweating, nausea and vomiting, and sharply elevated blood pressure are common prodromal symptoms. It has been estimated that one death in 100,000 patients treated with MAOI's has occurred after such crises. These reactions have been observed to follow the ingestion of sympathomimetic amines—for example, tyramine in certain cheeses—and pressor drugs.

Only in rare instances has *hepatitis* been associated with MAOI use. *Agranulocytosis* is an acute condition characterized by leukopenia with great reduction of polymorphonuclear leukocytes and is seen infrequently in association with phenothiazines. A *skin-eye syndrome* has been noted to be a side effect of lengthy treatment with high doses of phenothiazines. The symptoms of this reaction include progressive pigmentation of areas of the skin or conjunctiva, discoloration of the exposed sclera or cornea, and opacities of the anterior lens and cornea. *Acute dystonic reactions* may occur shortly after initiation of treatment with neuroleptics and are characterized by a broad range of bizarre movements of the tongue, face, and neck.

**27.17.  The answer is E** (*Synopsis*, ed. 4, page 681).

The manifestations of electrically induced convulsions resemble those of a spontaneous convulsion with certain differences. If the amount of current given is not sufficient, the nonanesthetized patient only loses consciousness (petit mal response). If somewhat more current is given, the patient may have a delayed convulsion—that is, the patient loses consciousness and, after only a few seconds of *apnea*, goes slowly into the tonic phase, followed by the clonic phase. If still more current is used, there is an immediate convulsion in which the tonic phase starts at the moment of the stimulation.

The tonic phase lasts for about 10 seconds, and the clonic phase for 30 to 40 seconds. It is important that the time relationship be watched carefully. In convulsions modified with muscle-relaxant drugs, it is sometimes difficult to see any movements. A *slight plantar extension of the feet*, however, can be noticed as evidence of the tonic phase; after about 10 seconds, some *toe, finger, or other movements* should indicate the clonic phase. If none of the manifestations is noted, it is wise to give a second stimulus. A nonmotor manifestation of a convulsion is the appearance of *gooseflesh.*

**27.18.  The answer is C** (*Synopsis*, ed. 4, page 632).

The major classes of antipsychotic drugs are as follows: phenothiazines, butyrophenones, thioxanthenes, dibenzoxazepines, dihydroindolones, and rauwolfia alkaloids. Unlike many drugs commonly used in psychiatry, these agents have little or no abuse potential and are thus not classified as controlled substances.

*Haloperidol* is a nonphenothiazine antipsychotic agent in the class of butyrophenones.

**27.19.  The answer is B** (*Synopsis*, ed. 4, page 689).

*The withdrawal of sleep for 1 night as a treatment for depression* was first described in 1970. A marked improvement in some patients with unipolar and bipolar depressions after 1 night of sleep deprivation was observed; some patients improve after two or more treatments, with the addition of 150 mg of amitriptyline. Elderly patients and patients suffering from involutional depression and neurotic depression without vegetative signs did not show any changes. Because depression may be associated with an increase in rapid eye movement (REM) sleep time (antidepressants, both tricyclics and MAOI's, cause a reduction in REM time), the effectiveness of the treatment may be attributed to a small-scale REM sleep deprivation.

Sleep withdrawal therapy has not appeared effective in *other psychiatric disorders*, perhaps due to the stage of sleep affected in other disorders. Specific medications affect different sleep stages. For instance, anxiolytics, such as benzodiazepines, do not suppress REM sleep but, rather, slow-wave sleep. Neuroleptic drugs, in contrast, tend to increase total sleep time. The serotonergic system seems to be pivotal in the development of non-REM sleep, especially slow-wave sleep, whereas REM sleep seems to rely on a complicated interaction among the serotonergic, noradrenergic, and cholinergic systems.

**27.20.  The answer is E (all)** (*Synopsis*, ed. 4, page 680).

Succinylcholine, an ultra *fast-acting depolarizing blocking agent*, has gained virtually universal acceptance for the purpose of producing muscle relaxation. The optimum succinylcholine dose is that which provides enough relaxation to *stop most, but not all, of the major ictal body movements*. A typical starting dose is 60 mg for a medium-sized adult. If musculoskeletal or cardiac disease necessitates the use of total relaxation, *the addition of curare* (3 to 6 mg IV) given several minutes prior to anesthetic induction, along with increased succinylcholine dosage, is indicated. If necessary, a peripheral nerve stimulator can be used to ascertain the presence of complete neuromuscular block. The presence of seizure activity under circumstances of complete relaxation can be monitored either by EEG or by the prevention of succinylcholine flow to one of the forearms, using an inflated blood pressure cuff.

Because succinylcholine is a depolarizing blocking agent, its action is marked by the presence of muscle fasciculations, or fine twitching movements, that move in a rostrocaudal progression. Clinically, this is a very useful phenomenon, as the disappearance of these movements indicates that maximal relaxation has been achieved.

Due to the short half-life of succinylcholine, the duration of apnea following administration generally is not longer than the delays in return to consciousness associated with the combined effects of anesthetic agent and postictal state. In cases of inborn or acquired pseudocholinesterase deficiency, however, or where the metabolism of succinylcholine is disrupted by drug interaction, a *prolonged apnea may occur*, and the treating physician should always be prepared to manage such an eventuality.

**27.21.    The answer is A (1, 2, 3)** (*Synopsis*, ed. 4, pages 650 and 651).

Many pharmacological agents, such as *levodopa, estrogen*, and *cocaine*, can induce severe depression with chronic use. *Lithium*, however, may act as a prophylactic against depression in a certain subgroup of patients. That subgroup is made up of bipolar patients who have not yet experienced a manic episode and are therefore diagnosed as depressed unipolar patients.

*Levodopa (L-Dopa)* is a catecholamine derived from the oxidation of the amino acid phenylalanine and tyrosine, and it serves as the precursor to dopamine, norepinephrine, and epinephrine. These metabolic derivatives of L-dopa are important neurotransmitters and are useful as sympathomimetic drugs. L-dopa has been reported to produce depression, but the mechanism is unclear.

*Estrogen* is a steroid compound that plays a vital physiological role in the development and maintenance of female sexual characeristics. Therapeutically, estrogens have a number of applications, including oral contraception and the treatment of menopausal symptoms. Some patients report depression with prolonged use of estrogen.

*Cocaine* is an amino alcohol structurally related to atropine. Its clinical importance lies in the local anesthetic action mediated by blockage of nerve conduction. Systematic ingestion produces a number of effects, however, including extreme cerebral nervous system stimulation (followed by depression) and potentiation of sympathetic response. Cocaine is a common drug of abuse.

*Lithium* is a salt that replaces sodium in the intracellular space and has a marked beneficial effect on the manic phase of bipolar disorder.

**27.22    The answer is B (1, 3)** (*Synopsis*, ed. 4, page 641).

The anticholinergic and antiadrenergic properties of phenothiazines may result in autonomic side effects, including *paralytic ileus, urinary retention, dry mouth and throat, orthostatic hypotension* blurred vision, cutaneous flushing, constipation, and confusion. Dry mouth and orthostatic hypotension—a drop in blood pressure on rising from a lying or sitting position—are among the more frequent complaints, but tolerance is readily developed for these and other autonomic symptoms.

*Paralytic ileus* refers to paralysis of the ileum that causes obstruction of the bowel, resulting in severe colicky pain, vomiting, and often fever and dehydration. *Urinary retention* refers to failure to pass urine as a result of paralysis of the bladder muscle or constriction of the bladder sphincter.

**27.23.    The answer is A (1, 2, 3)** (*Synopsis*, ed. 4, pages 644, 645, and 646).

The patient is experiencing tardive dyskinesia, which is an extrapyramidal syndrome that can emerge relatively late during the course of treatment with antipsychotic compounds, particularly when these drugs have been used in high doses over several years. It sometimes appears after the drug has been discontinued and may persist for years, although it is absent during sleep. It can be relatively treatment resistant. Tardive dyskinesia is characterized by grimacing and buccofacial-mandibular or buccolingual movements—for example, sucking, smacking movements of the lips, lateral or fly-catching movements of the tongue, and lateral jaw movements—choreiform-like jerky movements of the arms; athetoid movements of the upper extremities or fingers, ankles, and toes; and tonic contractions of the neck and back. The symptoms may occur or become intensified a few days to a few weeks after the drug has been stopped or reduced, although they may also appear during drug therapy. Their reappearance or intensificaiton with reduction of the dosage or cessation of drug treatment may be an unmasking of the symptom, because the phenothiazine-induced rigidity can dampen the dystonic movements. *Paradoxically, the symptom may be suppressed by putting the patient on large doses of phenothiazines or butyrophenones.* The symptoms may persist for long periods of time in some patients; in others, they may disappear weeks or months after the cessation of treatment. They are not particularly helped by antiparkinsonian medication; indeed, such treatment occasionally aggravates them. Reserpine-like drugs may produce a beneficial effect. Drugs that release dopamine, such as *levodopa*, worsen tardive dyskinesia. Drugs that raise brain acetylcholine—physostigmine, *choline, lecithin*—may help it.

**27.24.   The answer is A (1, 2, 3)** (*Synopsis,*
ed. 4, page 677).

Treatment failures of lithium therapy with
manic patients usually range between 20 and *40
percent.* These nonresponders cannot be easily
identified on clinical or biochemical grounds.
Nevertheless, several factors have been implicated, including family history, inadequate dose,
*low plasma lithium levels,* previous failure of
lithium treatment, *rapid cycling* (four or more
episodes of mania per year), and misdiagnosis.
For example, *patients who are suffering from
schizophreniform disorders will not respond to
lithium,* but will respond to a major tranquilizer,
such as phenothiazine.

**27.25.   The answer is E (all)** (*Synopsis,* ed.
4, page 658).

Even though there is no good clinical data to
support the rare case reports of hypertensive

crises following the ingestion of *chocolate* and
*canned figs,* these foods should probably be eaten
in only limited amounts. Certain foods high in
tyramine, such as *fava beans* and *aged cheese,*
however, should be avoided entirely because of
the possibility of severe hypertension.

See the table below for the dietary restrictions
that must be placed on a patient receiving
MAOI's.

**27.26.   The answer is C (2, 4)** (*Synopsis,*
ed. 4, page 676).

Lithium is an alkali metal similar to sodium,
potassium, magnesium, and calcium. Following
ingestion, it is *completely absorbed by the gastrointestinal tract. Serum levels peak in 1.5 to 2.0
hours* (lithium carbonate) or 4.0 to 4.5 hours
(slow-release preparation). *Lithium does not
bind to plasma proteins* and is distributed non-
uniformly throughout body water. It reaches

---

**Example of an Instruction Sheet Given to Patients who are on Monoamine Oxidase Inhibitor (MAOI) Drugs***

The drug you are taking may react to tyramine, a component of certain foods, and may produce unpleasant
side effects. Therefore, a diet omitting tyramine-containing foods is necessary. Certain other drugs should
also be avoided.

*Omit entirely the following foods containing tyramine:*

Alcohol (particularly beer and wines and especially Chianti). A little pure spirit is permissible, e.g. Scotch,
    gin, or vodka, or a small glass of sherry.
Fava or broad bean pods
Aged cheese. Creamed cheeses and cottage cheeses *are* permitted.
Beef or chicken liver
Orange pulp
Pickled herring or smoked fish
Soups (packaged)
Yeast vitamin supplements
Summer (dry) sausage

*Eat no more than two servings a day of the following foods, which contain smaller amounts of tyramine:*

Soy sauce
Sour cream
Bananas. Green bananas can only be included if cooked in their skins; ordinary peeled bananas are fine.
Avocados
Eggplant
Plums
Raisins
Spinach
Tomatoes
Yogurt

*Take no other medication without informing me. Do not take cough or cold medications or any of the following:*

Pain relievers (especially meperidine or morphine)
Tonics
Stimulants or diet pills
Nasal decongestants
Local anesthetics, e.g. those given by your dentist. First tell him that you are on a MAOI, which can produce
    side effects with certain local anesthetics that contain added vasoconstrictors.

---

* Table prepared by Daniel L. Crane, M.D., and Peter M. Kaplan, M.D.

equilibrium after about 5 to 7 days of regular intake. Lithium *has an elimination half-life of almost 24 hours.* Although nonsignificant losses occur through the skin and in the feces, about one-fifth of the lithium ion is eliminated through renal excretion. During each circulatory phase, plasma sodium levels—resulting from diuretics, excessive sweating, reduced sodium intake—initiate a compensatory increase in sodium reabsorption accompanied by lithium reabsorption. Considering these pharmacological properties, as well as the well-known potential of lithium to adversely affect the CNS, thyroid, heart, and kidneys, it is necessary that candidates for lithium undergo a thorough physical examination in which particular attention is given to the evaluation of the above systems. Aside from poorly-functioning kidneys, there are no absolute contraindications to lithium therapy.

**27.27.   The answer is E (all)** (*Synopsis*, ed. 4, page 673).

Antacids can delay the absorption of both chlordiazepoxide and diazepam. *They may also interfere with the absorption of antipsychotics.* Agents that slow gut motilities, such as anticholinergics, alcohol, and food, can potentially interfere with absorption, either by delaying or by impairing it.

The clinician should be aware of potential interactions, such as diazepam on muscle relaxants used in anesthesia, benzodiazepines' possible effect on dopa in the treatment of Parkinson's disease, and the influence of loxapine on phenytoin levels.

Drug-drug interactions can be complicated, particularly in drugs with several active metabolites. For example, acute alcohol intoxication can prolong elimination of chlordiazepoxide.

The *benzodiazepines can elevate phenytoin levels.* Disulfiram can elevate serum phenytoin levels and, furthermore, by interfering with the demethylation of chlordiazepoxide and diazepam, can prolong the half-life of those drugs. The hypertensive action of *guanethidine is interfered with by tricyclic antidepressants.*

The table below lists a variety of drug-drug interactions.

**27.28.   The answer is A (1, 2, 3)** (Synopsis, ed. 4, page 648).

The patient may be experiencing phenothiazine-induced agranulocytosis, which can occur in older female patients; however, its occurrence is rare. It generally appears within the first 6 to 8 weeks of phenothiazine treatment, its onset being abrupt and consisting of the sudden appearance of sore throat, ulcerations, and fever. When it occurs, the mortality rate is generally high, often 30 percent or more. *Phenothiazine medication should be immediately discontinued,* and the patient should be transferred to a medical facility. *A blood and throat culture* and *blood count* should be obtained. In the absence of a

## Drug-Drug Interactions

| Type | Interaction | Comment |
|---|---|---|
| Absorption | Some antacids may delay or interfere with absorption of benzodiazepines and chlorpromazine. | Because clinicians should adjust dose to clinical effect, they should not see this interaction clinically except when they need to use a slightly higher dose. |
| Metabolism | 1. Barbiturates plus nonbarbiturate sedative and alcohol speed up metabolism of phenothiazines. | Another reason why clinicians need to adjust dose to clinical response. |
| | 2. Disulfiram can prolong the half-life of benzodiazepines by interfering with desmethylation. | Oxazepam or lorazepam may be preferred in patients needing disulfiram, because those drugs are directly excreted as conjugates. |
| | 3. Methylphenidate or phenothiazines can increase plasma levels of tricyclics. | |
| | 4. Tricyclics can increase plasma levels of antipsychotics. | |
| Excretion | *Acid urine increases and basic urine decreases excretion of amphetamine, phenelzine, tranylcypromine, or PCP* | Applies to any drug or diet that alters urine pH. |
| Distribution | Antipsychotics and antidepressants (including doxepin) interfere with the therapeutic action of guanethidine. | Clinically important, particularly for chlorpromazine and tricyclics, because it can render guanethidine useless for hypertension. |
| Receptor site | Both sedative and anticholinergic side effects of several drugs can produce toxicity. | A simple summation of a common pharmacological effect. |

diagnosed infection, *prophylactic antibiotic therapy may not necessarily be indicated*, because of the danger of propagation of drug-resistant organisms.

There is no value in obtaining routine, complete blood counts to pick up agranulocytosis in patients on phenothiazines. Agranulocytosis develops so rapidly that daily blood counts would be necessary to pick up what is an extraordinarily rare complication.

**27.29.   The answer is E (all)** (Synopsis, ed. 4, page 659).

The MAOI's potentiate a great variety of drugs, including sympathomimetic amines (such as *ephedrine*), *opioids, barbiturates*, methyldopa, ganglionic-blocking agents, procaine, anesthetic agents, chloral hydrate, and *aspirin*.

*Opioids* consist of morphine or other alkaloids derived from opium, an extractable product of the poppy plant *Papaver somniferum*. *Barbiturate* is one of a class of sedative-hypnotic drugs derived from barbituric acid. The drug acts as a central nervous system depressant and readily produces psychic and physical dependence. Phenobarbital, secobarbital, and thiopental sodium are commonly used barbiturates. *Aspirin* contains acetylsalicylic acid and is widely utilized as an analgesic, antipyretic, and anti-inflammatory agent. *Ephedrine* is an adrenergic (sympathomimetic) agent and has similar actions to epinephrine. It is used as a bronchodilator, mydriatic, pressor agent and topical vasoconstrictor.

**27.30.   The answer is E (all)** (Synopsis, ed. 4, page 632).

In general, psychopharmacologists tend to divide schizophrenic symptoms into positive and negative ones. Phenothiazines tend to exert their most pronounced effects on the positive symptoms and exert lesser effects on the negative ones. Positive symptoms include the more florid psychotic signs, such as paranoid delusions, *hallucinations*, and agitation. Negative signs include flattened affect, withdrawal, social isolation, *retardation*, and *thought disorder*.

Phenothiazine therapy brings about cognitive restoration—with a decrease in psychotic and paranoid thinking, projection, suspiciousness, pathological hostility, perplexity, and ideas of reference—and a relative normalization of psychomotor behavior in both retarded and hyperactive patients. There is a reduction of hallucinations, paranoid identification, hostility, belligerence, resistiveness, uncooperativeness, and a reduction in thought disorder, including overinclusive thinking and bizarre, inappropriate response.

The antipsychotic drugs have a normalizing effect. In addition to lessening typical schizophrenic symptoms, such as hallucinations and delusions, they also normalize various other abnormal behaviors. For example, they speed up retarded schizophrenics and *slow down excited schizophrenics*. Hence, they are not uniformly sedatives in the sense of slowing down all symptoms of all patients.

The aim of drug treatment should be to achieve maximum therapeutic improvement in the patient. In some sense, one should be treating the whole patient or the underlying disease process, rather than a given symptom. That is particularly important for a retarded schizophrenic patient. Those patients often respond dramatically to antipsychotic drugs, even though troublesome target symptoms, such as agitation and aggression, are completely absent. The goals should be maximum cognitive reorganization and lessening of the underlying schizophrenic process, not control of a particular symptom. Evaluation of the severity of typical psychotic symptoms is a convenient benchmark for monitoring drug effects.

**27.31.   The answer is D (4)** (Synopsis, ed. 4, page 681).

The use of unilateral nondominant electrode placement *is associated with much less confusion and acute amnesia than bilateral placement*. For most patients, *unilateral ECT is as effective as bilateral ECT*, although there remains the possibility that an as yet undefined subgroup of patients may respond either better or quicker to bilateral ECT. To deal with this uncertainty, some clinicians now routinely start patients on unilateral ECT and switch to bilateral placement if no significant improvement is forthcoming after six or more treatments.

With unilateral ECT, one stimulus electrode is typically *placed over the nondominant frontotemporal area* for bilateral placement. Although a number of locations for the second stimulus electrode have been proposed, placement on the nondominant centroparietal scalp, just lateral to the midline vertex, appears to provide a configuration associated with a relatively low seizure threshold in terms of stimulus intensity.

The selection of which cerebral hemisphere is dominant can generally be accomplished by a simple series of performance tasks, i.e. to determine handedness and footedness, along with the patient's stated side of preference. Right body responses correlate very highly with left brain dominance. If the responses are mixed or if they clearly indicate left body dominance, there is no noninvasive way to unequivocally establish the side of brain dominance. In such cases, the clinician should alternate the polarity of unilateral stimulation at successive treatments while monitoring the time that it takes the patient to recover consciousness and to answer simple orientation and naming questions. The side of stimulation associated with less rapid recovery and return of function can be considered dominant.

**27.32. The answer is E (all)** (*Synopsis*, ed. 4, page 659).

*Amphetamine*, *dextroamphetamine*, methylphenidate, *deanol*, and *pemoline* are classified as psychomotor stimulants.

*Amphetamine* is a central nervous system (CNS) stimulant. Its chemical structure and action are closely related to ephedrine and other sympathomimetic amines. Although *deanol* is classified with the amphetamines, its action on neurotransmitters appears to be different. Investigators have found from studies with hyperactive children that deanol is effective in reducing tantrums, aggressive behavior, and restlessness. It is contraindicated in patients with grand mal epilepsy. *Dextroamphetamine* consists of two forms: a sulfate and a phosphate. Both have the same actions and uses as a sympathomimetic agent and appetite depressant. The sulfate form, however, is more stimulating to the CNS. *Pemoline*, as do the above sympathomimetic agents, acts primarily as a stimulant to the CNS.

**27.33. The answer is C (2, 4)** (*Synopsis*, ed. 4, page 657).

In recent years, there has been considerable interest in phenelzine *as an effective MAOI antidepressant*. A number of studies show that phenelzine *is effective in treating depression, panic attacks, and agoraphobia*. Phenelzine has amphetamine-like properties and is, in fact, *metabolized to amphetamine*. It also *inhibits the reuptake of norepinephrine*.

**27.34. The answer is A (1, 2, 3)** (*Synopsis*, ed. 4, page 672).

The *barbiturates, chlordiazepoxide, diazepam*, and meprobamate have been clearly shown to produce physical dependence of the barbiturate type, as evidenced by human studies. Glutethimide and methaqualone or Quaalude (the latter drug has been withdrawn from the market) clearly have that same property, as documented by cases of patients experiencing the usual withdrawal syndrome. It must be assumed that the other nonbarbiturate hypnotics and the benzodiazepines share that undesirable pharmacological property. Alcohol certainly has shown that property for centuries, as evidenced by delirium tremens.

The sedative antihistamines lack this potential for abuse or dependence, as do *phenothiazines* and tricyclic antidepressants.

**27.35. The answer is A (1, 2, 3)** (*Synopsis*, ed. 4, page 649).

Eye changes (opacities) have been noticed after long-term high-dose chlorpromazine treatment. The occurrence and the severity of the opacities are related to the duration and the total dose of chlorpromazine. These changes have been described as whitish brown, granular deposits concentrated in the *anterior lens* and *posterior cornea*, visible only by slit-lens examination. They progress to opaque white and yellow-brown granules, often stellate in shape. Occasionally, *the conjunctiva is discolored by a brown pigment*. These lens changes are quite different from those of senile cataracts, and are in no way related to them. Statistically, these opacities occur more frequently in patients with skin discoloration than in other patients. Retinal damage is not seen in these patients, and vision is almost never impaired.

*Retinitis pigmentosa* is a progressive atropy of the neuroepithelium with atrophy and pigmentary infiltration of the inner layers. It is not caused by chlorpromazine.

**27.36. The answer is C (2, 4)** (*Synopsis*, ed. 4, page 655).

When administered in their usual therapeutic doses, the tricyclic drugs may cause *tachycardia, flattened T-waves, prolonged Q-T intervals*, and *depressed S-T segments* in the electrocardiogram. Imipramine has been shown to have a quinidine-like effect at therapeutic plasma levels and, indeed, may reduce the number of premature ventricular contractions. Because these drugs prolong conduction, their use in patients with preexisting conduction defects is relatively contraindicated. The clinician must remain alert to the possibility of impaired conduction. At high plasma levels, the drugs become arrhythmogenic.

**27.37. The answer is B (1, 3)** (*Synopsis*, ed. 4, page 637).

The most common side effects of chlorpromazine—sedation and extrapyramidal symptoms—do not usually make a shift to another drug necessary. Sedation can be handled by *dose reduction* or by *administering most of the drug at bedtime*.

Extrapyramidal side effects present a quandary; one can block them with an antiparkinsonian agent, reduce the dose, or both. No clear evidence favors either strategy. *Antiparkinsonian drugs do not block the sedative effects of chlorpromazine*. The therapeutic decision should probably rest on the patient's level of improvement. If the patient is much better, decrease the dose. If the patient is still psychotic, add an antiparkinsonian drug and raise the dose of the antipsychotic drug if that decision seems clinically necessary.

Most clinicans will gradually reduce the dose of the antipsychotic drug once the patient appears maximally improved, and raise the dose again if symptoms recur. Sometimes a modest prophylactic elevation of dosage is used when the patient is about to undergo a special stress, such as returning home or starting a new job.

The antipsychotic effects are of relatively long duration, on the order of days, but their sedative effects generally last only a few hours. For this reason, the common medical practice of administering medication 3 times a day may make patients oversedated when they should be working or learning. The same total dose given at bedtime may well promote better sleep and leave patients calm but not sedated during the day.

Chlorpromazine *cannot be given as a sustained-release or long-acting preparation.* The only neuroleptic that can be administered in such a way is fluphenazine decanoate. Sedation is also a common and significant side effect of this sustained-release medication, with onset of action generally appearing between 24 and 72 hours after injection, and the effects of the drug becoming significant within 48 to 96 hours.

**27.38. The answer is E (all)** (*Synopsis*, ed. 4, page 676).

Because lithium is known to affect thyroid physiology, it is recommended that all patients have baseline measurements of triiodotyronine ($T_3$), thyroxine ($T_4$), and thyroid-stimulating hormone (TSH) before starting therapy. Most commonly, if lithium does alter thyroid function, there is found after the onset of therapy an *elevated serum TSH measurement* with normal $T_3$ and $T_4$ levels.

Recent reports of renal function in lithium treatment suggest that a number of renal disorders may appear as part of the treatment. These adverse kidney manifestations include oliguric (no urine output) *renal failure*, which results from acute intoxication; chronic tubulointerstitial nephropathy, which is seen during long-term therapy; and vasopressin-resistant diabetes insipidus, which may be seen early in therapy where blood levels of lithium are below the toxic range. In addition to these conditions, there may be transient *polydipsia* (excessive intake of fluid) and *polyuria* (excessive output of urine), symptoms that resolve spontaneously after the patient is stabilized on the drug. In cases of the

diabetes insipidus-like syndrome, discontinuation of lithium therapy should reverse the disorder. If lithium treatment is necessary, however, it is possible to eliminate the syndrome through use of thiazide diuretics. For example, 500 to 600 mg per day of chlorthiazide paradoxically has an antidiuretic effect.

Because of the myriad of renal conditions that may result from lithium carbonate therapy, all patients should have blood urea nitrogen or serum creatinine measurements or both taken before the onset of therapy.

**27.39. The answer is D (4)** (*Synopsis*, ed. 4, page 644).

The patient is experiencing an acute dystonic reaction. The acute dystonias, which typically occur in the first few days or weeks of treatment, can appear in patients receiving small amounts of phenothiazines and are not uncommon in children treated with a single dose of prochlorperazine for nausea. The patients sometimes present themselves in emergency rooms, and frequently the patients and their families make no connection between the medication and the symptom. As a result, they often neglect to tell the examining physician that the patients have taken a phenothiazine-type medication. The syndrome is often rather alarming and can cause considerable concern until the diagnosis is made. Although dystonias can disappear spontaneously, it is generally advisable to treat them with *antiparkinsonian medication,* because they are often painful and are always psychologically upsetting. Benztropine, 1 mg, or biperiden, 2 mg, can be injected intramuscularly. The therapeutic trial provides important diagnostic information by confirming the diagnosis with a dramatic response. Dystonias also respond to diphenhydramine 50 mg IV.

*Hospitalization is not indicated* in acute dystonic reactions, and *haloperidol is an antipsychotic agent that can produce dystonia* and that is, therefore, contraindicated. *Phenytoin is an anticonvulsant, and seizures are not part of the dystonic reaction.*

**27.40. The answer is A (1, 2, 3)** (*Synopsis*, ed. 4, pages 650 and 654).

The tricyclic antidepressants—imipramine, amitriptyline, desipramine, nortriptyline, protriptyline—are structurally similar to the phenothiazines, the sulfur atom in the phenothiazine molecule having been replaced by a dimethyl bridge. This similarity emphasizes the importance of minor structural changes in the production of critical differences in pharmacological activity. The drugs all appear to be active antidepressants, and *they do not have antipsy-*

chotic properties. Other drugs of this class that are slightly different in structure, such as chlorimipramine, doxepin, trimipramine, and opipramol, also appear to *have considerable antidepressant activity*. The tricyclic antidepressants are *readily absorbed from the gastrointestinal tract*. In human beings, *imipramine, amitriptyline, and chlorimipramine are partially metabolized to their respective desmethyl derivatives*, such as desmethylimipramine, desipramine, and nortriptyline.

The tricyclic drugs differ in their anticholinergic properties. In the case of a patient who has had difficulty with anticholinergic effects, such as urinary retention and constipation, the clinician may wish to consider a tricyclic with the fewest anticholinergic properties. Amitriptyline has the strongest anticholinergic properties, doxepin is intermediate in this respect, and *despramine has the weakest anticholinergic properties*.

**27.41.   The answer is E (all)** (*Synopsis*, ed. 4, page 644).

Akathisia is one of the major potential side effects of neuroleptic medication. In akathisia, the patients are driven by motor restlessness and are usually not verbally preoccupied with the psychological content of whatever they are agitated about. The symptoms are primarily motor and cannot be controlled by the patients' will. *Akathisias are worsened by increasing the dose and are alleviated by decreasing the dose and adding an antiparkinsonian medication*. The reverse occurs with agitation. Akathisia often responds dramatically to treatment with antiparkinsonian agents, such as piperidine, artane, tropine cogentin, and ethanolamine; however, sometimes it is resistant to treatment, but can be controlled by reducing the dosage or *by switching to a different medication*. The β-blocker propranolol may also be effective in treating akathisia. In rare cases, no treatment is effective.

**27.42.   The answer is E (all)** (*Synopsis*, ed. 4, pages 649 and 650).

There is extensive basic research literature on the effects of large doses of antipsychotic agents on a wide variety of endocrine systems in obscure animal species. In practical terms, the clinically important effects are impotence and *lactation*. Phenothiazines elevate prolactin, which is a hormone produced by the anterior lobe of the pituitary that stimulates the secretion of milk and possibly breast growth. That may account for the *gynecomastia* that is sometimes seen in male patients receiving phenothiazines. Gynecomastia is the excessive development of the male mammary glands, which some-

times secrete milk. The impotence is presumably autonomic in origin.

*The glucose tolerance curve* measures the absorption and metabolism of glucose over a period of time and is useful in diagnosing diabetes mellitus. The phenothiazines interfere with that metabolic pathway and distort the normal curve. Similarly, they can produce a *false positive pregnancy test* because of their effects on the pituitary hormones, such as chorionic gonadotropin that is tested for in various immunological pregnancy tests.

**27.43.   The answer is A (1, 2, 3)** (*Synopsis*, ed. 4, page 684).

Psychosurgery was introduced solely on the basis of the results of animal experimentation without a theoretical anatomical or physiological rationale. The *results were attributed to sectionings of the connections of the frontal cortex with other parts of the brain, particularly with the thalamus*. Clinical experience soon indicated that the prefrontal operations that avoided the connections of the lateral cortex produced benefits little different from those by more extensive procedures, but eliminated or reduced the severe adverse psychological effects of the extensive procedures.

The limbic system plays a major role in regulating the emotions and integrating the functions of cortical and subcortical structures. The reported beneficial outcome of *small lesions in different portions of the limbic system* is at least as favorable as that of the earlier prefrontal lobotomies. Especially important is the absence of adverse effects, such as intellectual deterioration and personality changes.

*One of the major problems in the evaluation of recent psychosurgery arises from the different procedures and sites of the lesions by individual neurosurgeons, resulting in small numbers in comparable groups of patients.*

The total number of lobotomies that have been performed in the United States is unknown, as is the number of other psychosurgical procedures. In any case, the vast majority of lobotomies were done before 1955. By that time, the serious limitations of the procedure were well recognized, and more limited operations were being pursued. Further, the introduction of the phenothiazines, beginning in 1952, provided pharmacological measures that, in a large majority of cases, were effective in controlling or reducing the disturbed, aggressive, and assaultive behavior in chronically ill patients hitherto not responsive to other available therapeutic efforts except psychosurgery.

Although precise figures are not available, *psychosurgery is clearly on the wane*, with less than 100 operations performed in the United

States each year. The figure that follows shows various psychosurgical techniques.

**27.44.   The answer is B (1, 3)** (*Synopsis, ed. 4, page 656*).

An overdose of an imipramine-type antidepressant produces a clinical picture known as the central anticholinergic syndrome or anticholinergic delirium. The syndrome is characterized by temporary agitation, delirium, convulsions, high fever, hyperactive tendon reflexes, bowel and bladder paralysis, orthostatic hypotension, and disturbances of cardiac rhythm, such as tachycardia, atrial fibrillation, ventricular flutters, and atrioventricular or intraventricular block. Stupor and coma may ensue. Many of these features are more severe forms of the typical autonomic effects expected from the tricyclics as a result of their anticholinergic or atropine-like properties; those autonomic ef-

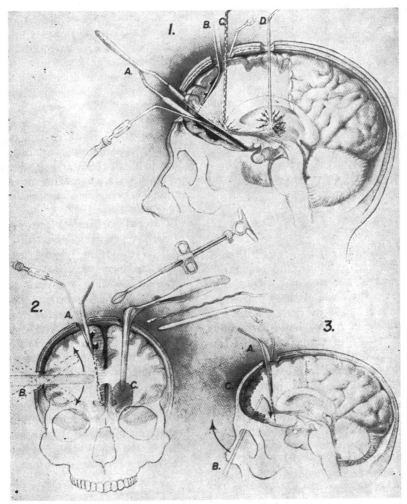

American leukotomy techniques (Scoville, *Diagram 1 A* Scoville's orbital undercutting; *B* Scoville's undercutting of superior convexity; *C* Grantham's electrocoagulation of inferior medial quadrant; *D* Spiegel and Wycis's stereotoxic electrocoagulation of thalamic nucleus. *Diagram 2 A* Scoville's cingulate gyrus undercutting. Livingston's cingulate gyrus subcortical sectioning; *B* Freeman and Watts's "closed" standard lobotomy; *C* medial inferior quadrant section by McKenzie's leukotome method, Schwartz's nasal speculum method. Grantham's electrocautery method, and Poppen's direct vision suction and spatula method. *Diagram 3 A* Poppen's "open" standard lobotomy under direct vision; *B* Freeman's transorbital lobotomy; *arrow* indicates deep frontal cut; *C* Pool's topectomy operation. (From Sargant W, Slater E: *An Introduction to Physical Methods of Treatment in Psychiatry.* Reprinted with permission of E and S Livingstone, London, 1963.)

fects include dry mouth, palpitations, tachycardia, postural hypotension, fainting, dizziness, vomiting, constipation, urinary retention, and, rarely, paralytic ileus.

Physostigmine—0.25 to 4.0 mg, intravenously or intramuscularly—is useful in preventing or reversing anticholinergic *tachycardia*. Physostigmine has a dramatic effect in counteracting anticholinergic toxicity or coma produced by tricyclics. It slows the atropine-induced tachycardia and wakes the patients from atropine coma. Because this effect can be dramatic, physostigmine can be overused. In a patient thought to have an atropine coma, but actually suffering from other toxicity and not protected by an anticholinergic, physostigmine can produce cholinergic toxicity. *Excess secretions*, such as profuse salivation, *respiratory depression*, seizures, or *bradycardia*—slowed heart rate—are signs of physostigmine-induced cholinergic toxicity, which can be reversed by small doses of atropine. In addition, if too much physostigmine is given to reverse the atropine coma, physostigmine toxicity can result. Physostigmine should be used selectively and judiciously by those who are aware of its toxicity, with proper attention to the use of minimal doses.

**27.45.   The answer is E (all)** (*Synopsis*, ed. 4, pages 650 and 651).

*In normal persons, imipramine and amitriptyline produce slight sedation.* In severely depressed psychotic patients, however, those medications produce a striking improvement in behavior and a *marked lessening of depression, generally 3 to 10 days after the onset of treatment.* Consequently, patients who do not respond after receiving an adequate dose of the drugs for a 3-week period probably will not respond at all. Furthermore, the degree of response in the first 3 weeks of treatment predicts the ultimate therapeutic response: *65 to 80 percent of the depressed patients substantially benefit from tricyclic antidepressants*, in contrast to 30 to 35 percent who are helped by a placebo in the same time period. When examined from the patient's point of view, *the patient's chance of recovering after 3 or 4 weeks of treatment is doubled if the tricyclic drugs, instead of a placebo, are taken.*

**27.46.   The answer is A (1, 2, 3)** (*Synopsis*, ed. 4, pages 641 and 642).

*Orthostatic (postural) hypotension occurs most frequently during the first few days of treatment,* and *patients readily develop a tolerance to it.* It is *most apt to occur when acute, high doses of intramuscular medications are given,* and it can occasionally be troublesome. The chief dangers of the side effect are that patients may faint, fall, and injure themselves, although such occur-

rences are rare. In susceptible patients—those taking a high dose of parenteral medication—it is sometimes prudent to measure blood pressure (lying and standing) after the first dose and during the first few days of treatment. Support hose may help. When appropriate, the patient should be warned of the side effect and given the usual instruction: Rise from bed gradually, sit at first with legs dangling, wait for a minute, and sit or lie down if you feel faint. A patient who is severely ill psychiatrically and needs antipsychotic medication can be kept in bed for several days. For a person with a cardiovascular disease, the doses should be increased very slowly, and blood pressure should be very carefully monitored to avoid clinically significant episodes of hypotension.

In general, postural hypotension is not troublesome, particularly when the dose is given orally. When it does occur, it can usually be managed by having the patients lie down with their feet higher than their head. On rare occasions, volume expansion or vasopressor agents, such as norepinephrine, may be indicated. Because phenothiazines are $\alpha$-adrenergic blockers, they block the $\alpha$-stimulating properties of epinephrine, leaving the $\beta$-stimulating properties untouched. Therefore, *the administration of epinephrine results in a paradoxical hypotension and is contraindicated in cases of phenothiazine-induced hypotension.*

**27.47.   The answer is D (4)** (*Synopsis*, ed. 4, page 668).

Phenobarbital deserves special attention. First, it is said to be an *excellent anticonvulsant*, and second, it is a potent inducer of hepatic enzymes. *Phenobarbital is further known to accelerate the body's metabolism of coumarin-type drugs, thus decreasing its half-life*, so that adjustment of anticoagulant dose is often needed if barbiturates are added or discontinued.

Phenobarbital is one of the *strongest-acting barbiturates*. In addition to having excellent anticonvulsant properties, it is also used for its hypnotic effects and as an antiepileptic. *It has no analgesic effects.*

**27.48.   The answer is B (1, 3)** (*Synopsis*, ed. 4, page 656).

*Physostigmine*—0.25 to 4.0 mg, intravenously or intramuscularly—is useful in preventing or reversing tricyclic overdose that produces anticholinergic tachycardia. Physostigmine has a dramatic effect in counteracting other anticholinergic toxic effects or coma produced by tricyclics.

Treatment of tricyclic overdoses should also include vomiting or gastric aspiration and lavage with activated charcoal, the use of intramuscular anticonvulsants—such as paraldehyde or *diaze-pam*—coma care, and support of respiration. Activated charcoal is important because it reduces tricyclic absorption.

Although tricyclic coma is generally of short duration—less than 25 hours—it can result in death due to cardiac arrhythmia; thus, management of cardiac function is critical. If the patient survives this period, recovery without sequelae is probable, and vigorous resuscitative measures—such as cardioversion—continuous electrocardiogram monitoring, and chemotherapy to prevent and manage arrhythmias should be applied in an intensive care unit. The tricyclics are direct myocardial depressants. Arrhythmias may be mediated, in part, by the tricyclic's quinidine and anticholinergic properties, and the uptake blockade may play a role. The myocardial depressant and quinidine-like properties are particularly important.

*Atropine* is an alkaloid with specific anticholinergic effects. Because it would aggravate tricyclic overdose, it is contraindicated. *Trihexyphenidyl* is also an anticholinergic drug. It is used to treat tremors associated with Parkinson's disease and is contraindicated in tricyclic toxicity.

**27.49.    The answer is E (all)** (*Synopsis*, ed. 4, pages 682 and 683).

There are no absolute contraindications to electroconvulsive therapy (ECT) but only situations for which there is increased risk. Patients with *intracranial masses, including tumors*, hematomas, and evolving strokes, are likely to undergo profound neurological deterioration with ECT because of an ECT-associated transient breakdown of the blood-brain barrier and increase in intracranial pressure. ECT for such patients should only be done in the presence of measures, such as antihypertensives and steroids, designed to minimize the likelihood and severity of these adverse sequelae.

The presence of an acute myocardial infarction raises the risk of further cardiac decompensation with ECT, due to the increased cardiovascular demands associated with the procedure. Severe underlying *hypertension* can be of concern, because ECT by itself increases blood pressure to a marked degree. Bringing the blood pressure under control, at least at the time of each treatment, is essential. *Pregnancy* is not an absolute contraindication to ECT, but depending on the stage of gestation, there is risk of premature labor.

*Osteoporosis* is a condition marked by a reduction in the quantity of bone or the atrophy of skeletal tissue. It occurs in postmenopausal women and elderly women. Severe convulsive movements with ECT may cause fractures, but that risk is minimized with the use of muscle relaxants.

**27.50.    The answer is B (1, 3)** (*Synopsis*, ed. 4, page 662).

The first of the benzodiazepine derivatives, synthesized in 1957, was *chlordiazepoxide*. Eleven other derivatives of this class are now available in the United States: *diazepam*, oxazepam, *clorazepate*, *lorazepam*, prazepam, temazepam, alprazolam, triazolam, halazepam, flurazepam, and clonazepam. Other benzodiazepines are available on foreign markets and are undergoing study in the United States and elsewhere.

To understand the clinical efficacy and the pharmacology of the benzodiazepines, one must understand their metabolism and pharmacokinetics. Chlordiazepoxide, after a series of intermediate changes, is converted to oxazepam which is conjugated to its glucuronic acid. Diazepam is also converted to oxazepam, which is then converted to its glucuronic acid.

Prazepam is nearly completely metabolized in a first-pass effect to desmethyldiazepam, suggesting that desmethyldiazepam is the active substance responsible for the antianxiety effect of the drug. Prazepam is essentially a prodrug or precursor of desmethyldiazepam. Clorazepate is also a prodrug and is rapidly and completely converted to desmethyldiazepam. From the point of view of clinical efficacy, clorazepate and prazepam are almost identical, because they are products of the same drug.

**27.51.    The answer is E (all)** (*Synopsis*, ed. 4, page 655).

Atropine-like psychosis, the so-called central anticholinergic syndrome, produces a characteristic symptom profile of *florid visual hallucinations*, such as hallucinations of bugs or colors, *loss of immediate memory*, *confusion*, and *disorientation*. Evidence that the syndrome, when observed after the administration of tricyclics, is the central anticholinergic syndrome is indicated by its emergence as the typical symptom picture. Further important evidence is that empirically it is reversible by the administration of physostigmine, an agent that increases brain acetylcholine and pharmacologically overcomes the atropine blockade. Generally, the usual clinical treatment is the discontinuation of anticholinergics, causing the syndrome to subside within a day. In selected cases, physostigmine can be used to produce this dramatic reversal.

*A visual hallucination* is a hallucination involving sight. *Loss of immediate memory* affects the reproduction, recognition, or recall of perceived material within a period of not more than 5 seconds after presentation. *Confusion* is a disturbance of consciousness manifested by a disordered orientation in relation to time, place, or person. *Disorientation* is the impairment of awareness of time, place, and the position of the self in relation to other persons, i.e. confusion. It is characteristic of organic mental disorders.

**27.52.    The answer is E (all)** (*Synopsis*, ed. 4, page 670).

Flurazepam, the first benzodiazepine to be marketed as a hypnotic, is less frequently used since the availability of newer benzodiazepines—temazepam and triazolam. *Benzodiazepines, unlike the barbiturates, do not alter liver microsomal enzymes. There is no evidence that they are dangerous in suicide attempts.* There have been almost no successful well-documented suicides with any benzodiazpines alone. It appears quite likely that *benzoadiazepines pose much less liability for abuse than do the barbiturates* and nonbarbiturate sedatives. *Its hypnotic effects are approximately equal to those of barbiturates.*

**27.53.    The answer is C (2, 4)** (*Synopsis*, ed. 4, page 643).

With cardiac patients, a predrug electrocardiogram (EKG) for baseline purposes is indicated. An EKG abnormality consisting of *broadened, flattened, or clove T-waves* and *increased Q-R intervals* of uncertain clinical significance has been described in patients receiving thioridazine at doses as low as 300 mg a day. The abnormality is not associated with any significant clinical problem. *Decreased P-R intervals and S-T segment elevation* are not associated with phenothiazine treatment.

**27.54.    The answer is E (all)** (*Synopsis*, ed. 4, page 682).

The most common indication for electroconvulsive therapy (ECT) is the presence of a *major depressive episode.* It is likely that over 80 percent of ECT patients in the United States now carry such a diagnosis. The closer a patient's presentation fits with a diagnosis of severe major depressive episode with melancholia, the more likely it is that a satisfactory response to ECT will take place.

This is equally true for severe depressions of old age, as long as they are not caused by arteriosclerotic or senile brain changes. It is one of the most gratifying therapeutic experiences to examine apparently senile patients with agitation to find that they actually do not suffer from senility but from an affective psychosis (*pseudodementia*) and then to remove their psychiatric symptoms with a few electroconvulsive treatments. In practice, 80 to 90 percent of such persons will show marked improvement, a significantly higher figure than with pharmaco-

logical intervention. The presence of psychotic symptomatology, usually a poor prognostic sign for antidepressant drug treatment by itself, does not appear to attenuate the changes of a good response to ECT.

Approximately 15 to 20 percent of patients receiving ECT are being treated for *schizophrenia.* ECT induces a remission in a sizable proportion of such persons who have an acute presentation, particularly if it is accompanied by catatonic or affective symptomatology. Its efficacy in such cases appears roughly equivalent to that of neuroleptics. In chronic schizophrenia, only 5 to 10 percent of patients will show a major improvement, although it should be noted that much of these data are based on drug nonresponders.

Although not well established by controlled studies, ECT is quite effective in *mania.* Because of the high likelihood of response to pharmacological management, however, only around 3 percent of ECT patients carry such a diagnosis.

*Pseudodementia* is a dementia-like disorder that can be reversed by appropriate treatment. It is not caused by organic brain disease but by major depression that interferes with cognitive functioning. *Mania* is a mood disorder characterized by elation, agitation, hyperactivity and hyperexcitability, and accelerated thinking and speaking (flight of ideas). It characterizes the manic phase of bipolar affective disorder. *Schizoprenia* refers to a psychotic mental disorder characterized by disturbances in thinking, mood, and behavior. *Major depression* is a severe affective disorder characterized by one or more depressive episodes but no history of a manic episode. This is a DSM-III diagnosis and replaces the DSM-II term of manic-depressive illness, depressed type.

**27.55.    The answer is B (1, 3)** (*Synopsis*, ed. 4, page 657).

The *therapeutic effect of tranylcypromine is greater than that of a placebo.* There is evidence from well-controlled studies that phenelzine and pargyline are also therapeutically effective. On the basis of the evidence, one may classify the MAOI's in terms of their clinical effectiveness as follows: *Isocarboxazid may be least effective*; phenelzine and *tranylcypromine occupy an intermediate position. Iproniazid* is no longer marketed in the United States.

**27.56–27.61.    The answers are 27.56–D, 27.57–C, 27.58–A, 27.59–B, 27.60–A, and 27.61–E** (*Synopsis*, ed. 4, page 675).

The Drug Enforcement Administration control levels were established to limit the abuse of various substances prescribed by physicians or obtained illicitly. For example, such drugs as *heroin and marijuana* are listed on Schedule I

**Characteristics of Drugs at Each Drug Enforcement Administration (DEA)**
**Control Level**

| DEA Control Level (Schedule) | Characteristics of Drug at Each Control Level | Examples of Drugs at Each Control Level |
|---|---|---|
| I | High abuse potential<br>*No accepted use in medical treatment in the United States at the present time* and therefore not for prescription use | LSD, *heroin, marijuana*, peyote, mescaline, psilocybin, tetrahydrocannabinols, nicodeine, nicomorphine, and others |
| II | High abuse potential<br>Severe physical dependence liability<br>Severe psychological dependence liability | *Amphetamine*, opium, *morphine*, codeine, hydromorphine, phenmetrazine, cocaine, amobarbital, secobarbital, pentobarbital, methylphenidate, and others. |
| III | Abuse potential less than levels I and II<br>*Moderate or low physical dependence liability*<br>*High psychological liability* | Glutethimide, methyprylon, phencyclidine, nalorphine, sulfonmethane, benzphetamine, phendimetrazine, clortermine, mazindol, chlorphentermine, compounds containing codeine, morphine, opium, hydrocodone, dihydrocodeine, and others. |
| IV | *Low abuse potential*<br>*Limited physical dependence liability*<br>*Limited psychological dependence liability* | Barbital, phenobarbital, benzodiazepines, chloral hydrate, ethchlorvynol, ethinamate, meprobamate, paraldehyde, and others |
| V | *Lowest abuse potential of all controlled substances* | Narcotic preparations containing limited amounts of nonnarcotic active medicinal ingredients |

and have *no accepted medical use in the United States* and are associated with a high abuse potential. There is a movement, however, to make heroin available for terminal cancer patients in severe pain and to make marijuana available to patients receiving cancer chemotherapy, because it eliminates nausea and vomiting in some patients who are receiving that treatment.

The table above lists the various schedules and gives examples of drugs and their characteristics at each control level.

**27.62–27.66. The answers are 27.62–C, 27.63–C, 27.64–A, 27.65–C, and 27.66–C** (*Synopsis*, ed. 4, pages 642 and 645).

Both the tricyclic antidepressants and the phenothiazines produce side effects relating to their anticholinergic actions. These include such symptoms as *dry mouth and throat*, blurred vision, and hypotension, among others. *Jaundice* is a rare complication of phenothiazine treatment and also has been reported with tricyclic administration. *Flattened T-waves* are produced by both classes of drugs, and the *antihypertensive effects of quanethidine are also impaired*. *Hallucinations* may be associated with the tricyclic antidepressants.

The following tables (shown below and on page 376) list some of the many reported side effects of the major tranquilizers and the antidepressant drugs.

**Side Effects of Antidepressant Agents**

| | |
|---|---|
| Dry mouth | Hallucinations and delusions (in latent psychotics) |
| Palpitations | Diarrhea |
| Tachycardia | Black tongue |
| Heart block | Edema |
| Myocardial infarction | Aggravation of narrow-angle glaucoma (not chronic simple glaucoma) |
| Loss of accommodation | |
| Orthostatic hypotension | Urinary retention (caution in benign prostatic hypertrophy) |
| Fainting | |
| Dizziness | Paralytic ileus |
| Nausea | Peculiar taste |
| Vomiting | Skin rash |
| Constipation | Galactorrhea |
| Sedation | Gynecomastia (in males) |
| Agitation | Bone marrow depression |

## Reported Side Effects of Major Tranquilizers

Dry mouth and throat
Blurred vision
Cutaneous flushing
Constipation
Urinary retention
Paralytic ileus
Mental confusion
Miosis
Mydriasis
Postural hypotension
Broadened, flattened, or clove T-waves and increased Q-R intervals on electrocardiogram
Parkinsonian syndrome
  Mask-like face
  Tremor at rest
  Rigidity
  Shuffling gait
  Motor retardation
  Drooling
Dyskinesias
  Bizarre movements of tongue, face, and neck
  Buccofacial movements
  Salivation
  Torticollis
  Oculogyric crisis
  Opisthotonos
  Akathisia
Lowered seizure threshold
Convulsive seizures
Sedation
Insomnia
Bizarre dreams
Impaired psychomotor activity
Somnambulism
Confusion
Paradoxical aggravation of psychotic symptoms
Skin eruptions (urticarial, maculopapular, petechial, or edematous)
Contact dermatitis
Photosensitivity reaction
Blue-gray metallic discoloration of the skin over areas exposed to sunlight
Deposits in the anterior lens and posterior cornea (visible only by slit-lens examination)
Retinitis pigmentosa
Abnormal glucose tolerance curve
Breast engorgement and lactation in female patients
Weight gain
Delayed ejaculation
Loss of erectile ability
Agranulocytosis
Eosinophilia
Leukopenia
Hemolytic anemia
Thrombocytic purpura
Pancytopenia
Jaundice

# References

Appleton, W S: Fourth psychoactive drug usage guide. J Clin Psychiatry *43:* 12, 1982.

Campbell, R J: Miscellaneous organic therapies. In *Comprehensive Textbook of Psychiatry*, ed 4, H I Kaplan, B J Sadock, editors, p 1569. Williams & Wilkins, Baltimore, 1985.

Craig T J, Mehta R M: Clinician-computer interaction: Automated review of psychotropic drugs. Am J Psychiatry *141:* 267, 1984.

Davis J M: Antidepressant drugs. In *Comprehensive Textbook of Psychiatry*, ed. 4, H I Kaplan, B J Sadock, editors, p 1513. Williams & Wilkins, Baltimore, 1985.

Davis J M: Minor tranquilizers, sedatives, and hypnotics. In *Comprehensive Textbook of Psychiatry*, ed 4, H I Kaplan, B J Sadock, editors, p 1537. Williams & Wilkins, Baltimore, 1985.

Davis J M: Other pharmacological agents. In *Comprehensive Textbook of Psychiatry*, ed 4, H I Kaplan, B J Sadock, editors, p 1553. Williams & Wilkins, Baltimore, 1985.

Donnelly J: Psychosurgery, In *Comprehensive Textbook of Psychiatry*, ed 4, H I Kaplan, B J Sadock, editors, p 1563. Williams & Wilkins, Baltimore, 1985.

Klein, D F, Gittelman, R, Quitkin, F, Rifkin, A: *Diagnosis and Drug Treatment of Psychiatric Disorders: Adults and Children*. Williams & Wilkins, Baltimore, 1980.

Lipton, M A, DiMascio, A, Killam, K F, editors: *Psychopharmacology: A Generation of Progress*. Raven Press, New York, 1978.

Shader R I, editor: *Manual of Psychiatric Therapeutics*. Little, Brown, and Co, Boston, 1975.

Weiner, R D: Convulsive therapies. In *Comprehensive Textbook of Psychiatry*, ed 4, H I Kaplan, B J Sadock, editors, p 1558. Williams & Wilkins, Baltimore, 1985.

# 28

# Child Psychiatry: Normal Development

As a subspecialty that addresses itself to the developmental and behavioral problems of children, child psychiatry has an important substantive role in psychiatry, and in fact, childhood experiences have long been considered of crucial significance in the genesis of adult psychopathology. Of great importance in the consideration of childhood is the awareness of the constant change that is taking place within the matrix of children's relationships to their families and society: Both children and their external world are in a continual state of flux. It follows, then, that the psychiatric evaluation of children will include an assessment of their total functioning, including their level of physical and psychological development, in any given situation, as well as the degree to which their functioning reflects the impact of their environment.

Until very recently, theoretical concepts regarding the development and behavior of children were derived from clinical data on adult psychopathology, rather than from the direct, intensive observation of children. Psychiatrists must understand normal as well as atypical reactions in childhood if they are to comprehend fully the pathogenesis of adult deviations. Concomitantly, there has been an increasing awareness of the importance of training in child psychiatry for all students of medicine and for all trainees in psychiatry, whatever their particular area of interest. Thus the study of child psychiatry is not the exclusive province of the specialist, but part of a sound education in general medicine, neurology, and the behavioral sciences, including psychiatry.

Because awareness of the criteria of "healthy" development is a *sine qua non* of child psychiatry, a section on normal child development precedes consideration of psychiatric evaluation, clinical descriptions, and treatment.

The reader should review Chapter 28, "Child Psychiatry: Normal Development," of *Modern Synopsis-IV*, and should then study the questions and answers below to test his or her knowledge of the subject. Of particular importance are the various ages at which biological, psychological, and social events take place or first appear.

# Questions

**DIRECTIONS:** Each of the statements or questions below is followed by five suggested responses or completions. Select the *one* that is *best* in each case.

**28.1.** The single measureable variable that correlates most highly with academic success in childhood is

A. motivation
B. intelligence quotient (I.Q.)
C. parental encouragement
D. work habits
E. creativity

**28.2.** The epigenetic theory of intelligence was formulated by

A. Jean Piaget
B. Otto Rank
C. Erik Erikson
D. Sigmund Freud
E. Alfred Binet

**28.3.** If strabismus is not corrected before the fifth or sixth year of life, which of the following results:

A. Astigmatism
B. Tunnel vision
C. Amblyopia ex anopsia
D. Diplopia
E. Blurred vision

**28.4.** Social smiling by an infant is elicited by the face or voice of the caretaker at

A. 1 to 4 weeks
B. 4 to 8 weeks
C. 8 to 12 weeks
D. 3 to 4 months
E. more than 4 months

**28.5.** Endogenous smiling is present in the infant by

A. 2 weeks
B. 4 weeks
C. 6 weeks
D. 2 months
E. 3 months

**28.6.** Which of the following is reflex behavior present in the infant at birth:

A. Sucking
B. Defecating
C. Head turning
D. Swallowing
E. All of the above

**DIRECTIONS:** For each of the incomplete statements below, *one* or *more* of the completions given is correct. Choose answer:

A. if only **1**, **2**, and **3** are correct
B. if only **1** and **3** are correct
C. if only **2** and **4** are correct
D. if only **4** is correct
E. if all are correct

**28.7.** The greater frequency of aggressive behavior in the abnormal child has been correlated with

1. brain injury
2. faulty identification models
3. the child's cultural environment
4. violence in movies

**28.8.** Congenital differences among human infants are expressed

1. as temperamental differences evident by the third month of life
2. as differences in autonomic reactivity
3. in their responses to stimulation
4. in their distractibility

**28.9.** Which of the following statements apply to the second and third years of life:

1. The ability to walk gives children a degree of control over their own actions.
2. It is a negativistic stage.
3. Boundaries of acceptable behavior have to be set.
4. Children must be protected when challenges are beyond them.

**28.10.** Adolescents who show overt behavioral problems in the school and in the home

1. come from unstable backgrounds
2. have a history of mental illness in the family
3. have parents who cannot separate from the child
4. are not overly dependent on peer culture

**28.11.** Trust in others

1. is a congenital trait of the infant
2. develops in the infant as a result of regular, predictable care
3. is unaffected by the social responses to the child's acts
4. must be continuously reinforced during childhood and adolescence if it is to become a prevailing trait

**28.12.** In the fourth year of life,

1. the child is capable of anticipating events
2. acquiring mastery is a central psychological activity
3. the child is curious about anatomical sex
4. toilet training is a central issue

**28.13.**   The normal adolescent copes with trauma through which of the following mechanisms:

1. Adaptive action
2. Denial
3. Isolation
4. Delayed gratification

**28.14.**   Social isolation in subhuman species produces which of the following:

1. Inadequate response to pain
2. Difficulty in mating
3. Inability to mother their young
4. Inability to be effectively socialized

**DIRECTIONS:** Each group of questions below consists of five lettered headings followed by a list of numbered words or statements. For each numbered word or statement, select the *one* lettered heading that is most closely associated with it. Each lettered heading may be selected once, more than once, or not at all.

**Questions 28.15–28.19**
A.  Under 4 weeks
B.  16 weeks
C.  28 weeks
D.  40 weeks
E.  52 weeks

**28.15.**   Makes alternating crawling movements

**28.16.**   Laughs aloud

**28.17.**   Says "da-da" or equivalent

**28.18.**   Stands alone briefly

**28.19.**   Pats mirror image

**Questions 28.20–28.24**
Match the lettered emotional capacities with the age at which the emotion first appears.
A.  Distress
B.  Shame
C.  Anger
D.  Fear
E.  Guilt

**28.20.**   Birth

**28.21.**   3–4 months

**28.22.**   8–9 months

**28.23.**   18 months

**28.24.**   3–4 years

**Questions 28.25–28.29**
A.  18 months
B.  2 years
C.  3 years
D.  4 years
E.  5 years

**28.25.**   Copies a square

**28.26.**   Repeats four digits

**28.27.**   Builds tower of three or four cubes

**28.28.**   Alternates feet going upstairs

**28.29.**   Uses three-word sentences

**DIRECTIONS:** Each set of lettered headings below is followed by a list of numbered words or phrases. For each numbered word or phrase, select

    A. if the item is associated with **A** *only*
    B. if the item is associated with **B** *only*
    C. if the item is associated with *both* **A** *and* **B**
    D. if the item is associated with *neither* **A** *nor* **B**

**Questions 28.30–28.34**
A. Continuous growth in adolescence
B. Surgent growth in adolescence
C. Both
D. Neither

**28.30.** Marked by problems and traumas

**28.31.** Unmarked by stressful or upsetting events

**28.32.** Marked by parental conflicts

**28.33.** Less prone to depression

**28.34.** Least commonly encountered

# Answers

# Child Psychiatry: Normal
# Development

**28.1. The answer is B** (*Synopsis*, ed. 4, page 696).

The *intelligence quotient (I.Q.)* is a numerical measure of mental capability determined by dividing a mental age (MA) score achieved on a specific test, such as the Stanford-Binet Test, by the patient's chronological age (CA) and multiplying by 100. Although the child's intelligence as measured by I.Q. tests is the single variable that correlates most highly with academic success, the coefficient of correlation between I.Q. and grades does not exceed 0.6 to 0.7, thus accounting for no more than one-third to one-half of the variance. Equally salient are *motivation, work habits, creativity, parental encouragement*, and other traits for which there are as yet no quantitative measures.

*Motivation* is the force or energy associated with an internal state that propels a person to engage in behavior to satisfy a need or desire. *Creativity* is the ability to produce something new. Silvano Arieti described creativity as the tertiary process, a balanced combination of primary and secondary processes, in which materials from the id are used in the service of the ego.

**28.2. The answer is A** (*Synopsis*, ed. 4, page 694).

The epigenetic theory of intelligence was formulated by *Jean Piaget*. To Piaget, intelligence was but a special instance of biological adaptation within the context of life, which he viewed as a continuous creative interaction between the organism and its environment. The outer manifestation of this interaction is coping behavior; the inward reflection is the functional organization of the mental apparatus. Adaptive coping continuously reorganizes the structures of the mind.

Piaget divided the development of intelligence into three major periods: sensorimotor, birth to 2 years; concrete operations, 2 to 12 years; and formal operations, 12 years through adult life. The sensorimotor period is one in which the congenital sensorimotor schemata or reflexes are generalized, related to one another, and differentiated to become the elementary operations of intelligence.

*Otto Rank* is known for his theory of the birth trauma as the prototype of anxiety. *Erik Erikson* developed an epigenetic theory of emotional development, rather than a theory of intellectual development. With Theodore Simon, *Alfred Binet* formulated a test of intelligence for children that is known as the Binet-Simon Intelligence Test. *Sigmund Freud* is the father of psychoanalysis.

**28.3. The answer is C** (*Synopsis*, ed. 4, page 691).

In the child, strabismus—a manifest lack of parallelism of the visual axes of the eyes—that is not corrected before the fifth or sixth year of life results in *amblyopia ex anopsia*. In that condition, blindness results from cortical suppression of central vision due to disuse. The severely limited vision in the unused eye cannot be rectified by optical or surgical procedures. Even relatively restricted interference with access to visual experience has telling effects.

*Astigmatism* is a condition of unequal curvatures along the different meridians in one or more of the refractive surfaces of the eye; for example, the cornea or anterior or posterior surface of the lens. As a result, rays are not focused at a single point on the retina, and blurred vision results. *Tunnel vision* consists of a narrowing of the visual field, as though one were looking through a hollow tube; it may be a symptom of conversion, hysteria, or malingering. *Diplopia* is defined as double vision, the condition in which a single object is perceived as two objects. *Blurred vision* is a condition in which objects are perceived in a hazy, blurred state.

**28.4. The answer is B** (*Synopsis*, ed. 4, page 694).

By *4 to 8 weeks*, social smiling is elicited by the face or the voice of the caretaker.

**28.5. The answer is A** (*Synopsis*, ed. 4, pages 693 and 694).

By *1 to 2 weeks of* age, the infant smiles; this response is endogenously determined, as evident by smiling in blind infants.

**28.6.  The answer is E** (*Synopsis*, ed. 4, page 693).

At birth, all infants have a repertoire of reflex behaviors—breathing, crying, *defecating, head turning* toward the stimulated cheek, mouthing of a nipple touching the lips, *sucking,* and *swallowing.*

**28.7.  The answer is E (all)** (*Synopsis*, ed. 4, page 696).

In the normal child, aggression can be effectively understood in terms of the motives—defense, mastery, curiosity—for which aggressiveness is a suitable mediator. Its greater frequency in the abnormal child can be correlated with defects in the organism, as in the case of *brain injury*, or with distortions in the child's environment, as in the case of *faulty identification models*. Moreover, the frequency of the display of aggressive behavior is a *function of the culture in which the child is reared*. Aggressive fantasy materials—*movies*, crime comics, television, and so on—rather than affording catharsis for instinctual aggressiveness, generate the very tensions they profess to release.

A central issue is the meaning to be ascribed to the term aggression. If a boy is observed taking apart a watch, this behavior can be described as aggressive. In a given instance, it may be aggressive—if, for example, the watch belongs to the child's father, and the father has just punished him. If the watch is an old one in his stock of toys, however, the boy's motive may be curiosity about its mechanism—a belief more readily accepted if his delight as he is able to reassemble it in working order is observed. If he strikes another child, this can be an act of aggression. It well may be motivated by aggression if the victim is the baby sister his parents have just embraced. Or it may be defensive if the victim has made a threatening gesture or has tried to seize a favorite toy. Homely anecdotes serve to make the point, but documented experimental examples of aggressive behavior are readily available, such as children emulating adult models, children systematically subjected to frustration, and children watching films or television of aggressive behavior—all of whom show predictable increases in aggressiveness.

**28.8.  The answer is E (all)** (*Synopsis*, ed. 4, page 693).

Although a definitive answer to this question is not possible with present evidence, there are strong suggestions that congenital differences exist. Investigators have demonstrated wide individual differences among infants in *autonomic reactivity*, differences that persist over the newborn period but whose long-range consequences are not yet known. The studies of Alexander Thomas and Stella Chess demonstrated *temperamental characteristics already evident by the third month of life*. In a careful longitudinal study of 130 middle-class infants, the researchers were able to identify nine behavioral dimensions on which reliable ratings can be obtained: activity-passivity, regularity-irregularity, intensity, approach-withdrawal, adaptive-nonadaptive, high-low threshold of *response to stimulation*, positive-negative mood, high-low selectivity, and high-low *distractibility*. The ratings on individual children showed substantial correlations between 3 months and 2 years, but much lower correlations at 5 years. During this course of the study, 27 of the children presented clinical psychiatric problems.

**28.9.  The answer is E (all)** (*Synopsis*, ed. 4, pages 694 and 695).

The second and third years of life are marked by acceleration of motor and intellectual development. *The ability to walk confers on toddlers a degree of control over their own actions that allows them to determine when to approach and when to withdraw.* The acquisition of speech profoundly extends their horizons. Typically, children learn to say "no" before they learn to say "yes." Correspondingly, infants know what they do not want long before they are able to formulate what they do want. The *negativism of the toddler is a vital stage* in individuation.

This time period poses changing tasks for parents of toddlers. Whereas in the stage of infancy, the major responsibility for parents is to meet the infant's needs in a sensitive and giving fashion, without overanticipating and overfulfilling those needs so that the baby never experiences tension, the parental task at the toddler stage is a requirement for *firmness about the boundaries of acceptable behavior* and encouragment of the progressive emancipation of the child. Children must be allowed to do for themselves insofar as they are able, b... .hey *must be protected and assisted when the challenges are beyond them.*

**28.10.  The answer is A (1, 2, 3)** (*Synopsis*, ed. 4, page 699).

Adolescents demonstrating tumultuous-growth patterns may come from *less stable backgrounds* than do other adolescents. Some of the parents of this group have overt marital conflicts, and others may have a *history of mental illness in the family*. Hence, the genetic and environmental backgrounds of the adolescents in the tumultuous-growth group are decidedly different from those of the other two groups. Some, however, may have a reasonably normal environmental and family background.

*Separation of the adolescent from the family is*

painful for the parents, and it becomes a source of continuing conflict for the adolescents. That forms much of the basis for the adolescent's identity crisis.

These adolescents are *considerably more dependent on peer culture* than are their age-mates, possibly because they receive fewer gratifications from their relationships within the family.

## 28.11. The answer is C (2, 4) (Synopsis, ed. 4, page 694).

Parallel to the stages of cognitive development are the stages of emotional development. Erik Erikson described the first phase of life as trust versus mistrust. *It is in relation to regular and, hence, predictable events of caretaking that an affectional tie between infant and caretaker develops*; the infant's behavioral repertoire expands, as his or her acts *have consequences in the form of social responses* from the caretakers.

As perceptual and cognitive maturation occurs, the infant is able to relate these initially disconnected and separate experiences to the person who provides them and is able to distinguish that person from other persons in the environment.

*The basis for trust in others begins to emerge from good care in infancy*, but trust is in no sense a final acquisition of this first year; *it must be continuously reinforced during all of childhood and adolescence if it is to become a prevailing trait.*

## 28.12. The answer is A (1, 2, 3) (Synopsis, ed. 4, page 695).

In the fourth year of life, there is further augmentation of children's capacities, which, however, still run well behind their aspirations; they often undertake things they cannot complete successfully. They become *capable of anticipation* as a basis for accepting the postponement of immediate gratification. There is a flowering of imagination, as revealed in controlled fantasy and play. Play is a central psychological activity for this period. It is, to begin with, fun—the sheer pleasure of exercising new executive capacities and *acquiring mastery*. It serves the function of releasing tension and energy. After stress, it can provide emotional catharsis. Perhaps most important of all, the trial roles assumed in dramatic play allow children to try out the adult identities they will one day have to understand and to assume. It is during this era that sexual identity is firmly established.

*Children exhibit active curiosity about anatomical sex.* If this curiosity is recognized as healthy and is met with honest and age-appropriate replies, they acquire a sense of the wonder of life and are comfortable about their own role in it. If the subject is taboo and their questions are rebuffed, they respond with shame and discomfort.

*Toilet training is a central issue in the second and third years of life.* This issue is generally resolved by age 4.

## 28.13. The answer is E (all) (Synopsis, ed. 4, page 698).

Normal adolescents are able to cope with external trauma, usually through an *adaptive action* orientation. When difficulties arise, they use the defenses of *denial* and *isolation* to protect their egos from being bombarded with affects. They can *postpone immediate gratification* and work in a sustained manner toward a future goal. They do not experience prolonged periods of anxiety or depression.

An *adaptive action* orientation implies that the person can mobilize a coping mechanism to deal effectively with the environment. *Denial* is a defense mechanism in which the existence of unpleasant realities is disavowed. The term refers to a keeping out of conscious awareness any aspects of either internal or external reality that, if acknowledged, would produce anxiety. *Isolation* is a defense mechanism involving the separation of an idea or memory from its attached feeling tone. Unacceptable ideational content is thereby rendered free of its disturbing or unpleasant emotional charge. *Delayed gratification* refers to a postponement in satisfaction of one's needs or desires.

## 28.14. The answer is E (all) (Synopsis, ed. 4, pages 691 and 693).

The effects of total social isolation in subhuman species are of great interest in studying the socialization process. Puppies isolated in individual cages for 6 months exhibit a peculiar syndrome characterized by overactivity, distractibility, *inadequate response to pain*, whirling fits, inferiority to pet-reared and colony-reared dogs in problem solving and in food competition, and *inability to be effectively socialized* thereafter. Monkeys reared as isolated, even when offered surrogate mothers (objects for clinging), are subsequently unable to adjust to a colony existence and have *extraordinary difficulty in learning to mate*. When impregnated, isolate-reared females *fail to mother their young*. The behavioral peculiarities of these isolates were initially attributed to the lack of mothering in infancy, but Harry Harlow's studies demonstrated that an opportunity for peer interaction between two nonmothered infant monkeys apparently suffices for the development of social behavior.

Harry Harlow is best known for his studies of social deprivation in animals. His experiments involved rhesus monkeys who were taken from their mothers at birth and brought up in an environment of total or partial social deprivation.

Some of the monkeys were placed with two artificial surrogate mothers. One surrogate mother was made of wire; the other was covered with terry cloth and had a more rhesus-looking face. Both "mothers" could be equipped with baby bottles inserted through a hole in the chest, which allowed nursing to take place. Regardless of which mother provided food, the baby rhesus spent as much time as possible cuddling and hugging the cloth surrogate mother.

Other monkeys were placed only with the wire mother, and these monkeys appeared chronically fearful and anxious. The important factor differentiating the two surrogates was the presence of terry cloth, which stimulated the monkeys sense of touch, and proprioception, which was comforting. The figure below illustrates an infant rhesus monkey with a cloth surrogate.

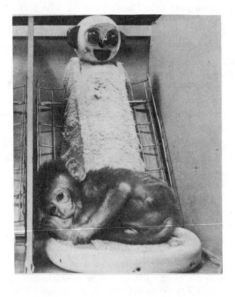

**28.15–28.19. The answers are 28.15–A, 28.16–B, 28.17–D, 28.18–E, and 28.19–C** (*Synopsis*, ed. 4, page 692).

Landmarks of normal behavioral development have been determined for the average infant and are outlined below. It is important to remember that individual variations exist and that there is a range of normal behavior that falls within the bell-shaped curve of normal distribution.

**28.20–28.24. The answers are 28.20–A, 28.21–C, 28.22–D, 28.23–B, and 28.24–E** (*Synopsis*, ed. 4, page 695).

Certain emotional capacities are present at birth and progress and expand as the child gets older. The small table on page 387 lists the average ages at which various feelings arise.

**28.25–28.29. The answers are 28.25–E, 28.26–D, 28.27–A, 28.28–C, and 28.29–B** (*Synopsis*, ed. 4, pages 692 and 693).

The normal child is able to accomplish specific tasks at certain ages. For example, a square can be copied at 5 years. Some children may be able to perform a task at an earlier or later age and still fall within the range of normal. Other landmarks of normal behavioral development are listed on pages 387 and 388.

**28.30–28.34. The answers are 28.30–B, 28.31–A, 28.32–B, 28.33–A, and 28.34–A** (*Synopsis*, ed. 4, pages 698 and 699).

The adolescents described within the continuous-growth grouping *are the least commonly encountered*. The following description may be considered to be ideal, and in it, perfection is extremely uncommon. The continuous-growth group progresses throughout adolescence with a smoothness of purpose and a self-assurance of their progression toward a meaningful and fulfilling adult life. They are favored by circumstances and master previous developmental stages without serious setbacks. Their genetic and environmental backgrounds are excellent. *Their family lives do not involve extremely stressful and upsetting events.* Their childhoods are unmarked by death or serious illness of a parent or sibling.

The parents of this group are able to encourage their children's independence; the parents themselves grow and change with their children. During the high school years, the parent of the opposite sex is the one who is most important for the healthy development of the adolescent. Through that parent, the teenager tests her or his sexuality, identity, and potential worth as an adult.

In their interpersonal relationships, these adolescents show a capacity for good object relationships. Adolescents described by the continuous-growth pattern act in accordance with their consciences, manifesting little evidence of superego problems and developing meaningful ego ideals, often identifying with persons they know and admire within the family or school communities.

Members of the continuous-growth group share many of the qualities of mental health when it is viewed in an ideal sense. These adolescents do not portray all these qualities, however, and they usually have some difficulties in one or another area. What is more distinctive about members of the continuous-growth group is their over-all contentment with themselves and their place in life. They are *relatively happy human beings*.

The surgent-growth group, although functioning as adaptively as the first group, is characterized by important enough differences in ego

## Landmarks of Normal Behavioral Development (Birth to 52 weeks)

| Age | Motor Behavior | Adaptive Behavior | Language | Personal and Social Behavior |
|---|---|---|---|---|
| Birth to 4 weeks | Hand to mouth reflex, grasping reflex, digital extension reflex | Anticipatory feeding approach behavior at 4 days | Crying as a sign of distress<br>Vocal reciprocity between mother and infant | Responsiveness to mother's face, eyes, and voice within first few hours of life |
| Under 4 weeks | *Makes alternating crawling movements*<br>Moves head laterally when placed in prone position | Responds to sound of rattle and bell<br>Regards moving objects momentarily | Small; throaty, undifferentiated noises | Quiets when picked up<br>Impassive face |
| 4 weeks | Tonic neck reflex positions predominate<br>Hands fisted<br>Head sags but can hold head erect for a few seconds | Follows moving objects to the midline<br>Shows no interest and drops objects immediately | Beginning vocalization, such as cooing, gurgling, and grunting | Regards face and diminishes activity<br>Responds to speech<br>Smiles preferentially to mother |
| 16 weeks | Symmetrical postures predominate<br>Holds head balanced<br>Head lifted 90 degrees when prone on forearm | Follows a slowly moving object well<br>Arms activate on sight of dangling object | *Laughs aloud*<br>Sustained cooing and gurgling | Spontaneous social smile<br>Aware of strange situations |
| 28 weeks | Sits steadily, leaning forward on hands<br>Bounces actively when placed in standing position | One-hand approach and grasp of toy<br>Bangs and shakes rattle<br>Transfers toys | Vocalizes "m-m-m" when crying<br>Makes vowel sounds, such as "ah" | Takes feet to mouth<br>*Pats mirror image* |
| 40 weeks | Sits alone with good coordination<br>Creeps<br>Pulls self to standing position<br>Points with index finger | Matches two objects at midline<br>Attempts to imitate scribble | *Says "da-da" or equivalent*<br>Responds to name or nickname | Separation anxiety manifest when taken away from mother<br>Responds to social play, such as "pat-a-cake" and "peek-a-boo"<br>Feeds self cracker and holds own bottle |
| 52 weeks | Walks with one hand held<br>*Stands alone briefly* | | Uses expressive jargon<br>Gives a toy on request | Cooperates in dressing |

## Landmarks of Normal Emotional Development

| Age | Emotional Capacity and Feeling |
|---|---|
| Birth | Pleasure, surprise, *distress* |
| 6–8 weeks | Joy |
| 3–4 months | *Anger* |
| 8–9 months | Sadness, *fear* |
| 12–16 months | Tenderness |
| 18 months | *Shame* |
| 2 yr | Pride |
| 3–4 yr | *Guilt* |
| 5–6 yr | Humility, confidence, envy |
| Adolescence | Romantic passion, philosophical brooding |

structure, in background, and in family environment to constitute a different—although normal—subgroup. Developmental spurts are illustrative of the pattern of growth of the surgent-growth group. This pattern is the most common one that adolescents follow.

One of the major differences between the surgent-growth adolescents and those in the continuous-growth group is that *the genetic and environmental backgrounds of the surgent-growth adolescents are not as free of problems and traumas*; the nuclear families in the surgent-growth group are more likely to have been affected by frequent and common life events, such as separation, death, or severe illnesses.

For the adolescents in the surgent-growth category, *relationships with parents are marked*

## Landmarks of Normal Emotional Development (15 months to 5 years)

| Age | Motor Behavior | Adaptive Behavior | Language | Personal and Social Behavior |
|---|---|---|---|---|
| 15 months | Toddles<br>Creeps up stairs | | Says three to five words meaningfully<br>Pats pictures in book<br>Shows shoes on request | Points or vocalizes wants<br>Throws objects in play or refusal |
| 18 months | Walks, seldom falls<br>Hurls ball<br>Walks up stairs with one hand held | *Builds a tower of three or four cubes*<br>Scribbles spontaneously and imitates a writing stroke | Says 10 words, including name<br>Identifies one common object on picture card<br>Names ball and carries out two directions—for example, "put on table" and "give to mother" | Feeds self in part, spills<br>Pulls toy on string<br>Carries or hugs a special toy, such as a doll<br>Imitates some behavioral patterns with slight delay |
| 2 yr | Runs well, no falling<br>Kicks large ball<br>Goes up and down stairs alone | Builds a tower of six or seven cubes<br>Aligns cubes, imitating train<br>Imitates vertical and circular strokes | *Uses three-word sentences*<br>Carries out four simple directions | Pulls on simple garment<br>Domestic mimicry<br>Refers to self by name<br>Says "no" to mother<br>Separation anxiety begins to diminish |
| 3 yr | Rides tricycle<br>Jumps from bottom steps<br>*Alternates feet going upstairs* | Builds tower of nine or 10 cubes<br>Imitates a three-cube bridge<br>Copies a circle and a cross | Gives sex and full name<br>Uses plurals<br>Describes what is happening in a picture book | Puts on shoes<br>Unbuttons buttons<br>Feeds self well<br>Understands taking turns |
| 4 yr | Walks down stairs one step per tread<br>Stands on one foot for 5 to 8 seconds | Copies a cross<br>*Repeats four digits*<br>Counts three objects with correct pointing | Names colors, at least one correctly<br>Understands five prepositional directives: "on," "under," "in," "in back of" or "in front of," and "beside" | Washes and dries own face<br>Brushes teeth<br>Plays cooperatively with other children |
| 5 yr | Skips, using feet alternately<br>Usually has complete sphincter control | *Copies a square*<br>Draws a recognizable man with a head, body, limbs<br>Counts 10 objects accurately | Names the primary colors<br>Names coins; pennies, nickels, dimes<br>Asks meaning of words | Dresses and undresses self<br>Prints a few letters<br>Plays competitive exercise games |

*by conflicts of opinions and values*. These adolescents are not as confident as those in the continuous-growth group; their self-esteem wavers. They rely on positive reinforcements from the opinions of important others, such as parents and peers. When this reinforcement is not forthcoming, they often become discouraged about themselves and their abilities. As a group, they are able to form meaningful interpersonal relationships similar to those of the adolescents in the continuous-growth group, but the relationships are maintained with a greater degree of effort. Some adolescents in this group are afraid of emerging sexual feelings and impulses. For them, meaningful relationships with the opposite sex begin relatively late.

These adolescents differ from the continuous-growth group in the amount of emotional conflict experienced and in their patterns of resolving conflicts. More concentrated energy is directed toward mastering developmental tasks than is obvious for members of the continuous-growth group. A cycle of progression and regression is more typical of this group than of the continuous-growth group. The defenses used—anger and projection—are different from the defenses used by the first group.

Although adolescents in this category are able to cope successfully with their average expectable environment, their ego development is not adequate for coping with unanticipated sources of anxiety. Affects that are usually flexible and available will, at a time of crisis, such as the death of a close relative, become stringently controlled. This, together with the fact that they

are not as action-oriented as the first group, makes them slightly more prone to depression. On some occasions, when their defense mechanisms falter, they experience moderate anxiety and a short period of turmoil. When disappointed in themselves or others, they show a tendency to use projection and anger.

The adolescents work toward their vocational goals sporadically or with a lack of enthusiasm; but they are able to keep their long-range behavior in line with their general expectations for themselves.

## References

Brunstetter R W, Silver L B: Normal adolescent development. In *Comprehensive Textbook of Psychiatry*, ed 4, H I Kaplan, B J Sadock, editors, p 1608. Williams & Wilkins, Baltimore, 1985.

Call J D, Noshpitz J D, Cohen R L, Berlin I N: Development. In *Basic Handbook of Child Psychiatry*, vol 1, J D Noshpitz, editor. Basic Books, New York, 1979.

Cohen R S: *Parenthood*. Guilford Press, New York, 1984.

Erikson E H: *Childhood and Society*, ed 2. Norton, New York, 1963.

Fraiberg S H: *The Magic Years: Understanding and Handling the Problems of Early Childhood*. Scribner, New York, 1959.

Freud A: *Normality and Pathology in Childhood: The Writings of Anna Freud*, vol 6. International Universities Press, New York, 1965.

Greenspan S I: Normal child development. In *Comprehensive Textbook of Psychiatry*, ed 4, H I Kaplan, B J Sadock, editors, p 1592. Williams & Wilkins, Baltimore, 1985.

Group for the Advancement of Psychiatry: *Normal Adolescence: Its Dynamics and Impact*, vol 6. GAP Report No 68, Washington, DC, 1968.

Piaget J, Inhelder B: *The Psychology of the Child*. Basic Books, New York, 1969.

# 29

# Child Psychiatry: Assessment, Examination, and Psychological Testing

The psychiatric assessment and examination of a child is a step in a process in which the clinician is responsible both to the child and to the child's parents, who are ultimately accountable for the child. The patient unit consists of the child and the parents—a child in a family. Understanding the parents is as important as the direct examination of the child. Interviews with the child are the culmination of an evaluative process illuminated by historical information and an appraisal of the child's current adjustment. The evaluation includes psychological tests and measurements and physical examination, with indicated biological studies.

The psychiatrist usually encounters the child through the parents, who have initiated the move to seek help. Work is carried out with their approval and assistance. They have been intimately involved in the development of the difficulties over which they are concerned, and their feelings and attitudes influence the evaluative review. The clinician is in the unique position of carrying out a service for the parents while endeavoring to study and understand them. The clinician must weigh the manner in which their personal needs and inclinations color the information they provide and must estimate how they will influence steps that are to be undertaken in diagnosis, treatment, or management. Some of the most important information about children derives from the manner in which the parents participate in the clinical procedures.

Another important source of information in the assessment of children is psychological testing. Because of their focused and objective nature, psychological tests help to identify some of the contributing factors in a particular case. Such tests make up one part of the total psychiatric evaluation.

Students should read Chapter 29 of *Modern Synopsis-IV*, which covers assessment, examination, and psychological testing of children. By studying the questions and answers below, they can assess their knowledge of these areas.

# Questions

**DIRECTIONS:** Each of the statements or questions below is followed by five suggested responses or completions. Select the *one* that is *best* in each case.

**29.1.** The illustration below is part of a series of drawings used to test children for which of the following:

A. Depression
B. Elation
C. Frustration
D. Anger
E. All of the above

I'm going to keep the swing all afternoon.

2 ┃

(Reproduced by permission of Saul Rosenzweig.)

**29.2.** Which of the following statements about play therapy is incorrect:

A. Play therapy was originally introduced by child psychiatrist David Levy.
B. Toys and materials should be abundant so that the child has the opportunity to become distracted or overwhelmed, which is an important part of the therapy.
C. Toys and materials should be available to suit children of different ages, sexes, and interests.
D. Offering boy toys to boys and girl toys to girls is not appropriate because this may preclude the expression of important elements in the patient's inner life.
E. The clinician should try to exclude toys that may involve the child in play that cannot come to a comfortable conclusion during a brief interview.

**29.3.** Most psychological tests used for infants focus on which of the following:

A. Language skills
B. Sensorimotor development
C. Cognitive development
D. Communication skills
E. Interaction skills

**DIRECTIONS:** For each of the incomplete statements below, *one* or *more* of the completions given is correct. Choose answer:

A. if only **1**, **2**, and **3** are correct
B. if only **1** and **3** are correct
C. if only **2** and **4** are correct
D. if only **4** is correct
E. if all are correct

**29.4.** When performing a psychiatric examination of a child, the psychiatrist should

1. encourage the child to sit quietly in a chair
2. avoid looking at the child
3. always have the parent in the same room with the child
4. use a conversational approach and encourage the child to take the initiative

**29.5.** In the examination of the child, play

1. helps elucidate the child's problems
2. is related to linguistic abstraction
3. bridges the gap between actions and their meanings
4. reduces tension in the child

**29.6.**  Anna Freud viewed psychiatric symptoms of children in which of the following ways:

1. They result from compromise formation between the id and the ego.
2. They result from changes in libido economy.
3. They result from changes in the quality or the direction of aggression.
4. They result from organic causes.

**29.7.**  A classification of diagnostic categories developed by the Group for the Advancement of Psychiatry for use with children

1. includes healthy responses as a diagnostic category
2. sees signs that may cause concern as manifestations of adaptation
3. includes developmental deviations
4. focuses on both the total personality and organ systems

**29.8.**  In comparison with tests of ability, personality tests

1. are less reliable and less valid
2. need to be supplemented from other sources
3. should be augmented by direct observation of behavior
4. are of little use in screening and identifying children in need of further investigation

**DIRECTIONS:** Each group of questions below consists of five lettered headings followed by a list of numbered words or statements. For each numbered word or statement, select the *one* lettered heading that is most closely associated with it. Each lettered heading may be selected once, more than once, or not at all.

**Questions 29.9–29.13**

A.  Children's Apperception Test
B.  Blacky Pictures
C.  Rorschach test
D.  Rosenzweig Picture-Frustration Study
E.  Toy tests and dolls

**29.9.**  Bilaterally symmetrical inkblots

**29.10.**  Reveals through play the child's attitudes toward the family, sibling rivalry, fears, aggressions, and conflicts

**29.11**  Pictures of various animal characters that are designed to evoke fantasies related to feeding and aggression

**29.12.**  Cartoons of a small dog, its parents, and a sibling are designed to elicit sexual conflicts

**29.13.**  The child writes in a blank space what he or she would reply to a frustrating situation

# Answers

# Child Psychiatry: Assessment, Examination, and Psychological Testing

**29.1.** The answer is C (*Synopsis*, ed. 4, page 707).

The illustration is part of the Rosenzweig Picture-Frustration Study. This test presents a series of cartoons in which the person *frustrates* another. In the blank space provided, the child writes what the frustrated person would reply. From that reply, the examiner determines the impact of frustration on the child, ranging from extreme passivity to extreme violence.

**29.2.** The answer is B (*Synopsis*, ed. 4, page 703).

*Toys and materials should be available to suit children of different ages, sexes, and interests.* The room should be furnished and arranged so that toys and materials inappropriate for a particular child can be removed from view. *Too great a choice may be overstimulating or distracting; too little may fail to accommodate important fantasies or concerns.* Toys and materials made available to the spontaneous interests of the child being examined should not be edited rigidly according to preconceived goals of the examiner. *Attempting, for example, to offer boy toys to boys and girl toys to girls may preclude the expression of important elements in the patient's inner life.*

*Play therapy was initially introduced and developed by the child psychiatrist David Levy.*

If the following toys and materials are included, the range should be adequate for the great majority of children up to the age of 8 or 10 years: facilities for water play; clay, paints, and crayons; kitchen equipment; building blocks; a furnished doll house with a doll family; puppets; trains, trucks, cars, and planes; a sandbox; dolls with anatomically perceptible body parts; and assorted table games. The play equipment in a well-equipped office-playroom is substantially the same for the diagnostic interview as it is for interviews in the course of play therapy, but certain materials are more strongly associated than others with continuity. *The clinician should try to exclude toys that may involve the child in play that cannot come to a comfortable conclusion during a brief diagnostic process.*

**29.3.** The answer is B (*Synopsis*, ed. 4, pages 704 and 705).

Tests applicable prior to school entrance are subdivided into infant tests, designed for the first 18 months of life, and preschool tests, covering the ages of 18 to 60 months. Infants must be tested while lying down or supported on someone's lap. *Speech is of little or no use* in giving test instructions, although each child's speech development provides relevant data. Most of the tests at this level are actually controlled observations of *sensorimotor development*: the ability of infants to lift their heads, turn over, reach for and grasp objects, and follow a moving object with their eyes. At the preschool level the children can walk, sit at a table, use their hands in manipulating test objects, and *communicate* by language. Preschool children are also *much more responsive to the examiner as a person.*

*Cognitive development* is the progressive acquisition of conscious thought and problem-solving abilities that follows an orderly sequence of more or less discrete stages.

**29.4.** The answer is D (4) (*Synopsis*, ed. 4, pages 701 and 702).

It is the clinician's task to provide an emotional setting within which both the clinician and each child who is interviewed may interact, so that the children can express directly or by implication what they are concerned about and what kind of a person they are. A child's behavior in the interview is observed, appraised, and evaluated in the light of the history and the social milieu. The manner of the interview depends on a child's age. Adolescents may seek help themselves and be the principal informant, especially if they are attempting to be independent of their parents.

No child should be expected to sit quietly in a chair throughout the interview. *A conversational approach should be attempted* with all children who are old enough. The examiner will be well-rewarded for any success that can be achieved in identifying with the mundane things that preoccupy the children, even or especially when under stress.

Whether in play or in conversation, each child should be allowed and *encouraged to take the initiative*. The children's self-protective need, out of anxiety, to adapt their communication to the examiner, is very strong. It is important, especially at the outset, for children to perceive the psychiatrist as a responsive human being. Time should be allocated to drawing the children out about their satisfying experiences and interests and to responding empathically to them. The examiner who shows signs of enjoyment in sharing these interests, before focusing attention on less pleasant matters, will be rewarded in the long run. It is virtually useless to push diagnostic questions at a child who is unready or unable to lower his or her guard.

**29.5. The answer is E (all)** (*Synopsis*, ed. 4, pages 702 and 703).

Through play, children attempt to *regulate the stimuli affecting them*. The play of a child with personality problems is directed perforce toward these problems and contains both expressive and defensive reflections. What the child says in connection with such play represents the partially developed capacity for *linguistic abstraction* commensurate with the child's age, personality, and emotional state; it *bridges the gap between actions and their meaning*, and helps the examiner fathom what is troubling the child and, of equal importance, why the child cannot bring it out more directly.

The examinating room should be open enough to allow for the physical activity required to *reduce tension*, but not so large as to attenuate a reasonably intimate contact between the examiner and the patient.

**29.6. The answer is E (all)** (*Synopsis*, ed. 4, pages 703 and 704).

The system of classification suggested by Anna Freud divides the psychiatric disorders of children into two major groups (see the table in column 2). Symptoms are defined more narrowly than in the Group for the Advancement of Psychiatry (GAP) scheme, which gives parity to symptoms of all the specific manifestations of disorder in childhood. For Anna Freud, symptoms are only those manifestations of disorder that result from the failure of an essential step in mental development to take place at the normal time. Symptoms are defined in terms of the specific step that failed and at which the child's development took its pathological turn. These true symptoms are viewed as the results of psychopathology, as defined in accord with psychoanalytic theory.

## Anna Freud's System of Classification

*Symptoms*

Symptoms resulting from initial nondifferentiation between somatic and psychological processes: psychosomatics

*Symptoms resulting from compromise formation between id and ego: neurotic symptoms*

Symptoms resulting from the irruption of id derivatives into the ego: psychotic or delinquent symptoms if complete irruption, borderline symptoms if partial irruption

Symptoms *resulting from changes in the libido economy* or direction of cathexis: symptoms of some personality disorders and hypochondriasis

Symptoms *resulting from changes in the quality or direction of aggression*: inhibited or destructive symptoms

Symptoms resulting from undefended regressions: infantile symptoms

Symptoms *resulting from organic causes*

*Other signs of disturbance and other reasons for a child's referral*

Fears and anxieties

Delays and failures in development

School failures

Failures in social adaptation

Aches and pains

The *id* is part of Freud's structural theory of mental functioning. The id is that part of the psychic apparatus that operates unconsciously; harbors the innate, biological, instinctual drives; and is the source of psychic energy (libido). It follows the pleasure principle, seeks immediate reduction of drive tension without regard for external reality, and is under the influence of the primary-process mental activity that characterizes the unconscious.

The *ego* refers to one of the three components of the psychic apparatus in the Freudian structural framework. The other two components are the id and the superego. Although the ego has some conscious components, many of its operations are automatic. It occupies a position between the primal instincts and the demands of the outer world; therefore, it mediates between the person and external reality. In so doing, it performs the important functions of perceiving the needs of the self, both physical and psychological, and the qualities and attitudes of the environment. It evaluates, coordinates, and integrates those perceptions so that internal demands can be adjusted to external requirements. It is also responsible for certain defensive functions to protect the person against the demands of the id and the superego. It has a host of functions, but adaptation to reality is perhaps the most important one.

In psychoanalysis, the superego is the part of the personality structure that represents the internalized values, ideals, and moral attitudes of society. Its psychic functions are expressed in guilt, self-criticism, and conscience. It develops through a child's identification with the parents, and the severity of the superego's prohibitions or demands is said to be related to the intensity and extent of resolution of the Oedipus complex. It has a rewarding function, referred to as the ego ideal, and a critical and punishing function, which evokes the sense of guilt.

The *libido* in psychoanalysis refers to the psychic energy associated with the sexual drive or life instinct.

**29.7.   The answer is E (all)** (*Synopsis*, ed. 4, page 703).

The Committee on Child Psychiatry of the Group for the Advancement of Psychiatry (GAP) proposed a classification that separates the disorders into 10 major diagnostic categories (see the table below). It is the first system to *include healthy responses as a diagnostic category*, pointing up the need in diagnostic work to recognize when *signs that may cause concern are manifestations of adaptation* and do not indicate failure to maintain mental growth. Whereas the first six categories, arranged more or less in ascending order of seriousness, deal essentially with the *total personality*, hewing as closely as possible to the unitary view underlying the system, the next three categories reflect end organ or *organ system responses*, even though the personality of the child with such a disorder may be and almost always is significantly involved.

**Group for the Advancement of Psychiatry
Classifications\***

---

1. *Healthy responses*
2. Reactive disorders
3. *Developmental deviations*
4. Psychoneurotic disorders
5. Personality disorders
6. Psychotic disorders
7. Psychosomatic disorders
8. Brain syndromes
9. Mental retardation
10. Other disorders

---

\* Based on Group for the Advancement of Psychiatry: *Psychopathological Disorders in Childhood*, Report No. 62. Group for the Advancement of Psychiatry, New York, 1966.

**29.8.   The answer is A (1, 2, 3)** (*Synopsis*, ed. 4, pages 706 and 707).

In comparison with tests of ability, personality tests are much *less satisfactory with regard to norms, reliability, and validity*. Any information obtained from personality tests should be verified and *supplemented from other sources*, such as interviews with the child and the child's associates, *direct observation of behavior*, and case history.

These *tests are of use, however, in identifying children who are in need of further investigation*.

**29.9–29.13.   The answers are 29.9–C, 29.10–E, 29.11–A, 29.12–B, and 29.13–D** (*Synopsis*, ed. 4, pages 707 and 708).

In projective techniques, the subject is assigned an unstructured task that permits an almost unlimited variety of possible responses. The test stimuli are typically vague and equivocal, and the instructions are brief and general. These techniques are based on the hypothesis that the way in which the person perceives and interprets the test materials reflects basic characteristics of that person's personality. The test stimuli serve as a screen on which the subject projects his or her own ideas.

One of the most widely used projective techniques is the Rorschach test, in which the subjects are shown a set of *bilaterally symmetrical inkblots* and asked to tell what they see or what the blot represents. Rorschach norms have been developed for children between the ages of 2 and 10 years and for adolescents between the ages of 10 and 17.

A somewhat more structured test is the Children's Apperception Test (CAT), an adaptation of the Thematic Apperception Test (TAT). In the CAT, pictures of animals are substituted for pictures of people on the assumption that children respond more readily to animal characters. *The pictures are designed to evoke fantasies relating to problems of feeding and other oral activity, sibling rivalry, parent-child relations, aggression*, toilet training, and other childhood experiences. Another example is the Blacky Pictures, a set of *cartoons showing a small dog, its parents, and a sibling*. Based on a psychoanalytic theory of psychosexual development, the cartoons depict situations suggesting various types of sexual conflicts. Still another type of picture test is illustrated by the Rosenzweig Picture-Frustration Study. This test presents a series of cartoons in which one person frustrates another. *In a blank space provided, the child writes what the frustrated person would reply*.

Drawings, toy tests, and other play techniques represent other applications or projective methods. Play and dramatic objects, such as puppets, dolls, toys, and miniatures, have also been used. The objects are usually selected because of their associative value, often including dolls representing adults and children, bathroom and kitchen fixtures, and other household furnishings. *Play with such articles is expected to reveal the child's attitudes toward the family, sibling rivalries, fears, aggressions, and conflicts.* They are of particular use in eliciting sexual abuse problems in children.

When evaluated as standardized tests, most projective techniques have fared quite poorly. They should be regarded not as tests but as aids to the clinical interviewer.

## References

Benton A L, Sines J O: Psychological testing of children. In *Comprehensive Textbook of Psychiatry*, ed 4, H I Kaplan, B J Sadock, editors, p 1625. Williams & Wilkins, Baltimore, 1985.

Call J D: Psychiatric evaluation of the infant and the child. In *Comprehensive Textbook of Psychiatry*, ed 4, H I Kaplan, B J Sadock, editors, p 1614. Williams & Wilkins, Baltimore, 1985.

Cohen R L: Development. In *Basic Handbook of Child Psychiatry*, J Noshpitz, R L Cohen, editors, vol 1, p 485. Basic Books, New York, 1979.

Dowling J, Wesner D: The concept of an infant mental status examination. Psychiatry *47:* 172, 1984.

Kaufman A S, Kaufman N L: *Kaufman Assessment Battery for Children: Interpretive Manual.* American Guidance Service, Circle Pines, MN, 1983.

Sattler J M: *Assessment of Children's Intelligence*, ed 2. W B Saunders, Philadelphia, 1982.

Simmons J E: *Psychiatric Examination of Children*, ed 3. Lea & Febiger, Philadelphia, 1981.

Wechsler D: *Wechsler Intelligence Scale for Children—Revised.* Psychological Corporation, New York, 1974.

Winnicott D W: *Therapeutic Consultation in Child Psychiatry.* Basic Books, New York, 1971.

# 30

# Mental Retardation

As stated in the fourth edition of the *Comprehensive Textbook of Psychiatry,* mental retardation is a behavioral syndrome that does not have a single cause, mechanism, course, or prognosis. Particularly when it is of a severe degree, it may have as a background one of many disorders that are known to affect human development, such as phenylketonuria, Down's syndrome, or congenital hypothyroidism.

The diagnosis of mental retardation includes the determination that retardation exists, classification of its severity, and medical diagnosis of the underlying disorder, if possible. The definition of mental retardation has evolved through the years and is still in the process of refinement. It has reflected society's attitude toward mental subnormality, as well as the state of diagnostic techniques and medical knowledge. According to the third edition of the *Diagnostic and Statistical Manual of Mental Disorders* (DSM-III), the essential features of mental retardation are (1) subaverage general intellectual functioning, (2) resulting in, or associated with, defects or impairments in adaptive behavior, (3) with onset before the age of 18.

The student should read Chapter 30, "Mental Retardation," of *Modern Synopsis-IV* and should then study the questions and answers below to test his or her knowledge of the subject.

# Questions

**DIRECTIONS:** Each of the statements or questions below is followed by five suggested responses or completions. Select the *one* that is *best* in each case.

**30.1.** According to DSM-III, mental retardation should not be diagnosed unless the I.Q. is below

A. 20
B. 40
C. 70
D. 90
E. 100

**30.2.** The child shown on page 400 has bushy eyebrows, thick lips, a large tongue, and coarse features. X-rays show elongation of the sella turcica and marked skull malformations. She is suffering from an autosomal recessive disease called

A. Hunter's disease
B. Hurler's syndrome
C. Sanfilippo's syndrome
D. Down's syndrome
E. none of the above

**30.3.** The percentage of all children with cerebral palsy who have normal intelligence is

A. 5 percent
B. 15 percent
C. 25 percent
D. 50 percent
E. 75 percent

**30.4.** Children may reach, but are unlikely to progress beyond, the second-grade level in academic subjects if their degree of mental retardation is

A. profound
B. severe
C. moderate
D. mild
E. none of the above

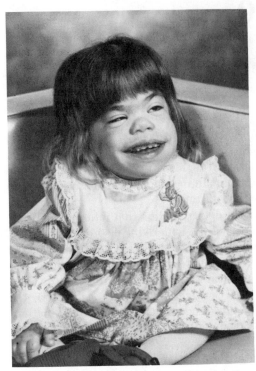

**(Courtesy of L S Szymanski, MD, and A C Crocker, M D)**

**30.5.** What percentage of mental retardation may be caused by biochemical metabolic disorders:

A. 5 percent
B. 10 percent
C. 15 percent
D. 20 percent
E. 25 percent

**30.6.** What percentage of the preschool population is classified as mentally retarded:

A. 1 percent
B. 3 percent
C. 5 percent
D. 7 percent
E. 10 percent

**30.7.** The incidence of Down's syndrome in the United States is about one in every

A. 250 births
B. 700 births
C. 1,000 births
D. 1,400 births
E. 5,000 births

**30.8.** Mental deterioration, hepatosplenomegaly, abdominal and cranial enlargement, hypotonia, and opisthotonos complete the clinical picture of

A. Tay-Sachs disease
B. Gaucher's disease
C. fructose intolerance
D. citrullinuria
E. Schilder's disease

**30.9.** The frequency of patients with Down's syndrome in institutions for the mentally retarded approximates

A. 1 percent
B. 5 percent
C. 10 percent
D. 15 percent
E. 20 percent

**DIRECTIONS:** For each of the incomplete statements below, *one* or *more* of the completions given is correct. Choose answer:

A. if only **1, 2,** and **3** are correct
B. if only **1** and **3** are correct
C. if only **2** and **4** are correct
D. if only **4** is correct
E. if all are correct

**30.10.** Which of the following statements about mental retardation are accurate:

1. Intelligence exists independent of cultural setting.
2. One can be retarded in some areas and normal for others.
3. The real number of retarded people can be scientifically determined.
4. Intelligence is relative to the requirements of the particular social system.

**30.11.** The genetic findings most likely to be associated with advancing maternal age are

1. translocation between chromosome 14 and 21
2. mitotic nondisjunction of chromosome 21
3. partially trisomic karyotype
4. meiotic nondisjunction of chromosome 21

**30.12.** Tay-Sachs disease

1. is a form of cerebromacular degeneration
2. begins in infants 4 to 8 months of age
3. occurs chiefly in Jewish infants
4. is treatable

**30.13.** Amniocentesis

1. is carried out intravaginally
2. is performed between the 14th and 16th week
3. is not recommended until the woman is at least 45 years old
4. can be used to diagnose Down's syndrome

**30.14.** Rubella (German measles)

1. is the major maternal infection producing mental retardation
2. will produce mental retardation in 50 percent of children of mothers infected during the first month of pregnancy
3. produces abnormalities in the newborn that are in inverse proportion to the duration of pregnancy at the time of maternal infection
4. rarely produces defects other than mental retardation

**30.15.** Which of the following diseases in the mother can produce mental retardation:

1. Toxoplasmosis
2. Cytomegalic inclusion body disease
3. Hepatitis
4. Breast cancer

**30.16.** Neurofibromatosis (Recklinghausen's disease) is associated with

1. epilepsy
2. large skin polyps
3. *café au lait* spots
4. meningiomas

**30.17.** Down's syndrome (mongolism)

1. is associated with increased age of the mother
2. occurs when there are three of chromosome 21 instead of the usual two (trisomy 21)
3. may have asymptomatic carriers
4. can be caused by translocation of two chromosomes

**30.18.** Important signs of Down's syndrome (mongolism) in a newborn are

1. oblique palpebral fissures
2. palmar transversal crease
3. protruding tongue
4. cat-like cry

**30.19.** In the treatment of phenylketonuria (PKU),

1. the results are equally good whether treatment is started before or after 6 months of age
2. a low phenylalanine diet is used
3. dietary treatment must continue throughout life
4. treatment decreases abnormal encephalogram changes

**30.20.** Cretinism is associated with

1. iodine deficiency in the diet
2. hypothyroidism
3. depressed protein-bound iodine
4. high cholesterol level

**30.21.** Hepatolenticular degeneration (Wilson's disease)

1. is a disorder of copper metabolism
2. is treated with penicillamine
3. is associated with a greenish-brown ring in the iris
4. may show personality changes before other clinical manifestations

**30.22.** Phenylketonuria (PKU)

1. is transmitted as a simple recessive autosomal Mendelian trait
2. is caused by the inability to convert phenylalanine to tyrosine
3. is associated with eczema
4. is most common in those of Mediterranean descent

**30.23.** Maple syrup urine disease

1. is transmitted by a single autosomal recessive gene
2. appears after the first year of life
3. is treated by dietary regimen
4. has a poor prognosis even with timely treatment

**30.24.** Hartnup disease

1. is transmitted by a single dominant autosomal gene
2. produces transient personality changes and psychoses
3. involves a defect in glucose metabolism
4. may not show itself until adolescence

**30.25.** Hurler's syndrome (gargoylism)

1. leads to death before adolescence
2. produces dwarfism
3. can be differentiated from cretinism by X-rays
4. is transmitted by an autosomal recessive trait

**DIRECTIONS:** Each group of questions below consists of five lettered headings followed by a list of numbered words or statements. For each numbered word or statement, select the *one* lettered heading that is most closely associated with it. Each lettered heading may be selected once, more than once, or not at all.

**Questions 30.26–30.30**

A. Hyperglycinemia
B. Histidinemia
C. Homocystinuria
D. Oculorenal dystrophy
E. Cystathioninuria

**30.26.** Cataracts

**30.27.** Severe ketosis

**30.28.** Positive ferric chloride test

**30.29.** Treatment with pyridoxine

**30.30.** Patients resemble those with Marfan's syndrome

# Answers

# Mental Retardation

**30.1. The answer is C** (*Synopsis*, ed. 4, page 710).

Mental deficiency is often used interchangeably with mental retardation. The World Health Organization, however, has recommended the use of the term mental subnormality, which is divided into two separate and distinct categories: mental retardation and mental deficiency. According to this nosology, mental retardation is reserved for subnormal functioning due to pathological causes. Mental deficiency is often used as a legal term, applied to people with an I.Q. of *less than 70* (see table below).

The degrees or levels of retardation are expressed in various terms. According to DSM-III, the following classification is used: mild mental retardation (I.Q. 50 to 70), moderate mental retardation (I.Q. 35 to 49), severe mental retardation (I.Q. 20 to 34), and profound mental retardation (I.Q. less than 20).

**30.2. The answer is B** (*Synopsis*, ed. 4, page 717).

The patient has *Hurler's syndrome*, which is a disease transmitted by an autosomal recessive gene. Biochemical abnormalities include the following: (1) accumulation of dermatan sulfate and heparitin sulfate in urine and tissue, (2) increased level of gangliosides in the brain, and (3) decreased $\beta$-galactosidase activity. X-rays show elongation of the sella turcica, kyphosis, club-shaped lower ribs, thickening of the long bones, and skull malformations. The disease has an onset at a very early age leading to death before adolescence. Mental deterioration is common.

*Hunter's disease* affects only males. *San Filippo's syndrome* involves only mild skeletal changes and has a different physiognomy than does Hurler's syndrome. *Down's syndrome* is the result of a chromosomal aberration, trisomy 21. Facial appearance is vastly different from that of Hurler's syndrome.

**30.3. The answer is C** (*Synopsis*, ed. 4, page 724).

About *25 percent* of all children with cerebral palsy have normal intelligence.

**30.4. The answer is C** (*Synopsis*, ed. 4, page 710).

*Moderate mental retardation* prevents children from progressing beyond the second-grade level in academic subjects. These patients can learn to communicate, but require moderate supervision and can work in unskilled or semiskilled jobs under sheltered conditions.

The table on page 404 lists the developmental characteristics of the mentally retarded.

**30.5. The answer is B** (*Synopsis*, ed. 4, page 711).

The total of all the known hereditary metabolic defects probably accounts for only a minority of mental defectives. Further biochemical research may bring the number of metabolic disorders to *at least 10 percent* of the mentally retarded.

**30.6. The answer is A** (*Synopsis*, ed. 4, page 711).

The incidence of mental retardation ultimately determines the prevalence of the condition.

*About 1 percent* of the preschool population is classified as mentally retarded, because only the severe forms of the disorder are recognized on routine examination. The highest incidence

---

### Diagnostic Criteria for Mental Retardation*

A. Significantly subaverage general intellectual functioning: an *I.Q. of 70 or below* on an individually administered I.Q. test (for infants, since available intelligence tests do not yield numerical values, a clinical judgment of significant subaverage intellectual functioning)

B. Concurrent deficits or impairments in adaptive behavior, taking the person's age into consideration

C. Onset before the age of 18

---

*From American Psychiatric Association: *Diagnostic and Statistical Manual of Mental Disorders*, ed 3. American Psychiatric Association, Washington, DC, 1980. Used with permission.

**Developmental Characteristics of the Mentally Retarded\*†**

| Degree of Mental Retardation | Preschool Age 0–5 Maturation and Development | School Age 6–20 Training and Education | Adult 21 and Over Social and Vocational Adequacy |
|---|---|---|---|
| *Profound* | Gross retardation; minimal capacity for functioning in sensorimotor areas; needs nursing care; constant aid and supervision required | Some motor development present; *may respond to minimal or limited training in self-help* | Some motor and speech development; may achieve very limited self-care; needs nursing care |
| *Severe* | Poor motor development; speech minimal; generally unable to profit from training in self-help; little or no communication skills | Can talk or learn to communicate; *can be trained in elemental health habits*; profits from systematic habit training; unable to profit from vocational training | May contribute partially to self-maintenance under complete supervision; can develop self-protection skills to a minimal useful level in controlled environment |
| *Moderate* | Can talk or learn to communicate; poor social awareness; fair motor development; profits from training in self-help; can be managed with moderate supervision | Can profit from training in social and occupational skills; *unlikely to progress beyond 2nd-grade level in academic subjects*; may learn to travel alone in familiar places | May achieve self-maintenance in unskilled or semiskilled work under sheltered conditions; needs supervision and guidance when under mild social or economic stress |
| *Mild* | Can develop social and communication skills, minimal retardation in sensorimotor areas; often not distinguished from normal until later age | Can *learn academic skills up to approximately 6th-grade level* by late teens; can be guided toward social conformity | Can usually achieve social and vocational skills adequate to minimum self-support, but may need guidance and assistance when under unusual social or economic stress |

\* This table integrates chronological age, degree of retardation, and level of intellectual, vocational, and social functioning.

† Adapted from *Mental Retardation Activities of the U.S. Department of Health, Education, and Welfare*, p 2. United States Government Printing Office, Washington, DC, 1963. DSM-III criteria are adapted essentially from this chart.

is found in school-aged children, with the peak at ages 10 to 14.

**30.7.   The answer is B** (*Synopsis*, ed. 4, page 718).

The incidence of Down's syndrome in the United States is about *1 in every 700 births*. Down's syndrome is a form of mental retardation caused by a chromosomal abnormality (trisomy 21). It was formerly referred to as mongolism.

**30.8.   The answer is B** (*Synopsis*, ed. 4, page 715).

*Gaucher's disease* is a lipidosis that occurs mostly in Jewish children and has an autosomal recessive mode of genetic transmission.

Clinically, the illness occurs in two forms. The acute infantile form has its onset in infancy, after several months of normal development, and is characterized by progressive mental deterioration and developmental arrest. Hepatosplenomegaly, abdominal and cranial enlargement, hypotonia, and opisthotonos complete the clinical course, which is usually fatal before the end of the first year of life.

The chronic form has an insidious onset, usually any time before the tenth year of life, but occurs occasionally in adolescents and young adults. The course is chronic, characterized mainly by chronic physical handicaps.

*Tay-Sachs disease* begins in infants 4 to 8 months of age. The infants become hypotonic, slow down in their developmental progress, and become weak and apathetic. In addition, the infants show spasticity, accompanied by persistent primitive postural reflexes, cherry-red spots in the macula lutea of each retina, convulsions, and progressive physical and mental deterioration leading to death in 2 to 4 years.

*Citrullinuria* is one of the rare disorders involving the urea cycle. It involves an enzymatic defect in the conversion of citrulline into argininosuccinic acid because of an argininosuccinate synthetase deficiency. As a result, the level of citrulline in the blood, cerebrospinal fluid, and urine is elevated. The disorder is accompanied by mental retardation.

*Fructose intolerance*, an autosomal recessive disorder, is characterized by episodes of hypoglycemia after the intake of fructose or sucrose. The nature of the biochemical defect involves a deficiency in liver aldolase. In unrecognized and untreated cases, mental retardation results, but it may be prevented by dietary measures, which consist of a sucrose- and fructose-free diet.

*Schilder's disease* may begin at any age, but is more common in older children and adults. There is demyelination of cerebral white matter to sudanophilic natural fat. Personality and behavioral changes often precede the neurological manifestations. Long-tract signs, such as spastic paraparesis and tetraparesis, are usually the first neurological symptoms, followed by cortical blindness and deafness, convulsions, and dementia. Some cases are reported as responding to steroids, but caution is indicated in the evaluation of those reports. The disease is chemically identical to, but clinically different from, multiple sclerosis.

**30.9.   The answer is C** (*Synopsis*, ed. 4, page 718).

The frequency of patients with Down's syndrome in institutions for the mentally retarded today approximates *10 percent.*

**30.10.   The answer is E (all)** (*Synopsis*, ed. 4, page 709).

There are two approaches to understanding mental retardation. The first is the clinical perspective, which approaches the disorder in a scientific manner, using I.Q. tests and biological markers. The second approach is from the social systems perspective, which views intelligence as relative to the person's cultural setting. Both views have validity and need to be considered in evaluating the individual patient. They are outlined more thoroughly in the table below.

**30.11.   The answer is D (4)** (*Synopsis*, ed. 4, page 718).

*Trisomy 21, resulting from meiotic nondisjunction,* not only produces the majority of cases of Down's syndrome—almost 85 percent—but also has been most closely linked to advancing maternal age. Paternal age has also been implicated as a factor in some studies.

*Translocation events,* by contrast, constitute only 5 percent of Down's cases. Furthermore, in many cases where an asymptomatic parent carries the aberrant chromosome in the genotype, the incidence of Down's is obviously unrelated to parental age. If the translocation, for example, occurs between chromosomes 14 and 21 (14/21), the proband carries 46 chromosomes, including two normal 21's, one normal 14, and the 14/21 translocation, which carries parts of both chromosomes. Any asymptomatic parent or sibling who is a carrier of the translocation will have only 45 chromosomes—missing one chromosome 21 and thus being spared the excessive genetic complement.

*Mitotic nondisjunction*—1 percent of all cases—occurs after fertilization of a presumably healthy ovum and may thus be considered independent of maternal age.

*Partial trisomy* may refer to the mosaicism—some cells normal, others with trisomy 21—seen in mitotic nondisjunction or to the excessive complement of chromosome 21 produced by translocation. Neither case is as closely tied to maternal age as is meiotic nondisjunction.

**30.12.   The answer is A (1, 2, 3)** (*Synopsis*, ed. 4, page 715).

Tay-Sachs disease, *occurring chiefly among Jewish infants* of Eastern European descent, *begins at 4 to 8 months of age* and has the earliest onset of the four types of *cerebromacular degenerations.* These are a group of disturbances in which there is progressive mental deterioration and loss of visual function. They are all transmitted by an autosomal recessive gene.

The other three types of cerebromacular degeneration are found in all races and include Jansky-Bielschowsky type, early juvenile or late infantile form with onset at 2 to 4 years; Spielmeyer-Stock-Vogt-Koyanagi disease, juvenile form with onset in early school years; and Kufs' disease, late juvenile form with onset after 15 years. All these variants of cerebromacular degeneration are progressive, and *there is no treatment available to date.*

**Two Views of Mental Retardation**

| Clinical Perspective | Social Systems Perspective |
| --- | --- |
| Intelligence is an entity that exists independent of cultural setting | Intelligence is relative to the requirements of the particular social system |
| If one is retarded according to standard statistical or medical tools, then one is indeed retarded | One can be retarded for some systems (such as school) and normal for others (such as family life) |
| A clinician can detect abnormalities not apparent to laymen. These unseen abnormalities can be proof of retardation. | Retardation cannot be undetected, because a person is retarded only by virtue of being labeled as such in a particular setting |
| The real number of retarded people in an area can be scientifically determined without considering the area's social structure | The number of people labeled retarded in an area is determined by the social structure of that area (What is expected of persons? How much, or how well, is difference tolerated?) |

**30.13.  The answer is C (2, 4)** (*Synopsis,* ed. 4, pages 718 and 719).

Amniocentesis, a procedure in which a small amount of amniotic fluid is removed from the amniotic cavity *transabdominally* between the *14th and 16th week of gestation,* has been of use in *diagnosing various infant abnormalities, especially Down's syndrome.* Amniotic fluid cells, mostly fetal in origin, are cultured for cytogenetic and biochemical studies. Many serious hereditary disorders can be predicted with this method, and then positive therapeutic abortion is the only method of prevention. Amniocentesis is recommended for *all pregnant women over the age of 35.* Fortunately, most chromosomal anomalies occur only once in a family.

The figure below illustrates the procedure.

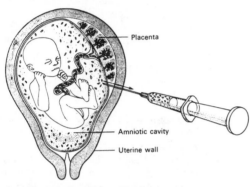

Amniocentesis. (From Moment G B, Haberman H M: *Biology: A Full Spectrum.* Williams & Wilkins, Baltimore, 1973.)

**30.14.  The answer is A (1, 2, 3)** (*Synopsis,* ed. 4, page 723).

This viral disease has replaced syphilis as *the major cause of congenital malformations and mental retardation due to maternal infection. The children of affected mothers may present a number of abnormalities,* including congenital heart disease, mental retardation, cataracts, deafness, microcephaly, and microphthalmia. Timing is crucial, because *the extent and the frequency of the complications are in inverse proportion to the duration of pregnancy at the time of maternal infection. When mothers are infected in the first trimester of pregnancy, 10 to 15 percent of the children will be affected, and the incidence rises to almost 50 percent when the infection occurs in the first month of pregnancy.* The situation is often complicated by subclinical forms of maternal infection, which often go undetected.

Syphilis is a venereal disease caused by an anaerobic spirochete bacteria, *Treponema pallidum,* and can lead to organic psychosis if left untreated. A congenital condition is one that is present at birth, including hereditary conditions and those resulting from prenatal development or the process of birth itself. A cataract is a condition in which the lens develops an opacity, usually grayish-white in color. In microcephaly, the head is unusually small as a result of defective brain development and premature ossification of the skull. Microphthalmia (microphthalmos) is a congenital condition associated with aberrant embryonic development of the eye, usually manifesting itself unilaterally. The malformation results in underdevelopment of the face and orbit of the affected side, and it produces an undersized eye.

**30.15.  The answer is A (1, 2, 3)** (*Synopsis,* ed. 4, page 723).

Brain damage due to *toxoplasmosis* and *cytomegalic inclusion body disease* transmitted from the pregnant mother to the fetus is another universally recognized but relatively rare complication of pregnancy that often results in mental retardation and a variety of brain malformations. Damage to the fetus from maternal *hepatitis* has also been reported.

The role of the other maternal infections during pregnancy, such as influenza, cold viruses, pneumonia, and urinary tract infections, in the causation of mental retardation is at present under extensive investigation. The results are still inconclusive. *Breast cancer* in the mother is not related to mental retardation in the child.

*Toxoplasmosis* results from the presence in various tissues of *Toxoplasma gordii,* usually acquired from the feces of cats, undercooked meat, and aerosol or mucus contamination. Except in immunologically depressed persons and in fetuses, most infections exhibit mild symptomatology.

*Cytomegalic inclusion body disease* results from viral infection—cytomegalovirus, a member of the herpetovirus family—which causes enlargement of the cells of certain organs, as well as the development of inclusion bodies in the nucleus and cytoplasm. It is noted in about one in every 200 live births and is thought to cause mental retardation in 10 percent of all cases.

*Hepatitis* is a viral disease affecting the liver. Commonly resulting from blood transfusions contaminated with the virus, it occurs in drug addicts who use contaminated needles.

**30.16.  The answer is E (all)** (*Synopsis,* ed. 4, pages 720 and 721).

The main features of Neurofibromatosis (Recklinghausen's disease) are small brown patches distributed over the entire body along the course of the subcutaneous nerves, autonomic nerves, and nerve trunks. Sensory nerves are usually more affected than other nerves. Astrocytomas, ependymomas, and *meningiomas* may be found in the brain. The skin manifestations usually begin in childhood and may include *large skin polyps* and *café au lait spots* over the trunk and the extremities. Acoustic or optic nerve glioma may also occur. Bilateral acoustic neurinomas are almost diagnostic of the disease. In addition to the skin manifestations, *epilepsy* and, in about 10 percent of cases, mental retardation are also seen. Anticonvulsant medication and neurosurgery may sometimes be effective because of the benign nature of the tumors.

*Epilepsy* is a neurological disorder resulting from a sudden, excessive, disorderly discharge of neurons in either a structurally normal or a diseased cerebral cortex. It is characterized by the paroxysmal recurrence of short-lived disturbances of consciousness, involuntary convulsive muscle movements, psychic or sensory disturbances, or some combination thereof. It is termed idiopathic epilepsy when there is no identifiable organic cause.

*Polyps* consist of tissue masses, which grow upward from a broad base or slender stalk and may arise from a variety of causes, such as neoplasms, inflammations, or a degenerative lesion. *Café au lait* spots are coffee-colored superficial pigmented discolorations of the skin scattered around the body and found particularly on the throat. *Meningiomas* are benign, encapsulated neoplasms of arachnoidal origin that occur in adults.

**30.17. The answer is E (all)** (*Synopsis*, ed. 4, page 718).

Since the classical description of mongolism by the English physician Langdon Down in 1866, this syndrome has remained the most discussed, most investigated, and most controversial in the field of mental retardation. Its cause still remains obscure, despite a plethora of theories and hypotheses advanced with variable acclaim in the past 100 years. There is agreement on very few predisposing factors in chromosomal disorders—among them, *the increased age of the mother* and possibly the increased age of the father, and X-ray radiation. The problem of cause is complicated even further by the recent recognition of three distinct types of chromosomal aberrations in Down's syndrome:

1. Patients with *trisomy 21—three of chromosome 21, instead of the usual two*—represent the overwhelming majority of mongoloid patients; they have 47 chromosomes, with an extra chromosome 21. The karyotypes of the mothers are normal. A nondisjunction during miosis, occurring for yet unknown reasons, is held responsible for the disorder.

2. Nondisjunction occurring after fertilization in any cell division results in mosaicism, a condition in which both normal and trisomic cells are found in various tissues.

3. In *translocation*, there is a fusion of two chromosomes, mostly 21 and 15, resulting in a total of 46 chromosomes, despite the presence of an extra chromosome 21. The disorder, unlike trisomy 21, is usually inherited, and the translocation chromosome may be found in unaffected parents and siblings. These *asymptomatic* carriers have only 45 chromosomes.

The figure on page 408 illustrates the clinical features associated with Down's syndrome.

**30.18. The answer is A (1, 2, 3)** (*Synopsis*, ed. 4, pages 719 and 720).

The diagnosis of Down's syndrome is made with relative ease in an older child, but is often difficult in newborn infants. The most important signs in a newborn include general hypotonia, *oblique palpebral fissures*, abundant neck skin, a small flattened skull, high cheek bones, and a *protruding tongue*. The hands are broad and thick, with a single *palmar transversal crease*, and the little fingers are short and curved inward. Moro reflex is weak or absent.

*Cat-cry syndrome* (*cri-du-chat*) consists of a missing part of the fifth chromosome whereas Down's syndrome usually involves a trisomy of chromosome 21.

**30.19. The answer is C (2, 4)** (*Synopsis*, ed. 4, pages 711 and 714).

Early diagnosis is of extreme importance in the treatment of phenylketonuria (PKU) because *a low phenylalanine diet*, in use since 1955, results in significant improvement in both behavior and developmental progress. *The best results seem to be obtained with early diagnosis and the start of the dietary treatment before the child is 6 months of age.*

Dietary treatment is not without dangers. Phenylalanine is an essential amino acid, and its complete omission from the diet may lead to such severe complications as anemia, hypoglycemia, edema, and even death. *Dietary treatment of PKU can often be discontinued at the age of 5 or 6 years*, although no alternate metabolic pathway capable of keeping the blood phenylalanine levels in the normal range has been discovered as yet.

In untreated older children and adolescents with PKU, a low phenylalanine diet does not influence the level of mental retardation. These children, however, do show a decrease in irritability and *a decrease in abnormal EEG changes*, and their social responsiveness and attention span increase.

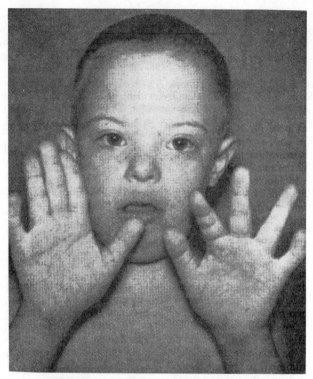

Child with Down's syndrome (mongolism).
Note the facial features, the single palmar
crease, and the short and incurvated little
fingers. (Courtesy of Beale H Ong, MD,
Children's Hospital, Washington, DC)

**30.20.  The answer is E (all)** (*Synopsis*, ed.
4, page 716).

Cretinism is a condition associated with mental retardation that has been known since antiquity. Up to the middle of the 19th century, all forms of mental retardation were considered as variants of cretinism.

The classical endemic variety occurs in certain regions as a result of *iodine deficiency in the diet*. Endemic goitrous cretinism is treated and prevented by the ingestion of small amounts of iodine.

The clinical signs in all varieties include *hypothyroidism*, goiter, dwarfism, coarse skin, disturbances in ossification, hypertelorism, and a large tongue. Mental retardation becomes a part of the clinical picture if the disease is unrecognized and untreated in infancy. This fact is explained by the essential role that thyroxin plays in the formation of structural proteins and lipids in the central nervous system during early infancy. Children with the disorder are sluggish, their voices are hoarse, and speech does not develop. Among the laboratory findings are a low basal metabolism rate, *depressed protein-bound iodine*, and a *high cholesterol level*. The radioactive iodine uptake is low, except in the inherited varieties. In these familial disorders, the serum thyroid-stimulating hormone is often abnormal.

Treatment with thyroid extract may avert most of the symptoms if instituted early in life, but it is not effective in adult cretins.

**30.21.  The answer is E (all)** (*Synopsis*, ed.
4, pages 716 and 717).

Wilson's disease (hepatolenticular degeneration) is a *disorder of copper metabolism* that has a recessive mode of inheritance. The two variants of the disease, the juvenile and the adult forms, are inherited independently as separate entities.

The biochemical changes are similar in both forms and consist of a diminished blood level of copper-containing ceruloplasmin. The low blood level is accompanied by excessive copper deposits in various tissues, chiefly in the liver and the brain. The resulting liver cirrhosis and degeneration of the lenticular nucleus gave the disease its name. Other laboratory findings include an elevated copper excretion in the urine and aminoaciduria involving primarily the aromatic amino acids—phenylalanine, tyrosine, and threonine. The aminoaciduria is explained on the basis of kidney damage due to copper deposits or blamed on a defect in a copper-containing enzyme, tyrosinase.

Heterozygous carriers are asymptomatic, but often manifest abnormal levels of ceruloplasmin in the blood and a tendency to various hepatic difficulties. A copper-loading test is available for the detection of heterozygous carriers.

*Personality changes may precede other clinical manifestations*, which include cirrhosis of the liver, progressive emotional and mental deterioration, pseudobulbar palsy, fatuous facial expression, spasticity, and *a greenish-brown ring in the iris* (Kayser-Fleisher ring). In some cases, there are only manifestations of liver involvement, without neurological symptoms.

The juvenile form begins between the ages of 7 and 15. Inattentiveness in school and dystonia, often with bizarre wing-flapping movements, are usually the first signs. This form is usually unresponsive to treatment, because the dystonia is related not to copper deposits but to hepatic dysfunction, which causes damage to the basal ganglia of the brain. The nature of the relationship between the hepatic disorder and the brain damage, found also in other liver diseases, is unknown.

The adult form usually begins with tremors and dysarthria, but may begin with psychiatric symptoms. It has a good prognosis. Several treatment methods are available, all aimed at lowering the serum copper level and increasing the urinary copper excretion. *Penicillamine, a copper-chelating amino acid derived from penicillin, is presently the most effective therapeutic agent.* Penicillin-sensitive patients may require the concomitant administration of steroids. Dimercaprol is also used with fair results. The administration of L-dopa may improve the rigidity and akinesis.

**30.22. The answer is A (1, 2, 3)** (*Synopsis*, ed. 4, page 711).

Phenylketonuria (PKU) has become known as the paradigmatic inborn error of metabolism associated with mental retardation.

*PKU is transmitted as a simple recessive autosomal Mendelian trait.* Its frequency in the United States and various parts of Europe ranges from 1 in 10,000 to 1 in 20,000. Although *the disease is reported predominantly in people of North European origin*, sporadic cases have been described in blacks, Yemenite Jews, and members of Mongolian races. The frequency among institutionalized defectives is about 1 percent.

The basic metabolic defect in PKU is an *inability to convert phenylalanine, an essential amino acid, to tyrosine*, because of the absence or inactivity of the liver enzyme phenylalanine hydroxylase, which catalyzes the conversion.

The majority of patients with PKU are severely retarded, but some patients are reported to have borderline or normal intelligence. *Eczema and convulsions are present in about one-third of all cases.* Although the clinical picture varies, typical PKU children are hyperactive and exhibit erratic, unpredictable behavior that makes them difficult to manage. They have frequent temper tantrums and often display bizarre movements of their bodies and upper extremities, as well as twisting hand mannerisms, and their behavior sometimes resembles that of autistic or schizophrenic children. Verbal and nonverbal communication is usually severely impaired or nonexistent. Coordination is poor, and there are many perceptual difficulties.

**30.23. The answer is B (1, 3)** (*Synopsis*, ed. 4, page 714).

Maple syrup urine disease (Menkes' disease) is an inborn error of metabolism, *transmitted by a rare single autosomal recessive gene.* The biochemical defect interferes with the decarboxylation of the branched chain amino acids—leucine, isoleucine, and valine. As a result, these amino acids and their respective keto acids accumulate in the blood and cause overflow aminoaciduria. The urine has a characteristic odor, which gives the condition its name, and which is due to the derivatives of the keto acids.

The diagnosis can be suspected by the use of ferric chloride or dinitrophenylhydrazine, each of which interacts with the urine to give, respectively, a navy blue color or a yellow precipitate.

The clinical symptoms *appear during the first week of life*. The infant deteriorates rapidly and develops decerebrate rigidity, seizures, respiratory irregularity, and hypoglycemia. If untreated, most patients die in the first months of life, and the survivors are severely retarded. Some variants have been reported, with transient ataxia and only mild retardation.

Treatment follows the general principles established for PKU, and *consists of a diet very low in the three involved amino acids*. With timely treatment, the prognosis is good.

**30.24. The answer is C (2, 4)** (*Synopsis*, ed. 4, page 714).

Hartnup disease is a rare disorder that took its name from the family in which it was detected. *It is transmitted by a single recessive autosomal gene.* The symptoms are intermittent and variable and tend to improve with age. They include a photosensitive pellagra-like rash on extension surfaces, episodic cerebellar ataxia, and mental deficiency. Of particular importance to psychiatrists is the fact that *transient personality changes and psychoses* may be the only manifestations of the disease, and *mild cases do not come to medical attention until late childhood or adolescence.*

The metabolic defect involves *defective tryptophan transport.*

**30.25.   The answer is E (all)** (*Synopsis*, ed. 4, pages 717 and 718).

Hurler's syndrome is a disorder *transmitted by an autosomal recessive trait.* The basic disturbance consists of the accumulation of dermatan sulfate and heparitin sulfate in the urine and tissues, increased levels of gangliosides in the brain, and decreased activity of $\beta$-galactosidase.

The lymphocytes contain metachromatic inclusions, and X-rays show several characteristic abnormalities, such as elongation of the sella turcica, beaking of the thoracic spine on the lateral view (kyphosis), club-shaped lower ribs, thickening of the long bones, misshapen metacarpal bones and phalanges, and skull malformations.

The clinical course is slow and progressive, and usually starts at a very early age, *leading to death before adolescence.* The hepatosplenomegaly causes abdominal enlargement. The *stature is dwarfed*, and the face acquires a peculiar appearance that gave rise to the name of gargoylism. The facial characteristics include bushy confluent eyebrows, thick lips, large tongue, and coarse features. Spade-like hands and sometimes hypertelorism and hydrocephalus complete the picture. There is nearly always a progressive mental deterioration, which often precedes the characteristic facial appearance. No treatment is available.

The differential diagnosis may present some problems. *The superficial resemblance to cretins is easily ruled out by X-ray findings* and by the hepatosplenomegaly, as well as by biochemical findings.

**30.26–30.30.   The answers are 30.26–D, 30.27–A, 30.28–B, 30.29–E, and 30.30– C** (*Synopsis*, ed. 4, page 714).

Hyperglycinemia, a nonketotic hyperglycinemia, is an autosomal recessive inborn error of metabolism in which large amounts of glycine are found in body fluids. The clinical picture includes severe mental retardation, seizures, spasticity, and failure to thrive. Ketotic hyperglycinemia is characterized by *severe ketosis.* The hyperglycinemia is secondary to blood elevation of several amino acids. The clinical picture includes seizures, mental retardation, vomiting, dehydration, ketosis, and coma.

Histidinemia, which is characterized by a defect in the histidine metabolism, is transmitted by a single autosomal recessive gene and involves a block in the conversion of histidine to

urocanic acid. The urine gives a *positive ferric chloride test* (green). Mild mental retardation and sometimes speech defects are part of the clinical picture.

Homocystinuria is a disorder that comprises a group of inborn errors of metabolism, each of which may lead to the accumulation of homocysteine. The patients are mentally retarded and *resemble those with Marfan's syndrome* in outward appearance.

Lowe's oculorenal dystrophy, a sex-linked disorder, presents a varied clinical picture that includes some of the following eye defects: buphthalmos, microphthalmos, *cataracts*, and corneal opacities. Renal ammonia production is decreased, and a generalized aminoaciduria is found.

Cystathioninuria is marked by a metabolic defect that consists of a block at the site of cleavage of cystathionine to cysteine and homoserine. Patients with the disease are mentally retarded. Prolonged *administration of pyridoxine* may improve intellectual performance.

The figure that follows illustrates a child with Lowe's oculorenal dystrophy.

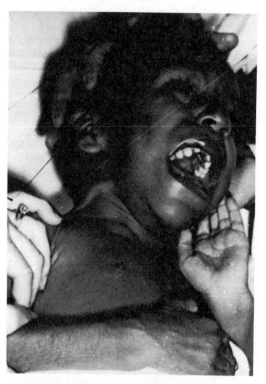

**Lowe's oculorenal dystrophy. (Courtesy of Michael Malone, MD, Children's Hospital, Washington, DC)**

# References

Crocker A C: Current strategies in prevention of mental retardation. Pediatr Ann *11:* 450, 1982.

Crocker A C, Nelson R P: Mental retardation. In *Developmental-Behavioral Pediatrics*, M D Levine, M D Levine, W B Carey, A C Crocker, R T Gross, editors, p 756. W B Saunders, Philadelphia, 1983.

Featherstone H: *A Difference in the Family Life with a Disabled Child*. Basic Books, New York, 1980.

Forness S R: Serving children with emotional or behavioral disorders. Am J Orthopsychiatry *54:* 22, 1984.

President's Committee on Mental Retardation. *Mental Retardation: The Leading Edge Service Programs That Work*. MR78, Government Printing Office, Washington, DC, 1979.

Pueschel S M, Rynders J E, editors: *Down's Syndrome: Advances in Biomedicine and Behavioral Sciences*, Ware Press, Cambridge, 1982.

Reiss S, Benson B A: Awareness of negative social conditions among mentally retarded, emotionally disturbed outpatients. Am J Psychiatry *141:* 88, 1984.

Syzmanski L S, Crocker A C: Mental retardation. In *Comprehensive Textbook of Psychiatry*, ed 4, H I Kaplan, B J Sadock, editors, p 1635. Williams & Wilkins, Baltimore, 1985.

# 31

# Pervasive Developmental Disorders of Childhood

The pervasive developmental disorders of childhood appear for the first time in the third edition of the *Diagnostic and Statistical Manual of Mental Disorders* (DSM-III), the official nomenclature of the American Psychiatric Association. These disorders are characterized by distortions, deviations, and delays in the development of social, language, and motor behaviors and of attention, perception, and reality testing.

DSM-III distinguishes among five diagnostic possibilities in this subclass: (1) infantile autism, full syndrome present; (2) infantile autism, residual state; (3) childhood onset pervasive developmental disorder, full syndrome present; (4) childhood onset pervasive developmental disorder, residual state; and (5) atypical pervasive developmental disorder.

There is controversy about the role of schizophrenia in childhood, with some workers believing that a small subgroup of autistic children may be early-onset schizophrenics who have not yet reached developmental stages where the symptomatology necessary for the diagnosis of schizophrenic disorder can be expressed. A few cases have been reported of children who, at a young age, fulfilled the criteria for infantile autism and, when older, fit diagnostic criteria for schizophrenia, with the possible exception of lack of deterioration from a previous level of functioning.

The reader is referred to Chapter 31 of *Modern Synopsis-IV*, which covers these disorders, and should then study the questions and answers below to assess his or her knowledge of the subject.

# Questions

**DIRECTIONS:** Each of the statements or questions below is followed by five suggested responses or completions. Select the *one* that is *best* in each case.

**31.1.** Atypical pervasive developmental disorder is the same as
A. childhood onset of schizophrenic disorder
B. mental retardation with behavioral symptoms
C. developmental reading disorder
D. disintegrative psychosis
E. none of the above

**31.2.** The phrase "obsessive insistence on sameness" has been used to describe children with
A. compulsive disorder
B. infantile autism
C. childhood schizophrenia
D. organic mental syndrome
E. seizure disorder

**31.3.** The drug used to treat the marked apathy and hypoactivity of the psychotic child is

A. diazepam
B. phenytoin
C. trifluoperazine
D. barbiturate
E. imipramine

**DIRECTIONS:** For each of the incomplete statements below, *one* or *more* of the completions given is correct. Choose answer:

A. if only **1**, **2**, and **3** are correct
B. if only **1** and **3** are correct
C. if only **2** and **4** are correct
D. if only **4** is correct
E. if all are correct

**31.4.** Pervasive developmental disorders are
1. more common in girls than in boys
2. marked by hallucinations and delusions
3. associated with a characteristic formal thought disorder
4. fully developed before the age of 12

**31.5.** Which of the following statements apply to infantile autism:
1. Up to 80 percent of autistic patients show electroencephalogram (EEG) abnormalities specific to infantile autism.
2. A significant number of autistics will develop grand mal seizures at some point in their lives.
3. Computed tomography scans are normal in autistics.
4. Approximately 2 percent of siblings of autistics are afflicted by autism.

**31.6.** Treatment of infantile autism involves
1. parental training
2. the use of fenfluramine
3. classroom training
4. the use of haloperidol

**31.7.** Childhood onset pervasive developmental disorder is characterized by
1. excessive clinging
2. lack of empathy
3. inappropriate emotional interactions
4. meager or primitive conscience

**31.8.** Epidemiological investigators of the infantile psychoses have noted
1. a high proportion of parents from lower social classes
2. an excess of boys over girls
3. an occurrence in 25 children per 10,000
4. increased case finding among the lower social classes

**DIRECTIONS:** Each set of lettered headings below is followed by a list of numbered words or phrases. For each numbered word or phrase, select

A. if the item is associated with **A** only
B. if the item is associated with **B** only
C. if the item is associated with *both* **A** *and* **B**
D. if the item is associated with *neither* **A** *nor* **B**

**Questions 31.9–31.13**
A. Infantile autism
B. Childhood onset pervasive developmental
   disorder
C. Both
D. Neither

**31.9.** Onset after 30 months of age

**31.10.** Onset after 12 years of age

**31.11.** Absence of delusions and hallucinations

**31.12.** Pervasive lack of responsiveness to other people

**31.13.** Gross deficits in language development

**Questions 31.14–31.18**
A. Schizophrenic disorder with onset before
   puberty
B. Infantile autism
C. Both
D. Neither

**31.14.** Age of onset not under 5 years of age

**31.15.** Family history of schizophrenia

**31.16.** Majority of cases have severely impaired intelligence

**31.17.** Male/female ratio is nearly equal

**31.18.** Incidence is rare

# Answers

# Pervasive Developmental Disorders of Childhood

**31.1. The answer is E** (*Synopsis*, ed. 4, page 736).

Atypical pervasive developmental disorder is defined as a separate diagnostic entity in order to diagnose childhood disorders that contain features similar to, but not identical with, infantile autism or childhood onset pervasive developmental disorder.

*Childhood onset of schizophrenic disorder* is the childhood version of adult onset schizophrenia, with onset generally occurring before puberty but after 5 years of age.

*Mental retardation with behavioral symptoms* differs from infantile autism and pervasive developmental disorder mainly in that mentally retarded children usually relate to adults and other children in accord with their mental age and use the limited language they have to communicate with others. According to DSM-III, the I.Q. of such children must be under 70 in order to make the diagnosis.

*Developmental reading disorder* is also known as "dyslexia," and has as its essential feature an impairment in reading skills, with associated difficulties in spelling and writing.

*Disintegrative psychoses* have also been termed symbiotic psychoses, a term introduced by Margaret Mahler. The child's development in these disorders is usually within normal limits until the onset of illness, usually between the ages of 3 to 5, when severe regression and decline in intelligence and all areas of behavior occur and are accompanied by stereotypes and mannerisms.

The following table gives the DSM-III definition of atypical pervasive developmental disorder.

### Atypical Pervasive Developmental Disorder*

This category should be used for children with distortions in the development of multiple basic psychological functions that are involved in the development of social skills and language and that cannot be classified as either infantile autism or childhood onset pervasive developmental disorder.

* From American Psychiatric Association: *Diagnostic and Statistical Manual of Mental Disorders*, ed 3. American Psychiatric Association, Washington, DC, 1980. Used with permission.

**31.2. The answer is B** (*Synopsis*, ed. 4, pages 732 and 734).

The phrase "obsessive insistence on sameness" has been used to refer to many varieties of fixed, stereotyped, perseverative behavior, particularly as seen in *autism*. Certain subjects are often pursued obsessively. Remarkable rote memory of poems and stories can be observed. Typically, there is fascination for objects in motion—for example, spinning toys—and intense, concentrated attention to music may also be seen.

Such resistance to unfamiliarity and change is a key problem in the rearing and comprehensive treatment of autistic children because the children tend to resist all changes.

**31.3. The answer is C** (*Synopsis*, ed. 4, page 739).

The major tranquilizers have been used to influence specific behaviors of psychotic children—for example, chlorpromazine for reducing hyperactivity, and *trifluoperazine* for overcoming marked apathy and hypoactivity. Both drugs are neuroleptics in the phenothiazine class.

The antidepressants, such as *imipramine*, and the antianxiety agents, such as *diazepam*, are not used in these disorders. *Phenytoin* and *barbiturates* play a role in the treatment of epilepsy in both children and adults.

**31.4. The answer is D (4)** (*Synopsis*, ed. 4, pages 737, 738, and 739).

As defined in DSM-III, the essential features of pervasive developmental disorders refer to an extreme and pervasive disturbance in human relations and to a wide range of bizarre behaviors, all becoming the full syndrome in children between *30 months of age and age 12*.

Associated with these essential features are many bizarre beliefs and fantasies without insight on the part of the child, as well as strange inner obsessions. There are also abnormal and fixed preoccupations with objects and with their use.

For diagnosis, the criteria include a gross and unchanging impairment in relationships, manifestations of bizarre behavior, and onset of the full syndrome after the child reaches 30 months of age. *A formal thought disorder, delusions, and hallucinations are absent.*

The syndrome is very rare and is *more common in boys than in girls.*

At the present time, childhood onset pervasive developmental disorders need to be differentiated from schizophrenia beginning in childhood, as well as from infantile autism. Schizophrenia is likely to be characterized by delusions, hallucinations, formal thought disorders, and incoherence. The childhood onset disorder may be differentiated from infantile autism by its later age of recognition and onset and by the absence of the full syndrome of infantile autism.

A *hallucination* is a false sensory perception occurring in the absence of any relevant external stimulation of the sensory modality involved. A *delusion* is a false belief that is firmly held, despite objective and obvious contradictory proof or evidence and despite the fact that other members of the culture do not share the belief. Neither hallucinations nor delusions are present in these disorders.

**31.5.   The answer is C (2, 4)** (*Synopsis*, ed. 4, page 733).

Most reports indicate that at least 10 percent and *up to 83 percent of autistic patients show electroencephalogram (EEG) abnormalities. There is no EEG finding specific to infantile autism;* however, there is suggestion that some abnormalities are indicative of failure of cerebral lateralization.

From *4 to 32 percent of autistic children will develop grand mal seizures* at some point in their lives. In addition, *about 20 to 25 percent of autistics show ventricular enlargement on computed tomography scans.*

All reports agree that *approximately 2 percent of siblings of autistics are afflicted by infantile autism,* a rate 50 times greater than in the general population. Concordance of infantile autism in monozygotic twins is significantly greater than in dizygotic twins. Clinical reports and studies suggest that nonautistic members of families of autistics share various language or other cognitive problems with the autistic individual, although of much lesser severity.

**31.6.   The answer is E (all)** (*Synopsis*, ed. 4, page 737).

The goals of treatment in autistic children are to decrease behavioral symptoms and to promote the development of delayed, rudimentary, or nonexistent functions, such as language and self-care skills. In addition, the parents, often distraught, need support and counseling. *Structured classroom training* in combination with intrusive behavioral methods is the most effective treatment method for many autistic children and is superior to other types of behavioral approaches. Well-controlled studies indicate that gains in the areas of language and cognition, as well as decreases in maladaptive behaviors, are achieved using this method. Careful *parental training,* individual tutoring of parents in the concepts and skills of behavior modification, and focusing on individual parent problems and concerns, within a problem-solving format, may yield considerable gains in the language, cognitive, and social areas of behavior; however, the training programs are rigorous, and a great deal of parental time is involved. The autistic child requires an all-day structure and a daily program for as many hours as feasible.

Pharmacotherapy, in addition to the educational/behavioral methods, seems to be a valuable adjunct to the comprehensive treatment programs for many autistic children.

Administration of the potent dopamine antagonist *haloperidol* yields both significant decreases in behavioral symptoms and significant acceleration in learning in the laboratory. The main improvements are as follows: decreases in hyperactivity, stereotypies, withdrawal, fidgetiness, abnormal object relations, irritability, and labile affect. There is supportive evidence that haloperidol, when given judiciously, remains an effective drug on a long-term basis. Under careful clinical monitoring, tardive and withdrawal dyskinesias are infrequent, and in prospective studies to date they always have been reversible.

*Fenfluramine,* a drug with antiserotonergic properties, has been reported to produce a marked decrease in behavioral symptoms and over-all improvement in this disorder, and it shows promise as an effective treatment.

**31.7.   The answer is E (all)** (*Synopsis*, ed. 4, page 738).

Pervasive developmental disorder is a disorder characterized by severe distortions in the development of social skills, language, and contact with reality. Many psychological functions are involved, and a child with a pervasive developmental disorder displays abnormalities that are not normal for any stage of development.

The disturbance in human relationships is profound and persistent. *Emotional interactions with others are inappropriate and inept.* There may be a marked absence of social response, or excessive and inappropriate *clinging* without the achievement of genuine caring or a relationship. *Manifestations of conscience are primitive and meager.* During the early school years and later, the disordered social behavior is expressed in an absence of friendships, difficulties in participating in a cooperative fashion in play with other children, a *pervasive lack of empathy,* and a striking insensibility with regard to the feelings of others.

**31.8.   The answer is C (2, 4)** (*Synopsis*, ed. 4, page 732).

Infantile autism is a syndrome that begins in infancy. It is characterized by withdrawal and self-absorption, failure to develop attachment to a parental figure, ineffective communication and mutism, preoccupation with inanimate objects, and an obsessive demand for sameness in the environment. It is also known as Kanner's syndrome. Infantile autism *occurs in 2 to 4 children per 10,000 children* (or 0.02 to 0.04 percent) under the age of 12 or 15. It begins before the child is 30 months of age, but may not be evident to the parents until later, depending on their acuity and the severity of the disease.

*Infantile autism is found more frequently in boys* in all samples studied. Over-all, a reasonable estimate would be that 3 to 5 times more boys than girls have autism.

Many studies report an overrepresentation of the upper classes, whereas some more recent reports have not found this to be the case. Over the past 20 years, *an increasing proportion of cases has been found in the lower social classes.* This may well be because of increased awareness of the syndrome, as well as increasing availability of child mental health workers for the lower classes.

**31.9–31.13. The answers are 31.9–B, 31.10–D, 31.11–C, 31.12–C, and 31.13– A** (*Synopsis*, ed. 4, page 733).

Childhood onset pervasive developmental disorder refers to an *extreme and pervasive disturbance* in human relations and to a wide range of bizarre behaviors, with an *onset in children between 30 months and age 12.* There may be abnormalities of speech and a monotonous voice, but there are *not the gross deficits or deviances in language development that are seen in infantile autism.* The syndrome is very rare and is more common in boys than in girls. The tables in column 2 list the DSM-III diagnostic criteria for this disorder and its residual state.

**31.14–31.18. The answers are 31.14–A, 31.15–A, 31.16–B, 31.17–A, and 31.18– C** (*Synopsis*, ed. 4, pages 732, 733, 734, and 735).

Infantile autism is defined as a pervasive lack of responsiveness to other people and gross deficits in language development, with an onset in children under 30 months of age. There has been confusion about whether infantile autism is the earliest possible manifestation of schizophrenia or whether it is a discrete clinical entity; but currently, the evidence weighs heavily in the direction of distinguishing infantile autism from schizophrenia. *Autism appears to be 3 to 4 times more common in males than in females, whereas the schizophrenic ratio is almost equal.* About 70 percent of autistic children have *I.Q.'s that are less than or equal to 70,* whereas only 15 percent

### Diagnostic Criteria for Childhood Onset Pervasive Developmental Disorder*

A. Gross and sustained impairment in social relationships, e.g. lack of appropriate affective responsivity, inappropriate clinging, asociality, lack of empathy

B. At least three of the following:

1. Sudden excessive anxiety manifested by such symptoms as free-floating anxiety, catastrophic reactions to everyday occurrences, inability to be consoled when upset, unexplained panic attacks;

2. Constricted or inappropriate affect, including lack of appropriate fear reactions, unexplained rage reactions, and extreme mood lability;

3. Resistance to change in the environment (e.g. upset if dinner time is changed), or insistence on doing things in the same manner every time (e.g. putting on clothes always in the same order);

4. Oddities of motor movement, such as peculiar posturing, peculiar hand or finger movements, or walking on tiptoe;

5. Abnormalities of speech, such as question-like melody, monotonous voice;

6. Hyper- or hypo-sensitivity to sensory stimuli, e.g. hyperacusis;

7. Self-multilation, e.g. biting or hitting self, head banging.

C. Onset of the full syndrome after 30 months of age and before 12 years of age

D. Absence of delusions, hallucinations, incoherence, or marked loosening of associations

---

* From American Psychiatric Association: *Diagnostic and Statistical Manual of Mental Disorders*, ed 3. American Psychiatric Association, Washington, DC, 1980. Used with permission.

### Diagnostic Criteria for Childhood Onset Pervasive Developmental Disorder, Residual State*

A. Once had an illness that met the criteria for childhood onset pervasive developmental disorder

B. The current clinical picture no longer meets the full criteria for the disorder, but signs of the illness have persisted to the present, such as oddities of communication and social awkwardness

---

* From American Psychiatric Association: *Diagnostic and Statistical Manual of Mental Disorders*, ed 3. American Psychiatric Association, Washington, DC, 1980. Used with permission.

of schizophrenic children have I.Q.'s that are less than or equal to 70. Schizophrenic children experience the classic adult schizophrenic symptoms of hallucinations, delusions, and thought disorder, but with onset before puberty *and not under 5 years of age.* Autistic children have an absence of hallucinations, delusions, or loosening of association. *There is no apparent increase in the incidence of schizophrenia in the families of autistic children, whereas there is an increased evidence in the families of childhood schizophren-*ics. Infantile autism occurs in *2 to 4 children per every 10,000 (or in 0.02 to 0.04 percent); the occurrence of childhood schizophrenia* is unknown, due to the paucity of data, but *is possibly even more rare* than infantile autism.

The tables on this page list the DSM-III diagnostic criteria for infantile autism and its residual state. The DSM-III criteria for adult schizophrenia apply also to schizophrenia with an onset before puberty.

### Diagnostic Criteria for Infantile Autism*

A. Onset before 30 months of age

B. Pervasive lack of responsiveness to other people (autism)

C. Gross deficits in language development

D. If speech is present, peculiar speech patterns, such as immediate and delayed echolalia, metaphorical language, pronominal reversal

E. Bizarre responses to various aspects of the environment, e.g. resistance to change, peculiar interest in or attachments to animate or inanimate objects

F. Absence of delusions, hallucinations, loosening of associations, and incoherence as in schizophrenia

* From American Psychiatric Association: *Diagnostic and Statistical Manual of Mental Disorders*, ed 3. American Psychiatric Association, Washington, DC, 1980. Used with permission.

### Diagnostic Criteria for Infantile Autism, Residual State*

A. Once had an illness that met the criteria for infantile autism

B. The current clinical picture no longer meets the full criteria for infantile autism, but signs of the illness have persisted to the present, such as oddities of communication and social awkwardness

* From American Psychiatric Association: *Diagnostic and Statistical Manual of Mental Disorders*, ed 3. American Psychiatric Association, Washington, DC, 1980. Used with permission.

## References

Anderson L T, Campbell M, Grega D M, Perry R, Small A M, Green W H: Haloperidol and infantile autism: Effects on learning and behavioral symptoms. Am J Psychiatry *141:* 999, 1984.

Campbell M: Autistic and schizophrenic disorders. In *Psychopharmacology in Childhood and Adolescence*, ed 2, J M Wiener, editor, p 323. Basic Books, New York, 1985.

Campbell M, Minton J, Green W H, Jennings S J, Samit C: Siblings and twins of autistic children. In *Biological Psychiatry 1981*, C Perris, G Struwe, B Jansson, editors, p 993. Elsevier/North-Holland Biomedical Press, Amsterdam, 1981.

Campbell M, Rosenbloom S, Perry R, George A E, Kricheff I I, Anderson L, Small A M, Jennings S J: Computerized axial tomography in young autistic children. Am J Psychiatry *139:* 510, 1982.

Fish B, Ritvo E R: Psychoses of childhood. In *Basic Handbook of Child Psychiatry*, J D Noshpitz, editor-in-chief, vol 2, p 249. Basic Books, New York, 1979.

Green, W H, Campbell M, Hardesty A S, Grega D M, Padron-Gayol M, Shell J, Erlenmeyer-Kimling L: A comparison of schizophrenic and autistic children. J Am Acad Child Psychiatry *23:* 399, 1984.

Kanner L: Autistic disturbances of affective contact. Nervous Child *2:* 217, 1943, and reprinted in Kanner L: *Childhood Psychosis: Initial Studies and New Insights*, p 1. John Wiley & Sons, New York, 1973.

Rosenbloom S: High resolution CT scanning in infantile autism. J Am Acad Child Psychiatry *23:* 72, 1984.

Rutter M, Schopler E, editors: *Autism: A Reappraisal of Concepts and Treatment*. Plenum Press, New York, 1978.

Special Issue on Neurobiological Research in Autism. J Autism Dev Disord *12:* 2, 1982.

# 32

# Attention Deficit Disorders

A significant number of children and adolescents are brought to health and mental health professionals because of difficulties in the school and at home that relate to learning and behavior. The children may be unable to sit still or attend to tasks sitting still; many have problems with academic requirements. Although these children constitute as many as half the referrals to the nation's mental health clinics, the literature that deals with their difficulties is confusing, particularly in regard to terminology. The literature on children with learning disabilities often refers to the related clinical finding of distractibility or hyperactivity, whereas the literature on the distractible or hyperactive child often notes the related learning disabilities. It is never certain what the degree of overlap is nor what its significance may be. In clinical practice, it is common to see children with emotional problems that are the consequence, but not the cause, of academic difficulties.

For some time, the term "minimal brain dysfunction" was used to describe children in whom learning disabilities, hyperactivity, distractibility, and other signs of central nervous system (CNS) dysfunction occurred together. Such children often had emotional problems that were the result of the frustrations and failures they experienced in school and with peers and family; others had emotional problems that researchers thought may be another reflection of CNS dysfunction, e.g. some forms of conduct disorder or oppositional disorder.

The term "minimal brain dysfunction" is no longer in official use. The third edition of the *Diagnostic and Statistical Manual of Mental Disorders* (DSM-III) approach requires separate diagnoses for each aspect of the problem. One can classify a child or adolescent as having learning disabilities (specific developmental disorders) or as being distractible or hyperactive or both (attention deficit disorder). One can use a third diagnosis to clarify any related emotional disorder. It is important that the clinician keeps in mind the possibility that the child may have other related disorders, as well as attention deficit disorder.

The reader is referred to Chapter 32 of *Modern Synopsis-IV*, which covers attention deficit disorder. By studying the questions and answers, students can test their knowledge of this area.

# Questions

**DIRECTIONS:** Each of the statements or questions below is followed by five suggested responses or completions. Select the *one* that is *best* in each case.

**32.1**  The epidemiology of attention deficit disorder with hyperactivity (hyperkinetic syndrome) indicates that

A. it is most common in high socioeconomic groups
B. it affects more than 30 percent of school-age children
C. it is more common in boys than in girls
D. there is no correlation among family members
E. all of the above

**32.2.**  An 8-year-old boy is doing poorly in his schoolwork. He exhibits excessive motor activity, restlessness, and an inability to sit still. He disrupts other students and shows little frustration tolerance when studying. He is easily distracted. On the basis of these observations, a physician may recommend a trial treatment with which one of the following drugs:

A. Phenytoin
B. Haloperidol
C. Chlorpromazine
D. Diazepam
E. Methylphenidate

**32.3.**  The most frequently found characteristic among children with an attention deficit disorder with hyperactivity is

A. emotional lability
B. disorders of memory and thinking
C. disorders of speech and hearing
D. hyperactivity
E. short attention span

**32.4.**  The most likely outcome of the hyperactive syndrome is

A. that remission is unlikely before the age of 12
B. remission of overactivity before distractibility
C. a decreasing need for medication as the child grows older
D. a tendency toward eventual sociopathic behavior
E. all of the above

**DIRECTIONS:** For each of the incomplete statements below, *one* or *more* of the completions given is correct. Choose answer:

A. if only **1, 2,** and **3** are correct
B. if only **1** and **3** are correct
C. if only **2** and **4** are correct
D. if only **4** is correct
E. if all are correct

**32.5.**  Infants afflicted with an attention deficit disorder with hyperactivity

1. have a delayed development schedule
2. are unduly sensitive to stimuli
3. may sleep excessively
4. cry past the traditional first 3 months of colic

**32.6.**  Attention deficit disorder, residual type,

1. is seen in patients under the age of 18
2. has signs of hyperactivity still present
3. has signs of the illness persisting to the present, but with periods of remission
4. is a disorder in which attentional deficits and impulsivity are present

**32.7.**  Essential characteristics of attention deficit disorder without hyperactivity include
1. difficulty in sustaining attention
2. more marked difficulties in unstructured situations or in unsupervised performance
3. disorganized, impulsive aspects manifested by, for instance, poor frustration tolerance
4. absence of excessive gross motor activity

**32.8.**  In attention deficit disorder with hyperactivity,
1. signs of the disorder may be absent when the child is in a one-on-one situation
2. the peak age range for referral is between the ages of 8 and 10
3. the behavioral disturbances must be present for at least 6 months and appear before the age of 7 for the diagnosis to be made
4. the child is generally incapable of attending any stimulus for more than 10 seconds

**32.9.**  In attention deficit disorders, a neurological examination may show which of the following:
1. Visual impairment
2. Auditory impairment
3. Problems in copying age-appropriate figures
4. Increased ability to perform rapid alternating movements

**32.10.**  The hyperactive child is
1. impulsive and irritable
2. accident-prone
3. fascinated with spinning objects
4. unimpaired in left-right discrimination tests

# Answers

# Attention Deficit Disorders

**32.1. The answer is C** (*Synopsis*, ed. 4, page 741).

Clinical observation and epidemiological surveys of attention deficit disorder with hyperactivity *report a greater incidence in boys than in girls*, the ratio being 10:1. It is more common in first-born boys.

This disorder *has been observed in children of varying socioeconomic status* and countries. Reports on the incidence in this country have varied from *4 to 20 percent of school-age children*. A conservative figure, and one more likely to be accepted, is 3 percent of prepubertal elementary school children.

A *significant familial pattern* seems to be present, at least in a minority. There is a significant appearance in the parents of hyperkinetic children of sociopathy, alcoholism, and hysteria. A correspondence appears in the studies of parents of hyperkinetic children concerning the earlier presence of the hyperkinetic syndrome in the parents.

**32.2. The answer is E** (*Synopsis*, ed. 4, pages 744 and 745).

The child is suffering from an attention deficit disorder. His essential difficulty in concentration may be shown by not completing tasks, shifting rapidly and unpredictably from one activity to another, seeming to be inattentive or uncomprehending, making careless and impulsive errors in daily schoolwork or in tests, and misperforming work of which he is entirely capable. This may be the case even when he is motivated and desires to do well.

One of the most common methods of treatment calls for the use of medications, amphetamine or dextroamphetamine. The medication probably most used now is *methylphenidate*.

Many studies indicate that stimulants reliably reduce overactivity and distractibility, and often irritability, impulsiveness, and explosive irritability. There is no evidence, however, that the medications directly improve any existing impairments in learning.

The stimulants are expected to enable such children to deal with schoolwork more efficiently, not to provide them magically with what they had not previously learned, and certainly not to overcome the developmental learning disorders; tutoring is needed to provide what they

have not previously learned, and structured forms of education are needed to overcome developmental learning disorders. Medication alone may not improve academic performance, but it does provide the preconditions for it.

*Phenytoin* is an anticonvulsant most commonly used in the treatment of grand mal epilepsy. *Haloperidol* is a butyrophenone antipsychotic drug. *Chlorpromazine* is a phenothiazine derivative used primarily as an antipsychotic agent and in the treatment of nausea and vomiting. The drug was synthesized in 1950 and was used in psychiatry for the first time in 1952. At present, chlorpromazine is one of the most widely used drugs in medical practice. *Diazepam* is a skeletal muscle relaxant. It is most commonly used as an antianxiety agent.

**32.3. The answer is D** (*Synopsis*, ed. 4, page 743).

The characteristics most often found among children with an attention deficit disorder with hyperactivity are, in order of frequency, (1) *hyperactivity*; (2) perceptual motor impairment; (3) *emotional lability*; (4) general coordination deficit; (5) disorders of attention (*short attention span*, distractibility, perseveration, failure to finish things off, not listening, poor concentration); (6) impulsivity (action before thought, abrupt shifts in activity, poor organizing, jumping up in class); (7) *disorders of memory and thinking*; (8) specific learning disabilities; (9) *disorders of speech and hearing*; and (10) equivocal neurological signs and electroencephalographic irregularities.

*Emotional lability* refers to an excessive emotional responsiveness, characterized by unstable and rapidly changing emotions.

**32.4. The answer is E** (*Synopsis*, ed. 4, page 743).

The course of the hyperactive syndrome is highly variable: Symptoms persist into adolescence or adult life; the symptoms disappear at puberty; or the hyperactivity disappears, but attention and impulse problems persist.

Over-all, clinical experience suggests that the condition *is not likely to remit before the age of 12*; in many children, various components, or the total picture but not its complications or sequelae, are likely to have disappeared by 20 years of age. *The overactivity is usually the first symptom to remit, and distractibility is the last to remit.*

*Some children with the condition outgrow the need for medication,* achieve adequately in adolescence and adult life, have happy and satisfying interpersonal relationships, and show no significant sequelae. Unfortunately, this is not the most frequent outcome reported in the literature. Hyperactive children may have learning difficulties, *along with a tendency to develop antisocial behavior,* personality disorder, schizophrenia, or depression. These effects may persist into adult life, despite the general diminution and final disappearance of the motor hyperactivity in adolescence.

**32.5. The answer is E (all)** (*Synopsis,* ed. 4, page 742).

Attention deficit disorder is a DSM-III category for a childhood mental disorder characterized by developmentally inappropriate short attention span and poor concentration. Hyperactivity (hyperkinesis) may or may not be present. The category subsumes abnormal behavior patterns that had been referred to by a variety of names, including hyperkinetic syndrome, hyperactive child syndrome, and minimal brain dysfunction.

A newborn who is already afflicted with an attention deficit disorder *may be unduly sensitive to stimuli* and may respond in an undifferentiated, massive, aversive manner.

Frequently, the converse occurs, and the child is placid, limp, and floppy, *sleeping excessively* and *developing slowly during the initial months.* It is more common, however, for the infant to be active in the crib, have a rapid development schedule, sleep little, and *cry much past the traditional first 3 months of colic.* Such infants often climb out of the crib on their own very early, undissuaded by the parents' attempts to bar their exit. Once out of the crib and able to get about, they are apt to do so relentlessly, getting into everything and generally fingering, breaking, or disintegrating objects. As times goes on, their sphere of activity widens and rapidly encompasses the neighboring territory and street.

**32.6. The answer is D (4)** (*Synopsis,* ed. 4, pages 746 and 747).

In the residual type of attention deficit disorder, *the patients must be 18 years of age or older.* Their history indicates that the patient had an illness during childhood that met the criteria for attention deficit disorder (with or without hyperactivity). *Signs of the illness persist, with no period of remission,* as demonstrated by *signs of both impulsivity and attention deficit;* for example, difficulty in organizing and completing work, inability to concentrate, increased distractibility, and sudden decision making without thought of consequences. The inattention and impulsive behavior cause impairment in both occupational and social functioning. *Signs of hyperactivity are no longer present.* These patients are sometimes helped by amphetamine or methylphenidate.

The table below gives the DSM-III diagnostic criteria for this disorder.

**32.7. The answer is E (all)** (*Synopsis,* ed. 4, pages 746 and 747).

Attention deficit disorder without hyperactivity is found in children who display, for their age, an impairment in the ability to concentrate without associated increased gross motor activity.

Essentially, little is yet known concerning this syndrome as differentiated from attention deficit disorder with hyperactivity. It is thought to be common, but not generally diagnosed before the age of 4. It is more common in boys than in girls. A familial pattern is not yet known.

This disorder is more marked in group and

---

**Diagnostic Criteria for Attention Deficit Disorder, Residual Type***

A. The individual once met the criteria for attention deficit disorder with hyperactivity. This information may come from the individual or from others, such as family members.

B. Signs of hyperactivity are no longer present, but other signs of the illness have persisted to the present without periods of remission, as evidenced by signs of both attentional deficits and impulsivity, e.g. difficulty organizing work and completing tasks, difficulty concentrating, being easily distracted, making sudden decisions without thought of the consequences

C. The symptoms of inattention and impulsivity result in some impairment in social or occupational functioning.

D. Not due to schizophrenia, affective disorder, severe or profound mental retardation, or schizotypal or borderline personality disorders.

---

*From American Psychiatric Association: *Diagnostic and Statistical Manual of Mental Disorders,* ed 3. American Psychiatric Association, Washington, DC, 1980. Used with permission.

unstructured situations, in class or out, and less so in one-to-one situations and where external structure is provided. This translates, in part, to being worse off in open classrooms than in traditional classrooms.

In young children especially, there may be restless sleep and restless figdeting, but the children can sit still and not show gross motor activity. Their distractibility, however, may hamper their ability to function in organized games.

Impaired academic performance secondary to distractibility may be present, and there may also be associated specific learning disorders.

Essential characteristics of attention deficit disorder without hyperactivity are as follows: (1) *difficulty, for the child's age, in sustaining attention*; (2) *more marked difficulties in unstructured situations or in unsupervised performance*; (3) *disorganized, impulsive aspects* manifested by at least two of the following: (a) sloppy work despite intent to perform otherwise; (b) demanding of attention; (c) frequent interruption or inappropriate intrusion into another's activity or conversation; (d) finding it hard to wait one's turn; and (e) *poor frustration tolerance*; (4) duration of at least 1 year; and (5) *absence of excessive gross motor activity*.

Insufficient data are available to differentiate the syndrome from attention deficit disorder with hyperactivity by means of the psychiatric examination or psychological tests. Only the presence of overactivity in attention deficit disorder with hyperactivity differentiates the two syndromes.

The table below gives the DSM-III diagnostic criteria for this disorder.

**32.8.   The answer is E (all)** (*Synopsis*, ed. 4, page 742).

The DSM-III definition of attention deficit disorder with hyperactivity states that the child displays signs of developmentally inappropriate inattention, impulsivity, and hyperactivity and that these signs must be reported by adults in the child's environment, such as parents and teachers. *The child is usually unable to pay attention to a stimulus for more than 10 seconds.* Because the child is typically worse in a situation that requires self-application, as in the classroom, *signs of the disorder may be absent when the child is in a new or one-on-one situa-*

*tion.* Thus, the clinician may not always observe the symptoms directly. *The peak age range for referral is between the ages of 8 and 10*, and the number of symptoms specified in the table on page 427 is for children between the ages of 8 and 10. (In younger children, more severe forms and a greater number of symptoms are usually present, whereas the opposite is true of older children.)

**32.9.   The answer is A (1, 2, 3)** (*Synopsis*, ed. 4, page 744).

A neurological examination may show *visual-perceptual or auditory-perceptual impairments, problems with coordination and with copying age-appropriate figures, decreased ability to perform rapid alternating movements*, reflex asymmetries, and a variety of soft signs. Sometimes no abnormality is seen at all.

**32.10.   The answer is A (1, 2, 3)** (*Synopsis*, ed. 4, pages 742 and 743).

Although hyperactivity is one of the hallmarks of attention deficit disorder, it does not always mean that quantitatively the degree of activity is greater than that of other children, although this may be so. Rather, the activity may be relatively continuous and not turned off in appropriate situations, such as in school and in church. Hyperkinetic children are far less likely than are normal children to reduce their locomotor activity when their environment is structured by social limits.

Such children are often *accident-prone*. In school, they may rapidly attack a test and do only the first two questions. They may be unable to wait to be called on in school and may answer for everyone else, and at home they cannot be put off for even a minute.

They are often explosively *irritable*. This irritability may be set off by relatively minor stimuli, and they may seem puzzled and dismayed over that phenomenon. They are frequently emotionally labile, easily set off to laughter and to tears, and their mood and performance are apt to be variable and unpredictable.

Not all the phenomena described are always seen together; just one or two of these characteristics may be seen. If so, distractibility is often the only characteristic present.

Other manifestations are often seen, includ-

---

**Diagnostic Criteria for Attention Deficit Disorder without Hyperactivity\***

The criteria for this disorder are the same as those for attention deficit disorder with hyperactivity except that the individual never had signs of hyperactivity.

---

\* From American Psychiatric Association: *Diagnostic and Statistical Manual of Mental Disorders*, ed 3. American Psychiatric Association, Washington, DC, 1980. Used with permission.

**Diagnostic Criteria for Attention Deficit Disorder with Hyperactivity***

The child displays, for his or her mental and chronological age, signs of developmentally inappropriate inattention, impulsivity, and hyperactivity. The signs must be reported by adults in the child's environment, such as parents and teachers. Because the symptoms are typically variable, they may not be observed directly by the clinician. When the reports of teachers and parents conflict, primary consideration should be given to the teacher's report because of greater familiarity with age-appropriate norms. Symptoms typically worsen in situations that require self-application, as in the classroom. Signs of the disorder may be absent when the child is in a new or a one-to-one situation.

The number of symptoms specified is for children between the ages of 8 and 10, the peak age range for referral. In younger children, more severe forms of the symptoms and a greater number of symptoms are usually present. The opposite is true of older children.

A. *Inattention.* At least three of the following:
   1. Often fails to finish things he or she starts;
   2. Often doesn't seem to listen;
   3. Easily distracted;
   4. Has difficulty concentrating on schoolwork or other tasks requiring sustained attention;
   5. Has difficulty sticking to a play activity.

B. *Impulsivity.* At least three of the following:
   1. Often acts before thinking;
   2. Shifts excessively from one activity to another;
   3. Has difficulty organizing work (this not being due to cognitive impairment);
   4. Needs a lot of supervision;
   5. Frequently calls out in class;
   6. Has difficulty awaiting turn in games or group situations.

C. *Hyperactivity.* At least two of the following:
   1. Runs about or climbs on things excessively;
   2. Has difficulty sitting still or fidgets excessively;
   3. Has difficulty staying seated;
   4. Moves about excessively during sleep;
   5. Is always "on the go" or acts as if "driven by a motor."

D. *Onset before the age of 7.*

E. *Duration of at least 6 months.*

F. Not due to schizophrenia, affective disorder, or severe or mental retardation.

* From American Psychiatric Association: *Diagnostic and Statistical Manual of Mental Disorders*, ed 3. American Psychiatric Association, Washington, DC, 1980. Used with permission.

ing a preoccupation with water play and a *fascination with spinning objects. There may be disturbances in left-right discrimination*; internal time telling or clock time telling; visual or auditory perception; visuomotor performance and hand-eye coordination; fine motor coordination; figure-background discrimination; the abilities to abstract, conceptualize, and generalize; and the abilities to assimilate, retain, and recall.

# References

Brunstetter R W, Silver L B: Attention deficit disorders. In *Comprehensive Textbook of Psychiatry*, ed 4, H I Kaplan, B J Sadock, editors, p 1684. Williams & Wilkins, Baltimore, 1985.

Comings D E, Comings B G: Syndrome and attention deficit disorder with hyperactivity: Are they genetically related? J Am Acad Child Psychiatry 23: 138, 1984.

Dykman R A, Ackerman P: Long-term follow-up studies of hyperactive children. Adv Behav Ped 1: 128, 1980.

Rubinstein R A, Brown R T: An evaluation of the validity of the diagnostic category of attention deficit disorder. Am J Orthopsychiat 54: 398, 1984.

Rutter M: Syndromes attributed to "minimal brain dysfunction" in childhood. Psychiatry 139: 21, 1982.

Varley C K: Diet and the behavior of children with attention deficit disorder. J Am Acad Child Psychiatry 23: 182, 1984.

Wender P H: *Minimal Brain Dysfunction in Children.* Wiley-Interscience, New York, 1971.

# 33

# Specific Developmental Disorders of Childhood and Adolescence

Specific developmental disorders include the following conditions, characterized by a disorder in a specific area of development: reading disorders (alexia and dyslexia), arithmetic disorder, language disorder, articulation disorder, and coordination disorder. According to the third edition of the *Diagnostic and Statistical Manual of Mental Disorders* (DSM-III), this classification is for disorders of specific areas of development not due to another disorder. For example, a delay in language development in an otherwise normal child would be classified as a specific developmental disorder, whereas a delay in language development in a child with infantile autism would be attributed to the infantile autism and therefore would not be classified as a specific developmental disorder. Similarly, a person with general delays in development would receive a diagnosis of mental retardation, not a specific developmental disorder.

Each aspect of development is related to biological maturation. There is no assumption, however, regarding the primacy of biological etiological factors, and nonbiological factors are clearly involved in these disorders.

The inclusion of these categories in a classification of mental disorders is controversial, because many of the children with these disorders have no other signs of psychopathology, and the detection and treatment of the most common category, developmental reading disorder, take place mainly within the educational system, rather than the mental health system.

The reader should review Chapter 33 of *Modern Synopsis-IV*, which covers these various disorders, and should then study the questions and answers below to test his or her knowledge of these subjects.

# Questions

**DIRECTIONS:** Each of the statements or questions below is followed by five suggested responses or completions. Select the *one* that is *best* in each case.

**33.1.** Developmental articulation disorder is related to

A. maturational delay
B. genetic factors
C. twinning
D. low socioeconomic status
E. all of the above

**33.2.** A phoneme is

A. a constellation of sounds
B. a genetic marker on a chromosome
C. a chemical mediator
D. the smallest sound unit
E. an artificial language device

**33.3.** When a young child presents with a delay or disorder of language development, the possible diagnoses to be considered include which of the following:

A. Mental retardation
B. Elective mutism
C. Receptive dysphasia
D. Hearing impairment
E. All of the above

**DIRECTIONS:** For each of the incomplete statements below, *one* or *more* of the completions given is correct. Choose answer:

A. if only **1, 2,** and **3** are correct
B. if only **1** and **3** are correct
C. if only **2** and **4** are correct
D. if only **4** is correct
E. if all are correct

**33.4.** The child with an arithmetic disorder
1. has little difficulty in learning to count
2. usually cannot master cardinal and ordinal systems
3. is able to envision clusters of objects as groups
4. has difficulty in performing arithmetic problems

**33.5.** The cardinal feature of developmental articulation disorder is an articulation defect characterized by
1. omissions
2. substitutions
3. distortions
4. inflections

**33.6.** Coordination disorder
1. begins in infancy
2. presents no complications to the child after birth
3. presents complications before, during, and after birth
4. is more common in girls than in boys

**33.7.** Which of the following associated features apply to coordination disorder:
1. Speech disorders
2. Inattentiveness
3. School difficulties
4. Rapid mood swings

**33.8.** The causes of arithmetic disorders are which of the following:
1. Right-sided brain lesions
2. Inborn deficiency to manipulate spatial relationships
3. Faulty teachers
4. Socioeconomic factors

**33.9.** Which of the following terms have been used synonymously with developmental reading disorder:
1. Alexia
2. Dyslexia
3. Word blindness
4. Specific reading disability

**33.10.** Which of the following are classified as *essential* features of dyslexia in DSM-III:
1. Poor spelling
2. Dysgraphia
3. Motor problems—awkwardness, dyspraxia
4. Impaired development of reading skills

**33.11.** Dyslexia has been associated with a
1. higher-than-average occurrence in juvenile offenders
2. higher occurrence in girls than in boys
3. family history of reading disorders
4. lower-than-average rate among the socially disadvantaged

**33.12.** Which of the following statements are applicable to the specific impairment called developmental language disorder:

1. It is present in less than 1 percent of all children.
2. It is more common in girls than in boys.
3. Siblings of those affected are usually normal.
4. The expressive disorder is less common than the receptive disorder.

**33.13.** Features of dyslexia include which of the following:

1. Reading impairment
2. Difficulty in spelling
3. Letter transpositions
4. A dislike of reading and writing

**DIRECTIONS:** Each set of lettered headings below is followed by a list of numbered words or phrases. For each numbered word or phrase, select

    A. if the item is associated with **A** only
    B. if the item is associated with **B** only
    C. if the item is associated with *both* **A** *and* **B**
    D. if the item is associated with *neither* **A** *nor* **B**

**Questions 33.14–33.18**
    A. Developmental language disorder, expressive type
    B. Developmental language disorder, receptive type
    C. Both
    D. Neither

**33.14.** Failure to develop comprehension (decoding)

**33.15.** Failure to develop vocal expression (encoding)

**33.16.** Underlying impairment in auditory discrimination

**33.17.** Presence of age-appropriate concepts

**33.18.** Due to a hearing impairment

# Answers

# Specific Developmental Disorders of Childhood and Adolescence

**33.1. The answer is E** (*Synopsis*, ed. 4, page 756).

The cause of developmental articulation disorder is unknown. It is commonly believed that a *maturational delay* in the neurological processes underlying speech may be at fault.

A disproportionately high number of children with developmental articulation disorder are found to be second-borns, *twins*, or of *low socioeconomic status*. It is now believed that these children, rather than being at risk for the disorder, are the recipients of inadequate speech stimulation and reinforcement.

Constitutional factors, rather than environmental factors, seem to be of major importance in determining whether a child has developmental articulation disorder. The high proportion of children with developmental articulation disorder who have relatives with a similar disorder suggests that there is a *genetic component* to the disorder.

See the table below for the DSM-III diagnostic criteria for developmental articulation disorder.

**33.2. The answer is D** (*Synopsis*, ed. 4, page 756).

Developmental articulation disorder cannot be accounted for by structural, physiological, or neurological abnormalities. Language is within normal limits. The term actually refers to a number of different articulation problems that range in severity from mild to severe. Only one speech sound or phoneme (*the smallest sound unit*), may be affected, or many phonemes may be involved. The child may be completely intelligible, partially intelligible, or unintelligible.

A phoneme in linguistics is a speech sound that serves to distinguish words from one an-

other; for example: the vowels in *tan, ten, tin, ton, tun*. There is a rigid sequence in the process of acquisition of new phonemes by a child learning to speak, and accordingly, this process is reversed in various types of aphasic speech disorders.

Different terms used to describe this disorder have included dyslalia, baby talk, infantile perseveration, lalling, delayed speech, lisping, oral inaccuracy, lazy speech, mild specific developmental speech disorder, and defective articulation.

**33.3. The answer is E** (*Synopsis*, ed. 4, page 754).

When a young child presents with a delay or disorder of language development, a number of possible diagnoses must be considered. These include *mental retardation, hearing impairment,* infantile autism, *elective mutism*, developmental articulation disorder, and *receptive and expressive dysphasia* due to brain damage.

The mentally retarded child has normal hearing and responds appropriately to sounds; however, his or her articulation is consistently poor. Motor milestones, only slightly delayed in the dysphasic child, are clearly delayed in the child with mental retardation. Performance intelligence is seriously impaired in the child who is mentally retarded.

An audiogram is the best way to establish the presence of a hearing impairment in a child, although sometimes this diagnosis is clear from the child's behavior.

A differential diagnosis between autism and severe developmental language disorder is generally made on behavioral grounds, rather than on linguistic grounds. The most striking feature that distinguishes the two disorders is the lack

---

**Diagnostic Criteria for Developmental Articulation Disorder\***

A. Failure to develop consistent articulations of the later-acquired speech sounds, such as r, sh, th, f, z, l, or ch.

B. Not due to developmental language disorder, mental retardation, childhood onset pervasive developmental disorder, or physical disorders.

---

\* From American Psychiatric Association: *Diagnostic and Statistical Manual of Mental Disorders*, ed. 3. American Psychiatric Association, Washington, DC, 1980. Used with permission.

of interest in communication in the autistic child. The autistic child does not watch the faces of speakers, does not make eye contact, and does not attempt to communicate through the use of gestures. Inner language, slightly impaired in the dysphasic child, is severely impaired or totally absent in the autistic child. In older children who have acquired some language, the child with infantile autism may have inappropriate intonation, delayed echolalia, and stereotyped utterances.

The electively mute child's mother reports that the child had a normal developmental history and can speak normally but that the child is shy and speaks only to certain persons.

Examination of the language of a child with developmental articulation disorder reveals that comprehension and expression are normal and that only articulation is disturbed.

Children with developmental language disorder score better on performance intelligence tests than on verbal intelligence tests.

**33.4.   The answer is C (2, 4)** (*Synopsis*, ed. 4, pages 751 and 752).

Developmental arithmetic disorder is usually diagnosed when a child's performance falls significantly below age-expected norms in school. Some children may make progress at first in the early years of mathematics by the use of rote memory, but as the need for discrimination and manipulation of spatial and numerical relationships becomes greater, they encounter difficulties.

Investigators have described certain cardinal characteristics of the child with specific arithmetic disorder: (1) *difficulty in learning to count meaningfully*, (2) *difficulty in mastering cardinal and ordinal systems*, (3) *difficulty in performing arithmetic operations*, and (4) *difficulty in envisioning clusters of objects as groups*. In addition, they described difficulties in associating auditory and visual symbols, understanding the conservation of quantity, remembering sequences of arithmetic steps, and choosing principles for problem-solving activities. These children, however, were presumed to have good auditory and verbal abilities.

**33.5.   The answer is A (1, 2, 3)** (*Synopsis*, ed. 4, page 757).

The cardinal feature of developmental articulation disorder is an articulation defect characterized by *omission, substitution*, or *distortion* of phonemes that generally involves the late-learned phonemes. The disorder is not attributable to structural or neurological abnormalities, and it is accompanied by language development that is within normal limits.

It is generally thought that omissions are the most serious type of misarticulation, with substitutions the next most serious type, and distortion the least serious type.

The articulation of the child with developmental articulation disorder is often inconsistent. A phoneme may be correctly produced in one phonetic environment and incorrectly produced in another phonetic environment. Errors are most likely to occur in the final consonant of a word and are least likely to occur in the initial consonant of a word. Another type of inconsistency in the speech of children with developmental articulation disorder is that their articulation of single words in isolation may be normal, whereas articulation of the same word in longer utterances is quite disturbed. Generally, articulation is worse during an increased rate of speech.

Omissions, distortions, and substitutions also occur normally in the speech of a young child learning to talk. Whereas the young normal child soon replaces these misarticulations, the child with developmental articulation disorder does not. Even as children with developmental articulation disorder grow and finally acquire the correct phoneme, they may use it only in newly acquired words and may not correct earlier learned words that they have been mispronouncing for some time.

*Inflections* are grammatical markers that are added to the end of words to change their meaning. For example, the possessive "s," as in "baby's chair," or the noun, as in "baby chairs."

The following table gives the essential and associated features of developmental articulation disorder.

**Essential and Associated Features of Developmental Articulation Disorder**

| Essential Features | Associated Features |
| --- | --- |
| Defective articulation— omissions, distortions, or substitutions—of later acquired speech sounds not attributable to structural or neurological abnormalities | Delay in first beginning to speak |
| | Lack of firmly established laterality |
| | Enuresis |
| | Dysfluencies of speech (stuttering) |
| Language within normal limits | General immaturity, dependency, shyness, or hyperactivity |
| | Problems with school, especially with reading |

**33.6.   The answer is B (1, 3)** (*Synopsis*, ed. 4, page 759).

The exact prevalence of coordination disorder is not known, but it appears to be a relatively common disorder. It is generally accepted that the disorder is *more common in boys than in girls*, as most developmental disorders are, but the exact boy-to-girl ratio is not known. No evidence suggests that coordination disorder runs in family members of children with this disorder.

Some studies suggest that children with coordination disorder have an *increased frequency of complications before, during, and after birth.* Other predisposing factors are thought to include *hypoxia during pregnancy, low birth weight*, and malnutrition. No specific causative factor, however, can be pinpointed for coordination disorder. It is likely that the factors suggested as playing a causative role probably do so in a multifactorial way. They may also lead to other problems, and they are not specific for coordination disorder.

Coordination disorder *begins in infancy.* Generally, recognition is early, occurring as soon as the child attempts tasks requiring motor coordination. The one single essential feature is a serious impairment in the development of motor coordination. The manifestations may vary with age and with the severity of the disorder. Children with motor coordination disorder are looked on as having motor learning difficulties. They display inefficient motor behavior and asynchronous motor behavior when commonly expected movement tasks are carried out. Thus, they may be clumsy, they may drop things, and they may trip over their own feet and fall frequently. Developmental milestones, such as tying shoelaces, buttoning shirts, and zipping up pants, are late in being learned. Most movements are uncoordinated and awkward, leading to difficulties in such activities as doing table games that require putting together puzzles, building models, building blocks, and playing any kind of ball game. Difficulties in handwriting may be noted in a school-age child.

**33.7.   The answer is E (all)** (*Synopsis*, ed. 4, page 759).

A number of associated features are present in some but not all children with coordination disorder. For instance, there is a high incidence of *speech disorders*, and developmental milestones may be delayed in areas other than motor coordination. Secondary problems, such as *school difficulties*, may often be presenting complaints. *Rapid mood swings* and *inattentiveness* may also occur as associated features.

**33.8.   The answer is E (all)** (*Synopsis*, ed. 4, page 751).

Developmental arithmetic disorder, as diagnosed in DSM-III, probably has many causes. Some children are probably *born with a deficiency in the ability to discriminate and manip-* *ulate numerical relationships and spatial relationships.* This deficiency, in some cases, may be due to *lesions on the right side of the brain.* These children lack the fundamental tools necessary for mathematics attainment. Emotional factors, *socioeconomic factors, teaching methods*, and other cognitive factors, however, are likely to interact to produce children who have varying degrees of severity of problems with mathematics. Certainly no one cause can be pinpointed for all children with developmental arithmetic disorder.

See the table below for the DSM-III diagnostic criteria for developmental arithmetic disorder.

### Diagnostic Criteria for Developmental Arithmetic Disorder*

Performance on standardized, individually administered tests of arithmetic achievement is significantly below expected level, given the individual's schooling, chronological age, and mental age (as determined by an individually administered I.Q. test). In addition, in school, the child's performance on tasks requiring arithmetic skills is significantly below his or her intellectual capacity.

* From American Psychiatric Association: *Diagnostic and Statistical Manual of Mental Disorders*, ed 3. American Psychiatric Association, Washington, DC, 1980. Used with permission.

**33.9.   The answer is E (all)** (*Synopsis*, ed. 4, page 748).

The terms *alexia*, developmental *dyslexia*, *word blindness*, and *specific reading disability* have all been used to refer to a significant interference with the development of reading proficiency that cannot be explained by inadequate intelligence and poor schooling. Most physicians use the term alexia to refer to reading disabilities, of whatever severity, resulting from brain lesions, whereas they use dyslexia to designate an innate inability to learn to read. Psychologists and educators, in contrast, use the term alexia according to its linguistic derivations to refer to a total inability to learn to read.

In general, one should confine the definition of dyslexia to the presenting problem, reading failure. The several definitions all agree on the point that, in developmental dyslexia, there is a discrepancy between the child's actual reading performance and the expected performance, given the child's mental age, schooling, and intelligence. In addition, in school the child's performance on tasks requiring reading skills is below his or her intellectual capacity.

*Alexia* is a loss of the power to grasp the meaning of written or printed words and sentences. *Dyslexia* is a specific learning disability syndrome involving an impairment of the ability to read, unrelated to the person's intelligence. *Word blindness* is a term that was introduced in 1877 by Kussmase to refer to a type of reading disability. A *specific reading disability* refers to specific delays in the person's reading development.

**33.10. The answer is D (4)** (*Synopsis*, ed. 4, page 749).

The *impaired development of reading skills* is considered to be the defining and *essential* feature of dyslexia, which is known in DSM-III as developmental reading disorder.

*Dysgraphia* (difficulty in writing), *poor spelling*, and *motor problems* are often seen in dyslexic persons, but these problems are considered by DSM-III to be associated features.

The table below gives the clinical features of dyslexia, according to DSM-III.

**33.11. The answer is B (1, 3)** (*Synopsis*, ed. 4, page 748).

A positive *family history of speech, reading, spelling, and writing disability* has often been observed by those who work with the reading disabled. The large percentage of affected parents speaks in favor of a dominant mode of inheritance. One study found that 45 percent of first-degree relatives of poor readers showed a history of reading problems. Another study found that the reading and spelling performance of siblings of poor readers was significantly lower than that of controls. Twin studies more

conclusively suggest a genetic component, but there is little agreement as to what it is that is inherited.

Estimates of the incidence of reading disability in the general United States population of school children generally vary between 3 and 15 percent. Estimates for Canada seem to be in the same range.

The prevalence is *higher than average in groups of juvenile offenders and among the socially disadvantaged.*

*The incidence of specific reading retardation is higher among boys than among girls*, 3 or 4 to 1, but there is no significant difference in the proportion of males and females among backward readers.

**33.12. The answer is B (1, 3)** (*Synopsis*, ed. 4, page 753).

There have been several studies in which the incidence of developmental language disorder was *reported as 1 in 1,000 (0.1 percent) for the expressive type and 1 in 2,000 (0.5 percent) for the receptive type. The receptive disorder is less common than the expressive disorder.*

Developmental language disorder *is more common in boys than in girls.* The ratio is two to three boys for each girl.

A family history of developmental language disorder is rare, and *siblings are usually normal.* Nonetheless, a family history of related disorders is common. There is often a history in first-degree relatives of difficulty in the early stage of learning to read and write, a family history of

**Clinical Features of Dyslexia***

| Essential Features | Associated Features | Other Features† |
|---|---|---|
| Impaired development of reading skills: faulty oral reading, misreading of graphemes, omissions and additions of words | Poor spelling and dictation; bizarre spelling errors, letter transposals, reversals<br>Poorly formulated compositions<br>Dysgraphia<br>Poor oral language skills: impaired sound discriminations, problems with word sequencing, dysnomia, mildly deficient grammar<br>Comprehension problems in oral and printed language<br>Anomalies of hand-eye preference and impaired left-right discrimination<br>Motor problems: awkwardness, dyspraxia<br>Behavioral problems: impulsiveness, short attention span, immaturity<br>Finger agnosia (less common) | Variability in cognitive efficiency<br>Aversion to reading and writing<br>Soft neurological signs |

* Adapted from American Psychiatric Association: *Diagnostic and Statistical Manual of Mental Disorders*, ed 3. American Psychiatric Association, Washington, DC, 1980.

† Not cited as a clinical feature in DSM-III, but may be present in this disorder.

slow speech development, articulation problems, and of difficulties in learning to read and spell. Ambidexterity occurs in a larger number of relatives than might ordinarily be expected.

**33.13.  The answer is E (all)** (*Synopsis*, ed. 4, page 750).

The cardinal features of dyslexia are varying degrees of *impairment of reading, spelling,* and writing in intelligent, healthy children. Characteristic disorders include *difficulties with the recall, evocation, and sequencing of printed letters and words*, with the processing of sophisticated grammatical constructions, and with the making of inferences.

Most dyslexic children *dislike reading and writing* and avoid these activities. Their anxiety is heightened when they are confronted with demands that involve printed language.

**33.14–33.18.  The answers are 33.14–B, 33.15–C, 33.16–B, 33.17–A, and 33.18–D** (*Synopsis*, ed. 4, pages 752, 753, and 754).

Developmental language disorder, according to DSM-III, is described as (1) a failure to acquire any language, (2) an acquired language disability as a result of trauma or neurological disorder, and (3) delayed language acquisition. It is the most common of all the disorders affecting language. (See the tables below.)

Delayed language acquisition is the most common type of developmental language disorder and is divided into two types: *expressive type and receptive type*. The expressive subtype of the disorder involves an impairment in the *encoding* or production of language, with the understanding of language remaining relatively intact. The receptive subtype of the disorder, which is more serious and inclusive, involves impairment of both language production (*encoding*) and *language comprehension* (*decoding*). Children with the receptive type appear to have an *underlying impairment in auditory discrimination*. They are more responsive to environmental sounds than to speech sounds.

### Diagnostic Criteria for Developmental Language Disorder, Expressive Type*

A. Failure to develop vocal expression (encoding) of language despite relatively intact comprehension of language.

B. Presence of inner language (*the presence of age-appropriate concepts*, such as understanding the purpose and use of a particular household object).

C. Not due to mental retardation, childhood onset pervasive developmental disorder, *hearing impairment*, or trauma.

* From American Psychiatric Association: *Diagnostic and Statistical Manual of Mental Disorders*, ed 3. American Psychiatric Association, Washington, DC, 1980. Used with permission.

### Diagnostic Criteria for Developmental Language Disorder, Receptive Type*

A. Failure to develop comprehension (decoding) and vocal expression (encoding) of language.

B. Not due to hearing impairment, trauma, mental retardation, or childhood onset pervasive developmental disorder.

* From American Psychiatric Association: *Diagnostic and Statistical Manual of Mental Disorders*, ed 3. American Psychiatric Association, Washington, DC, 1980. Used with permission.

## References

Arnheim D D, Sinclair W A: *The Clumsy Child.* C V Mosby, St. Louis, 1975.

Baker L, Cantwell D P: Developmental arithmetic disorder. In *Comprehensive Textbook of Psychiatry*, ed 4, H I Kaplan, B J Sadock, editors, p 1697. Williams & Wilkins, Baltimore, 1985.

Baker L, Cantwell D P: Developmental articulation disorder. In *Comprehensive Textbook of Psychiatry*, ed 4, H I Kaplan, B J Sadock, editors, p 1705. Williams & Wilkins, Baltimore, 1985.

Baker L, Cantwell D P: Developmental language disorder. In *Comprehensive Textbook of Psychiatry*, ed 4, H I Kaplan, B J Sadock, editors, p 1700. Williams & Wilkins, Baltimore, 1985.

Cantwell D P, Baker L: Coordination disorder. In *Comprehensive Textbook of Psychiatry*, ed 4, H I Kaplan, B J Sadock, editors, p 1709. Williams &

Wilkins, Baltimore, 1985.

Eisenson J, Ogilvie M: *Communicative Disorders in Children.* Macmillan, New York, 1983.

Jansky J J: Developmental reading disorder (alexia and dyslexia). In *Comprehensive Textbook of Psychiatry*, ed 4, H I Kaplan, B J Sadock, editors, p 1691. Williams & Wilkins, Baltimore, 1985.

Kose L: Neuropsychological implications of diagnoses and treatment of mathematical learning disabilities. Topics Lang Learning Dis *1:* 19, 1981.

Myklebust H R: Childhood aphasia: Identification, diagnosis, and remediation. In *Handbook of Speech Pathology and Audiology*, L E Travis, editor, p 1203. Appleton-Century-Crofts, New York, 1971.

Shapiro B K: Issues in the early identification of specific learning disability. J Develop Behav Ped *5:* 15, 1984.

# 34

# Movement and Speech Disorders of Childhood and Adolescence

The stereotyped movement disorders of childhood and adolescence include transient tic disorder, chronic motor tic disorder, Tourette's disorder, and atypical stereotyped movement disorder. Atypical stereotyped movement disorder includes head banging, rocking, and other repetitive voluntary movements.

The disorders that are present with the behavior of tics may lie on a clinical continuum from simple to multiple motor tics to the fuller syndrome of Tourette's disorder. Thus, at the onset of the disorder, the differential diagnosis is difficult. Although interventions may be initiated, one may not be able to establish a diagnosis until the full clinical picture has developed.

Speech disorders are classified in three categories, each of which is subdivided into one or more types. The categories are (1) articulation disorders, divided into substitution, omission, addition, and distortion; (2) voice disorders, divided into pitch, intensity, and quality; and (3) dysfluency disorders, such as stuttering.

The reader should review Chapter 34 of *Modern Synopsis-IV*, which covers the disorders mentioned above. By studying the questions and answers below, students can test their knowledge of these areas.

# Questions

**DIRECTIONS:** Each of the statements or questions below is followed by five suggested responses or completions. Select the *one* that is *best* in each case.

**34.1.** A slow, rhythmic, backward-and-forward swaying of the trunk from the hips is known as

A. chorea
B. jactatio capitis nocturnus (head banging)
C. nocturnal myoclonus
D. body rocking
E. transient tic

**34.2.** The drug of choice in the treatment of Tourette's disorder is

A. chlorpromazine
B. diazepam
C. haloperidol
D. amphetamine
E. phenobarbital

**34.3.** Soon after the start of the school year, teachers noticed that a 7-year-old girl had not spoken in any of her classes. Although her written work was excellent, she did not speak to either teachers or students when questioned. The student's parents reported that she appeared normally active at home and spoke normally. The most probable disorder in this student is

A. dyslalia
B. elective mutism
C. catatonic schizophrenia
D. expressive aphasia
E. stuttering

**34.4.** A recurrent, repetitive, rapid, purposeless motor movement is known as a

A. clonus
B. hypnic jerk
C. transient tic
D. ballismus
E. chorea

**34.5.** The modern treatment of stuttering emphasizes the use of

A. hypnosis
B. group therapy
C. psychoanalysis
D. speech therapy
E. distraction

**34.6.** Tourette's disorder

A. does not show minimal brain dysfunction
B. is more common in males than in females
C. is found more frequently in low socioeconomic groups than in high socioeconomic groups
D. does not run in families
E. usually shows a normal EEG

**34.7.** The incidence of stuttering in the United States is

A. 1 percent
B. 3 percent
C. 5 percent
D. 7 percent
E. 10 percent

**DIRECTIONS:** For each of the incomplete statements below, *one* or *more* of the completions given is correct. Choose answer:

    A. if only **1, 2,** and **3** are correct
    B. if only **1** and **3** are correct
    C. if only **2** and **4** are correct
    D. if only **4** is correct
    E. if all are correct

**34.8.** Which of the following statements about tics are accurate:

1. The average age of onset is 7 years.
2. The face is most frequently involved.
3. Hiccoughing is classified as a tic.
4. Tics may be a reflection of diffuse anxiety.

**34.9.** Children classified as having a coordination disorder

1. are usually mentally retarded
2. often show specific neurological diseases
3. are usually girls
4. are seriously impaired in the development of motor coordination

**34.10.** In Tourette's disorder,

1. there is rapid, purposeless motor movement
2. vocal tics are present in more than 95 percent of the patients
3. echolalia is present in 35 percent of cases
4. coprolalia is always present

**34.11.** Rhythmic head banging in children

1. is more common in boys than in girls
2. usually begins between the ages of 6 and 12 months
3. may be associated with pica
4. is best treated by pharmacotherapy

**34.12.** Theories to explain stuttering emphasize

1. conflict between the right half and the left half of the brain for dominance
2. constitutional predisposition
3. family problems, such as harsh parental criticism
4. learned pathological speech patterns

**DIRECTIONS:** Each set of lettered headings below is followed by a list of numbered words or phrases. For each numbered word or phrase, select:

    A. if the item is associated with **A** only
    B. if the item is associated with **B** only
    C. if the item is associated with *both* **A** *and* **B**
    D. if the item is associated with *neither* **A** *nor* **B**

**Questions 34.13–34.16**
A. Chronic motor tic disorder
B. Transient tic disorder
C. Both
D. Neither

**34.13.** Ability to suppress movements voluntarily for minutes to hours

**34.14.** Duration of at least 1 month

**34.15.** Unvarying intensity over weeks and months

**34.16.** Onset during childhood or early adolescence

# Answers

# Movement and Speech Disorders of Childhood and Adolescence

**34.1.   The answer is D** (*Synopsis*, ed. 4, page 766).

*Body rocking* is characterized by a slow, rhythmic, backward-and-forward swaying of the trunk from the hips, usually while in a sitting position. At times, the rocking is so violent that the child's bed is moved from one side of the room to the other. The rocking may be accompanied by low humming or crooning noises. Some children accelerate the tempo of rocking to a peak of activity and then decelerate slowly to a calmer pace. These movements are most common in infancy and early childhood, but may persist into adult life. Although such rhythmic habit patterns are more common with children of low intelligence and developmental disabilities, they are also seen in children of normal intelligence and functioning.

*Chorea* is a movement disorder, characterized by random and involuntary quick, jerky, purposeless movements. *Jactatio capitus nocturnus (head banging)* is a rare condition that occurs in children. It is voluntary and often seems enjoyable to the child. *Nocturnal myoclonus* is a neuromuscular abnormality that manifests itself in sudden, repeated contractions of one or more muscle groups—usually the leg muscle—during sleep. A *transient tic* is a recurrent, repetitive, rapid, purposeless motor movement that can be voluntarily suppressed for minutes to hours.

**34.2.   The answer is C** (*Synopsis*, ed. 4, page 765).

*Haloperidol*, which is a butyrophenone antipsychotic drug, is generally acknowledged to be the drug of choice in the treatment of Tourette's disorder. Psychotherapy may help the patient cope with his or her illness, but is ineffective as a primary treatment modality. Behavioral therapy has been successful in minimizing some of the symptoms.

*Chlorpromazine* is a phenothiazine derivative used primarily as an antipsychotic agent and in the treatment of nausea and vomiting. *Diazepam* is used for relaxation of the skeletal muscles and as an antianxiety agent. *Amphetamine* is a central nervous system stimulant. Its chemical structure and action are closely related to ephedrine and other sympathomimetic amines.

*Phenobarbital* is a long-acting barbiturate used as a sedative and hypnotic.

**34.3.   The answer is B** (*Synopsis*, ed. 4, page 770).

The primary clinical picture in *elective mutism* is the pervasive and persistent refusal to speak in social or school situations. Children with this disorder are able and willing to speak to selected persons, usually family or selected peers. They may communicate through gestures by nodding or shaking their head.

Onset of the mutism is usually between the ages of 3 and 5 years. Before starting school, the child's reluctance to speak to people outside of the family may be seen as normal shyness; thus, referral often does not occur until the child starts school and his or her failure to speak to anyone is noticed by the teachers and the other children. The child's behavior in school is often in contrast to the parents' report that the child talks and plays freely at home.

*Dyslalia* is faulty articulation due to structural abnormalities of the articulatory organs or impaired hearing. *Catatonic schizophrenia* is a state of stupor characterized by muscular rigidity, stupor, and negativism. *Aphasia* is a disturbance in language function due to organic brain disorder. The disturbance cannot be explained on the basis of a defect in sensory pathways, in motor mechanisms of phonation and articulation, or in sensorium. Aphasia may be classified as receptive, expressive, or mixed (global). *Stuttering* is the repetition of words, syllables, or sounds that disrupt the flow of speech.

The table on the facing page gives the DSM-III diagnostic criteria for elective mutism.

**34.4.   The answer is C** (*Synopsis*, ed. 4, page 761).

*Transient tics* are defined in DSM-III as recurrent, repetitive, rapid, purposeless motor movements. These movements can be voluntarily suppressed for minutes to hours. The total clinical picture usually lasts for weeks or months with varying intensity of symptoms. If the tics last for longer than 1 year, they should be classified as a chronic motor tic disorder.

## Diagnostic Criteria for Elective Mutism*

A. Continuous refusal to talk in almost all social situations, including at school.

B. Ability to comprehend spoken language and to speak.

C. Not due to another mental or physical disorder.

* From American Psychiatric Association: *Diagnostic and Statistical Manual of Mental Disorders*, ed 3. American Psychiatric Association, Washington, DC, 1980. Used with permission.

Leo Kanner first described tics as sudden, quick, involuntary, and frequently repeated movements of circumscribed groups of muscles, serving no apparent purpose. This description has been the standard used by clinicians and is the basis for the DSM-III definition.

A *clonus* is a rhythmic series of contractions in response to the maintenance of tension in a muscle, often appearing in pyramidal lesions as a manifestation of exaggerated tendon reflexes. A *hypnic jerk* is a generalized body twitch that some people exhibit occasionally as they fall asleep. A *ballismus* is characterized by lively jerking or shaking movements, especially as observed in chorea. *Chorea* is a movement disorder, characterized by random and involuntary quick, jerky, purposeless movements.

**34.5.   The answer is D** (*Synopsis*, ed. 4, page 769).

Most of the modern treatments of stuttering are based on the view that, essentially, stuttering is a learned form of behavior that is not necessarily associated with a basic neurotic personality or atypical neurology. The objective of this group of approaches has been to work directly with the speech difficulty by using *speech therapy* to (1) minimize the issues that maintain and strengthen the stuttering, (2) modify or decrease the severity of the stuttering by eliminating the secondary symptoms, and (3) encourage the stutterer to speak, even if stuttering, in a relatively easy and effortless fashion, avoiding fears and blocks.

The treatment of stuttering goes back to classical antiquity. The most common measures used until the end of the 19th century were distraction, suggestion, and relaxation. Demosthenes' famous use of pebbles, if the story is true, was an example of *distraction*. More recent approaches using distraction have included teaching the stutterer to talk in time to rhythmic movements of the arm, hand, or fingers. Stutterers have been advised to speak slowly in a sing-song or monotone. These approaches remove the stuttering only temporarily. Suggestion techniques, such as *hypnosis*, also stop stuttering but, again, only temporarily. Relaxation techniques are based on the premise that it is almost impossible to be relaxed and to stutter

in the usual manner at the same time. Because of the lack of long-term benefits, distraction, suggestion, and relaxation approaches as such are now not in use.

Stutterers have been treated by classical *psychoanalysis*, analytically oriented psychotherapy, *group therapy*, nondirective therapy, and other varieties of psychotherapy. Although such approaches may improve the patient's self-image and level of anxiety, no form of such therapy has proved successful in producing long-term effects.

*Hypnosis* is an artificially induced alteration of consciousness characterized by increased suggestibility and receptivity to direction. *Group psychotherapy* is the application of psychotherapeutic techniques to a group of patients, using interpatient interactions to effect changes in the maladaptive behavior of the individual members. *Psychoanalysis* is a theory of human mental phenomena and behavior, a method of psychic investigation and research, and a form of psychotherapy originally formulated by Sigmund Freud. As a technique for exploring the mental processes, psychoanalysis includes the use of free association and the analysis and interpretation of dreams, resistances, and transferences. *Speech therapy* is a therapeutic mode encompassing all abnormalities in language production that are not due to faulty innervation of speech muscles or organs of articulation. A *distraction* is defined as difficulty in concentrating or a fixation of the mind.

**34.6.   The answer is B** (*Synopsis*, ed. 4, pages 763 and 764).

Surveys of the sex distribution in Tourette's disorder have consistently reported a *greater percentage of males*. The lifetime prevalence rate ranges from 0.1 to 0.5 per 1,000. The ratio of males to females is 3 to 1.

Tourette's disorder is *found in all social classes*. Its incidence *in the same family is higher* than statistically expected.

Tourette's disorder is probably caused by a disorder of the central nervous system. This concept is supported by the following data: (1) There is a high *incidence of minimal brain dysfunction* (57.9 percent) in such patients. (2) Such patients show a high incidence of soft neurological signs. (3) There is a high incidence (50 to 60 percent) of *abnormal electroencephalograms.* (4) There is a higher than normal incidence of left-handedness. (5) Haloperidol suppresses the tics.

**34.7.   The answer is A** (*Synopsis*, ed. 4, page 767).

About *1 percent* of the population are stutterers. The incidence is slightly higher in Europe. About one-half of all stutterers are children.

The incidence of stuttering appears to vary markedly in different cultures. In many primitive societies, it is not seen. There is consistent evidence that the cultures in which relatively large numbers of stutterers are seen are those characterized by competitive pressures. In Western cultures, stuttering appears to be more common in certain socioeconomic levels, especially those marked by upward mobility, than in others.

Stuttering is noted more frequently and persists longer in boys than in girls; this ratio increases with age. The ratio of boys to girls appears to vary between 2 to 1 and 5 to 1. Most studies report the ratio of 4 to 1, males to females.

**34.8.   The answer is E (all)** (*Synopsis*, ed. 4, pages 761 and 762).

*Tics may be a reflection of diffuse anxiety* or may have a more specific meaning; they may be used as a defense against another motor activity or may symbolically represent a condensed ego function. Psychogenic tics seem to increase in severity during emotional excitement, decrease as a result of distraction or concentration, and disappear during sleep.

The *average age of onset of tics is 7 years*, but tics may occur as early as 2 years; the great majority of patients have an onset before the age of 10. The *face and the neck are the most frequently involved* parts of the body. The most common tics involve the face, and there is a descending gradient of frequency from face to feet.

Types of body movements and types of tics include the following:

1. Face and head: Grimacing, puckering of forehead, raising eyebrows, blinking eyelids, winking, wrinkling nose, trembling nostrils, twitching mouth, displaying teeth, biting lips and other parts, extruding tongue, protracting lower jaw, nodding, jerking, or shaking the head, twisting neck, looking sideways, and head rolling.

2. Arms and hands: Jerking hands, jerking arms, plucking fingers, writhing fingers, and clenching fists.

3. Body and lower extremities: Shrugging shoulders, shaking foot, knee, or toe, peculiarities of gait, body writhing, and jumping.

4. Respiratory and alimentary: *Hiccoughing*, sighing, yawning, snuffing, blowing through nostrils, whistling inspiration, exaggerated breathing, belching, sucking or smacking sounds, and clearing throat.

**34.9.   The answer is D (4)** (*Synopsis*, ed. 4, page 758).

Coordination disorder is a disorder of development. In developmental sequence, perceptual motor skills are acquired first, then spoken language is acquired, and, with rare exceptions, only after these functions have been acquired does the child learn how to read. Coordination disorder may be considered a subset of the developmental disorders of perceptual motor skills.

Although clumsy children or children with coordination disorder have been described for at least the past 15 years, only in the most recent editions of the classification manuals has a specific disorder been so delineated. The operational definition for coordination disorder includes *a serious impairment in the development of motor coordination* and *the absence of general mental retardation or any neurological disorder* that would account for the motor coordination problems. ICD-9 also includes the term coordination disorder as one of its developmental disorders. *More boys* have coordination disorder than girls, although the exact incidence is unknown.

**34.10.   The answer is B (1, 3)** (*Synopsis*, ed. 4, pages 763 and 764).

Gilles de la Tourette's disease (now known simply as Tourette's disorder) is characterized by recurrent, involuntary, repetitive, *rapid, purposeless motor movements* (tics) and multiple vocal tics. The movements can be voluntarily suppressed for minutes to hours, and the intensity of the symptoms may vary over weeks or months. The motor tics typically involve the head, but frequently also involve other parts of the body—torso, upper and lower limbs. The *vocal tics are present in 60 percent of all cases* and include various complicated sounds and words and coprolalia.

*Coprolalia occurs in only 60 percent of all patients*; it may appear an average of 6.3 years after the onset of the disorder and may spontaneously disappear in some patients on an average of 10.3 years after onset. *Echolalia occurs in only 35 percent of all patients*, and intellectual deterioration is infrequent. Also contributing to the underdiagnosis of this disorder is the fact

**Diagnostic Criteria for Tourette's Disorder***

A. Age at onset between 2 and 15 years.

B. Presence of recurrent, involuntary, repetitive, rapid, purposeless motor movements affecting multiple muscle groups.

C. Multiple vocal tics.

D. Ability to suppress movements voluntarily for minutes to hours.

E. Variations in the intensity of the symptoms over weeks or months.

F. Duration of more than 1 year.

* From American Psychiatric Association: *Diagnostic and Statistical Manual of Mental Disorders*, ed 3. American Psychiatric Association, Washington, DC, 1980. Used with permission.

that physicians may interpret the initial symptoms as transient or habit tics of childhood.

The above table gives the DSM-III diagnostic criteria for Tourette's disorder.

**34.11. The answer is A (1, 2, 3)** (*Synopsis*, ed. 4, pages 765 and 766).

Head banging is characterized by repetitive movement marked by a definite rhythm and monotonous continuity. The head is struck rhythmically against the head board, side railing of the crib, or on other objects.

It is useful to distinguish between autoerotic head banging and tantrum head banging. With the autoerotic head banger, the child's head banging consists of knocking his or her head against a hard surface in a vigorous, noisy, absorbing, rhythmic manner. The child finally becomes exhausted and falls asleep. This type of head banging *may begin between the ages of 6 and 12 months* and continue into latency; it is often associated with severe ego disturbances or developmental disability. It may be seen in association with other self-stimulating activities, such as thumb sucking, rocking, tongue chewing, hair twirling, crib biting, and *pica.*

Tantrum head banging begins about the time that children are able to talk. When frustrated, children throw themselves on the ground, arms and legs extended, thrashing, kicking, and banging their heads vigorously. Tantrum head banging often results in secondary gains, which may perpetuate the pattern.

In a study of 130 children with rhythmic patterns, *about 5 percent more boys than girls* were noted. With some of the children, the rhythmic movements were transitory; with others, the movements continued for months or years.

*Increased contact with the child by his or her mother is the treatment of choice.* Unfortunately, this approach often fails because mothers of head bangers are often unable to carry out the recommendation. Counseling or therapy with

the mother may make her more available to her child. An alternative proposal abandons the concept of treatment and recommends that the mother find a soft place for her child to bang his or her head. If mothers are able to pick up a head banger and hold the child for a long enough period of time, the head banging disappears. *Pharmacotherapy is not indicated.*

**34.12. The answer is E (all)** (*Synopsis*, ed. 4, page 767).

Theories related to the stuttering block fall into three groups—genogenic, psychogenic, and semantogenic.

The basic premise in the genogenic models is that the stutterer is biologically different from the nonstutterer. An example is the theory of cerebral dominance, which states that *children are predisposed to stutter by a conflict between the two halves of the cerebrum for control of the activity of the speech organs.* The current consensus is that there may be some sort of *constitutional predisposition* toward stuttering but that environmental stresses work in conjunction with this somatic variant to produce stuttering.

Most psychogenic theories emphasize obsessive-compulsive mechanisms and a variety of psychosocial factors, such as a dysfunctional family. Stuttering is seen as a neurosis caused by the persistence into later life of early pregenital oral-sadistic and anal-sadistic components.

With the semantogenic theories, stuttering is seen as a *learned pathologic response* to the mislabeling of normal early syllable and word repetitions. Johnson, for instance, observed that stuttering is induced by *undue parental criticism.*

**34.13–34.16. The answers are 34.13–C, 34.14–B, 34.15–A, and 34.16–B** (*Synopsis*, ed. 4, pages 761, 762, and 763).

The *ability to suppress movements voluntarily for minutes to hours* is indicative of both transient and chronic motor tic disorders. A *duration of 1 month* is characteristic of a transient tic disorder, whereas the criteria for chronic motor tic disorder is a duration of at least 1 year. An *unvarying intensity over weeks and months* is indicative of a chronic motor tic disorder; however, in transient tic disorder, there is a variation in intensity. The age of onset for a transient tic is *childhood or early adolescence*, although there is no epidemiology listed under chronic motor tic disorder.

The tables below give the DSM-III diagnostic criteria for transient tic disorder and chronic motor tic disorder.

### Diagnostic Criteria for Transient Tic Disorder*

A. Onset during childhood or early adolescence.

B. Presence of recurrent, involuntary, repetitive, rapid, purposeless, motor movements (tics).

C. Ability to suppress the movements voluntarily for minutes to hours.

D. Variation in the intensity of the symptoms over weeks or months.

E. Duration of at least 1 month but not more than 1 year.

* From American Psychiatric Association: *Diagnostic and Statistical Manual of Mental Disorders*, ed 3. American Psychiatric Association, Washington, DC, 1980. Used with permission.

### Diagnostic Criteria for Chronic Motor Tic Disorder*

A. Presence of recurrent, involuntary, repetitive, rapid, purposeless movements (tics) involving no more than three muscle groups at any one time.

B. Unvarying intensity of the tics over weeks or months.

C. Ability to suppress the movements voluntarily for minutes to hours.

D. Duration of at least 1 year.

* From American Psychiatric Association: *Diagnostic and Statistical Manual of Mental Disorders*, ed 3. American Psychiatric Association, Washington, DC, 1980. Used with permission.

## References

Cohen D J, Detlor J, Shaywitz B A, Leckman J F: Interaction of biological and psychological factors in the natural history of Tourette syndrome: A paradigm for childhood neuropsychiatric disorders. In *Gilles de la Tourette Syndrome*, A J Friedhoff, T N Chase, editors. Raven Press, New York, 1982.

Cohen D J, Leckman J F: Tourette's syndrome: Advances in the treatment and research. J Am Acad Child Psychiatry 23: 123, 1984.

Diedrich W M, Carr D B: Identification of speech disorders. J Develop Behav Ped 5: 38, 1984.

Hayden T L: Classification of elective mutism. J Am Acad Child Psychiat 19: 118, 1980.

Shapiro A K, Shapiro E: Tourette syndrome: History and present status. In *Gilles de la Tourette Syndrome*, A J Friedhoff, T N Chase, editors. Raven Press, New York, 1982.

Silver L B: Speech disorders. In *Comprehensive Textbook of Psychiatry*, ed 4, H I Kaplan, B J Sadock, editors, p 1716. Williams & Wilkins, Baltimore, 1985.

Silver L B: Stereotyped movement disorders. In *Comprehensive Textbook of Psychiatry*, ed 4. H I Kaplan, B J Sadock, editors, p 1711. Williams & Wilkins, Baltimore, 1985.

# 35

# Other Disorders of Infancy, Childhood, and Adolescence

This chapter covers a broad range of disorders that relate to different stages of the life cycle from birth through adolescence. The attachment disorders of infancy, for example, occur before 8 months of age and are due to inadequate parenting and faulty caretaking of the infant. The disorder is not due to a physical condition, but in severe cases, physical changes result in conditions known as failure to thrive, hospitalism, and marasmus—the last of which often results in death. At the other end of the cycle are the identity disorders of adolescence, in which adolescents are unable to define their sense of self, set long-term goals, or establish a value system acceptable to both themselves and the society around them. If the identity disorder is not resolved, such persons may be fated for a life without lasting emotional attachments, intimacy, or vocational adjustment.

Between the two stages of infancy and adolescence range the entire spectrum of emotional disorders, many of which are covered in this section. Among those included are the eating disorders, such as anorexia nervosa; the personality disorders, such as schizoid disorder; the anxiety disorders, which include separation anxiety disorders; and finally, the conduct disorders—a group of disorders that, left untreated, may evolve into physical violence, stealing, truancy, and other forms of antisocial behavior.

The reader should refer to Chapter 35 in *Modern Synopsis-IV*, which covers these various disorders, and should then study the questions and answers below to gain an understanding of this area.

# Questions

**DIRECTIONS:** Each of the statements or questions below is followed by five suggested responses or completions. Select the *one* that is *best* in each case.

**35.1.** The child shown on the right is 5 years old and has a height of 35 inches (89 cm). Legs are short, head is normal-sized, and bodily proportions are infantile. Shortly after hospitalization, growth began in the absence of medical intervention.

The most likely diagnosis is

A. achondroplastic dwarfism
B. mesomelic dwarfism
C. hypothyroid dwarfism
D. psychosocial dwarfism
E. tryptophanuric dwarfism

**35.2.** All of the following are clinical features of bulimia *except*

A. an episodic pattern of binge eating
B. the ability to stop eating voluntarily
C. termination of binge by induced vomiting
D. weight fluctuations
E. rapid eating with little chewing

**35.3.** Habit disturbances that stem from separation anxiety include

A. nail biting
B. thumb sucking
C. masturbation
D. temper tantrums
E. all of the above

**35.4.** The treatment approach to socialized conduct disorder and delinquency that has been most effective is

A. the attempt to deal directly with delinquent gangs in their neighborhoods
B. traditional individual psychotherapy
C. welfare programs
D. drug therapy
E. various forms of group therapy

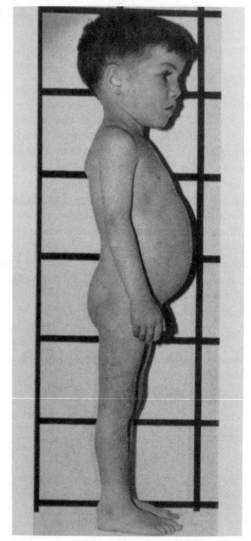

(Reproduced with permission from Davis J A, Dobbing J, editors: *Scientific Foundations of Paediatrics*, ed 1. William Heinemann Medical Books, London, 1974.)

**DIRECTIONS**: For each of the incomplete statements below, *one* or *more* of the completions given is correct. Choose answer:

A. if only **1, 2,** and **3** are correct
B. if only **1** and **3** are correct
C. if only **2** and **4** are correct
D. if only **4** is correct
E. if all are correct

**35.5.** Children with a schizoid disorder

1. are introverted
2. have a constricted affect
3. are with younger children when they make friendships
4. are generally aggressive and hostile

**35.6.** The 6-month-old infant illustrated below may be suffering from

1. malnourishment
2. failure to thrive
3. dehydration
4. psychosocial deprivation

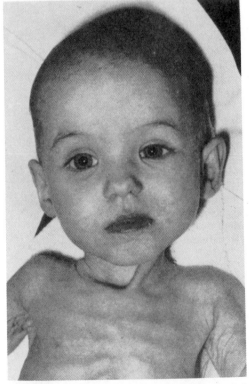

(Reproduced with permission from Davis J A, Dobbing J, editors: *Scientific Foundations of Paediatrics*, ed 1. William Heinemann Medical Books, Philadelphia, 1974.)

**35.7.** Separation anxiety in children is characterized by

1. fears that a loved one will be hurt
2. fears about getting lost
3. irritability
4. animal and monster phobias

**35.8.** Reactive attachment disorder of infancy

1. may be reversed shortly after institution of adequate caretaking
2. includes a normal head circumference and a failure to gain weight disproportionately greater than the failure to gain length
3. is usually associated with gross emotional neglect or imposed social isolation in an institution
4. is indicated by a lack of developmentally appropriate signs of social responsivity

**35.9.** Therapies for rumination (regurgitation disorder) include

1. devices to keep the mouth securely closed
2. the use of electric shocks
3. squirting lemon juice in the mouth
4. thickening the child's formula

**35.10.** A major affective episode in children under 6 years of age may present with

1. poor or increased appetite
2. insomnia or hypersomnia
3. psychomotor agitation or retardation
4. a persistently sad facial expression

**35.11.** Attachment to the mothering figure

1. appears to be an inherent tendency
2. depends on the intensity and quality of interaction
3. gradually develops during the first year of life
4. is defined as having the quality of a bilateral, reciprocal affectionate relationship

**35.12.** Rumination (regurgitation disorder)

1. occurs equally in males and females
2. may result in death
3. causes weight loss
4. is not seen in adults

| Directions Summarized | | | | |
|---|---|---|---|---|
| A | B | C | D | E |
| 1, 2, 3 | 1, 3 | 2, 4 | 4 | All are |
| only | only | only | only | correct |

**35.13.**  Oppositional disorder

1. is diagnosed only as negativistic behavior
2. is more common in girls than in boys
3. shows distinct familial patterns
4. is more common in unwanted children

**35.14.**  An avoidant disorder is diagnosed in children

1. who avoid contact with strangers
2. who have symptoms for at least 6 months
3. who are able to relate well to family members only
4. who refuse to play with other children by 1 year of age

**35.15.**  Infants with adequate multiple caretakers

1. develop feelings of severe depression
2. develop failure to thrive
3. develop poor social responsivity
4. do not develop attachment disorder

**35.16.**  Clinical evidence supports which of the following as predisposing toward overanxious disorders in children:

1. Large families
2. First-born children
3. Low socioeconomic status
4. High expectations

**35.17.**  Identity disorders of adolescence

1. result from transitory regression
2. are associated with uncertainty regarding long-term goals
3. are common in members of revolutionary groups and cults
4. are usually diagnosed as secondary to another mental disorder

**35.18.**  The diagnosis of bulimia includes

1. a depressed mood and self-deprecating thoughts following eating binges
2. the disorder being due to anorexia nervosa
3. physical discomfort terminating the episode
4. a lack of awareness that the eating pattern is abnormal

**35.19.**  Pica

1. is more commonly seen in white children than in black children
2. increases in prevalence with increasing age
3. is seen more commonly in girls than in boys
4. occurs most frequently between the ages of 12 months to 6 years

**35.20.**  According to DSM-III, conduct disorders in children are divided into which of the following types:

1. Aggressive, undersocialized
2. Unaggressive, undersocialized
3. Unaggressive, socialized
4. Aggressive, socialized

**35.21.**  Oppositional disorder is characterized by

1. continuous argumentativeness
2. unwillingness to respond to persuasion
3. negativism
4. disobedience to all in authority

**35.22.**  Psychoanalytic bases for anxiety in the child have been ascribed to

1. dependency
2. fear of the superego
3. symbiosis
4. castration fears

**35.23.**  Schizoid disorder in children must be differentiated from

1. avoidant disorder
2. psychoses
3. depression
4. adjustment disorder

**DIRECTIONS:** Each set of lettered headings below is followed by a list of numbered words or phrases. For each numbered word or phrase, select

    A. if the item is associated with **A** only
    B. if the item is associated with **B** only
    C. if the item is associated with *both* **A** *and* **B**
    D. if the item is associated with *neither* **A** *nor* **B**

**Questions 35.24–35.28**
A. Bulimia
B. Pica
C. Both
D. Neither

**35.24.** Predominance in females

**35.25.** Chronic, remitting course

**35.26.** Strong familial pattern

**35.27.** Differentiated from somatization disorder

**35.28.** Disturbance in eating behavior

# Answers

# Other Disorders of Infancy, Childhood, and Adolescence

**35.1. The answer is D** (*Synopsis*, ed. 4, pages 773 and 778).

The child is suffering from a condition known as *psychosocial dwarfism*. The disorder results from psychosocial deprivation in early childhood that may lead to growth failure of psychogenic origin. The various physical and behavioral symptoms of psychosocial dwarfism are briefly outlined in the table below.

*Achondroplastic dwarfism* results from growth retardation due to abnormal ossification of cartilage in the epiphyses of the long bones. This condition, mediated by mutation or autosomal dominant inheritance, is characterized by short extremities with normally proportioned trunk, enlarged head, and flattened nose.

*Mesomelic dwarfism* is characterized by an abnormal shortness of the forearm and lower legs.

*Hypothyroid dwarfism* is associated with cretinism—infantile hypothyroidism. In addition to typical behavioral and physiological symptoms, its physical features include protruding tongue, flat nose, wide-set eyes, sparse hair, dry skin, and protuberant abdomen with umbilical hernia.

*Tryptophanuric dwarfism* results from an inherited deficiency—autosomal recessive—in tryptophan pyrrolase and is characterized by a constellation of symptoms, including short stature, mental deficiency, cutaneous photosensitivity, and gait disturbance.

Other distinguishing symptoms notwithstanding, the key feature in this particular case is the rapid onset of growth—and correspondingly elevated levels of growth hormone—on removal from the pathological psychosocial environment.

---

### Diagnostic Criteria for Classical Psychosocial Dwarfism*

A. Age at onset usually between 2 and 3 years.

B. Severe retardation of growth. Marked linear growth retardation well below the third percentile for age and significantly delayed epiphysical maturation are usually present. (Although not a disqualifier, malnutrition is *not* felt to be contributory in the majority of cases.)

C. Severe disturbances in the mother(ing figure)/child dyad. (Mothers are heterogeneous regarding their psychopathologies.)

D. Emotional disturbance in the child as evidenced by some of the following:

　1. Bizarre behavior involving abnormal acquisition and intake of food and water, e.g. polyphagia, polydipsia, gorging and vomiting, eating from garbage pails, drinking toilet water;

　2. Apathy, withdrawal, chronic grief;

　3. Poor peer relations;

　4. Accident proneness, self injury, pain agnosia;

　5. Developmental lags, e.g. psychomotor retardation and delayed language, and I.Q.'s in the borderline or retarded ranges.

E. Abnormal endocrine functioning is present in over 50 percent of the children (decreased growth hormone (GH) and somatomedin levels and abnormal pituitary-adrenal axis findings).

F. Not due to a physical disorder, e.g. idiopathic hypopituitarism, mental retardation, or infantile autism.

G. The diagnosis is confirmed when growth promptly begins with no medical, hormonal, or psychiatric treatment following the child's removal to a new domicile or hospitalization.

---

* Adapted from Green W H, et al: Psychosocial dwarfism: A critical review of the evidence. J Am Acad Child Psychiatry *23:* 39, 1984.

**450**

**35.2.   The answer is B** (*Synopsis*, ed. 4, page 780).

According to DSM-III, there are essential features that are always present in a person suffering from bulimia. There is always an *episodic pattern of binge eating* that involves rapid consumption of a large amount of food in a discrete period of time. Also present is a *fear of not being able to stop eating voluntarily*. Most bulimic patients will *terminate a binge by induced vomiting*, abdominal pain, sleep, or social interruption. *Weight fluctuations* are seen, within a range of mildly underweight to mildly overweight. Food is eaten as inconspicuously as possible or secretly during a binge; there is also rapid eating with little chewing and consumption of high-caloric, sweet-tasting food with a texture that facilitates rapid eating.

The following table gives the DSM-III outline of the clinical features of bulimia.

### Clinical Features of Bulimia*

*Essential features that are always present:*

1. Episodic pattern of binge eating—rapid consumption of a large amount of food in a discrete period of time, usually less than 2 hours.
2. Fear of not being able to stop eating voluntarily.
3. Awareness of the eating disorder and great concern about weight demonstrated by repeated attempts to control weight by diet, vomiting, or use of cathartics.
4. Food eaten as inconspicuously as possible or secretly during a binge; rapid eating with little chewing; consumption of high-caloric, sweet tasting food with a texture that facilitates rapid eating.
5. Termination of a binge with abdominal pain, sleep, social interruption, or induced vomiting.
6. Disparaging self-criticism and depressive mood after episodes of binge eating.
7. Dieting, often quite severe between episodes of bingeing.
8. Weight fluctuations within a range of mildly underweight to mildly overweight.

*Associated features that are commonly but not invariably present:*

1. History of intermittent substance abuse; substances most frequently abused: barbiturates, amphetamines, alcohol.
2. Disturbed sexual adjustment ranging from promiscuity to a restricted sexual life.
3. Manifest concern with body image and emphasis on appearance, with often intense concern as to how others see and react to the patient.

* Adapted from American Psychiatric Association: *Diagnostic and Statistical Manual of Mental Disorders*, ed 3. American Psychiatric Association, Washington, DC, 1980.

**35.3.   The answer is E** (*Synopsis*, ed. 4, page 794).

Many habit disturbances, such as *nail biting, thumb sucking, temper tantrums*, eating problems, *masturbation*, and stuttering, stem from a common base of separation anxiety.

Transient experiences of separation anxiety are quite frequent, and as the organism cannot tolerate anxiety for any length of time, the anxiety tends to crystallize into other kinds of disorders. The transformation of anxiety into compulsive mechanisms, phobias, and other symptoms occurs frequently. Therefore, a mixed picture of neurotic symptoms and free anxiety is often seen.

*Nail biting* is also known as onychophagy and is a habitual manipulation in which one's inner tension is released. *Thumb sucking* is one of the earliest and most common manipulations of one's body used by young children. During the first month, thumb sucking is common, but is not a universal characteristic of the infant. It is classified as abnormal if it continues to persist through early childhood. *Masturbation* is a self-stimulation of the genitals for sexual pleasure. A *temper tantrum* is an outburst of crying, screaming, and kicking produced by a child in response to frustrations.

**35.4.   The answer is E** (*Synopsis*, ed. 4, page 807).

Treatment approaches to delinquency may be divided into preventive efforts and treatment methods designed for children already officially declared delinquent.

Only a small percentage of delinquent youngsters respond favorably to the typical permissive, dynamically oriented counseling approach. There is some evidence that reality therapy may be *most effective in a group setting*, either in self-help groups or in professionally directed groups. The treatment is effective *when it takes place in the neighborhood of the delinquent gang*. Basically, these groups use a core of reformed delinquents who understand the rationalizations, denials, and self-justifications of the gang member and vigorously confront the youngster with the realities of his or her predicament and the inevitability of eventual negative consequences if delinquency continues.

Although the evidence to this point is anecdotal and inconclusive, the consensus in the literature seems to *favor various forms of group therapy* for the child with socialized conduct disorder. Group-oriented approaches capitalize on the gang member's natural proclivity to turn to peers for direction and emotional support. The crucial task is to convert the group orientation toward more conventional values. This conversion may require separation from the previous peer group and transplantation to an entirely new environment, as in training schools, Outward Bound, and Therapeutic camping programs.

*Drug therapy* is of use when there is an underlying mental disorder contributing to the delinquent behavior.

One element of the preventive approach to delinquency is the variety of general *welfare programs* that have been mounted over the years in an effort to ameliorate the sociological conditions that seem to produce a high incidence of delinquent behavior. It is obvious that delinquency continues in spite of such programs, but the programs' proponents can argue with justification that efforts have been inadequate and, at any rate, may have prevented the delinquency statistics from being worse than they are.

Experiments in which potential delinquents received *traditional individual psychotherapy* have produced disappointing results. Individual outpatient psychotherapy appears to be relatively ineffective in problems of this kind, although it should be noted that the psychotherapy was brief and relatively superficial in these studies.

**35.5.   The answer is A (1, 2, 3)** (*Synopsis*, ed. 4, pages 784 and 785).

Schizoid disorder of childhood is described in DSM-III as a defect in the capacity to form social relationships, *introversion*, and bland or *constricted affect* that cannot be attributed to another disorder. Children with this disorder show little desire for social involvements, prefer to be loners, and have few, if any, friends. When placed in social situations, they are inept and awkward. *Their friendships tend to be with younger or other poorly functioning children.*

These children often appear reserved, withdrawn, and seclusive, and they pursue solitary interests or hobbies. They may seem vague about their goals, indecisive in their activities,

absentminded, and detached from their environment ("not with it" or "in a fog"). They do not appear distressed by their isolation.

Children with this disorder usually lack the capacity for emotional display and *are unable to express aggressiveness or hostility.* They usually appear cold, aloof, and distant, although attachment to a parent or other adult is not unusual. They especially avoid competitive activities and sports.

See the table below for the DSM-III diagnostic criteria for schizoid disorder in children or adolescence.

**35.6.   The answer is E (all)** (*Synopsis*, ed. 4, pages 774 and 775).

In *psychosocially deprived* infants, hypokinesis, dullness, listlessness, or apathy with a poverty of spontaneous activity are usually seen. The children look sad, unhappy, joyless, or miserable. Some infants also appear frightened, and an appearance of watchfulness or radar-like gaze has been described. Despite this, these children may exhibit delayed responsiveness to a stimulus that would elicit fright or withdrawal in a normal child.

Some older infants who are psychosocially deprived continue to exhibit infantile postures. They may hold their arms in a characteristic position with elbows flexed to a right angle or more, the upper arm held close to the body but rotated outward, and the hands pronated and held up in front of the chest or behind the head. Normally, this posture is not seen in infants over 4 to 5 months of age.

Most of the children appear significantly *malnourished*, and many have characteristically protruding abdomens. Occasionally, foul-smelling, celiac-like stools are reported. In unusually severe cases, a clinical picture of marasmus may appear. Weight is often below the third percentile and markedly below appropriate weight for height. If serial weights are available, it may be

### Diagnostic Criteria for Schizoid Disorder of Childhood or Adolescence*

A. No close friend of similar age other than a relative or a similarly socially isolated child.

B. No apparent interest in making friends.

C. No pleasure from usual peer interactions.

D. General avoidance of nonfamilial social contacts, especially with peers.

E. No interest in activities that involve other children (such as team sports, clubs).

F. Duration of the disturbance of at least 3 months.

G. Not due to pervasive developmental disorder; conduct disorder, undersocialized, nonaggressive; or any psychotic disorder, such as schizophrenia.

H. If 18 or older, does not meet the criteria for schizoid personality disorder.

* From American Psychiatric Association: *Diagnostic and Statistical Manual of Mental Disorders*, ed 3. American Psychiatric Association, Washington, DC, 1980. Used with permission.

noted that weight percentiles have progressively decreased because of actual weight loss or a failure to gain weight as height increases. If strict criteria for weight gain in infants are adhered to, *failure to thrive* may become evident within the first month, as indicated by the infant's failing to regain birthweight by day 14 and by failing to average a weight gain of 18.7 g/day (0.66 oz/day) from days 15 to 60. Head circumference is usually normal for age. Poor muscle tone may be present. The skin may be colder and more pale or mottled than the normal child's. Laboratory values are usually within normal limits except those abnormal findings are coincident with malnutrition, *dehydration,* or intercurrent illness. Bone age is usually retarded. Growth hormone levels are usually normal or elevated, and pituitary functioning is normal. This is in agreement with suggestions that growth failure in these children is secondary to caloric deprivation and malnutrition. Both physical improvement of the child and concomitant weight gain usually occur rapidly following hospitalization.

**35.7.  The answer is E (all)** (*Synopsis*, ed. 4, page 792).

Morbid fears, preoccupations, and ruminations are characteristic of separation anxiety in children. Children become fearful that *someone close to them will be hurt* or that something terrible will happen to them when they are away from important caring figures. Many children worry that accidents or illness will befall their parents or themselves. *Fears about getting lost* and about being kidnapped and never again finding their parents are common. Young children express less specific, more generalized concerns because their immature cognitive development precludes the formation of well-defined fears. In older children, fears of getting lost may include elaborate fantasies around kidnappings, being harmed, being raped, or being made slaves.

When separation from an important figure is imminent, children show many premonitory signs, such as *irritability,* difficulty in eating, and complaining and whining behavior. Physical complaints, such as vomiting or headaches, are common when separation is anticipated or actually happens. These difficulties increase in intensity and organization with age because the older child is able to anticipate anxiety in a more structured fashion. Thus, there is a continuum between mild anticipatory anxiety before a threatened separation and pervasive anxiety after the separation has occurred.

*Animal and monster phobias* are common, as are concerns about dying. The child, when threatened with separation, may become fearful that events related to muggers, burglars, car accidents, or kidnapping may occur.

See the table below for a list of the DSM-III diagnostic criteria for separation anxiety.

---

**Diagnostic Criteria for Separation Anxiety Disorder\***

A. Excessive anxiety concerning separation from those to whom the child is attached, as manifested by at least three of the following:

1. Unrealistic worry about possible harm befalling major attachment figures or fear that they will leave and not return;

2. Unrealistic worry that an untoward calamitous event will separate the child from a major attachment figure, e.g. the child will be lost, kidnapped, killed, or be the victim of an accident;

3. Persistent reluctance or refusal to go to school in order to stay with major attachment figures or at home;

4. Persistent reluctance or refusal to go to sleep without being next to a major attachment figure or to go to sleep away from home;

5. Persistent avoidance of being alone in the home and emotional upset if unable to follow the major attachment figure around the home;

6. Repeated nightmares involving theme of separation;

7. Complaints of physical symptoms on school days, e.g. stomachaches, headaches, nausea, vomiting;

8. Signs of excessive distress upon separation, or when anticipating separation, from major attachment figures, e.g. temper tantrums or crying, pleading with parents not to leave (for children below the age of 6, the distress must be of panic proportions);

9. Social withdrawal, apathy, sadness, or difficulty concentrating on work or play when not with a major attachment figure.

B. Duration of disturbance of at least 2 weeks.

C. Not due to a pervasive developmental disorder, schizophrenia, or any other psychotic disorder.

D. If 18 or older, does not meet the criteria for agoraphobia.

---

\* From American Psychiatric Association: *Diagnostic and Statistical Manual of Mental Disorders,* ed 3. American Psychiatric Association, Washington, DC, 1980. Used with permission.

## Diagnostic Criteria for Reactive Attachment Disorder of Infancy*

A. Age at onset before 8 months.

B. Lack of the type of care that ordinarily leads to the development of affectional bonds to others, e.g. *gross emotional neglect, imposed social isolation in an institution.*

C. *Lack of developmentally appropriate signs of social responsivity*, as indicated by at least several of the following (the total number of behaviors looked for will depend on the chronological age of the child, corrected for prematurity):

    1. Lack of visual tracking of eyes and faces by an infant more than 2 months of age;

    2. Lack of smiling in response to faces by an infant more than 2 months of age;

    3. Lack of visual reciprocity in an infant of more than 2 months; lack of vocal reciprocity with caretaker in an infant of more than 5 months;

    4. Lack of alerting and turning toward caretaker's voice by an infant of more than 4 months;

    5. Lack of spontaneous reaching for the mother by an infant of more than 4 months;

    6. Lack of anticipatory reaching when approached to be picked up, by an infant of more than 5 months;

    7. Lack of participation in playful games with caretaker by an infant of more than 5 months.

D. At least three of the following:

    1. Weak cry;

    2. Excessive sleep;

    3. Lack of interest in the environment;

    4. Hypomotility;

    5. Poor muscle tone;

    6. Weak rooting and grasping in response to feeding attempts.

E. Weight loss or failure to gain appropriate amount of weight for age unexplainable by any physical disorder. In these cases, usually *the failure to gain weight (falling weight percentile) is disproportionately greater than failure to gain length; head circumference is normal.*

F. Not due to a physical disorder, mental retardation, or infantile autism.

G. The diagnosis is confirmed if the clinical picture is *reversed shortly after institution of adequate caretaking,* which frequently includes short-term hospitalization.

* From American Psychiatric Association: *Diagnostic and Statistical Manual of Mental Disorders*, ed 3. American Psychiatric Association, Washington, DC, 1980. Used with permission.

**35.8. The answer is E (all)** (*Synopsis*, ed. 4, page 772).

The essential features of reactive attachment disorder of infancy are signs of poor emotional and physical development, with onset before 8 months of age, and are due to a lack of adequate caretaking. The disturbance is not due to a physical disorder, mental retardation, or infantile autism.

The table above lists the DSM-III diagnostic criteria for this disorder in more detail.

**35.9. The answer is E (all)** (*Synopsis*, ed. 4, page 783).

Many therapies have been advocated for treating rumination. Treatment includes fostering a loving relationship between parent and infant and parental training. There are case reports of ruminating infants who gradually gave up this behavior as they were given love and attention from an attentive nurse.

Various devices have been invented to *keep the mouth securely closed.* This form of treatment has seldom been successful, however, nor has *thickening the infant's formula* met with dramatic results. In three ruminating children

with hiatus hernias, one was treated successfully by feeding the child in an upright position and by maintenance of this upright position for prolonged periods of time. The other two were successfully treated with surgical repair of the hernias.

Behavior therapy techniques have been reported to be successful in stopping rumination. Aversive conditioning with *electric shock* has been able to eliminate rumination within a 3- to 5-day period. In all the above aversion conditioning reports on rumination, the infants were doing well at 9- or 12-month follow-ups, with no recurrence of the rumination and with weight gains, increased activity levels, and greater general responsiveness to people. Another form of aversive conditioning reported was that of *squirting a small amount of lemon juice into the mouth of an infant* whenever rumination activity was detected. This approach was as effective as electric shock therapy.

It is extremely difficult to evaluate the variety of treatments that have been used for rumination, because most are single case reports and because none of the treatments has been evaluated by a randomly assigned controlled study.

See the following table for a list of the DSM-III clinical features of rumination.

### Clinical Features of Rumination*

*Essential features that are always present:*

1. Regurgitation of food, with failure to thrive after a period of normal functioning.
2. Food brought up to the mouth without nausea, retching, or disgust, and then rejected from the mouth or chewed and reswallowed.
3. Characteristic position of straining and arching the back with the head held back.
4. Sucking movements of the tongue; infant gives impression of gaining considerable satisfaction from the activity.

*Associated feature that is commonly but not invariably present:* Irritability and hunger between episodes of rumination.

* Adapted from American Psychiatric Association: *Diagnostic and Statistical Manual of Mental Disorders*, ed 3. American Psychiatric Association, Washington, DC, 1980.

**35.10.   The answer is E (all)** (*Synopsis*, ed. 4, pages 776 and 777).

DSM-III specifically recommends considering the diagnosis of major depressive episode if a picture clinically similar to attachment disorder develops after 8 months of age. Criteria for this diagnosis in children under 6 years of age differ from those in older children and adults. The primary differentiating feature from a reactive attachment disorder would be a history of normal development and attachment behavior up to at least the age of 8 months. The rationale for diagnosing an 8-month-old as major depressive episode and a 7-month-old as attachment disorder is not clear.

The specific DSM-III diagnostic criteria for a major affective episode in children under 6 years of age are listed in the table below.

**35.11.   The answer is E (all)** (*Synopsis*, ed. 4, page 771).

Attachment is *the quality of a bilateral, reciprocal affectionate relationship* between the infant and parent, especially the mother or primary caretaker, *which gradually develops during the first year of life.*

John Bowlby has suggested *there is an inherent tendency* for an infant to attach to one person, which he called monotropy. Although there is clinical evidence that this is usually the case, the primary attachment is not necessarily with the mother, and multiple attachments can occur. Although mother and infant must spend a certain minimum amount of time interacting with each other, after this has been satisfied, *it is the intensity and quality of the interaction* that appear to be the most important factors in establishing attachment.

**35.12.   The answer is A (1, 2, 3)** (*Synopsis*, ed. 4, page 782).

Rumination is an extremely rare but fascinating illness that has been recognized for hundreds of years. This regurgitation disorder, which is *potentially fatal*, occurs predominantly in infancy and seldom in adults. An awareness of the disorder is important so that it may be correctly diagnosed and so that unnecessary surgical procedures or inappropriate treatment can be avoided.

Rumination is derived from the Latin word ruminare, which means to chew the cud. The Hellenic equivalent is merycism, which describes the act of regurgitation of food from the stomach into the mouth, chewing the food again, and reswallowing.

The association of this behavior with malnutrition and death in children has been reported for many years. Usually, children with this affliction will suffer from *weight loss*, although *adults who are afflicted maintain a normal weight.*

### Diagnostic Criteria for a Major Affective Episode in Children under Six Years of Age*

A. Dysphoric mood, which may have to be inferred from a *persistently sad facial expression.*

B. At least three of the following symptoms present nearly every day for a period of at least 2 weeks:

1. *Poor appetite* or significant weight loss or *increased appetite* or significant weight gain or failure to make expected weight gains;
2. *Insomnia or hypersomnia:*
3. *Psychomotor agitation or retardation* or hypoactivity;
4. Loss of interest or pleasure in usual activities or signs of apathy.

C. Neither bizarre behavior nor preoccupation with a mood-incongruent delusion or hallucination is present before or after the major depressive episode.

D. Schizophrenia, schizophreniform disorder, or a paranoid disorder is not present.

E. It is not due to any organic mental disorder or uncomplicated bereavement.

* Adapted from American Psychiatric Association: *Diagnostic and Statistical Manual of Mental Disorders*, ed 3. American Psychiatric Association, Washington, DC, 1980

Rumination has been reported *equally in males and females.* Although familial cases, including rumination in five generations and in a man and his six children, have been reported, the bias of selective case reporting does not allow any conclusion about the existence of a familial pattern in this disorder.

The first table below lists the DSM-III diagnostic criteria for rumination.

**35.13.   The answer is D (4)** (*Synopsis*, ed. 4, pages 786, 787, and 788).

Oppositional negativistic behavior in children is fairly common, but because a good deal of it is normative, temporarily reactive, cultural, or a symptom of another disorder, its presence is not diagnostic. Epidemiological studies of the trait of negativism in nonclinical populations indicate an incidence of between 16 and 22 percent in the over-all school-age population. The disorder can begin at 3 years of age, but is more common during late childhood or early adolescence. *In many cases, the patients were unwanted children.*

*Both the trait of negativism and the diagnosis of oppositional disorder are much more common in boys than in girls,* with estimates of the occurrence in boys ranging from twice to 10 times the occurrence in girls.

There are *no distinct family patterns,* but almost all parents of oppositional children are themselves overconcerned with issues of power, control, and autonomy. Some families contain a large number of obstinate characters, a larger number of controlling and depressed mothers, and fathers who tend to be passive-aggressive.

The second table below lists the DSM-III diagnostic criteria for oppositional disorder.

**35.14.   The answer is A (1, 2, 3)** (*Synopsis*, ed. 4, pages 796 and 797).

Avoidant disorder is diagnosed on the basis of *a persistent shrinking from contact and involvement with strangers* and on avoidance behavior that interferes with peer functioning. These *symptoms must be present for at least 6 months* in a child at least 2½ years of age who has *generally warm and satisfying relationships with family members.* In the mild disorder, there may be *an ability to function comfortably with a few close friends,* but there is some impairment in general peer functioning without any adverse effect on school performance. In the moderate disorder, there is difficulty in participation in class activities and some impairment in school work, together with alienation from friends due to inability to join them in other activities. Severe cases manifest marked interference with the development of peer relationships and serious impairment in class work or social participation.

The table at the top of the facing page gives the DSM-III diagnostic criteria for avoidant disorder of childhood and adolescence.

---

### Diagnostic Criteria for Rumination Disorder of Infancy*

A. Repeated regurgitation without nausea or associated gastrointestinal illness for at least 1 month following a period of normal functioning.

B. Weight loss or failure to make expected weight gain.

* From American Psychiatric Association: *Diagnostic and Statistical Manual of Mental Disorders,* ed 3. American Psychiatric Association, Washington, DC, 1980. Used with permission.

---

### Diagnostic Criteria for Oppositional Disorder*

A. Onset after 3 years of age and before age 18.

B. *A pattern, for at least 6 months, of disobedient, negativistic, and provocative opposition to authority figures,* as manifested by at least two of the following symptoms:
   1. Violations of minor rules;
   2. Temper tantrums;
   3. Argumentativeness;
   4. Provocative behavior;
   5. Stubbornness.

C. No violation of the basic rights of others or of major age-appropriate societal norms or rules (as in conduct disorder); and the disturbance is not due to another mental disorder, such as schizophrenia or a pervasive developmental disorder.

D. If 18 or older, does not meet the criteria for passive-aggressive personality disorder.

* From American Psychiatric Association: *Diagnostic and Statistical Manual of Mental Disorders,* ed 3. American Psychiatric Association, Washington, DC, 1980. Used with permission.

## Diagnostic Criteria for Avoidant Disorder of Childhood or Adolescence*

A. Persistent and excessive shrinking from contact with strangers.

B. Desire for affection and acceptance, and generally warm and satisfying relations with family members and other family figures.

C. Avoidant behavior sufficiently severe to interfere with social functioning in peer relationships.

D. Age at least 2½. If 18 or older, does not meet the criteria for avoidant personality disorder.

E. Duration of the disturbance of at least 6 months.

*From American Psychiatric Association: *Diagnostic and Statistical Manual of Mental Disorders*, ed 3. American Psychiatric Association, Washington, DC, 1980. Used with permission.

**35.15. The answer is D (4)** (*Synopsis*, ed. 4, page 774).

The disastrous effects that institutionalization or prolonged hospitalization may have on infants and young children have been studied and reviewed by René Spitz, John Bowlby, and others. This condition has been called hospitalism or *failure to thrive*. These researchers have emphasized the need of infants for intimate emotional involvement with their caretakers and adequate sensory stimulation for their physical well-being and resistance to infection, as well as their long-term emotional health. Because of their research, institutions today assign more stable or permanent caretakers to specific infants and children, and hospitals encourage increased parental visitation and rooming in. *Infants with adequate multiple caretakers do not develop attachment disorder* or signs of poor physical development, such as feelings of *severe depression* or *poor social responsivity*.

**35.16. The answer is C (2, 4)** (*Synopsis*, ed. 4, page 798).

The onset of overanxious disorder may be sudden or gradual, with exacerbations associated with stress. Some clinical evidence suggests that this disorder is most common in *small families of upper socioeconomic status, in first children, and in situations in which there is unusual concern about performance*, even when the child is functioning at an adequate level. In such families, children who develop the overanxious disorder come to feel that they must earn their acceptance in the family by high-level, conforming behavior. They tend to be "goody-two-shoes" children. Although both boys and girls develop this disorder, it has been seen more frequently in boys than in girls.

See the table below for a list of DSM-III diagnostic criteria for overanxious disorder.

**35.17. The answer is A (1, 2, 3)** (*Synopsis*, ed. 4, pages 809 and 810).

The clinical picture of acute identity disorder is recognized in young people who are unable to use the social or intrapsychic moratoriums provided. The normal intrapsychic transformations necessary in ego mastery result in persistent regressive phenomena leading to crisis formation and, if not relieved by adequate growth responses, identity diffusion.

## Diagnostic Criteria for Overanxious Disorder*

A. The predominant disturbance is generalized and persistent anxiety or worry (not related to concerns about separation), as manifested by at least four of the following:
1. Unrealistic worry about future events;
2. Preoccupation with the appropriateness of the individual's behavior in the past;
3. Overconcern about competence in a variety of areas, e.g. academic, athletic, social;
4. Excessive need for reassurance about a variety of worries;
5. Somatic complaints, such as headaches or stomachaches, for which no physical basis can be established;
6. Marked self-consciousness or susceptibility to embarrassment or humiliation;
7. Marked feelings of tension or inability to relax.

B. The symptoms in A have persisted for at least 6 months.

C. If 18 or older, does not meet the criteria for generalized anxiety disorder.

D. The disturbance is not due to another mental disorder, such as separation anxiety disorder, avoidant disorder of childhood or adolescence, phobic disorder, obsessive-compulsive disorder, depressive disorder, schizophrenia, or a pervasive developmental disorder.

*From American Psychiatric Association: *Diagnostic and Statistical Manual of Mental Disorders*, ed 3. American Psychiatric Association, Washington, DC, 1980. Used with permission.

## Diagnostic Criteria for Identity Disorder*

A. Severe subjective distress regarding uncertainty about a variety of issues relating to identity, including three or more of the following:
   1. Long-term goals;
   2. Career choice;
   3. Friendship patterns;
   4. Sexual orientation and behavior;
   5. Religious identification;
   6. Moral value systems;
   7. Group loyalties.

B. Impairment in social or occupational (including academic) functioning as a result of the symptoms in A.
C. Duration of the disturbance of at least 3 months.
D. Not due to another mental disorder, such as affective disorder, schizophrenia, or schizophreniform disorder.
E. If 18 or older, does not meet the criteria for borderline personality disorder.

* From American Psychiatric Association: *Diagnostic and Statistical Manual of Mental Disorders*, ed 3. American Psychiatric Association, Washington, DC, 1980. Used with permission.

The clinical features of identity disorder are summarized in a serious struggle with the question: "Who am I?" The *resulting transitory regression* is manifested by being unable to make decisions, a sense of isolation and inner emptiness, an inability to achieve relationships and sexual intimacy, a distorted time perspective resulting in a sense of great urgency and a loss of consideration for time as a dimension of living, an acute inability to work, and, at times, choosing of a negative identity, one that is a hostile parody of the usual roles in one's family or community.

The *uncertainty regarding long-term goals* may be expressed as inability to choose a life pattern (material success versus service to the community) and conflict regarding career choice. Conflict regarding friendship patterns may manifest itself as attraction to particular groups characterized by uncommon interests or styles (*revolutionary or drug-oriented movements or cults*). Conflict regarding values and loyalties may include concerns over religious identification, patterns of sexual behavior, and moral issues.

*Identity disorder should not be diagnosed if the identity problems are secondary to another mental disorder.* Identity disorder must also be differentiated from the ordinary conflicts associated with maturing.

The DSM-III diagnostic criteria for identity disorder are described in the table above.

**35.18.   The answer is B (1, 3)** (*Synopsis*, ed. 4, pages 779 and 780).

Bulimia is an episodic, uncontrolled, compulsive, rapid ingestion of large quantities of food over a short period of time (binge eating). *Physical discomfort, such as abdominal pain or feelings of nausea, terminates the bulimic episode*, which is followed by feelings of guilt, depression, or self-disgust.

No epidemiological survey has been done of this disorder. The prevalence is not known, but appears to be common in adolescents and young adults. A few current reports indicate that bulimia may be far more prevalent, especially in young women, than previously was thought. No studies investigating a familial pattern in this disorder have been reported to date, but obesity may be found in other family members. There is no substantive evidence to support any causative hypothesis for this disorder.

The onset of the illness is usually in adolescence or early adult life. The usual course is chronic over a period of many years, with occasional remission. Bulimia is seldom incapacitating, except in a few persons who spend their entire day in binge eating and self-induced vomiting. Electrolyte imbalance and dehydration can occur in persons who vomit excessively.

Definite precipitating factors are unknown, but the onset of binge eating often occurs during the senior year in high school, when the patient is having to make important decisions about leaving home, getting a job, or going on to further schooling.

Bulimic patients are concerned about their body image and their appearance, they worry about how others see them, they are concerned about sexual attractiveness, and they fear getting obese. During a binge, these patients eat food that is sweet, high in calories, generally of smooth texture or soft, such as cakes or pastry. The binge episodes are usually planned, and the food is eaten secretly, rapidly, and sometimes not even chewed.

Once the binge starts, the patient may be unable to stop until vomiting is induced. The patient feels better after having vomited, and abdominal fullness or pain is relieved. The patient may then begin to binge again or may terminate bingeing temporarily. *Depression often follows the episode*, which has been called post-binge anguish.

*Bulimic episodes may occur in anorexia nervosa; but bulimia is not due to anorexia nervosa.* A diagnosis of bulimia cannot be made if anorexia nervosa is present, but episodic bulimic symptoms can occur in anorexia nervosa. If a patient meets all the criteria for the diagnosis of anorexia nervosa, then a diagnosis of anorexia nervosa should be given. Severe weight loss does not occur in bulimia, and amenorrhea seldom occurs. These two symptoms are necessary for the diagnosis of anorexia nervosa.

There is a paucity of published information about the treatment of bulimia. The treatment of bulimia in obese patients by psychotherapy is frequently stormy and always prolonged, although some obese bulimics who had prolonged psychotherapy did surprisingly well. Effective positive reinforcement, informational feedback, and contingency contracting with bulimic women with anorexia nervosa have been reported. A program of desensitization to the thoughts and feelings a bulimic patient has just before binge eating, in conjunction with a behavioral contract, may be a promising approach to the treatment of bulimia.

Several investigators have reported good results with imipramine. Pharmacotherapy requires further study.

The table below gives the DSM-III diagnostic criteria for bulimia.

**35.19. The answer is D (4)** (*Synopsis*, ed. 4, page 781).

DSM-III gives the diagnostic criteria for pica as evidence of regular eating of nonnutritive substance(s) for at least 1 month and not due to another mental disorder.

*There is a slight preponderance of black children with pica compared with white children. The prevalence of pica and the range of articles ingested decrease with increasing age. Investigators have reported that pica affects both sexes equally*, and age of onset can be from 12 to 24 months or even earlier. Some studies have found that the siblings of children with pica were more likely to have pica than are the siblings of unaffected children.

There are two commonly expounded theories about the causes of pica. One states that a specific nutritional deficit is present in the patient and this deficit causes the indiscriminate ingestion of nonnutritive substances. The other theory postulates that the inadequate relationship with the patient's mother produces unmet oral needs, which are expressed in the persistent search for inedible substances. In addition, poor supervision and neglect of the child are often found.

Generally, the practice of eating nonedible substances is regarded as abnormal after the age of 12 months. *Pica occurs most frequently between the ages of 12 to 24 months and 6 years*, but it can occur in any age group. Typically, young children ingest paint, plaster, string, hair, and cloth; older children have access to dirt, animal feces, stones, and paper.

Different forms of pica with varying complications and varying outcomes have been described. Lead poisoning is a major hazard for children who eat plaster and can result in mental retardation. Parasitic infestations are common in children who eat contaminated soil. Geophagia has been associated with anemia and zinc deficiency. Amylophagia—the ingestion of large quantities of starch, such as Argo starch—has

---

### Diagnostic Criteria for Bulimia*

A. Recurrent episodes of binge eating (rapid consumption of a large amount of food in a discrete period of time, usually less than 2 hours).

B. At least three of the following:

    1. Consumption of high-caloric, easily ingested food during a binge;

    2. Inconspicuous eating during a binge;

    3. Termination of such eating episodes by abdominal pain, sleep, social interruption, or self-induced vomiting;

    4. Repeated attempts to lose weight by severely restrictive diets, self-induced vomiting, or use of cathartics or diuretics;

    5. Frequent weight fluctuations greater than 10 pounds due to alternating binges and fasts.

C. *Awareness that the eating pattern is abnormal* and fear of not being able to stop eating voluntarily.

D. Depressed mood and self-deprecating thoughts following eating binges.

E. The bulimic episodes are not due to anorexia nervosa or any known physical disorder.

*From American Psychiatric Association: *Diagnostic and Statistical Manual of Mental Disorders*, ed 3. American Psychiatric Association, Washington, DC, 1980. Used with permission.

been associated with severe iron deficiency anemia. Rare forms of pica, such as trichophagia (hair ingestion) and stone or gravel ingestion (lithophagia), have been associated with intestinal obstruction, such as hair-ball tumors. Low serum iron levels have been found in patients who have pagophagia or who ingest large amounts of ice. A life-threatening hyperkalemia and chronic renal failure were described in five patients who had geophagia. In summary, the deleterious effects of pica are related to the type and the amount of ingested materials.

The pica of childhood usually remits by the time of adolescence, and the pica associated with pregnancy remits with the termination of the pregnancy. This disorder is rare in adults.

Pica may be treated from several approaches—environmental, behavioral, and directive guidance or family counseling. For children who are eating lead plaster, it is obviously necessary to alter the physical environment. In some patients, correction of an iron or zinc deficiency has resulted in the elimination of pica behavior. Several behavior therapy techniques have been effective in stopping pica. Aversion therapy has consisted of using mild electric shock, unpleasant noise, or an emetic drug. Positive reinforcement, such as social recognition or object rewards, has been effective, but it usually produces slower results compared with aversion therapy. Behavior shaping, having the child imitate the preferred behavior from a model, also produces behavioral changes more slowly than do negative reinforcements. Involving parents in a positive reinforcement behavior therapy program may allow the children to get attention that was previously lacking from their parents.

The table below gives the DSM-III diagnostic criteria for pica.

**35.20.   The answer is E (all)** (*Synopsis*, ed. 4, pages 800, 801, 803, and 804).

DSM-III divides the conduct disorders into four major types: *aggressive conduct disorder, undersocialized type; unaggressive conduct disorder, undersocialized type; unaggressive conduct disorder, socialized type; and aggressive conduct disorder, socialized type.* Children who cannot be fitted into one of the specific categories of conduct disorder because of lack of information or a mixed symptom picture may be classified as having an atypical conduct disorder.

DSM-III defines conduct disorders as follows: The essential feature of this group of disorders is repetitive and persistent patterns of antisocial behavior that violates the rights of others, beyond the ordinary mischief and pranks of children and adolescents. The diagnosis is only given to persons below the age of 18 years.

The tables on pages 461 and 462 describe in detail the DSM-III diagnostic criteria for each of the four major types of conduct disorder.

**35.21.   The answer is E (all)** (*Synopsis*, ed. 4, page 786).

Oppositional disorder is of interest for its resemblance to normal periods of development in early childhood and for its relationship to the passive-aggressive and compulsive personality disorders in adulthood. Oppositional disorder can be seen as an interim diagnostic phase between a period of greater plasticity and one of fixity.

Oppositional disorder is defined in DSM-III as follows: The essential features are a *pervasive opposition and disobedience to all in authority regardless of self-interest, a continuous argumentativeness*, and an *unwillingness to respond to reasonable persuasion*. Children with this disorder express their aggressiveness by oppositional patterns of behavior, especially toward parents and teachers. The oppositional behavior should be present for at least 6 months before the diagnosis is made.

*Negativism* is a verbal or nonverbal opposition or resistance to outside suggestions and advice. It is commonly seen in catatonic schizophrenia in which the patient resists any effort to be moved or does the opposite of what is asked.

**35.22.   The answer is E (all)** (*Synopsis*, ed. 4, pages 790 and 791).

In the course of development, various stresses were conceptualized by Freud as triggers for the occurrence of anxiety in the child.

Each period of the person's life has its appropriate determinant of anxiety. Thus, the danger of psychical helplessness is appropriate to the period of life when the ego is immature; the danger of loss of object, to early childhood when the child is still *dependent on others; the danger of castration*, to the phallic phase; and *the fear of the superego*, to the latency period. Nevertheless, all these danger situations and determi-

---

**Diagnostic Criteria for Pica\***

A. Repeated eating of a nonnutritive substance for at least 1 month.

B. Not due to another mental disorder, such as infantile autism or schizophrenia, or a physical disorder, such as Kleine-Levin syndrome.

---

\* From American Psychiatric Association: *Diagnostic and Statistical Manual of Mental Disorders*, ed 3. American Psychiatric Association, Washington, DC, 1980. Used with permission.

## Diagnostic Criteria for Conduct Disorder, Undersocialized, Aggressive*

A. A repetitive and persistent pattern of aggressive conduct in which the basic rights of others are violated, as manifested by either of the following:

    1. Physical violence against persons or property (not to defend someone else or oneself), e.g. vandalism, rape, breaking and entering, fire-setting, mugging, assault;

    2. Thefts outside the home involving confrontation with the victim, e.g. extortion, purse-snatching, armed robbery.

B. Failure to establish a normal degree of affection, empathy, or bond with others as evidenced by *no more than one* of the following indications of social attachment:

    1. Has one or more peer-group friendships that have lasted over 6 months;
    2. Extends himself or herself for others even when no immediate advantage is likely;
    3. Apparently feels guilt or remorse when such a reaction is appropriate (not just when caught or in difficulty);
    4. Avoids blaming or informing on companions;
    5. Shares concern for the welfare of friends or companions.

C. Duration of pattern of aggressive conduct of at least 6 months.

D. If 18 or older, does not meet the criteria for antisocial personality disorder.

* From American Psychiatric Association: *Diagnostic and Statistical Manual of Mental Disorders*, ed 3. American Psychiatric Association, Washington, DC, 1980. Used with permission.

## Diagnostic Criteria for Conduct Disorder, Undersocialized, Nonaggressive*

A. A repetitive and persistent pattern of nonaggressive conduct in which either the basic rights of others or major age-appropriate societal norms or rules are violated, as manifested by any of the following:

    1. Chronic violations of a variety of important rules (that are reasonable and age-appropriate for the child) at home or at school, e.g. persistent truancy, substance abuse;
    2. Repeated running away from home overnight;
    3. Persistent serious lying in and out of the home;
    4. Stealing not involving confrontation with a victim.

B. Failure to establish a normal degree of affection, empathy, or bond with others as evidenced by *no more than one* of the following indications of social attachment:

    1. Has one or more peer-group friendships that have lasted over 6 months;
    2. Extends himself or herself for others even when no immediate advantage is likely;
    3. Apparently feels guilt or remorse when such a reaction is appropriate (not just when caught or in difficulty);
    4. Avoids blaming or informing on companions;
    5. Shows concern for the welfare of friends or companions.

C. Duration of pattern of nonaggressive conduct of at least 6 months.

D. If 18 or older, does not meet the criteria for antisocial personality disorder.

* From American Psychiatric Association: *Diagnostic and Statistical Manual of Mental Disorders*, ed 3. American Psychiatric Association, Washington, DC, 1980. Used with permission.

## Diagnostic Criteria for Conduct Disorder, Socialized, Aggressive*

A. A repetitive and persistent pattern of aggressive conduct in which the basic rights of others are violated, as manifested by either of the following:

    1. Physical violence against persons or property (not to defend someone else or oneself), e.g. vandalism, rape, breaking and entering, fire-setting, mugging, assault;

    2. Thefts outside the home involving confrontation with a victim, e.g. extortion, purse-snatching, armed robbery.

B. Evidence of social attachment to others as indicated by at least two of the following behavior patterns:

    1. Has one or more peer-group friendships that have lasted over 6 months;
    2. Extends himself or herself for others even when no immediate advantage is likely;
    3. Apparently feels guilt or remorse when such a reaction is appropriate (not just when caught or in difficulty);
    4. Avoids blaming or informing on companions;
    5. Shows concern for the welfare of friends or companions.

C. Duration of pattern of aggressive conduct of at least 6 months.

D. If 18 or older, does not meet the criteria for antisocial personality disorder.

* From American Psychiatric Association: *Diagnostic and Statistical Manual of Mental Disorders*, ed 3. American Psychiatric Association, Washington, DC, 1980. Used with permission.

---

### Diagnostic Criteria for Conduct Disorder, Socialized, Nonaggressive*

A. A repetitive and persistent pattern of nonaggressive conduct in which either the basic rights of others or major age-appropriate societal norms or rules are violated, as manifested by any of the following:

1. Chronic violations of a variety of important rules (that are reasonable and age-appropriate for the child) at home or at school, e.g. persistent truancy, substance abuse;
2. Repeated running away from home overnight;
3. Persistent serious lying in and out of the home;
4. Stealing not involving confrontation with a victim.

B. Evidence of social attachment to others as indicated by at least two of the following behavior patterns:

1. Has one or more peer-group friendships that have lasted over 6 months;
2. Extends himself or herself for others even when no immediate advantage is likely;
3. Apparently feels guilt or remorse when such a reaction is appropriate (not just when caught or in difficulty);
4. Avoids blaming or informing on companions;
5. Shows concern for the welfare of friends or companions.

C. Duration of patterns of nonagressive conduct of at least 6 months.

D. If 18 or older, does not meet the criteria for antisocial personality disorder.

---

* From American Psychiatric Association: *Diagnostic and Statistical Manual of Mental Disorders*, ed 3. American Psychiatric Association, Washington, DC, 1980. Used with permission.

---

nants of anxiety can persist side by side and cause the ego to react to them with anxiety at a period later than the appropriate one; or again, several of them can come into operation at the same time.

These views have been elaborated conceptually and clinically by a number of workers. During the period of *symbiosis*, described by Margaret Mahler as occurring at about 3 to 18 months of age, the mother functions as an auxiliary ego and helps the infant develop ego boundaries that define and delimit reality testing, frustration tolerance, and impulse control. The traumatic loss of a mothering figure, or the rejection of the infant by the mothering figure early in life, may result in fear of total annihilation, followed later by a fear of the loss of the mothering figure or object. These anxieties must border on panic and be among the most powerful and terror-ridden ones experienced by a human. Anna Freud emphasized the concept of anxiety in the recognition of the strength of the instincts of the infant. In this dim, early developmental period, the strength of their rage and destructive impulses may leave infants with a feeling of overwhelming anxiety.

During the maximal development of early self-awareness or object constancy, the 2-year-old child has internalized experiences of goodness and badness from the mother and is able to retain an internalized memory of the mother figure and of others in a rudimentary way. Under stress, the child may regress and lose this sense of self-awareness or object constancy; terror and panic result. These fears of the loss of self-boundaries and of annihilation are in many ways similar to the overwhelming adult anxiety at loss of identity and loss of impulse control.

A fear of loss of body parts and loss of body functions, often conceptualized as castration fears, can be demonstrated most clearly in the child who is 3 to 6 years old.

As the sense of self develops, the 3- to 6-year-old child, under the stress of dealing with oedipal transformations, gradually encompasses a beginning sense of personal responsibility. An internalized superego develops, and the child becomes prone to anxiety and dread at the internalized anger and harsh thoughts directed toward the self.

*Dependency* refers to a state of reliance on another, as for security, love, protection, or mothering. *Symbiosis* refers to a dependent, mutually reinforcing relationship between two persons. It is generally a normal, constructive characteristic of the infant-mother relationship, but it can also occur in a destructive context, as between two mentally ill persons who reinforce each other's pathology or in a mother-infant relationship that induces in the child intense separation anxiety, autism, and severe regression (symbiotic psychosis).

*Castration anxiety* is that anxiety concerning a fantasied loss of or injury to the genitalia.

**35.23.   The answer is E (all)** (*Synopsis*, ed. 4, page 785).

Schizoid disorder must be differentiated from several conditions. In *avoidant disorder*, the anxious, inhibited child shows extreme shyness, submissiveness, inhibition of initiative, and constriction of personality functions, including speech, under selected circumstances. Such children enjoy relationships at home or with familiar persons and may give evidence of desiring social interaction when it is available under nonthreatening conditions, enjoying it once it has been established. They express doubts about their abilities and are dependent on others. Their behavior is more responsive to environmental shift than is that of the schizoid child.

In adolescence and, less often, in childhood, there is often some overlap between withdrawal and depression, and often the two conditions coexist. Both may show inhibition and isolation. Diagnosis is especially difficult in cases in which the affective components of the *depression* are masked by alienation. The depressed adolescent is likely to have had better relationships in the premorbid state than the schizoid adolescent had. The differential diagnosis can be extremely difficult, however, and may ultimately depend on outcome or response to medication.

*Psychotic children* and adolescents tend to demonstrate a greater break with reality, have wider affective swings, and show more bizarre qualities than do schizoid children and adolescents.

*Adjustment disorder* with withdrawal is a response to an identified stressor that remits when the stress ceases.

Aggressive conduct disorder, undersocialized type, is marked by persistent antisocial behavior, such as lying or manipulation. Children with this disorder, unlike schizoid children, at one time or another become attached to antisocial groups.

In DSM-III, *avoidant disorder* is a disorder of childhood or adolescence characterized by a persistent or excessive shrinking from strangers. *Psychosis* is a mental disorder in which a person's thoughts, affective response, ability to recognize reality, and ability to communicate and relate to others are sufficiently impaired to grossly interfere with that person's capacity to deal with reality. The classical characteristics of psychosis are: impaired reality testing, hallucinations, delusions, illusions. Although used less in DSM-III than in DSM-II, the term is still in common usage. *Depression* refers to a mental state characterized by feelings of sadness, loneliness, despair, low self-esteem, and self-reproach. The term refers either to a mood that is so characterized or to an affective disorder. Accompanying signs include psychomotor retardation or at times agitation, withdrawal from interpersonal contact, and vegetative symptoms, such as insomnia and anorexia. *Adjustment disorder* is a maladaptive reaction to identifiable circumstances or life events that is expected to remit when the stress ceases.

**35.24–35.28.   The answers are 35.24–A, 35.25–A, 35.26–D, 35.27–C, and 35.28–C** (*Synopsis*, ed. 4, pages, 779, 780, and 781).

The eating disorders include bulimia, pica, rumination, and anorexia nervosa. They are characterized by a conspicuous *disturbance in eating behavior*. Bulimia usually has a *chronic, remitting course*, whereas the other three disorders most often have a single episode. Anorexia and rumination may have a gradually deteriorating course, leading to death. *No familial pattern is known for the eating disorders except for anorexia nervosa*, which occurs with a higher prevalence in relatives of the afflicted patient than in the general population. Anorexia nervosa and bulimia occur *predominantly in females*, whereas pica and rumination have no sex preference. The onset of anorexia nervosa and bulimia occurs in adolescence or early adulthood. The onset of rumination is usually in infancy. Pica occurs predominantly in early childhood, but can begin during pregnancy.

The eating disorders must be distinguished from peculiar eating behavior in patients with *somatization disorders*, affective disorders, and schizophrenic disorders.

Bulimia refers to a morbidly increased appetite, whereas pica is the craving and eating of nonfood substances, such as paint and clay.

## References

Bowlby J: *Attachment and Loss*, vols 1, 2, 3. Basic Books, New York, 1969, 1973, 1980.

Feinstein S C: Identity and adjustment disorders of adolescence. In *Comprehensive Textbook of Psychiatry*, ed 4, H I Kaplan, B J Sadock, editors, p 1760. Williams & Wilkins, Baltimore, 1985.

Green W H: Attachment disorders of infancy and early childhood. In *Comprehensive Textbook of Psychiatry*, ed 4, H I Kaplan, B J Sadock, editors, p 1722. Williams & Wilkins, Baltimore, 1985.

Halmi K A: Eating disorders. In *Comprehensive Textbook of Psychiatry*, ed 4, H I Kaplan, B J Sadock, editors, p 1731. Williams & Wilkins, Baltimore, 1985.

LaVietes R L: Schizoid disorder. In *Comprehensive Textbook of Psychiatry*, ed 4, H I Kaplan, B J Sadock, editors, p 1744. William & Wilkins, Baltimore, 1985.

Lewis D O: Conduct disorder and juvenile delinquency. In *Comprehensive Textbook of Psychiatry*, ed 4, H I Kaplan, B J Sadock, editors, p 1754. Williams & Wilkins, Baltimore, 1985.

Rutter M: Prevention of children's psychosocial disorders. In *Annual Progress Child Psychiatry Child Development 1983*, S Chess, A Thomas, editors, p 271. Year Book Medical Publishers, Chicago, 1984.

Thomas A, Chess S: Genesis and evolution of behavioral disorders: From infancy to early adult life. Am J Psychiatry *141:* 1, 1984.

Werkman S L: Anxiety disorders. In *Comprehensive Textbook of Psychiatry*, ed 4, H Kaplan, B J Sadock, editors, p 1746. Williams & Wilkins, Baltimore, 1985.

# 36

# Child Psychiatry and Psychiatric Treatment

Evidence of direct therapeutic contact with children before the 20th century is rare. Until this century, formal efforts to cope with emotional and mental disturbances in children generally took the form of advising the parents about alternate means of handling their children. The experts rarely confronted the children directly in an effort to alter their clinical course. A noteworthy exception was the celebrated efforts of the French otologist Jean Marc Gaspard Itard in the latter part of the 18th century. Itard adopted Victor, a prepubertal boy who was assumed to have lived the bulk of his life as a savage with animals in the forests of Aveyron. Itard undertook to civilize and educate Victor in a manner that conceivably might be considered psychotherapy.

The modern era of child psychotherapy is generally thought to begin with Sigmund Freud's famous case report of little Hans, a 5-year-old phobic child. Although the approach employed with little Hans should unquestionably be labeled psychotherapy, it is of historical significance to note that it was the young patient's father, a physician, who, under Freud's direction, was the psychotherapist.

After it was recognized that a child's play could be considered a valid means of communication, child psychoanalysis was developed as a direct psychotherapeutic approach to the child. The central role of play in the development of modern child psychotherapy has been compared to the historical significance of hypnosis in adult psychiatry. Each has contributed considerably to the understanding of unconscious mental phenomena. In addition, family therapy and group therapy are being used more extensively than ever before in the treatment of children.

Since 1940, amphetamines and anticonvulsants have been used to treat children with behavior disorders. The introduction of chlorpromazine increased the range of effective pharmacotherapy. Drugs are as important an adjunct in the comprehensive treatment of disturbed children as they are in the treatment of adults. The fact that the child is a growing organism creates special problems in evaluating the effects of drugs.

Experience has demonstrated, however, that drugs can control symptoms that do not readily respond to other measures, if appropriate agents are chosen and if the dosage is regulated properly. Drugs can then facilitate the educational and experiential aspects of treatment if the psychological meaning of the medication to children and their parents is treated with understanding.

A trial of drug therapy is indicated for such symptoms when appropriate psychotherapeutic and environmental measures do not quickly relieve the child's subjective distress and restore optimal functioning. This judgment differs from adult therapy in that children are more dependent on and responsive to the adults who care for them. One must evaluate the relation of the children and their symptoms to their families before introducing drugs.

Finally, increasing attention has been focused on the need for more residential centers to provide a specialized program for children with behavioral symptoms not amenable to out-patient psychiatric care. Under the pressure of this need, it has been assumed that there is greater uniformity in such specialized facilities than is the case. A lack of uniformity exists not only in terms of which child is best served by which facility, but also in terms of the pattern of organization, administration, staffing, and programs to be found in these institutions. Such a lack of uniformity is not a criticism of the residential treatment center, but is best viewed as a symptom of the historical evolution of the facilities. Successful treatment requires strong attachments and commitment by the staff to the child.

Students should review Chapter 36 of *Modern Synopsis-IV*, which covers child psychiatry and psychiatric treatment, and should then study the questions and answers below to test their knowledge of this area.

# Questions

**DIRECTIONS:** Each of the statements or questions below is followed by five suggested responses or completions. Select the *one* that is *best* in each case.

**36.1.** Children usually selected for group therapy include all the following *except*

A. phobic children
B. effeminate boys
C. withdrawn children
D. extremely aggressive children
E. children with primary behavior disorders

**36.2.** In attention deficit disorder with hyperactivity (hyperkinetic syndrome), the drug of choice is

A. diazepam
B. alprazolam
C. amphetamine
D. chlorpromazine
E. thioridazine

**DIRECTIONS:** For each of the incomplete statements below, *one* or *more* of the completions given is correct. Choose answer:

A. if only **1, 2,** and **3** are correct
B. if only **1** and **3** are correct
C. if only **2** and **4** are correct
D. if only **4** is correct
E. if all are correct

**36.3.** Which of the following statements are accurate about the pharmacokinetics of childhood psychotropic drug therapy:

1. Depressed children require a higher plasma level of imipramine than do adults to achieve the same therapeutic effect
2. Higher drug tolerance in children than in adults may reflect greater renal clearance
3. Stimulants have a longer half-life in children than in adults
4. Higher drug tolerance in children than in adults is due to a greater liver/body weight ratio in the former.

**36.4.** Which of the following medications have been used with positive results in patients with infantile autism:

1. Fenfluramine
2. Methylphenidate
3. Haloperidol
4. Propranolol

**36.5.** Organic therapy in children is influenced by which of the following factors:

1. Psychiatric disorder in one or both parents
2. Attitudes about drugs
3. History of drug response in a parent
4. Diagnosis

**36.6.**  Children who are likely to benefit from day treatment include those with

1. infantile autism
2. personality disorders
3. minimal brain dysfunction
4. chronic physical illnesses

**36.7.**  Which of the following are indicated in the treatment of major depression in children:

1. Monoamine oxidase inhibitors
2. Electroconvulsive therapy
3. Imipramine
4. Amphetamine

**36.8.**  Most children referred for residential treatment

1. have that as the first type of intervention
2. are usually more than 16 years old
3. are more frequently girls than boys
4. usually have severe learning disabilities in addition to other disorders.

**DIRECTIONS:** Each group of questions below consists of five lettered headings followed by a list of numbered words or statements. For each numbered word or statement, select the *one* lettered heading that is most closely associated with it. Each lettered heading may be selected once, more than once, or not at all.

### Questions 36.9–36.13
A. Relationship therapy
B. Remedial or educational psychotherapy
C. Supportive psychotherapy
D. Release therapy
E. Child psychoanalysis

**36.9.**  Teaches new patterns of behavior

**36.10.**  Helps well-adjusted children cope with crises

**36.11.**  Facilitates the abreaction of pent-up emotions

**36.12.**  Interpretation of transference neurosis

**36.13.**  Positive, friendly, helpful attitude is the primary therapeutic ingredient, as in the Big Brother Organization

# Answers

# Child Psychiatry and Psychiatric Treatment

**36.1. The answer is D** *(Synopsis,* ed. 4, page 820).

The children selected for group treatment show in common a social hunger, the need to be like their peers and to be accepted by them, which would exclude *children who are extremely aggressive* and show little need to be accepted. Usually, the therapist excludes children who have never realized a primary relationship, as with their mother, inasmuch as individual psychotherapy can better help these children. Usually, the children selected include those with *phobic reactions, effeminate boys,* shy and *withdrawn children,* and *children with primary behavior disorders.*

**36.2. The answer is C** *(Synopsis,* ed. 4, pages 823 and 824).

The most well-documented indication for pharmacological treatment in child psychiatry is attention deficit disorder with hyperactivity. The symptoms usually prompting therapy are developmentally inappropriate inattention and impulsivity that respond insufficiently to social control. Although research has focused on those children with motoric excess, clinically it is probable that those who have a pure attention disorder are likely to benefit from stimulant drugs as well.

The clear first choice among organic therapies is a stimulant, such as *amphetamine* or methylphenidate. The dosage of the stimulant can be titrated upward about every 3 to 5 days (every week in the case of pemoline) until either therapeutic benefit is achieved or side effects prohibit further increase. This is done with the aim of using the lowest dose that is efficacious. Doses are usually administered during the day, with frequency based on the drug's half-life. All of the stimulants are short acting when compared to the long half-lives of the antidepressants and neuroleptics. Methylphenidate has the shortest half-life (2.5 hours is about the mean). As a consequence, it is frequently administered twice daily. Amphetamine's half-life is intermediate, and pemoline has the longest half-life in this drug group (about 12 hours).

Stimulants are contraindicated in children with thought disorder or psychosis as they may exacerbate those conditions. These drugs are relatively contraindicated for mental retardates, those with tics, and highly anxious children. Stimulants have been associated with precipitation or aggravation of Tourette's disorder. The common side effects of stimulants are listed in the table below.

*Diazepam* and *alprazolam* are antianxiety agents, and *chlorpromazine* and *thioridazine* are phenothiazine antipsychotic agents. These drugs are not used in hyperkinetic disorders.

**Common Dose-Related Side Effects of Stimulants**

1. Insomnia
2. Decreased appetite
3. Irritability or nervousness
4. Weight loss

**36.3. The answer is C (2, 4)** *(Synopsis,* ed. 4, pages 822 and 823).

*Children appear to be more efficacious metabolizers of psychoactive drugs than are adults.* They may require or tolerate slightly higher doses on milligram per kilogram body weight basis than adults. This is clearly the case with lithium, which *may reflect greater renal clearance.* A possible explanation for other differential effects is the *greater liver/body weight ratio present in childhood;* that is, 30 percent greater for a 6-year-old child than for an adult. *Stimulants seem to have a somewhat shorter half-life in children* than in adults. Children convert imipramine to desmethylimipramine more actively than do adults. In children, it is expected that the desmethylated metabolite is the predominant active moiety. Although children clear imipramine more rapidly through demethylation than do adults, their clearance of the sum of imipramine and desmethylimipramine following a dose of imipramine is at a rate similar to that of adults.

Studies of serum levels of both of these different classes of drugs demonstrate wide variability of serum levels among subjects receiving the same milligram per kilogram dose. Similarly, this same variation has been seen in adults with the above-mentioned drugs, as well as with most other psychotherapeutic agents. At least with imipramine, another similarity with adult pharmacology is seen: *Depressed children require the same plasma levels associated with a favorable response in adults.*

**36.4   The answer is B (1, 3)** (*Synopsis*, ed. 4, page 824).

Drugs can provide only symptomatic behavioral management of children with infantile autism. Hyperactivity, agitation, crying, screaming, and lability of mood make the care of these children very difficult. The main symptoms of gross deficits in communication and social unresponsiveness, however, will not be relieved by neuroleptics. Low doses of relatively less sedating neuroleptics—for example, *haloperidol* 2 mg/day—seem to best ameliorate the secondary symptoms.

*Fenfluramine*, a sympathomimetic amine, has been claimed to be beneficial when used in some trials.

*Methylphenidate* is a psychostimulant used in attention deficit disorders, and *propranolol* is a β-adrenergic drug used primarily as an antihypertensive agent.

**36.5.   The answer is E (all)** (*Synopsis*, ed. 4, page 822).

The use of organic therapy in children is influenced by several factors. First, *a thorough diagnostic assessment* needs to be made. Does the child have a disorder of type and severity that warrants this kind of intervention? Other medical or social conditions causing such symptoms need to be considered. Equally important are evaluation and understanding of the social and family context of the patient, which may influence the choice of therapy in a major way: *Psychiatric disorders in one or both parents* may require intervention at the same time as or even before the child is placed on medication. *Parental or school opposition to medication* can prevent its use, and careful evaluation must take this fact into account. Preexistent causal attributions held by the family and child may be powerful features that influence attitudes about medicating the child. Thus, social and psychological factors are important parts of this determination. The *history of drug response in other family members* may be helpful in assessing the risk-benefit ratio, as well as being helpful in deciding which drug to select within a particular class of drugs.

The table in column 1 outlines the stepwise process taken by the psychiatrist in planning organic therapy.

**36.6.   The answer is E (all)** (*Synopsis*, ed. 4, page 829).

Children who are likely to benefit from day treatment may have a wide range of diagnoses, including *infantile autism*, borderline conditions, *personality disorders, minimal brain dysfunction*, and mental retardation.

The lessons learned from day treatment programs have moved the mental health disciplines in the direction of having the services follow the children, rather than toward discontinuities of care. An increasing number of residential treatment centers have added day treatment programs.

Day treatment programs have become increasingly valuable for children with *chronic physical illnesses*. Psychological and economic factors converge advantageously in promoting effective treatment while the children remain with their families.

*Infantile autism* is a syndrome beginning in infancy and characterized by withdrawal and self-absorption, failure to develop attachment to a parental figure, ineffective communication and mutism, preoccupation with inanimate objects, and an obsessive demand for sameness in the environment. It is also known as Kanner's syndrome. *Personality disorder* is a mental disorder characterized by inflexible, deeply ingrained, maladaptive patterns of adjustment to life that cause either subjective distress or significant impairment of adaptive functioning. The manifestations are generally recognizable in adolescence, or even earlier. *Minimal brain dysfunction* is a behavioral syndrome of childhood characterized by learning difficulties, decreased attention span, distractibility, hyperactivity, impulsiveness, emotional lability, and, often, disturbances in perceptuomotor and language development. The term minimal brain dysfunction implies neurological causation, but in most cases there are no major unequivocal neurological signs, and there has been an unfortunate tendency to apply the term as a convenient explanatory label to any child presenting with a specific learning difficulty or behavioral dysfunction.

**Stepwise Process of Organic Therapy**

1. Diagnostic evaluation
2. Symptom measurement
3. Risk/benefit ratio analysis
4. Establishment of a contract of therapy
5. Periodic reevaluation
6. Termination/tapered drug withdrawal

**36.7.   The answer is B (1, 3)** (*Synopsis*, ed. 4, page 824).

Major depression has recently been recognized to occur in children and adolescents, not just adults. The role of pharmacological therapy in this disorder is not entirely sorted out. Depressed children with endogenous features may respond to *imipramine*, in dosages ranging from 1.5 to 5 mg/kg/day, with improvement in mood. The side effects are similar to those experienced by adults. The margin of benefit over placebo does not appear to be as clear in children as it is in adults. Whether *monoamine oxidase inhibitors* are any more effective than imipramine remains to be seen.

There is *no current indication for electroconvulsive therapy in depressed children.* Also, *amphetamine* is not indicated in major depression, but rather it is a psychostimulant of use in attention deficit disorder with hyperactivity.

From bipolar patients' retrospective accounts, a sizable minority (30 percent) experience the onset of their illness in adolescence or earlier. Although lithium has had very limited study, a trial is warranted in those patients who meet the DSM-III criteria for the disorder and have not responded to more conservative management. Administration to achieve blood levels of 0.6 to 1.2 meq/l (similar to adult patients) are suggested, and doses may approximate adult dose to achieve this result. Side effects and complications can occur that are similar to those seen in adults.

**36.8.   The answer is D (4)** (*Synopsis*, ed. 4, page 827).

Most, if not all, children referred for residential treatment *have severe learning disabilities and have been seen previously by one or more professional persons,* such as a school psychologist or pediatrician, or by members of a child guidance clinic, juvenile court, or state welfare agency. Unsuccessful previous attempts at outpatient treatment and foster home or other custodial placement often precede residential treatment. The age range of the children varies from institution to institution, but most children are *between 5 and 15 years of age. Boys are referred more frequently than girls.*

Children who are likely to benefit from residential treatment include children with antisocial and aggressive behaviors, such as stealing, truancy, running away, firesetting, bedwetting, and destructive behavior. The child may have psychotic symptoms, including loose associations, hallucinations, and precipitous, severe regression.

**36.9–36.13.   The answers are 36.9–B, 36.10–C, 36.11–D, 36.12–E, and 36.13–A** (*Synopsis*, ed. 4, pages 814 and 815).

Among the common bases for classification of child therapy is identification of the element presumed to be helpful for the young patient.

Isolating a single therapeutic element as the basis for classification tends to be somewhat artificial, because most, if not all, of the factors are present in varying degrees in every child-psychotherapeutic undertaking. For example, there is no psychotherapy in which the relationship between therapist and patient is not a vital factor; nevertheless, child psychotherapists commonly talk of relationship therapy to describe a form of treatment in which a *positive, friendly, helpful relationship is viewed as the primary, if not the sole, therapeutic ingredient.* Probably one of the best examples of pure relationship therapy is to be found outside of a clinical setting in the work of the *Big Brother Organization.*

Remedial, educational, and patterning psychotherapy endeavors to *teach new attitudes and patterns of behavior* to children who persist in using immature and inefficient patterns, which are often presumed to be due to a maturational lag.

Supportive psychotherapy is particularly helpful in enabling a *well-adjusted child to cope with the emotional turmoil engendered by a crisis.* It is also used with those quite disturbed children whose less than adequate ego functioning may be seriously disrupted by an expressive-exploratory mode or by other forms of therapeutic intervention. At the beginning of most psychotherapy, regardless of the patient's age and the nature of the therapeutic interventions, the principal therapeutic elements perceived by the patient tend to be the supportive ones, a consequence of therapists' universal efforts to be reliably and sensitively responsive. In fact, some therapy may never proceed beyond this supportive level, whereas others develop an expressive-exploratory or behavioral-modification flavor on top of the supportive foundation.

Release therapy, described initially by David Levy, *facilitates the abreaction of pent-up emotions.* Although abreaction is an aspect of many therapeutic undertakings, in release therapy the treatment situation is structured to encourage only this factor. It is indicated primarily for preschool-age children who are suffering from a distorted emotional reaction to an isolated trauma.

Psychotherapy with children is often psychoanalytically oriented, which means that it endeavors through the vehicle of self-understanding to enable the children to develop their potential further. This development is accomplished by liberating for more constructive use the psychic energy that is presumed to be expended in defending against fantasied dangers. Children are generally unaware of these unreal dangers, their fear of them, and the psychological defenses they use to avoid both the danger and the fear. With the awareness that is facilitated, the patients can evaluate the usefulness of their defensive maneuvers and relinquish the unnecessary ones that constitute the symptoms of their emotional disturbance.

This form of psychoanalytic psychotherapy is to be distinguished from child psychoanalysis, a more intensive and less common treatment, in which the unconscious elements are interpreted systematically from outside in, resulting in the orderly sequence of affect-defense-impulse. Under these circumstances, the therapist anticipates unconscious resistances and *allows transference manifestations to mature to a full transference neurosis, through which neurotic conflicts are resolved.*

# References

Gadpaille W J: Psychiatric treatment of the adolescent. In *Comprehensive Textbook of Psychiatry*, ed 4, H I Kaplan, B J Sadock, editors, p 1805. Williams & Wilkins, Baltimore, 1985.

Group for the Advancement of Psychiatry: *The Process of Child Therapy*. Group for the Advancement of Psychiatry, New York, 1982.

Harrison S I: Individual psychotherapy. In *Comprehensive Textbook of Psychiatry*, ed 4, H I Kaplan, B J Sadock, editors, p 1766. Williams & Wilkins, Baltimore, 1985.

Kraft I A: Group therapy with children and adolescents. In *Comprehensive Textbook of Psychiatry*, ed 4, H I Kaplan, B J Sadock, editors, p 1785. Williams & Wilkins, Baltimore, 1985.

Lewis M: Day treatment. In *Comprehensive Textbook of Psychiatry*, ed 4, H I Kaplan, B J Sadock, editors, p 1803. Williams & Wilkins, Baltimore, 1985.

Lewis M: Residential treatment. In *Comprehensive Textbook of Psychiatry*, ed 4, H I Kaplan, B J Sadock, editors, p 1798, Williams & Wilkins, Baltimore, 1985.

Lourie R S: Child and Adolescent Psychiatry. In *The Year Book of Psychiatry and Applied Mental Health*. Year Book Medical Publishers, Chicago, 1983.

Noshpitz J D, editor: *Basic Handbook of Child Psychiatry*. Basic Books, New York, 1979.

Rapaport J L, Kruesi M J P: Organic therapies. In *Comprehensive Textbook of Psychiatry*, ed 4, H I Kaplan, B J Sadock, editors, p 1793. Williams & Wilkins, Baltimore, 1985.

# 37

# Child Psychiatry:
# Special Areas of Interest

There are special areas of interest in the field of child psychiatry that are of concern to doctors regardless of their specialty. Among these areas are children's reactions to illness, hospitalization, and surgery and child abuse, especially the so-called battered child syndrome. The last of these problems, child abuse, required that a National Center on Child Abuse and Neglect be established to evaluate the extent of the problem. It has been found that over 300,000 instances of child maltreatment are reported each year in the United States. Recent scandals involving sexual assaults on children in day care centers, nurseries, and school settings have served to make the public even more aware of the problem of child maltreatment.

The sick child, regardless of whether or not hospitalization is required, creates a stress for the child's entire family. The existing family equilibrium is upset, and the illness and the way in which it is handled can have important and long-lasting effects on the child's biological, psychological, and social adaptation. Related to these areas are the affective disorders that occur in children who show signs and symptoms of depression not unlike that seen in adults, e.g. insomnia, psychomotor retardation, feelings of guilt, low self-esteem, and, in some instances, suicide. Although successful suicide in children under age 12 is rare, approximately 12,000 children are admitted each year to psychiatric hospitals because of suicidal ideation. Among adolescents, however, suicide is the third leading cause of death, with approximately 6,000 adolescents killing themselves each year. Thus, affective disorders in children are major mental health problems.

Of lesser import than the conditions mentioned above are the developmental disorders, such as enuresis, encopresis, nail biting, and thumb sucking. Nevertheless, these disorders may be one of the earliest signs that the child is experiencing stress and, in some cases, may be masking a more serious emotional disorder.

The student should read Chapter 37 of *Modern Synopsis-IV*, which covers these areas, and should then study the questions and answers below to test his or her knowledge of these subjects.

# Questions

---

**DIRECTIONS:** Each of the statements or questions below is followed by five suggested responses or completions. Select the *one* that is *best* in each case.

**37.1.** True statements about cyclothymia in adolescents do not include which of the following:

A. Episodes of dysthymia and hypomania may occur in the same patient in either an alternating or simultaneous manner.

B. The duration of the disorder must exceed 24 months before this diagnosis is made.

C. There are no psychotic symptoms.

D. There have been at least several ill periods, even with symptom-free intervals lasting for months.

E. It is unlikely that a majority of these adolescents will develop bipolar illness in the future.

**37.2.** Which of the following statements concerning the epidemiology of affective disorders in children is correct:

A. The prevalence rate among 10-year-olds for the combined diagnoses of major depression and dysthymic disorder is approximately 1.5 to 2.0 percent.

B. In adolescents, the prevalence rate for major depression and dysthymia is probably higher than it is for 10-year-olds.

C. Affective disorders comprise approximately 10 percent of intakes on general child psychiatric services in a general hospital.

D. Approximately 5 percent of prepubertal children and 15 percent of adolescents examined by general child psychiatric services will present with affective disorders.

E. All of the above

**37.3.** Which of these statements concerning neuroendocrine markers in children with major affective disorders is not applicable:

A. Prepubertal children in an episode of major depression have been shown to secrete significantly more growth hormone during sleep than do normal children.

B. Prepubertal children in an episode of major depression secrete significantly more growth hormone in response to insulin-induced hypoglycemia than normal children.

C. The majority of prepubertal children in a major depressive episode have normal cortisol secretion during and after the depressive episode.

D. There may be a supersensitivity to acetylcholine in some children born of parents with bipolar or unipolar depression.

E. Growth hormone abnormalities in children with a major depressive episode have been found to remain abnormal after at least 4 months full antidepressant response.

**37.4.** Enuresis can be defined as clothes or bed wetting in children over the age of

A. 2 years
B. 3 years
C. 4 years
D. 5 years
E. 6 years

**37.5.** The best single indication of a cause-and-effect relationship between the type of mothering received and symptoms of infant abuse can be established

A. if the child appears to be afraid

B. if the child shows evidence of skin injuries

C. if the child is undernourished

D. if significant recovery occurs in the infant when the mothering is altered

E. if the child is dressed inappropriately for weather conditions

**37.6.** The estimated number of deaths from child maltreatment throughout the country each year is

A. 1,000
B. 2,000
C. 5,000
D. 7,000
E. 10,000

**37.7.** In making the diagnosis of mania in children, which of the following statements is incorrect:

A. Diagnostic criteria for mania in children are different from those in adults.
B. DSM-III requires at least one distinct period of persistent elevation or irritability of mood.
C. At least three symptoms in the manic syndrome need to be present.
D. There is no bizarre behavior once the affective symptomatology has remitted.
E. There is no prominent preoccupation with a psychotic symptom that is incongruous with a manic mood.

**37.8.** True statements about the treatment of childhood or adolescent onset depressive disorders do not include which of the following:

A. If the patient is suicidal, hospitalization is indicated.
B. Antidepressant response of prepubertal children with major depressive disorder who are treated with imipramine is dependent on maintenance plasma levels.
C. The best indication for individual or group treatment is the lack of spontaneous gradual improvement in relationships after the affective symptoms have remitted.
D. Tricyclic antidepressants in children can generally be discontinued immediately, as opposed to a schedule of gradual weaning from the medication.
E. In prepubertal depressives, it is advisable to continue antidepressant treatment at the same dose for 3 to 4 months after the patients' initial recovery.

**37.9.** The diagnosis of affective disorders in children may be confused with the diagnosis of

A. schizophrenia
B. conduct disorders
C. substance abuse
D. attention deficit disorder with hyperactivity
E. all of the above

**37.10.** Depression in children is characterized by

A. disturbances of sleep
B. suicidal ideas
C. psychomotor retardation
D. episodes of anxiety
E. all of the above

**37.11.** The treatment that has been most effective in the management of enuresis is

A. hypnosis
B. sleep interruption
C. electric shocks
D. imipramine
E. psychotherapy

**37.12.** Children who receive inadequate care in institutions for a prolonged period of time

A. appear, developmentally, to be most vulnerable to language retardation
B. appear to be least affected in the area of early motor functions
C. suffer from anaclitic depression
D. appear to recover from acquired emotional and cognitive difficulties if returned to their mothering figure within 3 months
E. all of the above

**37.13.** The most common reaction in children to acute illness or injury is

A. depression
B. regression
C. conversion disorder
D. hyperventilation
E. amnesia

**DIRECTIONS:** For each of the incomplete statements below, *one* or *more* of the completions given is corect. Choose answer:

A. if only **1, 2,** and **3** are correct
B. if only **1** and **3** are correct
C. if only **2** and **4** are correct
D. if only **4** is correct
E. if all are correct

**37.14.** Reactions of parents to the hospitalization of their children include which of the following:
1. Fear of criticism from the hospital staff
2. Rivalry with nurses or physicians
3. Feelings of guilt
4. Noncompliance with treatment programs

**37.15.** Childhood onset affective illness
1. tends to follow a more chronic course than its adult onset counterpart
2. tends to appear in families with higher pedigree density for alcoholism
3. may represent the most severe forms of affective illness
4. often presents with academic failure and is misdiagnosed as learning disorder

**37.16.** Affective disorders with childhood or adolescent onset are likely
1. to produce poor academic achievement
2. to lead to arrest in psychosocial development
3. to lead to drug and alcohol abuse
4. not to be recurrent

**37.17.** True statements about suicide among children include which of the following:
1. Suicide is generally ranked as the third leading cause of death in adolescents.
2. The suicide rate is higher among male children.
3. The suicide rate is higher among children whose families have recently moved.
4. Girls attempt suicide more often than boys.

**37.18.** A clinical description of childhood affective disorders would include which of the following statements:
1. Children who do not develop their first depressive episode until adolescence are likely to present more acute or clearly delineated episodes than do children with prepubertal onset.
2. A significant percentage of adolescent affective disorders first present as substance abuse disorders.
3. Children may refer to dysphoria with a variety of labels, which often may not include sadness.
4. Children tend to give unreliable reports concerning their own behavior and emotions.

**37.19.** For the diagnosis to be made of dysthymic disorder in children, there should be evidence
1. that the child has presented with persistent depressed mood
2. that there is marked loss of interest in almost all of the usual activities
3. that there is functional impairment at home or in school
4. that there are possible psychotic symptoms

**37.20.** Which of the following would support a diagnosis of suspected child abuse and neglect:
1. The date of the injury precedes the date of admission to the hospital; that is, there has been a delay in seeking medical care.
2. Ocular damage and old healed lesions are observed.
3. Epiphyseal separation can be seen on the X-ray.
4. The child is under 3 years of age.

**37.21.** Children who risk developing depression include those who
1. are disfigured in some way
2. have a chronic disease
3. have physically ill parents
4. have a depressed parent

**37.22.** Organic causes of enuresis include which of the following conditions:

1. Obstructive uropathy
2. Urinary infection
3. Diabetes mellitus
4. Epilepsy

**37.23.** Encopresis is characterized as being

1. more frequent in girls than in boys
2. associated with enuresis in some cases
3. most common in low socioeconomic groups
4. associated with constipation in some cases

**37.24.** Encopretic children are frequently found to have

1. depressed mothers
2. critical fathers
3. excessive emphasis placed on bowel habits
4. gastrointestinal lesions

**37.25.** According to psychoanalytic theory, nail biting is thought to be

1. caused by competitive impulses toward a parent
2. a form of self-punishment
3. an expression of aggression
4. related to birth trauma

**37.26.** Thumb sucking

1. is socially offensive
2. may cause finger necrosis
3. adversely affects dentition
4. damages the child's self-image

**37.27.** During a major depressive episode,

1. there are frequent subjective sleep complaints from children
2. prepubertal children show polysomnographic abnormalities
3. REM latency is shortened in adolescents
4. it has been shown that the shortening of REM latency persists in the drug-free recovered state

**DIRECTIONS:** Each set of lettered headings below is followed by a list of numbered words or phrases. For each numbered word or phrase, select

A. if the item is associated with **A** only
B. if the item is associated with **B** only
C. if the item is associated with *both* **A** *and* **B**
D. if the item is associated with *neither* **A** *nor* **B**

**Questions 37.28–37.31**
A. Psychotic affective disorders (depressive or manic) in children
B. Schizoaffective disorders in children
C. Both
D. Neither

**37.28.** Generally characterized by delusions and hallucinations thematically consistent with mood

**37.29.** Psychotic symptoms present when the mood disorder is no longer manifest

**37.30.** Conversing and commenting hallucinations

**37.31.** Delusions of thought insertion, broadcasting, or withdrawal

**Questions 37.32–37.35**
A. Atypical depression in children
B. Adjustment disorder with depressive mood
   in children
C. Both
D. Neither

**37.32.**   Duration of episode is the same as with dysthymic disorder.

**37.33.**   Duration of episode is less than 1 year.

**37.34.**   Episodes follow a significant stressful life event by less than 3 months.

**37.35.**   Episode is likely to have high predictive value for future more severe affective disorder episodes.

# Answers

# Child Psychiatry:
# Special Areas of Interest

**37.1.   The answer is E** (*Synopsis*, ed. 4, page 850).

In the same way that, in bipolar illness, episodes of major depression and mania or hypomania occur in the same patient—either separately, alternating, intermixed, or simultaneously—*some adolescent patients present full hypomanic and dysthymic symptomatic pictures in any of the above temporal combinations. These patients receive a diagnosis of cyclothymia if the duration of the disorder exceeds 24 months, if there have been no psychotic symptoms whatsoever, and if there have been at least several ill periods, even with symptom-free intervals lasting for months.* It is likely that adolescents with a cyclothymic picture lasting for at least a year should also receive the cyclothymia diagnosis. *It is also likely that a majority of cyclothymic adolescents will go on to develop a full fledged bipolar illness on follow-up.*

**37.2.   The answer is E** (*Synopsis*, ed. 4, page 850).

Through use of a detailed, semistructured interview with the child, a *1.7 percent prevalence rate has been found among 10-year-olds for the combined DSM-III diagnoses of major depression and dysthymic disorder. No similar study exists on adolescents, but there are good reasons to expect that the rate will be higher.* In surveys that utilized modern assessment techniques and diagnostic criteria, a conservative consensual figure for affective disorders of all types on general child psychiatric services in a general hospital would be *10 percent of intakes: approximately 5 percent of children before puberty and 15 percent of adolescents.* It should be obvious that affective disorders constitute a relatively frequent clinical set of psychiatric diagnoses in youngsters and a sizable public mental health problem to be considered in policymaking.

**37.3.   The answer is B** (*Synopsis*, ed. 4, pages 851 and 852).

Prepubertal children in an episode of major depression have been shown to *secrete significantly more growth hormone during sleep than normal children* and than those with nondepressed emotional disorders. *They also secrete significantly less growth hormone in response to* insulin-induced hypoglycemia than the latter group. *Both abnormalities have been found to remain abnormal and basically unchanged after at least 4 months of full, sustained clinical response,* the last month in a drug-free state. Similar work in adolescents is ongoing.

In contrast, although occasional cases of cortisol hypersecretion are found among prepubertal children in a major depressive episode, when compared to themselves after recovery, *the majority of these children have normal cortisol secretion during and after the depressive episode.*

Other putative neuroendocrine markers are being studied at the present time. These include growth hormone responses to desmethylimipramine and clonidine, thyrotropin response to thyrotropin-releasing hormone, and cortisol response to d-amphetamine.

Investigators have reported recently on an inherited biochemical trait that may be present *in some children born of parents who suffer from bipolar or unipolar depression. There may be a receptor abnormality*—specifically a supersensitivity—*to the neurotransmitter acetylcholine* in those children who would then be at risk for developing a major affective disorder later in life.

The test consists of demonstrating that skin cells, especially fibroblasts grown *in vitro*, show an increased density of muscarine cholinergic receptors, which are then shown to be sensitive to acetylcholine.

The test needs to be validated by further studies, but is important because 25 percent of children with a manic-depressive parent develop either a bipolar or unipolar depression later in life. Early detection would target this subgroup and enable the clinician to more easily differentiate depression from substance abuse and antisocial behavior, which often mask or are confused with depression. In addition, clinicians are reluctant to use medications such as antidepressants for either children or adolescents unless there is a clear indication for their use, and this test would provide such an indication.

**37.4.   The answer is D** (*Synopsis*, ed. 4, page 843).

Enuresis is manifested as a repetitive, inappropriate, involuntary passage of urine. Operationally, enuresis can be defined as bed wetting or clothes wetting in persons *over the age of 5* who fail to inhibit the reflex to pass urine when the impulse is felt during waking hours, and in those who do not rouse from sleep of their own accord when the process is occurring during the sleeping state.

The table below lists the DSM-III diagnostic criteria for functional enuresis.

### Diagnostic Criteria for Functional Enuresis*

A. Repeated involuntary voiding of urine by day or at night

B. At least two such events per month for children between the ages of 5 and 6, and at least one event per month for older children.

C. Not due to a physical disorder, such as diabetes or a seizure disorder.

---

* From American Psychiatric Association: *Diagnostic and Statistical Manual of Mental Disorders*, ed 3. American Psychiatric Association, Washington, DC, 1980. Used with permission.

**37.5.   The answer is D** (*Synopsis*, ed. 4, pages 837 and 838).

The only way to establish an unchallengeable cause-and-effect relationship between the infant's mothering and his or her symptoms is to demonstrate *significant recovery when the mothering is altered*. This single criterion can make the diagnosis of maternal deprivation syndrome possible and, once made, calls for the development of a treatment plan based on immediate intervention and continued persistent surveillance. All infants diagnosed as markedly deprived should have an investigation of the social-environmental condition of the family and the psychological status of the mother to determine the factors responsible for inefficient mothering.

Child abuse and neglect may be suspected when several of the following factors are in evidence: the *child seems unduly afraid*, especially of the parents; the child is kept confined—as in a crib, playpen, or cage—for overlong periods of time; the child shows *evidence of repeated skin or other injuries;* the child's injuries are inappropriately treated in terms of bandages and medication; *the child appears undernourished;* the child is given inappropriate food, drink, or medicine; *the child is dressed inappropriately for the weather conditions;* the child shows evidence of over-all poor care; the child cries often; the child takes over the role of a parent and tries to be protective or otherwise to take care of parent's needs.

**37.6.   The answer is B** (*Synopsis*, ed. 4, page 834).

The National Center on Child Abuse and Neglect in Washington, D.C., has estimated that there are more than 300,000 instances of child maltreatment reported to central registries throughout the country every year, and about *2,000 deaths from abuse annually.*

Not all neglected and abused children are taken to physicians or hospitals for medical attention. Many maltreated children who are seen by physicians go unrecognized, undiagnosed, and, hence, not reported. With all the statistics, probably only the upper portion of a submerged iceberg is seen.

**37.7.   The answer is A** (*Synopsis*, ed. 4, page 849).

The diagnostic criteria for mania in children are *no different than in adults.* DSM-III requires that at least *one distinct period* characterized by relatively persistent elevated, elated, expansive or irritable mood be present. In addition, a *minimum of three symptoms* in the manic syndrome should also be present (four if the mood is only irritable); once the affective symptomatology remits, there should be *neither bizarre behavior nor a prominent preoccupation with a psychotic symptom the content of which was incongruous with manic mood*; and the episode should not be due to any organic cause, nor should it follow a preexisting nonorganic, nonaffective psychotic disorder.

**37.8.   The answer is D** (*Synopsis*, ed. 4, pages 853 and 854).

The aims of the treatment of depressive episodes in children and adolescents include the following:

Immediate protection is made against the patient's own self-destructive impulses or behaviors. *If the patient is suicidal, hospitalization is indicated.*

There is substantial evidence that the *antidepressant response of prepubertal children with major depressive disorder treated with imipramine is dependent on maintenance plasma levels.*

The imipramine dose can be as high as 6 mg/kg/day, preferably administered in three roughly equal daily doses. Dosage can be increased relatively quickly, beginning at 1.5 mg/kg/day and going up to 3, 4, 5, and 6 mg/kg/day every third or fourth day. Systematic assessment of clinical response is done 5 weeks after the beginning of treatment. The imipramine-sensitive symptoms are the symptom criteria for major depression and depressive hallucinations.

In prepubertal depressives, *it is advisable to continue successful antidepressant treatment at the same dose for 3 to 4 months after initial recovery.* Following the guideline, only about one of every five cases will present a relapse in the 30 days after the last pill. There are two exceptions to this: (1) When during psychopharmacological maintenance a patient receives also a course of any modality of psychotherapy, it is probably well to continue the medication until the end of the psychotherapeutic trial as there is some suggestion from adult work that a depressive relapse could erase psychotherapeutic gains during the course of treatment; and (2) when a child has been found to be prone to relapses in the past, it is advisable to treat the child for longer time periods. *Discontinuation of tricyclic antidepressants in children should be carried out on a progressive schedule over a 10-day period in order to avoid a withdrawal syndrome.*

Child psychotherapy as generally practiced does not appear to be very effective in treating the depressive symptomatology, or any other aspect of the child's psychopathology, as long as the youngster is severely depressed.

Based on work with ambulatory adult depressives and on clinical experience with child affective patients, it appears sensible to defer a decision for psychotherapeutic intervention until after the youngster has recovered from major depressive disorder. *The best indication for individual or group treatment is the lack of spontaneous gradual improvement in relationships after the affective picture remitted.* Other times, familial crises are precipitated by the child's recovery, indicating that the patient's depression had taken on a dysfunctional significance to several family members. The indication for family therapy in such cases is obvious.

**37.9.   The answer is E** (*Synopsis*, ed. 4, page 853).

Psychotic forms of depression and mania and schizoaffective disorders should be differentiated from *schizophrenia*. This diagnosis of mania and hypomania is very rare in prepuberty. This may be because prepubertal children only very rarely will experience elation.

Anxiety symptoms and conduct-disordered behavioral patterns not infrequently coexist with depression and can pose problems in differentiating these cases from nondepressed emotional and *conduct disorders*. The differentiation of depression or mania from different forms of delirious drug intoxication and *substance abuse* most frequently will have to await inpatient detoxification for affective assessment to be possible.

More clinically relevant is the differentiation between agitated depression and *attention deficit disorder with hyperactivity*. Prepubertal children do not present classical forms of agitated depression with handwringing and pacing. Instead, inability to sit still and frequent temper tantrums are the most common symptoms of agitation when the latter is present. On the basis of these signs alone, it is not possible to differ-

entiate agitation from hyperactivity. In dysthymic or depressive disorders, it is frequently impossible to determine if the hyperactivity preceded and coexists with the affective disorder or if, simply, agitation was noted by the parents before the other symptoms of mood disorder. Sometimes the correct answer only becomes apparent after successful tricyclic antidepressant treatment is discontinued. If the child has no difficulty concentrating and is not hyperactive while recovered from the depressive episode in a drug-free state, it is highly likely he or she had never suffered from attention deficit disorder with hyperactivity.

**37.10.   The answer is E** (*Synopsis*, ed. 4, page 849).

The symptom clusters in the depressive syndrome in children are appetite or weight changes corrected for normal growth; *sleep difficulty or sleeping too much; psychomotor agitation or retardation;* loss of interest or pleasure in usual activities, including sexual drive in adolescents; fatigue, tiredness; thoughts of self-reproach, feelings of guilt that are excessive or inappropriate, low self-esteem; difficulty concentrating or slowed thinking; morbid preoccupation with death, *suicidal ideation,* or behavior; and *episodes of anxiety.*

*Suicidal ideation* involves thoughts regarding the act of self-inflicted, self-intentioned taking of one's own life. Successful suicide is rare in children, but suicidal ideas are not uncommon. Children will threaten to jump in front of a car or to cut themselves with a knife.

*Psychomotor retardation* consists of a slowing of mental and physical activity and is common in depression. *Anxiety* is an unpleasurable emotional state associated with psychophysiological changes in response to an intrapsychic conflict. In contrast to fear, the danger or threat in anxiety is unreal. Physiological changes consist of increased heart rate, disturbed breathing, trembling, sweating, and vasomotor changes. Psychological changes consist of an uncomfortable feeling of impending danger, an overwhelming awareness of being powerless, the inability to perceive the unreality of the threat, prolonged feeling of tension, and exhaustive readiness for the expected danger.

**37.11.   The answer is D** (*Synopsis*, ed. 4, page 845).

The drug used for the treatment of functional enuresis is the antidepressant anticholinergic drug *imipramine* hydrochloride. The usual dosage for 6- to 12-year-olds is 25 mg, although some children may require as much as 75 mg. At the present time, imipramine is the most effective choice in the treatment of enuresis.

Often, drug therapy is used in conjunction

with other management methods. *Sleep interruption* involves waking the child every few hours to voluntarily void. *Electric shocks* involve the use of a device that, on becoming wet with urine, causes the child to receive an electric shock. It is a form of aversive conditioning, but is not considered humane. An alternative is to have the child awakened by a bell after voiding. That technique has been effective in some cases. *Hypnosis* is an artificially induced alteration of consciousness characterized by increased suggestibility and receptivity to direction. Hypnosis is not effective in enuresis of childhood primarily because children are not easily hypnotizable. *Psychotherapy* is a form of treatment in which a trained person through therapeutic communication, both verbal and nonverbal, attempts to reverse or change maladaptive patterns of behavior and to encourage personality growth and development. It has not been effective in the treatment of enuretic children.

**37.12.   The answer is E** (*Synopsis*, ed. 4, page 842).

Hospitalism or *anaclitic depression* (the latter term coined by René Spitz) refers to the syndrome manifested by infants separated from their mothers for long time periods, usually because the child was placed in an institution where children were given inadequate individual attention and where they were rarely held or played with.

At first, they show distress and crying; after 3 months of separation, weepiness subsides and stronger stimuli are necessary to provoke it. The children sit with expressionless eyes, unresponsive, and they are retarded in motor, cognitive, and language development. They act as if in a daze, not aware of their environment. Spitz studied 6- to 8-month-old children who had been separated from their mothers for at least 3 months.

These early deviations in personal-social behavior are considered precursors of personality disturbances in adolescents and adults, characterized by poor impulse control, lack of appropriate guilt feelings associated with aggressive and destructive behavior, and an inability to establish close interpersonal relationships. All aspects of development are not equally affected by early environmental deprivation. *Early motor functions that are most dependent on maturation seem to be least affected*; cognitive functions, especially *language, seem to be most vulnerable. Intellectual and language retardation is evident early in infancy* and becomes intensified with continued institutionalization.

Hospitalism occurs in inadequate institutions with a rapid turnover in caretakers who do not become emotionally involved with the children. The syndrome is also associated with listlessness, pallor, emaciation, and absence of sucking habits. *It is reversible if the child is returned to the mother within 3 months.*

The following illustration shows a child suffering from marasmus, a condition considered to be the end to anaclitic depression. This condition most often results in death.

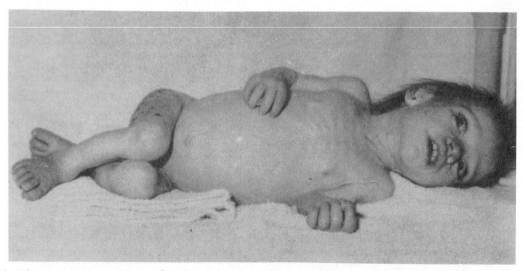

**Marasmus precipitated by a mild chest infection in an infant with failure to thrive secondary to maternal deprivation. (Reproduced with permission from J A Davis, J Dobbing, editors:** *Scientific Foundations of Paediatrics*, **ed 1. William Heinemann Medical Books, London, 1974.)**

**37.13. The answer is B** (*Synopsis*, ed. 4, page 839).

Certain broad patterns of response to acute illness or injury are characteristic of children, with some differences related to individual variations and to developmental level. The most ubiquitous response pattern is that of *emotional or behavioral regression*. The child undergoes a partial or total return to earlier patterns of behavior, e.g. a child who is already toilet-trained may return to wetting the bed.

Other emotional responses, often related to regressive trends, include the reemergence of primitive fears and feelings of helplessness or inadequacy. These responses can lead to *depressive* feelings in children, complete at times with vegetative signs, such as anorexia, anhedonia, and insomnia. This level of response, however, is not the most common reaction of children to illness or injury. Stereotyped behavior of a compulsive or ritualized nature may be seen, as may transient hypochondriacal concerns.

Other psychological reactions, seen frequently in school-age children or adolescents in relation to physical illness, include *conversion disorders*. These disturbances affect the voluntarily innervated striated musculature and the somatosensory apparatus, with their unconsciously symbolic expression of emotional conflict. They are to be distinguished from psychophysiological disorders, which affect involuntarily innervated systems and visceral end organs, without symbolic significance. Dissociative reactions, such as *amnesia*, somnambulism, fugue states, and pseudodelirious states, may also occur. These reactions may compound or be compounded by an actual delirium, which is often of a subclinical nature.

*Hyperventilation* is excessive breathing generally associated with anxiety. A reduction in blood carbon dioxide produces symptoms of lightheadedness, palpitations, numbness and tingling periorally and in the extremities, and, occasionally, syncope. It is a very rare response in children to illness. *Amnesia* is a disturbance in memory manifested by partial or total inability to recall past experiences; it might occur in children who have a head injury.

**37.14. The answer is E (all)** (*Synopsis*, ed. 4, page 842).

Many parents *fear criticism from the hospital staff* regarding their role in the child's illness or their effectiveness as parents. Some parents may show strong *rivalry with nurses or physicians*, misinterpreting professional competence in handling the child as a threat to their own parental capacities. Feeling left out or unwanted is also common among parents. A few may project their *own guilt onto the hospital staff and blame them for minor difficulties*. Difficulty in accepting recommended treatment occasionally leads to their signing the child out of the hospital against advice or to *noncompliance with post-hospitalization treatment plans*.

Parents who have newborn infants in high-risk nurseries are in a special situation. They have not had a chance to assume responsibility for the care of their infant and must delegate this care to the hospital staff.

The need to delegate care, and the paucity of communication between parents and staff members, may have a significant detrimental effect on the eventual emotional adjustment and bonding between child and parents. There is a growing concern that hospital care practices that do not take into consideration the importance of the early contacts between infants, parents, and hospital staffs could be contributing to the onset of parent-child relationships that lead to the syndromes of battered child, failure to thrive, and the vulnerable child.

**37.15. The answer is E (all)** (*Synopsis*, ed. 4, pages 852 and 853).

Childhood onset affective illness, compared with its adult onset counterpart, *tends to follow a generally more chronic course, appears in families with higher pedigree density for affective illness and alcoholism*, and is more likely to develop secondary complications (conduct disorder, alcoholism, substance abuse, and antisocial personality) in the short and the long run. Such very early onset disorders *may represent the most severe forms of affective illness*.

Functional impairment associated with depressive disorders in childhood extends to practically all areas of the child's psychosocial world: school performance and behavior, peer relationships, and family relations. Only highly intelligent and scholastically oriented children with no more than moderate depression can compensate for their difficulty in learning by substantially increasing time and effort. Otherwise, school performance is invariably affected by a combination of concentration difficulty, slowed thinking, lack of interest and motivation, tiredness, sleepiness, depressive ruminations, and preoccupations. Thus, it is not surprising that *academic failure* is one of the presenting complaints of children with major depression. A *misdiagnosis of learning disorder* in a depressed child is not an uncommon occurrence. It usually indicates that no symptom-oriented interview with the child was carried out. Learning problems secondary to depression, even when longstanding, always correct themselves quickly after recovery from the affective episode.

**37.16.   The answer is A (1, 2, 3)** (*Synopsis,* ed. 4, page 853).

Affective disorders with childhood or adolescent onset *are likely to be recurrent* and, if not properly treated, will produce considerable short- and long-term difficulties and complications: *poor academic achievement, arrest in psychosocial developmental patterns,* complicating negative reinforcement, suicide, *drug and alcohol abuse* as a means of self-treatment, and development of conduct disorder. Long-term follow-up studies have not been long enough to follow the subjects into adulthood. The follow-up studies so far do, on the whole, indicate continued liability for affective disorder as predicted.

**37.17.   The answer is E (all)** (*Synopsis,* ed. 4, page 852).

Suicide and, more commonly, suicidal ideas occur frequently in children and adolescents. *The third leading cause of death in adolescents is suicide.* Accidents are the prime cause; however, many feel that a number of such accidents may actually be disguised suicides. *The suicide rate is higher among male children and in children whose families have recently moved* or been dislocated. The tendency, however, is for *females of all ages to attempt suicide more often than males,* but females, including adolescents, succeed less often. Successful suicide also tends to be more frequent in persons of higher socioeconomic status and intelligence. In one major study of 100 children referred for psychiatric hospitalization, one-third of the children had threatened or attempted suicide.

**37.18.   The answer is A (1, 2, 3)** (*Synopsis,* ed. 4, page 852).

The onset of major affective disorder in children tends to be insidious and retrospectively difficult to pinpoint.

*Patients who do not develop their first depressive episode until adolescence are more likely than those with prepubertal onset of affective illness to present episodes with more clearly delineated or acute onset.* Nevertheless, a dysthymic course of illness can also occur in adolescent onset affective illness. Typically, mania, hypomania, and cyclothymia begin in or after puberty, although the onset of affective illness (depressive or dysthymic) is likely to have occurred in prepuberty in a substantial proportion of these youngsters.

If there have been attempts at self-medication with either illicit drugs or alcohol, adolescent onset of affective disorder may be very difficult to diagnose when the patient is first seen. In a recent study, *17 percent of the affective youngsters first presented to medical attention as having substance abuse disorders.* Only after detoxification could the patients' psychiatric symptoms be properly assessed and the correct affective diagnosis be made.

A child's negative reply to a question about feeling sad is unlikely to be tantamount to absence of depressed mood. *Children may refer to dysphoria with a variety of labels, which often may not include sadness.* Thus, it is advisable to inquire about feeling sad, empty, low, down, blue, very unhappy, like crying, or having a bad feeling inside which is with the child most of the time and is a feeling the child "cannot get rid of." Depressed children will usually identify one or more of these terms as the persistent dysphoric feeling they have had no name for. The duration and periodicity of depressive mood throughout the day and week should be carefully assessed in order to differentiate relatively universal, short-lived, sometimes frequent periods of sadness, usually following a frustrating event, from true, persistent depressive mood. The younger the child, the more imprecise time estimates are likely to be.

It is clinically sound to use a minimum duration of 3 consecutive hours of reported dysphoria at least 3 times a week. This cut-off usefully separates true depressive mood from sad affect.

Contrary to common wisdom, *children are, in fact, reliable reporters about their own behavior, emotions, relationships, and difficulties in psychosocial functions.* What neither children nor adolescents can even attempt to do is to talk freely, without direction—almost like free-associating—about their troubles, difficulties, and inner feelings. In a semistructured interview, however, where the clinician asks direct questions in a professional yet sensitive manner, youngsters can and do provide the information needed for a psychiatric diagnosis.

**37.19.   The answer is A (1, 2, 3)** (*Synopsis,* ed. 4, page 849).

Some youngsters with depressive symptomatology do not quite meet criteria for major depression. If the episode has persisted for at least 12 months in either a chronic or intermittent fashion (symptom-free intervals are no more than a few months at a time, so that the child has been suffering from these symptoms all or most of the time), such an episode is highly likely to fit the DSM-III diagnostic criteria for dysthymic disorder. For this diagnosis to be made, *there should be evidence that the child has presented persistent depressed mood or marked loss of interest or pleasure in almost all of the usual activities* and pastimes; *no psychotic symptoms whatsoever;* and other signs—*such as functional impairment at home, in school, or with peers*—pessimism or brooding, crying or tearfulness, irritability and anger, social withdrawal, and low self-esteem or feelings of inadequacy. It is probably a mistake to deemphasize psychomotor agitation in children as it is relatively frequent.

### 37.20.   The answer is E (all) (*Synopsis*, ed. 4, page 837).

The physician's index of suspicion for child abuse and neglect might include the following: *the child being under 3 years of age; the delay in seeking medical care* following the actual time of the injury; physical manifestations, such as hematomas, bites, *ocular damage, or old healed lesions*; and radiological manifestations, such as periosteal shearing, subperiosteal hemorrhages, and *epiphyseal separations*. A number of diagnoses may mimic the picture of child abuse or neglect and should be ruled out in the differential diagnosis. These include scurvy and rickets, syphilis of infancy, ostrogenesis imperfecta, and accidental trauma. The table below gives an extensive listing of the manifestations and differential diagnosis of child abuse.

### 37.21.   The answer is E (all) (*Synopsis*, ed. 4, pages 850 and 851).

Children with acute disabilities include those suffering from hospitalization, immobilization, pain, and *disfigurement*. Such children almost invariably have at least a single episode of depression. Children with *chronic disabilities*— such as paralysis, renal disease, severe allergies, and heart disease—tend to have single or multiple episodes of depression, depending on their family background, personality, biological substrate, and psychosocial stressors. Children of *chronically physically ill parents* often suffer episodic depression because of the loss of the parent through periodic hospitalization and because of identification with the parent's depressive state, which is frequent in this group.

Affective disorders in children, adolescents, and adult patients tend to cluster in the same families. The more densely and more deeply (second-degree relatives) a family is loaded with affective disorders, the higher the proportion of offspring likely to be affected and the younger their age of onset is likely to be. The current consensus is that *having one depressed parent probably doubles the risk to the offspring of developing an affective episode before age 18 years*, over the risk in children from two nondepressive parents. In addition, at least four times as many

## Differential Diagnosis and Manifestations of Child Abuse

| History | Physical Examination |
|---|---|
| Characteristic age—usually under 3 years | Signs of general neglect, failure to thrive, poor skin hygiene, malnutrition, withdrawal, irritability, repressed personality |
| General health of child—indicative of neglect | |
| Characteristic distribution of fractures | |
| Disproportionate amounts of soft tissue injury; evidence that injuries occurred at different times, with lesions in various stages of resolution | Bruises, abrasions, burns, soft tissue swellings, bites, hematomas, ocular damage, old healed lesions |
| | Evidences of dislocation of fractures of the extremities |
| Cause of recent trauma not known | |
| Previous history of similar episodes and multiple visits to various hospitals | Unexplained symptoms of an acute abdomen— ruptured viscera |
| Date of injury before admission to hospital— delay in seeking medical help | Neurological findings associated with brain damage |
| Child brought to hospital for complaint other than one associated with abuse or neglect, such as cold, headache, stomachache | Coma, convulsions, death |
| | Symptoms of drug withdrawal or drug intoxication |
| Reluctance of parents or caretaker to give information | *Differential Diagnosis* |
| | Scurvy and rickets |
| History related by parents or caretakers is usually at complete variance with the clinical picture and the physical findings noted on examination of the child | Infantile cortical hyperostosis |
| | Syphilis of infancy |
| | Osteogenesis imperfecta |
| | Neurological, organic brain damage |
| Parents' inappropriate reaction to severity of injury | Accidental trauma |
| | *Radiological Manifestations* |
| Family discord or financial stress, alcoholism, psychosis, drug addiction, and inconsistent social history that varies according to intake worker | Subperiosteal hemorrhages |
| | Epiphyseal separations |
| | Periosteal shearing |
| | Metaphyseal fragmentation |
| | Previously healed periosteal calcifications |
| | Squaring of the metaphysis |

children from two depressive parents as those from normal parents are likely to present an affective disorder during the same time period. The studies that have investigated the effects of dual parental matings in pedigrees of adult depressive probands have found results very consistent with those in children. It should be noted that the timing of such parental depressive episodes is irrelevant to the analyses. Even if the parent had had a major depressive episode before the children were conceived, the results of these analyses would not change. There is some evidence to indicate that the number of recurrences of parental depression do increase the likelihood of the children being affected, but this may be related, at least in part, to affective loading of that parent's own side of the family.

**37.22.   The answer is E (all)** (*Synopsis*, ed. 4, page 844).

The combination of nocturnal and diurnal enuresis, especially in the patient with frequency and urgency, should signal the high possibility of an organic basis for the complaint.

Another possibility to be ruled out is *epilepsy*, a neurological disorder resulting from a sudden, excessive, disorderly discharge of neurons in either a structurally normal or a diseased cerebral cortex. It is characterized by the paroxysmal recurrence of short-lived disturbances of consciousness, involuntary convulsive muscle movements, psychic or sensory disturbances, or some combination thereof. It is termed idiopathic epilepsy when there is no identifiable organic cause. The loss of urine or feces during the seizure is common.

Bed wetting may be the presenting symptom in children with *obstructive uropathy*, which is a physical blockage of the urinary tract. *Urinary infections* are often associated with enuresis.

Many enuretics are sleepwalkers, and they attempt to urinate during somnambulism. Therefore, sleepwalking must be differentiated from both enuresis and epilepsy.

In young children, the sudden development of enuresis is a common presentation of *diabetes mellitus*, which is characterized by polyuria (excessive output of urine), polydypsia (excessive intake of fluid), and polyphagia (excessive food intake). Diabetes mellitus is caused by insulin deficiency.

Diagnoses to be considered when a child presents with enuresis include diabetes insipidus, spina bifida, lumbosacral myelodysplasia, sickle-cell anemia, foreign body, calculus, paraphimosis, vaginitis, mental retardation, the presence of intestinal parasites, and spinal tumors. Spinal tumors have a low incidence in childhood, but the loss of sphincter control in a child with progressive weakness, clumsiness, pain, and gait

disturbance should alert the doctor to the possibility.

**37.23.   The answer is C (2, 4)** (*Synopsis*, ed. 4, page 846).

*Encopresis is found much more frequently in boys than in girls.* The ratio is about 5 to 1. Even so, in terms of large samples of the general population, the malady is found in relatively few persons. About 1 percent of 5-year-old children are encopretic. In some cases, encopresis has been *associated with enuresis.*

Cases of encopresis are found throughout Western civilization. There seem to be *no social or class barriers to encopresis.*

About one-fourth of all encopretics *have an associated constipation*, which results in an overflow encopresis. Most cases of encopresis are not associated with voluminous fecal impaction.

The DSM-III diagnostic criteria for functional encopresis are listed below.

---

**Diagnostic Criteria for Functional Encopresis***

A. Repeated voluntary or involuntary passage of feces of normal or near-normal consistency into places not appropriate for that purpose in the individual's own sociocultural setting.

B. At least one such event a month after the age of 4.

C. Not due to a physical disorder, such as aganglionic megacolon.

---

* From American Psychiatric Association: *Diagnostic and Statistical Manual of Mental Disorders*, ed 3. American Psychiatric Association, Washington, DC, 1980. Used with permission.

**37.24.   The answer is E (all)** (*Synopsis*, ed. 4, pages 846 and 847).

The child who fails to attain bowel control may soon suffer from hostile behavior by one or more family members. As the child mixes with others outside the home, there is ridicule by peers and alienation from teachers.

There appears to be *excessive emphasis placed on bowel habits*, and many encopretics seem to lack the sensory cues as to when they need to defecate. Psychologically, the patient remains blunted to the effect the disorder has on other people. Nevertheless, the child comes to feel unwanted and to have a low self-concept. Dynamically, the *mother is frequently depressed*, often dissatisfied with her marriage and maternal roles, compulsive, and emotionally unavailable. In such a household, the *father is found to be critical*, emotionally distant, and often absent physically or psychologically or both.

A rash of mechanical problems may result in *organic defects in the lower gastrointestinal tract* as the condition continues. The sufferer may require treatment for fissures, rectal prolapse, rectal excoriations, or impaction.

Nevertheless, the child who is encopretic can be obedient and tractable and is frequently well liked by adults. This attitude is important because the disorder may last for years, although it usually disappears by adolescence. The natural history of the disorder seems to be self-limited.

**37.25.   The answer is A (1, 2, 3)** (*Synopsis*, ed. 4, page 848).

In psychoanalytic theory, nail biting is thought to be caused by *intense or competitive impulses toward a parent.* If such impulses were actualized, these children would destroy their source of dependency gratification. To resolve the conflict, the children bite their nails, thus denying their hostility, injuring themselves, and *demonstrating self-punishment.* At the same time, they are able to *express aggression* but spare the object of their aggression.

Finger sucking and thumb sucking are thought to be the result of regression to oral satisfactions when a person is placed under the duress of tension or fatigue.

*Birth trauma* is a term used to describe what Otto Rank considered the basic source of anxiety in human beings, the birth process.

**37.26.   The answer is E (all)** (*Synopsis*, ed. 4, page 848).

Nail biting, thumb sucking, and finger sucking are considered *socially offensive.* In a few cases, nail biting or finger sucking is so severe that it causes physical discomfort or even *finger necrosis.* Thumb sucking after age 3½ should elicit concern relative to the possibility of *damage to dentition.* Similarly, children past age 7 who continue to finger suck may adversely affect their teeth, particularly in the anterior region.

In cases so severe that the children have physical discomfort, meet frequent social disapproval, or damage their bite, there may be psychological *damage to their self-image.*

**37.27.   The answer is B (1, 3)** (*Synopsis*, ed. 4, page 852).

The technology by which sleep is assessed and diagnosed is called polysomnography. A polysomnogram includes an electroencephalogram (which measures brain waves), an electromyogram (which measures action potentials in muscles), and eye movements and other nocturnal events.

*In spite of frequent subjective sleep complaints, prepubertal children do not show polysomno-* *graphic abnormalities* during a major depressive episode. Rapid eye movement (REM) sleep is the stage during which dreaming occurs and the dreamer exhibits coordinated rapid eye movement. REM latency is that period of time between the onset of sleep and the beginning of the first REM sleep period. In adolescents, *REM latency is shortened* during major depressive episodes, as it is in adults. *It is not known at present if this abnormality persists in the drug-free recovered state.*

**37.28–37.31.   The answers are 37.28–A, 37.29–B, 37.30–B, and 37.31–B** (*Synopsis*, ed. 4, page 850).

Children and adolescents with major depressive disorder, which is not superimposed on a preexisting, nonaffective, nonorganic psychotic disorder, will quite frequently be *found to suffer from hallucinations and delusions.* In the wide majority of cases, *these psychotic symptoms are thematically consistent with depressive mood, occur within the depressive episode and not outside it* (usually during the times the depression is at its worst), and do not include types of hallucinations that are somewhat specific to schizophrenia, such as conversing voices or a commenting voice. These cases are referred to as psychotic depressions. Depressive hallucinations usually consist of a single voice speaking to the subjects from outside their head, with derogatory or suicidal content when the youngsters are most depressed. Depressive delusions are centered on themes of guilt, physical disease, death, nihilism, deserved punishment, personal inadequacy, or sometimes persecution if related by the patients to their own imagined or exaggerated fault. These delusions are very rare in prepuberty, probably because of cognitive immaturity, but present in about half the psychotically depressed adolescents. Depressive hallucinations are almost the sole psychotic depressive symptom presented by prepubertal children, and they are also quite frequent in adolescents with psychotic depression.

A parallel description can be made for psychotic mania. It is characterized by delusions and hallucinations thematically consistent with manic mood—that is, involving grandiose evaluation of the patient's own power, worth, knowledge, family or relationships, or even persecutory delusions if related to the youngster's grandiosity—or flight of ideas with gross impairment of reality testing, which occur at the same time as frank mania and usually during the worst periods. Conversing and commenting hallucinations are not included.

In a subgroup of youngsters with major depression or mania plus psychotic symptoms, the latter do not strictly conform to the pattern described and cannot be characterized as clearly depressive. For example, when any of the following are present: *conversing or commenting voices*; delusions of persecution not related to guilt or grandiosity; delusions *of thought insertion, broadcasting or withdrawal*, delusions of being controlled; or catatonia. For another example, *psychotic symptoms are present when mood disorders are no longer manifest*, especially if they are not mood congruous. Such cases are usually diagnosed as schizoaffective disorder. Adolescents, and probably also children, who fit criteria for schizoaffective disorder do exist, but little is known at present about the course of the illness, family history, psychobiology, and treatment.

**37.32–37.35.  The answers are 37.32–D, 37.33–C, 37.34–B, and 37.35–C** (*Synopsis*, ed. 4, page 849).

It is not unusual to find that a youngster presents a clinical picture that does not fit criteria for major depression but could be diagnosed as dysthymia, *except that the duration of the episode is under 1 year*. Sometimes there are two or three episodes, each lasting anywhere from 2 weeks to 11 months, but the *symptom-free interval is simply too long (over 2 or 3 months) for the dysthymic diagnosis to be applicable* on strict grounds. DSM-III classifies these and other clinical presentations under the overall rubric of atypical depression. *When such episodes follow a significant stressful life event by less than 3 months*, the diagnoses of adjustment disorder with depressive mood or uncomplicated bereavement should be made. As the expressivity of the genetic predisposition to affective disorders is highly likely to be negatively correlated with age, minor affective *presentations in children are likely to have high predictive value for future more severe affective disorder episodes.*

## References

Fontana V J: Child maltreatment and battered child syndrome. In *Comprehensive Textbook of Psychiatry*, ed. 4, H I Kaplan, B J Sadock, editors, p 1816. Williams & Wilkins, Baltimore, 1985.

Pfeffer C R: Children's reactions to illness, hospitalization, and surgery. In *Comprehensive Textbook of Psychiatry*, ed. 4, H I Kaplan, B J Sadock, editors, p 1836. Williams & Wilkins, Baltimore, 1985.

Pierce C M: Encopresis. In *Comprehensive Textbook of Psychiatry*, ed. 4, H I Kaplan, B J Sadock, editors, p. 1847. Williams & Wilkins, Baltimore, 1985.

Pierce C M: Enuresis. In *Comprehensive Textbook of Psychiatry*. ed. 4, H I Kaplan, B J Sadock, editors, p 1842. Williams & Wilkins, Baltimore, 1985.

Pierce C M: Other developmental disorders. In *Comprehensive Textbook of Psychiatry*, ed 4, H I Kaplan, B J Sadock, editors, p 1849. Williams & Wilkins, Baltimore, 1985.

Puig-Antich J: Affective disorders. In *Comprehensive Textbook of Psychiatry*, ed. 4, H I Kaplan, B J Sadock, editors, p 1850. Williams & Wilkins, Baltimore, 1985.

Wolman B B, Egan J, Ross A O: Handbook of Treatment of Mental Disorders in Childhood and Adolescence, Prentice-Hall, Englewood Cliffs, NJ, 1978.

# 38

# Conditions Not Attributable to a Mental Disorder

As defined in the third edition of the American Psychiatric Association's *Diagnostic and Statistical Manual of Mental Disorders* (DSM-III), conditions not attributable to a mental disorder have led to contact with the mental health care system, but without sufficient evidence to justify a diagnosis of mental illness. In some instances, one of these conditions will be noted because, following a thorough evaluation, no mental disorder is found to be present. In other instances, the scope of the diagnostic evaluation was not such as to adequately determine the presence or absence of a mental disorder, but there is a need to note the primary reason for contact with the mental health care system.

Conditions not attributable to a mental disorder represent an interface between psychiatry and sociology. Many of the situations covered in this section are culturally engendered and can produce severe emotional distress in otherwise psychiatrically normal persons. The psychiatrist must be alert to the extent of the environmental stress and must offer help through supportive therapy or suggestions for environmental manipulation. At the same time, the psychiatrist must remain aware of the psychodynamics that may have led the patient into that situation or that contribute to the difficulties of the situation and that may require more traditional psychotherapy.

The categories covered include the following: academic problem, previously called underachievement; occupational problem, such as job dissatisfaction; phase of life problem, such as changing careers; marital problem, such as impending divorce; parent-child problem, such as methods of discipline; family circumstance problem, such as sibling rivalry; and other interpersonal problem, such as difficulties with co-workers. Also included in this classification are noncompliance with medical treatment, in which the patient for one or several reasons refuses to follow the doctor's advice; borderline intellectual functioning, in which the I.Q. is between 71 and 84 (according to DSM-III, an I.Q. below 70 is diagnosed as mental retardation); and uncomplicated bereavement, the normal reaction to the death of a loved one.

Finally, malingering and antisocial behavior are covered in this section. Both are classified in DSM-III as conditions not attributable to a mental disorder. The essential feature of malingering is the voluntary production and presentation of false or grossly exaggerated physical or psychological symptoms. The category of adult antisocial behavior is a vague grouping for antisocial persons without readily demonstrable psychopathology to account for their undesirable behaviors, such as robbery, violent crimes, prostitution, and other illegal acts.

The reader should review these conditions in Chapter 38 of *Modern Synopsis-IV* and should then study the questions and answers below to test his or her knowledge of these areas.

# Questions

**DIRECTIONS:** Each of the statements or questions below is followed by five suggested responses or completions. Select the *one* that is *best* in each case.

**38.1.** Which of the following statements about environmental factors influencing antisocial behavior is not true:

A The occurrence of serious psychopathology among parents is an important factor in the development of delinquent children.

B. The incidence of broken homes is the same in delinquent and in nondelinquent children.

C. Homes broken by divorce or separation seem to produce higher rates of delinquency than do homes disrupted by the death of a parent.

D. Socioeconomic class is a factor in determining antisocial behavior.

E. Techniques of discipline are important factors in the development of delinquent behavior.

**38.2.** Which of the following statements about the epidemiology of antisocial behavior is not correct:

A. Over 80 percent of property crime arrests in the United States in 1981 were of persons 18 years of age or younger.

B. Males commit 8 times the number of violent crimes and 4 times as many property crimes as do females.

C. Crime, in general, has been increasing, especially crime committed by females.

D. Statistics on crime are not necessarily synonymous with statistics on antisocial behavior.

E. Estimates of the prevalence of antisocial personality disorder used to include those people currently classified as having antisocial behavior.

**38.3.** A very effective method of treatment for antisocial behavior is

A. the therapeutic community
B. group therapy
C. individual therapy
D. medication
E. none of the above

**38.4.** Holmes' social readjustment scale of stressful life events indicates that, of the changes listed below, the one that produces the greatest stress is

A. being fired at work
B. marriage
C. being sent to jail
D. divorce
E. death of a spouse

**38.5.** Malingering may be differentiated from more purely neurotic behavior on the basis of

A. a past history of irresponsibility, dishonesty, or inadequacy

B. an unwillingness to accept alternate employment of which the person is capable

C. a preserved capacity for play

D. bizarre and inconsistent psychological test results

E. all of the above

**38.6.** Which of the following statements about marital stress is not correct:

A. If the partners are from similar backgrounds, conflicts are less likely to arise.

B. The birth of children often precipitates a problem period in marriages.

C. Abortion is not generally included as a potential conflict in a seemingly healthy marriage.

D. Sexual dissatisfaction is involved in most cases of marital maladjustment.

E. Complaints of anorgasmia or impotence are usually indicative of deeper problems.

**DIRECTIONS:** For each of the incomplete statements below, *one* or *more* of the completions given is correct. Choose answer:

A. if only **1, 2,** and **3** are correct
B. if only **1** and **3** are correct
C. if only **2** and **4** are correct
D. if only **4** is correct
E. if all are correct

**38.7.** The relationship between life stress and illness indicates that

1. specific life events in and of themselves do not necessarily produce a mental disorder
2. the evolution of a person's adaptive style is more dependent on internal growth than on the interpersonal environment
3. the number of stresses occurring within a period of time is potentially more injurious than the stress itself
4. it is irrelevant whether the event is expected or unexpected

**38.8.** In dual-career families in which both spouses are working,

1. mothers are vulnerable to guilt about child rearing
2. there is a tendency to use physical punishment as a child-rearing mechanism
3. the value of producing psychological health in the child is given a high priority
4. there is minimal stress for the woman

**38.9.** Maladaptation at work may arise from psychodynamic conflicts that include

1. problems with authority figures
2. competitive rivalries
3. pathological envy
4. fear of hostility from others

**38.10.** Persons with borderline intellectual functioning

1. have an I.Q. of between 90 and 100
2. make up about 7 percent of the population
3. are usually vocationally well adjusted
4. can be helped by psychiatric treatment

**38.11.** The DSM-III category of academic problems should be used

1. only after a thorough psychiatric examination
2. when no mental disorder is found
3. when the academic problem is not caused by a coexisting mental disorder
4. when it occurs before the child is formally enrolled in school

**38.12.** Antisocial behavior is generally characterized by

1. lack of social charm and poor intelligence
2. heightened nervousness with neurotic manifestations
3. often successful suicide attempts
4. lack of remorse or shame

**38.13.** The differential diagnosis of antisocial behavior includes

1. alcoholism and drug abuse
2. manic phases of cyclothymic disorder
3. schizophrenia
4. temporal lobe epilepsy

**38.14.** Psychological theories relating to antisocial behavior have included which of the following themes:

1. The child feels significant emotional deprivation and resents it.
2. The parents' lack of limits on the child have prevented the child from developing his or her own skills.
3. The parents are overstimulating and inconsistent.
4. The child's behavior represents a vicarious source of pleasure for the parent.

**38.15.** Malingering is characterized by

1. an unwillingness to work
2. a good record of payment to doctors
3. ill-defined symptoms
4. secondary gain

**38.16.** The category of adult antisocial behavior

1. is considered the same as the DSM-III diagnosis of antisocial personality disorder
2. is usually used as an intermediate designation on the way to a more useful diagnosis
3. gives a good indication of absence of mental illness in the antisocial person
4. should be utilized only in the absence of evidence of organic, psychotic, neurotic, or intellectual impairment

| Directions Summarized | | | | |
|---|---|---|---|---|
| A | B | C | D | E |
| 1, 2, 3 only | 1, 3 only | 2, 4 only | 4 only | All are correct |

**38.17.** Academic problems

1. can best be alleviated through the use of psychological means
2. are often related to poor motivation, poor self-concept, and underachievement
3. frequently compound themselves and precipitate more severe difficulties
4. should rarely be treated with behavioral deconditioning techniques

**38.18.** Factors most often associated with job-related stress include

1. unclear work objectives
2. conflicting demands
3. responsibility for the professional development of others
4. too much or too little work

**38.19.** Personality characteristics of the lower classes as compared to the upper classes include which of the following:

1. They are visual, rather than aural.
2. They are less introspective.
3. They are games- and action-oriented, rather than test-oriented.
4. They are more impulsive.

# Answers

# Conditions Not Attributable to a Mental Disorder

**38.1.** **The answer is B** (*Synopsis*, ed. 4 page 858).

One aspect of the family that does emerge as particularly important in delinquent children is the occurrence of serious psychopathology. Several studies have noted that *the parents of delinquents, when compared with the parents of nondelinquents, manifest more severe psychopathology*. These studies raise questions about the quality of the parenting in the development of delinquent children; however, antisocial behavior in such patients may be a manifestation of a genetic schizophrenic tendency. *There is a higher incidence of broken homes in delinquent children.* The critical factor seems to relate more to the quality of the home life; *homes broken by divorce or separation seem to produce higher rates of delinquency than do homes disrupted by the death of a parent.* Thus, the important factor seems to be family discord and disharmony, rather than parental absence.

*Studies note that the sons of unskilled workers brought up in neighborhoods in which families of this socioeconomic class predominate are more likely to commit more numerous and more serious criminal offences than are the sons of middle-class or skilled working-class parents*, at least during adolescence and early adulthood. These data are not as clear for females, but the findings are generally similar in studies from many different countries. Areas of family training that have been particularly cited as differing by social class from the techniques seen in middle-class parents are the use of more love-oriented techniques in disciplining, the withdrawal of affection versus physical punishments, parental attitudes toward aggressive behavior and attempts to curb it, parental values in general, and the verbal ability to communicate the various reasons for the values and proscriptions of behavior.

**38.2.** **The answer is A** (*Synopsis*, ed. 4, page 857).

In 1981, in the United States with a population of over 200 million persons, there were over 10 million arrests. Although the nation has focused attention on youth crime, *over 80 percent of arrests were of persons 18 years of age or older.* Adults 18 years of age or older accounted for 81.5 percent of violent crime, but only 62.6 percent of property crime. *That males in today's society are more violent than females is clear from the fact that they commit 8 times the number of violent crimes and 4 times as many property crimes*, according to federal arrest data. Violent crime in cities is 10 times as frequent as it is in rural areas. The incidence of violent crime in suburbia falls somewhere between the incidence in cities and in rural areas.

It is noteworthy that, within cities, the crime rate for males increased 4.7 percent between 1980 and 1981, whereas the rate for females increased 7.9 percent. Thus *crime, in general, has been increasing, especially crime committed by females.*

*Statistics regarding crime, however, are not necessarily synonymous with statistics either on antisocial personality or on antisocial behavior.* Clearly, many intelligent, devious, well-functioning criminals do not appear in these statistics, whereas a fair number of psychotic, neurologically impaired, and retarded persons do add to them. *Estimates of the prevalence of the disorder of antisocial personality, which, until the new classification in DSM-III, included those persons currently classified as having antisocial behavior* (and which was often called sociopathic personality), have ranged from 5 to 15 percent of the population, depending on criteria and sampling. Even within the prison population, different investigators have reported prevalence figures of between 20 and 80 percent. The higher percentage is most likely due to using previous arrests and incarcerations as important criteria for diagnosing a person as having an antisocial personality.

**38.3.** **The answer is E** (*Synopsis*, ed. 4, pages 859 and 860).

In general, great therapeutic pessimism surrounds the term antisocial behavior. It is difficult for a therapist not to feel that there is little hope of changing a pattern of behavior that has been present almost throughout the patient's life. In part, the literature bears out this therapeutic pessimism.

There have been no major breakthroughs with biological treatments nor any overwhelming success with the use of *medications*.

More enthusiasm has been expressed for various *therapeutic communities* and *group treatment* of delinquents and adult criminals. The data, however, provide little basis for enthusiasm.

Treatment of outpatients with antisocial behavior is extremely difficult, and such patients should be *treated individually*, primarily in an institutional center, where they can be prevented from running away. Once immobilized in an institutional setting, the patient becomes less alien to the therapist and less difficult to understand.

The natural history of violence and of criminal and antisocial behavior seems to decrease after age 40, and recidivism also decreases after age 40. Several authors have suggested that perhaps one way of treating these patients is to isolate them from society until after age 40. Although this position may be overly pessimistic, it is important to recognize that antisocial behavior is a repetitive pattern that seems to limit itself after age 40 and that has been unresponsive to most therapeutic interventions.

A *therapeutic community* is an institutional treatment setting designed with an emphasis on the importance of socioenvironmental and interpersonal influences in the therapy, management, and rehabilitation of the hospitalized mental patient. A *therapeutic group* is a group of patients joined together under the leadership of a therapist for the purpose of working together for psychotherapeutic ends—specifically, for the treatment of each patient's mental disorders. *Individual therapy* refers to the traditional dyadic therapeutic technique in which a psychotherapist treats one patient during a given therapeutic session. Newer techniques, however, deal with more than one patient during these sessions.

**38.4.    The answer is E** (*Synopsis,* ed. 4, pages 863 and 864).

T. Holmes quantified life events, assigning a point value to life changes that require adaptation. His Social Readjustment Rating Scale is shown in the table below.

**38.5.    The answer is E** (*Synopsis,* ed. 4, page 856).

To differentiate malingering from neurosis, several criteria can be used:

1. *Past history of irresponsibility, dishonesty, or inadequacy.*

2. *Unwilling to accept alternate employment for which capable.*

3. Reluctant to have psychiatric hospitalizations, surgery, or other treatment.

4. Symptoms are present only during the period when the patient is aware of being observed.

5. Resists reexamination, especially by groups of doctors.

6. Poor compliance with therapy and symptoms not influenced by suggestion.

7. Typical psychological testing. (Psychological testing may reveal suspiciously *bizarre responses and inconsistencies* throughout.)

8. Lack of preoccupation with the event in dreams, thoughts, or speech.

9. *Preserved capacity for play.*

Often, the physician experiences the malingerer as being hostile or unfriendly or even suspicious and may, in turn, feel hostile, especially if the patient is uncooperative with the evaluation and noncompliant with attempted treatment. Thus, the physician's emotional reaction to such behavior may be a diagnostic clue.

**38.6.    The answer is C** (*Synopsis,* ed. 4, pages 862 and 863).

Marriage involves many stressful situations that tax the adaptive capacities of the partners.

Economic stresses, moves to new areas, unplanned pregnancies, and *abortions may upset a seemingly healthy marriage.* Differing attitudes toward religion can also present a problem.

*If the partners are of different backgrounds and have been raised within different value systems, conflicts are more likely to arise* than if they came from similar backgrounds. The areas of potential conflict that should be explored include sexual relations; attitudes toward contraception, childbearing, and child rearing; handling of money; relation with in-laws; and attitudes toward social life.

**The Social Readjustment Rating Scale**

| Life Event | Mean Value |
| --- | --- |
| 1. *Death of spouse* | 100 |
| 2. *Divorce* | 73 |
| 3. Marital separation from mate | 65 |
| 4. *Detention in jail* or other institution | 63 |
| 5. Death of a close family member | 63 |
| 6. Major personal injury or illness | 53 |
| 7. *Marriage* | 50 |
| 8. *Being fired at work* | 47 |
| 9. Marital reconciliation with mate | 45 |
| 10. Retirement from work | 45 |

*A problem period in a marriage is often precipitated by the birth of children,* especially the first child. It is a stressful time for both parents.

*Complaints of anorgasmia or impotence by marital partners are usually indicative of deeper disturbances,* although sexual dissatisfaction is involved in most cases of marital maladjustment. Some marriages can survive without sexual relations, but poor sexual functioning frequently reflects disturbances in other areas of the relationship.

The institution of marriage is itself being stressed by cultural changes. Some workers feel that the family is being scapegoated because of pressures from other rapid changes in the social system.

### 38.7. The answer is A (1, 2, 3) *(Synopsis, ed. 4, page 863).*

Psychological development throughout the life cycle has been studied and conceptualized by numerous workers. Specific attention is currently focused on the relationship between life stresses and illness to determine what brings people without a mental disorder into the mental health care system.

Emerging from this research is the concept that *specific life events in and of themselves do not necessarily produce a mental disorder.* A person's adaptive style evolves and matures throughout life, but *its evolution is more dependent on internal growth than on the interpersonal environment.*

*External events are most likely to overwhelm the person's adaptive capacities if they are unexpected,* if they are overwhelming in number—that is, *a number of stresses occurring within a short time span*—if the strain is chronic and unremitting, or if one loss actually heralds a myriad of concomitant adjustments that strain a person's recuperative powers.

### 38.8. The answer is B (1, 3) *(Synopsis, ed. 4, page 868).*

A particular stress arises in dual-career families. The mothers in these families—defined as families in which both spouses have careers, rather than jobs—are found to be particularly *vulnerable to guilt and anxiety regarding their maternal role.* These women usually accept middle-class or upper middle-class values that emphasize the individual development and *psychological health of the child* as very important. They espouse middle-class child-rearing practices that use sensitivity and verbal communication in imparting values to the child, *rather than using physical punishment to enforce demands to behave and conform.* The middle-class family system is particularly demanding of the wife and mother, and *it is especially stressful for the career wife and mother* who has significant time commitments outside the home.

### 38.9. The answer is E (all) *(Synopsis, ed. 4, pages 864 and 865).*

Maladaptation at work may, of course, arise from psychodynamic conflicts. These conflicts can be reflected in *the patient's inability to accept the authority of competent superiors or, conversely, in an overdependency on authority figures to fulfill infantile needs.* People with unresolved *conflicts over their competitive and aggressive impulses* may experience great difficulty in the work area. They may suffer from a *pathological envy of success of others, or fear success for themselves because of their inability to tolerate envy from others.* These conflicts are manifest in other areas of the patient's life as well, and the maladaptation is not limited to job performance.

An authority figure is a real or projected person in a position of power; transferentially, it is a projected parent.

### 38.10. The answer is C (2, 4) *(Synopsis, ed. 4, page 862).*

As described in DSM-III, the category may be used when a focus of attention or treatment is on a deficit in adaptive functioning associated with borderline intellectual functioning; that is, an *I.Q. in the 71 to 84 range.* The problem is often masked when a mental disorder is present that comes to the attention of the psychiatrist.

The premise behind the inclusion of this category is that these persons may experience difficulties in their adaptive capacities, which may ultimately produce *impaired social and vocational functioning.* Thus, in the absence of specific intrapsychic conflicts, developmental traumas, biochemical abnormalities, or other factors that are linked to mental disorders, they may experience severe emotional distress. Frustration and embarrassment over their difficulties may shape life choices and lead to circumstances warranting psychiatric intervention.

Once the underlying problem is known to the therapist, *psychiatric treatment can be quite useful.* Many persons with borderline intellectual functioning are able to function at a superior level in some areas, while being markedly deficient in others. By directing them to appropriate areas of endeavor, by pointing out socially acceptable behavior, and by teaching living skills, the therapist can act as a force that improves their self-esteem.

Only *about 6 to 7 percent of the population are found to have a borderline I.Q.,* as determined by the Stanford-Binet Test or the Wechsler scales.

### 38.11. The answer is A (1, 2, 3) *(Synopsis, ed. 4, page 860).*

Appropriate use of the category of academic problems for diagnostic purposes is limited to one of the following three circumstances: (1) the absence of evidence of a mental disorder that accounts for the academic problem, as determined by a *complete and adequate psychiatric evaluation;* (2) the *absence of evidence of a mental disorder* that accounts for the academic problem, as determined by an incomplete and inadequate psychiatric evaluation, but one in which some notation is required stating the reason for contact with the mental health care system; (3) the presence of a mental disorder is noted, but it is felt that the focus of attention or treatment— *the academic problem—is not caused by that disorder.*

Academic problems may result from a variety of causes and may arise at any time in life. *They occur most often between the ages of 5 and 21, a span that includes the school years.*

**38.12.   The answer is D (4)** *(Synopsis,* ed. 4, page 858).

Perhaps the most important clinical point to emphasize in the designation of antisocial behavior is that this is a diagnosis based primarily on the historical description of behavior. Hervey Cleckley, one of the major investigators of antisocial behavior, described the clinical picture of antisocial behavior that is summarized in the following table.

Included in this description are the presence of *a superficial charm and good intelligence, an absence of nervousness and neurotic manifestations, rarely successful suicide attempts,* and *lack of remorse or shame.*

### Clinical Profile of Antisocial Behavior*

Superficial charm and good intelligence
Absence of delusions and other signs of irrational thinking
Absence of nervousness and psychoneurotic manifestations
Unreliability
Untruthfulness and insincerity
Lack of remorse or shame
Inadequately motivated antisocial behavior
Poor judgment and failure to learn by experience
Pathological egocentricity and incapacity for love
General poverty in major affective reactions
Specific loss of insight
Unresponsiveness in general interpersonal relations
Fantastic and uninviting behavior with drink and sometimes without
Suicide rarely carried out
Sex life impersonal, trivial, and poorly integrated
Failure to follow any life plan

* Data from Cleckley H: *The Mask of Sanity,* ed 4. C V Mosby, St. Louis, 1964.

**38.13.   The answer is E (all)** *(Synopsis,* ed. 4, page 859).

The intertwining of alcoholism and drug dependence in the descriptive behaviors of antisocial behavior often makes it difficult to distinguish antisocial behavior, related primarily to drug abuse or alcoholism, from disordered behavior that occurred before the *drug abuse or alcoholism* or that occurred during episodes unrelated to alcoholism or drug abuse.

During *manic phases of cyclothymic disorder,* certain aspects of behavior, such as wanderlust, sexual promiscuity, and financial difficulty, can be similar to antisocial behaviors. The early onset of antisocial behavior and acts before the age of 15 is most often absent in cyclothymic disorder. The episodic and cyclic nature of cyclothymic disorder is also characteristic and discernible; the mental status symptoms noted in the manic patient of flight of ideas, pressure of speech, grandiosity, and euphoria are most often absent in antisocial behavior.

*Schizophrenia,* especially in childhood, may often manifest as antisocial behavior. In the adult schizophrenic patient, however, episodes of antisocial behavior may occur, but the symptom picture is usually clear, especially with regard to thought disorders, delusions, and hallucinations noted during the mental status examination.

Neurological conditions may cause antisocial behavior. EEG's, CT scans, and a complete neurological examination should be done. *Temporal lobe epilepsy* is often considered in the differential diagnosis. When a clear-cut diagnosis of temporal lobe epilepsy or encephalitis can be made, that may account for the antisocial behavior.

**38.14.   The answer is E (all)** *(Synopsis,* ed. 4, page 858).

The psychological theories pertaining to antisocial behavior have focused on two major themes: (1) the quality of the parental experience, particularly the quality of the mothering, and (2) the development of conscience. The psychological theories are as follows: (1) Such children feel *significant emotional deprivation and strongly resent it;* (2) *children cannot establish their own range of skills because their parents have not set limits for them;* (3) *the parents, especially the mother, are very often overstimulating and inconsistent* in their attitudes toward the child; and (4) *the child's behavior usually represents a vicarious source of pleasure* and gratification for a parent and is often an expression of the parent's unconscious hostility toward the child, as the behavior is either overtly or covertly self-destructive to the child.

**38.15.   The answer is E (all)** *(Synopsis*, ed. 4, pages 855 and 856).

Malingering is classified in DSM-III as a condition not attributable to a mental disorder that is a focus of attention or treatment. The essential feature is the voluntary production and presentation of false or grossly exaggerated physical or psychological symptoms.

The artifice disorder may follow a planned or accidental event, usually resulting in a complaint, request, or claim. Malingerers seeking compensation often choose an event that commonly results in disability. Timing is important. Many express vague, *ill-defined symptoms* that are mostly subjective—for example, headache; pains of the neck, lower back, chest, or abdomen; dizziness; vertigo; amnesia; anxiety and depression; and symptoms often having a family history, in all likelihood not organically based but incredibly difficult to refute. Malingerers may complain bitterly, describing how much the symptoms impair normal function and how much they are disliked. They may use the very best doctor who is most trusted (and perhaps most easily fooled), *and promptly and willingly pay all bills*, even if excessive, to impress the doctor with their integrity. To seem credible, they must invariably give the same report of symptoms, but tell the physician as little as possible. Often, however, they complain of misery without objective signs or other symptoms congruent with recognized diseases or syndromes; if symptoms are described, they come and go. Malingerers are often preoccupied with cash, rather than cure, and have a knowledge of the law and precedents relevant to their claims.

In malingering, the action is conscious, voluntary, and goal directed. There is always *secondary gain*, the obvious advantage that a person gains from an illness, such as gifts, attention, and release from responsibility. Malingerers are usually *unwilling to work*. Self-esteem is usually intact.

**38.16.   The answer is C (2, 4)** *(Synopsis*, ed. 4, page 857).

The category of adult antisocial behavior, except perhaps in the case of certain racketeers, embezzlers, forgers, and others who have made crime an organized profession, is usually *an interim designation on the way to a more useful diagnosis. The category of adult antisocial behavior is intended to be distinct from the DSM-III diagnosis of antisocial personality disorder.*

There are at least two difficulties with the designation of adult antisocial behavior. First, persons so designated may have manifested diverse behaviors, ranging from repeated cheating, lying, forgery, and embezzlement to arson, rape, and murder. Second, *the term gives no indication* of whether it is being used to convey the absence of mental illness in the antisocial person or that the person has not yet been adequately evaluated.

Antisocial behaviors in childhood and adulthood are characteristic of persons with a variety of psychopathology, ranging from the psychotic to the characterological. Moreover, antisocial behavior is often characteristic of persons whose functioning is on the border of several other kinds of disorders, including psychosis, organic brain syndromes, and retardation. A comprehensive neuropsychiatric assessment of antisocial persons usually reveals a myriad of more and less serious, potentially treatable psychiatric and neurological impairments that can easily be overshadowed by offensive behaviors and thus be overlooked. When the clinician leaves the patient in the category "antisocial behavior," it is usually because the time has not been taken to complete a thorough evaluation, rather than because, in a comprehensive assessment, the clinician has found no significant disturbance other than the antisocial behavior itself. Because of the negative connotations of any designation that includes the term "antisocial" in its name, be it antisocial personality or simply antisocial behavior, it is imperative that no patient be left in these categories simply for want of a careful assessment. *Only in the absence of evidence of organic, psychotic, neurotic, or intellectual impairment should the patient be so categorized.*

**38.17.   The answer is A (1, 2, 3)** *(Synopsis*, ed. 4, page 861).

Academic problems, although not a diagnosable psychiatric disorder, *can best be alleviated through use of psychological means.* Psychotherapeutic techniques can be used successfully for scholastic difficulties, including those *related to poor motivation, poor self-concept, and underachievement.*

Early efforts at the relief of the problem should outweigh all other considerations, because sustained problems in learning and school performance *frequently are compounded and precipitate more severe difficulties.* Feelings of anger, frustration, shame, loss of self-respect, and helplessness—emotions that most often accompany school failures—have an emotionally and cognitively damaging effect on self-esteem, disabling future performance and clouding expectations for success.

Tutoring is an extremely effective technique in dealing with academic problems and should be considered for use in all cases. In dealing with the stigma attached to having a tutor—for many students, having a tutor is a humiliating concession to their perception of being dumb—the therapist may find it helpful to explain to the student that he or she probably holds to the self-serving hypothesis of academic performance—the concept that success in school work is due to internal factors but that failure is due to chance or other forces. Thus, success is attributed to ability or disposition, and failure is attributed to extenuating circumstances. That attitude is exemplified by the saying "good students are born, not made" and by the general reluctance of students to admit that they study hard. Clarification of this outlook, if present, is often important in getting a student to accept tutoring. Tutoring is of special proven value in preparing for objective multiple choice examinations, such as the SAT, MCAT, and National Boards. Diminishing anxiety by repetitively taking such type of examination questions is *a behavioral deconditioning technique.*

**38.18.   The answer is E (all)** (*Synopsis*, ed. 4, pages 864 and 865).

Important questions to ask concerning work stress include how the occupation was chosen. Was it a childhood goal? Was it chosen in emulation of a model and hero? Was it forced or encouraged by the patient's family? Was it an outgrowth of a special talent? Was it well prepared for? Was it arrived at by trial and error? Was it an impulsive decision? Was it forced by financial need? With a young patient, what are the expectations regarding advancement? Are they realistic? With an older patient, what is the record of success? What is the frequency of changing employment? What are the frequency and the duration of unemployment?

Along with these questions, it is important to keep in mind that recent research has suggested that job-related stress is most likely to develop when *work objectives are not clear, when workers are pressured by conflicting demands, when they have too much or too little to do, and when they are responsible for the professional development of others* and have little control over decisions that affect them.

Special problems to be considered are the adjustments of those about to face retirement, the dissatisfaction of the housewife, and the minority group member blocked from position or advancement because of sex, race, religion, or ethnic background.

**38.19.   The answer is E (all)** (*Synopsis*, ed. 4, page 867).

Poverty is conventionally defined in terms of a family's financial resources. Most workers, however, agree that this arbitrary form of definition is inadequate and unrealistic. The related variables of low income, family size, age, low occupational level, high unemployment rate, local cost of living, and geographic location have come to be used in measuring poverty.

Mental health workers have attempted to describe those personality traits that are most frequently found among the poor. The poor are said to be (1) *physical and visual, rather than aural;* (2) content-centered, rather than form-centered; (3) *externally oriented, rather than introspective;* (4) problem-centered, rather than abstract-centered; (5) inductive, rather than deductive; (6) spatial, rather than temporal; (7) slow, careful, patient, perservering (in areas of importance), rather than quick, facile, clever; (8) *games- and action-oriented, rather than test-oriented;* (9) expressive-oriented, rather than instrumental-oriented; (10) geared to one-tract thinking and unorthodox learning, rather than other-directed flexibility; and (11) prone to use words in relation to action, rather than being word-bound.

The poor are also characterized as being *impulsive;* oriented in terms of time to the present and, to a lesser extent, the immediate past, a quality that manifests itself in failure to plan for the future and to delay gratification; and resigned and fatalistic, a characteristic that results in a tolerance of somatic and psychological pathology far in excess of that accepted by the more affluent.

## References

Bliss E L: Hysteria and hypnosis. J Nerv Ment Dis *172:* 203, 1984.

Blumstein P, Schwartz P: *American Couples.* Morrow, New York, 1983.

Lewis D O: Adult antisocial behavior and criminality. In *Comprehensive Textbook of Psychiatry,* ed 4, H I Kaplan, B J Sadock, editors, p 1865. Williams & Wilkins, Baltimore, 1985.

Long, J V F, Vaillant G E: Natural history of male psychological health. XI: Escape from the underclass. Am J Psychiatry *141:* 341, 1984.

Sadock V A: Other conditions not attributable to a

mental disorder. In *Comprehensive Textbook of Psychiatry,* ed 4, H I Kaplan, B J Sadock, editors, p 1872. Williams & Wilkins, Baltimore, 1985.

Sussman N: Academic problem and borderline intellectual functioning. In *Comprehensive Textbook of Psychiatry,* ed 4, H I Kaplan, B J Sadock, editors, p 1870. Williams & Wilkins, Baltimore, 1985.

Yudosky S C: Malingering. In *Comprehensive Textbook of Psychiatry,* ed 4, H I Kaplan, B J Sadock, editors, p 1862. Williams & Wilkins, Baltimore, 1985.

# 39

# Community Psychiatry

Community psychiatry denotes the body of knowledge required by psychiatrists who participate in organized community programs for the promotion of mental health, the prevention and treatment of mental disorders, and the rehabilitation of former psychiatric patients in the population. It supplements the clinical knowledge and skills that equip the psychiatrist to diagnose and treat individual patients. It requires the psychiatrist to relate to the community-at-large in addition to the individual.

The emergence of the theory and practice of community psychiatry was coupled with an attempt to establish coordinated community services and facilities that would provide comprehensive care for the mentally ill. This movement achieved the status of a national program with the passage of the Community Mental Health Centers (CMHC) Act of 1963.

The original goal of that act was to establish 2000 CMHC's around the country, with each one serving a particular geographic area composed of up to 200,000 people, called a catchment area. Currently, there are approximately 700 CMHC's in operation. The basic model of community psychiatry is to provide a range of comprehensive services, such as inpatient care, outpatient care, and education and consultation to local groups involved in health care and health maintenance. The community mental health movement has been called the third psychiatric revolution, the first being the recognition after the Middle Ages that mental illness was not the result of witchcraft and the second being the origin of psychoanalysis by Freud.

Preventive psychiatry encompasses measures to diminish the frequency, incidence, and degree of mental illness. Its goal is to reduce the number of persons suffering from mental illness, which is estimated to be 15 percent of the general population, not counting the 6 million persons who are mentally retarded. Within the scope of preventive psychiatry are measures to prevent mental disorders (primary prevention); measures to limit the severity of illness, as through early case finding and treatment (secondary prevention); and measures to reduce disability after a disorder (tertiary prevention).

The reader should review Chapter 39, "Community Psychiatry," in *Modern Synopsis-IV* and should then study the questions and answers below to test his or her knowledge of the subject.

# Questions

**DIRECTIONS:** Each of the statements or questions below is followed by five suggested responses or completions. Select the *one* that is *best* in each case.

**39.1.** The maximum number of persons in a catchment area served by a community mental health center (CMHC) is

A. 25,000
B. 75,000
C. 100,000
D. 200,000
E. 500,000

**39.2** Community mental health centers have historically given low priority to the needs of which of the following groups:

A. Blacks
B. Infants
C. Schizophrenic patients
D. Elderly persons
E. Neurotic patients

**39.3.** Which one of the following statements does not apply to general health care in the United States:

A. Young adults (20 to 30 years of age) are high users of all health care services.
B. Persons over 65 years of age have more illness than persons in middle adulthood.
C. Heart disease, arthritis, and cancer are the three major illnesses of the elderly.
D. Men seek health care more often than women, regardless of age.
E. Psychiatric illness is a major factor in days lost from work.

**39.4.** Primary prevention programs

A. reduce the incidence of psychiatric disorders
B. do not diminish the number of persons who are ill at one point in time (point prevalence)
C. decrease the duration of the disorder
D. treat long-term complications of the disorder
E. none of the above

**39.5.** Projections made through the 1990s indicate that there will be a shortage of physicians in which of the following specialties:

A. Neurology
B. Ophthalmology
C. Obstetrics and gynecology
D. Psychiatry
E. Otolaryngology

**39.6.** The services required by legislation to be provided by a community mental health center include all the following *except*

A. emergency services
B. outpatient services
C. inpatient services
D. psychosurgery
E. consultation-education services

**DIRECTIONS:** For each of the incomplete statements below, *one* or *more* of the completions given is correct. Choose answer:

    A. if only **1, 2,** and **3** are correct
    B. if only **1** and **3** are correct
    C. if only **2** and **4** are correct
    D. if only **4** is correct
    E. if all are correct

**39.7.** Examples of primary prevention in psychiatry include
1. the use of iodized salt
2. serological testing for syphilis
3. drunk-driver prevention programs
4. lead control programs

**39.8.** Which of the following statements apply to the ways in which hospitals are organized in the United States:
1. The state mental hospital system has about 200,000 patients.
2. Investor-owned hospitals are increasing nationally.
3. Veterans Administration (VA) hospitals are affiliated with medical schools.
4. Special hospitals are less regulated than are voluntary hospitals.

**39.9.** Which of the following statements regarding utilization of health care—psychiatric and nonpsychiatric—service are true:
1. Rates of hospitalization increase with age.
2. Men are hospitalized more frequently than women.
3. Physician services account for 20 percent of every health dollar spent.
4. There is an undersupply of hospital beds in the United States.

**DIRECTIONS:** Each set of lettered headings below is followed by a list of numbered words or phrases. For each numbered word or phrase, select

    A. if the item is associated with **A** *only*
    B. if the item is associated with **B** *only*
    C. if the item is associated with *both* **A** *and* **B**
    D. if the item is associated with *neither* **A** *nor* **B**

**Questions 39.10–39.15**
    A. Secondary prevention
    B. Tertiary prevention
    C. Both
    D. Neither

**39.10.** Emphasizes rehabilitation

**39.11.** Reduces residual defect of chronic mental illness

**39.12.** Early treatment of school phobia

**39.13.** Dietary deficiency in niacin

**39.14.** Shortens the course of illness

**39.15.** Lowers the prevalence of disease

**Questions 39.16–39.20**
A. Medicare (Title 18)
B. Medicaid (Title 19)
C. Both
D. Neither

**39.16.**   The program applies only to persons 65 or older.

**39.17.**   Money comes from both federal and state governments.

**39.18.**   Services vary from state to state.

**39.19.**   The program potentially covers both hospital and individual physician services.

**39.20.**   There are no requirements for eligibility.

**DIRECTIONS:** Each group of questions below consists of five lettered headings followed by a list of numbered words or statements. For each numbered word or statement, select the *one* lettered heading that is most closely associated with it. Each lettered heading may be selected once, more than once, or not at all.
   Match the following organizational abbreviations with the descriptions below.

**Questions 39.21–39.25**
A. JCAH
B. HMO
C. BCA
D. PSRO
E. HSA

**39.21.**   Nonprofit organizations mandated by the federal government to promote or limit the development of health services, depending on the need of a particular area

**39.22.**   Multispecialty association of physicians who provide both inpatient and outpatient care on a prepaid basis

**39.23.**   Series of agencies that influence and monitor the standards of hospital care and performance

**39.24.**   Organization made up of doctors elected by local medical societies to review and monitor care received by patients that was paid for with government funds

**39.25.**   Association of over 80 independent insurance plans that pay primarily for inpatient services

# Answers

# Community Psychiatry

**39.1.   The answer is D** (*Synopsis*, ed. 4, page 871).

A catchment area is a designated geographic area served by a community mental health center (CMHC) and has a population between 75,000 and *200,000* people. The CMHC has the responsibility to provide care to all persons in this population, including children, the aged, minorities, the chronically ill, and the acutely ill.

The concept of the catchment area has produced a number of problems. Often, the catchment area does not reflect political boundaries, natural communities, or realistic geographic-political definitions. In thinly populated and rural regions, the catchment area's size is so huge that service delivery is very difficult. In cities, the requirement for totally separate catchment areas ignores the realistic political requirements of government. The President's Commission on Mental Health recommended flexibility in delineating catchment area boundaries, sharing of cross-catchment area programs, and flexibility in delineating required services in a community mental health program.

**39.2.   The answer is D** (*Synopsis*, ed. 4, page 870).

Community mental health centers (CMHC's) have tended to neglect the elderly. Because of negative attitudes toward the aged and a false belief that psychiatric conditions in the elderly are untreatable, *mental health centers do not give the elderly a high priority*, and so the aged are significantly underrepresented in terms of service delivered. Many elderly persons could be maintained in the community within their own families or with minimal supervision; instead, large numbers are relegated to nursing homes and institutional care.

*Schizophrenia* is a psychotic mental disorder characterized by disturbances in thinking, mood, and behavior. Schizophrenic patients are now well served by most CMHC's, as are members of minority groups, such as *blacks* and Hispanics. *Infant care* is attended to by the CMHC primarily through parental education about child-rearing practices. A *neurosis* is a mental disorder characterized primarily by anxiety. Although neuroses are not accompanied by gross distortion of reality or severe personality disor-

ganization, normal functioning is impaired by the person's symptoms. In general, neurotic patients do not make use of CMHC's.

**39.3.   The answer is D** (*Synopsis*, ed. 4, page 876).

The use of all health care services is influenced by age. For example, *young adults (20 to 30 years)* and *persons over age 65 have more illness than persons in middle adulthood*. Among the elderly, chronicity of illness is a major factor, and *heart disease, arthritis*, and *cancer are the three major chronic conditions of old age*. Regardless of age, *women seek health care more often than do men*.

The causes of death have varied through the years, with pneumonia, tuberculosis, and gastrointestinal disease being the three leading causes of death at the beginning of the 20th century. In 1983, the three leading causes of death were heart disease, cancer, and stroke. Although psychiatric illness does not play a major role in the mortality rate, it is probably the major factor in the morbidity rate and is also a *major factor in days lost from work and employment*.

**39.4.   The answer is A** (*Synopsis*, ed. 4, page 876).

The goal of prevention measures in psychiatry is similar to those of medical specialties, which is to *diminish the incidence of illness* and to diminish the prevalence of illness. Measures directed at incidence aim at the prevention of new cases. Measures directed at prevalence are intended *to diminish the number of persons ill at one point in time (point prevalence)* or in any one year (yearly prevalence). Reducing the incidence of new cases of the disorder (primary prevention), *decreasing the duration of the disorder through effective early intervention* (secondary prevention), *preventing the long-term complications* (tertiary prevention)—all reduce the prevalence of the disorder in a population.

Primary prevention is the prevention of a specific undesirable state, whether it is a state of disturbed feelings, a state of disturbed thoughts, a reaction pattern that is undesirable, a stress reaction, a formal illness, or a disease state.

**39.5.   The answer is D** (*Synopsis*, ed. 4, page 880).

Projections made through the 1990s indicate that there will be shortages, balances, and surpluses in the number of physicians in various specialties. For example, by 1990 it is estimated that *48,000 psychiatrists will be needed in the United States, but there will only be 38,000 trained.* The only other fields in which there will be a shortage include emergency medicine and preventive medicine.

Other specialties will have a surplus, e.g. 24,000 surgeons will be needed in 1990, and there will be 35,000 available. There will be a similar surplus in the fields of *neurology, ophthalmology, obstetrics and gynecology,* internal medicine, and neurosurgery.

Fields in which supply will equal demand in 1990 include dermatology, family practice, *otolaryngology,* and pediatrics.

Physician services tend to be underutilized, with 40 percent of the population not seeing a physician at all in a given year. Of the 60 percent who do see a physician, most are either very young or old, or women, and they average about 5 visits per year.

**39.6.   The answer is D** (*Synopsis*, ed. 4, page 869).

According to the legislation passed in 1963, the community mental health center (CMHC) must provide a range of services. The original legislation called for five required services— *emergency services, outpatient services,* partial hospitalization, *inpatient services,* and *consultation-education services.* Public Law 94-63, which was passed in 1975, required the addition of services for children, services for the aged, screening before hospitalization, follow-up services for those who had been hospitalized, transitional housing services, alcoholism services, and drug abuse services.

Consultation-education services vary from attention to or even treatment of the emotional problems of the consultee to using knowledge about human behavior to help the consultee achieve his or her professional goals with the program and its patients. Program-centered consultation focuses on the total system or program, offering whatever assistance the mental health professional can give in regard to programs, systems, and agencies.

*Psychosurgery* is a neurosurgical intervention to treat a mental disorder for which no organic pathological cause can be demonstrated. It is not a required service that must be provided by a CMHC.

**39.7.   The answer is E (all)** (*Synopsis*, ed. 4, pages 876 and 877).

Primary prevention techniques may be roughly classified into two broad groups: biotechnical methods and psychosocial methods. Biotechnical methods emphasize such things as somatic interventions, engineering, blood tests, removal of toxic substances, and vitamin supplementation. Psychosocial methods require changes in individual habits or life-styles, group interventions, family interventions, and the development of community support systems. *Drunk-driving prevention programs* are an example of primary prevention through psychosocial methods.

The major successes in prevention have resulted from biotechnical interventions. The dietary supplementation that led to the virtual elimination of pellagra, the *use of iodized salt* to prevent hypothyroidism, *serological testing* and penicillin treatment that led to the sharp reduction in tertiary syphilis, the *lead control* programs that resulted in the reduced incidence and prevalence of lead encephalopathy—all these were related to specific biotechnical prevention methods.

Lead encephalopathy is a disease of the brain, caused by an intake of lead. This disease is mostly seen in early childhood. Tertiary syphilis is the third stage of syphilis, which is marked by the formation of cardiovascular and central nervous system lesions. It is commonly associated with an organic brain syndrome characterized by dementia with delusions, often of a grandiose nature. Hypothyroidism refers to a decrease in the production of thyroid hormone. As a result, a thyroid insufficiency, known as myxedema, develops.

**39.8.   The answer is E (all)** (*Synopsis*, ed. 4, page 873).

The census in state mental hospital beds has been steadily declining and *at present is about 200,000.* Of that group, about 60 percent of patients have been hospitalized for over 1 year.

*Investor-owned hospitals are increasing* in importance and numbers. They provide voluntary short-term treatment and are run for profit.

*Veterans Administration (VA) hospitals are usually affiliated with medical schools.* They provide inpatient care for medical and psychiatric patients, especially for Vietnam veterans suffering from posttraumatic stress syndrome.

Special hospitals are set up to treat patients who have a single medical condition and include obstetrical and gynecologic hospitals. They do not include psychiatric hospitals or substance abuse hospitals and are *generally less regulated than other types of hospitals.*

For an overview of hospital organization, see the table on the facing page.

**Aspects of Hospital Organization***

| Criteria | Voluntary Hospital | Investor-owned Hospitals | State Mental Hospital System | Municipal Hospital System | Federal Hospital System | Special Hospital |
|---|---|---|---|---|---|---|
| Patient population | All illnesses | All illnesses, although hospital may specialize | Mental illness | All illnesses | All illnesses | 70 percent of facility must be for single diagnosis |
| Number of hospitals | 6,000 | 750 | 280 (20,000 beds nationally) | Variable per city | See below | 150 |
| Profit orientation | Nonprofit | For profit | Nonprofit | Nonprofit | Nonprofit | For profit or nonprofit |
| Ownership | Private management board | Private corporation; may be owned by MD's | State | City government | Federal government | Private or public |
| Affiliation | 1200 church-affiliated; remainder are privately owned or university sponsored | May be owned by large chains, such as Hospital Corporation of America or Humana Corporation | Free-standing or affiliated with various medical schools | Voluntary teaching hospitals and medical schools | Department of Defense (190); Public Health Service, Coast Guard, Prison, Merchant Marine, Indian Health Service; Veterans Administration (129) | Optional affiliation with medical schools |
| Other | Provide bulk of care in U.S. | Increasing in importance nationally | Deinstitutionalization— number of patients has been reduced | Most physicians at municipal hospitals are employed by their affiliated medical school | VA Hospitals usually have affiliations with medical schools | Less regulated than other types of hospitals (see note 5) |

* *Notes.* (1) To be designated a teaching hospital, at least four types of approved residencies must be offered, clinical experiences for medical students must be provided, and an affiliation with a medical school must be maintained. (2) As of 1982, there were 364 state-operated facilities and approximately 60,000 community facilities for the mentally retarded. (3) In 1981, there were 139 investor-owned for profit hospitals for psychiatric patients in the United States. That number is growing. The total number of psychiatric hospitals (public and private) is about 600. (4) Short-term hospitals have an average patient stay of less than 30 days; long-term, an average of longer duration. (5) Special hospitals include obstetrics and gynecology; eye, ear, nose, and throat; etc. They do not include psychiatric hospitals or substance abuse hospitals.

**39.9. The answer is B (1, 3)** (*Synopsis*, ed. 4, page 877).

*Rates of hospitalization for all illness increase with age,* and within the last decade 75 percent of adults have been in a hospital at one time or another, with *women being hospitalized more often than men.* Twenty-five percent of hospital costs are made up of laboratory and X-ray bills, and the remaining costs are for management, nursing, drugs, and other support services.

*Physician services account for 20 percent of every health dollar spent* (within or out of a hospital), and 50 percent of physician fees are covered by some form of health insurance, except in the case of psychiatry. At present there is a 10 percent *oversupply of hospital beds in this country* that must be paid for even though they remain empty. The average general hospital stay is just over 8 days in all specialties.

**39.10.–39.15.   The answers are 39.10–B, 39.11–B, 39.12–A, 39.13–D, 39.14–A, and 39.15–A** (*Synopsis*, ed. 4, pages 876, 877, and 879).

Preventive psychiatry is a branch of preventive medicine dealing with mental disorders. Encompassed within its scope are measures to prevent mental disorders (primary prevention); measures to limit the severity of illness, as through early case finding and treatment (secondary prevention); and measures to reduce disability after a disorder (tertiary prevention). The goal of prevention measures in psychiatry is similar to those of other medical specialties, which is to diminish the incidence of illness and to diminish the prevalence of illness.

Secondary prevention decreases the prevalence of psychiatric illness by *shortening the course of the illness.* This level of prevention is often characterized as therapeutic or curative medicine or psychiatry. An example would be the *quick and effective treatment of school phobia* in which the goal is to get the child to return to school as quickly as possible. Early and effective secondary intervention may reduce not only the duration but also the severity of the morbidity and the mortality from the disorder. In general medicine, early and effective intervention in infections, neoplasms, cardiovascular disease, shock, hemorrhage, and numerous other states reduces risk, complications, duration of illness and discomfort. Considerable evidence indicates that secondary prevention is one of the most effective techniques for *lowering the prevalence of psychiatric disorders.* Providers at this level are almost always psychiatrists; but psychologists, social workers, and other mental health workers are also involved.

Tertiary prevention is directed at *reducing the residual defect of chronic mental illness* in two related ways. One way is through the prevention of the complications of the disorders. The other way is through an *active program of rehabilitation.* In the care of the chronically mentally ill, the two are closely interrelated. Tertiary prevention, however, *does not lower the prevalence of disease as does secondary prevention.*

Rehabilitation refers to all methods and techniques used in an attempt to achieve maximal function and optimal adjustment in a given patient and the physical, mental, social, and vocational preparation of a patient for the fullest possible life compatible with his abilities and disabilities. Inasmuch as the process aims also to prevent relapses or recurrences of the patient's condition, it is sometimes called tertiary prevention.

*A diet deficient in niacin* can produce pellagra, which is characterized by three D's—dementia, diarrhea, and dermatitis—and which can be fatal. Adding niacin to the diet prevents pellagra and is a good example of primary prevention.

**39.16.–39.20.   The answers are 39.16–A,  39.17–B,  39.18–B,  39.19–C, and 39.20–D** (*Synopsis*, ed. 4, pages 872 and 874).

Medicare provides both hospital and medical insurance under the Federal Social Security Act. It *applies to persons 65 or older*, in addition to certain disabled persons, such as the blind and those needing renal dialysis. There are two parts to Medicare: Part A *covers hospital care, extended care (after care)*, and home health services. Part B is an option to *cover physicians fees* that can be purchased by the patient. Medicare is an insurance program with money coming from federal trust funds. *Standards of Medicare are uniform throughout the United States.*

Medicaid is a program *financed by both the federal and state governments* that provides comprehensive medical care (including psychiatric services) to needy and low-income persons. It is an assistance rather than *insurance program, and each state defines the requirements for eligibility*; consequently, *Medicaid services vary from state to state* and *potentially include both hospital and individual physician services.*

**39.21.–39.25.   The answers are 39.21–E, 39.22–B, 39.23–A, 39.24–D, and 39.25–C** (*Synopsis*, ed. 4, page 872).

There is a series of agencies, such as the American Medical Association Council on Medical Education and the Joint Commission on Accreditation of Hospitals (*JCAH*), *that influence the standards of hospital care and performance.* In addition to city and state health rules with which hospitals must comply, the Council on Medical Education and the JCAH inspects hospitals every 2 years. JCAH accreditation, however, is on a voluntary basis.

Currently, there is a trend toward monitoring all the hospitals in a community as a single health entity and community resource. That means that each unit does not have the prerogative to develop new facilities without concern for the services offered by the other hospitals in the area.

The Professional Standards Review Organization (PSRO) was created by the federal government to review and *monitor the care received by patients that was paid for with government funds.* PSRO's have been established by local medical associations and serve several functions: They attempt to assure high-quality care, control cost, determine maximum length of stay by patients in hospitals, and censure physicians who do not adhere to established guidelines. The *PSRO is made up of doctors elected by local medical societies.*

The Health Maintenance Organization *(HMO) is a multispecialty association of physicians who provide both inpatient and outpatient care* in all specialties, including psychiatry. Physicians are paid a salary by the HMO, and patients pay a *prepayment fee* for all health care services provided for a fixed period of time. Primary prevention is emphasized by HMOs, of which there are about 300 in the United States at this time.

The *Health Systems Agencies (HSA's) are nonprofit organizations mandated by the federal government to promote or limit the development of health services and facilities, depending on the needs of a particular area* of the country. HSA's are made up of consumers, and these agencies have much power in medicine. To build a new hospital, for example, the HSA must approve a certificate of need (CON); thereby, it controls the availability of medical care.

The *Blue Cross Association (BCA) is an association of over 80 independent insurance plans around the country that pay primarily for inpatient hospital services.* Blue Shield pays for physician services during the patient's hospital stay. BCA is a nonprofit organization and is regulated by state insurance agencies. Psychiatric benefits are limited compared to other medical illnesses. Inpatient psychiatric care is less curtailed than outpatient psychiatric care, the latter being the most constricted.

## References

Barofsky I, Budson R D, editors: *The Chronic Psychiatric Patient in the Community: Principles of Treatment.* SP Medical and Scientific Books, New York, 1983.

Caplan G: *Principles of Preventive Psychiatry.* Basic Books, New York, 1964.

Craig TJ: The dynamics of hospitalization in a defined population during deinstitutionalization. Am J Psychiatry *141:* 802, 1984.

Okin R L: How community mental health centers are coping. Hosp Comm Psychiatry *35:* 1118, 1984.

Langsley D G: Community psychiatry. In *Comprehensive Texbook of Psychiatry.* ed 4, H I Kaplan, B J Sadock, editors, p 1885. Williams & Wilkins, Baltimore, 1985.

Langsley D G: Prevention in psychiatry: Primary, secondary, and tertiary. In *Comprehensive Textbook of Psychiatry,* ed 4, H I Kaplan, B J Sadock, editors, p 1878. Williams & Wilkins, Baltimore, 1985.

Mollica R F: From asylum to community: The threatened disintegration of public psychiatry. N Engl J Med *308:* 367, 1983.

President's Commission on Mental Health: *Report to the President from the President's Commission on Mental Health,* vol 1. US Government Printing Office, Washington, DC, 1978.

# 40

# Geriatric Psychiatry

Geriatric psychiatry deals with the psychopathology associated with that period of life—old age—that is an end product of an ongoing life process. Old age is not static, and the defensive responses to the emerging deficits—physical and psychosocial—vary from person to person. The need to provide health services to the elderly is a major health issue because this group represents a large proportion of the over-all population. For example, at the present time approximately 25 million people are 65 years of age or older, and that segment of the population is growing at a faster rate than any other age group.

Although old age in itself is not a disease, it is a time marked by new issues, many of which are related to the physical manifestations that accompany the aging process—a decline in physical health and reduced sensory acuity. Negative stereotypes about being old—held by society and the elderly themselves—are important aspects of this period. Also important is the need to adapt to major losses, such as the work role, friends, or a spouse. Old age may present special difficulties for women, who are widowed longer than men, institutionalized more frequently, and are usually poorer than men of the same age. For both sexes, there is, as Erikson stated, the need to deal with issues of death and dying so that the final stage of the life cycle encompasses a sense of integrity, rather than a sense of despair.

The reader should refer to Chapter 40 of *Modern Synopsis-IV* on geriatric psychiatry and should then study the questions and answers below to test his or her knowledge of this area.

# Questions

**DIRECTIONS:** Each of the statements or questions below is followed by five suggested responses or completions. Select the *one* that is *best* in each case.

**40.1.** Abnormalities of cognitive functioning in the aged are most often the result of

A. affective disorders
B. schizophrenic disorders
C. medication
D. cerebral deterioration or dysfunction
E. hypochondriasis

**40.2.** Toxic confusional states in the elderly may result from

A. minor tranquilizers
B. barbiturates
C. tricyclic antidepressants
D. antiparkinsonian drugs
E. all of the above

**40.3.** Manic disorders in the elderly

A. are more frequent than depression
B. may be part of an unrecognized bipolar disorder
C. are almost always caused by organic changes in the brain
D. are rarely associated with paranoid behavior
E. do not respond to lithium

**40.4.** It is projected that, by the year 2030, of the approximately 300 million people in the United States, about how many will be 65 years of age and older:

A. 8 million
B. 20 million
C. 30 million
D. 50 million
E. None of the above

**40.5.** The yearly death rate associated with Alzheimer's disease is approximately

A. 50,000 per year in the United States
B. 100,000 per year in the United States
C. 50,000 per year world-wide
D. 100,000 per year world-wide
E. none of the above

**40.6.** Psychiatric disorders in the elderly may manifest themselves by

A. change in mood
B. loss of weight
C. perceptual changes
D. constipation
E. all of the above

**40.7.** A 72-year-old man, 2 months after the removal of his prostate gland for benign prostatic hypertrophy, begins to suspect his 68-year-old wife of being unfaithful to him. The most likely reason for his suspicion is that

A. he has seen her in the company of strange men
B. he has a lifelong pattern of denial as a defense
C. it is a restitutive attempt to mask the blow to his sense of masculinity and mastery
D. he is unhappy in his marriage
E. he is becoming disoriented

**40.8.** Alzheimer's disease is seen in what percentage of nursing home populations:

A. 5 percent
B. 25 percent
C. 50 percent
D. 75 percent
E. Unknown

**DIRECTIONS:** For each of the incomplete statements below, *one* or *more* of the completions given is correct. Choose answer:

A.   if only **1, 2,** and **3** are correct
B.   if only **1** and **3** are correct
C.   if only **2** and **4** are correct
D.   if only **4** is correct
E.   if all are correct

**40.9.** Psychotropic drugs prescribed for the elderly

1. are best given in a single nighttime dose
2. should be given in equally divided doses 3 or 4 times over a 24-hour period
3. should be given along with antiparkinsonian drugs that are prescribed prophylactically
4. frequently cause changes in blood pressure

**40.10.** Which of the following are likely side effects resulting from the use of major tranquilizers in the elderly:

1. Pavor nocturnus
2. Tardive dyskinesia
3. Paresthesia of the extremities
4. Akathisia

**40.11.** Patients who develop a depressive disorder for the first time in later life (late-onset depressions)

1. usually have had well-adjusted personalities earlier in life
2. usually develop their first attack after age 65
3. do so after some traumatic event
4. respond only to electroconvulsive therapy

**40.12.** Which of the following statements about psychiatric disorders in the elderly (over age 65) are accurate:

1. Depression is the most common diagnosis.
2. Schizophrenia may first appear in patients over age 65.
3. The suicide rate is highest among elderly white males.
4. The suicide rate is highest among elderly white females.

**40.13.** Alzheimer's disease is associated with

1. progressive structural abnormality of certain neurons
2. age-specific psychosocial trauma
3. a hippocampal location
4. conversion disorder

**40.14.** Sleep disturbances in the elderly

1. develop because elderly persons need less sleep than they did when they were younger
2. are common
3. should not be treated with benzodiazepines
4. may be due to decreased bladder capacity

**40.15.** Side effects of tricyclic antidepressants in the elderly include

1. exacerbation of psychotic symptoms
2. central anticholinergic syndrome
3. cardiotoxicity
4. parkinsonism

**40.16.** Features of the normal aging process include

1. slowness of thinking
2. reduction of episodes of enthusiasm
3. tendency to take daytime naps
4. progressive impairment of recent memory

**40.17.** Which of the following physical conditions are known to cause mental symptoms in the elderly:

1. Urinary infection
2. Diabetes
3. Emphysema
4. Vitamin deficiencies

**DIRECTIONS:** Each set of lettered headings below is followed by a list of numbered words or phrases. For each numbered word or phrase, select

**A. if the item is associated with A** *only*
B. if the item is associated with **B** *only*
C. if the item is associated with *both* **A** *and* **B**
D. if the item is associated with *neither* **A** *nor* **B**

**Questions 40.18–40.21**
A. Functional depression in the elderly
B. Depression associated with organic mental disorder
C. Both
D. Neither

**40.18.** Disorientation to time and place

**40.19.** Confabulation

**40.20.** Better response to antidepressant medication

**40.21.** Respond to chlorpromazine

# Answers

## Geriatric Psychiatry

**40.1.  The answer is D** (*Synopsis*, ed. 4, page 882).

Abnormalities of cognitive functioning in the elderly may be the result of many *depressive* or *schizophrenic disturbances*, but they are most often due to some *cerebral dysfunctioning or deterioration*. In many instances, intellectual difficulties are not obvious, and a searching evaluation is necessary to detect them. The elderly are sensitive to the effects of *medication*, and in some instances, cognitive impairment may occur as a result of overmedication. *Hypochondriasis* is the fear or preoccupation that one has a disease. It is not uncommon in the elderly, but does not cause cognitive impairment.

Cognitive functions include those involved in the ability to recognize and understand reality, such as perception, recognition, judgment, and reasoning. The inability to think abstractly, to reproduce geometric designs, and to name objects correctly are examples of cognitive abnormalities. Intact memory and a general fund of information are also important cognitive functions that may be disturbed by cerebral dysfunctioning.

An *affective disorder* is any mental disorder in which disturbance of mood is the primary characteristic; disturbances in thinking and behavior are secondary characteristics. *Schizophrenia* is a psychotic mental disorder characterized by disturbances in thinking, mood, and behavior. The thinking disturbance is manifested by a distortion of reality, sometimes with delusions and hallucinations, accompanied by a fragmentation of associations that results in characteristic disturbances of speech. The mood disturbance includes ambivalence and inappropriate or constricted affective response. The behavior disturbance may be manifested by apathetic withdrawal or bizarre activity. *Hypochondriasis*, also known as hypochondriacal neurosis, is a somatoform disorder characterized by excessive, morbid anxiety about one's health. The term is derived from the belief that the state was caused by some dysfunction in the hypochondrium, especially the spleen. Hypochondriacal patients exhibit a predominant disturbance in which their physical symptoms or their complaints are not explainable on the basis of demonstrable organic findings and are apparently linked to psychological factors.

**40.2.  The answer is E** (*Synopsis*, ed. 4, pages 885 and 886).

A major side effect of psychotropic drugs is a toxic confusional state, resulting from the anticholinergic properties of a single drug or a combination of psychotropic drugs, such as a neuroleptic, an *antiparkinsonian drug*, and a *tricyclic antidepressant*.

The elderly patient with mild to moderate anxiety may be a candidate for a mild tranquilizer. The effective dosage is usually less than in other adult patients. Chlordiazepoxide or diazepam, in doses of 5 or 10 mg, two or three times a day, is often effective. A mild tranquilizer can also be used at bedtime for its hypnotic effect. Compared with the *barbiturates*, the minor tranquilizers have a higher ratio of therapeutic effectiveness to side effects and are considered safer. The *minor tranquilizers*, although to a lesser extent than the barbiturates, can also be addictive, however, and can produce paradoxical reactions characterized by confusion, disorientation, excitement, and the exacerbation of psychiatric symptoms.

The drugs most commonly used in the treatment of depression are the tricyclics (named for their common three-ringed structural element) and the monoamine oxidase inhibitors (named for their pharmacological effect in preventing the deamination of the neurotransmitter norepinephrine). Both classes of drugs appear, at least in part, to increase the concentration of norepinephrine and, thus, to produce anticholinergic side effects.

Antiparkinsonian drug therapy is used to treat parkinsonism, a motor disorder based on a central nervous system imbalance of acetylcholine dopamine levels. The side effects produced are the result of anticholinergic or dopaminergic stimulation, both of which may lead to a toxic confusional state that is marked by delirium, disorientation, hallucinations, or delusions. Antiparkinsonian drugs are also used to prevent or reverse the extrapyramidal side effects of the major tranquilizers.

Although increasingly replaced by safer drugs, barbiturates, a class of compounds derived from barbituric acid, have long been used for their sedative-hypnotic effects.

Tranquilizers are classified as major (neuroleptic or antipsychotic) or minor (primarily antianxiety).

**40.3. The answer is B** (*Synopsis*, ed. 4, page 883).

In the elderly, the manic disorders *are less frequent than are depressions.* Nevertheless, they may make an appearance in late life. The patient and family may fail to recognize *the hypomanic phase of a bipolar disorder.* It may be incorrectly ascribed to the aggressiveness, overactivity, and poor judgment of a senile brain, or to *other organic changes.* Hypomania is the less intense, usually nonpsychotic form of full-blown mania and is characterized by increased energy, irritability, and impaired judgment. It usually follows a depressive disorder, which may have been so brief as to have escaped the attention of those about the patient. *Hostile* or *paranoid behavior is usually present.* The response to treatment is usually good. *Lithium, which is effective* in the treatment and prophylaxis of bipolar disorders, *has been used successfully* in these conditions in the elderly.

Bipolar depressions, in contrast to the unipolar type, are diagnosed in depressed patients who have also experienced at least one manic episode; patients in the unipolar group experience episodes of depression only. Certain, more subtle distinctions may also be made on familial, behavioral, physiological, and pharmacological bases.

**40.4. The answer is D** (*Synopsis*, ed. 4, page 881).

In 1985, according to the U.S. Bureau of the Census, there are approximately 230 million people in this country, of whom about 25 million are 65 years of age and older. It is projected that by the year 2030 there will be a little over 300 million people in this country, of whom approximately *50 million* will be 65 years of age and older.

The figure below illustrates this point graphically.

**40.5. The answer is B** (*Synopsis*, ed. 4, page 882).

Alzheimer's disease is a common type of senile brain disorder that affects millions of people throughout the world; it is associated with more than *100,000 deaths* in the United States each year.

Alzheimer's is a primary, progressive demen-

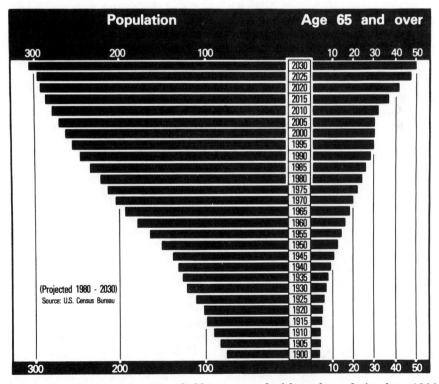

**Bars show number of persons age 65 and older compared with total population from 1900. The chart extends to the year 2030. (From US Bureau of the Census, 1983.)**

tia, characterized in its early phase by recent memory and attention defects, general failure of efficiency, and defects in sensory perception leading to episodes of disorientation to time and place. In the later phase, disorientation becomes complete, rigidity of muscles becomes apparent, and the patient shows purposeless hyperactivity, confusion, and agitation. The patient appears dull and apathetic. In the terminal phase, dementia is profound, and the patient declines to a vegetative existence. The pathology consists of generalized brain atrophy with Alzheimer's neurofibrillary whorls, senile plaques, and granulovascular degeneration in the hippocampal pyramidal neurons. There is no known treatment for the disorder, and the average duration of life once symptoms appear is 6½ years.

**40.6.   The answer is E** (*Synopsis*, ed. 4, page 881).

Mental disorders in old age are quite common. The causes are multiple, complex, and complicated by the frequent presence of organic brain involvement.

Psychiatric diagnosis in the elderly, in order to be precise, may not be at all simple. Psychiatric illnesses may manifest themselves by physical symptoms and signs, such as *loss of weight, constipation*, dry mouth, changes in heart rate and blood pressure, and tremors. Disorders of awareness, *mood, perception*, thinking, and thought content are usually present and prominent.

Overt behavior may manifest itself in the motor activity, walk, expressive movements, and the form of talk of the patient. It can be observed by the examining physician, and the history can be obtained from meaningful others.

Mood disorder may be inferred from the patient's movements; but one must be aware of the presence of euphoria, sadness, despair, anxiety, tension, loss of feelings, and a paucity of ideation. The patient often complains of somatic sensations that may, in a sense, be substituted for an expression of emotional state.

The evaluation of the mental content should be extensive and detailed. One should obtain the patient's own description of his or her feelings and account of the onset.

**40.7.   The answer is C** (*Synopsis*, ed. 4, pages 882 and 883).

On the whole, *paranoid symptoms seem to be a defense against the gradual loss of mastery* that some patients experience as a result of various life stresses. Thus some elderly men, especially those with prostatism or prostatic postoperative conditions, may express *delusions about their wives' infidelity*, as in the case presented.

Prostatism is a syndrome caused by enlarge-ment of the prostate gland, in which the patient experiences significant obstruction to urinary flow and often an increase in urinary frequency. Psychologically, some men view any illness of the genitourinary tract as a *threat to their masculinity*.

It is important to rule out an *organic mental disorder* in the patient in view of his being 72 years of age. A delusion of jealousy is *not caused by a lifelong pattern of denial nor by an unhappy marriage*. Both may be incidental findings, however.

**40.8.   The answer is C** (*Synopsis*, ed. 4, page 882).

Alzheimer's disease patients constitute *50 percent* of the 1.3 million people in nursing homes.

**40.9.   The answer is C (2, 4)** (*Synopsis*, ed. 4, page 885).

The following principles are useful guidelines regarding the use of psychotropic drugs for the elderly.

Most psychotropic drugs should be given in *equally divided doses 3 or 4 times over a 24-hour period*, because elderly patients may be intolerant of a sudden rise in drug blood level, which can lead to uncomfortable and potentially dangerous side effects, such as significant lowering of blood pressure and dizziness. There should be careful monitoring for *changes in blood pressure*, pulse rate, and other side effects.

An *antiparkinsonian drug to counteract the extrapyramidal side effects of a major tranquilizer should be used only as needed and not prophylactically*; it may further aggravate the anticholinergic side effects of the major tranquilizer and other medications.

Disturbances of the extrapyramidal system—either occurring naturally or induced by medication—result in impairment of its functions concerned with automatic movements involved in postural adjustment and with autonomic regulation. Various movement disorders may also result, as well as significant blood pressure problems.

The psychotropics are defined as drugs with an effect on psychic function, behavior, or experience. The term is a broad one and includes a wide variety of pharmacological agents. Six groups of psychotropic agents can be differentiated. These include the following:

1. Neuroleptics—also known as antipsychotics, ataractics, or major tranquilizers. They have antipsychotic and sedative effects, particularly on the extrapyramidal system.
2. Anxiolytic sedatives—also known as minor tranquilizers, psycholeptics, or antianxiety

agents. They reduce pathological anxiety, tension, and agitation without therapeutic effects on disturbed cognitive or perceptual processes. They usually do not produce autonomic or extrapyramidal effects, but they have a high potential for drug dependency.

3. Antimanic agents—lithium. This drug reduces hypomania and mania.
4. Antidepressants—also known as thymoleptics. They reduce pathological depression.
5. Psychostimulants—increase the level of alertness or motivation. The amphetamines are included.
6. Psychodysleptics—also known as hallucinogens, psychedelics, or psychotomimetics. They produce abnormal mental phenomena, particularly in the cognitive and perceptual spheres.

**40.10.   The answer is C (2, 4)** (*Synopsis*, ed. 4, page 885).

The elderly person, particularly one with an organic brain disease, is especially susceptible to the extrapyramidal side effects of the major tranquilizers, which include the following: (1) *tardive dyskinesia*, which is characterized by disfiguring and involuntary buccal and lingual masticatory movements. Examination of the patient's protruded tongue for fine tumors and vermicular (worm-like) movements is a useful diagnostic procedure because these manifestations are one of the earliest signs of tardive dyskinesia; (2) *akathisia*, which is a restlessness marked by a compelling need for constant motion; and (3) choreiform body movements, which are spasmodic and involuntary movements of the limbs and face, and rhythmic extension and flexion of the fingers. There is evidence that extrapyramidal symptoms are the result of a dopamine deficiency, particularly in the limbic system.

*Pavor nocturnus* (night-terrors) and *paresthesia* (spontaneous tingling sensation) are not side effects of the major tranquilizers.

**40.11.   The answer is B (1, 3)** (*Synopsis*, ed. 4, page 883).

Depressions are unusually common in later life. Late-onset depressives, in comparison with early-onset depressives, *had better adjusted personalities emotionally, socially, and psychosexually*. The majority of first depressive attacks, especially severe attacks, appear in the second half of life. The highest *first incidence occurs between ages 55 and 65 in men, and between 50 and 60 in women*. Regardless of the presence of predominantly neurotic or psychotic symptoms, the *onset follows closely the occurrence of some traumatic event*. These precipitating events can all be classified as various kinds of loss, such as bereavement, the moving away of children, loss of status, retirement from a job, threatened loss through physical illness, and the illness of the spouse. The precipitants occur more frequently in late-onset depression than in early-onset depression.

*Electroconvulsive therapy (ECT)* involves the artificial induction of a tonic-clonic seizure by application of a regulated electrical current to the temporal areas. It is thought to exert its effects by altering the metabolism release and activity of central neurochemicals, as well as mediating changes in receptor sensitivity. Alternatives to ECT in the treatment of affective disorders are psychotherapy and antidepressant drugs, often given in combination. Generally, unless the depression is extremely severe and unresponsive to other treatments, or unless the potential for dangerous side effects with antidepressants is very great, ECT is considered the treatment of last resort. Elderly people, perhaps more than others, might require ECT for the treatment of depression primarily because of the potentially toxic side effects of antidepressants.

**40.12.   The answer is B (1, 3)** (*Synopsis*, ed. 4, page 886).

*Depression is the most common* psychiatric disorder of the elderly. Elderly *white men have the highest suicide rate* of any group. Depressions are fairly common among the elderly and are generally responsive to psychotherapy.

According to DSM-III criteria, the diagnosis of *schizophrenia* may be made only if onset is before 45 years of age.

**40.13.   The answer is B (1, 3)** (*Synopsis*, ed. 4, page 882).

The most serious symptom of Alzheimer's disease closely correlates with the accumulation within *neuronal cells of abnormal protein structures* known as neurofibrillary tangles. These structures are destroyed and replaced by neuritic plaques, which are the replacement of the dead nerve cells. The damage is confined to the hippocampus, according to most recent evidence. Experimental destruction of the *hippocampus* has been linked to a profound and lasting memory impairment that affects all types of learning. Progressive impairment in recent memory is a hallmark of Alzheimer's.

Alzheimer's disease is classified as an organic mental disorder, the mental changes of the disease being secondary to an organic etiology. Psychogenic factors, such as *psychosocial trauma* and hysteria-like mechanisms, are not considered as important etiological factors. A *conversion disorder* is a somatoform disorder in which the patient experiences an involuntary limitation or alteration of physical function that is an expression of psychological conflict or need, not physical disorder. In the older terminology, it was referred to as a hysterical neurosis.

**40.14. The answer is C (2, 4)** (*Synopsis*, ed. 4, page 884).

Contrary to the popular myth, *elderly persons need as much if not more sleep than they did in their earlier mature years. Complaints about sleeplessness*, however, *are common*. To some extent, these complaints can be traced to sleep disturbances, rather than to sleeplessness. The sleep disturbances may be due to *the need for more frequent visits to the bathroom*, with resulting problems in again falling asleep. Furthermore, many of the elderly—retired, unemployed, not active, and noninvolved—succumb to the practice of taking catnaps during their waking hours, a habit that may interfere with what they describe as a good night's sleep.

When insomnia does occur and is unaccompanied by delirium or a psychotic reaction, it usually responds to standard hypnotics. When insomnia is accompanied by a psychotic or depressive reaction, phenothiazine or tricyclic medication often induces sleep. Insomnia *may also be treated with a bedtime dose of an antianxiety benzodiazepine* medication, such as diazepam or triazolam. The patient should be reassessed at frequent intervals to determine the need for maintenance medication, changes in dosage, and the development of side effects.

Before prescribing a medication for sleep, the physician should perform a comprehensive evaluation that includes a review of the patient's medical and psychiatric history, current stress factors, use of prescribed and over-the-counter medications, mental status and physical examination results, and other test results as indicated. It is especially useful to have the elderly patient or family bring to the physician all currently used medications because multiple drug usage may be contributing to the patient's symptoms.

The comprehensive evaluation may reveal a recent stress, such as a death in the family, that may account for a change in the patient's behavior. The patient's symptoms may, therefore, respond better to environmental support or psychotherapy than to sleep medication.

**40.15. The answer is E (all)** (*Synopsis*, ed. 4, page 886).

The tricyclic antidepressants, like other psychotropic drugs, have more side effects in old patients than in younger patients. The side effects include anticholinergic side effects: *exacerbation of psychotic symptoms*, extrapyramidal symptoms, and tremors; the *central anticholinergic syndrome*; and *cardiotoxicity*. The primary cardiotoxic effect of tricyclics is a life-threatening heart block, which is manifested by a prolongation of the PR interval on the electrocardiogram. Tricyclics appear also to exert a suppressive effect on arrhythmias, sometimes referred to as a quinidine-like effect after the drug quinidine, which acts to suppress atrial fibrillation and flutter and paroxysmal ventricular tachycardias (PVC's).

*Parkinsonism* (paralysis agitans) is a chronic progressive CNS disease, with onset between 50 and 70 years of age, that results in a variety of motor disturbances—tremors, propulsive gait, and mask-like facies. It appears to be related to a depression of central dopamine and serotonin levels.

Elderly patients show considerable variability with regard to the optimal dosage and the development of side effects. Patients unresponsive to one tricyclic antidepressant may respond to another. If a patient is still significantly depressed, despite intensive psychotherapy and a trial on one or more antidepressants, hospitalization should be considered. In the hospital, a monoamine oxidase inhibitor, such as phenelzine, or electroconvulsive therapy may be considered.

**40.16. The answer is A (1, 2, 3)** (*Synopsis*, ed. 4, page 881).

Psychological changes accompany the passing of years. These changes include such well-known features as *slowness of thinking*, mild nonprogressive impairment of recent memory, *reduction of surgency of enthusiasm*, an increase in cautiousness, changes in sleep patterns with a *tendency to daytime naps*, and a relative libidinal shift from genitality to the alimentary tract and interior of the body.

*Progressive impairment of recent memory is not a feature of normal aging* and, if present, is evidence of an organic mental disorder, such as Alzheimer's disease. In fact, Alzheimer's is characterized in its early phase by primary progressive impairment of recent memory associated with attention defects.

**40.17. The answer is E (all)** (*Synopsis*, ed. 4, page 881).

A number of common and important physical conditions should be kept in mind when examining an elderly psychiatric patient, because these conditions are known to cause mental symptoms. Toxins of bacterial and metabolic origins are common in old age. Bacterial toxins usually originate in occult or inconspicuous foci of infection, such as suspected pneumonic conditions and *urinary infections*. The most common metabolic intoxication causing mental symptoms in the aged is uremia; *mild diabetes,* hepatic failure, and gout may easily be missed as causative agents. Uremia is an excess of urea and other nitrogenous waste products in the blood. Disturbances in nitrogen metabolism and excretion, as seen in diabetes (diabetic nephropathy is a fairly common complication), hepatic failure (the liver being an important location of detoxification and nitrogen metabolism), and gout (in which uric acid accumulates in the blood) may produce uremic conditions and the attendant psychiatric complications.

Cerebral anoxia, resulting from cardiac insufficiency or *emphysema,* or both, often precipitates mental symptoms in old people. Anoxic confusion may follow surgery, a cardiac infarct, gastrointestinal bleeding, or occlusion or stenosis of the carotid arteries. Nutritional deficiencies may not only be symptomatic of emotional illness but may also cause mental symptoms. *Vitamin deficiencies* may occur, but they are infrequent. All in all, various deficiencies need to be taken into consideration in the physical assessment of the aged.

Alcohol and drug misuse cause many mental disturbances in late life, but these abuses, with their characteristic effects, are easily determined by the history taking.

**40.18–40.21.   The answers are 40.18–B, 40.19–B, 40.20–A, and 40.21–D** (*Synopsis,* ed. 4, page 883).

The following differential points are important in distinguishing an affective depressive disorder or functional depression from depression associated with an organic mental disorder.

1. In the history, the depressed patient does not usually show evidences of memory loss or disorientation, nor is there habit deterioration, such as incontinence, self-exposure, or masturbation.
2. In the mental status examination, *the depressed patient does remain oriented,* if contact can only be made, in contrast to the patient with chronic organic mental disorder.
3. In the depressed patient, the mood disturbance is primary and is often accompanied by irritability and hostility. The organically ill patient, in contrast, makes some attempt to respond to questions, even though his or her replies may be irrelevant, *confabulatory,* or nonsensical.
4. The depressed patient ordinarily is free of signs of a clear neurological deficit or abnormal primitive reflexes and has a better integrated electroencephalogram, with preservation of basic rhythms.
5. The depressed patient may respond to a therapeutic trial of *antidepressant medication*; the organically ill patient is likely to react with an increase of confusion because of the central anticholinergic effect.
6. Psychological testing may be helpful in difficult cases.

*Chlorpromazine* has antiemetic, antiadrenergic, and anticholinergic effects and is used as an antipsychotic agent, not as an antidepressant.

## References

Albert M: Assessment of cognitive function in the elderly. Psychosom *25:* 310, 1984.

Bergener M: *Geropsychiatric Diagnostics Treatment: Multidimensional Approaches.* Springer Publishers, New York, 1983.

Birren J E, Sloan R B, editors: *Handbook of Mental Health and Aging.* Prentice Hall, Englewood Cliffs, NJ, 1980.

Butler R N: Geriatric psychiatry. In *Comprehensive Textbook of Psychiatry,* ed 4, H I Kaplan, B J Sadock, editors, p 1953. Williams & Wilkins, Baltimore, 1985.

Butler R N: Stress of the retirement years. Med Aspects Hum Sex *18:* 158, 1984.

Feigenbaum L Z: An introduction to geriatric medicine. Bull Menninger Clin *48:* 251, 1984.

Pollock G H *Old age: The last developmental challenge* [Reprint no. 9737]. Smith Kline & French, 1984.

Popkin M K, Mackenize T B, Callies A L: Psychiatric consultation to geriatric medically ill inpatients in a university hospital. Arch Gen Psychiatry *41:* 703, 1984.

Salzman C: *Clinical Geriatric Psychopharmacology.* McGraw-Hill Inc, New York, 1984.

Webb W B, Schneider-Helmert D: A categorical approach to changes in latency, awakening, and sleep length in older subjects. J Nerv Men Dis *172:* 291, 1984.

# 41

# Forensic Psychiatry

Forensic psychiatry is the branch of psychiatry that is concerned with the legal aspects of mental illness and represents the intermix between psychiatry and the law. That intermix includes problems of credibility of witnesses, culpability of accused persons, competency to make a will or contract or to take care of one's self or one's property or to stand trial, compensation of injured persons, and custody of children. The intermix of psychiatry and law is not limited to those areas, but they constitute the major part of forensic work. Other notable areas involve assisting in the process of jury selection and preparing presentencing evaluations for probationary status.

At various stages in their historical development, psychiatry and law have converged. Both disciplines are concerned with the social deviant, the person who has violated the rules of society and whose behavior presents a problem, not only because it diminishes that person's ability to function effectively but also because it adversely affects the functioning of the community. Traditionally, the psychiatrist's efforts are directed toward elucidation of the causes and, through prevention and treatment, reduction of the self-destructive elements of harmful behavior. The lawyer, as the agent of society, is concerned with the fact that the social deviant represents a potential threat to the safety and security of other people within the deviant's environment. Both psychiatry and law seek to implement their respective goals through the application of pragmatic techniques, based on empirical observations. The interaction between law and psychiatry, however, does not occur in a vacuum. Rather, it is marked by pervasive governmental regulation. The state—through its elected officials, judges, legislators, and administrators—says when, where, and why psychiatry and law interact.

The reader should refer to Chapter 41 of *Modern Synopsis-IV*, "Forensic Psychiatry," and should then study the questions and answers below to test his or her knowledge of this area.

# Questions

**DIRECTIONS:** Each of the statements or questions below is followed by five suggested responses or completions. Select the *one* that is *best* in each case.

**41.1.** The Gault decision applies to

A. minors
B. *habeas corpus*
C. informed consent
D. battery
E. none of the above

**41.2.** Product rule is concerned with

A. testimonial privilege
B. involuntary admission
C. criminal responsibility
D. competency to stand trial
E. none of the above

**DIRECTIONS:** For each of the incomplete statements below, *one* or *more* of the completions given is correct. Choose answer:

A. if only **1, 2,** and **3** are correct
B. if only **1** and **3** are correct
C. if only **2** and **4** are correct
D. if only **4** is correct
E. if all are correct

**41.3.** Informed consent requires that there be

1. an understanding of the risks of a procedure
2. a knowledge of alternate procedures for the same condition
3. an understanding of the consequences of not going along with the recommended procedure
4. consent that is voluntary

**41.4.** Involuntary admission to a mental hospital

1. requires that the patient be a danger to others or to self
2. can be done by one psychiatrist
3. requires that the next of kin be notified
4. allows the patient to be involuntarily hospitalized for a maximum of 120 days

**41.5.** The Model Penal Code states which of the following about reduced criminal responsibility:

1. The person must have a mental illness.
2. The criminal act must result from a mental illness.
3. The person cannot conform his or her conduct to the requirements of the law.
4. Antisocial behavior is a mental disorder.

**41.6.** In the case of *O'Connor v. Donaldson,* the Supreme Court ruled that mental patients cannot be confined in a hospital against their will unless

1. they are a danger to themselves
2. they receive treatment
3. they cannot survive outside a hospital
4. they are mentally ill

**41.7.** A 23-year-old male student seen in consultation by a university health service psychiatrist states that he has plans to kill a fellow student who formerly was his girlfriend. He explains his reasons on the basis of her having rejected him. The patient states that he has already purchased a gun. In this instance, the psychiatrist should

1. treat the patient's plans as a confidential communication
2. notify the police of the patient's dangerousness
3. advise the patient to begin a course of psychotherapy
4. warn the intended victim of the plan so that she can protect herself

**41.8.** A wife accuses her husband of having incestuous relations with their 16-year-old daughter. Both the husband and the daughter deny any such relationship. In this instance a psychiatrist

1. can help eliminate the confusion by a thorough psychiatric examination of the family
2. can be appointed by the court to perform a psychiatric examination of the family
3. may testify that one or more of the persons are lying
4. has no role to play in the situation

**41.9.** A person is declared to be incompetent if he or she

1. has a diagnosed mental disorder
2. is a psychiatric inpatient
3. is undergoing psychotherapy
4. has an impairment of judgment resulting from a mental disorder

**41.10.** *Wyatt v. Stickney* established minimum requirements for

1. staff-patient ratios
2. individualized treatment plans
3. the physical hospital plant
4. nutritional standards

**41.11.** A psychiatrist may be held liable for
1. breach of confidence
2. faulty diagnosis
3. failure to prevent suicide
4. drug toxicity

**41.12.** Competency to make a will is based on the finding that persons wishing to do so know

1. that they are making a will
2. the natural beneficiaries of their bounty
3. the nature and the extent of their property
4. the state in which they are domiciled

**41.13.** The M'Naghten rule holds that individuals are not guilty of a crime by reason of insanity if

1. they were aware of the nature, quality, or consequences of their act
2. they suffer from hallucinations
3. they did not realize the act was wrong
4. they are schizophrenic

**41.14.** In order to stand trial, a person
1. must understand the nature of the proceedings against him or her
2. must have the capacity to consult with a lawyer
3. must be able to assist in preparing the defense
4. must not have a mental illness

**41.15.** Testimonial privilege
1. gives the psychiatrist the right to maintain secrecy
2. does not exist in military courts
3. is waived when patients mention that they are or have been in treatment
4. does not apply in malpractice claims by patients

**41.16.** Reporting by physicians is mandated by law when patients

1. have epilepsy and operate a motor vehicle
2. are suspected of child abuse
3. have firearm or knife wounds
4. are enrolled in drug-abuse programs

**41.17.** In which of the following situations should the psychiatrist break confidentiality and notify the authorities:

1. The psychiatrist believes that the patient will probably commit murder.
2. The psychiatrist believes that the patient is actively suicidal.
3. The patient has severely impaired judgment and is in a responsible position, e.g. an airline pilot.
4. The patient has aggressive fantasies.

# Answers

# Forensic Psychiatry

**41.1. The answer is A** (*Synopsis*, ed. 4, pages 892 and 893).

The Gault decision applies to *minors*, those under the care of a parent or guardian and usually under the age of 18. In the case of minors, the parent or guardian is the person legally empowered to give consent to medical treatment. Most states by statute, however, list specific diseases or conditions that a minor can consent to have treated, such as venereal disease, pregnancy, contraception, drug dependency, alcoholism, and contagious diseases. In an emergency situation, a physician can treat a minor without parental consent. The trend is to adopt what is referred to as the mature minor rule, allowing minors to consent to treatment under ordinary circumstances. As a result of the Gault decision, the juvenile must now be represented by counsel, must be able to confront witnesses, and must be given proper notice of any charges. Emancipated minors have the rights of adults when it can be demonstrated that they are living as adults with control over their own lives.

A writ of *habeas corpus* may be proclaimed on behalf of anyone who claims he or she is being deprived of liberty illegally. This legal procedure asks a court to decide whether hospitalization has been accomplished without due process of the law, and the petition must be heard by a court at once, regardless of the manner or form in which it is filed. Hospitals are obligated to submit these petitions to the court immediately.

*Informed consent* is a knowledge of the risks and alternatives of a treatment method.

Under classical tort (a tort is a wrongful act) theory, an intentional touching to which one has given no consent is a *battery*. Thus, the administration of electroconvulsive therapy or chemotherapy, although it may be therapeutic, is a battery when done without consent. Indeed, any unauthorized touching outside of conventional social intercourse constitutes a battery. It is an offense to the dignity of the person, an invasion of the right of self-determination, for which punitive and actual damages may be imposed.

**41.2. The answer is C** (*Synopsis*, ed. 4, page 896).

In 1954 in the case of *Durham v. United States*, a decision was handed down by Judge David Bazelon, a pioneering jurist in forensic psychiatry in the District of Columbia Court of Appeals, that resulted in the *product rule of criminal responsibility*: An accused is not criminally responsible if his or her unlawful act was the product of mental disease or defect.

Judge Bazelon in the *Durham* case expressly stated that the purpose of the rule was to get good and complete psychiatric testimony. He sought to break the criminal law out of the theoretical straightjacket of the M'Naghten test.

*Testimonial privilege* is the right to maintain secrecy or confidentiality in the face of a subpoena. The privilege belongs to the patient, not to the physician, and it is waivable by the patient. *Involuntary admission* involves the question of whether or not the patient is a danger to self, such as in the suicidal patient, or a danger to others, such as in the homicidal patient. Because these individuals do not recognize their need for hospital care, application for admission to a hospital may be made by a relative or friend and is involuntary. *Competency to stand trial* refers to the person being able to understand the nature and the object of the proceedings against him or her, to consult with counsel, and to assist in preparing the defense to stand trial.

**41.3. The answer is E (all)** (*Synopsis*, ed. 4, page 893).

Simultaneously with the growth of consumer law, the courts began to require that the physician relate sufficient information to allow the patient to decide whether a medical procedure is acceptable in light of its risks and benefits and to understand the available alternatives, including no treatment at all. This duty of full disclosure gave rise to the phrase informed consent. In general, informed consent requires that there be (1) *an understanding of the nature and foreseeable risks and benefits of a procedure*, (2) *a knowledge of alternative procedures*, (3) *an understanding of the consequences of withholding consent*, and (4) *consent that is voluntary*. If the consent is coercive—that is, given under some kind of duress—it is not considered informed consent.

**41.4. The answer is B (1, 3)** (*Synopsis*, ed. 4, page 891).

Involuntary admission involves the question

of whether or not the *patient is a danger to self, such as in the suicidal patient, or a danger to others, such as in the homicidal patient.* Because these persons do not recognize their need for hospital care, application for admission to a hospital may be made by a relative or friend.

Once the application is made, the patient must *be examined by two physicians,* and if they confirm the need for hospitalization, the patient can then be admitted.

There is an established procedure for written *notification to the next of kin* whenever involuntary hospitalization is involved. Furthermore, the patient has access at any time to legal counsel, who can bring the case before a judge. If hospitalization is not felt to be indicated by the judge, he or she can order the patient's release from the hospital.

*Involuntary admission allows the patient to be hospitalized for 60 days.* After this time, the case must be reviewed periodically by a board consisting of psychiatrists, nonpsychiatric physicians, lawyers, and other citizens not connected with the institution, if the patient is to remain hospitalized. In New York State this board is called the Mental Health Information Service. The power of the state to involuntarily commit mentally ill persons in need of care is known as *parens patriae* and sometimes as police power, in that it prevents mentally ill persons from doing harm to themselves or to others.

Despite the clear-cut procedures and safeguards for hospitalization available to the patient and family, as well as to the medical and legal profession, involuntary admissions are viewed by some as an infringement of civil rights.

**41.5.   The answer is A (1, 2, 3)** (*Synopsis,* ed. 4, page 896).

The American Law Institute in its Model Penal Code recommended the following test of criminal responsibility: (1) Persons are not responsible for criminal conduct if at the time of such conduct as a *result of mental disease or defect* they lack substantial capacity either to appreciate the criminality [wrongfulness] of their conduct or to conform their conduct to the requirement of the law. (2) As used in this Article, the terms "mental disease or defect" do not include an abnormality manifested only by repeated criminal or otherwise antisocial conduct.

There are five operative concepts in the first subsection of the American Law Institute rule: (1) mental disease or defect, (2) lack of substantial capacity, (3) appreciation, (4) wrongfulness, and (5) *conformity of conduct to the requirements of law.* The second subsection of the rule, stating that repeated criminal or antisocial conduct is

not of itself to be taken as mental disease or defect, aims to keep the sociopath or psychopath within the scope of criminal responsibility.

The test of criminal responsibility and other tests grading criminal liability refer to the time of the commission of the offense, whereas the test of competency to stand trial refers to the time of trial.

*Antisocial behavior is not considered a mental disorder* according to DSM-III. It is characterized by the inability to get along with other members of society and by repeated conflicts with authorities, the law, individual persons, and groups. There may be an underlying mental disorder in persons with antisocial behavior, which should then be diagnosed. DSM-III does define an antisocial personality disorder, however, as a mental illness that is characterized by impulsiveness, egocentricity, hedonism, low frustration tolerance, irresponsibility, inadequate conscience development, exploitation of others, and rejection of authority and discipline.

**41.6.   The answer is A (1, 2, 3)** (*Synopsis,* ed. 4, page 892).

In the 1976 case of *O'Connor v. Donaldson,* the Supreme Court ruled that *harmless mental patients cannot be confined against their will without treatment if they can survive outside the hospital.* A finding of *mental illness alone cannot justify a state's confining persons in a hospital against their will* according to the Court. Instead, patients must *be considered dangerous to themselves or others.*

This case raised the question of the psychiatrist's ability to accurately predict dangerousness and the risk to the psychiatrist who might be sued for monetary damages if a person is deprived of civil rights as a result of this difficulty in accurately assessing dangerousness in some cases. That question, however, was not answered by the Supreme Court.

**41.7.   The answer is C (2, 4)** (*Synopsis,* ed. 4, page 890).

The consulting psychiatrist must *notify both the authorities and the intended victim* when he or she believes a patient is dangerous to others.

This issue was clearly raised in the case of *Tarasoff v. Regents of University of California* in 1966. In this case, Prosenjit Poddar, a student and a voluntary outpatient at the mental health clinic of the University of California, related to his therapist his intention to kill a girl readily identifiable as Tatiana Tarasoff. Realizing the seriousness of the intention, the therapist, with the concurrence of a colleague, concluded that Poddar should be committed for observation under a 72-hour emergency psychiatric detention provision of the California commitment law. The therapist notified the campus police both orally and in writing that Poddar was dangerous and should be committed.

The discharge of the duty imposed on the therapist to protect the intended victim against such danger may take one or more various steps, depending on the nature of the case. Thus, said the court, it may call for the therapist to warn the intended victim or others likely to apprise the victim of the danger, to notify the police, or to take whatever other steps are reasonably necessary under the circumstances.

The Tarasoff ruling does not require a therapist to report a fantasy. It simply means that when therapists are realistically convinced that a homicide is in the making, it is their duty to exercise good judgment.

Advising imminently dangerous patients *to enter psychotherapy is not likely to be an effective control* on their dangerousness. In such cases, it is best to first hospitalize such patients and afterward begin psychotherapy.

**41.8.   The answer is A (1, 2, 3)** (*Synopsis,* ed. 4, page 888).

In incest cases, the father and the daughter may jointly deny the incest that the mother persistently alleges, as in the case presented. In other cases, the father may steadfastly deny the act, and the mother may support his denial; or after accusing her father, the daughter may retract the accusation. Psychiatrists say that only a *thorough psychiatric examination of the family can eliminate such confusion.* Recognizing that false sex charges may stem from the psychic complexes of a victim who appears normal to the layman, *courts have permitted psychiatrists to expose mental defects, hysteria, and pathological lying in complaining witnesses.* The liberal attitude in the area is probably due to the gravity of the charge, to the general lack of corroborating evidence, and perhaps to a popular feeling that sex is peculiarly within the ken of psychiatrists.

It is within the discretion of the trial judge to decide whether a psychiatric examination should be granted. Before ordering such an examination, the trial judge requires a substantial showing that the examination is necessary to determine the merits of the case properly and that the imposition on or inconvenience to the witness does not outweigh the value of the examination. Many courts limit psychiatric examination to complaining witnesses in rape and other sex offense cases, in which corroborative proof is nearly always circumstantial.

**41.9.   The answer is D (4)** (*Synopsis,* ed. 4, page 894).

Competency is determined on the basis of the person's ability to have sound judgment. The *diagnosis of a mental disorder is not, in and of itself, sufficient to warrant a finding of incompetency.* The mental disorder must cause an *impairment in judgment regarding the specific issues involved.* Once declared incompetent, persons are deprived of certain rights: They cannot make contracts, marry, start a divorce action, drive a vehicle, handle their own property, or practice their profession. Incompetency is decided at a formal courtroom proceeding, and the court usually appoints a guardian who will best serve the interests of the patient. Once declared incompetent, another hearing is necessary to declare the patient competent. It should be noted that *admission to a mental hospital does not automatically mean the person is incompetent.* A separate hearing is usually required. Also, the fact that the patient *is undergoing psychotherapy* has no bearing on competency.

In reference to contracts, competency is essential because a contract is an agreement between parties to do some specific act. The contract will be declared invalid if, when it was signed, one of the parties was unable to comprehend the nature of his or her act. The marriage contract is subject to the same standard and will be voidable if either party did not understand "for want of understanding" the nature, duties, obligations, and other characteristics entailed. In general, courts are unwilling to declare a marriage void on the basis of incompetency.

Whether the competence relates to wills, contracts, or the making or breaking of marriages, the fundamental concern is the person's state of awareness and capacity to comprehend the significance of the specific subject of the particular commitment being made—at the time the person made it.

**41.10.   The answer is E (all)** (*Synopsis,* ed. 4, page 892).

In 1971, Federal District Court Judge Frank Johnson, sitting in Alabama, made an important ruling in *Wyatt v. Stickney.* The *Wyatt* case was a class action proceeding, brought under newly developed rules, that sought not release but treatment. Judge Johnson ruled that persons civilly committed to a mental institution have a constitutional right to receive such individual treatment as will give each of them a reasonable opportunity to be cured or to improve his or her mental condition.

Judge Johnson set out minimum requirements for *staffing,* specified *physical facilities and nutritional standards,* and required *individualized treatment plans.* Shortly thereafter, Federal District Judge William Justice, sitting in

Texas, set out standards for state training schools.

The new codes, more detailed than the old, include the right to be free from excessive or unnecessary medication, the right to privacy and dignity, the unrestricted right to be visited by attorneys and private physicians, the right not to be subjected to experimental research, the right to wear one's own clothes, and the right not to be subjected to lobotomy, electroshock treatments, or other procedures without fully informed consent. Patients can be required to perform therapeutic tasks but not hospital chores unless they volunteer for them and are paid the federal minimum wage. This is an attempt to eliminate the practice of peonage, in which psychiatric patients were forced to work at menial tasks for the benefit of the state, without payment.

**41.11. The answer is E (all)** (*Synopsis*, ed. 4, pages 897 and 898).

Psychiatrists have been sued for malpractice mainly for *faulty diagnosis* or screening, improper certification in commitment, failure to prevent *suicide, harmful effects of convulsive treatments and psychotropic drugs, improper divulgence of information*, and sexual intimacy with patients.

In relative frequency of malpractice suits, psychiatry ranks eighth among medical specialties, and in almost every suit for psychiatric malpractice in which liability was imposed, tangible physical injury was demonstrated. The number of suits against psychiatrists is said to be small because of the patient's reluctance to expose a psychiatric history, the skill of the psychiatrist in dealing with the negative feelings of the patient, and the difficulty in linking injury with treatment.

**41.12. The answer is E (all)** (*Synopsis*, ed. 4, pages 893 and 894).

The psychiatrist may be called on to evaluate a patient's testamentary capacity, i.e. competency to make a will. Three psychological abilities are necessary to demonstrate this competency; patients must know (1) *the nature and extent of their bounty* (property); (2) *that they are making a will; and* (3) *who their natural beneficiaries are*; that is, their wife, children, and relatives. If the patients *do not know in which state they live*, their competency to make a will is in question.

**41.13. The answer is B (1, 3)** (*Synopsis*, ed. 4, pages 894 and 895).

The precedent for determining legal responsibility was established in the British courts during 1843. The so-called M'Naghten rule, which has, until recently, determined responsibility in most of the United States, holds that people are not guilty by reason of insanity if they labored under a mental disease such that they were *unaware of the nature, quality, and consequences of their act*, or if they were *incapable of realizing that their act was wrong*. Moreover, to absolve people from punishment, a delusion has to be one, which if true, would be an adequate defense. If the deluded idea does not justify the crime, then presumably such persons are to be held responsible, guilty, and punishable. The M'Naghten rule is known commonly as the right-wrong test.

The M'Naghten rule derives from the famous M'Naghten case dating back to 1843. At that time Edward Drummond, the private secretary of Sir Robert Peel, was murdered by Daniel M'Naghten. M'Naghten had been suffering from delusions of persecution for several years. He had complained to many people about his delusional persecutors, and finally he decided to correct the situation by murdering Sir Robert Peel. When Drummond came out of Peel's home, M'Naghten shot Drummond, mistaking him for Peel. He was later adjudged insane and committed to a hospital. The case aroused great interest, causing the House of Lords to debate the problems of criminality and insanity. In response to questions about what guidelines could be used to determine whether a person should plead insanity as a defense against criminal responsibility, the English judiciary wrote:

"1. To establish a defense on the ground of insanity it must be clearly proved that, at the time of committing the act, the party accused was laboring under such a defect of reason, from disease of the mind, as not to know the nature and quality of the act he was doing, or if he did know it, he did not know he was doing what was wrong.

"2. Where a person labors under partial delusions only and is not in other respects insane and as a result commits an offense he must be considered in the same situation as to responsibility as if the facts with respect to which the delusion exists were real."

The jury, as instructed under the prevailing law, found the defendant not guilty by reason of insanity.

In view of the above discussions, patients *may be suffering from hallucinations and be schizophrenic and still be considered legally responsible for their acts*.

**41.14. The answer is A (1, 2, 3)** (*Synopsis*, ed. 4, page 897).

It has long been accepted that a person who lacks the capacity to *understand the nature and the object of the proceeedings against him or her, to consult with counsel,* and to *assist in preparing the defense* is not competent to stand trial.

The Supreme Court has said that "the prohibition [against trying a mental incompetent] is fundamental to an adversary system of justice." Accordingly, the Court has approved a test of incompetence that seeks to ascertain whether a criminal defendent "has sufficient present ability to consult with his lawyer with a reasonable degree of rational understanding—and whether he has a rational as well as factual understanding of the proceedings against him."

The failure to observe procedures adequate to protect a defendant's right not to be tried or convicted while incompetent to stand trial deprives the defendant of the due-process right to a fair trial.

A person *may have a mental illness, such as schizophrenia, and still meet the criteria for competency to stand trial.*

**41.15.   The answer is E (all)** (*Synopsis*, ed. 4, page 889).

Testimonial privilege is the *right to maintain secrecy* or confidentiality in the face of a subpoena. The privilege belongs to the patient, not to the physician, and it is waivable by the patient. Currently, 38 of the 50 states have statutes providing some kind of physician-patient privilege. Psychiatrists, licensed in the practice of medicine, fall under the medical privilege, but they have come to find that it is so riddled with qualifications that it is practically meaningless. In purely federal cases, there is no psychotherapist-patient privilege. Moreover, the privilege *does not exist at all in military courts,* regardless of whether the physician is military or civilian, or whether the privilege is recognized in the state where the court-martial is sitting. The exceptions to the privilege, often viewed as implied waivers, are numerous. In the most common exception, *patients are said to waive the privilege by injecting their condition into the litigation,* making their condition an element of their claim or defense. Another exception involves proceedings for hospitalization, in which the interests of both patient and public are said to call for a departure from confidentiality. Yet another exception is made in child custody and child protection proceedings, out of regard for the best interests of the child.

Furthermore, the privilege does not apply in actions between a therapist and a patient. Thus, in a fee dispute or a *malpractice claim, the complainant's lawyer can obtain the therapist's records* necessary to the resolution of the dispute.

**41.16.   The answer is E (all)** (*Synopsis*, ed. 4, pages 889 and 890).

In a number of situations, reporting by the physician to the authorities is specifically required by law. The classic example of mandated reporting is of a patient *having epilepsy and operating a motor vehicle.* Another example of mandated reporting, one in which penalities are imposed for failure to report, involves child abuse. By law, therapists are obliged to report *suspected cases of child abuse* to public authorities. Expanded definitions of what constitutes child abuse under the law have been amended in some jurisdictions to include emotional as well as physical child abuse. Under this legislation a practitioner who learns that a patient is engaged in sexual activity with his or her child would be obliged to report it, although nothing may be gained by notifying the authorities.

Other notable examples of mandated reporting include dangerous or contagious diseases, *firearm and knife wounds,* and the reporting on *patients in drug-abuse treatment programs.*

**41.17.   The answer is A (1, 2, 3)** (*Synopsis*, ed. 4, page 890).

Confidentiality is the ethical principle by which physicians are bound to hold secret all information given them by their patients. Legally, certain states do not recognize confidentiality and can require physicians to divulge such information if needed in a legal proceeding.

According to the American Psychiatric Association, confidentiality may, with careful judgment, be broken in the following ways: (1) *A patient will probably commit murder*; the act can be stopped only by the intervention of the psychiatrist. (2) *A patient will probably commit suicide*; the act can be stopped only by the intervention of the psychiatrist. (3) *A patient, such as a bus driver or airline pilot, who is charged with serious responsibilities, shows marked impairment of judgment.*

*Aggressive fantasies* about harming someone need not be reported to the authorities. Such fantasies are considered part of the psychotherapeutic process, and unless the psychiatrist believes that the fantasy will be acted on, it remains a confidential communication.

## References

American Bar Association Standing Committee on Association Standards for Criminal Justice: *Policy on the Insanity Defense.* American Bar Association, Washington, DC, 1983.

American Medical Association Committee on Medicolegal Problems: Insanity defense in criminal trials and limitation of psychiatric testimony. JAMA *251:* 2967, 1984.

American Psychiatric Association: Statement on the insanity defense. Am J Psychiatry *140:* 681, 1983.

Ciccone J R, Clements C: Forensic psychiatry and applied clinical ethics Am J Psychiatry *141:* 395, 1984.

Davidson H A: *Forensic Psychiatry,* ed 2. Ronald Press, New York, 1965.

Drane, J F: Annotations on informed consent for psychiatry. Bull Menninger Clinic *48:* 111, 1984.

Freedman D X: Law and psychiatry. In *Year Book of Psychiatry and Applied Mental Health,* D X Freedman, J A Talbott, R S Lourie, H Y Meltzer, J C Nemiah, H Weiner, editors, p 327. Year Book Medical Publishers, Chicago, 1984.

Gutheil T G, Appelbaum P S: *Clinical Handbook of Psychiatry and the Law.* McGraw-Hill, New York, 1982.

Sadoff R L: *Forensic Psychiatry: A Practical Guide for Lawyers and Psychiatrists.* Charles C Thomas, Springfield, IL, 1975.

Slovenko R: Law and psychiatry. In *Comprehensive Textbook of Psychiatry,* ed 4, H I Kaplan, B J Sadock, editors, p 1960. Williams & Wilkins, Baltimore, 1985.

# Index